AN INSTITUTIONAL APPROACH TO THE RESPONSIBILITY TO PROTECT

Covering the State, the main political organs of the UN, important regional and security organisations, international judicial institutions and the regional human rights protection systems, *An Institutional Approach to the Responsibility to Protect* examines the roles and responsibilities of the State and the international community regarding the responsibility to protect, and proposes improvements to the current system of collective security and human rights protection.

GENTIAN ZYBERI is Associate Professor of International Law at the Norwegian Centre for Human Rights, University of Oslo, Norway.

G000068539

AN INSTITUTIONAL APPROACH TO THE RESPONSIBILITY TO PROTECT

Edited by

GENTIAN ZYBERI

Assistant editor

KEVIN T. MASON

CAMBRIDGE
UNIVERSITY PRESS

CAMBRIDGE
UNIVERSITY PRESS

University Printing House, Cambridge CB2 8BS, United Kingdom

Cambridge University Press is part of the University of Cambridge.

It furthers the University's mission by disseminating knowledge in the pursuit of education, learning and research at the highest international levels of excellence.

www.cambridge.org
Information on this title: www.cambridge.org/9781316603437

© Cambridge University Press 2013

This publication is in copyright. Subject to statutory exception and to the provisions of relevant collective licensing agreements, no reproduction of any part may take place without the written permission of Cambridge University Press.

First published 2013
First paperback edition 2015

A catalogue record for this publication is available from the British Library

Library of Congress Cataloguing in Publication data
An institutional approach to the responsibility to protect / edited by Gentian Zyberi ; assistant editor Kevin T. Mason.
pages cm
ISBN 978-1-107-03644-4
1. Responsibility to protect (International law)   I. Zyberi, Gentian.   II. Mason, Kevin T.
KZ4082.I577   2013
341.4′8–dc23
2012050468

ISBN 978-1-107-03644-4 Hardback
ISBN 978-1-316-60343-7 Paperback

Cambridge University Press has no responsibility for the persistence or accuracy of URLs for external or third-party internet websites referred to in this publication, and does not guarantee that any content on such websites is, or will remain, accurate or appropriate.

CONTENTS

NOTES ON CONTRIBUTORS

MAHASEN M. ALJAGHOUB is Associate Professor of International Law, University of Jordan, Jordan.

DIANA AMNÉUS is Associate Senior Researcher, Raoul Wallenberg Institute, Lund University, Sweden and Senior Legal Adviser, Temporary International Presence in Hebron (TIPH).

SUSAN C. BREAU is Professor of International Law, School of Law, Flinders University, Australia.

MICHAEL CONTARINO is Associate Professor of Politics and Director of the Politics and Society programme at the University of New Hampshire at Manchester, United States of America.

HANNE CUYCKENS is Ph.D. candidate, Catholic University of Leuven, Belgium.

SOLOMON A. DERSSO is senior researcher with the Peace and Security Council Project of the Institute for Security Studies and adjunct professor of human rights at Addis Ababa University, Ethiopia.

DANIEL FIOTT is Ph.D. researcher, Institute for European Studies, Vrije Universiteit Brussels, Belgium.

NIKI FRENCKEN is an international consultant; MA in conflict studies and human rights and LL.M in public international law, Amsterdam, the Netherlands.

TERRY D. GILL is Professor of Military Law at the University of Amsterdam and at the Netherlands Defence Academy and Associate Professor of International Law at the University of Utrecht, the Netherlands.

CONALL MALLORY is lecturer in law, University of Northumbria, United Kingdom.

IBRAHIM MASHOUR ALJAZY is Associate Professor of International Law, University of Jordan, Jordan.

NOEL M. MORADA is Senior Research Fellow, School of Political Science and International Studies and Executive Director, Asia-Pacific Centre for the Responsibility to Protect, University of Queensland St Lucia, Brisbane, Australia.

MELINDA NEGRÓN-GONZALES is Assistant Professor of Politics at the University of New Hampshire at Manchester, United States of America.

JODY M. PRESCOTT is Senior Fellow, West Point Center for the Rule of Law; adjunct professor, University of Vermont, Political Science Department, United States of America.

ARNOLD N. PRONTO is Senior Legal Officer, United Nations Office of Legal Affairs, member of the Secretariat of the International Law Commission, New York, United States of America.

CEDRIC RYNGAERT is Associate Professor of International Law at Leuven University and Utrecht University.

MAYSA SAID BYDOON is Assistant Professor of International Law, Al al-Bayt University, Jordan.

DENNIS J. D. SANDOLE is Professor of Conflict Resolution and International Relations at the School for Conflict Analysis and Resolution (S-CAR) at George Mason University in Arlington, Virginia, United States of America.

GÖRAN SLUITER is Professor in the Law of International Criminal Procedure at the University of Amsterdam and Lawyer at Böhler Advocaten, Amsterdam, the Netherlands.

RHONA SMITH is Professor of International Human Rights, University of Northumbria, United Kingdom.

OLIVER HILAIRE SOBERS is a human rights specialist, Inter-American Commission on Human Rights, Organization of American States, Washington, DC, United States of America.

LYAL S. SUNGA is Visiting Professor, Raoul Wallenberg Institute for Human Rights and Humanitarian Law, Lund, Sweden.

PAULO DE TARSO LUGON ARANTES is a Ph.D. candidate, Catholic University of Leuven, Belgium.

NICHOLAS TURNER is Senior Programme Coordinator, United Nations University–Institute for Sustainability and Peace, Tokyo, Japan.

RAPHAËL VAN STEENBERGHE is a postdoctoral researcher, Belgian National Fund for Scientific Research (FNRS); visiting lecturer in humanitarian law at the University of Louvain (Belgium) and the University of Lille (France); visiting professor at the Royal Military School of Belgium; member of the International Law Centre at the University of Louvain.

FRANS VILJOEN is Professor of International Human Rights Law and Director of the Centre for Human Rights, University of Pretoria, South Africa.

MARIE VINCENT is former project manager at the Madariaga – College of Europe Foundation, Brussels, Belgium.

GENTIAN ZYBERI is Associate Professor of International Law at the Norwegian Centre for Human Rights, University of Oslo, Norway; *pro bono* defence lawyer at the International Criminal Tribunal for the former Yugoslavia.

PREFACE

Preventing mass atrocity crimes requires a proper and synchronised functioning of all existing international and regional mechanisms – political, judicial and military – as well as strong involvement on the part of the civil society. The 'Responsibility to Protect' concept, as first espoused in the December 2001 report of the International Commission on Intervention and State Sovereignty (ICISS) and widely referred to with the acronyms 'R2P' or 'RtoP' was created as a response to the challenge of ending mass atrocities in the face of the failures in Rwanda, Bosnia-Herzegovina, the Democratic Republic of Congo, Kosovo and other places. Over the last ten years the initial concept has gone through considerable scrutiny and fine-tuning in an open and inclusive process, culminating in the debates held at the UN General Assembly on the basis of several reports submitted by the Secretary-General. The debate surrounding the operationalisation and the institutionalisation of the responsibility to protect should be informed by a complex legal framework of norms of conduct for States, international and regional organisations, non-State actors and individuals, embodied in a number of international and regional human rights and international humanitarian law treaties, customary international law, the statutes of international courts and tribunals and other relevant guidelines adopted or presently under consideration by the International Law Commission (ILC). Such a debate takes place within an international legal and institutional framework which has developed quite extensively since the establishment in 1945 of the United Nations.

This book aims at providing a general picture of existing institutional mechanisms and practices relevant to the responsibility to protect, while at the same time also exploring ways of improving the current systems of collective security and enforcement of fundamental human rights. While there is considerable literature on the responsibility to protect, a book which takes the comprehensive institutional approach adopted here has been missing thus far. Moreover, the discussion of important legal aspects from the perspectives of the law of international responsibility, human rights, humanitarian law, and international criminal law has tended to be somewhat superficial and scattered. The depth of the discussion, its institutional angle, and the possibility to include therein recent responsibility to protect situations as that in Sudan, Libya, Ivory Coast and other unfolding situations as that in Syria are part of this book's strengths.

The book explores the potential role and contribution with regard to the responsibility to protect of a wide variety of actors that make up what is generally, though ineptly, referred to as the international community. That mixture of selected relevant actors includes not only some of the main organs and entities of the UN, which logically are a focal point, but also a considerable number of regional and security organisations. A complete picture of the possibilities and limitations with regard to turning responsibility to protect into reality will emerge by looking at some of the most important components of the present-day international system. Thus, the book addresses from an institutional perspective the potential role and contribution of the State, the main political organs of the UN, important regional and security organisations, the main international judicial institutions, the regional human rights protection systems and the civil society in the process of institutionalisation and implementation of the responsibility to protect. Indeed, the main strengths of this book, compared to others on this very topic, lay in its institutional emphasis and close inquiry into how to achieve a better implementation of responsibility to protect obligations through the proper institutionalisation of this overarching principle. The chapters are written by a number of highly qualified and well-known authors, coming from different parts of the world. The contributors have chosen themselves which acronym (that is, R2P or RtoP) to use in their respective chapters.

By dealing with most of the key international and regional actors in one volume, this book aims to provide a comprehensive institutional perspective on the state of affairs with regard to operationalising the responsibility of States and the institutional capabilities and limitations of the international community to protect populations from genocide, war crimes, ethnic cleansing and crimes against humanity. The effort towards comprehensiveness of the book is clearly reflected in the five parts composing it.

Part I of the book is entitled 'Theoretical and practical perspectives on the responsibility to protect'. In large part, the three chapters of this part lay the foundation for the discussion that follows. The first chapter provides a discussion of the coining and evolution of the responsibility to protect from the 2001 ICISS report to its endorsement by the High-Level Summit of the UN in the 2005 World Summit Outcome Document and the most recent discussions in the General Assembly. This chapter discusses the scope and content of the international legal obligations to protect populations against mass atrocity crimes incumbent upon States under the three RtoP pillars. The second chapter deals with the role of non-State actors in implementing the responsibility to protect, focusing on NGOs, the ICRC and armed groups. The third chapter deals with peacekeeping operations as an important component of the international response to the plight of populations at risk from mass atrocity crimes. This last chapter serves as a prelude to the next part of the book which focuses on the work of the UN.

Part II is entitled 'The United Nations system'. The first three chapters of this part focus on the work of the main UN organs, namely the Security Council, the General Assembly and the Secretary-General. The relevance of these bodies to properly frame and implement the responsibility to protect is fairly evident. The fourth chapter focuses on the work of the Human Rights Council – a subsidiary body of the General Assembly – whose activity is central to human rights protection from mass atrocities. The Human Rights Council has responded swiftly to a number of situations which fall under the responsibility to protect, including that in Libya. The last chapter focuses on the work of the International Law Commission, an international body entrusted with the codification and progressive development of international law. A part of the work of the ILC, especially that on the law of international responsibility is highly relevant to a proper understanding of the obligations and the ensuing responsibility for States and international organisations for implementing the responsibility to protect populations from genocide, war crimes, ethnic cleansing and crimes against humanity.

Part III is entitled 'Regional and security organisations'. This part deals with key regional and security organisations; thereby analysing and highlighting the regional dimension of the responsibility to protect. This dimension was recently explored in the 2011 report of the Secretary-General to the General Assembly. Regional and security organisations have played a key role in protecting populations from mass atrocities in a number of situations, past and present. This part includes seven chapters, which focus respectively on the European Union, the African Union, the Association of Southeast Asian Nations, the Organisation of American States, the Arab League, the Organization for Security and Co-operation in Europe and the North Atlantic Treaty

Organization. The selection of these regional organisations is based mainly on their weight and membership, their capacities and their activity with regard to RtoP. Another factor influencing this selection has been maintaining a regional balance and representation.

Part IV of the book focuses on international courts and tribunals. This part, composed of three chapters, deals with the main international courts and tribunals. The first chapter deals with the International Court of Justice (ICJ). This court is entrusted with resolving inter-State disputes, besides its important advisory jurisdiction to the UN, and in a number of cases has clarified several important issues relating to the obligations of States to protect populations from mass atrocities. The second chapter discusses the relationship to RtoP of the two ad hoc tribunals, in view of their ground-breaking findings and important place within the international criminal justice system. The third chapter of this part shall focus on the work of the International Criminal Court (ICC). As a permanent court tasked with prosecuting persons accused of having committed genocide, war crimes and crimes against humanity, its close connection with RtoP is fairly evident. Among others, the preventive function of the activity of the ICC with regard to the internationally recognised crimes falling under RtoP will receive the necessary attention. A difficult choice needed to be made to leave out of this part of the book hybrid or national criminal judicial bodies.

Part V is entitled 'Regional human rights protection mechanisms'. This part is important because it shows the relevance of the regional human rights protection systems to strengthening relevant RtoP components. The contribution of these regional human rights mechanisms to strengthening RtoP comes not only through the inter-State cases and the individual complaints brought before the operating regional human rights courts and commissions, but also through the activity of other human rights protection mechanisms which operate alongside them. By focusing on the European, African and Inter-American human rights' systems, it will be shown that regional human rights courts and other human rights enforcement agencies have played an important civilising role in entrenching respect for human rights standards at the domestic level. By ensuring State compliance with commonly agreed human rights standards, regional human rights mechanisms have given a direct contribution to implementing the responsibility to protect at the regional level. While there is some potential for overlap between this part and Part III of the book, it is kept to the necessary minimum.

The chapter included in the last part tries to tie together the discussion of relevant institutional actors and mechanisms by identifying certain achievements and highlighting certain trends and proposals put forward in order to improve the work of a number of actors with regard to implementing RtoP. While obviously the debate on RtoP continues, it is hoped that this book will further understanding of the possibilities and limitations of important actors and the work that remains to be done in turning the promise of RtoP into practice.

Gentian Zyberi

ACKNOWLEDGEMENTS

Preparing this book for publication has been an interesting and lessons-filled journey that has taken about two years to complete. I have been quite fortunate to share this journey with a large number of well-known authors, who generously agreed to contribute and kept to tight deadlines. From them I have learned a great deal about the place of the responsibility to protect (RtoP) in the agenda of different institutions, these institutions possibilities and limitations and potential improvements to their work in this regard.

The format and other details of the book were discussed first with my mentor and good friend, Terry Gill, sometime in August 2010 near Utrecht's famous Domtower. His remarks and suggestions were very helpful at that early stage and throughout the process. Further preparations and the first invitations to potential contributors to get the project off the ground were sent while I was a visiting scholar at Peking University's Research Center for Human Rights and Humanitarian Law in the period September–December 2010. I am very grateful to Professors Bai Guimei, Gong Renren and Li Hongyun of Peking University for welcoming me to the Center, for the interesting discussions on different international law subjects and for being such great hosts. While working at the Amsterdam Center for International Law of the University of Amsterdam, I had the benefit of discussing several RtoP-related issues with a number of colleagues, including Professor André Nollkaemper, who very kindly provided feedback, even on rather short notice. The discussions I have had with a number of colleagues at Utrecht University, Peking University, the University of Amsterdam and the University of Oslo have been very useful and enriching and I'll have to apologise if I am not able to mention everyone by name. Last, but not least, my colleagues at the Norwegian Centre for Human Rights of Oslo University were kind enough to give me the necessary time to complete the project, before assigning me other duties.

The book and its contents were further shaped in the course of 2011 through a dialogue with a number of Cambridge University Press reviewers, whom I thank wholeheartedly for supporting the idea and for giving me their excellent feedback. Their suggestions have done much to improve the book. The editors of Cambridge University Press, Nienke van Schaverbeke, Finola O'Sullivan, Juliet Binns, Sarah Roberts and Richard Woodham have been a delight to work with and I'm very grateful for their assistance throughout the process. Martin Barr's sharp eye for detail has helped to avoid errors and has added clarity.

Special thanks and a great deal of gratitude go to my able assistant editor, Kevin T. Mason. Kevin is a diligent young professional whose skills and hard work have been very useful in completing this book for publication. And, as we share an interest in international criminal justice, I'm sure we will continue our cooperation in the future.

Obviously, some final words of gratitude go to my parents Xhemal and Fetije and brothers Klodian and Ermir for their continuous support and encouragement. But, above all, the laughs and joy of my small nephews, Elion and Erlind, are a real source of inspiration. My life partner, Lila Zotou, deserves special praise for her love and support and occasional poignant remarks on RtoP.

PART I

Theoretical and practical perspectives
on the responsibility to protect

The coining and evolution of responsibility to protect: the protection responsibilities of the State

DIANA AMNÉUS

> While RtoP in some aspects may reinforce or reiterate existing law, its strength lies in the framework it establishes – unearthing, interpreting, and crystallising the obligation to act in the face of mass atrocity crimes.[1]

Since 2005 the idea that each State has a responsibility to protect its own population from genocide, war crimes, crimes against humanity and ethnic cleansing has been embraced by the international community in the principle of Responsibility to Protect (RtoP). It is uncontroversial that this primary RtoP flows from already existing legal obligations of States under international law. A variety of treaty and customary obligations of States under human rights law, humanitarian law and international criminal law as well as under the United Nations (UN) Charter, the law on State responsibility, peremptory norms and *erga omnes* obligations, prescribe diverse duties for States to protect populations and prevent and punish these grave crimes. It is less clear and under debate how to interpret these obligations with regard to the implementation of RtoP, the scope and thresholds for their applicability for States, individually and collectively, and the ensuing measures to be taken. What is the content of the duties to protect, prevent and punish mass atrocity crimes and what measures of positive action or acts of omissions are embedded in these obligations for individual States as well as States collectively through the UN, regional and sub-regional organisations and other entities? What is the remit of such obligations for the State and to what extent do these differ for each of the four crimes?

I wish to thank my research assistant Annabel Raw (LLM, Lund University) for her dedicated research assistance and language revision.

[1] Sheri Rosenberg, 'Responsibility to Protect: A Framework for Prevention', in Alex Bellamy, Sara Davies and Luke Glanville (eds.), *The Responsibility to Protect and International Law* (Leiden: Martinus Nijhoff, 2011), pp. 157–92, at p. 163.

This chapter will in the *first section* begin by giving an overview of the events and conceptual developments of RtoP based on the reframing of the principle of sovereignty that enfolded the notion and led to its endorsement in 2005, and give an account of the subsequent efforts to implement and operationalise RtoP. The lingering tensions and debates on contested issues and interpretations of the concept are briefly displayed as well as the views on the legality of RtoP. The following main analysis in the *second section* will examine the scope and content of the legal obligations of individual States to protect their populations under pillar one. The *third section* will similarly analyse the individual legal obligations of third States but also of States collectively through intergovernmental organisations under pillars two and three. Finally, in the *last section* there will be a brief reflection on the issue of multiple and variable responsibilities under RtoP. The merging of the principle of RtoP with international law gives rise to a variability of responsibilities and obligations. This marriage creates uncertainties on the content, scope, thresholds, responses and actions that are morally, politically and legally imposed by RtoP as well as under international law.

The coining and evolution of RtoP

Several prominent scholars and norm entrepreneurs for RtoP have given lengthy and detailed accounts on *the journey from idea to norm*:[2] covering the broadening and widening of the security discourse by the introduction of the notion of human security and the evolution of 'sovereignty as responsibility' in the 1990s; the developments through its antecedents in the doctrine on a right to humanitarian intervention linked to just war criteria;[3] the launch of the RtoP report of the International Commission on

---

[2] Gareth Evans, *The Responsibility to Protect: Ending Mass Atrocity Crimes Once and for All* (Washington, DC: Brookings Institution Press, 2008), pp. 31–54; Alex Bellamy, *Global Politics and the Responsibility to Protect: From Words to Deeds* (London; New York: Routledge, 2011), pp. 9–25; Ekkehard Strauss, *The Emperor's New Clothes? The United Nations and the Implementation of the Responsibility to Protect* (Baden-Baden: Nomos, 2009), pp. 11–40.

[3] See for example Diana Amnéus, 'Responsibility to protect by military means – emerging norms on humanitarian intervention', doctoral thesis, Stockholm University (2008); also summarised in Amnéus, 'Has Humanitarian Intervention Become Part of International Law under the Responsibility to Protect Doctrine?', in Julia Hoffmann and André Nollkaemper (eds.), *Responsibility to Protect: From Principle to Practice* (Amsterdam University Press, 2012), pp. 157–72; Bellamy, *Just Wars: From Cicero to Iraq* (Cambridge, UK: Polity Press, 2006).

Intervention and State Sovereignty (ICISS) in 2001;[4] its support in the UN High-Level Panel report (2004)[5] and the UN Secretary-General's report 'In Larger Freedom' (2005);[6] the negotiation history that led to the endorsed principle of RtoP in the World Summit Outcome Document in New York in 2005;[7] the follow-up report by the UN Secretary-General on the implementation of RtoP in 2009[8] and its subsequent reports on RtoP which were debated in the General Assembly in the summers of 2009 to 2012; the work of the Joint Office of the UN Secretary-General's Special Advisers for the prevention of genocide and RtoP; and so on. The presentation of these developments and events will in this context therefore take a slightly shifted viewpoint by its emphasis on those aspects that are related to the protection responsibilities of *States*. Viewing this evolution from this specific lens or angle will, it is hoped, shed some distinctive light on these processes.

In general, the majority of these benchmark documents and conceptual frameworks have had a tendency to focus their main analysis and policy agendas on the protection against mass atrocities by different agents in the international community, leaving the protection responsibilities and legal obligations of each State less explored and under-examined in relation to RtoP. Much of the initial prescriptions in the initiatives taken by the international community in the 1990s to address mass atrocities and humanitarian catastrophes were based on the idea of a 'right to intervene' in response of mass atrocities, with varying degrees of success and failure in cases like Somalia, Bosnia, Northern Iraq, Rwanda, Haiti, East Timor and Kosovo. The right to undertake humanitarian interventions became the single most debated foreign policy issue of that decade.[9]

The use of the concept of *'human security'* in the 1994 *Human Development Report*[10] by Mahbub ul Haq was an influential attempt to bridge the North and South positions in international affairs as well as the

---

[4] International Commission on Intervention and State Sovereignty, *The Responsibility to Protect* (Ottawa: International Research Centre, 2001), p. 8.

[5] United Nations Secretary-General, *A More Secure World: Our Shared Responsibility* (New York: United Nations, 2004).

[6] UNSG, 'In Larger Freedom: Towards Development, Security and Human Rights for All', UN Doc. A/59/2005, 21 March 2005.

[7] '2005 World Summit Outcome', UN Doc. A/RES/60/1, 24 October 2005 (WSOD).

[8] UNSG, 'Implementing the Responsibility to Protect', UN Doc. A/63/677, 12 January 2009, para. 61.

[9] Evans, *The Responsibility to Protect*, p. 32.

[10] UN Development Programme, *Human Development Report* (Oxford University Press, 1994), p. 23; Roland Paris, 'Human Security: Paradigm Shift or Hot Air?', *International Security*, 26 (2001), 87–102.

traditionally separated security and development agendas.[11] The report mainly dealt with the *freedom from want* aspect of human security in relation to human development, while the *freedom from fear* aspect of human security referring to physical violence was considered under the category of 'personal security'. Mass atrocity crimes were addressed under 'community security', or as serious forms of State repression under 'political security'. The analysis was not agent or responsibility oriented but needs based and had an emphasis on early prevention in general.

In 1996 Francis Deng, the UN Secretary-General's Representative on Internally Displaced Persons, and scholars at the Brookings Institution elaborated on the idea of '*sovereignty as responsibility*' in *Sovereignty as Responsibility: Conflict Management in Africa*.[12] The traditional view where international law empowers a sovereign State to exercise exclusive, absolute jurisdiction within its territorial borders and where other States and multilateral actors have a corresponding duty not to interfere in a State's internal affairs has been questioned, contested and somewhat abandoned.[13] The contemporary interpretations of sovereignty display pragmatic attempts at reconciling 'State sovereignty' with 'responsibility'.[14] The UN Secretary-General Kofi Annan recognised this development of sovereignty in an article in *The Economist* in 1999 when stating that '[s]tate sovereignty, in its most basic sense, is being redefined – not least by the forces of globalisation and international co-operation. States are now widely understood to be instruments at the service of their peoples, and not vice versa.'[15]

The modern understanding of sovereignty in which the State does not have unlimited power, was also central in the ICISS report on RtoP. The ICISS report acknowledged that 'sovereignty as responsibility has become the minimum content of good international citizenship', and that this

---

[11] The concept had been in use in academic circles long before, dating back to the 1960s. See for example William Blatz, *Human Security: Some Reflections* (Toronto University Press, 1966).

[12] Francis Deng, Sadikiel Kimaro, Terrence Lyons, Donald Rothchild and I. William Zartman (eds.), *Sovereignty as Responsibility: Conflict Management in Africa* (Washington, DC: Brookings Institution, 1996).

[13] Christopher Joyner, '"The Responsibility to Protect": Humanitarian Concern and the Lawfulness of Armed Intervention', *Virginia Journal of International Law*, 47 (2007), 693–723, at 703.

[14] Deng *et al.*, *Sovereignty as Responsibility: Conflict Management in Africa*, p. 2. See also, a later essay on its evolution by Deng, 'From "Sovereignty as Responsibility" to the "Responsibility to Protect"', *Global Responsibility to Protect*, 2 (2010), 353–70.

[15] Kofi Annan, 'Two concepts of sovereignty', *The Economist*, 18 September 1999.

implies a 'dual responsibility'. First, internally, to respect the dignity and basic rights of all the people within the State, and second, externally, to respect the sovereignty of other States.[16] This approach is based upon the premise that sovereignty is conditional and defined in terms of a State's willingness and capacity to provide protection for its citizens.

The ICISS report on RtoP was a response to the call by the UN Secretary-General to the international community to find a new consensus on how to approach and respond to situations of massive violations of human rights and humanitarian law within a State.[17] Its main aim was to look into the legal, moral, operational and political questions on humanitarian intervention following the NATO intervention in Kosovo in 1999. The report supported the security shift from State security and built the notion of RtoP on human security.[18] It set forward bold proposals regarding how the international community could deal with the 'gap' between the legality and the legitimacy of unauthorised humanitarian interventions that emerged as a critical issue after Kosovo,[19] and introduced a set of precautionary principles, a just cause threshold and right authority for military intervention elaborated upon just war doctrine. The ICISS report has been met with much approval and praise, but it also has been criticised as confined to a liberal international discourse.[20] Concern has also been forwarded by sceptical and resistant States regarding the consistency and selectivity in real world application of RtoP by the Security Council, and the risk of abuse of the concept by powerful States, serving as a justification or pretext for inappropriate interventions.[21]

The introduction of the responsibility of each State based on sovereignty as responsibility in the first basic principle of the ICISS report marked an important break with the previous humanitarian intervention discourse and

---

[16] ICISS, *The Responsibility to Protect*, para. 1.35.   [17] *Ibid.*, p. 81.   [18] *Ibid.*, p. 15.

[19] Independent International Commission on Kosovo, *Kosovo Report: Conflict, International Response, Lessons Learned* (Oxford University Press, 2000), pp. 4 and 10.

[20] S. Neil MacFarlane, Carolin Thielking and Thomas Weiss, 'The Responsibility to Protect: Is Anyone Interested in Humanitarian Intervention?', *Third World Quarterly*, 25 (2004), 977–92, at 981.

[21] For analysis and critique on the assumptions and controversies of the findings in the ICISS report, see Welsh *et al.*, 'The Responsibility to Protect: Assessing the Report of the International Commission on Intervention and State Sovereignty', *International Journal*, 57 (2002), 489–512. On the selectivity, see Nicole Deller, 'Challenges and Controversies', in Jared Genser and Irwin Cotler, *The Responsibility to Protect: The Promise of Stopping Mass Atrocities in Our Time* (Oxford University Press, 2011), pp. 62–84, at pp. 78ff.

was seen as another potential bridge builder between the Global North and South on the mass atrocity issue.[22] But vesting the primary responsibility in the State itself is not unproblematic. With it follows the great worries of failed and fragile States, being some of the greatest sources of national and international instability.[23] The second basic principle of RtoP therefore provided that the principle of non-intervention yields to the international RtoP when the State in question is 'unwilling or unable' to halt or avert a population suffering serious harm, as a result of internal war, insurgency, repression or State failure.[24] But the shifting of RtoP to the international community entails more than humanitarian intervention, and it was proposed that RtoP comprise three constitutive elements: the responsibility to prevent, react and rebuild.[25]

The ICISS declared that the foundations of RtoP are embedded in a miscellany of legal provisions in human rights and humanitarian law as well as in State practice and the practice of the Security Council.[26] *'Sovereignty as responsibility'* was suggested to have a threefold significance: First, responsibility for providing for the safety and lives of the citizens; second, responsibilities owed to the international community through the UN; third, State responsibility and accountability for acts of both commission and omission.[27] RtoP was seen as a correlative collective duty or responsibility of States in relation to individuals' rights to protection.[28] The report did not, however, go further into elaborating on these specific duties and obligations, and most of its analysis and focus was on the criteria and guidelines for external responses when a State is unable or unwilling to protect its populations.

The *High-Level Panel* (HLP) was set up by the UN Secretary-General in November 2003 with the mandate to examine contemporary global

---

[22] Evans, *The Responsibility to Protect*, pp. 42 and 47.

[23] Welsh *et al.*, 'The Responsibility to Protect', 497.

[24] ICISS, *The Responsibility to Protect*, p. xi.

[25] This continuum of elements was, however, not explicitly endorsed in the WSOD, nor were the ICISS report's principles of precaution and other proposals on the right authority for military interventions.

[26] ICISS, *The Responsibility to Protect*, pp. xi and 50.   [27] *Ibid.*, paras. 2.14 and 2.15.

[28] See ICISS, *The Responsibility to Protect: Research, Bibliography, Background: Supplementary Volume to the Report of the International Commission on Intervention and State Sovereignty* (Ottawa: International Development Research Centre, 2001), pp. 147–50. Several bearers of obligation were identified: the State being the primary one; the international community and multilateral bodies having a residual responsibility; and ultimately 'everyone' bears an ethical or moral responsibility when a State fails to fulfil its obligations to protect.

threats, provide analysis of future challenges to international peace and security, and recommend necessary changes to ensure effective collective action by the UN. Its 2004 report, which brought forward new ideas of institutional reform of the UN to meet the new global security threats, endorsed the concept of RtoP as an emerging norm of collective international responsibility to protect, exercisable by the Security Council authorising military intervention as a last resort when governments have proved powerless or unwilling to prevent.[29] Although it reiterated that governments have the primary responsibility to protect, it turned its attention to the shifting of responsibility to the international community when a State is unable or willing to protect, and the following analysis was concerned with the issue of legitimacy and guidelines for the use of military force by the Security Council.

Similarly, the Secretary-General's report, *In Larger Freedom*, which formulated his agenda of proposals for UN reform to be considered at the 2005 UN Summit, also embraced the emerging norm of RtoP and the primary responsibility to protect.[30] The report drew heavily on the HLP report, but at the same time exercised more moderation on RtoP.[31] Annan placed stronger emphasis on the need to implement RtoP through peaceful means and did not endorse the notion under the chapter on the rules on the use of force but in the chapter on the rule of law.[32] This move was made to mitigate the concerns by some States against the military dimension of the concept of RtoP and the risk of its abuse.[33]

> [I]f national authorities are unable or unwilling to protect their citizens, then the responsibility shifts to the international community to use diplomatic, humanitarian and other methods to help protect the human rights and well-being of civilian populations. When such methods appear insufficient, the Security Council may out of necessity decide to take action under the Charter of the United Nations, including enforcement action, if so required.[34]

---

[29] UNSG, *A More Secure World*, para. 203.

[30] UNSG, 'In Larger Freedom', p. 49. The report took a comprehensive approach to human security, uniting the twin tracks of 'freedom from want' and 'freedom from fear'.

[31] Peter Hilpold, 'The Duty to Protect and the Reform of the United Nations – A New Step in the Development of International Law', *Max Planck Yearbook of United Nations Law*, 10 (2006), 35–69, at 37.

[32] Carsten Stahn, 'Responsibility to Protect: Political Rhetoric or Emerging Legal Norm?', *American Journal of International Law*, 101 (2007), 99–120, at 107.

[33] The Iraq intervention in 2003, based partly on humanitarian justifications, had damaging effects on the evolving concept of RtoP (Bellamy, *Global Politics*, pp. 11–12).

[34] UNSG, 'In Larger Freedom', para. 135.

The placing opened up for a more elaborate discourse on what RtoP may entail for each State. For example, Annan urged States to ratify and implement all treaties relating to the protection of civilians, stressed the need to re-establish effective national judicial institutions providing for rule of law and accountability through transitional justice in conflict and post-conflict societies, and encouraged States to cooperate fully with the International Criminal Court (ICC) and other war crimes tribunals, as well as to strengthen the work of the International Court of Justice (ICJ).[35] The Secretary-General's modest question with regard to the use of military force simply stated: '[a]s to genocide, ethnic cleansing and other such crimes against humanity, are they not also threats to international peace and security, against which humanity should be able to look to the Security Council for protection?'[36] The choice to link to legal definitions in international criminal law came to influence the negotiations on RtoP at the UN Summit and dismissed the earlier, more open formulations of the ICISS report.[37]

The Heads of States and governments endorsed the principle of RtoP in the 2005 World Summit Outcome Document (WSOD),[38] and the provisions have been hailed as one of the few true successes of the Summit in New York.[39] It provided for a primary responsibility of States to protect their own populations against genocide, war crimes, crimes against humanity and ethnic cleansing, including their incitement, through appropriate and necessary means, but also a subsidiary responsibility of the international community to assist States in exercising that responsibility and in building their protection capacities. The international community declared itself prepared to take collective action when a State 'manifestly fails' to protect its population from these four crimes 'in a timely and decisive manner' through the Security Council and in accordance with the UN Charter, including Chapter VII on a case-by-case basis and in cooperation with relevant regional organisations as appropriate.[40] The bar was raised from 'unable and unwilling' to 'manifestly fails' for the shift to subsidiary responsibility. Stahn regards the inclusion of RtoP in the WSOD as a testimony of

---

[35] *Ibid.*, paras. 136–9.   [36] *Ibid.*, para. 125.   [37] *Ibid.*, para. 126.

[38] '2005 World Summit Outcome', paras. 138–40.

[39] William Pace and Nicole Deller, 'Preventing Future Genocides: An International Responsibility to Protect', *World Order*, 36 (2005), 15–32, at 27; cf. Bellamy, 'Whither the Responsibility to Protect? Humanitarian Intervention and the 2005 World Summit', *Ethics and International Affairs*, 20 (2006), 143–69.

[40] '2005 World Summit Outcome', para. 139.

a broader systemic shift in international law where the principle of State sovereignty finds its limits in the protection of human security.[41]

However, the WSOD endorsement was followed by a few years of backlash in the debates on RtoP.[42] To advance the RtoP agenda the Secretary-General Ban Ki-moon sought, and in December 2007 received, assent from the Security Council to appoint Edward Luck as his Special Adviser on the Responsibility to Protect. Initially there was resistance among some States to appoint an adviser on RtoP, by arguing that the idea was premature as the General Assembly had not begun its deliberations on RtoP.[43] Luck assumed the position on 21 February 2008 and has since been working closely with the Special Adviser for the Prevention of Genocide and Mass Atrocities, Francis Deng, who was succeeded by Adama Dieng on 17 July 2012. The Special Adviser on the Prevention of Genocide was expressly and fully supported by States already in paragraph 140 of the WSOD.

The aim of the *Secretary-General's Report on the Implementation of RtoP* presented on 12 January 2009, was to forge a common strategy and renewed political commitment. Through it Ban Ki-moon strongly encouraged the General Assembly to begin the political process of considering the overall strategy suggested in the report, including the ideas for bolstering the UN early warning capacity.[44] The report called for a Joint Office for the Special Advisers on the Prevention of Genocide and RtoP to conduct independent early warning assessment, institutionalise the collaboration between the Special Advisers, and act as a focal point that could mobilise the UN system in developing a coordinated response.[45] In December 2010 the General Assembly's Fifth Committee agreed on the necessary funding for the office.

The 2009 report introduced three pillars for advancing the authoritative framework and agenda of RtoP, corresponding with the formulations of the principle mandated in the WSOD: pillar one, the protection responsibilities of the State; pillar two, international assistance and capacity-building; and pillar three, timely and decisive

---

[41] Stahn, 'Responsibility to Protect', 101.   [42] Bellamy, *Global Politics*, pp. 28–31.

[43] The resistance to Luck's appointment was a low point in the debate on RtoP (see *ibid.*, pp. 32–3). In the General Assembly debate Cuba, India, Pakistan, Venezuela, Egypt, China and Nicaragua expressed negative positions on this appointment. See UN General Assembly Verbatim Record, UN Doc. A/C.5/62/SR.23, 7 February 2008.

[44] UNSG, 'Implementing the Responsibility to Protect', para. 69.

[45] See more on the Joint Office in Bellamy, *Global Politics*, pp. 135–41; and Turner, Chapter 6 in this book.

response. The report outlined a broad-based approach to the prevention and protection responsibilities of States, the UN, regional and sub-regional organisations and civil society partners, and the need for a cross-sectoral approach and sharing of burdens in a common effort to eliminate mass atrocities.[46] The report acknowledged that the State remains the bedrock of the RtoP principle and that the protection of populations is a defining attribute of sovereignty and Statehood in the twenty-first century.[47] The Secretary-General explained that '[t]his entails the building of institutions, capacities and practices for the con-structive management of tensions so often associated with the uneven growth or rapidly changing circumstances that appear to benefit some groups more than others.'[48]

The lively debate in the General Assembly among Member States on the Secretary-General's 2009 report, that took place at the end of July 2009, confirmed a continued endorsement of the RtoP principle under the formula of 'three pillars – four crimes', and a 'narrow but deep' approach to RtoP.[49] The majority of States expressed continued support for the prevention and early warning elements of pillars one and two, which were seen as the most important pillars of RtoP. But States shied away from commenting on how to exercise the responsibility under the primacy of pillar one.[50]

The second General Assembly debate on RtoP, on 9 August 2010, concerning the Secretary-General's 2010 report *Early Warning, Assessment and the Responsibility to Protect*, displayed continued but limited disagreement among some States on the status and application of RtoP and some unresolved issues and lingering concerns on the selec-tivity and double standards of application, the legality and legitimacy of the different forms of military force, the lack of clarity between the roles of the Assembly and Council and fear of misuse and abuse of RtoP.[51] The focus on strengthening early warning mechanisms was primarily direc-ted towards the UN, international and regional systems of early warning. One possible venue for strengthening the States' own early warning

---

[46] UNSG, 'Implementing the Responsibility to Protect', para. 68.
[47] *Ibid.*, paras. 13–14.   [48] *Ibid.*, para. 14.
[49] Bellamy, *Global Politics*, pp. 43–4. For a detailed discussion of the relevant debates and the role of the General Assembly, see Ryngaert and Cuyckens, Chapter 5 in this book.
[50] Bellamy, *Global Politics*, p. 44.
[51] UNSG, 'Early Warning, Assessment and the Responsibility to Protect', UN Doc. A/64/864, 14 July 2010.

capacity could be to establish and mandate national human rights institutions (NHRIs) to take on such a role.[52]

The 2011 General Assembly debate on RtoP addressed the Secretary-General's report entitled 'The Role of Regional and Sub-regional Arrangements in Implementing the Responsibility to Protect'.[53] The report also emphasised that the ultimate goal is that States institutionalise and internalise their legal responsibilities in a sustainable manner, and it encouraged States to partner with civil society to prevent mass atrocities.[54] Bottom-up learning processes with regard to self-protection at the village and family levels were mentioned as good practices together with State-to-State and region-to-region learning as means to help States address tension and conflicts through training, education and awareness raising. Regional and sub-regional arrangements were viewed as means of encouragement for State recognition of their obligations under international law and support for identification of sources of friction before these lead to violence or atrocities.[55] Complementarity work at the national level under the Statute of the ICC was further mentioned as an important measure of law enforcement.[56]

With regard to *the legal status of RtoP*, most observers have concluded through the years that RtoP has not yet become a binding 'norm of international law'.[57] This claim still holds and it would be more correct to speak of the 'norm of RtoP' as an international social, political and moral norm which comprises various legal rules as well as various *lex ferenda* (the law as it ought to be) propositions of rules that have not (yet) attained the status of legally binding hard law.[58] Stahn has argued that some of the features of RtoP are already well embedded in

---

[52] See also Bellamy *et al.*, 'Conclusion', in Bellamy *et al.* (eds.), *The Responsibility to Protect and International Law*, pp. 217–22, at p. 218. One possible venue for strengthening the States' own early warning capacity could be to establish and mandate national human rights institutions (NHRIs) to take on such a role.

[53] UNSG, 'The Role of Regional and Sub-regional Arrangements in Implementing the Responsibility to Protect', UN Doc. A/65/877–S/2011/393, 27 June 2011, pp. 3–6.

[54] *Ibid.*, paras. 11–12.   [55] *Ibid.*, paras. 15–17.   [56] *Ibid.*, paras. 19.

[57] Alex Bellamy and Ruben Reike, 'The Responsibility to Protect and International Law', in Bellamy *et al.* (eds.), *The Responsibility to Protect and International Law*, pp. 81–100, at pp. 81–2; Stahn, 'Responsibility to Protect', 101 and 118; Strauss, 'A Bird in the Hand is Worth Two in the Bush', in Bellamy *et al.* (eds.), *The Responsibility to Protect and International Law*, pp. 25–58, at p. 33. On the differences between RtoP as a *concept*, *principle* or *norm*, see Bellamy, *Responsibility to Protect* (Cambridge, UK: Polity Press, 2009), p. 6.

[58] From a legal positivist perspective, the concept of 'norm' or 'rule' within law is a narrower notion than in international relations or in inter-disciplinary scholarship.

contemporary international law, while others are so innovative that it might be premature to speak of crystallising practice.[59] Despite the apparent lack of legal status of the 'norm of RtoP', the endorsed RtoP principle could make existing legal obligations more effective and overcome the fundamental deficit in the current application of legal obligations to protect under international law.[60]

The question, whether the endorsed RtoP principle has created *new legal obligations* apart from the already existing obligations has been answered in the negative by most commentators.[61] The negotiation history of RtoP in the WSOD reveals that the choice of the term 'responsibility' was meant not to imply, include or add new legal obligations apart from those already in existence.[62] The claim of a new right to intervene to halt mass atrocity crimes has neither gained express or sufficient support nor *opinio juris* with regard to non-authorised military interventions.[63] At best it could be argued that the RtoP principle formulation does not expressly prohibit unilateral humanitarian intervention – which is not the same as granting a legal right thereto.[64]

It is not the intention of this chapter to answer the question whether the international political and moral norm of RtoP is also an *'emerging norm' in international law*.[65] Instead the following analysis on the

See Amnéus, 'Responsibility to Protect by Military Means', pp. 30, 48–50 and 53–8. Compare with Jutta Brunnée and Stephen Toope, 'The Responsibility to Protect and the Use of Force', *Global Responsibility to Protect*, 2 (2010), 191–212, at 193 and 203, which take a much broader approach. Submitting to the fact that law can never fully be separated from morality and politics and to a great degree overlaps or is intertwined, I will in this context refer to 'norm' or principle to denote the wider political and moral principle of RtoP as endorsed in the WSOD and 'rule' to refer to some of the more specific legal obligations or rights contained in this norm.

[59] Stahn, 'Responsibility to Protect', 110; cf. Bellamy and Reike, 'International Law', in Bellamy *et al.* (eds.), *The Responsibility to Protect and International Law*, p. 83.

[60] Strauss, *Emperor's New Clothes?*, p. 37.

[61] UNSG, 'Implementing the Responsibility to Protect', para. 11(a); Strauss, *Emperor's New Clothes?*, pp. 37–8; cf. Louise Arbour, 'The Responsibility to Protect as a Duty of Care in International Law and Practice', *Review of International Studies*, 34 (2008), 445–58.

[62] Strauss, 'A Bird in the Hand', in Bellamy *et al.* (eds.), *The Responsibility to Protect and International Law*, p. 48; Bellamy, *Responsibility to Protect*, pp. 84–5.

[63] Amnéus, 'Responsibility to Protect: Emerging Rules on Humanitarian Intervention?', *Global Society*, 26 (2012), 241–76.

[64] Bellamy, *Responsibility to Protect*, pp. 85 and 91, who reveals that it was clear that 'creative ambiguity' was the order of the day in relation to authority during the WSOD negotiations on RtoP.

[65] Compare with Jonah Eaton, 'An Emerging Norm? Determining the Meaning and Legal Status of the Responsibility to Protect', *Michigan Journal of International Law*, 23 (2011), 765–804.

protection responsibilities of the State under RtoP will address the existing or possibly emerging *international legal obligations of States* to protect, prevent and punish grave crimes under pillars one to three.

The primary responsibility to protect under pillar one

The *individual State responsibilities* under pillar one of RtoP were formulated in paragraph 138 of the WSOD. This responsibility reflects obligations under international law such as the treaty and customary obligations to prevent and punish genocide, to respect and ensure respect of international humanitarian law, and the 'duty to respect, protect and fulfil' under international human rights law. Embedded in already existing obligations to prevent grave crimes in international law, the pillar one protection responsibilities of States are considered the least controversial pillar of RtoP.

Not all of the Secretary-General's 2009 suggestions on how to implement pillar one could easily be subsumed under States' international *legal obligations* to prevent genocide, war crimes, or crimes against humanity. Some of the *responsibilities* under pillar one are legal obligations, while others remain at the moral or political level. The manifold examples of practices that may strengthen pillar one implementation comprise both measures to be undertaken by the State itself and also by the State in cooperation with external actors, for example through UN organs, other international and regional organisations and civil society. The report suggests that States may wish to review their achievements of their human rights obligations and to cooperate with the various UN human rights mechanisms, including: assisting the Human Rights Council with the Universal Periodic Review mechanism; acceding to and implementing all relevant international instruments for the protection of human security in domestic laws; strengthening the rule of law, enhancing access to justice and combating impunity through judicial processes (including preventing sexual and gender-based violence); conducting justice and security sector reforms; promoting a lively civil society; receiving technical assistance from the UN on the crafting of legislation; establish independent national institutions and monitoring mechanisms; nurturing NHRIs; participating in peer review mechanisms such as State-to-State learning; carrying out training, learning and educational programmes; giving support to NGOs supporting victims and survivors of mass atrocity crimes; facilitating the creation of networks; and making constructive use of the lessons learned from survivors.[66] The report indicates that the protection responsibilities of the State under RtoP are broader than the *legal* obligations to protect against grave crimes under international law. The following sections will however for the purpose of this book focus on the legal obligations.

Protection obligations of States under international law

State obligations to protect people from genocide, war crimes, ethnic cleansing and crimes against humanity are derived from a State's treaty and customary obligations under international human rights law, international humanitarian law and international criminal law, but also other areas of international law.[67] These may entail obligations of protection, prevention or punishment and may vary in content and scope for each respective crime. The prohibitions on genocide, war crimes and crimes against humanity have also attained the status of *jus cogens*, and the obligations to refrain from and prevent their commission are *erga omnes* – owed to the international community as a whole.[68]

The obligation to protect populations from genocide

The risk and occurrence of the 'crime of genocide'[69] confers legal obligations on States to 'prevent and punish' under the Genocide

---

[66] UNSG, 'Implementing the Responsibility to Protect', paras. 16–26.

[67] On other areas, see Charter of the United Nations, adopted 24 October 1945, 1 UNTS XVI; case law from the International Court of Justice (ICJ), for example *Barcelona Traction, Light and Power Company, Limited (Belgium* v. *Spain), Second Phase, Judgment*, ICJ Reports 1970, paras. 33–4; International Law Commission, 'Draft Articles on Responsibility of States for Internationally Wrongful Acts', in 'Report of the International Law Commission on the Work of Its Fifty-Third Session (23 April–1 June and 2 July–10 August 2001)', UN Doc. A/56/10, ch. IV(E)(1).

[68] 'Such obligations derive, for example, in contemporary international law, from the outlawing of acts of aggression, and of genocide, as also from the principles and rules concerning the basic rights of the human person, including protection from slavery and racial discrimination' (*Barcelona Traction*, para. 34).

[69] See the definition in Convention on the Prevention and Punishment of the Crime of Genocide, adopted 9 December 1948 and entered into force 12 January 1951, UN Doc. A/RES/260 (III), 78 UNTS 277, art. 2. See also the identical definitions in Statute of the International Criminal Tribunal for the Former Yugoslavia, UNSC Res. 808, UN Doc. S/25704, 3 May 1993, annex, art. 4; Statute of the International Criminal Tribunal for Rwanda, UNSC Res. 955, UN Doc. S/RES/955, 8 November 1994, annex, art. 2; and Rome Statute of the International Criminal Court, adopted 17 July 1998 and entered into force 1 July 2002, 2187 UNTS 90.

Convention as well as under customary international law.[70] The ICJ Advisory Opinion on the Reservations to the Genocide Convention affirmed that the general provisions of the Genocide Convention express binding universal principles recognised by civilised nations,[71] and reiterated the condemnation of genocide and of the cooperation required in order to liberate humankind from such an odious scourge. The outlawing of genocide has been considered to constitute *jus cogens*,[72] creating *erga omnes* obligations vis-à-vis other States.[73]

The legal obligations to '*prevent and punish*' genocide are regulated by Article I of the Convention, affirming genocide as a crime under international law, whether committed in time of peace or in time of war. The article does not explicitly prohibit States from committing genocide themselves, but the ICJ has confirmed that such a prohibition follows from the obligation to 'prevent and punish' and from the fact that genocide is a crime under international law.[74] The State must thus ensure that its own organs and officials as well as other individuals or groups under its control do not commit genocide.[75] The Genocide Convention is not specific on what the legal obligation to prevent genocide exactly entails, but the case law from the ICJ elucidates the content of this obligation.[76] According to Strauss, these clarifications should also apply under customary international law.[77]

---

[70] See Convention on Genocide, art. 1; William Schabas, *Genocide in International Law: The Crime of Crimes* (Cambridge University Press, 2000), pp. 495–6.

[71] *Reservations to the Convention on the Prevention and Punishment of the Crime of Genocide, Advisory Opinion*, ICJ Reports 1951, p. 15; Hanne Cuyckens and Philip De Man, 'The Responsibility to Prevent: On Assumed Legal Nature of Responsibility to Protect and its Relationship with Conflict Prevention', in Hoffmann and Nollkaemper (eds.), *From Principle to Practice*, pp. 111–24, at pp. 113–14; this was also confirmed in case law by the two ad hoc tribunals.

[72] Bellamy and Reike, 'International Law', in Bellamy *et al.* (eds.), *The Responsibility to Protect and International Law*, p. 90; Strauss, *Emperor's New Clothes?*, p. 29.

[73] Strauss, 'A Bird in the Hand', in Bellamy *et al.* (eds.), *The Responsibility to Protect and International Law*, p. 50; see also *Barcelona Traction*, paras. 33–4.

[74] *Case Concerning the Application of the Convention on the Prevention and Punishment of the Crime of Genocide (Bosnia and Herzegovina v. Serbia and Montenegro), Judgment*, ICJ Reports 2007, para. 166.

[75] Strauss, *Emperor's New Clothes?*, p. 31.

[76] Siobhán Wills, 'Military Interventions on Behalf of Vulnerable Populations: The Legal Responsibilities of States and International Organizations Engaged in Peace Support Operations', *Journal of Conflict & Security Law*, 9 (2004), 387–418, at 410; for more details, see Zyberi, Chapter 16 in this book.

[77] Strauss, *Emperor's New Clothes?*, p. 30.

In the *Application of the Genocide Convention* case the 'obligation to prevent' genocide was seen as 'unqualified', compelling and free standing from the obligation to punish and other Articles under the Convention.[78] The obligation entails a duty to take positive anticipatory measures and *'employ all means reasonably available'* to prevent genocide so far as possible.[79] As noted by the ICJ, the obligation is one of 'conduct' and not of 'result'.[80] A violation may result from mere failure to adopt suitable preventive measures, but State responsibility for such omissions is only incurred if genocide is actually committed.[81]

The positive obligation arises as soon as 'the State was *aware, or should normally have been aware,* of the serious danger that acts of genocide would be committed'.[82] A relevant factor for assessing whether a State has fulfilled such due diligence is its 'capacity to influence effectively' the action of persons likely to commit, or already committing, genocide. This capacity depends among other things on the geographical distance to the scene of the events and the strength of the political and other links between the authorities of that State and the main actors.[83] When an international criminal law tribunal or court has been given jurisdiction to prosecute individuals for committing genocide, State obligations would also include a duty to cooperate with the tribunal with regard to arrest and transfer of indictees to the court.[84]

---

[78] *Bosnia and Herzegovina* v. *Serbia and Montenegro*, paras. 162 and 427; cf. *ibid.*, para. 159; Sandesh Sivakumaran, 'Application of the Convention on the Prevention and Punishment of the Crime of Genocide (*Bosnia and Herzegovina* v. *Serbia and Montenegro*), Judgment of 26 February 2007', *International and Comparative Law Quarterly*, 56 (2007), 695–708, at 701–5.

[79] *Bosnia and Herzegovina* v. *Serbia and Montenegro*, paras. 428–38. The court stated that 'the ban on genocide and the other acts listed in Article III, including complicity, places States under a negative obligation ... while the duty to prevent places States under positive obligations, to do their best to ensure that such acts do not occur' (*ibid.*, para. 432).

[80] *Ibid.*, para. 430 (emphasis added).

[81] *Ibid.*, paras. 431–2; Marko Milanović, 'State Responsibility for Genocide: A Follow-up', *European Journal of International Law*, 18 (2007), 669–94, at 687.

[82] *Bosnia and Herzegovina* v. *Serbia and Montenegro*, paras. 431–2. This statement has been met with scepticism for not being supported by international practice. See Andrea Gattini, 'Breach of the Obligation to Prevent and Reparation thereof in the ICJ's Genocide Judgment', *European Journal of International Law*, 18 (2007), 695–713, at 702.

[83] *Bosnia and Herzegovina* v. *Serbia and Montenegro*, para. 430.

[84] Strauss, *Emperor's New Clothes?*, p. 31.

The obligation to respect and ensure respect for humanitarian law: preventing war crimes

A variation of definitions on what constitutes 'war crimes' can be found in several international instruments such as the four Geneva Conventions (1949), the Statutes of the two ad hoc tribunals,[85] and most recently in the ICC Statute. War crimes are serious violations of customary or treaty-based international humanitarian law, binding on the parties to an armed conflict at the time of the offence,[86] and generally refer to grave breaches of the four Geneva Conventions and other serious violations of the laws and customs applicable in armed conflict.[87] A violation is of a serious nature and treated as a war crime if it endangers protected persons or objects, or if it breaches a rule protecting important values.[88]

The legal obligation to '*respect and ensure the respect*' for humanitarian law is established in Common Article 1 of the Geneva Conventions and in customary international law. It applies independent of violations by adversaries and irrespective of the lawfulness of the war.[89] Common Article 1 and Article 1(1) of Additional Protocol I to the Geneva Conventions stipulate that States Parties have a legal obligation to respect and to ensure respect for the Conventions 'in all circumstances'.[90] The *Nicaragua* case asserted that the obligation to respect is binding also for non-States Parties under customary law, including in non-international armed conflicts where Common Article 3 is to be observed and respected 'in all circumstances'.[91] The extent of

---

[85] The International Criminal Tribunal for the Former Yugoslavia (ICTY) and the International Criminal Tribunal for Rwanda (ICTR).

[86] Jean-Marie Henckaerts and Louise Doswald-Beck (eds.), *Customary International Humanitarian Law: Volume I, Rules* (Cambridge University Press, 2009), rule 156.

[87] Strauss, *Emperor's New Clothes?*, p. 32.

[88] Henckaerts and Doswald-Beck (eds.), *Customary International Humanitarian Law*, pp. 569–70.

[89] Vienna Convention on the Law of Treaties, adopted 23 May 1969 and entered into force 27 January 1980, 1155 UNTS 331, art. 60; Henckaerts and Doswald-Beck (eds.), *Customary International Humanitarian Law*, rule 140.

[90] 'In all circumstances' does not cover the case of civil war, as the Common Article 3 applies to these situations.

[91] *Military and Paramilitary Activities in and against Nicaragua (Nicaragua v. United States of America)*, Merits, Judgment, ICJ Reports 1986, para. 220; Henckaerts and Doswald-Beck (eds.), *Customary International Humanitarian Law*, rule 139; Strauss, *Emperor's New Clothes?*, p. 33. The legal obligation to respect and ensure the respect of humanitarian law does, however, not have an explicit equivalence in Protocol Additional to the Geneva Conventions of 12 August 1949 and Relating to the

customary international law in non-international armed conflicts is less certain outside Common Article 3, but the fundamental principles of humanitarian law have been affirmed by the ICJ to constitute customary international law.[92] The ICJ furthermore asserted that these fundamental customary norms embody obligations that are essentially of *erga omnes* character.[93] The International Committee of the Red Cross (ICRC) study on customary international humanitarian law holds that many of the customary rules applicable in international armed conflict are applicable in non-international armed conflicts.[94] The customary obligation to respect IHL provides that States may not encourage violations of international humanitarian law and must exert their influence, to the extent possible, to stop such violations.[95]

The specific measures to be executed under the obligation to 'respect and ensure respect' have not been more closely defined other than by means of the examples in Articles 7 and 89 (see the section below on pillars two and three).[96] However, the ICRC Commentary to Common Article 1 is explicit in that a State must of necessity prepare in advance in peacetime, the legal, material or other means of ensuring the faithful enforcement of the Convention when the occasion arises, and to supervise the execution of the orders it gives.[97] States must make available legal advisers to military commanders and impose command

Protection of Victims of Non-International Armed Conflicts, adopted 8 June 1977 and entered into force 7 December 1978, 1125 UNTS 609.

[92] 'It is undoubtedly because a great many rules of humanitarian law applicable in armed conflict are so fundamental to the respect of the human person and "elementary considerations of humanity" as the Court put it in its Judgment of 9 April 1949 in the *Corfu Channel* case (ICJ Reports 1949, p. 22), that the Hague and Geneva Conventions have enjoyed a broad accession. Further these fundamental rules are to be observed by all States whether or not they have ratified the conventions that contain them, because they constitute intransgressible principles of international customary law' (*Legality of the Threat or Use of Nuclear Weapons, Advisory Opinion*, ICJ Reports 1996, para. 79).

[93] *Legal Consequences of the Construction of a Wall in the Occupied Palestinian Territory, Advisory Opinion*, ICJ Reports 2004, para. 157.

[94] Henckaerts and Doswald-Beck (eds.), *Customary International Humanitarian Law*; Strauss, 'A Bird in the Hand', in Bellamy *et al.* (eds.), *The Responsibility to Protect and International Law*, p. 48.

[95] Henckaerts and Doswald-Beck (eds.), *Customary International Humanitarian Law*, rule 144.

[96] Hanna Brollowski, 'The Responsibility to Protect and Common Article I of the 1949 Geneva Conventions and Obligations of Third States', in Hoffmann and Nollkaemper (eds.), *From Principle to Practice*, pp. 93–110, at p. 97.

[97] Jean Pictet (ed.), *Commentary on the Geneva Conventions of 12 August 1949: Relative to the Protection of Civilian Persons in Time of War* (Geneva: International Committee of the Red Cross, 1960), p. 16.

responsibility for violations by subordinates under their control.[98] It furthermore conveys that the duty means to ensure 'respect by civilian and military authorities, the members of the armed forces, and in general, by the population as a whole'.[99] Moreover, the contracting parties are no longer merely required to take the necessary legislative action to prevent or repress violations but are under an obligation to seek out and prosecute the guilty parties, and cannot evade their responsibility.[100] The obligation thus includes a duty to ensure that grave breaches are not committed and to enact necessary legislation for the criminalisation of such acts, including the duty to prosecute or extradite responsible persons.[101] It is an obligation for States to do all in their power to ensure that humanitarian law is respected *universally*,[102] as will be explained further below in the section on obligations under pillars two and three.

The prohibition on crimes against humanity

The expression 'crimes against humanity' was used first to describe the atrocities committed against the Armenian population in the Ottoman Empire. However, the first prosecution of 'crimes against humanity' would not be until the Nuremberg Trials following the Second World War.[103] Various definitions of crimes against humanity appear throughout history,[104] and the normative uncertainties regarding what may constitute such a crime have not been mitigated by the diverging and somewhat

---

[98] Strauss, *Emperor's New Clothes?*, p. 33.

[99] The duty covers 'armed forces and other persons or groups acting in fact on its instructions, or under its direction or control' (Yves Sandoz, Christophe Swinarski and Bruno Zimmermann (eds.), *Commentary on the Additional Protocols of 8 June 1977 to the Geneva Conventions of 12 August 1949* (Geneva: International Committee of the Red Cross/Martinus Nijhoff, 1987), p. 35). See also Henckaerts and Doswald-Beck (eds.), *Customary International Humanitarian Law*, rule 139.

[100] Pictet (ed.), *Civilian Persons in Time of War*, p. 17, fn. 2.

[101] The duty to 'prosecute or extradite' suspected perpetrators does not cover other prohibited acts which are not grave breaches under the relevant treaties, however, the duty to prosecute or extradite war crimes is also a rule under customary international law. Strauss, *Emperor's New Clothes?*, p. 36.

[102] Pictet (ed.), *Civilian Persons in Time of War*, p. 16; Sandoz et al. (eds.), *Additional Protocols of 8 June 1977*, p. 36.

[103] Schabas, *The International Criminal Court: A Commentary on the Rome Statute* (Oxford University Press, 2010), p. 139.

[104] The crime was first included in an international instrument through the Charters of the Military Tribunals at Nuremberg and Tokyo, and has been incorporated in several domestic penal codes. Leila Nadya Sadat (ed.), *Forging a Convention for Crimes against Humanity* (Cambridge University Press, 2011), pp. xix–xxii; Gerhard Werle, *Principles of International Criminal Law* (The Hague: TMC Asser, 2005), para. 641.

contradictory definitions in the Statutes of the ad hoc tribunals and Special Court for Sierra Leone, one example being the nexus to an armed conflict. The definition in the ICC Statute has come to provide the most refined, clear and broad definition, intended for universal acceptance.

The ICC definition of crimes against humanity in Article 7 represents both a codification and progressive development of international law and has a similar structure to those in the ICTY and ICTR Statutes.[105] The ICTY and ICTR have reaffirmed the customary law character of 'crimes against humanity',[106] and its prohibition is also considered to be part of *jus cogens*.[107] The peremptory norm establishes a prohibition to commit crimes against humanity and an ensuing *erga omnes* obligation to prevent the crime and the international community as a whole has a legal interest in the prosecution of such crimes.[108] States must thus ensure that their officials and organs as well as groups or individuals under their overall control refrain from committing crimes against humanity, and must take measures to prevent the commission of such crimes.[109] This would arguably include the obligation to criminalise, investigate and punish individual perpetrators of crimes against humanity.[110]

States may also have obligations to cooperate with an international tribunal or court prosecuting crimes against humanity, including to arrest and transfer indictees. The ICTY jurisprudence suggests, however, more limited cross-border obligations for crimes against humanity and there are no generalised legal duties beyond the obligation to refrain from and prevent its commission.[111]

---

[105] Kai Ambos, 'Crimes Against Humanity and the ICC', in Sadat (ed.), *Crimes against Humanity*, pp. 279–304, at pp. 280–3; cf. Jann Kleffner, 'The Scope of the Crimes Triggering the Responsibility to Protect', in Hoffmann and Nollkaemper (eds.), *From Principle to Practice*, pp. 85–92, at p. 88.

[106] Werle, *International Criminal Law*, para. 641.

[107] Lauri Hannikainen, *Peremptory Norms (Jus Cogens) in International Law* (Helsinki: Finnish Lawyers' Publishing Company, 1988), p. 434; Strauss, *Emperor's New Clothes?*, p. 34; Bellamy and Reike, 'International Law', in Bellamy *et al.* (eds.), *The Responsibility to Protect and International Law*, p. 93.

[108] Alexander Orakhelashvili, *Peremptory Norms in International Law* (Oxford University Press, 2006), p. 288.

[109] Strauss, *Emperor's New Clothes?*, p. 34.

[110] Compare with obligations of States under Article 8 of the Proposed International Convention on the Prevention and Punishment of Crimes. Sadat (ed.), *Crimes Against Humanity*, p. 363.

[111] Tarun Chhabra and Jeremy Zucker, 'Defining the Crimes', in Genser and Cotler (eds.), *The Promise of Stopping Mass Atrocities*, pp. 37–61, at p. 52.

'Crimes against humanity might usefully be viewed as an implementation of human rights norms within international criminal law.'[112]
Since the legal foundations of RtoP comprise international human rights
law, another line of argumentation that may be pursued is to draw on
States' obligations under human rights law to *respect, protect and fulfil*
human rights.[113] States are obliged to *respect* human rights by the
negative obligation to refrain from such violations by their agents and
organs, and also have a positive *'duty to protect'* human rights by taking
measures to ensure that human rights are enforced between private
actors and prevent breaches by third parties, and are furthermore
under a positive obligation to *fulfil* the human rights through the adoption of comprehensive legal, institutional and procedural measures for
their full realisation.[114]

The *'duty to protect'* human rights can be either preventive or remedial
post hoc and arises only in so far as the State is *aware or should have been
aware* of the violation or threat of violation and has the legal means to
prevent it. While there is no explicit treaty obligation in human rights
law to protect against violations by private, non-State actors, the positive
obligations under the 'duty to protect' have evolved through the *principle
of due diligence* to prevent, investigate, prosecute, punish and provide
remedies. The principle can be identified in various soft law instruments
as well as in case law from the Inter-American Court of Human Rights
starting with the *Velásquez Rodríguez* case, later confirmed and developed by other human rights courts and bodies.[115] The question of which
exact human rights give rise to a claim for protection and to what extent

---

[112] Schabas, *International Criminal Court*, p. 139.

[113] Rosenberg, 'A Framework for Prevention', in Bellamy *et al.* (eds.), *The Responsibility to
Protect and International Law*, pp. 165–75; Dorota Gierycz, 'The Responsibility to
Protect: A Legal and Rights-Based Perspective', in Bellamy *et al.* (eds.), *The
Responsibility to Protect and International Law*, pp. 101–18, at pp. 104–17.

[114] Walter Kälin and Jörg Künzli, *The Law of International Human Rights Protection*
(Oxford University Press, 2010), pp. 96–7.

[115] *Velásquez Rodríguez v. Honduras, Judgment*, IACtHR, Series C, No. 4, 29 July 1988;
*Case of González et al. ('Cotton Field') v. Mexico, Preliminary Objection, Merits,
Reparations and Costs, Judgment*, IACtHR, Series C, No. 205, 16 November 2009;
Opuz v. Turkey, Judgment, ECtHR, Application No. 33401/02, 9 June 2009; *M.C. v.
Bulgaria, Judgment*, ECtHR, Application No. 39272/98, 4 December 2003; *Sudan
Human Rights Organisation and Centre on Housing Rights and Evictions v. Sudan*,
African Commission on Human and Peoples Rights (ACHPR), Communication Nos.
279/03 and 296/05, 2009; *Saadia Ali v. Tunisia*, Committee Against Torture (CAT),
Communication No. 291/2006, CAT Doc. CAT/C/41/291/2006, 21 November 2008;
Ms. A. T. v. Hungary, Committee on the Elimination of Discrimination Against

has not yet been conclusively resolved, but many of the fundamental and other human rights provide for such a duty.[116]

The obligation to prevent ethnic cleansing

The term *ethnic cleansing* has been defined as 'rendering an area ethnically homogenous by using force or intimidation to remove persons of given groups from that area'.[117] The term has no immediate legal significance: instead, the acts may under certain circumstances be subsumed under each of the other three crimes defined in international law.[118] Different acts and practices may constitute ethnic cleansing, such as deportation, forcible transfer, displacement, killings, destruction of houses and so on, and may qualify as either crimes against humanity, war crimes or even genocide when the required subjective and material elements of the specific crime are met.[119] The obligations to protect and prevent ethnic cleansing consequently arise under the obligations to prevent the respective crimes accounted for in the previous sections.[120]

State obligations to protect under pillars two and three

The important and varying roles of international and regional actors in the implementation of RtoP are taking shape and root in the international political practice and security discourse on mass atrocity prevention and management. An overwhelming majority of States are supportive of the collective responsibility to assist other States in capacity-building under 'pillar two',[121] while a minority of States are continuously resistant or

Women (CEDAW), Communication No. 2/2003, 26 January 2005. See also Rosenberg, 'A Framework for Prevention', in Bellamy *et al.* (eds.), *The Responsibility to Protect and International Law*, pp. 168–75. However, this principle should be distinguished from the very specific treaty-based notion of due diligence used by the ICJ in the *Bosnia* v. *Serbia* case to assess the extra-territorial obligations to prevent genocide.

[116] Kälin and Künzli, *The Law of International Human Rights Protection*, pp. 106ff.; see also Carin Benninger-Budel, *Due Diligence and Its Application to Protect Women from Violence* (Leiden: Martinus Nijhoff, 2008).

[117] *Bosnia and Herzegovina* v. *Serbia and Montenegro*, para. 190.

[118] Strauss, 'A Bird in the Hand', in Bellamy *et al.* (eds.), *The Responsibility to Protect and International Law*, pp. 49–50.

[119] Kleffner, 'The Scope of the Crimes', in Hoffmann and Nollkaemper (eds.), *From Principle to Practice*, p. 87.

[120] See for example Strauss, *Emperor's New Clothes?*, p. 36.

[121] According to the Secretary-General's 2009 report, pillar two responsibilities builds on the request and express consent of the host State. See the four forms presented in UNSG, 'Implementing the Responsibility to Protect', para. 28; and on specific measures, Bellamy, *Global Politics*, pp. 37–8.

sceptical towards the application of more robust and coercive action under 'pillar three' as timely and decisive response.[122]

The differing positions taken on RtoP by States are to some extent related to the lack of clarity in the more specific content, scope, remit, thresholds and application of the respective collective responsibilities under these pillars, for States, international organisations and other actors, be it diplomatic, political, economic or military. These variable responsibilities will be analysed further in the following chapters of this book with regard to distinct actors. This section of the chapter will therefore pay exclusive attention to the collective *State* responsibilities under these pillars that can be traced to the *legal* domain – the specific legal obligations of States to protect also outside their own territory.[123] The following analysis confirms previous scholarly identification of normative weaknesses in the international legal rules with regard to extra-territorial duties to prevent crimes against humanity, while for the prevention of genocide and war crimes all States are under strong treaty and customary legal obligations, to undertake a wide range of measures for their prevention also in other States.[124]

The *extra-territorial obligations to prevent genocide* under the Genocide Convention impose far-reaching obligations outside the territories of States when there are links to the perpetrators and the commission of genocide. The ICJ asserted already in 1996 that the rights and obligations enshrined in the Convention are *erga omnes*, and not territorially limited.[125] In the 2007 judgment the ICJ delineated the scope of the extra-territoriality,[126] asserting that Articles I and III apply to a State 'wherever it may be acting or may be able to act in ways appropriate to

---

[122] Pillar three responsibilities can be exercised in two steps, the first referring to peaceful, diplomatic, humanitarian and other measures under Chapters VI and VIII of the UN Charter, while the second involves a range of coercive measures under Chapter VII, including use of military force as a last resort when a State manifestly fails to protect. Part of the toolkit of responsive measures was illustrated by the Security Council resolutions in the Libya case, UNSC Res. 1970, UN Doc. S/RES/1970, 26 February 2011 (non-military) and UNSC Res. 1973, UN Doc. S/RES/1973, 17 March 2011 (military).

[123] Compare with Luke Glanville, 'The Responsibility to Protect Beyond Borders', *Human Rights Law Review*, 12 (2012), 1–32.

[124] Cuyckens and De Man, 'The Responsibility to Prevent', in Hoffmann and Nollkaemper (eds.), *From Principle to Practice*, p. 114.

[125] *Case Concerning Application of the Convention on the Prevention and Punishment of the Crime of Genocide (Bosnia and Herzegovina v. Yugoslavia), Preliminary Objections, Judgment*, ICJ Reports 1996, para. 31.

[126] *Bosnia and Herzegovina v. Serbia and Montenegro*, para. 154; see also Bellamy and Reike, 'International Law', in Bellamy *et al.* (eds.), *The Responsibility to Protect and*

meeting the obligations in question'.[127] The obligation is directly proportionate to the State's 'capacity to effectively influence' the actions[128]
indicating the necessary level of control over the actors.[129]

When it comes to measures for the implementation of the duty to
prevent genocide beyond State territory, the possibility to use military
force must comply with the general rules on the use of force under
international law.[130] The Genocide Convention does not expressly vest
States Parties or the UN with such a legal right, and the ICJ case law does
not extend the duty to include the use of military force in another State
even if there are links to the perpetrator. It has been argued that limited
State practice of responses when links are lacking may suggest that this
represents a practice of permissibility of inactivity.[131]

The *obligation to enforce humanitarian law universally* embedded in
the obligation to respect and ensure respect for humanitarian law provides a strong legal basis for States to take positive measures under RtoP
outside its own territories. States have extra-territorial obligations under
Common Article 1 to the Geneva Conventions to take wide-ranging
measures to ensure the respect of humanitarian law in *international*
armed conflicts. The ICRC Commentary states that:

> In the event of a member state failing to fulfil its obligations, the other
> contracting parties (neutral, allied or enemy) may, and should, endeav-
> our to bring it back to an attitude of respect for the Convention, and
> should not be content merely to apply its provisions themselves, but
> 'should do everything in their power to ensure that the humanitarian
> principles underlying the Conventions are applied universally'.[132]

International Law, p. 95; Rosenberg, 'A Framework for Prevention', in Bellamy *et al.*
(eds.), *The Responsibility to Protect and International Law*, pp. 175ff.

[127] *Bosnia and Herzegovina* v. *Serbia and Montenegro*, para. 183.

[128] *Ibid.*, para. 430; Milanović, 'State Responsibility for Genocide', 686.

[129] The ICJ rejected the 'overall control' test adopted by ICTY in the *Tadić* case, and instead
used its own test on 'effective control' and attribution for acts by non-State actors
applied in the *Nicaragua* case. The 'overall control' test was considered to overly
broaden the scope of State responsibility (*Nicaragua* v. *The United States of America*,
para. 115); *Prosecutor* v. *Tadić*, ICTY, Case No. IT-94-1-A, 15 July 1999, para. 120;
Cassese, 'The *Nicaragua* and *Tadić* Tests Revisited in Light of the ICJ Judgment on
Genocide in Bosnia', *European Journal of International Law*, 18 (2007), 649–68, at
652–3 and 665; Milanović, 'State Responsibility for Genocide', 670.

[130] Milanović, 'State Responsibility for Genocide', 687; *Bosnia and Herzegovina* v. *Serbia
and Montenegro*, para. 430.

[131] Schabas, *Genocide in International Law*, p. 495.

[132] Pictet (ed.), *Civilian Persons in Time of War*, p. 16; Sandoz *et al.* (eds.), *Additional
Protocols of 8 June 1977*, p. 36.

Supported by various examples of current State practice of measures to be taken, Brollowski argues in line with Kalshoven that Common Article 1 of the Geneva Conventions creates obligations also for *third* States to fulfil the obligation to 'ensure respect of humanitarian law'.[133] This also applies in non-international armed conflict with regard to Common Article 3 and customary law.[134] Rule 144 of the 2005 ICRC customary international humanitarian law study provides that States must exert their influence to the degree possible to stop violations of humanitarian law in all types of armed conflicts.[135]

Furthermore, States Parties have a legal obligation to repress breaches of humanitarian law in *international* armed conflicts under Article 89 of the Additional Protocol I, stipulating that '[i]n situations of serious violations of the Conventions or of this Protocol, the High Contracting Parties undertake to act, jointly or individually, in co-operation with the United Nations and in conformity with the United Nations Charter.' However, international law imposes legal limitations on action under Article 89, 'particularly the prohibition on the use of force' and requires conformity with the UN Charter.[136] Nor does Common Article 1 constitute an independent legal right to use military force,[137] even if the obligation to 'respect and ensure respect' leaves the measures to be taken to the discretion of States.[138]

The *erga omnes obligations owed under peremptory norms* is another area of law influencing the responsibilities under pillars two and three. Stahn has noted that the protection responsibilities of 'every' State under RtoP is a simple reminder of the *erga omnes* nature of international obligations on the 'prohibition on genocide and torture, and grave breaches of the Geneva Conventions'.[139] It is generally accepted that 'obligations towards the international community as a whole' arise under 'peremptory norms' of general international

[133] See Brollowski, 'Common Article I', in Hoffmann and Nollkaemper (eds.), *From Principle to Practice*, pp. 97–103.

[134] Henckaerts and Doswald-Beck (eds.), *Customary International Humanitarian Law*, rule 144.

[135] *Ibid.*

[136] Sandoz *et al.* (eds.), *Additional Protocols of 8 June 1977*, p. 36; See Brollowski, 'Common Article I', in Hoffmann and Nollkaemper (eds.), *From Principle to Practice*, p. 101.

[137] Henckaerts and Doswald-Beck (eds.), *Customary International Humanitarian Law*, p. 512. Chhabra and Zucker, 'Defining the Crimes', in Genser and Cotler (eds.), *The Promise of Stopping Mass Atrocities*, p. 50.

[138] *Ibid.*   [139] Stahn, 'Responsibility to Protect', 105.

law.[140] No treaty law regulates the legal consequences of *erga omnes* obligations but some case law has elucidated the matter.[141] Following the *Barcelona Traction* case, the International Law Commission (ILC) has taken the view that *erga omnes* obligations and peremptory norms are essentially two sides of the same coin.[142] There is a substantial overlap, but the difference lies in the focus, on the scope and priority accorded to a certain number of fundamental obligations (peremptory norms)[143] and the legal interests of all States in their compliance (*erga omnes* obligations).[144] Peremptory norms entail obligations owed to the international community as a whole, to respect and ensure such norms.

By and large *erga omnes* obligations can be viewed as secondary rules but the two concepts also overlap to a certain extent in that the primary rules are basically the same, according to Kadelbach.[145] The interlinkage between a breach of a peremptory norm and the applicable secondary rules varies greatly, that is why the conceivable sanctions must be specifically ascertained in each instance.[146] *Erga omnes* obligations are arguably not only obligations owed by every State vis-à-vis all other States, but several scholars also argue that they are shared by all States as 'collective obligations'.[147]

---

[140] ILC, 'Fifty-Third Session', *Yearbook of the International Law Commission, 1966*, vol. II, UN Doc. A/CN.4/SER.A/1966/Add.l, pp. 281–2, para. 7. See also André de Hoogh, *Obligations Erga Omnes and International Crimes: A Theoretical Inquiry into the Implementation and Enforcement of the International Responsibility of States* (The Hague: Kluwer Law International, 1996); Christian Tams, *Enforcing Obligations Erga Omnes in International Law* (Cambridge University Press, 2005); Christian Tomuschat and Jean-Marc Thouvenin (eds.), *The Fundamental Rules of the International Legal Order: Jus Cogens and Obligations Erga Omnes* (Leiden: Martinus Nijhoff, 2006).

[141] Stefan Kadelbach, 'Jus Cogens, Obligations *Erga omnes*, and Other Rules – The Identification of Fundamental Norms', in Tomuschat and Thouvenin (eds.), *International Legal Order*, pp. 21–40, at pp. 35–9.

[142] Ian Scobbie, 'The Invocation of Responsibility for the Breach of "Obligations under Peremptory Norms of General International Law"', *European Journal of International Law*, 13 (2002), 1201–20, at 1210.

[143] Among the examples mentioned of peremptory norms are the prohibition of genocide, slavery and slave trading, the principle of self-determination, the unlawful use of force and violations of human rights. ILC, 'Fifty-Third Session', pp. 281–2, para. 7, fn. 675.

[144] ILC, 'Fifty-Third Session', pp. 281–2, para. 7.

[145] Kadelbach, 'Jus Cogens, Obligations *Erga Omnes*, and Other Rules', in Tomuschat and Thouvenin (eds.), *International Legal Order*, pp. 26–7 and 35–8, who mentions the prohibitions on genocide, crimes against humanity, war crimes, aggression, etc.

[146] Tomuschat, 'Reconceptualizing the Debate on *Jus Cogens* and Obligations *Erga Omnes* – Concluding Observations', in Tomuschat and Thouvenin (eds.), *International Legal Order*, pp. 425–36, at p. 429.

[147] Cf. Hannes Peltonen, 'Modelling International Collective Responsibility: The Case of Grave Humanitarian Crises', *Review of International Studies*, 36 (2010), 239–55, at 249;

While the 'obligation to prevent genocide' may be referred to as an *erga omnes* obligation with extra-territorial reach,[148] and humanitarian law creates universal *erga omnes* obligations towards the international community as a whole, including in internal armed conflicts,[149] the obligation to prevent crimes against humanity does not have a similar extra-territorial or universal reach.[150] The obligation to prevent crimes against humanity outside the State territory has no explicit treaty basis and is thus more limited in scope.[151] However, since its prohibition is a peremptory norm, it may be argued that it carries ensuing *erga omnes* obligations and that all States have a legal interest on its prevention and suppression based on customary law and *jus cogens*. However, an extra-territorial obligation to prevent crimes against humanity based on *erga omnes* has not expressly been accepted by States yet.[152]

The *obligation to cooperate to end serious breaches of peremptory norms under the secondary rules on State responsibility* has not yet been fully confirmed under international law. The legal consequences flowing from such serious breaches were considered progressive in the International Law Commission (ILC) Draft Articles on State

referring to the EU, Christian Tams and Alessandra Asteriti, '*Erga Omnes, Jus Cogens, and Their Impact on the Law on State Responsibility*', in Malcolm Evans and Panos Koutrakis (eds.), *The International Responsibility of the European Union* (Oxford: Hart Publishing, 2013).

[148] Toope, 'Does International Law Impose a Duty upon the United Nations to Prevent Genocide?', *McGill Law Journal*, 46 (2000–1), 187–94, at 193. A breach of the obligation to prevent genocide does not, however, in itself constitute a violation of *jus cogens*, according to Gattini ('ICJ's Genocide Judgment', at 697).

[149] Sandoz *et al.* (eds.), *Additional Protocols of 8 June 1977*, p. 36; Henckaerts and Doswald-Beck (eds.), *Customary International Humanitarian Law*, p. 512; Orakhelashvili, *Peremptory Norms in International Law*, p. 61. The view that this entails obligations also for non-parties to a conflict is not shared by all States according to Strauss (*Emperor's New Clothes?*, p. 33); see also Chhabra and Zucker, 'Defining the Crimes', in Genser and Cotler (eds.), *The Promise of Stopping Mass Atrocities*, p. 50. But State practice shows an overwhelming use of diplomatic protests and collective measures through which States exert their influence to stop violations, such as international conferences, resolutions, international tribunals, Commissions of Inquiry, peace-enforcement operations, sanctions and other coercive measures through the Security Council.

[150] Cuyckens and De Man, 'The Responsibility to Prevent', in Hoffmann and Nollkaemper (eds.), *From Principle to Practice*, p. 114. See however, the recent initiative to fill this gap with a new convention: Sadat (ed.), *Crimes Against Humanity*.

[151] Strauss, *Emperor's New Clothes?*, p. 35; Bellamy and Reike, 'International Law', in Bellamy *et al.* (eds.), *The Responsibility to Protect and International Law*, p. 93.

[152] On the scope and structure of *erga omnes* obligations and its relationship to *jus cogens*, see Maurizio Ragazzi, *The Concept of International Obligations Erga Omnes* (Oxford: Clarendon Press, 2000), pp. 133–4, 189–90 and 200.

Responsibility and beyond established customary international law.[153] These secondary rules provide that any State may invoke State responsibility for such breaches since all States are considered injured parties when a peremptory norm is breached.[154] The obligations of third States entail a 'duty to co-operate' to put an end to a serious breach by lawful means, an obligation of non-recognition as well as non-assistance to maintaining the situation created by the breach.[155] However, State practice on the negative duties of non-recognition and non-assistance has been confirmed for a long time,[156] while the positive duty to cooperate to put an end to a serious breach has not matured into hard law yet.[157]

There are no specified procedures for determining when a serious breach has been committed, but the ILC argues that they are likely to be addressed by the competent international organisation such as the Security Council and the General Assembly.[158] The decision of responses to genocide or war crimes remains a choice, not a duty imposed on States.[159] On the choice of consequences, both *individual and collective* responsibility have been envisaged:

> Co-operation could be organised in the framework of a competent international organisation, in particular the United Nations. However, paragraph 1 also envisages the possibility of non-institutionalised co-operation ... Neither does paragraph 1 prescribe what measures States should take in order to bring an end to serious breaches in the sense of article 40. Such co-operation must be through lawful means, the choice of which will depend on the circumstances of the given situation.[160]

---

[153] ILC, 'Fifty-Third Session', pp. 281–2, para. 7. A breach is serious if it involves a gross or systematic failure by the responsible State to fulfil its obligations. See ILC, 'Draft Articles on Internationally Wrongful Acts', art. 40(2).

[154] See ILC, 'Draft Articles on Internationally Wrongful Acts', art. 48(1)(b). Article 48(2) provides that a State may claim cessation of the wrongful act, assurances and guarantees of non-repetition and reparation in the interest of the injured State or of the beneficiaries of the obligation breached.

[155] ILC, 'Draft Articles on Internationally Wrongful Acts', art. 41.

[156] Hannikainen, *Peremptory Norms*, pp. 301–7; *Wall in the Occupied Palestinian Territory*, para. 159.

[157] Tams and Asteriti, '*Erga Omnes, Jus Cogens*', in Evans and Koutrakis (eds.), *European Union*, p. 18.

[158] ILC, 'Fifty-Third Session', art. 40, commentary, p. 286, para. 9.

[159] Milanović, 'State Responsibility for Genocide', 603, with reference to the ILC, 'Draft Articles on Internationally Wrongful Acts', art. 41(3).

[160] ILC, 'Fifty-Third Session', art. 41, commentary, p. 287, paras. 2–3. The 'duty to cooperate' in cases of 'aggravated responsibility' admits lawful uses of military force.

Klein welcomes non-institutionalised cooperation as some established institutionalised responses carry legitimacy deficits,[161] while Glanville views collective State obligations through institutionalisation in the form of international organisations as the means to perfect the collective duty to cooperate and coordinate effective response, albeit recognising that this duty rests on very weak legal grounds.[162] Stahn has claimed that the 'duty of co-operation' comes close to the idea of the collective State 'responsibility to protect' envisaged in the concept of RtoP, but believes that RtoP marks an even more progressive development.[163]

Variable responsibilities under RtoP

As the analysis above has illustrated, 'State responsibility' in the context of RtoP could take several meanings from an *international law* perspective: first, it denotes an *individual State's* responsibility to protect its own population from mass atrocity crimes under pillar one, based on the obligations to prevent and punish genocide, war crimes and crimes against humanity. Second, the *individual State's* RtoP also extends outside the State territory under pillars two and three based on the extra-territorial obligations in the Genocide and Geneva Conventions and under customary international law (*erga omnes*). Third, *collective State* RtoP under pillars two and three, leaning on less clear or express legal obligations but on the peremptory character of the grave crimes, lend all States legal interests in their compliance and thus ensuing *erga omnes* obligations to prevent and halt the commission of such crimes – also collectively.[164] Furthermore, a progressive reading of the law on State responsibility in relation to serious breaches of peremptory norms provides a *lex ferenda* 'duty to cooperate'. Fourth, it necessarily includes the *attribution of State responsibility* and accountability for war crimes, crimes against humanity and genocide.[165]

---

[161] Pierre Klein, 'Responsibility for Serious Breaches of Obligations Deriving from Peremptory Norms of International Law and United Nations Law', *European Journal of International Law*, 13 (2002), 1241–55, at 1253.

[162] Glanville, 'On the Meaning of "Responsibility" in the "Responsibility to Protect"', *Griffith Law Review*, 20 (2011), 482–504; and Glanville, 'Beyond Borders', 28. Glanville also relates the collective RtoP to the responsibility of international organisations.

[163] Stahn, 'Responsibility to Protect', 115–16.

[164] Cf. Milanović, 'State Responsibility for Genocide', 688.

[165] See for example, ILC, 'Draft Articles on Internationally Wrongful Acts', arts. 4–11.

While only the first example of State responsibility falls under pillar one, both the second and third forms fall under pillars two and three. The manifold forms of individual State responsibility in international law in relation to the different crimes as well as the various responsibilities under the different pillars contribute to troublesome ambiguities on State and collective responsibilities under RtoP.[166] The variability is further enhanced by the multitude of perspectives on responsibilities viewed from the moral and political horizons influencing the policy, diplomatic and scholarly discourses.[167] The several meanings and applications of the term 'responsibility' within the norm of RtoP are sources of confusion and different understandings.[168] The specific contents, thresholds and scope of obligations for individual and collective responsibilities remain to be further examined, conceptualised and clarified with regard to the distinct crimes.[169] The following chapters of the book will elucidate the collective responsibilities and roles of specific actors under the different RtoP pillars, especially under pillars two and three.

[166] On the indeterminacy of the norm of RtoP, in particular of pillars two and three on what RtoP prescribes for States and other actors, see Bellamy, 'The Responsibility to Protect – Five Years On', *Ethics and International Affairs*, 24 (2010), 143–69; Bellamy, *Global Politics*, pp. 85–6; cf. Rosenberg, 'A Framework for Prevention', in Bellamy *et al.* (eds.), *The Responsibility to Protect and International Law*, p. 187.

[167] See for example, the analysis of the moral, legal and political responsibilities embedded in RtoP. Glanville, 'The International Community's Responsibility to Protect', *Global Responsibility to Protect*, 2 (2010), 287–306.

[168] Compare with the broader approaches in Chhabra and Zucker, 'Defining the Crimes', in Genser and Cotler (eds.), *The Promise of Stopping Mass Atrocities*, p. 57; and Glanville, 'On the Meaning of "Responsibility" in the "Responsibility to Protect"'.

[169] On 'variable responsibilities', see Chhabra and Zucker, 'Defining the Crimes', in Genser and Cotler (eds.), *The Promise of Stopping Mass Atrocities*, p. 56.

2

Non-State actors

RAPHAËL VAN STEENBERGHE

Introduction

The main actors which are generally envisaged in relation to the responsibility to protect (R2P) are States and international organisations. States are indeed the primary bearers of R2P, while the international community, mostly acting through the United Nations or regional organisations, is assumed to intervene when such responsibility is not (adequately) exercised. Yet, it is now an indisputable fact that non-State actors also have a role to play in international relations. This is particularly clear with respect to R2P, since this concept is primarily concerned with the protection of individuals rather than State interests. The first and most obvious type of non-State actors whose activities are related to such protection and, therefore, the implementation of R2P are non-governmental organisations (NGOs), especially those dedicated to the defence of human rights. The first and main section of this chapter will accordingly be devoted to studying the relationship between R2P and NGOs. However, some other types of non-State actors also seem to be good candidates for playing a role with respect to R2P, as they are significantly involved in protecting populations in times of crisis. One of those actors is the International Committee of the Red Cross (ICRC), which has received a specific mandate, under the four 1949 Geneva Conventions and their 1977 Additional Protocol I, to protect non-combatants in armed conflicts. It is also the case of armed groups, as they too are bound by all the relevant international humanitarian law (IHL) norms, including those obliging them to respect civilians in armed conflicts. As a result, the two last sections of this chapter will briefly examine the relationship between R2P and the ICRC as well as between R2P and armed groups, respectively.

Non-governmental organisations

Many NGOs have expressed their views on the concept of R2P. Such views will be first analysed, before discussing NGOs' concrete role with respect to the promotion and implementation of R2P and examining whether this role is exercised as bearers of this responsibility or merely as 'implementing' actors.

R2P as seen by NGOs

Every NGO is likely to have an opinion on R2P. It is impossible to know and detail the opinions of all NGOs. Yet, many international round-tables, in which important NGOs have participated, have been organised on the subject, and reports of such roundtables have been published.[1] Those reports enable one to have a general overview of NGOs' stance on R2P. Views have been expressed on three main aspects of this concept: its scope, its positive features as well as problematic aspects.

Scope

Many NGOs have expressed their opinion about what they consider to be the current scope of R2P. This scope is far from settled. It is still very much debated among States.[2] Nonetheless, one may identify some

---

[1] See the many roundtable consultations which have been organised with NGOs by the International Commission on Intervention and State Sovereignty (ICISS) during the drafting of the report on the responsibility to protect (R2P): ICISS, *The Responsibility to Protect: Research, Bibliography, Background* (Ottawa: International Development Research Centre, 2001); see also roundtables organised with NGOs by the World Federalist Movement–Institute for Global Policy (WFM–IGP) on the ICISS report on R2P available at www.responsibilitytoprotect.org: 'Civil Society Perspectives on the Responsibility to Protect: Final Report', 30 April 2003; 'Global Consultative Roundtables on the Responsibility to Protect: Civil Society Perspectives and Recommendations for Action', February–August 2008; 'Global Consultative Roundtables on the Responsibility to Protect: Western African Perspectives', 30–31 July 2008; 'Global Consultation on the Responsibility to Protect: Roundtable for SADC NGOs', 29–30 April 2008; 'Dialogue on the Responsibility to Protect: Latin Americas Perspectives', 31 March–1 April 2008; 'Prospects for an International Coalition on the Responsibility to Protect (R2P): Civil Society Consultation', 7 March 2008.

[2] See for example, concerning State debates on R2P, the Informal Interactive Thematic Dialogue of the United Nations General Assembly on the Responsibility to Protect. UNGA Verbatim Record, UN Doc. A/63/PV.97, 23 July 2009; UNGA Verbatim Record, UN Doc. A/63/PV.98, 23 July 2009; UNGA Verbatim Record, UN Doc. A/63/PV.99, 24 July 2009. See also, the UN Security Council debates on the Protection of Civilians in Armed Conflict. UNSC Verbatim Record, UN Doc. S/PV.6151, 26 June 2009; UNSC Verbatim Record, UN Doc. S/PV.6151 (Resumption 1), 26 June 2009; UNSC

evolution in that regard, in particular from the 2001 report of the International Commission on Intervention and State Sovereignty (ICISS),[3] which forged the notion of R2P, to the 2005 World Summit Outcome Document (WSOD),[4] in which this notion was approved by States, and especially the 2009 United Nations Secretary-General (UNSG) report on implementing R2P.[5] In the 2009 UNSG report, which reasserts and structures the relevant content of the WSOD, it is clearly acknowledged that R2P is only concerned with the protection of populations from four crimes: genocide, ethnic cleansing, crimes against humanity and war crimes. In addition, this report proposes an R2P concept based on three pillars: the responsibility of States to protect their populations; the responsibility of the international community to provide States with assistance and capacity-building in that regard; and the responsibility of the international community to take timely and decisive action in the event of manifest failure on the part of States to protect their populations. The 2009 UNSG report seems to provide the most comprehensive picture of the current scope of R2P. It takes its cue from the WSOD. Moreover, both the limitation of the scope of R2P to the four above-mentioned crimes as well as the very clear 'three pillars approach' developed therein have been endorsed by most States during the 2009 UN General Assembly (UNGA) debates on R2P.[6]

The scope that several NGOs have ascribed to R2P is broader in two respects. First, it includes a distinct responsibility borne by the international community to support the United Nations in establishing an early warning capability.[7] Such specific responsibility has indeed been emphasised mainly because NGOs consider prevention as the most

---

Verbatim Record, UN Doc. S/PV.6216, 11 November 2009; UNSC Verbatim Record, UN Doc. S/PV.6216 (Resumption 1), 11 November 2009; UNSC Verbatim Record, UN Doc. S/PV.6531, 10 May 2011; UNSC Verbatim Record, UN Doc. S/PV.6531 (Resumption 1), 10 May 2011.

[3] ICISS, *The Responsibility to Protect* (Ottawa: International Development Research Centre, 2001).

[4] '2005 World Summit Outcome', UN Doc. A/RES/60/1, 24 October 2005, paras. 138–40.

[5] UN Secretary-General, 'Implementing the Responsibility to Protect', UN Doc. A/63/677, 12 January 2009.

[6] See, for a similar observation, the summary of Executive Director of the Global Centre for the Responsibility to Protect Monica Serrano's comments in International Coalition for the Responsibility to Protect, 'Meeting Summary: Reflections on the UN General Assembly Debate on the Responsibility to Protect', 26 October 2009, p. 1, available at www.globalr2p.org.

[7] WFM–IGP, 'Recommendations for Action', p. 7; see also ICRtoP, 'The Coalition's Common Understanding of RtoP', available at www.responsibilitytoprotect.org.

important aspect of R2P and due to the fact that, as developed in more detail below, they are generally considered as key actors with respect to early warning about situations which risk leading to mass atrocities. Second, although the R2P rebuilding aspects, which form an important part of R2P under the ICISS report, were no longer mentioned in the 2005 WSOD nor in the 2009 UNSG report, many NGOs have still emphasised those aspects and, more particularly, asserted that they 'support[ed] a full spectrum of responsibility [under the R2P, including] the responsibility . . . to rebuild'.[8] This is again perfectly understandable in light of NGOs' activities. In general, the two above-mentioned extensions of the current agreed scope of R2P coincide with the interests and activities of NGOs. The latter are necessarily more involved in prevention, early warning and rebuilding activities than in carrying out concrete actions during occurrences of mass crimes. Such situations of high level of violence are obviously not favourable for the undertaking of field operations, especially by civil society organisations.

Positive features

NGOs are also concerned with the positive aspects of R2P. Generally speaking, many NGOs strongly support R2P and see it as a significant evolution related to the international protection of individuals.[9] An important evolution brought by the R2P concept is the shift away from the term 'humanitarian intervention', which was at the origin of the ICISS's reflections on the notion of 'responsibility to protect'. By no longer associating the term 'humanitarian' with the concept of military intervention, the notion of R2P helps to avoid any potential confusion between humanitarian and military activities.[10] NGOs have struggled against the tendency to mix humanitarian assistance with military intervention as this confusion has proved to be damaging to their activities. The very strong opposition expressed by humanitarian agencies, humanitarian organisations and humanitarian workers towards any militarisation of the word 'humanitarian' was duly noted by the ICISS.[11] This change of terminology is not the only specific positive aspect of the influence exercised by NGOs. Such aspects are various

---

[8] *Ibid.*   [9] See for example WFM–IGP, 'Final Report', p. 12.
[10] See for example, the statements of NGOs at the roundtable consultation with nongovernmental and other interested organisations on 14 January 2001 and 10 March 2001. ICISS, *Research, Bibliography, Background*, pp. 350 and 362.
[11] ICISS, *Responsibility to Protect*, para. 1.40.

and notably include the reinforcement of the notion of sovereignty, which is counterbalanced with responsibilities, and the continuum of responsibilities from prevention to reaction and rebuilding.[12]

Problematic aspects

Although supporting the emergence of a new global tool for protecting people from crisis situations, NGOs have expressed concern and scepticism about some R2P aspects. The first and most important concern is related to the part of R2P on the use of force. During the discussions preceding the drafting of the ICISS report, some NGOs expressed their doubts about the usefulness of using force, stating that 'military force can be as damaging as non-intervention and ha(s) long-term consequences'.[13] Similarly, after the release of the ICISS report, many NGOs pointed out that too much attention was given to the issue of use of force in the report.[14] More generally, NGOs were afraid that conclusions reached by the ICISS in that regard could be abused by powerful States in order to safeguard their national interests rather than to protect civilian populations in distress. Their fear was particularly justified in light of the political climate existing at that time – notably the US war on terror and the 2003 invasion of Iraq by the 'coalition of the willing' – and the lack of detailed definition of the situations under which R2P was to come into play. Many of those concerns diminished after the adoption of the 2005 WSOD and the 2009 UNSG report on implementing R2P. Indeed, NGOs now acknowledge that the risks of abusive or misused resorts to force under R2P have been severely limited in two respects. First, there is by now a clear and agreed limitation of R2P to four specific crimes. Second, it is clearly acknowledged, according to NGOs, that force is to be resorted to only in conformity with the UN Charter, in particular only following express UN Security Council (UNSC) authorisation.[15] This latter view shows that NGOs share the opinion held by the majority of States that R2P is not an autonomous basis for resorting to force alongside the two classically admitted exceptions to the prohibition on the use of force – that is, self-defence and force authorised by the UN Security Council.[16]

---

[12] WFM–IGP, 'Recommendations for Action', p. 8.

[13] See statement by NGOs in ICISS, *Research, Bibliography, Background*, p. 352.

[14] WFM–IGP, 'Final Report', p. 12.

[15] WFM–IGP, 'Recommendations for Action', p. 8.

[16] See on this subject Olivier Corten, *The Law Against War: The Prohibition on the Use of Force in Contemporary International Law* (Oxford: Hart Publishing, 2010), pp. 517–22.

Moreover, having nonetheless recognised that R2P had been misused by some powerful States in the past, including for justifying the use of force,[17] NGOs are satisfied by the fact that, when States approved R2P references in UNSC resolutions, no government or NGO criticised this inclusion.[18]

Although significantly reduced, some concerns in relation to the use of force under R2P remain, for two main reasons. Many NGOs consider, especially in light of the recent military intervention in Libya, that criteria for assessing the need and the way to resort to force under R2P should be adopted by the UN Security Council as guidelines for its actions in that field. Some NGOs, such as Médecins Sans Frontières, firmly reject R2P precisely because it is too vague with respect to the circumstances under which force can be resorted to, although they do not exclude that using force may be necessary in some instances.[19] In addition, mandates of most NGOs are not adapted to deal with that matter. NGOs often have a position of impartiality and neutrality which, although allowing them to express strong criticism on the conduct of hostilities, nonetheless prevents them from commenting on the legality of the conflict. That specific position makes it difficult for some NGOs, such as Amnesty International, to call for or endorse military responses to a crisis.[20] However, other NGOs, such as Oxfam International,[21] expressly support the military aspect of R2P and do not hesitate to refer to it in practice in order to persuade States to intervene in a specific

---

See also, for a confirmation of this view in the light of recent practice in Libya and the Ivory Coast, Raphaël van Steenberghe, 'The Law against War or *Jus contra Bellum*: A New Terminology for a Conservative View on the Use of Force?', *Leiden Journal of International Law*, 24 (2011), 747–88, at 786.

[17] For example, the invocation of R2P by Russia in the 2008 armed conflict with Georgia. Global Centre for the Responsibility to Protect, 'The Georgia Russia Crisis and the Responsibility to Protect: Background Note', 19 August 2008, at www.globalr2p.org/pdf/related/GeorgiaRussia.pdf.

[18] WFM–IGP, 'Recommendations for Action', p. 9.

[19] See Fabrice Weissman, 'Not in Our Name! Why MSF Does Not Support the Responsibility to Protect', *Criminal Justice Ethics*, 29 (2010), 194–207, at 201–2. Other civil society bodies have emphasized the need for such criteria without rejecting the third pillar of R2P. See for example, the reaction of GCR2P to the new concept 'Responsibility While Protecting', which was submitted by Brazil at the Informal UNGA discussion held on 21 February 2012. GCR2P, 'Statement by the Hon. Gareth Evans Co-Chair of the Global Centre for the Responsibility to Protect', 21 February 2012, available at www.globalr2p.org.

[20] Concerning Amnesty International, see WFM–IGP, 'Final Report', p. 17.

[21] Ekkehard Strauss, *The Emperor's New Clothes? The United Nations and the Implementation of the Responsibility to Protect* (Baden-Baden: Nomos, 2009), p. 71, fn. 225.

country. It is worth mentioning in this regard the call made in December 2008 by several NGOs, including Human Rights Watch, Oxfam International, Caritas France and CARE, to the European Union to deploy military forces in the Democratic Republic of Congo (DRC) in order to protect the civilian population.[22] Similarly, in the context of the more recent Libyan crisis, a significant group of NGOs, members of the International Coalition for the R2P, urged governments to take timely and decisive measures, including use of force if necessary and under some specific conditions, to put an end to the violent repression of Libyan civilians in February 2011.[23]

Other major concerns have been expressed by NGOs regarding R2P, including the scope of its prevention aspect.[24] Given the current tendency, as will be seen below,[25] to link R2P to the responsibility to protect civilians in armed conflicts, are prevention measures similar to those already provided for the prevention of armed conflicts? Or do these measures involve a wider range of actions and include measures addressing structural as well as root causes of mass crimes, such as the structural ones envisaged in the ICISS report?[26] These questions are important since, as emphasised above, NGOs' activities are mainly devoted to the prevention of mass atrocities. If one adopts an expansive approach with regard to prevention, many NGOs may be considered R2P implementers. Alongside their concern relating to the scope of prevention under R2P, NGOs have also expressed doubts about the effective implementation of this new concept by States. More particularly, that concern has to do with the political willingness as well as the operational readiness of governments to work towards such implementation.[27] Finally, and more

---

[22] Action des Chrétiens pour l'abolition de la Torture – France *et al.*, 'RD Congo/Conseil Européen: La France doit montrer l'exemple', 10 December 2008, available at www.acatfrance.fr.

[23] ICRtoP, 'Open Letter to the Security Council on the Situation in Libya', 4 March 2011, available at www.globalr2p.org.

[24] See for example WFM–IGP, 'Recommendations for Action', p. 10.

[25] See for example UNSC Res. 1674, UN Doc. S/RES/1674, 28 April 2006; UNSC Res. 1894, UN Doc. S/RES/1894, 11 November 2009.

[26] See ICISS, *Responsibility to Protect*, pp. 22–3. In his 2010 report on early warning, assessment and R2P, UN Secretary-General Ban Ki-moon expressly considered that '[p]reventing the incitement or commission of one of the four proscribed crimes or violations [was] not necessarily the equivalent of preventing the outbreak of armed conflict'. According to him, '[s]ometimes such egregious acts are associated with armed conflicts, but sometimes they are not' (UNSG, 'Early Warning, Assessment and the Responsibility to Protect', UN Doc. A/64/864, 14 July 2010).

[27] See for example WFM–IGP, 'Recommendations for Action', pp. 11–12.

fundamentally, NGOs have expressed some scepticism about the added value of R2P in relation to their activities since, in their views, such activities could be perfectly carried out without invoking R2P.[28]

R2P as implemented by NGOs

Almost all the activities carried out by NGOs whose mandate is to protect civilians or safeguard human rights could be considered as contributing to the implementation of R2P, especially if, as just seen above, the notion of prevention were broadly construed. Many of these NGOs have emphasised that they were already implementing R2P, without calling it such. Their activities range from carrying out research, as well as launching advocacy campaigns, to undertaking on-the-ground actions designed to promote peace through mediation, capacity-building or confidence-building and conducting humanitarian relief operations.[29] While it might be unnecessary to describe here all these activities, it is noteworthy to identify some specific NGO functions that have been especially emphasised by States as well as in core R2P documents. NGO practice also evidences that some actions have been expressly undertaken as an application of R2P.

NGO roles envisaged by States and core R2P documents

There are specific as well as general NGO roles which have been emphasised by States and in some core R2P documents in relation to the implementation of R2P. A first specific role relates to the well-established and developed NGO function of early warning. As indicated in the ICISS's report,[30] it is well known that, although Article 99 of the UN Charter provides the UN Secretary-General with a specific legal basis for developing an early warning capacity, such capacity is still lacking. The absence of a centralised early warning system has pushed several NGOs, such as the International Crisis Group (ICG), to dedicate their activities on an almost exclusive basis to 'monitor and report on areas of the world where conflict appears to be emerging (and to alert) governments and media if they believe preventive action is urgently

[28] *Ibid.*, p. 12.
[29] See in this respect, Gareth Evans, *The Responsibility to Protect: Ending Mass Atrocity Crimes Once and for All* (Washington, DC: Brookings Institution, 2008), p. 198.
[30] See ICISS, *Responsibility to Protect*, para. 3.14; see also WFM–IGP, 'Latin Americas Perspectives', p. 3.

required'.[31] International human rights organisations, such as Amnesty International, Human Rights Watch and the Fédération Internationale des Ligues des Droits de l'Homme, also play a significant role in that regard because of their well-established monitoring and reporting capacity.[32]

Another specific role of NGOs relates to their capacity to collect and provide information about ongoing crises where mass crimes are occurring.[33] Indeed, in order to adequately react to failures by States to protect their populations, the international community must become aware of what is happening on the ground. In such crisis situations, competing facts and versions of events are generally produced, which render decision-making at an international level rather difficult. That is especially so, since there is no formal centralised agency fulfilling such a fact-finding task. Although recent practice evidences an increasing use of special inquiry missions in that respect,[34] mostly at the UN level, reports generated by those missions are generally produced after the facts. Relying on the ICRC for such purpose is not helpful either. Although physically present in most of the crises locations, the ICRC functions in accordance with the principles of confidentiality and neutrality, which prevent it from fulfilling such a task. As a result, most of the relevant information will become available through the media or NGO reports.

Besides the specific interrelated functions of early warning and information-collecting and providing, NGOs are often seen as important actors in lobbying governments in order to influence their decision-making.[35] This general function is additional to the even broader role which seems to have been recognised to NGOs by the UN

---

[31] ICISS, *Responsibility to Protect*, para. 3.13.   [32] *Ibid.*

[33] *Ibid.*, pp. 34–5; see also UNSG, 'Implementing the Responsibility to Protect', p. 31, para. 3; UNSG, 'Early Warning', p. 5.

[34] See for example, the recent International Commission of Inquiry appointed by the Human Rights Council to investigate human rights violations in Libya. UN Human Rights Council, 'Situation of Human Rights in the Libyan Arab Jamahiriya', UN Doc. A/HRC/RES/S-15/1, 25 February 2011, para. 11. For the commission's report, see UNHRC, 'Report of the International Commission of Inquiry to Investigate all Alleged Violations of International Law in the Libyan Arab Jamahiriya', UN Doc. A/HRC/17/44, 1 June 2011.

[35] See for example ICISS, *Responsibility to Protect*, para. 8.11; see also, declarations made by States during the 2009 UNGA debates on R2P, in particular those made by Ghana (UN Doc. A/63/PV.98, pp. 19–21); Czech Republic (*ibid.*, pp. 22–3); Nigeria (*ibid.*, pp. 26–9); Rwanda (UN Doc. A/63/PV.99, pp. 20–1). See also on the subject, Judy Large, *The War Next Door: A Study of Second-Track Interventions During the War in Ex-Yugoslavia* (Gloucestershire: Hawthorn Press, 1997); Mohammed Omar Maundi, 'Preventing Conflict Escalation in Burundi', in Chandra Lekha Sriam and Karin Wermester (eds.),

Secretary-General in his 2009 report on implementing R2P. Indeed, as explained below, the Secretary-General seems to have considered civil society, including NGOs, as direct bearers of R2P, in particular the responsibility under its second pillar to assist States in protecting their populations.

Specific actions undertaken by NGOs

Specific actions have been undertaken by NGOs expressly in relation to the implementation of R2P. Those actions have both institutional and substantial aspects. These aspects are dealt with in more detail below.

Institutional aspects   R2P has led to a huge mobilisation among civil society actors.[36] Very early in the formation process of the concept, NGOs appeared to be crucial actors in promoting and operationalising it. After the release of the ICISS's report, the government of Canada, which established and funded the ICISS, asked a prominent NGO, the World Federalist Movement–Institute for Global Policy (WFM–IGP), to become actively involved in reaching out to other NGOs and civil society actors. The WFM–IGP held a series of roundtable meetings with NGOs from all over the world.[37] As a result of the positive reaction from those NGOs and their willingness to take part in the implementation of R2P, the WFM–IGP launched in 2003 the 'Responsibility to Protect – Engaging Civil Society' (R2P–CS) project, with the support of other prominent NGOs, including Oxfam International, ICG, Human Rights Watch and Refugees International. The main objective of the project was 'to engage civil society in the advancement of [R2P] in order to achieve early and effective responses by governments and the international community to protect populations'.[38]

In September 2007, the WFM–IGP launched a new initiative under the R2P–CS to build a global civil society coalition for the responsibility to protect. It then organised a new series of consultative roundtables with NGOs. Seven global roundtables were held in 2008 in several countries, including Thailand, Canada, Argentina, Uganda, South

From Promise to Practice: Strengthening UN Capacities for the Prevention of Violent Conflict (Boulder, CO: Lynne Rienner, 2003), pp. 327–48.

[36] For a similar view, see Alex Bellamy, Sara Davies and Luke Glanville, 'Introduction', in Alex Bellamy, Sara Davies and Luke Glanville (eds.), *The Responsibility to Protect and International Law* (Leiden; Boston, MA: Martinus Nijhoff, 2011), pp. 1–12, at p. 1, fn. 2.

[37] See the roundtable discussions held by WFM–IGP, at n. 1, above.

[38] ICRtoP, 'About the R2PCS Project at WFM–IGP', available at www.responsibilityto-protect.org.

Africa, France and Ghana.[39] It has been rightly emphasised that 'the summaries of these roundtables are a unique source of insight into the political, legal and cultural considerations of civil society in different regions that often contrast with the position of their respective government'.[40] These summaries provide a general overview of the NGOs' understanding of the notion of R2P and the possible means for promoting and implementing it.

The project of building a global civil society coalition for the responsibility to protect gave birth to two important civil society bodies: the Global Centre for the Responsibility to Protect (GCR2P), established in February 2008,[41] and the International Coalition for the Responsibility to Protect (ICRtoP), created in January 2009.[42] These bodies share common features, as they were both established under the auspices of prominent NGOs, mainly those involved in the R2P–CS project. Both of them work for the promotion and implementation of R2P and include advocacy as well as advisory activities. Yet, the main difference is that unlike the ICRtoP, the GCR2P is not composed only of NGOs. The Global Centre's staff includes mostly academic researchers, while its international advisory board, which is charged with providing the Centre's Executive Director with advice on strategy, policy and management, is composed of different representatives of the civil society, including policymakers and academics, representatives of associated centres and leaders in the NGO community. This composition explains why, although also playing an advocacy role, the Global Centre has a particular capacity as regards carrying out research projects on R2P. This is evidenced among others by the numerous workshops, seminars and conferences it has organised and hosted. In contrast, the ICRtoP appears to be more of an NGO coalition, whose primary function is to advocate for the promotion and implementation of R2P by States and other governmental institutions. In addition, the ICRtoP is more representative as its members include NGOs from all over the world.[43]

---

[39] For the report of those roundtables, see WFM–IGP, 'Recommendation for Action'.

[40] Strauss, *Emperor's New Clothes?*, p. 71.

[41] For more information on the Global Centre for the Responsibility to Protect, see www.globalr2p.org.

[42] For more information on ICRtoP, see www.responsibilitytoprotect.org.

[43] ICRtoP, 'Current Members', available at www.responsibilitytoprotect.org. ICRtoP is also associated with other centres established in different regions of the world, including the Asia-Pacific Centre for the Responsibility to Protect (Brisbane), the Instituto de Investigación en Ciencias Sociales (Santiago), the Kofi Annan International Peacekeeping

The creation of such an important coalition is a significant phenomenon regarding the role played by NGOs and, more generally, non-State actors with respect to R2P. This phenomenon may have a great impact on the development of R2P, since it is not the first time that NGOs work through coalitions. This strategy has already been adopted in the past and has yielded significant results, such as the establishment of the International Criminal Court[44] and the adoption of treaties banning antipersonnel landmines.[45] The current expanding civil society mobilisation with respect to R2P is likely to have a similar boosting effect on this concept. Indeed, the ICRtoP serves as a central hub from which many NGOs carry out substantial actions regarding R2P, including organising scientific events such as conferences on the subject,[46] pushing States towards normative endorsement of R2P,[47] or even calling on States to adopt military measures against specific countries.[48]

Substantial aspects   NGOs increasingly invoke R2P while carrying out their activities. Over time NGOs have agreed to pursue a number of general objectives in relation to R2P which are likely to guide their actions in this regard. The first objective is to further the understanding of R2P among civil society, policymakers and the public.[49] This implies raising awareness of R2P among those actors, explaining the precise scope and meaning of this concept, as well as pushing for its promotion. This task amounts to disseminating and pushing for dissemination of

Training Centre (Accra), the Norwegian Institute of International Affairs (Oslo) and the African Leadership Centre (Nairobi).

[44] On this subject, see Gaëlle Breton-le-Goff, 'NGO's Perspectives on Non-State Actors', in Jean d'Aspremont (ed.), *Participants in the International Legal System: Multiple Perspectives on Non-State Actors in International Law* (London: Routledge, 2011), pp. 248–66, at p. 250. For information on the Coalition for the International Criminal Court, see www.iccnow.org.

[45] For information on the international campaign to ban landmines, see www.icbl.org.

[46] For information on the many conferences organised by ICRtoP or in which it was actively involved, see ICRtoP, 'Latest from the Coalition Secretariat', available at www.responsibilitytoprotect.org.

[47] See for example, the open letters of ICRtoP and other members of civil society to the Security Council and General Assembly available at www.responsibilitytoprotect.org. Oxfam International *et al.*, 'Inclusion of Responsibility to Protect in Security Council Resolution Protection of Civilians in Armed Conflict', undated; ICRtoP, 'Untitled Letter to the Members of the Security Council in Advance of the Protection of Civilians Debates', 6 November 2009; ICRtoP, 'Civil Society Organizations Send Open Letter to Governments in Advance of the General Assembly Debate on the Responsibility to Protect', 20 July 2009.

[48] See ACAT France, 'RD Congo: La France doit montrer l'exemple', 10 December 2008; ICRtoP, 'Situation in Libya', 4 March 2011, available at www.globalr2p.org.

[49] See for example WFM–IGP, 'Recommendations for Action', p. 13.

precise and adequate information about R2P. NGOs fulfil such a task mainly by organising or actively participating in conferences, workshops and seminars on R2P. Such events take place regularly in many regions of the world before diverse audiences.[50]

A second objective is to strengthen normative consensus for R2P at the international, regional, sub-regional and national levels.[51] This implies pushing for additional normative endorsement of R2P. Such a concept has already been endorsed in international instruments, notably, in the 2005 WSOD,[52] two UNSC resolutions concerning the protection of civilians in armed conflicts[53] and five UNSC resolutions dealing with specific crises.[54] Many of those endorsements have been pushed for by NGOs. For example, on 7 December 2005[55] and 6 November 2009,[56] the ICRtoP and its members sent official letters to the Member States of the Security Council in order to call for the inclusion of a reference to R2P in the UNSC resolutions on the protection of civilians in armed conflicts. Similarly, ICRtoP sent an official letter to States in advance of the UNGA debate on R2P, held in July 2009, in order to urge them to refer to and endorse R2P in their declarations before the General Assembly.[57] Such endorsements, which NGOs are pushing for, are significant. They may have both practical and normative effects. As emphasised by NGOs themselves,[58] a widespread institutional acceptance of R2P is likely to legitimise this concept and to push governments to establish effective mechanisms to specifically prevent and halt genocide, war crimes, crimes against humanity and ethnic cleansing. References to R2P in international instruments as well as in State declarations may also have a normative impact and, in particular, contribute to the emergence of a customary R2P rule. This is particularly true with respect to references in UNSC resolutions dealing with specific

---

[50] See ICRtoP, 'Latest from the Coalition Secretariat'.

[51] See for example WFM–IGP, 'Recommendations for Action', p. 14.

[52] '2005 World Summit Outcome'.

[53] UNSC Res. 1674, para. 4; UNSC Res. 1894, pmbl., para. 7.

[54] UNSC Res. 1706, UN Doc. S/RES/1706, 31 August 2006, pmbl., para. 2; UNSC Res. 1970, UN Doc. S/RES/1970, 26 February 2011, pmbl., para. 9; UNSC Res. 1973, UN Doc. S/RES/1973, 17 March 2011, pmbl., para. 4; UNSC Res. 1975, UN Doc. S/RES/1975, 30 March 2011, pmbl., para. 9; UNSC Res. 2085, UN Doc. S/RES/2085, 20 December 2012, para. 9(d).

[55] Oxfam International et al., 'Inclusion of Responsibility to Protect'.

[56] ICRtoP, 'Untitled Letter to the Members of the Security Council'.

[57] ICRtoP, 'Open Letter to Governments in Advance of the General Assembly Debate'.

[58] See for example WFM–IGP, 'Recommendations for Action', pp. 10–11.

situations, such as the UNSC resolutions concerning Libya[59] and the Ivory Coast,[60] since those general references materialised into physical acts. Those references could potentially be seen as expressing the *opinio juris* of the States having voted in favour of the resolutions and the actions concretely undertaken on the basis of those resolutions as the *State practice* element of the customary rule, as this element is classically construed – that is, as involving material conduct. In other words, the two main elements of customary law could be identified in this case. Yet, a customary R2P rule could also be derived from references to R2P in international instruments unrelated to specific situations, such as the UNSC resolutions on the protection of civilians in armed conflicts, or in State declarations preceding the adoption of such instruments, like those made during the 2009 UNGA debates, even if no material act may support such declarations. Indeed, in accordance with a modern conception of the formation process of customary law,[61] which is particularly defended in the fields of human rights and humanitarian law because of the lack of State material conduct in those fields,[62] such abstract references to R2P could be considered as a form of State practice and, if sufficiently repeated over time by the majority of States, as expressing the *opinio juris* of those States.[63]

Admittedly, it is clear that no customary R2P rule can be claimed to have emerged on the basis of all those references to R2P, since an important requirement, the widespread acceptance and repetition of the relevant State practice, must still be met. More fundamentally, the notion of R2P has not gained an autonomous and normative content yet and it is far from being established that the above-mentioned references to R2P evidence the *opinio juris* of States – that is, the belief to act in accordance with law – rather than a mere political endorsement of this

---

[59] UNSC Res. 1970; UNSC Res. 1973.   [60] UNSC Res. 1975.

[61] On this subject, see Anthea Elizabeth Roberts, 'Traditional and Modern Approaches to Customary International Law: A Reconciliation', *American Journal of International Law*, 95 (2001), 757–91, at 757. For the application of such modern conception by the International Court of Justice, see *Legality of the Threat or Use of Nuclear Weapons*, ICJ Reports 1996, Advisory Opinion of 8 July 1996, pp. 254–5, paras. 70–3.

[62] On this subject, see Bruno Simma and Philip Alston, 'The Sources of Human Rights Law: Custom, *Jus Cogens*, and General Principles', *Australian Yearbook of International Law*, 12 (1988–9), 82–108, at 82.

[63] For further developments on this position, see Raphaël van Steenberghe, *La légitime défense en droit international public* (Brussels: Larcier, 2012), pp. 147–9; van Steenberghe, 'The Obligation to Extradite or Prosecute: Clarifying its Nature', *Journal of International Criminal Justice*, 9 (2011), 1089–118, at 1093–4.

concept. Yet, those references significantly open the door for potential normative developments of R2P. While raising concern regarding the non-binding nature of the 2005 WSOD, some NGOs have pushed for additional references to R2P in international instruments with the explicit hope of transforming R2P from an emerging norm into established customary international law.[64]

A third general objective guiding NGOs' activities is to encourage more effective international, sub-regional and national responses to genocide and mass atrocities.[65] This objective involves actions devoted to strengthening the capacity to prevent such atrocities, including the mechanisms with respect to which States and core R2P documents have emphasised the crucial role of NGOs – early warning and information gathering. It also implies taking actions for the application of R2P to country-specific situations in order to ensure the materialisation of R2P beyond the conceptual level. NGOs have already undertaken action for both strengthening prevention capacities and ensuring the application of R2P to specific situations. In this respect, one may mention, for example, the numerous letters or declarations by NGOs, in which the situation is described as falling within the concept of R2P and requiring urgent action from the international community.[66]

R2P as borne by NGOs?

Many activities carried out by NGOs may be seen as contributing to the promotion and implementation of R2P. The question is whether NGOs can be considered as proper bearers of the responsibilities arising under R2P, alongside States and international organisations.

It is uncontested that the primary responsibility to protect populations from mass atrocities rests upon the domestic authorities of the State where such mass atrocities are occurring or about to occur. Yet, R2P also entails a responsibility on the part of the *international community* to intervene, alongside or instead of the domestic authorities, whenever such authorities fail to exercise their primary responsibility or exercise it in an inadequate manner. This subsidiary responsibility is deemed to constitute the core element of the second pillar of R2P.

---

[64] See for example WFM–IGP, 'Recommendations for Action', p. 11.   [65] *Ibid.*, p. 15.

[66] ICRtoP maintains several informative lists of the reactions of civil society to current and past crises. ICRtoP, 'Crises', at www.responsibilitytoprotect.org/index.php/crises.

However, the notion of international community, which is referred to as the bearer of such responsibility, lacks any precise definition. This is particularly true in the political or moral sphere, which is important since R2P is still considered a political or moral instrument rather than a legal norm.[67] Moreover, the notion of international community is not clear even under international law.[68] While in the 1969 Vienna Convention on the Law of Treaties, the express reference is to the international community of *States*,[69] this limitation no longer appears in the international case law, in particular the *Barcelona Traction* case before the International Court of Justice,[70] or in other international texts, like the articles on State responsibility.[71] It is indicative that the International Law Commission has voluntarily deleted the terms 'of States' when deciding to refer to the notion of international community in the articles on State responsibility, even though these articles are dealing with State responsibility.[72]

As a result, nothing prevents interpreting the notion of international community in a broad sense, as encompassing a wide range of actors, including NGOs.[73] This understanding ultimately tends to assimilate the notion of international community with the concept of humanity.[74] Although such an understanding is not clearly apparent in the ICISS report, it is noticeable in core R2P documents, especially the 2005 WSOD and the 2009 UNSG report on implementing R2P. As mentioned above, the 'three-pillars approach' adopted in that report on the basis of

---

[67] For more on this subject, see Carsten Stahn, 'Responsibility to Protect: Political Rhetoric or Emerging Legal Norm', *American Journal of International Law*, 101 (2007), 99–102, at 99; Daniel Warner and Gilles Giaccia, 'Responsibility to Protect', in Vincent Chetail (ed.), *Post-Conflict Peacebuilding: A Lexicon* (Oxford University Press, 2009), pp. 291–306, at pp. 299–300.

[68] See on this subject Santiago Villalpando, *L'émergence de la communauté internationale dans la responsabilité des États* (Paris: Presses Universitaires de France, 2005), pp. 10–15.

[69] Vienna Convention on the Law of Treaties, adopted 23 May 1969 and entered into force 27 January 1980, 1155 UNTS 331, art. 53.

[70] *Barcelona Traction, Light and Power Company, Limited (Belgium v. Spain), Second Phase, Judgment*, ICJ reports 1970, p. 32, para. 33.

[71] UNGA Res. 56/83, UN Doc. A/RES/56/83, 12 December 2001, arts. 25, 42 and 48.

[72] See the commentary on Article 25 of the International Law Commission's (ILC) Articles on State responsibility. ILC, 'Report of the International Law Commission on the Work of Its Fifty-Third Session (23 April–1 June and 2 July–10 August 2001)', UN Doc. A/56/10, p. 84, para. 18; and *ibid.*, p. 127, fn. 726.

[73] See for a similar observation, Warner and Giaccia, 'Responsibility to Protect', in Chetail (ed.), *Post-Conflict Peacebuilding*, p. 298.

[74] See for example, Villalpando, *L'émergence de la communauté internationale*, p. 13, fn. 15.

the wording of the 2005 WSOD seems to reflect the agreed approach towards the scope of R2P. Under this approach, the international community bears two different kinds of responsibility: a responsibility *to assist* States in protecting their populations from mass atrocities and a responsibility *to react* when States fail to ensure such protection. The 2005 WSOD and the 2009 UNSG report suggest different conceptions of international community with respect to these two distinct kinds of responsibility. While the responsibility to react rests only upon States, the responsibility to assist rests on the international community construed in a broad sense, including NGOs. Indeed, the WSOD refers to the 'international community, through the United Nations' – that is, the international community *of States* – when considering the responsibility to react in paragraph 139, but uses the mere notion of 'international community', without any other specification, when envisaging the responsibility to assist in paragraph 138. The 2009 UNSG report is even more explicit. While repeating the language of the WSOD with respect to the responsibility to react,[75] the report indicates that the international community's responsibility to assist 'seeks to draw on the co-operation of Member States, regional and subregional arrangements, *civil society* and the private sector, as well as on the institutional strengths and comparative advantages of the United Nations system'.[76] This report clearly envisages the international community as encompassing all the relevant actors, including NGOs, which are able to assist States in implementing the primary responsibility to protect their populations from mass atrocities. This view is in line with declarations made by a number of States in relation to R2P.[77]

One may question, however, whether recognising that the responsibility to assist also bears upon NGOs changes anything in the debate. In any event, such responsibility could not be deemed as having a legal nature since that cannot be ascribed to R2P itself, as yet.[78] Therefore, no sanctions can be imposed against NGOs failing to exercise it. However,

---

[75] UNSG, 'Implementing the Responsibility to Protect', p. 22. Earlier in the report, the UN Secretary-General Ban Ki-moon expressly considers that '[p]illar three is the responsibility of *Member States*' (*ibid.*, p. 9, emphasis added).

[76] *Ibid.* (emphasis added).

[77] See statements of Guinea-Bissau (UN Doc. A/63/PV.98, p. 29) and Turkey (UN Doc. S/PV.6151, p. 26). Such clear declarations are limited. Most of the States refer to the international community without specifying whether it is the international community of States or the international community in a broader sense.

[78] See Stahn, 'Responsibility to Protect'.

this responsibility could have some concrete positive effects on NGOs' actions. If attributing responsibility is generally intended to put pressure on the bearers of this responsibility, it cannot be the case with respect to attributing a possible NGO's responsibility to assist under R2P. Per definition NGOs are willing to provide assistance to people in a vulnerable position, in accordance with their mandate. No political or moral pressure is needed to that end. Rather, this – arguably – NGO responsibility is likely to add more weight to NGOs' actions and facilitate the undertaking of such actions vis-à-vis the other bearers of R2P – that is, States and international organisations.

The International Committee of the Red Cross (ICRC)

Contrary to traditional NGOs, the ICRC has not taken a clear stance on R2P.[79] Does this mean that this particular non-State actor has no role to play in that regard? At first glance, its specific functions, which mainly consist in assisting belligerents in protecting civilian populations in armed conflicts, are definitely related to R2P, and should apparently make it a privileged actor with respect to the implementation of R2P. In this sense, it is logical that the ICRC has been involved at the initial stages of the formation of the R2P concept. In particular, it has been associated with the work of the ICISS[80] as well as invited to the round-tables organised by the WFM–IGP,[81] together with NGOs. Like the latter, the ICRC has strongly pushed for and welcomed the change in terminology from 'humanitarian intervention' to 'responsibility to protect', since such a change, as already emphasised, helps to avoid any potential confusion between military and humanitarian activities.[82] In addition, the ICRC has been mentioned in core R2P documents, alongside traditional NGOs, as a potentially important actor in implementing R2P.[83] More generally, as the ICRC is a well-known crucial

---

[79] Beat Schweizer, 'Responsibility to Protect: The Perspective of the ICRC', *Horizons et débats*, 20 (2008), at www.horizons-et-debats.ch/index.php?id=941.

[80] See for example, the roundtable consultations among the UN, international organisations, NGOs and other interested organisations in Geneva on 31 January 2001 (ICISS, *Research, Bibliography, Background*, p. 354); Maputo on 10 March 2001 (*ibid.*, p. 362); Washington, DC on 2 May 2001 (*ibid.*, p. 366); Cairo on 21 May 2001 (*ibid.*, p. 374); Paris on 23 May 2001 (*ibid.*, p. 383); New Delhi on 10 June 2001 (*ibid.*, p. 387).

[81] WFM–IGP, 'Final Report', p. 26, annex A.

[82] Schweizer, 'The Perspective of the ICRC'.

[83] See for example ICISS, *Responsibility to Protect*, pp. 21, 35 and 61.

actor in protecting civilians in armed conflicts, one could argue that it is intended to play a similar role in implementing R2P, given the current trend of assimilating R2P with the responsibility to protect civilians in armed conflicts (PoC). Indeed, after the 2005 WSOD, the notion of R2P has often been associated with the PoC, which has developed from the 1999 UNSG report on the subject.[84] Such association appears in many instances: in two UNSC resolutions dealing with PoC;[85] in all the four recent UNSC resolutions dealing with a specific crisis, namely, Darfur,[86] Libya[87] and the Ivory Coast;[88] in the 2007 UNSG report on PoC[89] as well as in the UNSC debates on PoC.[90] Many States,[91] like the UN Secretary-General,[92] have expressed themselves in favour of interlinking the two concepts. This is despite some fundamental differences between these concepts, in particular their different material scope of application, with R2P applying only in relation to the four specific crimes and PoC applying to any violation of IHL.

Yet, the ICRC's role with respect to R2P is actually limited. This limitation mainly comes from its specific neutral nature. The mandate that it received from States, enshrined in the four 1949 Geneva Conventions and their 1977 Additional Protocol I, requires the ICRC to adopt a totally neutral position. As acknowledged in the ICISS report

---

[84] UNSG, 'The Protection of Civilians in Armed Conflict', UN Doc. S/1999/957, 8 September 1999. This report is concerned with all the measures aiming at the protection of civilians in times of war on the basis of existing legal obligations, mainly those stemming from international humanitarian law, human rights law and refugee law. On this subject, see Jean-François Thibault, 'Protection des civils et responsabilité de protéger: les enjeux humanitaires d'une séparation du *jus in bello* et du *jus ad bellum*', *Bulletin du maintien de la paix*, 94 (2009), 1–4, at 1.

[85] UNSC Res. 1674; UNSC Res. 1894.   [86] UNSC Res. 1706.

[87] UNSC Res. 1970; UNSC Res. 1973.   [88] UNSC Res. 1975.

[89] UNSG, 'The Protection of Civilians in Armed Conflict', UN Doc. S/2007/643, 28 October 2007, p. 4.

[90] See for example, the statements of Burkina Faso (UN Doc. S/PV.6151, p. 24); France (UN Doc. S/PV.6216, p. 15); Russia (*ibid.*, p. 17); Libya (*ibid.*, p. 18); Sweden (*ibid.*, p. 30); Italy (*ibid.*, p. 31); Belgium (UN Doc. S/PV.6216 (Resumption 1), p. 26); Germany (UN Doc. S/PV.6531, p. 18); Nigeria (*ibid.*, p. 20); Uruguay (*ibid.*, p. 24); and Croatia (UN Doc. S/PV.6531 (Resumption 1), p. 15).

[91] See for example, the statements of Croatia (UN Doc. S/PV.6216, p. 11); Ireland (UN Doc. S/PV.6216 (Resumption 1), p. 19); Rwanda (*ibid.*, p. 53); and the Netherlands (UN Doc. S/PV.6531 (Resumption 1), pp. 23–5). For an opposite view, see Brazil (UN Doc. S/PV.6531, p. 11). For a more nuanced view, see Uruguay (*ibid.*, p. 24).

[92] UNSG, 'The Protection of Civilians in Armed Conflict', p. 4. The UN Secretary General seems to have changed his position in 2012; see UNSG, 'Protection of Civilians in Armed Conflict', UN Doc. S/2012/376, 22 May 2012, para. 21.

itself,[93] such requirement of absolute neutrality necessarily affects the role that the ICRC could directly play in relation to the implementation of R2P. Generally speaking, the ICRC must remain careful when giving its opinion on R2P. Contrary to the humanitarian law treaties of which the ICRC is generally considered to be the guardian,[94] the R2P concept is still a highly controversial notion whose content is much debated among States.[95] The neutral nature of the ICRC requires it to avoid entering such political discussions. This may actually be the reason why the ICRC has not given any clear official position on R2P yet and is merely attending debates on the matter 'out of concern that the developing world's suspicions about R2P's notion of protection ... do not spill over into hostility to the ICRC's humanitarian protection'.[96] In particular, its neutral nature prevents it from exercising most of the functions exercised by NGOs in relation to the implementation of R2P, such as to be an advocacy actor with respect to the application of R2P in a country-specific crisis,[97] to gather and communicate information to States in an ongoing crisis,[98] or to recommend States to use force as a last resort. More generally, as suggested by the positions adopted by some national Red Cross societies[99] and given the political nature of R2P, any assimilation of this concept with the responsibility under PoC is likely to be opposed by the ICRC.

Armed groups

In contrast with traditional NGOs and the ICRC, armed groups are generally absent from R2P discussions. They have never been mentioned as potential actors in implementing R2P. Reference has been made to

---

[93] *Ibid.*, p. 34.

[94] Yves Sandoz, *The International Committee of the Red Cross as Guardian of International Humanitarian Law* (Geneva: International Committee of the Red Cross, 1998).

[95] See for example, statements made by Venezuela at the 2009 UNGA dialogue on R2P (UN Doc. A/63/PV.99, pp. 3–6) as well as the 2009 UNSC debate on the protection of civilians in armed conflict (UN Doc. S/PV.6151 (Resumption 1), p. 30). See also, the statements made by China at the 2009 UNGA dialogue on R2P (UN Doc. A/63/PV.98, p. 23) as well as the 2011 UNSC debate on the protection of civilians in armed conflict (UN Doc. S/PV.6531 (Resumption 1), p. 20).

[96] Steven Ratner, 'Law Promotion Beyond Law Talk: The Red Cross, Persuasion, and the Laws of War', *European Journal of International Law*, 22 (2011), 459–506, at 466.

[97] For an emphasis on this aspect, see WFM–IGP, 'Final Report', p. 16.

[98] For an emphasis on this aspect, see ICISS, *The Responsibility to Protect*, p. 35.

[99] Australian Red Cross, 'International Humanitarian Law and the Responsibility to Protect: A Handbook', (2011), p. 18, available at www.redcross.org.au.

them mainly in relation to the situations triggering R2P. It has been emphasised that potential or actual crimes committed by armed groups should lead the State on the territory of which those groups are operating to act and protect its population from those crimes.[100] Although not recognising any role for armed groups in the implementation of R2P, such references are nonetheless important for two main reasons.

First, since the 2009 UNSG report on the matter, there is now a well-established consensus among States about the 'three-pillars approach' of R2P. However, this approach is meaningful only in situations where populations are threatened by armed groups (or others) rather than the military forces of the State on the territory of which those populations are located. Indeed, the specific responsibility of the international community to assist States in protecting their populations from mass atrocities, under the second pillar, can only be exercised in such situations. Once a State is itself responsible for the mass atrocities against its population, it becomes useless for the international community to propose its assistance, as provided under the second pillar of R2P. That situation directly triggers actions under the third pillar, which requires the international community to take timely and decisive measures, including the use of armed force. This is clearly acknowledged in the 2009 UNSG report.[101] Yet, in practice, especially at the UN level,[102] failures to uphold R2P have mainly been invoked in situations where the State was accused of committing – sometimes together with armed groups[103] – mass atrocities against its population. Therefore, only the first and third pillars of R2P were referred to in these cases.

Second, it is also only with respect to situations where populations are threatened by armed groups (or others) rather than the military forces of the State on the territory of which those populations are located that the

---

[100] UNSG, 'Implementing the Responsibility to Protect', pp.15–16.   [101] *Ibid.*, p. 15.

[102] See for example, concerning Libya, UNSC Res. 1970 and UNSC Res. 1973; concerning the Ivory Coast, UNSC Res. 1975. See also, concerning the current situation in Syria, GCR2P, 'Open Letter to the Security Council on the Situation in Syria', 9 June 2011, at www.globalr2p.org; declarations by States such as Italy (UN Doc. S/PV.6531, p. 26). See also, concerning the past situation in Guinea, in particular the events of 28 September 2009, GCR2P, 'The International Response to 28 September 2009 Massacre in Guinea and the Responsibility to Protect', 11 January 2010, available at www.globalr2p.org.

[103] See for example, the situation in the Democratic Republic of Congo. GCR2P, 'Open Letter to the United Nations Security', 3 November 2008, available at www.globalr2p. org. See also the situation in Sri Lanka. GCR2P, 'To: Members of the UN Security Council', 11 May 2009, available at www.globalr2p.org.

notion of responsibility to protect in its primary meaning – the responsibility of the States to protect their populations – is conceptually coherent. Admittedly, R2P assumes that States cannot mistreat their
own populations. However, the prohibition on such mistreatment
cannot be seen as embodied in the concept of R2P itself. Committing
not to adopt a specific behaviour, for example to kill or injure people,
is different from committing *to protect* persons against such
behaviour. In this latter case, the prohibited behaviour is supposed to
originate from a source other than that making the commitment. In
this sense, it seems conceptually inaccurate to assert that a State
has failed to exercise R2P because it is committing crimes against
its own population. Such a situation amounts to a violation by the
State of its primary obligation not to commit mass atrocities against
its own population, rather than the lack of fulfilling its responsibility
to protect that population against others. However, practice does not
seem to confirm such a conceptual view. Indeed, as already emphasised
above, references to R2P in specific crises, including at the UN level,
have mostly been made with respect to situations in which the State was
considered as having failed in exercising R2P, because it was
itself committing mass atrocities. This reinforces the idea that the
notion of responsibility under R2P was created especially for political
purposes and, originally, for reintroducing the notion of 'humanitarian
intervention' – whose primary concern is to protect populations
against the State where they are located – in a more acceptable
manner.[104]

Besides States, armed groups also bear responsibility with regard to
protecting civilians during an armed conflict. Indeed, it is generally
admitted that international humanitarian law, including obligations
related to the protection of civilians, is binding upon armed groups
once they are a party to an armed conflict,[105] although the mechanism

---

[104] See ICISS, *The Responsibility to Protect*, pp. 16–17.
[105] See Eric David, *Principes de droit des conflits armés*, 4th edn (Brussels: Bruylant, 2008),
pp. 245–6; Liesbeth Zegveld, *The Accountability of Armed Opposition Groups in
International Law* (Cambridge University Press, 2002), p. 11, fn. 5; see also
International Commission of Inquiry on Darfur, 'Report of the International
Commission of Inquiry on Darfur to the United Nations Secretary-General', 25
January 2005; *Case Concerning Military and Paramilitary Activities in and against
Nicaragua (Nicaragua v. United States of America)*, Merits, ICJ Reports 1986, p. 114,
para. 219; *Prosecutor v. Sam Hinga Norman*, Special Court for Sierra Leone, Case No.
SCSL-2004-14-AR72(E), Decision on Preliminary Motion Based on Lack of
Jurisdiction (Child Recruitment) of 31 May 2004, p. 14, para. 22.

through which they are bound is highly debated.[106] The primary responsibility to protect civilians during an armed conflict falls upon any party to such a conflict, whether a State or an armed group. As a result, the question arises as whether any role can be attributed to armed groups with respect to R2P in light of the above-mentioned trend to assimilate this concept with the responsibility under PoC. However, the concepts of R2P and PoC diverge to a considerable extent with respect to the primary bearers of the responsibility to protect, that difference being among the most significant obstacles against the assimilation of these concepts. Indeed, under R2P the primary bearers are States, while under PoC, both States and armed groups bear that responsibility.

It would be inapposite to argue, as some State declarations seem to suggest,[107] that the current tendency to assimilate R2P with the responsibility under PoC has led to the primary responsibility to protect civilians in armed conflicts being limited to States. Such a position goes against contemporary humanitarian law and would weaken the level of protection accruing to civilians under this branch of international law. The reverse idea that such a tendency has led to shifting the primary responsibility to protect populations under R2P to armed groups is also untenable. No State has ever claimed that such responsibility was borne by armed groups.[108] The fundamental reason is that the assertion of R2P is based upon the notion of sovereignty.[109] The responsibility of States to protect their populations is presented as an attribute of their sovereignty. This way of presenting R2P was certainly most helpful in ensuring the success of the concept and facilitated its endorsement by States. However, the same consistently prevents such a responsibility being attributed to non-State actors.

It is not difficult to envisage a particular situation in which armed groups control a significant part of the territory of a State and exercise State-like functions over it. Arguably, such functions should logically include the responsibility to protect populations located in the area that they control. Those armed groups could therefore be considered as

---

[106] On this subject, see van Steenberghe, 'Non-State Actors from the Perspective of the International Committee of the Red Cross', in d'Aspremont (ed.), *Participants in the International Legal System*, pp. 204–32, at pp. 217–24.

[107] See for example, the statements of France (UN Doc. S/PV.6151, p. 16); Austria (UN Doc. S/PV.6216, p. 29); Sudan (UN Doc. S/PV.6216 (Resumption 1), p. 42); China (UN Doc. S/V.6531, p. 20); the Netherlands (UN Doc. S/PV.6531 (Resumption 1), p. 24).

[108] See, nonetheless, the ambiguous declarations of Burkina Faso (UN Doc. S/PV.6151, p. 24).

[109] ICISS, *The Responsibility to Protect*, p. 13.

primary bearers of R2P, on an equal footing with States.[110] However, it is questionable whether imposing a primary responsibility to protect civilians upon armed groups under R2P would change much in the debate. In practice, States would still bear the responsibility to prevent or stop mass atrocities occurring in their territory. If such atrocities were committed by armed groups in some part of their territory, States should react and strive to stop them and, if they fail to do so, ask for or accept the assistance of external actors. Otherwise, if they do not ask for or consent to such external assistance, they might be subject to the timely and decisive measures undertaken by the international community. Additionally, the existing legal framework concerning PoC provides for enforcement mechanisms in case of failure by armed groups to respect their obligations to protect civilians during an armed conflict. The main mechanism is Article 1 common to the four 1949 Geneva Conventions, according to which States that are parties to these conventions must ensure their respect, including by armed groups.[111] Under this provision, States Parties are allowed to take action against armed groups when the latter do not respect their obligations under humanitarian law, such as those designed to protect civilians in armed conflicts.

Concluding remarks

Certainly, R2P is not only a matter for States and international organisations. Non-State actors have an obvious and significant role to play, especially NGOs, since their mandates generally include protecting people in distress. An increasing number of actions are currently undertaken by NGOs for the purpose of promoting and implementing R2P.

---

[110] The 1977 Additional Protocol II to the Geneva Conventions expressly contains such a control criterion as a requirement for its application. Protocol Additional to the Geneva Conventions of 12 August 1949 and Relating to the Protection of Victims of Non-International Armed Conflicts, adopted 8 June 1977 and entered into force 7 December 1978, 1125 UNTS 609. However, this criterion is also frequently referred to in legal literature as founding the attribution to armed groups of an international legal personality as well as some State-like capacities such as concluding international agreements or being bound by international obligations like the human rights ones. See in respect of international agreements, Antonio Cassese, 'The Special Court and International Law: The Decision Concerning the Lomé Agreement Amnesty', *Journal of International Criminal Justice*, 2 (2004), 1130–40, at 1134; see in respect of human rights obligations, Annyssa Bellal, Gilles Giacca and Stuart Casey-Maslen, 'International Law and Armed Non-State Actors in Afghanistan', *International Review of the Red Cross*, 93 (2011), 47–79, at 69.

[111] See in this sense, *Nicaragua* v. *United States of America*, pp. 114–15, para. 220.

Those actions range from raising public awareness and advocacy campaigns to undertaking concrete activities in the field. Interestingly, one of the main activities carried out by NGOs consists of pushing for the inclusion of R2P references in State declarations and international instruments, such as UNSC and UNGA resolutions. Potentially, this may have a significant impact on the normative status of R2P, since such endorsements by States may lead over time to the transformation of this still highly controversial concept to a norm of customary international law. In this sense it can even be said that NGOs play (or at least have the ability to play) a significant, although informal, role in international lawmaking in relation to R2P. Another specific feature of NGOs' mobilisation with respect to R2P is the creation of an international coalition of NGOs, following the models of international coalitions which have led to significant results such as the creation of the International Criminal Court. The potential effect of such an international coalition is to dramatically boost the development of R2P, both in terms of its operationalisation and normative aspects. This involvement is generally presented as a contribution to the implementation of the responsibilities that States and the international community formally bear under R2P. Yet, nothing prevents us from conceptually considering that NGOs, being part of the broader international community, are also direct bearers of R2P at least as far as the responsibility to assist States under the R2P second pillar is concerned.

NGOs are the main non-State actors to play a significant role regarding R2P. Although the ICRC and armed groups could be seen as playing a similar role, as they are significantly involved in the protection of persons in times of crisis, some major obstacles remain in considering them as relevant actors with respect to R2P. In general, their role and ensuing actions are not linked to R2P proper, but to the responsibility to protect civilians in armed conflicts. No equal sign can be placed between these two kinds of responsibility especially as far as these actors are concerned.

3

Peacekeeping operations

SUSAN C. BREAU

Introduction

This chapter discusses recently completed and current United Nations Peacekeeping Operations and assesses whether or not the consensus General Assembly resolution at the 60th anniversary UN Summit adopting the responsibility to protect has had any impact on these operations.[1] The resolution contained two levels of responsibility. The first level established an individual State responsibility to protect populations from genocide, war crimes, ethnic cleansing and crimes against humanity. The second level mandated that the international community, through the United Nations had the responsibility to use appropriate diplomatic, humanitarian and other peaceful means in accordance with Chapters VI and VIII of the Charter to protect these same populations. Moreover, the resolution states that the United Nations through the Security Council is prepared to take collective Chapter VII enforcement action 'in a timely and decisive manner' if peaceful means were inadequate and the national authorities manifestly failed to protect their populations from mass atrocity crimes. It is that second level of responsibility that results in a dramatic impact on the practice of United Nations peacekeeping.[2]

In an article completed just before the passing of this groundbreaking resolution, I argued that the three separate components of the responsibility to protect; the responsibility to prevent, react and rebuild, had already been incorporated into a number of peacekeeping operations.[3] Indeed, the Security Council has incorporated into its resolutions

---

[1] '2005 World Summit Outcome', UN Doc. A/RES/60/1, 24 October 2005.
[2] *Ibid.*, paras. 138 and 139.
[3] Susan Breau, 'The Impact of the Responsibility to Protect on Peacekeeping', *Journal of Conflict and Security Law*, 11 (2006), 429–64.

specific mandates to use force to protect civilian populations and also other mandates that assist in prevention, reaction and rebuilding of shattered societies. This chapter will bring that research up to date and will also examine in detail the change in mandate for the UN operation in Côte d'Ivoire (or Ivory Coast). This operation is probably the clearest example to date of providing a clear Security Council direction to ensure the responsibility to protect in a peacekeeping operation.

The first part of this chapter will review the ongoing peace-enforcement/ peacekeeping operations in the Democratic Republic of Congo (DRC), Darfur and the combined operation in the Central African Republic (CAR) and Chad. These have been characterised as 'peacekeeping with muscle' operations.[4] These operations incorporate and operationalise the second level of the responsibility to protect, the responsibility to react, meaning the use of armed force to respond to massive abuses of human rights.[5] This is defined as intervention measures by other members of the broader community of States which would include political, economic or judicial measures, and in extreme cases, they may also include military action.[6]

The second part of this chapter will review continuing peacebuilding operations in Afghanistan and Haiti incorporating obligations involved in the responsibility to rebuild. This means that after the use of force in a responsibility to react action there must be a genuine commitment to helping to build a durable peace by promoting good governance and sustainable development.[7] It is the case in these two examples that the rebuilding component does not follow a responsibility to react operation as the operation in Afghanistan was one justified on the law of self-defence and Haiti was a threatened rather than actual military intervention. However, the international activity in these countries incorporates the responsibility to rebuild; establishing that rebuilding can take place in isolation from prevention or reaction. The final part of this chapter will closely review the most recent operation in Côte d'Ivoire as the enabling Security Council resolution contains language incorporating the responsibility to protect.

Regrettably, there are no ongoing missions adopting or incorporating the first level of the responsibility to protect, which is the responsibility

---

[4] Alex Morrison, Douglas Fraser and James Kiras (eds.), *Peacekeeping with Muscle: The Use of Force in International Conflict Resolution* (Clementsport, NS: Canadian Peacekeeping Press, 1997), foreword.

[5] International Commission on Intervention and State Sovereignty, *The Responsibility to Protect* (Ottawa: International Development Research Centre, 2001), pp. 29–38.

[6] *Ibid.*, p. 29.   [7] *Ibid.*, p. 39.

to prevent. To date, the only true prevention operation was the United Nations Preventive Deployment Force (UNPREDEP) in the Former Yugoslav Republic of Macedonia (FYROM).[8] At a Security Council meeting on 25 February 1999 the UNPREDEP's mandate was not renewed beyond 28 February 1999 as the Council did not adopt a draft resolution on a six-month extension due to a veto by China. The mandate of that successful operation, to prevent conflict between potential warring forces, has most regrettably, never been repeated since. This critical gap has been recognised by the Secretary-General of the United Nations, Ban Ki-moon who released a report in 2010 entitled 'Early Warning, Assessment and the Responsibility to Protect'.[9] This report was a follow-up to the report 'Implementing the Responsibility to Protect' released a year earlier which also strongly favoured early warning and prevention of conflict activities, particularly in pillar two, on international assistance and capacity-building.[10]

Responsibility to react through peacekeeping

There can be a major debate as to whether peacekeeping operations should ever involve a robust enforcement mandate, as they were originally envisioned as operations established to maintain the peace between two parties. The colloquial expression for robust enforcement is 'crossing the Mogadishu line', reflecting the first operation that did so, the tragic and failed operation in Somalia.[11] However, with the horrific experiences in peacekeeping missions in Yugoslavia and Rwanda there was a realisation that peacekeeping often required a civilian protection mandate which would allow the peacekeepers to use force for the purpose of preventing the types of mass murders that took place at Srebrenica and in Rwanda.[12] This development is linked to the increased

[8] UN Security Council Res. 983, UN Doc. S/RES/983, 31 March 1995.
[9] UN Secretary-General, 'Early Warning, Assessment and the Responsibility to Protect', UN Doc. A/64/864, 14 July 2010.
[10] UNSG, 'Implementing the Responsibility to Protect', UN Doc. A/63/677, 12 January 2009, pp. 15–21.
[11] This refers to the operation in Somalia which for the first time incorporated civilian protection obligations in a peacekeeping mission. See UNSC Res. 794, UN Doc. S/RES/794, 3 December 1992, which authorised using 'all necessary means to establish a secure environment for humanitarian relief operations in Somalia'.
[12] UNSG, 'Identical Letters Dated 21 August 2000 from the Secretary-General to the President of the General Assembly and the President of the Security Council', UN Doc. A/55/305–S/2000/809, 21 August 2000.

role of the Security Council in the protection of civilians starting earlier in 1999 with a Security Council request to the Secretary-General to prepare a dedicated report on the protection of civilians in armed conflict which eventually resulted in Security Council Resolution 1674 entitled 'Protection of Civilians in Armed Conflict'.[13] There have been several subsequent reports on the protection of civilians including the 2009 independent study commissioned by the Office of Coordination of Humanitarian Affairs (hereafter OCHA) and the Department of Peacekeeping Operations (hereafter DPKO) entitled 'Protecting Civilians in the Context of UN Peacekeeping Operations'.[14]

In a parallel development, the concept of the responsibility to protect developed by the Canadian-funded International Commission for Intervention and State Sovereignty (ICISS) in 2001 was supported in a number of subsequent peace and security reports.[15] Research reveals that many peacekeeping operations have evolved towards receiving Chapter VII mandates to use force not just for self-defence, but also to protect the civilians within their field of operations. The High-Level Panel on Threats, Challenges and Change in their report entitled 'A More Secure World' supported Chapter VII mandates from the outset for any peacekeeping missions where there was a possibility of 'an explosion of violence'.[16] This recommendation seems to have been largely adopted in subsequent operations in the Democratic Republic of Congo, Burundi and Côte d'Ivoire. A question remains as to whether these operations with specific use of force mandates are no longer peacekeeping missions and instead are Chapter VII collective security actions. However, all of the peacekeeping operations examined in this chapter commenced within the legal mandate of a consensual peacekeeping mission.

---

[13] UNSC Res. 1674, UN Doc. S/RES/1674, 28 April 2006. See also the reports of the Secretary-General on the Protection of Civilians, UNSG, 'The Protection of Civilians in Armed Conflict', UN Docs. S/1999/957, 8 September 1999; UN Doc. S/2001/331, 30 March 2001; UN Doc. S/2002/1300, 26 November 2002; UN Doc. S/2004/431, 28 May 2004; and UN Doc. S/2005/740, 28 November 2005.

[14] Victoria Holt, Glyn Taylor and Max Kelly, *Protecting Civilians in the Context of UN Peacekeeping Operations* (New York: United Nations, 2009). See also UNSG, 'The Protection of Civilians in Armed Conflict', UN Doc. S/2010/579, 11 November 2010, paras. 58–72.

[15] ICISS, *The Responsibility to Protect*; UNSG, *A More Secure World: Our Shared Responsibility* (New York: United Nations, 2004); UNSG, 'In Larger Freedom: Towards Development, Security and Human Rights for All', UN Doc. A/59/2005, 21 March 2005.

[16] UNSG, *A More Secure World*, para. 212.

In practice there have been several peacekeeping missions with a specific Chapter VII mandate given for precisely the situation that engages the responsibility to protect; genocide, crimes against humanity and grave breaches of international humanitarian law directed against the civilian population. It is the argument of this chapter that the second level of the responsibility to protect, the responsibility to react, is now embedded into most peacekeeping operations. Due to the restrictions of space, only three of these missions will be examined here, but they reflect a continuing pattern of peace-enforcement, rather than peacekeeping.

Democratic Republic of Congo – October 2005 to the present

The conflict in the Democratic Republic of Congo involving armed groups from several different African countries has been labelled the world's deadliest since the Second World War, with estimates of between three million and seven million casualties.[17] Two months after the adoption of the General Assembly resolution adopting the responsibility to protect doctrine, the Security Council was called upon once again (as it has done regularly since the early 1960s) to deal with the situation in the DRC. As it had in several previous resolutions, the Security Council authorised its troops to protect civilians.[18] The key provision in Resolution 1649 (2005) stated:

> 11. *Emphasizes* that, as per resolution 1565, MONUC is authorized to use all necessary means, within its capabilities and in the areas where its armed units are deployed, to deter any foreign or Congolese armed group from attempting to use force to threaten the political process, and to ensure the protection of civilians under imminent threat of physical violence.

There is an important geographical limitation, as the conflict encompasses such a wide area it is impossible for the peacekeepers to exercise the responsibility to protect civilians everywhere, but this mandate has continued in the DRC since 2000.[19] It has to be acknowledged that imminent threat of physical violence may be a less stringent condition

---

[17] See, among others, Armed Activities on the Territory of the Congo (Democratic Republic of Congo v. Uganda), Declaration of Judge Koroma, ICJ Reports 2005, p. 284, para. 1. It has to be noted that most of these casualties are from illness and poverty caused by the conflict.

[18] Breau, 'Peacekeeping', 446–9.

[19] USNC Res. 1291, UN Doc. S/RES/1291, 24 February 2000.

than genocide, crimes against humanity and war crimes, but the reality is that the responsibility to protect has a threshold of physical violence.[20] Additionally, there is the condition of 'manifestly failing' to protect the population by the State concerned. This would mean that for outside intervention to occur, widespread and/or systematic violations of these serious crimes should be under way or imminent.[21]

The conflict in the DRC is part of a larger conflict, a long-standing war involving several States in the African Great Lakes region growing out of ethnic conflicts and genocides in Burundi and Rwanda and the attendant refugee flows. In tandem with peacekeeping operations in Burundi and the DRC, the nations involved in the Great Lakes conflict have been engaged in a comprehensive peace process. The African Union and the United Nations initiated the International Conference on the Great Lakes Region (ICGLR). This process culminated in the signing by eleven States of the Pact on Security, Stability and Development in the Great Lakes Region (the Great Lakes Pact). The Pact entered into force in June 2008 and has been ratified by the eleven Member States.[22] Part and parcel of the settlement is one of the several Protocols to the Pact which is entitled Protocol on Non-Aggression and Mutual Defence in the Great Lakes Region. The Protocol includes this clause:

> Member States agree that the provisions of this Article and Article 5 of this Protocol shall not impair the exercise of their responsibility to protect populations from genocide, war crimes, ethnic cleansing, crimes against humanity, and gross violations of human rights committed by, or within, a State. The decision of the Member States to exercise their responsibility to protect populations in this provision shall be taken collectively with due procedural notice to the Peace and Security Council of the African Union and the Security Council of the United Nations.[23]

---

[20] This is known as the just cause threshold in the original report, ICISS, *The Responsibility to Protect*, p. XII. '*(1) The Just Cause Threshold*. Military intervention for human protection purposes is an exceptional and extraordinary measure. To be warranted, there must be serious and irreparable harm occurring to human beings, or imminently likely to occur, of the following kind: A. *large scale loss of life*, actual or apprehended, with genocidal intent or not, which is the product either of deliberate state action, or state neglect or inability to act, or a failed state situation; or B. *large scale 'ethnic cleansing'*, actual or apprehended, whether carried out by killing, forced expulsion, acts of terror or rape.'

[21] '2005 World Summit Outcome'.

[22] The Member States are Angola, Burundi, Central African Republic, Democratic Republic of Congo, Republic of Congo, Kenya, Rwanda, Sudan, Tanzania, Uganda and Zambia.

[23] International Conference of the Great Lakes Region, 'Protocol on Non-aggression and Mutual Defence in the Great Lakes Region', 30 November 2006. For more information

This is an example of State practice among the African States indicating that they are prepared within their mandate to keep the peace on their continent, to intervene to ensure that the responsibility to protect is complied with.[24] Notwithstanding the Pact, the violence continues in this area, most particularly in the DRC which has resulted in a continuing civilian protection role for the United Nations troops, part of MONUC.

The international response in Darfur, Sudan

Events in the Darfur province have been by far the most violent, and have involved the most civilian casualties, in Sudan's twenty-two-year civil war. The Sudan Liberation Army/Movement (SLA) and Justice and Equality Movement (JEM) rebelled against the government beginning in February 2003. The rebels were made up of predominantly African tribes, such as Fur, Zaghawa and Massalit. After a string of rebel victories in spring 2003, the government responded to the rebellion by arming Arab 'Janjaweed' militia to clear civilian population bases of African tribes thought to be supporting rebellion. The policy led to displacement of between one-and-a-half to two million civilians in Darfur, and an estimated 200,000 deaths.[25] One of the major controversies in this long-standing conflict is whether the Sudanese government and Janjaweed militia are perpetrating genocide. A commission reporting to the Secretary-General of the United Nations characterised the activities of the militias and government as crimes against humanity rather than genocide, but the United States government supported a finding of genocide.[26]

Through Resolution 1590 (2005) the Security Council established a peacekeeping force to monitor the Comprehensive Peace Agreement that supposedly would end the long-standing civil war, but it did not incorporate any comprehensive solution to the Darfur crisis.[27] The

and documents on the situation in the Great Lakes, see www.lse.ac.uk/collections/law/projects/greatlakes/ihl-greatlakes-summary.htm.

[24] For a detailed discussion of the African Union and RtoP, see Dersso, Chapter 10 in this book.

[25] This number is disputed due to the lack of proper casualty recording mechanisms. See 'Death toll of 200,000 disputed in Darfur', MSNBC, 28 March 2008, at www.msnbc.msn.com/id/23848444/ns/world_news-africa/t/death-toll-disputed-darfur.

[26] International Commission of Inquiry on Darfur, 'Report to the United Nations Secretary-General', 25 January 2005; 'US House calls Darfur "genocide"', BBC, 24 July 2004, at news.bbc.co.uk/2/hi/africa/3918765.stm.

[27] UNSC Res. 1590, UN Doc. S/RES/1590, 24 March 2005.

resolution determined that the situation in Sudan was a threat to international peace and security. However, unlike operations conducted at the same time, namely Burundi, the Democratic Republic of Congo and Côte d'Ivoire there was *no* robust mandate given to protect civilians. The United Nations Mission in Sudan (UNMIS) was mandated to support the implementation of the Comprehensive Peace Agreement and monitor and verify the implementation of the Ceasefire Agreement including the disarmament, demobilisation and reintegration programme. In terms of civilian protection there was a mandate to ensure a human rights presence, but not the use of force to protect civilians. This was a disgraceful abdication of international responsibility. This operation ended as South Sudan is now an independent State, admitted as the 193rd Member State of the United Nations.[28] However, this has not resolved the situation in Darfur which is in Sudan proper and remains a continuing UN peacekeeping operation.

Following the adoption by the UN of the responsibility to protect doctrine in 2005, the Security Council acted belatedly in 2007 through Resolution 1769. This resolution authorised the deployment of a 26,000 strong United Nations–African Union Mission in Darfur known as UNAMID. Acting under Chapter VII of the Charter of the United Nations, the Security Council gave this mission a fairly robust mandate to protect civilians by providing as follows:

(a) *decides* that UNAMID is authorised to take the necessary action, in the areas of deployment of its forces and as it deems within its capabilities in order to:
   (i) protect its personnel, facilities, installations and equipment, and to ensure the security and freedom of movement of its own personnel and humanitarian workers,
   (ii) support early and effective implementation of the Darfur Peace Agreement, prevent the disruption of its implementation and armed attacks, and protect civilians, without prejudice to the responsibility of the Government of Sudan.[29]

It is evident from this enabling resolution that UNAMID had the protection of civilians as its core mandate, but was also tasked with contributing to security for humanitarian assistance, monitoring and

---

[28] UNMIS wound up its operations on 9 July 2011 with the completion of the interim period agreed on by the government of Sudan and Sudan People's Liberation Movement in the Comprehensive Peace Agreement (CPA), signed on 9 January 2005. See, for more details, unmis.unmissions.org. However, UNAMID continues.

[29] UNSC Res. 1769, UN Doc. S/RES/1769, 31 July 2007, para. 15.

verifying implementation of agreements, assisting an inclusive political process, contributing to the promotion of human rights and the rule of law, and monitoring and reporting on the situation along the borders with Chad and the Central African Republic. This mission has carried on until this day, but there is a major difficulty with the numbers of troops employed to police such a large area and there are still numerous fatalities and human rights abuses being perpetrated.[30] Arrest warrants were also issued by the International Criminal Court for Sudanese President al-Bashir, respectively in March 2009 and July 2010, charging him with genocide, war crimes and crimes against humanity with respect to the conflict in Darfur.[31]

There have been several efforts to secure the peace in Darfur, but as of yet the conflict has not ended.[32] Notwithstanding the continuing violence, Security Council 1769 (2007) is hailed as containing a responsibility to protect mandate, but in reviewing the debate that surrounded this resolution, it is evident that Security Council members refrained from mentioning the responsibility to protect.[33]

The Central African Republic and Chad

The humanitarian crisis in the Central African Republic (CAR) and Chad grew out of the violent conflict in Sudan. Since 2003, more than 240,000 Sudanese refugees have fled to eastern Chad from the conflict in Darfur, joined by approximately 45,000 refugees from the CAR. With around 180,000 Chadians displaced by the civil war in the east of the country, this generated increased tensions among the region's ethnic communities.[34]

Responding to this, and to the activities of armed groups based in eastern Chad and Darfur, including cross-border attacks, the United Nations Mission in Central African Republic and Chad (MINURCAT)

---

[30] Amnesty International, *Sudan: No End to Violence in Darfur* (London: Amnesty International Publications, 2012).

[31] The first arrest warrant against al-Bashir, issued in March 2009, is available at www.icc-cpi. int/iccdocs/doc/doc639078.pdf. The second arrest warrant, issued in July 2010, is available at www.icc-cpi.int/iccdocs/dsoc/doc907140.pdf. For more information on the situation in Darfur, see www.icc-cpi.int/Menus/ICC/Situations+and+Cases.

[32] See 'Sudan profile: timeline', BBC, 24 June 2012, at news.bbc.co.uk/2/hi/middle_east/ country_profiles/827425.stm; see also UNSC Res. 2063, UN. Doc. S/RES/2063, 31 July 2012, extending the mandate of the operation until 31 July 2013.

[33] UNSC Verbatim Record, UN Doc. S/PV.5727, 31 July 2007.

[34] For more information, see www.un.org/en/peacekeeping/missions/minurcat/background. shtml.

was established by Security Council Resolution 1778 on 25 September 2007.[35] The specific purpose of the mission was to contribute to the protection of civilians; the promotion of human rights and the rule of law; and to promote regional peace. The Council authorised a multi-dimensional presence intended to help to create the security conditions conducive to a voluntary, secure and sustainable return of refugees and displaced persons, by contributing to the protection of refugees, displaced persons and civilians in danger, by facilitating the provision of humanitarian assistance in eastern Chad and the north-eastern CAR and by creating favourable conditions for the reconstruction and economic and social development of those areas. By that resolution and acting under Chapter VII of the UN Charter, the Council also authorised the European Union to deploy a military force, which became known as EUFOR, in support of the MINURCAT mandate.[36] Prior to the completion of EUFOR's mandate in March 2009, Security Council resolution 1861 authorised the deployment of a military component of MINURCAT to follow up EUFOR in both Chad and the CAR. Based on a Chapter VII mandate, MINURCAT was to carry out a wide range of functions which included security and protection of civilians, human rights and the rule of law and regional peace support.[37] In adopting this resolution the Security Council expressed again its deep concern at armed activities and banditry in eastern Chad, the north-eastern Central African Republic and western Sudan which were threatening the security of the civilian population, the conduct of humanitarian operations in those areas and the stability of those countries, and which resulted in serious violations of human rights and international humanitarian law.

After the Chadian government had called in early 2010 for the withdrawal of MINURCAT and had committed itself to take full responsibility for the security of the civilian population in the eastern part of the country, the Security Council, by its Resolution 1923 of 25 May 2010, revised the mandate of the Mission and extended it for the final period until 31 December 2010. For the remainder of its mandate, the Council decided that MINURCAT should continue to assist with the organisation and training of Chad's Détachement Intégeré de Sécurité (DIS), in support of

---

[35] *Ibid.*
[36] For more information, see www.un.org/en/peacekeeping/missions/minurcat/mandate.shtml.
[37] UNSC Res. 1861, UN Doc. S/RES/1861, 14 January 2009.

efforts to relocate refugee camps away from the border; to liaise with other security structures in both Chad and the Central African Republic; and to contribute to the protection of civil rights and the rule of law in Chad.

The decision for MINURCAT to cease operations was met with criticism. On 24 May 2010, Amnesty International issued a press release indicating that the withdrawal of the peacekeeping forces from eastern Chad would put the safety of thousands of refugees and other vulnerable groups at risk. Amnesty International's Africa Director stated that, 'MINURCAT has demonstrated it is able to play a significant role in bolstering security and human rights protection in eastern Chad. This is not the time for the Chadian government to pull the plug on MINURCAT and the Security Council should stand up for the vulnerable women, men and young people in the region.'[38]

The Mission completed its mandate on 31 December 2010, in accordance with Security Council Resolution 1923 (2010) at the request of the Chadian government, which had pledged full responsibility for protecting civilians on its territory. Reporting to the Security Council at the end of this mission the Secretary-General stated that 'MINURCAT has been an unusual and unique United Nations peacekeeping operation in that it was devoted solely to contributing to the protection of civilians, without an explicit political mandate. It has gone through the stages of planning, deployment and withdrawal in the short span of less than four years, enduring adversities in each.'[39]

This mission, the last in our case studies review, was a clear responsibility to react mission. There had been serious violations of both human rights and humanitarian law and this mission had a comprehensive mandate of protecting civilians in cooperation with an armed European Union force.

Rebuilding shattered societies

The third aspect of the doctrine of the responsibility to protect as articulated in the original report is the responsibility to rebuild.[40] This aspect corresponds to pillar two in the Secretary-General's 2009 report

---

[38] Amnesty International press release, 'UN move to withdraw from Chad puts thousands at risk', 25 May 2010, at www.amnesty.org/en/news-and-updates/un-move-withdraw-chad-puts-thousands-risk-2010-05-24.

[39] UNSG, 'Report on the United Nations Mission in the Central African Republic and Chad', UN Doc. S/2010/611, 1 December 2010.

[40] ICISS, *Responsibility to Protect*.

on the implementation of the responsibility to protect, focusing on international assistance and capacity-building.[41] There had been a long-standing recognition of the necessity for a peacebuilding component to follow any armed intervention, as a critical component in the prevention of a repetition of the conflict. In his seminal report, *An Agenda for Peace*, Boutros Ghali provides the first definition of post-conflict peacebuilding, which is 'action to identify and support structures which will tend to strengthen and solidify peace in order to avoid a relapse into conflict'.[42] For peacemaking and peacekeeping operations to be truly successful, they have to include efforts to identify and support structures which would consolidate peace and advance a sense of confidence and well-being among people. This includes: disarming the previously warring parties and the restoration of order; the custody and possible destruction of weapons; repatriating refugees; advisory and training support for security personnel; monitoring elections; advancing efforts to protect human rights; reforming or strengthening governmental institutions and promoting formal and informal processes of political participation.[43] The 2001 ICISS report included post-conflict peacebuilding as a critical third phase in any international forcible intervention in human rights catastrophes. This was defined in that report as:

> 5.1 The responsibility to protect implies the responsibility not just to prevent and react, but to follow through and rebuild. This means that if military intervention action is taken – because of a breakdown or abdication of a state's own capacity and authority in discharging its 'responsibility to protect' – there should be a genuine commitment to helping to build a durable peace, and promoting good governance and sustainable development. Conditions of public safety and order have to be reconstituted by international agents acting in partnership with local authorities, with the goal of progressively transferring to them authority and responsibility to rebuild.

The ICISS report also asserts that, in previous operations, the responsibility to rebuild had been insufficiently recognised and the exit of the intervening forces poorly managed with the result that the underlying problems causing the conflict were left unresolved.[44]

---

[41] UNSG, 'Implementing the Responsibility to Protect', pp. 15–22.

[42] UNSG, 'An Agenda for Peace: Preventive Diplomacy, Peacemaking and Peace-keeping', UN Doc. A/47/277–S/24111, 17 June 1992, para. 21.

[43] *Ibid.*, para. 5.   [44] *Ibid.*, para. 5.7.

This component, of all the three suggested in the original ICISS report, has received the strongest vocal support from the UN Member States. The 2005 World Summit Outcome Document supported the establishment of the Peacebuilding Commission.[45] Prior United Nations practice for several years in Cambodia, Afghanistan, Bosnia, Haiti, Kosovo and East Timor had given strong support to the idea of the responsibility of the international community to assist in the rebuilding of post-conflict societies. If anything, that practice has increased since late 2005. The peacekeeping missions in the DRC, Darfur and CAR/Chad, previously discussed here, all contain peacebuilding elements. Our focus will be on two ongoing examples, namely Afghanistan and Haiti, both of which are clearly peacebuilding operations. There has also been significant international involvement in Iraq, but that is a complex situation that requires more substantial explanation.

It should be noted that there are several other countries now which are the subject of extensive activity by the Peacebuilding Commission and the Peacebuilding Fund. The African nations of Burundi, Sierra Leone, Guinea-Bissau, Liberia and the Central African Republic are on the agenda of the Commission. The Commission's mandate is to 'marshal resources at the disposal of the international community to advise and propose integrated strategies for post-conflict recovery, focusing attention on reconstruction, institution-building and sustainable development, in countries emerging from conflict'. In order to accomplish this task the Commission is to use the United Nations' capacities and experience in conflict prevention, mediation, peacekeeping, respect for human rights, the rule of law, humanitarian assistance, reconstruction and long-term development. In summary the Commission's aims are to:

- Propose integrated strategies for post-conflict peacebuilding and recovery;
- Help to ensure predictable financing for early recovery activities and sustained financial investment over the medium- to longer-term;

---

[45] '2005 World Summit Outcome', para. 97 reads: 'Emphasizing the need for a coordinated, coherent and integrated approach to post-conflict peacebuilding and reconciliation, with a view to achieving sustainable peace; and recognizing the need for a dedicated institutional mechanism to address the special need of countries emerging from conflict towards recovery, reintegration and reconstruction and to assist them in laying the foundation for sustainable development; and recognizing the vital role of the United Nations in that regard, we decide to establish a Peacebuilding Commission as an inter-governmental advisory body.'

- Extend the period of attention by the international community to post-conflict recovery;
- Develop best practices on issues that require extensive collaboration among political, military, humanitarian and development actors.[46]

These activities do not involve a Security Council mandate for a mission, although it is likely that the Peacebuilding Commission will assume much more of the task of the responsibility to rebuild. This mechanism will assist the Security Council to consider emerging threats to international peace and security.

Afghanistan

After the 11 September 2001 attacks in Washington and New York, a large coalition of forces from many countries invaded Afghanistan and the Taliban regime was defeated. After a conference in Bonn in December 2001 resulted in the 'Agreement on Provisional Arrangements in Afghanistan Pending the Re-Establishment of Permanent Government Institutions', it was decided that the United Nations would contribute to the task of rebuilding Afghanistan. The invasion of Afghanistan might at first glance take this situation out of the responsibility to protect framework, but it had been clear for several years that the Taliban regime has failed to protect its civilian population and the continuing non-international armed conflict in Afghanistan has been characterised by large numbers of civilian casualties particularly caused by the Taliban fighters, but also by coalition forces.[47]

The United Nations Assistance Mission for Afghanistan (UNAMA) was established on 28 March 2002. UNAMA's mandate has changed over the years, but its primary obligations include promoting national reconciliation; fulfilling the tasks and responsibilities entrusted to the

---

[46] Mandate as described on the website of the Peacebuilding Commission at www.un.org/peace/peacebuilding.

[47] Amnesty International, *Getting Away with Murder? The Impunity of International Forces in Afghanistan* (London: Amnesty International Publications, 2009); Amnesty International, *All Who Are Not Friends, Are Enemies: Taleban Abuses against Civilians* (London: Amnesty International Publications, 2007). See Zahir Tanin, Ambassador of Afghanistan, 'Statement of H. E. Dr Zahir Tanin Permanent Representative of Afghanistan to the UN', delivered at Security Council Debate on Children and Armed Conflict, New York, 8 July 2010, at www.afghanistan-un.org/category/afghanistan-at-the-un/statements-by-permanent-representative.

United Nations in the Bonn Agreement, including those related to human rights, the rule of law and gender issues, and managing all UN humanitarian, relief, recovery and reconstruction activities in Afghanistan in coordination with the Afghan Administration.[48] The UN describes the mission as 'a political mission established at the request of the Government to assist it and the people of Afghanistan in laying the foundations for sustainable peace and development'.[49]

Up until this date, there has been extensive involvement in rebuilding Afghanistan by UNAMA in almost every aspect of governance. Security Council Resolution 1662 passed in March 2006 acknowledged the growing role of the Afghan government in implementing obligations for disarmament and security and governance, but in paragraph 12 continued an important role for UNAMA in rebuilding the country:

> 12. *Calls for* full respect for human rights and international humanitarian law throughout Afghanistan; in this regard, *requests* UNAMA, with the support of the Office of the United Nations High Commissioner for Human Rights, to continue to assist in the full implementation of the human rights provisions of the Afghan constitution and international treaties to which Afghanistan is a State party, in particular those regarding the full enjoyment by women of their human rights; *commends* the Afghan Independent Human Rights Commission for its courageous efforts to monitor respect for human rights in Afghanistan as well as to foster and protect these rights; *welcomes* the adoption of the Action Plan on Peace, Justice and Reconciliation on 12 December 2005; and *encourages* international support for this Plan.[50]

In 2011 there was an extensive resolution on the continuation of rebuilding in Afghanistan including in paragraph 12:

---

[48] UNSC Res. 1401, UN Doc. S/RES/1401, 28 March 2002. There are several other UN agencies involved in the task of reconstruction including: UNDP (United Nations Development Programme), UNCC (United Nations Compensation Commission), UNCCD (United Nations Convention to Combat Desertification), UN–HABITAT (United Nations Centre for Human Settlements), UNCTAD (United Nations Conference on Trade and Development), UNEP (United Nations Environment Programme), UNESCO (United Nations Educational, Scientific and Cultural Organization), UNFPA (United Nations Population Fund for Afghanistan), UNHCR (United Nations High Commission for Refugees), UNICEF (United Nations Children's Fund), UNIDO (United Nations Industrial Development Organization), UNIFEM (United Nations Development Fund for Women) and UNODC (United Nations Office on Drugs and Crime).

[49] See unama.unmissions.org/Default.aspx?tabid=1742.

[50] UNSC Res. 1662, UN Doc. S/RES/1662, 23 March 2006.

12. *Stresses* the role of UNAMA in supporting the process of peace and reconciliation, including the Afghan Peace and Reintegration Programme, as mandated in this Resolution, and *encourages* the international community to assist the efforts of the Government of Afghanistan in this regard including through continued support to the Peace and Reintegration Trust Fund and, in this context, *notes* the conference on reintegration to be hosted by the Afghan Government in Kabul in the spring of this year.[51]

As Gheciu and Welsh argue, this mission is part of a 'proliferation of comprehensive international missions of peacebuilding and reconstruction, aimed not simply at bringing conflict to an end but also at preventing its recurrence.'[52] Afghanistan clearly remains in the middle of a non-international armed conflict, and the responsibility to rebuild is complicated by these further hostilities which are being conducted outside of the United Nations enforcement structure.[53] Nevertheless, on 22 March 2012, the Security Council adopted Resolution 2041, renewing UNAMA's mandate until March 2013.

Haiti

The United Nations has a long history of involvement with Haiti dating from 1991 when the Security Council began to meet to consider the military coup that took place in September 1991. Although the democratically elected government was eventually reinstated, Haiti has been a major failed State and on 30 April 2004 the United Nations dealt with the continuing problem of State collapse in Haiti. On that date they established a governance mission with all aspects of civilian administration supporting Haiti's transitional government.[54] While this might not seem to be a responsibility to protect situation, Haiti had been characterised for decades as a society where systematic human rights abuses were carried out and the regime manifestly failed to protect its population, particularly after the departure of the elected president in 2004.[55]

---

[51] UNSC Res. 1974, UN Doc. S/RES/1974, 22 March 2011.

[52] Alexandra Gheciu and Jennifer Welsh, 'The Imperative to Rebuild: Assessing the Normative Case for Postconflict Reconstruction', *Ethics and International Affairs*, 23 (2009), 121–46, at 121.

[53] The International Security Assistance Force (ISAF) is a NATO-led operation that continues to assist the Afghan government in fighting the resurgent Taliban.

[54] UNSC Res. 1542, UN Doc. S/RES/1542, 30 April 2004.

[55] Athena Kolbe and Royce Hutson, 'Human Rights Abuse and other Criminal Violations in Port-au-Prince, Haiti: A Random Survey of Households', *The Lancet*, 368 (2006),

Resolution 1542 (2004) established the United Nations Stabilization Mission in Haiti (MINUSTAH). Again acting under Chapter VII of the Charter, the Security Council established the mission to support the transitional government in ensuring a secure and stable environment; to assist in monitoring, restructuring and reforming the Haitian National Police; to help with comprehensive and sustainable Disarmament, Demobilization and Reintegration (DDR) programmes; to assist with the restoration and maintenance of the rule of law, public safety and public order in Haiti; to protect United Nations personnel, facilities, installations and equipment and to protect civilians under imminent threat of physical violence; to support the constitutional and political processes; to assist in organising, monitoring and carrying out free and fair municipal, parliamentary and presidential elections; to support the transitional government as well as Haitian human rights institutions and groups in their efforts to promote and protect human rights; and to monitor and report on the human rights situation in the country.[56] In extending the mission's mandate for another year on 13 October 2009, the Security Council, by its resolution 1892, further mandated MINUSTAH to support the Haitian political process, promoting an all-inclusive political dialogue and national reconciliation, and providing logistical and security assistance for elections anticipated for 2010.[57]

The last few resolutions on rebuilding followed the devastating earthquake that took place on 12 January 2010. On 19 January 2010 the force levels of MINUSTAH were increased to cope with the recovery efforts.[58] In June of 2010 the resolution recognised the 'critical role of MINUSTAH in ensuring stability and security in Haiti' and critically in paragraph 4:

> *Recognizes* the need for MINUSTAH to assist the Government of Haiti in providing adequate protection of the population, with particular atten- tion to the needs of internally displaced persons and other vulnerable groups, especially women and children, including through additional joint community policing in the camps along with strengthened mech- anisms to address sexual and gender-based violence; and to tackle the risk of a resurgence in gang violence, organized crime and trafficking of children.[59]

864–73, estimating 8,000 people murdered in the Port-au-Prince area in the twenty-two months after the departure of the elected regime.

[56] For more information, see www.minustah.org.
[57] UNSC Res. 1892, UN Doc. S/RES/1892, 13 October 2009.
[58] UNSC Res. 1908, UN Doc. S/RES/1908, 19 January 2010.
[59] UNSC Res. 1927, UN Doc. S/RES/1927, 4 June 2010.

Resolution 2012 on Haiti passed in October 2011 stressed the need for MINUSTAH to continue to focus its work on ensuring Haiti's security and stability as currently mandated by the Security Council. The mandate for the operation was extended for a further twelve months with an intention of renewal. There was evident recognition that this rebuilding operation would take a considerable amount of time because of the exacerbation caused by the January 2010 earthquake. The resolution reiterated the mandate concerning the protection of the civilian population, with particular attention to the needs of internally displaced persons and other vulnerable groups, especially women and children.[60]

These Security Council resolutions authorise a number of UN activities falling under pillar two of the responsibility to protect, namely international assistance and capacity-building, taking place in a State going through a very unstable situation while emerging from years of chaotic government and civil disturbance. This intervention is a clear example of the assumption of international responsibility for a clearly failed State and, in fact, extended this mandate after a natural disaster by providing even more troops to avoid a humanitarian disaster and get the country back onto its feet.

Implementing the responsibility to protect: Côte d'Ivoire and Libya

The activity of the Security Council concerning Côte d'Ivoire over 2011 is nothing short of astonishing. The same could be said with regard to the situation in Libya in early 2011. The Security Council Member States have exhibited willingness to act sooner rather than later in these two situations of grave danger to human life. On 17 March 2011, the Security Council approved a no-fly zone over Libya and gave a coalition of the willing a mandate to use 'all necessary means' to protect civilians under threat of attack.[61] This was not the establishment of a peacekeeping mission, but a Chapter VII peace-enforcement authorisation in a country that did not consent to any type of peacekeeping mission.

In the same month, on 30 March 2011, the Security Council acting under Chapter VII of the Charter adopted Resolution 1975 in order to deal with the escalation of violence in Côte d'Ivoire. The United Nations had been involved in that country since the establishment of the United

---

[60] UNSC Res. 2012, UN Doc. S/RES/2012, 14 October 2011.
[61] UNSC Res. 1973, UN Doc. S/RES/1973, 17 March 2011.

Nations Operation in Côte d'Ivoire in February of 2004 in response to ongoing civil conflict involving fights between groups of rebel forces.[62] From the beginning force was to be used to 'protect civilians under imminent threat of physical violence, within its capabilities and its areas of deployment'. This mandate contained again the limitation clause for the use of force. In addition the mission was 'to facilitate the free flow of people, goods and humanitarian assistance, *inter alia*, by helping to establish the necessary security conditions'.[63]

The mission established by this resolution in April 2004 authorised a large force of 7,000 UN peacekeepers and personnel to the country, alongside 4,000 French troops that would act in accordance with instructions by UN commanders. The mandate of both UN peacekeepers and Operation Licorne (the French operation) was extended by Resolution 1609 in June 2005 and then again in October of 2005 which set 30 September 2006 as the expiration date of the mission. However, in spite of a power-sharing deal in 2007 and him losing a democratic round of general elections President Gbagbo would not step down and was involved in shelling of areas that were loyal to the democratically elected Alassane Ouattara. The Human Rights Council estimated that, by 25 February 2011, about 300 civilians had been killed and more than 35,000 people had been forced to flee their homes and seek refuge elsewhere, including in neighbouring countries.[64]

Although Security Council Resolution 1073 (2011) was the latest in a long series of resolutions that had dealt with the peacekeeping mission in that country, this was a different type of resolution entirely. The resolution urged President Gbagbo, who had been defeated in a recent election, to immediately step aside and declared the situation in the Côte d'Ivoire to be a threat to international peace and security. The resolution also imposed targeted sanctions, namely the freezing of assets and travel bans against Laurent Gbagbo and other members of his regime. In its preamble it declared that the attacks currently taking place in Côte d'Ivoire against the civilian population could amount to crimes against humanity and that perpetrators of such crimes must be held accountable under international law and noting that the International Criminal Court may decide on its jurisdiction over the

---

[62] UNSC Res. 2004, UN Doc. S/RES/1528, 27 February 2004.   [63] *Ibid.*
[64] UN High Commissioner for Human Rights, 'Report on the Situation of Human Rights in Côte d'Ivoire', UN Doc. A/HRC/16/79, 25 February 2011; UN Doc. A/HRC/17/49, 14 June 2011; UN Doc. A/HRC/18/52, 20 September 2011.

situation in Côte d'Ivoire on the basis of article 12, paragraph 3 of the Rome Statute.

For the purposes of this analysis the resolution also authorized the United Nations Operation in Côte d'Ivoire (UNOCI) to use 'all necessary means to carry out its mandate to protect civilians' including preventing the use of heavy weapons against them. Surprisingly, the resolution specifically mentioned 'the French forces' supporting UNOCI, which indirectly authorised the use of force by French forces in assisting the UN operation to fulfil its mandate. Importantly, and uniquely the resolution referred to the 'primary responsibility' of each State to protect civilians, thus referring to the responsibility to protect, albeit in an oblique way. However, in the debate that considered the adoption of this unanimous resolution the Permanent Representative of Nigeria stated: 'Let there be no doubt that this situation is a collective global responsibility. We must act now.'[65] She went on to state that, 'The collective action that we have taken today by adopting this resolution is a significant step towards protecting the defenceless civilians, including women and children, in Côte d'Ivoire, who bear the brunt of the brutal attacks.'[66]

By the next Security Council meeting considering the situation in Côte d'Ivoire which took place on 28 April 2011, Gbagbo had been taken into custody by opposition forces with the assistance of more than 30 French armoured vehicles.[67] However, by a further resolution the Security Council moved into the rebuilding phase of the action and continued its extensive involvement, which was subsequently continued in a further resolution that continued the mandate of UNOCI until 31 July 2011.[68]

Alex Bellamy argues that the belated removal of Laurent Gbagbo signals another welcome step towards realising the responsibility to protect. He states: '[b]ut, as in Libya, decisive action in Côte d'Ivoire was premised on the need to protect civilians, lending further weight to the idea that the "responsibility to protect" has become more than just

---

[65] UNSC Verbatim Record, UN Doc. S/PV .6508, 30 March 2011.   [66] *Ibid.*

[67] For an account, see David Smith, Kim Willsher and Sam Jones, 'Laurent Gbagbo detained by Ivory Coast opposition force', *The Guardian*, 11 April 2011. Among others, the newspaper reported: 'it is possible that the French and UN soldiers attacked the building, surrounded it and then waited for Ouattara's forces to go in, as France may not have the mandate or legal basis to make the arrest.'

[68] UNSC Res. 1980, UN Doc. S/RES/1980, 28 April 2011; UNSC Res. 1981, UN Doc. S/RES/1981, 13 May 2011.

fine words'.[69] Yet, neither the Libyan, nor the Côte d'Ivoire resolutions specifically mention an international responsibility to protect. On the contrary, the resolutions remind the respective nations of their primary responsibility to protect their own civilians. However, it can be asserted that as a result of both resolutions authorising 'all necessary means to protect civilians', this is a specific acknowledgement of international responsibility towards civilians of any country, as was argued by the Nigerian member of the Security Council.

Conclusion

In the years since the adoption by consensus of the responsibility to protect by the General Assembly, the UN Security Council has incorporated the obligation in several United Nations peacekeeping missions, including those discussed in the last section above. This practice has continued the work begun several years earlier and, if anything, has confirmed that protection of civilians is part of the core obligations within peacekeeping missions. Even though each one of these missions can be criticized for lacking the resources to truly fulfil their mandates, the change in practice in the years since the end of the Cold War is astonishing. The first civilian protection mission was in Somalia in 1992 and since then civilian protection mandates have become the norm. In cases where a sovereign State *manifestly* fails to protect its own population from genocide, war crimes, ethnic cleansing and crimes against humanity it is likely that the Security Council will react as is evident by the two most recent missions in the Côte d'Ivoire and Libya. In traditional consensual peacekeeping missions there will be a routine protection of civilian mandate together with the other tasks. This is a truly welcome development which goes towards ensuring that genocides such as those committed in Srebrenica and in Rwanda will not be repeated.

The one unfortunate omission in these recent developments is the lack of prevention missions. Implementing the responsibility to prevent will involve a fundamental shift in understanding as to when a 'threat to the peace' might actually emerge, as the fact is that Chapter VII mandates are needed at a much earlier stage in the process. This would be assisted if the Security Council would acknowledge the specific criteria needed to engage the responsibility to protect which include the concept of imminence. Unless criteria are adopted which mandate early intervention to

---

[69] Alex Bellamy, 'Ivory Coast needs economic lifeline', *The Australian*, 13 April 2011.

prevent human rights catastrophes, peace-enforcing missions will be seen by many countries as an attack on the notion of State sovereignty.

Yet, if peacekeeping missions were to be constituted before mass murder begins, with a specific civilian protection mandate, the scenario of true civilian protection would finally be realised. The tragic situation that Roméo Dallaire, the Head of the Peacekeeping Mission in Rwanda found himself in by being denied a mandate to intervene to confiscate the arms to be used in the Rwandan genocide should never be repeated.[70] Unless the UN acts on its responsibility to prevent, this could happen over and over again.

In a previous article on this subject I had predicted that the term peacekeeping may no longer be appropriate as the operations discussed here are more aptly described as peacemaking or peace-enforcement. However, it is still premature to indicate that UN operations have evolved into true collective security actions to deal with threats to the peace posed by the human rights abuses that occur in intra-State conflicts. It will only be the case if the responsibility to protect in its full meaning is accepted that multidimensional activities will take place with the three essential elements: early warning and prevention; robust and timely reaction; and comprehensive rebuilding.

[70] Roméo Dallaire, *Shake Hands with the Devil* (London: Arrow Books, 2004).

PART II

The United Nations system

4

The Security Council

TERRY D. GILL

Introduction

The UN Security Council's (Council) relationship to and role in the implementation of the concept and doctrine of the Responsibility to Protect (R2P) is important and even crucial for a number of reasons. First, there can be little doubt that the failures of the Council in adequately responding to a number of major humanitarian crises in the closing decade of the last century were one of the main reasons for the development of the concept in the first place. The examples of such failures, on the part of the international community in general and the Security Council in particular, to adequately respond to widespread, systematic violations of fundamental human rights and humanitarian law in relation to the crimes and atrocities committed in the Balkans and Rwanda are well known and had a catalytic effect upon the efforts inside and outside the UN Organisation to redress this inadequacy and prevent future recurrence of such atrocities in the future.[1] One such initiative has been the development of R2P and its subsequent endorsement by the UN, including the Security Council itself.[2] Second, the primary role of

---

[1] See International Commission on Intervention and State Sovereignty, *The Responsibility to Protect* (Ottawa: International Development Research Centre, 2001), p. 17. See also the Organization for African Unity report, 'The Preventable Genocide', regarding the failure of the international community to intervene in Rwanda. OAU, 'International Panel of Eminent Personalities (IPEP): Report on the 1994 Genocide in Rwanda and Surrounding Events (Selected Sections)', *International Legal Materials*, 40 (2001), 141–236.

[2] The UN Secretary-General at the time approved and adopted the approach set out by the ICISS in his own report relating to reform of the UN. UNSG, 'In Larger Freedom: Towards Development, Security and Human Rights for All', UN Doc. A/59/2005, 21 March 2005. The R2P concept was also elaborated upon in relation to the UN Collective Security System in the report of the High-Level Panel on Threats, Challenges and Change. UNSG, *A More Secure World: Our Shared Responsibility* (New York: United Nations, 2004). In the 'World Summit Outcome Document' the UN General Assembly

the Council in the maintenance and restoration of international peace and security and its powers to do so under the UN Charter are a crucial component of R2P, in particular of its third pillar, the duty to take timely and adequate measures to respond to mass crimes and violations of human rights and humanitarian law, including the taking of coercive measures to halt such violations.

The UN Charter is predicated upon the prohibition of the use or threat of force, except within the exceptions laid out therein. One of these exceptions are the powers of the Council to take effective collective measures in response to threats to, or breaches of, the peace and there is ample evidence that such massive atrocities can have a major impact upon regional and wider international peace and stability, in addition to amounting to international crimes in their own right. Consequently, when a State fails to meet its obligations to prevent and halt such violations, either through a breakdown in its ability to do so, or because it is itself directly involved or implicated in the perpetration of such crimes, and other measures have proved to be inadequate or clearly would be inadequate to address the situation, the Security Council will have a crucial role to play in taking or authorising measures aimed at halting such violations. However, the Council does not operate alone, nor will it always be capable of adequately responding to all situations in which massive human rights violations occur. Its powers and prerogatives, while considerable, are not unlimited and will also depend upon a number of other actors and factors, including in particular the cooperation of regional organisations and Member States in implementing effective collective action. One question which R2P strives (understandably perhaps) to avoid is the extent to which R2P is synonymous with humanitarian intervention, or is rather a replacement or alternative thereof. Humanitarian intervention is a much older concept than R2P, but is highly controversial from both a legal and policy perspective and its relationship to R2P is likewise a point of controversy.[3]

incorporated the R2P concept in paragraphs 138 and 139 where, among other things, the role of the UNSC in taking enforcement measures is set out. 'World Summit Outcome', UN Doc. A/RES/60/1, 15 September 2005. The UN Security Council referred to the R2P concept in relation to the protection of civilians in UNSC Res. 1674, UN Doc. S/RES/1674, 28 April 2006. All documents relating to R2P and R2P within the UN framework can be found at www.responsibilitytoprotect.org.

[3] Humanitarian intervention is the subject of a vast amount of literature and as a proposed exception to the prohibition of the use of force alongside collective security measures and self-defence is highly controversial. Positions range from those who find it compatible with international law to those who find it so subject to abuse that it is unacceptable, with

This contribution will first examine the general relationship of R2P to the powers allocated to the Security Council under the Charter to maintain international peace and security and address the question whether R2P has altered the Charter provisions relating to (non-)intervention and the maintenance of international peace and security. It will then go on to examine the relationship of R2P to the question of humanitarian intervention and attempt to arrive at a conclusion as to whether R2P and humanitarian intervention are related or wholly different concepts and whether the former has supplanted the latter, or whether it is simply a question of 'old wine in new bottles', or perhaps something in between, and how this relates to the Security Council and its role in relation to both the maintenance of peace and security and in the implementation of R2P. In this context, some discussion of the recent impact of R2P on the way the Council and other actors have reacted to some recent humanitarian crises will be made, without pretending in any way that this constitutes empirical proof of a precedent which will determine how the Council may act in future situations. In the final section a number of conclusions will be submitted in relation to the foregoing questions and controversies.

differing shades of opinion in between these two positions. The former position representing a minority view is put forward by writers such as, among others, Fernando Teson, *Humanitarian Intervention: An Inquiry into Law and Morality*, 2nd edn (Ardsley, NY: Transnational Publishers, 1997); Richard Lillich, 'Humanitarian Intervention: A Reply to Ian Brownlie and a Plea for Constructive Alternatives', in John Moore (ed.), *Law and Civil War in the Modern World* (Baltimore, MD: Johns Hopkins University Press, 1974), pp. 229–51, at pp. 229ff. The majority opinion is that humanitarian intervention is not a recognised exception to the Charter ban on the use of force, but may be eligible for a greater or lesser degree of tolerance, provided it meets certain criteria. This group of writers includes, among others, Ian Brownlie, 'Thoughts on a Kind Hearted Gunman', in Richard Lillich (ed.), *Humanitarian Intervention and the United Nations* (University of Virginia Press, 1973), pp. 139ff.; Oscar Schachter, *International Law in Theory and Practice* (Dordrecht; Boston, MA: Martinus Nijhoff, 1991), pp. 123–6; Thomas Franck, *Recourse to Force: State Action against Threats and Armed Attacks* (Cambridge University Press, 2002), p. 189; Simón Chesterman, *Just War or Just Peace: Humanitarian Intervention and International Law* (Oxford University Press, 2001), pp. 112ff. The present author expressed a similar viewpoint in 'Humanitaire Interventie: Rechtmatigheid, Rechtvaardigheid en Legitimiteit', *Militair Rechtelijk Tijdschrift*, 94 (2001), 221–41, which was translated and updated as 'Humanitarian Intervention: Legality, Justice and Legitimacy', in *The Global Community Yearbook of International Law & Jurisprudence 2004* (Dobbs Ferry, NY: Oceana Publications, 2005), pp. 51–76. See also the section on humanitarian intervention, below.

The responsibility to protect in relation to the UN collective security system

R2P has developed quickly since its inception with the International Commission on Intervention and State Sovereignty (ICISS) report initiated by the Canadian government in December 2001, through its inclusion in the World Summit Outcome Document in 2005 and its subsequent endorsement and recognition by both the Security Council in 2006 in reference to the Protection of Civilians and by the General Assembly in 2009, following a report by the UN Secretary-General on the Implementation of R2P.[4] The legal status of R2P is commented upon elsewhere and will not receive extensive attention here.[5] Nevertheless, it is necessary to examine to some extent what its legal status is in relation to the role envisaged for the Security Council in implementing important components of R2P and the impact that R2P may have upon the powers of the Security Council in the context of maintaining international peace and security.

The starting point of such an examination is to note that R2P does not constitute a (new) binding rule of international law, although it undoubtedly reflects certain existing legal obligations. R2P has not been incorporated into either an international convention, nor does it at present reflect a rule of customary international law. It lacks both sufficient practice and, in particular, *opinio juris*, which would indicate that States consider it to be a binding rule of customary law.[6] The references to and endorsement of R2P in a number of UN resolutions and the above-mentioned report by the Secretary-General do, however, indicate that R2P has obtained the status of an important political principle and policy undertaking by both key UN organs and by a very large number of Member States. This may give it the potential to develop at some point into a binding rule of law, but that is at present no more than a possibility and need not concern us in the context of the present discussion on how it relates to the UN collective security system as laid out in the Charter and as developed in the practice of the Council over the past decades.

---

[4] See in addition to the sources cited in n. 2, above, UNSG, 'Implementing the Responsibility to Protect', UN Doc. A/63/677, 12 January 2009.

[5] See for example Carsten Stahn, 'Responsibility to Protect: Political Rhetoric or Emerging Legal Norm', *American Journal of International Law*, 101 (2007), 99–120, at 99ff. See also Amnéus, Chapter 1 in this book.

[6] *Ibid.*, 101; cf. Amnéus, Chapter 1 in this book.

The constituent documents mentioned above setting out the three pillars or layers of responsibility which are the core elements of R2P make reference to the role and primacy of the Security Council in relation to the implementation of any coercive measures of either a non-military or of a military nature, when the situation calls for it and the State fails to meet its primary responsibility to protect its population from genocide, crimes against humanity, ethnic cleansing and war crimes, and lesser measures have proved to be or would be inadequate.[7] These references reflect existing legal obligations incumbent upon States to prevent the occurrence of such crimes, as well as the fact that measures undertaken by the international community to help to prevent such crimes and to assist States in preventing such crimes and where necessary to recommend further measures where the State where they occur is unable or unwilling to carry out its responsibility, do not constitute unwarranted intervention in the domestic jurisdiction of the affected State. This, as stated, reflects existing legal obligations and is far from being revolutionary or imposing new obligations upon States, although the manner in which these responsibilities are presented within the context of R2P are novel to some extent. Likewise, the references to the role and primacy of the Security Council in taking any collective coercive measures necessary to implement R2P, including those involving the use of force, reflect the powers of the Council provided for under the Charter and the way the UN collective security system has evolved, particularly in the post-Cold War period. This calls for some explanation of how these powers are allocated and how R2P directly relates to the UN collective security system.

The UN Charter sets out the primary purposes and principles of the Organisation in Articles 1 and 2 of the Charter. Foremost among these are the prohibition of the use or threat of force in international relations and the maintenance and restoration of international peace through the implementation of effective collective measures and the pacific settlement of international disputes in accordance with international law and justice. This is collective security in the narrow sense of preserving the peace.[8] The Charter is essentially aimed at preventing unauthorised transboundary force and preserving the independence and territorial

---

[7] See n. 2, above.

[8] Rüdiger Wolfrum, in Bruno Simma, Andreas Paulus and Eleni Chaitidou (eds.), *The Charter of the United Nations: A Commentary*, 2nd edn (Oxford University Press, 2002), pp. 40–3.

integrity of its Member States and the use of collective measures is seen as the primary instrument to address threats to international peace and suppress breaches of the peace and acts of aggression. Alongside this strict component of collective security, and complementing it, is a wider notion of collective security aimed at promoting international cooperation, self-determination and human rights.[9] In this context, the promotion and protection of human rights has gained increasing importance since the Charter was adopted through the development of international human rights law in numerous instruments and conventions of both a universal and regional scope over the past half-century.

To implement the objective of collective security in the stricter sense referred to above, the Security Council has been allocated with the primary responsibility for the maintenance and restoration of international peace and security in Article 24 of the Charter and its powers are further worked out in Chapters VI and VII of the Charter relating to the pacific settlement of disputes and action aimed at the maintenance and restoration of international peace respectively. These include the power to take binding decisions and implement collective measures, ranging from measures not involving the use of force, to the taking or authorisation of coercive military measures aimed at maintaining or restoring international peace. Such non-forceful enforcement measures may include economic and diplomatic sanctions, the interruption of maritime and aerial transportation and even the establishment of ad hoc tribunals to prosecute core international crimes. Under the Rome Statute, the Security Council has powers of referral to the International Criminal Court and has made use of those powers in relation to widespread violations of human rights and humanitarian law in Sudan and, more recently, Libya.[10] As a consequence, the Council, while not

---

[9] *Ibid.*

[10] The International Criminal Tribunal for the former Yugoslavia (ICTY) and the International Criminal Tribunal for Rwanda (ICTR) have been established by the Security Council under its Chapter VII powers. A number of ad hoc so-called hybrid tribunals have been established on the basis of agreements between the UN and the countries concerned. Two situations where the power of the UNSC under Article 13(b) of the Rome Statute of the International Criminal Court (ICC) to refer a situation to the ICC Prosecutor has been exercised are the referral of the situation in Darfur/Sudan through UNSC Res. 1593, UN Doc. S/RES/1593, 31 March 2005 and more recently of the situation in Libya through UNSC Res. 1970, UN Doc. S/RES/1970, 26 February 2011. For a detailed discussion of these key judicial mechanisms, see Frencken and Sluiter, Chapter 17 and Contarino and Negrón-Gonzales, Chapter 18 in this book.

primarily an international law enforcement agency, does play a support-ing role in upholding international human rights and humanitarian law and preventing impunity for core international crimes.

Alongside the Council, other important players are involved in a secondary role within the UN collective security system. The General Assembly as the plenary organ of the Organisation has wide powers of recommendation, and plays an important, if secondary role, in the context of the maintenance of international peace through its recom-mendations, some of which are evidence of the emergence of new normative obligations and through the interpretation and development of existing obligations. Also of importance in understanding the system of collective security set out in the Charter are Article 2(7) which restricts the Organisation from intervening in matters which fall under the domestic jurisdiction of its Member States under international law, except in relation to the taking of collective measures to maintain or restore international peace and security, and Article 27, which deals with the voting procedure necessary within the Council for the adoption of any substantive decision by the Council. Finally, Chapter VIII sets out the relationship of Regional Organisations and Arrangements to the Council in relation to both the pacific settlement of disputes and the maintenance and restoration of international peace and security and Article 103 makes clear that obligations under the Charter, including decisions of the Council, take precedence over any conflicting obliga-tions arising under other international treaties.[11]

The system outlined above is relatively simple in a conceptual sense, but exceedingly complex in its implementation. Nevertheless, it basically boils down to a central concern with the maintenance of international peace and security, a primacy of the Council in effectuating this and a duty on the part of all Member States and regional organisations to cooperate with the Council in doing so. While this duty of cooperation does not go so far as to include an obligation to actively participate in collective (or collectively authorised) military measures, it does include

---

[11] On Article 24, see Simma *et al.* (eds.), *Charter of the United Nations*, pp. 445–9. On the Security Council's enforcement powers, see for example *ibid.*, pp. 727ff.; Leland Goodrich, Edvard Hambro and Anne Simons (eds.), *Charter of the United Nations: Commentary and Documents*, 3rd rev. edn (New York: Columbia University Press, 1969), pp. 301–17; Terry Gill, 'Operations and Peace Enforcement Operations under the Charter', in Terry Gill and Dieter Fleck (eds.), *The Handbook of the International Law of Military Operations* (Oxford University Press, 2010), pp. 81–93, at pp. 82–6.

the duty to take effective action to implement other measures decided upon by the Council and to at least not impede or interfere with measures involving the use of force decided upon or authorised by the Council in the context of the maintenance or restoration of international peace.[12] The Council is allocated with a wide degree of discretion in determining whether a particular situation constitutes a threat to or breach of international peace and security and its actions to address such situations are taken on behalf of the entire Organisation and its Member States, notwithstanding the limited membership of the Council. The Council has repeatedly made use of this discretionary power to characterise large-scale violations of human rights and humanitarian law as constituting a threat to international peace and security, starting with the measures taken in response to the apartheid policies of South Africa over half a century ago and continuing up to the present with the authorisation of military action to protect civilians in relation to the internal conflict in Libya.[13] There can be little doubt that such large-scale violations of human rights and humanitarian norms can have a major impact upon regional and wider international stability as the examples of the ethnic conflicts in the Balkans and the Great Lakes region of Africa, along with numerous others, clearly demonstrate. Consequently, there are sufficient grounds for the international community to treat such situations as matters which can affect international peace, as well as constituting violations of core norms of international law in their own right. Nevertheless, despite the wide powers allocated to the Council and the numerous examples of their application to large-scale violations of human rights, there are major impediments inherent to the system which will often stand in the way of effective responses to large-scale violations of human rights. One of the most important of these is the built-in requirement that the Council can only take action when two-thirds of its members are in favour of doing so and none of the permanent members of the Council are opposed. Another major impediment within the Charter system is the dependence of the Council upon the readiness and ability of Member States and regional organisations to actively participate in any type of military action aimed at halting widespread human rights violations and

---

[12] Goodrich *et al.* (eds.), *Charter of the United Nations: Commentary and Documents*, 311–12; Simma *et al.* (eds.), *Charter of the United Nations*, pp. 739–40.

[13] Regarding the Council's determination that South Africa's racial policies constituted a threat to the peace, see UNSC Res. 418, UN Doc. S/RES/418(1977), 4 November 1977. In relation to the Council's determination that large-scale repression in Libya constituted a threat to the peace, see UNSC Res. 1970.

atrocities. Since neither the Council, nor any other organ within the UN has any independent military capacity, all forms of coercive action involving the use of force which can be decided upon or authorised by the Council are wholly dependent upon the voluntary contribution and participation of Member States and regional actors to effectuate such a decision.[14] It is well known that the original conception of the UN collective security system included provisions for the Member States to provide the Council with the capacity to take rapid and effective military action through the provision of standing forces on the basis of Special Agreements and the allocation of command to a Military Staff Committee under the political control of the Council. Both of these provisions have remained dead letters, and there is little prospect that this original concept will be resuscitated in the foreseeable future.

Instead, the Council has been forced to find other ways to carry out its task of maintaining or restoring international peace and security than was originally intended when the Charter was adopted. These include the development and practice of UN peacekeeping and its evolution into a multifaceted instrument which often includes provisions relating to the protection of civilians from violence and assistance to humanitarian efforts and support for governmental authorities to establish a stable environment and promote the rule of law. Indeed, while the question of protection of civilians within the context of UN peacekeeping and R2P are distinct, they are nevertheless related. Protection of civilians has increasingly become an integral part of UN peacekeeping doctrine and practice and this development coincides to a considerable extent with the emergence of R2P and reflects the second pillar of it (the duty to assist a State to uphold and protect human rights when it is not capable of doing so on its own). This is in fact one of the main tasks of many contemporary peacekeeping operations.[15]

---

[14] Gill, 'Peace Enforcement', in Gill and Fleck (eds.), *Law of Military Operations*, p. 85.

[15] The Protection of Civilians (PoC) is referred to in the UN Peacekeeping doctrine, widely referred to as the 'Capstone Doctrine' with various references to PoC as a core component of contemporary peace operations. See 'The Core Business of United Nations Peacekeeping Operations', in *United Nations Peacekeeping Operations: Principles and Guidelines* (New York: United Nations, 2008), pp. 20–5. The issue of PoC was first referred to in UNSC Res. 1265 (1999); and since then in numerous other resolutions, including, among others, UNSC Res. 1296 (2000); UNSC Res. 1674 (2006); UNSC Res. 1738 (2006) and UNSC Res. 1894 (2009). The PoC is also included in most recent UNSC resolutions mandating Peace Operations with the conditions that the protection is not open ended, but limited to cases of imminent violence resulting from armed conflict and

In cases where the situation is even more serious and there is the prospect that serious armed opposition will be encountered and peace-keeping would not suffice, the practice of the Council has been to authorise Member States and/or regional organisations to militarily implement the decision of the Council under its overall political author-ity, often in conjunction with other measures of a non-military nature undertaken by the UN itself or in cooperation with other actors.[16] Although the Council has the legal capacity to set up a force under direct UN command to conduct such coercive military enforcement measures, this has remained the exception and most enforcement measures involv-ing the use of force have been carried out by Member States, often acting through regional organisations or arrangements under a variety of different command structures acting under the overall political authority of the Council.[17]

Alongside impediments of an institutional nature forming part of the system itself, there are others of a more political nature. These include differing perceptions on the part of Member States in relation to the propriety and acceptability of taking military measures against a govern-ment or without its full consent, even in cases where a government is directly involved or implicated in large-scale human rights violations, perceptions of imbalance and lack of representativeness within the Council and its membership, and perceptions that such coercive use of force in relation to human rights situations constitutes 'outside interfer-ence' and could potentially threaten the independence and sovereignty of Member States.[18] In addition to the above-mentioned institutional

breakdown of authority which is directed against civilians and then only in so far as this is within the capability of the mission and is not incompatible with the mandate. The first UN Peace Operation specifically charged with PoC was in relation to UNAMSIL in Sierra Leone in 1999. Since then, many UN Peace Operations have included PoC within the context of their mandates along the lines set out above. For a detailed discussion of UN peacekeeping operations, see Breau, Chapter 3 in this book.

[16] Franck, *Recourse to Force*, pp. 21–31.
[17] Gill, 'Peace Enforcement', in Gill and Fleck (eds.), *Law of Military Operations*, pp. 92–3.
[18] The debate in the UN General Assembly regarding R2P took place over three days (23, 24 and 28 July 2009) and over ninety States made statements which give a good general view of how States stand on the issue and the above-mentioned objections and concerns with regards to collectively authorised military intervention in relation to human rights violations were put forward by a number of them, including among others: China, Cuba, India, Nicaragua, Russia and Venezuela to name some of those expressing clear or implicit reservations in this connection. More information on the 2009 UNGA debate on R2P is available at www.responsibilitytoprotect.org.

and political impediments, there are also practical limitations as to what the Council and other actors, including Member States, can actually undertake and successfully carry out. Even if a necessary majority within the Council and the wider international community is forthcoming in relation to the necessity of taking or authorising coercive measures in relation to a particular situation, such measures will only be capable of being implemented if Member States are willing and able to actually commit themselves to the risks and burdens involved in such an undertaking. The more serious the situation is and the greater the prospect of active resistance, the greater the risks and burdens will be and the fewer States will be willing to or capable of taking on the task. If an important regional organisation or (group of) regional Power(s) is willing and capable of providing the bulk of military capacity necessary for successful implementation and bearing the economic burdens of such an operation, it will increase the likelihood of it being undertaken and its chances of ultimate success, as well as its acceptability within the Council and the wider international community. However, in some cases, no such regional actor will be available or willing to either undertake or actively support such far-reaching measures and as a result, the likelihood of any coercive action being undertaken decreases dramatically and will only be forthcoming if an outside Power has overriding interests in taking on the risks and burdens involved in such a military intervention. There are only a handful of States which have the capacity to carry out a large-scale military intervention outside their immediate region and few, if any, which would be ready to do so without significant support from other States, except perhaps in cases of (perceived) overriding national security interests and even then only if the risks involved in intervention, including the possibility of aggravating the situation and potentially widening the conflict did not outweigh the perceived threat to national security. There are few humanitarian crises which have risen to this level of perceived threat to national security resulting in military intervention from States which are geographically removed from and are not directly affected by the consequences of inaction. Consequently, any effective response will in most cases be dependent upon the effect a particular humanitarian crisis has upon regional stability and the willingness and capacity of regional actors, including both powerful or influential States within the region and regional organisations to effectively respond to the situation with at least the acquiescence of the wider international community, including the Permanent Members of the

Council.[19] The practice of the Council is to authorise such regional actors to take the necessary measures when the necessary majority for a Security Council decision exists. No action without Security Council authorisation will fall within the recognised exception to the prohibition of the use of force contained in the UN collective security system. Such authorisation has been forthcoming in a significant number of cases,[20] and the role of R2P and the legitimacy provided in the combination of such authorisation and the willingness of a regional actor to implement the Council's decision is an important factor in increasing the chances of its success. In any case, the Charter system of collective security outlined above does provide a recognised legal basis for the taking or authorisation of coercive measures, including the use of force in situations where this is required, and R2P may well increase the political acceptability of such action or authorisation in specific cases. In short, the Charter system of collective security and R2P are mutually compatible and in some cases mutually reinforcing. Nevertheless, the impediments and barriers of an institutional, political and practical nature to the taking of effective coercive action mentioned above have not been removed by the advent of R2P, and there (will) continue to be situations involving large-scale violations of core human rights and humanitarian norms which will either be responded to by States or regional actors acting outside the recognised legal and policy framework of the Charter system of collective security and contours of R2P, or not addressed at all. This brings us to the question of the relationship between R2P and humanitarian intervention.

---

[19] The role of regional and sub-regional organisations in the implementation of R2P was set out in UNSG, 'The Role of Regional and Sub-regional Arrangements in Implementing the Responsibility to Protect', UN Doc. A/65/877–S/2011/393, 27 June 2011. The aforementioned report was discussed in the General Assembly on 12 July 2011. UNGA Information Note, 'Informal Interactive Dialogue on the Role of Regional and Sub-regional Arrangements in Implementing the Responsibility to Protect', 12 July 2011, available at www.responsibilitytoprotect.org. A number of State representatives and representatives of regional organisations made statements and comments in relation to this theme and the UNSG report.

[20] Examples include the cooperation between the UN and ECOMOG in the civil conflict in Sierra Leone, with the UK intervening under UN Security Council mandate to assist UN peacekeepers when the ceasefire broke down in May 2000, the cooperation between NATO and the UN in the aftermath of NATO's unauthorised humanitarian intervention in Kosovo and the ongoing hybrid UN–African Union mission in Darfur.

The responsibility to protect and humanitarian intervention: incompatible concepts or 'two sides of the same coin'?

The starting point for a discussion of the relationship between R2P and humanitarian intervention is a clear definition of what each of these concepts entail, at least for the purposes of this particular discussion. R2P as it has developed over the past decade and is set out in its constituent instruments consists of three main pillars: the primary duty of States to protect their populations from genocide, crimes against humanity, war crimes and ethnic cleansing; the duty of other States to assist a State in carrying out this primary duty; and the responsibility of the international community to protect populations threatened by or subjected to these crimes through appropriate measures, including where necessary, the use of force when the situation calls for it and other measures have proved to be inadequate or would be inadequate to address the situation.[21] In relation to the third element involving the use of force in the most serious situations, the Security Council is named as the sole authority which is capable and responsible for authorising any measures involving the use of force. R2P is based on a number of non-binding instruments and reports and is of recent origin, although it reflects a number of well-established legal principles and long-standing ethical considerations.

Humanitarian intervention is a much older concept and traces its roots to the natural law just war tradition stretching back over centuries, as well as to nineteenth-century State practice, and is subject to both a wide variety of definitions and a considerable amount of legal controversy.[22] Some authors take a broad view of what constitutes humanitarian intervention and would

---

[21] See n. 2, above.

[22] See Gill, 'Humanitarian Intervention', 62–4, on the relationship of humanitarian intervention to natural law doctrine and nineteenth-century State practice. An extensive analysis of pre-1914 State practice relating to humanitarian intervention is given by Jean-Pierre Fonteyne, 'The Customary International Law Doctrine of Humanitarian Intervention: Its Current Validity under the UN Charter', *California Western International Law Journal*, 4 (1974), 203–70. For an example of a broad approach to humanitarian intervention, see for example, Oliver Ramsbotham and Tom Woodhouse, *Humanitarian Intervention in Contemporary Conflict* (Cambridge, UK: Polity Press, 1996), pp. 106–13. The classic definition of 'intervention' as 'dictatorial interference' signifying forcible interference without any form of authorisation is given by Lassa Oppenheim, *International Law*, 3rd edn (London; New York: Longmans, Green, and Co., 1920), p. 220. This strict approach is followed by, among others, Wil Verwey, 'Humanitarian Intervention', in Antonio Cassese (ed.), *The Current Legal Regulation of the Use of Force* (Dordrecht; Boston, MA: Martinus Nijhoff, 1986), pp. 57–78, at p. 59.

include measures not involving the use of force, such as diplomatic action, humanitarian assistance, and so forth, alongside more coercive measures as falling within its scope. However, the classical approach is to define intervention more strictly. Humanitarian intervention seen from that perspective would consist of measures involving coercion, particularly the use of force, in response to large-scale, acute and systematic violations of human rights, especially the right to life, without the consent of the State where the violations were taking place (or were imminent). To the extent that such coercive measures were authorised by the Security Council, they would have a recognised legal basis under international law and would constitute collective (or collectively authorised) enforcement measures within the Charter system of collective security. This is sometimes referred to as 'collective humanitarian intervention' in the literature and undoubtedly has a degree of convergence with R2P, as set out in the previous paragraph, notwithstanding the (understandable) reluctance on the part of many States to openly recognise this partial overlap.[23]

But the essence of humanitarian intervention and the reason for the controversy surrounding it lie in an even stricter definition as to what it is and what its legal consequences are, namely as a proposed or putative basis for the use of force in response to large-scale human rights violations in the absence of any consent on the part of the State where the intervention is carried out, or any form of authorisation by the Security Council or other body which has the power to collectively confer such authorisation. In short, it is usually seen by both its proponents and opponents as a (proposed) exception to the prohibition on the use of force across State boundaries, alongside self-defence and collectively authorised enforcement measures.

There are persuasive reasons for adopting this strict approach in defining humanitarian intervention. First, measures not involving the use of force are governed by other rules and principles of international law and do not constitute a (potential) violation of the prohibition of use of force. Second, to the extent military action is carried out with either the consent of the State where it is conducted, or under collective authorisation by the Security Council, it has a recognised legal basis. In the former case, it will not even constitute intervention in the correct sense of the term and in the latter case when duly authorised, will have a well-established legal basis. Only in the event either are lacking, will

---

[23] For a discussion of collectively authorised humanitarian intervention as an exercise of the enforcement powers of the UN Security Council, see Gill, 'Humanitarian Intervention', in Gill and Fleck (eds.), *Law of Military Operations*, pp. 221–8, at p. 223.

there be a need to put forward humanitarian intervention as a potential legal basis for taking military action in response to massive human rights violations.

In distinguishing humanitarian intervention from other possible reactions to violations of human rights and from collective enforcement measures, one is doing more than engaging in mere legal semantics. A strict definition makes it possible to concentrate upon what distinguishes humanitarian intervention from other concepts, including R2P and other possible grounds for intervention, namely the controversy surrounding its legal status and its potential impact upon the international system. The Charter is, as stated previously, predicated upon the prohibition of the use of force in international relations and has as its primary purpose the maintenance of peace and security, as well as the independence and integrity of Member States through the use of collective measures, except in cases of self-defence. These are the only two generally recognised exceptions to the abovementioned prohibition, and whatever the shortcomings of the system of collective security, there are good grounds for adhering to a strict interpretation of the prohibition of force, both from a legal as well as a policy standpoint. Not least of these is the fact that the Charter was intended to help to prevent the recurrence of large-scale international conflict, which as the Preamble of the Charter formulates it, 'has brought untold human suffering to mankind'. From a more legal perspective, the prohibition of the use of force is generally considered to constitute a peremptory rule of international law which can only be altered with the overwhelming consensus of the international community. There is scant evidence of any such consensus or any likelihood of it emerging within the foreseeable future. Consequently, humanitarian intervention has been and will remain a highly controversial proposed legal basis for the use of force and lacks the necessary widespread acceptance to qualify as a recognised rule of either customary law or gain acceptance as treaty law which would have the effect of amending the Charter. The legal consequence of this is that humanitarian intervention without State consent or collective authorisation as defined here is prima facie illegal under contemporary international law, whatever its status under natural law doctrine or the international legal system of the nineteenth century might have been.[24]

---

[24] Humanitarian intervention as defined here does not fall within either of the recognised exceptions to the prohibition of the use of force. It likewise is generally considered to fall outside of any of the circumstances precluding wrongfulness in the Articles on State

This partly explains the reluctance on the part of the framers of R2P and among most States to refer to R2P as a form of collectively authorised humanitarian intervention. The political controversy surrounding humanitarian intervention is another reason for distinguishing the two concepts from each other. Humanitarian intervention is often seen and portrayed by many States as (neocolonial) interference by outside parties in the internal affairs of States, and/or, as a threat to the Charter system limiting the use of force, whereas R2P seems to emphasise State sovereignty in conjunction with other existing legal obligations and rights, including in particular the duty of States to implement human rights obligations and the primacy of the UN collective security system, and is therefore seen as more acceptable by many States.[25]

In any case, while R2P, including collectively authorised measures of protection, are, in principle, more politically acceptable and are in conformity with existing international law, there is no guarantee that such measures will inevitably be approved and implemented where this is called for. In some cases, large-scale violations of human rights will occur without the international community being able to reach the necessary level of consensus to take effective collective or collectively authorised measures, including the use of force to halt them. In such situations, humanitarian intervention as defined here – that is, without collective authorisation – will remain as a possible response alongside other less far-reaching measures and in some extreme cases, the only available response, other than standing by while massive crimes are being perpetrated. How can the lack of a generally recognised and accepted legal basis for such intervention be reconciled with the moral imperative to take action when this is required and is a feasible alternative to inaction and the consequences thereof? Can such intervention be carried out, without potentially undermining the entire edifice of collective security or threatening international stability?

The answer to this can be determined by asking whether all violations of the prohibition of the use of force, which is after all a peremptory rule

---

Responsibility of the International Law Commission, including distress and necessity and under the definition here, consent would nullify the action as 'intervention'. See James Crawford, *The International Law Commissions Articles on State Responsibility: Introduction, Text and Commentaries* (Cambridge University Press, 2002), pp. 174–7. In relation to the exclusion of the grounds of 'distress' and 'necessity' from humanitarian intervention, see *ibid.*, p. 185.

[25] See Franck, *Recourse to Force*; and the statements of the representatives of the States named there as expressing reservations relating to the use of force and to the concept of humanitarian intervention.

of a *jus cogens* character, should be treated equally; or whether there is room in international law for accepting that there are degrees of wrongfulness attached to the commission of a wrongful act which take account of mitigating circumstances, and by recognising that the incapacity or unwillingness of the international community to take effective action to halt large-scale systematic and acute violations of core human rights can be treated as a mitigating circumstance in the event a humanitarian intervention is the only response available to prevent and halt such violations, provided a number of conditions are met. Put differently, are all violations of a rule of law equally reprehensible and damaging to society and to the legal system, or are some less egregious and even excusable, albeit still illegal, under certain conditions?

Most, if not all, legal systems are familiar with the concept of mitigating circumstances and with the notion that there are degrees of wrongfulness. Mitigation recognises the possibility that different degrees of wrongfulness can be attached to an illegal act and gives account to considerations of equity and fairness in assessing the legal consequences of what is otherwise an illegal or wrongful act. In this sense it differs from a justification, which removes entirely the wrongful character of an act. Instead it is a consideration which, while not removing the wrongful character of an act, limits or in some cases excuses wrongful conduct by taking into account extra-legal factors, such as the motivation behind and factual circumstances surrounding an act, the manner in which it is carried out, its intended consequences and its impact upon society and the legal system. Mitigation is normally applied in the context of a formal legal proceeding in most domestic legal systems and can influence a court in determining which legal consequences should result from a particular wrongful conduct. As such, it qualifies as a general principle of law and is integral to the legal system, although it often will take account of extra-legal factors.[26]

The consideration of mitigating circumstances as a general principle of law has also found its way into international law, alongside the recognition that there are degrees of wrongfulness which can be attached

---

[26] The distinction between exculpating and mitigating circumstances is well known and is to be found both in legal systems (primarily) based upon the Anglo-American common law tradition and those which are (primarily) based upon the continental European civil law tradition and as such qualifies as a general principle of law as one of the 'sources' of international law under Article 38(2)(c) of the Statute of the International Court of Justice. For a thorough discussion of the notion of mitigating circumstances as a general principle of law, see Franck, *Recourse to Force*, pp. 189ff.

to conduct in violation of a rule of international law. Examples of this can be found in various areas of international law, including the use of force. One well-known example relating to the use of force can be found in the famous *Corfu Channel* judgment of the International Court of Justice, where the Court rejected the argument put forward by the United Kingdom that its actions did not violate the rule of non-intervention; but at the same time took into account the factual and other circumstances related to the incident and determined that Albania's conduct had violated elementary considerations of humanity. The Court ruled that a finding of violation of the principle on non-intervention on the part of the United Kingdom provided appropriate satisfaction to Albania under the circumstances, while ordering that Albania provide financial compensation to the United Kingdom for the loss of life and damage resulting from its own wrongful conduct.[27]

While this example does not directly relate to humanitarian intervention as the term is generally used and is defined here, there is an obvious analogy. In a situation where large-scale, systematic and acute violations of core human rights are being violated, whereby the Security Council is unwilling to act or is prevented from acting or granting authorisation to one or more States or to a regional organisation to take remedial action, an intervention undertaken in the absence of collective authorisation which is aimed at halting or preventing such violations while undoubtedly constituting a violation of the prohibition of the use of force and the prohibition of non-intervention, could qualify for the application of mitigation in limiting or excusing the wrongful conduct, provided a number of well-known and generally accepted conditions are met. These conditions include considerations of necessity and proportionality within the context of such an intervention: humanitarian intervention only as a last resort in the face of large-scale atrocities, full compliance with human rights and humanitarian law in conducting it, limiting the impact of such an intervention upon the target State and its population to the maximum extent possible and the duty to refrain from action which would threaten international peace and security and lead to a wider conflict. It also includes a duty to limit the impact upon the international legal system to the maximum extent possible, by keeping the international community informed of its actions and objectives and paying due regard to the Security Council's primacy in the maintenance of international peace and security, as well as cooperating with other

---

[27] *Corfu Channel Case, Merits, Judgment*, ICJ Reports 1949, p. 35.

responsible organs of the United Nations and with the international community as a whole. When these or similar conditions are met, there are good grounds for limiting or excusing the consequences of wrongful conduct and while reaffirming the legal rules affected, not treating such intervention as a threat to or breach of the peace, or as an act of aggression.

How should this be seen in relation to and in the context of the emergence of R2P? There are clear differences between them and humanitarian intervention as defined here is clearly outside the parameters of R2P, which confers sole authority upon the Council to take or authorise collective military action. Nevertheless, there is a degree of convergence, in that humanitarian intervention is a possible measure of last resort, when all other remedies within the context of R2P are unavailable. If the intervening State does so in a way which minimises the impact of its intervention upon the international legal system and makes a clear effort to coordinate its action with the Council and the international community as a whole to the maximum extent possible, it is less likely that such an emergency measure will be seen as a threat to the system or as undermining the role of the Council and will increase the chances that the Council and the international community will at some point, become engaged and take up the responsibility of attempting to resolve the humanitarian crisis and promoting a return of at least some degree of stability to the affected State and region. Moreover, if an intervening State carried out such an intervention as an emergency measure in conformity with the conditions set out above it would be exceedingly difficult to ignore the fact that the inaction or inability of the Council was the underlying reason why the intervention was carried out without its formal authorisation in the first place. While neither R2P, nor humanitarian intervention imply an unconditional duty to take coercive measures in extreme situations, since this is not always possible or desirable where this would potentially result in an even greater threat to international stability or when military intervention is unlikely to be successful;[28] in cases where such an intervention was carried out without authorisation, but in a manner which conformed with the conditions set out above, the Council would be forced to confront the consequences of its own inaction. Not only would this make it difficult, if not impossible

---

[28] The consideration that humanitarian intervention must not result in 'more harm than good' is expressed by a variety of authors and reflects what Franck refers to as 'tactical realism' (*Recourse to Force*, p. 189).

to attach significant consequences to the breach of international law posed by such an intervention, it would in all likelihood act as a catalyst upon the Council to exercise its authority when this was necessary in future cases. This ultimately could end up strengthening, rather than undermining its authority and the legal system regulating the use of force as a whole. If, on the other hand, the Council were to clearly condemn a particular intervention as either a pretext for aggression or because it was unnecessary or potentially destabilising, it would also distinguish between an excusable breach of law and one which constituted a serious violation and posed a threat to international stability. This too would likely reaffirm the legal system regulating the use of force and make such an intervention untenable in the shorter or longer term.

In short, humanitarian intervention still has a potential place alongside R2P as an 'emergency exit' of last resort and while the two are distinct, they do to an extent potentially complement each other. The two concepts have a common purpose and can to at least some extent be seen as interlocking. If R2P works as it is intended, there will be little scope for humanitarian intervention without collective authorisation. Nevertheless, there have been and will continue to be situations where humanitarian intervention could potentially complement R2P and the primary role of the Security Council within it, in some, but not all cases where human rights are being systematically violated. This need not necessarily undermine the Security Council's central place within R2P, nor its primary role in maintaining international peace and security, provided such emergency recourse to humanitarian intervention is conducted in conformity with a number of conditions and the intervening State or organisation fully informs and cooperates with the Council and the wider international community to normalise the situation as quickly as possible, with the least possible negative impact upon the international system of collective security and the legal framework regulating the use of force.[29] However, it is an inescapable fact that not all such situations will be capable of being addressed by either of these instruments, no more than all violations of domestic law are capable of being prevented or effectively remedied. This does not make the effort to do so, when this is possible, any less worthwhile or necessary.

---

[29] See Gill, 'Humanitarian Intervention', 69, with accompanying notes.

Some recent trends in the (non-)application of R2P in the Security Council

A discussion in relation to the way the Council has responded to human rights violations in two current situations where large-scale violations of human rights may serve to help to illustrate the potentials and limitations of R2P and the role of the Council in implementing it. This discussion is not intended to serve as empirical proof of the effectiveness or lack thereof of R2P in a generic sense, nor does it pretend to provide a comprehensive study of the examples which will be briefly compared (the role of the Council in relation to the Libyan and Syrian situations), but simply as an illustration of the more theoretical considerations set out in the preceding sections.

The role of the Council in relation to the popular uprising in Libya and the influence that R2P may have exerted in helping to shape that role stands in stark contrast with the inaction of the Council in the face of comparable human rights violations in Syria. In the former case, after popular protests against the authoritarian regime of Colonel Gaddafi resulted in military repression, the Council took prompt action in condemning human rights violations and implementing sanctions. Noteworthy for the purposes of our discussion is the reference to R2P in the Council's response and the crucial role played by regional organisations and arrangements in providing a stimulus for the unprecedented swift response by the Council to the attempts by the Gaddafi regime to quell opposition through the use of military force. Within a short-time span the uprising had transformed into a civil war between the forces loyal to the regime and what had become an armed and reasonably organised opposition movement. As Colonel Gaddafi's forces initially regained control over most of the country and the opposition stronghold of Benghazi was surrounded and on the point of being retaken in early March 2011, the Council authorised military measures for the purpose of implementing a no-fly zone in Libyan airspace and the protection of civilians with the support of key regional organisations and NATO. NATO took on the role of implementing the military measures in an aerial campaign directed against loyalist Libyan armed forces and the command and communications facilities and functions of Colonel Gaddafi's regime helping turn the tide in the conflict. With NATO air support, by the middle of September 2011, opposition forces had gained control over most of the country and had been recognised as the government of Libya by most of the international community. Without the above-mentioned support of key regional organisations such as the Arab League, African Union and Islamic Conference, it is unlikely that the Council would have moved as far and as fast as it did in implementing its enforcement powers in response to the situation, and without the active role played by NATO, the opposition movement and forces would not have been able to achieve the overthrow of the regime and probably would have been defeated. While the response of the international community may well have been forthcoming in the absence of the R2P concept, it is probably fair to say that R2P in general and in particular the position taken by key regional organisations, facilitated and legitimised the role of the international community in not only condemning the violence, but also actually taking a proactive role in protecting the population and bringing about the ultimate demise of the Gaddafi regime and made it more difficult for States within the Council which were not in favour of a military response to block the measures taken, as is evidenced by the references to the legitimisation that regional organ-isations provided in relation to collective authorisation for intervention and the references to R2P in the Council's decisions regarding the situation.[30]

In relation to the situation in Syria, events have taken a very different turn and the role of the Council and of regional organisations has been limited and ineffectual in preventing massive repression by the Syrian armed forces of protests against the authoritarian regime of President Al Assad, despite verbal condemnations by a number of governments inside and outside the region. The Council in particular has been singularly incapable of reaching a consensus regarding any type of measures to be taken in response to the large-scale use of military force by the Syrian regime against (mostly unarmed) civilians and no organised opposition movement or large-scale defection by members of the armed forces has emerged to date. While there has been strong verbal condemnation of the repression, there seems to be little likelihood of any repetition of the international community's response with regard to Libya and equally little prospect of an end to the repression or chances of effective outside intervention. Most recently, a draft resolution which merely hinted at possible consequences to the Syrian government for its repression and

---

[30] The important role of the position taken by important regional organisations in backing authorisation for the use of force to protect civilians and enforce the no-fly zone over Libya is clearly set out in the official record of the meeting of the Council which adopted Resolution 1973. UNSC Verbatim Record, UN Doc. S/PV.6498, 17 March 2011.

omitted any reference to concrete measures was blocked by the negative vote of two Permanent Members, Russia and China, which made specific references to preventing a repeat of the type of response which had taken place in relation to the situation in Libya.[31] It seems likely that the scope of the collective intervention in Libya has reinforced the position of some States within and outside the Council which are reluctant to implement collective enforcement measures in response to human rights violations and has probably deepened the existing divisions within the international community relating to such action and to the use of R2P as a means to legitimise it.

Where does that leave the role of R2P as an instrument which can influence the Council and other important actors within the international community in taking action to prevent or halt large-scale violations of human rights and how can the contrast in the responses to these two humanitarian crises in relation to the role of the Council in implementing R2P be explained? While the reasons underlying the vastly different responses in these two situations involve many more considerations than the role that R2P may have played, and it is risky to draw general conclusions regarding the efficacy of R2P on the basis of two examples, the comparison does illustrate both the possibilities and limitations inherent in the R2P concept and the role of the Security Council in its implementation. In relation to the situation in Libya, where a government which had no important allies and little sympathy within the region or the wider international community engaged in massive repression, R2P provided a useful framework for generating a significant degree of political legitimacy to the implementation of collective enforcement measures (although this legitimacy was strained when the execution of the mandate by NATO was severely criticised by a number of States as exceeding the mandate). The fact that key regional organisations were willing to both approve such measures and were willing and able to carry them out, made the situation amenable to the taking of

---

[31] The international reaction to the humanitarian crisis in Syria is summarised on the ICRtoP website and can be found at www.responsibilitytoprotect.org/index.php/crises/crisis-in-syria. The vetoing of a draft resolution submitted by France, Germany, Portugal and the United Kingdom by China and the Russian Federation and the ensuing discussions and statements of the members of the Council can be found in UNSC Verbatim Record, UN Doc. S/PV.6627, 4 October 2011. Particularly the statements of the two Permanent Members voting against the draft resolution make clear that the example of Libya was crucial in motivating them in not allowing the Council to take any action which could constitute any form of sanctions, much less intervention in relation to the situation in Syria.

such far-reaching measures, albeit without the backing of several important States within the Council and only with their acquiescence in the
form of abstentions in the decisions relating to the authorisation of
the use of force. Without the backing of key regional organisations like
the Arab League and African Union, it is highly unlikely that collective
authorisation for military intervention would have been forthcoming.
Likewise, without the willingness of NATO and several other States to
undertake the risks and burdens involved in such an intervention, the
outcome would probably have been very different. While R2P did not
create these conditions or determine the positions of the various actors,
it probably did make the approval and facilitation of collective enforcement measures more acceptable from a political perspective, although it
in no way affected the Council's legal authority to take or not to take any
such measures. In contrast, the situation in Syria vividly demonstrates
that when there is no clear consensus within the region for taking action
of even the mildest sort, much less military intervention, and important
members of the Council are opposed to it, R2P has little or no impact
upon the situation. Moreover, the risks and potential spill-over effects
upon regional security are significantly greater in relation to the situation
in Syria, than they were in relation to the Libyan uprising. Not only does
the Syrian regime have long-standing close ties with several key States
both inside the region and the Council, but also military intervention
there is considerably more problematic and could well result in a widening of conflict and instability in the region, due to the possibility of
counter-intervention by Syria's ally Iran and/or the reopening of hostilities in Lebanon or between Syria and Israel if military intervention by an
actor such as NATO or one or more of its members were to take place.
This demonstrates that both R2P and the undertaking of any type of
humanitarian intervention are not always viable options in response to
even massive human rights violations, such as those which have
occurred and are (at the time of writing) still ongoing in Syria.

Some general conclusions

After discussion of the issues raised in the preceding sections, it is
possible to draw some conclusions regarding the relationship of R2P to
the Security Council and its powers under the UN collective security
system and to the relationship between R2P and the older notion of
humanitarian intervention, taking into account recent developments in
relation to the humanitarian crises in Libya and Syria.

Our examination of the relationship of R2P to the UN collective security system revealed that the two are quite compatible and that R2P neither alters the existing framework of international law relating to the use of measures of coercion, including the use of force in response to gross human rights violations, nor constitutes a binding rule of international law on its own. R2P is also compatible with other existing instruments within the UN collective security system, such as UN peacekeeping and related to the protection of civilians within the context of such peacekeeping operations. R2P reflects, moreover, existing legal obligations and provides a potentially useful policy framework for the Council to take or authorise the use of collective enforcement measures within the scope of the UN Charter. Such measures, while primarily aimed at the maintenance of international peace and security also have an increasingly important secondary objective of reinforcing international law in the area of respect for human rights and humanitarian law and preventing impunity for core international crimes. Where the Council is able to approve such measures, usually working in tandem with important regional actors, it has both the legal authority and the practical means to take or authorise a variety of measures, including the use of force, to respond to large-scale, acute violations of core human rights, which not only violate peremptory legal obligations incumbent upon States, but almost inevitably have an impact upon regional stability and security. Nevertheless, significant impediments of an institutional, political and practical nature remain to the taking of effective collective measures in response to such situations and the advent of R2P has not altered this.

In some cases, humanitarian intervention may serve as an 'emergency exit' alternative to collectively authorised action when no other alternatives are open and when such an intervention is feasible. We have also seen that while R2P and humanitarian intervention are to an extent complementary and share certain common objectives, they are nevertheless distinct concepts. One clear indication of this distinctness is that humanitarian intervention as defined above is a use of force which, in contrast to the use of enforcement measures by the Security Council under the guise of R2P, is *not* compatible with the contemporary legal regulation of the use of force, although under certain conditions it may qualify for far-reaching mitigation or excuse of wrongfulness. However, many of the same impediments which can prevent effective collective measures being implemented, can also stand in the way of a use of force for humanitarian purposes outside the UN collective security system, and there will unfortunately always be situations where human rights are violated on a large scale, where no remedy is readily available. The two recent examples of the international responses to the humanitarian crises in Libya and Syria serve to illustrate both the possibilities and limitations inherent in both concepts. In the first situation, R2P probably facilitated a virtually unprecedented response by the international community, which was made possible by the convergence of a number of factors which made this possible. In the other, neither R2P, nor humanitarian intervention offered a ready solution to an egregious violation of human rights due to the convergence of a number of inherent impediments to the taking of effective action, whether collectively authorised or not.

While this is a sobering conclusion, it is not a reason or an excuse to forgo the taking of action whenever and wherever this is possible to protect human life and uphold human dignity. Both R2P and humanitarian intervention have a role to play in doing so, albeit within the limitations and subject to the conditions which are an inevitable by-product of the international system.

5

The General Assembly

CEDRIC RYNGAERT AND HANNE CUYCKENS

Introduction

In its seminal report on the responsibility to protect (R2P), the Canadian-sponsored International Commission on Intervention and State Sovereignty (ICISS) referred at various junctures to the role of the UN General Assembly (GA) in assuming and implementing a responsibility to protect. As those references capture the policy rationale and legal basis of the GA's R2P role rather well, they can serve as a useful starting point for our analysis.

In its report, ICISS observes that the Security Council only has a 'primary' responsibility under the Charter for peace and security matters; the Charter gives a general or fall-back responsibility to the General Assembly, although the GA's power can only be recommendatory.[1] When assuming this responsibility, in the view of ICISS, the GA, meeting in an Emergency Special Session, may even recommend military action.[2] ICISS believed that such a GA decision would be imbued with a high degree of legitimacy and that 'the mere possibility that this action might be taken will be an important additional form of leverage on the Security Council to encourage it to act decisively and appropriately'.[3]

As often pointed out, the ICISS report set the conceptual terms of the R2P agenda, and led to a flurry of academic, civil society and institutional responses. In the 2005 World Summit Outcome Document, world leaders duly referred to the pre-eminent R2P role of the United Nations, and in particular the Security Council, but, interestingly, also emphasised the role of the GA:

[1] International Commission on Intervention and State Sovereignty, *The Responsibility to Protect* (Ottawa: International Development Research Centre, 2001), para. 6.7.
[2] *Ibid.*, para. 6.29.   [3] *Ibid.*, para. 6.30.

> We stress the need for the General Assembly to continue consideration of the responsibility to protect populations from genocide, war crimes, ethnic cleansing and crimes against humanity and its implications, bearing in mind the principles of the Charter and international law.[4]

The reference to 'the principles of the Charter and international law' is arguably a reference to the prerogatives of the Security Council with regard to authorising the use of force. But the very mentioning of the GA in the 2005 World Summit Outcome Document constitutes progress vis-à-vis the 2004 report of the UNSG's High-Level Panel, which failed to cite the GA's R2P role: this report limited itself to stating that 'there is a collective international responsibility to protect, exercisable by the *Security Council*'.[5] A similar reference to the apparent exclusivity of the Security Council's role could be found in the UN Secretary-General's (SG) report, *In Larger Freedom*.[6]

The GA's consideration of R2P, contemplated in the World Summit Outcome Document, was subsequently encouraged by the 2009 SG report entitled *Implementing the Responsibility to Protect*, which followed up on the outcome of the Millennium Summit.[7] In this report, the SG – like the ICISS – drew particular attention to the useful role which the *Uniting for Peace* Resolution could play, notably as regards sanctions to be taken against regimes failing to protect their own population (although such sanctions would not be binding, given the limited powers of the GA):

> 57. The General Assembly could also consider such measures under its resolution 377 (V), entitled 'Uniting for peace', although they would then not be legally binding. While sanctions may be inadequate to stop abuses

---

[4] 'World Summit Outcome 2005', UN Doc. A/RES/60/1, 24 October 2005, para. 139.

[5] 'We endorse the emerging norm that there is a collective international responsibility to protect, exercisable by the Security Council authorizing military intervention as a last resort, in the event of genocide and other large scale killing, ethnic cleansing or serious violations of international humanitarian law which sovereign Governments have proved powerless or unwilling to prevent' (UN Secretary-General, *A More Secure World: Our Shared Responsibility* (New York: United Nations, 2004), para. 203).

[6] 'Where threats are not imminent but latent, the Charter gives full authority to the Security Council to use military force, including preventively, to preserve international peace and security. As to genocide, ethnic cleansing and other such crimes against humanity, are they not also threats to international peace and security, against which humanity should be able to look to the Security Council for protection?' (UNSG, 'In Larger Freedom: Towards Development, Security and Human Rights for All', UN Doc. A/59/2005, 21 March 2005, para. 125).

[7] UNSG, 'Implementing the Responsibility to Protect', UN Doc. A/63/677, 12 January 2009.

by a determined authoritarian regime, if applied sufficiently early they can demonstrate the international community's commitment to meeting its collective responsibilities under paragraph 139 of the Summit Outcome and serve as a warning of possibly tougher measures if the violence against a population persists.

58. While the General Assembly has at times called for arms embargoes, only the Security Council has the authority to make them binding.

The SG did not hesitate to identify a responsibility of the GA in relation to the action-oriented pillar three of R2P, 'timely and decisive response'. Echoing the findings of ICISS as to the legal basis for GA action, the SG wrote:

63. The General Assembly has an important role to play, even under pillar three. Its peace and security functions are addressed in Articles 11, 12, 14, and 15 of the Charter. Article 24 of the Charter confers on the Security Council 'primary', not total, responsibility for the maintenance of peace and security, and in some cases the perpetration of crimes relating to the responsibility to protect may not be deemed to pose a threat to international peace and security. Moreover, under the 'Uniting for peace' procedure, the Assembly can address such issues when the Council fails to exercise its responsibility with regard to international peace and security because of the lack of unanimity among its five permanent members. Even in such cases, however, Assembly decisions are not legally binding on the parties.

The SG proceeded by brushing aside a restrictive interpretation of the GA's R2P role. Building on the ICISS's observation as to the added legitimacy of GA action in respect of R2P, the SG drew attention to the GA being the 'world's premier inclusive political forum' and to the 'public expectations and shared responsibilities' of all 192 UN Member States assembled in the GA, as opposed to the merely fifteen members of the Security Council.[8] Having made his case, the SG then urged the GA to consider carefully the strategy for implementing the R2P.[9]

In the second part of this chapter, the recent steps taken in this regard by the GA, following up on the SG report, also as regards early warning and assessment, will be discussed at length. In the first part, the legal basis for GA action in the field of R2P will be analysed. Particular attention will be devoted to the *Uniting for Peace* Resolution, a 1950 GA resolution which strengthened the powers of the GA vis-à-vis the Security Council as regards the maintenance of international peace and

---

[8] *Ibid.*, paras. 61 and 69.   [9] *Ibid.*, paras. 69 and 71.

security. This resolution may find its legal basis in the UN Charter, which contains a number of provisions that confer powers on the GA to address matters of peace and security, including R2P. In this first part, specific emphasis will be put on legal obstacles to potential GA authorisation to use force, that is, pillar three, rather than on the other pillars. It is hardly contentious that the GA, in exercising its general competences under the UN Charter, can recommend action that does *not* amount to authorising the use of force, but that is rather related to conflict prevention, confidence-building or post-conflict peace-building.

The *Uniting for Peace* Resolution

The famous 1950 GA's *Uniting for Peace* Resolution shifted, at least partially, the responsibility for maintaining international peace and security from the UN Security Council to the GA in case the Council does not exercise its – primary – responsibility in this regard. In such case, the GA could assume its responsibility to recommend – non-binding – collective measures.[10] Although the Resolution was adopted against the backdrop of a classic inter-State conflict (the Korea crisis), it has particular relevance for R2P situations, since (notably permanent) members of the Security Council may well decide to veto Council action even in the face of a clear case for intervention, when their geostrategic interests are considered to outweigh the moral imperative for intervention.

In spite of its early adoption, *Uniting for Peace* has so far hardly been invoked. Still, it is worth noting that some NATO members, notably the United Kingdom and Canada, entertained the idea of requesting authorisation for a humanitarian intervention in Kosovo (1999), that is, the intervention that sparked the intellectual debate on R2P.[11] This idea was

---

[10] 'The General Assembly ... 1. *Resolves* that if the Security Council, because of lack of unanimity of the permanent members, fails to exercise its primary responsibility for the maintenance of international peace and security in any case where there appears to be a threat to the peace, breach of the peace or act of aggression, the General Assembly shall consider the matter immediately with a view to making appropriate recommendations to Members for collective measures, including in the case of a breach of the peace or act of aggression the use of armed force when necessary, to maintain or restore international peace and security' (UN General Assembly Res. 377 (V), UN Doc. A/RES/377(V), 3 November 1950, p. 10, part A).

[11] Ian Brownlie and C. J. Apperley, 'Kosovo Crisis Inquiry: Memorandum on the International Law Aspects', *International and Comparative Law Quarterly*, 49 (2004), 878–905; Dominik Zaum, 'The Security Council, the General Assembly, and War: The Uniting for Peace Resolution', in Vaughan Lowe, Adam Roberts, Jennifer Welsh and

apparently abandoned for political and legal reasons, in particular the concern that a proposal for a GA resolution under *Uniting for Peace* would fail to command sufficient support among GA members,[12] concerns over the legality of *Uniting for Peace* in so far as it was invoked to buttress military enforcement action,[13] and the major powers' fear that applying *Uniting for Peace* to the situation in Kosovo would create an unwelcome precedent of eroding the prerogatives of the Security Council in maintaining international peace and security.[14]

The political and legal concerns over *Uniting for Peace* in the Kosovo crisis are bound to play out in other R2P contexts as well, and thus may dash the hopes for a R2P application of *Uniting for Peace*. As far as politics is concerned, while the growing unease with a Security Council perceived as 'unrepresentative' may theoretically inform a broader use of *Uniting for Peace* – which thus implies the GA taking on a higher profile[15] – it remains no less true that the GA is dominated by developing and emerging States that are wary of foreign intervention in their domestic affairs, which the international community dimension of R2P is after all about.[16] More importantly perhaps, the Security Council's hardly timid authorisation to use robust forcible action in recent times, as is for instance epitomised by the R2P-informed Resolutions 1973 and 1975 (2011) regarding the situations in respectively Libya and Côte d'Ivoire, has obviated the need for GA action.

Dominik Zaum (eds.), *The United Nations Security Council and War: The Evolution of Thought and Practice Since 1945* (Oxford University Press, 2008), pp. 154–74, at p. 165.

[12] Christian Tomuschat, '"Uniting for Peace": ein Rückblick nach 50 Jahren', *Die Friedens-Warte: Journal of International Peace and Organization*, 76 (2001), 289–303.

[13] See for concerns over the legality of *Uniting for Peace*, Mr Emyr Jones Parry, Political Director of the Foreign Office, Testimony to the House of Commons Foreign Affairs Committee, Fourth Report, 'Kosovo', 18 November 2000, pp. 63–4. See also Zaum, 'The Security Council, the General Assembly, and War', in Lowe *et al.* (eds.), *Security Council and War*, p. 166, citing House of Commons, 'Fourth Report of the Select Committee on Foreign Affairs', 23 May 2000, para. 128, which concluded that a UFP resolution could possibly have provided a legal basis for intervention.

[14] Nicholas Wheeler, *Operationalising the Responsibility to Protect: The Continuing Debate of where Authority should be Located for the Use of Force* (Oslo: Norwegian Institute of International Affairs, 2008), p. 21.

[15] Christina Binder, 'Uniting for Peace Resolution (1950)', in *Max Planck Encyclopedia of Public International Law* (Oxford University Press, 2006), para. 35.

[16] It is somewhat ironic in this respect that the *Uniting for Peace* Resolution was adopted in 1950 at the behest of the United States, which attempted to bypass the blockage of the Security Council by the Soviet Union.

The legality of *Uniting for Peace*-based R2P action

Since the adoption of *Uniting for Peace*, doubts have been voiced over the legality of the Resolution, concerning mainly its compatibility with the division of competences between the GA and the Security Council, as laid down in the UN Charter. Typically, Articles 11(2) and 12(1) of the UN Charter are invoked to challenge the Resolution's legality, notably to the extent that it would authorise enforcement action, albeit cloaked as a mere recommendation.[17] Article 11(2) allows the GA to 'discuss any questions relating to the maintenance of international peace and security brought before it', but adds that '[a]ny such question on which action is necessary shall be referred to the Security Council by the General Assembly either before or after discussion'. In so doing, it seems to bar GA recommendations as to the third pillar of R2P: enforcement action. Article 12(1), for its part, prohibits the GA from making any recommendation with regard to a dispute or situation, while the Security Council is exercising in respect of that dispute or situation the functions assigned to it in the present Charter. Pursuant to this provision, as long as a R2P situation is on the agenda of the Security Council, the GA may be precluded from making any recommendation with regard to the situation, whether it concerns prevention or enforcement.

As far as Article 11(2) of the UN Charter is concerned, much of the doctrinal debate has, not surprisingly, focused on the exact definition of 'action'. In the *Certain Expenses* Advisory Opinion – which related to the financing of UN peacekeeping operations – the International Court of Justice usefully considered that 'the kind of action referred to in Article 11, paragraph 2, is coercive or enforcement action'.[18] This, however, only raised the further question of what 'coercive or enforcement action' precisely is. Hailbronner and Klein have gone as far as to suggest that the provision only means that the GA cannot take binding enforcement actions and that accordingly, in their words, Article 11(2) 'does not effect a substantive limit to recommendations by the GA but rather one of a procedural nature'.[19] In their view, the GA could recommend

---

[17] It is hardly disputed that only the Security Council could adopt 'binding' resolutions, under Chapter VII of the UN Charter, and that the GA's resolutions are, accordingly, not binding, although they may be authoritative.

[18] *Certain Expenses of the United Nations (Article 17, Paragraph 2, of the Charter)*, *Advisory Opinion*, ICJ Reports 1962, pp. 164–65.

[19] Bruno Simma, Andreas Paulus and Eleni Chaitidou (eds.), *The Charter of the United Nations: A Commentary*, 2nd edn (Oxford University Press, 2002), pp. 266 and 283.

enforcement action under Chapter VII, short of taking binding measures. This view is echoed by Hervé Cassan, who while arguing that the
GA has the power to make an Article 39-like determination,[20] at the
same time notes that this interpretation 'est en contradiction totale avec
les intentions des rédacteurs de la Charte'.[21] Be that as it may, in fact the
GA has so far not recommended Article 42-like military enforcement
action, but it *has* recommended Article 41-like diplomatic and economic
sanctions with regard to situations that come close to present-day R2P
situations – for example, South Africa's occupation of Namibia.[22]

Alternatively, even if one were of the view that R2P-informed UNGA
sanctions do qualify as enforcement action that *is* prohibited by Article
11(2) of the UN Charter, the argument could still be made that the
wrongfulness of this violation of an international obligation is precluded
to the extent that the relevant GA recommendation could be characterised as a 'legitimate countermeasure in the collective interest'.[23] It is
noted, however, that the Articles on the Responsibility of States for
Internationally Wrongful Acts (2001) and on the Responsibility of
International Organisations for Internationally Wrongful Acts (2009),
while allowing for the invocation of responsibility by a State or an
international organisation other than an injured State or organisation,[24]
only seem to contemplate the taking of '*lawful* measures against [a] State
to ensure cessation of the breach and reparation in the interest of . . . the
beneficiaries of the obligation breached [in the case of R2P the civilian
population]',[25] irrespective of whether a 'General Assembly resolution

---

[20] Hervé Cassan, 'Article 11(2)', in Jean-Pierre Cot, Alain Pellet and Mathias Forteau
(eds.), *La Charte des Nations Unies: Commentaire article par article*, 3rd edn, 2 vols.
(Paris: Economica, 2005), vol. I, pp. 661–77, at pp. 669 and 674.

[21] 'is in total contradiction with the intentions of the drafters of the Charter' (*ibid.*,
p. 674).

[22] See UNGA Res. ES-8/2, which called upon all States 'in view of the threat to international
peace and security posed by South Africa, to impose against that country comprehensive
mandatory sanctions in accordance with the provisions of the Charter' (UN Doc. A/ES-
8/2, 14 September 1981, paras. 13–14).

[23] Binder, 'Uniting for Peace', para. 29.

[24] International Law Commission, 'Report of the International Law Commission on
the Work of Its Fifty-Third Session (23 April–1 June and 2 July–10 August 2001)', UN
Doc. A/56/10, p. 126, art. 48(1); ILC, 'Report of the International Law Commission:
Sixty-First Session (5 May–6 June and 7 July–8 August 2008)', UN Doc. A/64/10, p. 145,
art. 48(1).

[25] ILC, 'Fifty-Third Session', p. 137, art. 54; ILC, 'Sixty-First Session', p. 159, art. 54
(emphasis added).

recommending such measures might provide an essential additional basis of legitimacy', as Binder appears to believe.[26]

While a narrow interpretation of 'enforcement action' may allow *Uniting for Peace* to comport with Article 11(2), Article 12(1) of the UN Charter constitutes potentially a more formidable obstacle. As the Security Council typically discusses a panoply of humanitarian emergencies at any given moment, without necessarily taking much action – for example, as a result of a permanent member casting a veto – the very circumstance that such an emergency continues to appear on the Council's agenda may, in accordance with Article 12(1), bar any GA action. While this view may have been dominant in the early days of the UN,[27] it is now widely accepted that '[t]he GA may ... regard ... inactivity as evidence that the Security Council is no longer dealing with the matter, notwithstanding the fact that it remains formally on the list of items with which the Security Council is dealing.'[28] The ICJ appears to have confirmed this view – that GA and Security Council may deal in parallel with the same situation – in its *Wall* Advisory Opinion, which was triggered by a GA reference on the basis of *Uniting for Peace*.[29] As Simma and others have observed, as long as the GA does not directly contradict Security Council action, the overlapping action of GA and SC does not seem to be problematic.[30] In any event, if the SC is dealing quite actively with the military security aspects of an R2P situation, the GA could address the broader human security aspects of the situation.[31] After all, another provision of the Charter, Article 14, grants a very broad mandate to the GA to 'recommend measures for the peaceful adjustment of any situation, regardless of origin, which it deems likely to impair the general welfare or friendly relations among nations' – albeit subject to the provisions of Article 12. By providing that UN members 'confer on the Security Council primary responsibility for the maintenance of international peace and security', Article 24(1) of the UN Charter suggests the existence of a secondary or subsidiary responsibility

---

[26] Binder, 'Uniting for Peace', para. 29.

[27] Simma *et al.* (eds.), *Charter of the United Nations*, p. 290.

[28] *Ibid.*, p. 291 (references omitted). See also *Legal Consequences of the Construction of a Wall in the Occupied Palestinian Territory, Advisory Opinion, Opinion of Judge Kooijmans*, ICJ Reports 2004, p. 136, para. 16. In fact, as early as 1968, the UN Legal Counsel construed the words 'the Security Council is exercising' as 'is exercising at this moment'.

[29] *Wall in the Occupied Palestinian Territory*, p. 149; see also Leonardo Nemer, 'Article 12 (1)', in Cot *et al.* (eds.), *La Charte des Nations Unies*, vol. I, pp. 683–90, at p. 690.

[30] Simma *et al.* (eds.), *Charter of the United Nations*, p. 293.   [31] *Ibid.*, p. 292.

for another organ, logically the UN General Assembly, which has a general competence to discuss any questions or any matters within the scope of the Charter pursuant to Article 10 of the UN Charter.[32]

Article 14 of the UN Charter, in fact, may have specific relevance for GA action in a R2P context, as it not simply refers to GA competence over inter-State tensions ('friendly relations among nations'), but also cites 'the general welfare', irrespective of whether such welfare is threatened in an inter- or intra-State context.[33] Doubtless, measures to protect the civilian population, that is, the essence of R2P, further the general welfare. In any event, in scholarly writings Article 14 of the UN Charter has been considered as allowing for GA action furthering human rights and the right to self-determination,[34] which ultimately are among the norms that the R2P discourse aims to protect. As far as *practice* is concerned, it is of note that the situation in the Occupied Palestinian Territories was the subject of the seventh, eighth and tenth (and current) emergency special sessions convened by the GA in accordance with *Uniting for Peace*.[35]

---

[32] 'The General Assembly may discuss any questions or any matters within the scope of the present Charter or relating to the powers and functions of any organs provided for in the present Charter, and, except as provided in Article 12, may make recommendations to the Members of the United Nations or to the Security Council or to both on any such questions or matters' (Charter of the United Nations, adopted 24 October 1945, 1 UNTS XVI, art. 10).

[33] The provision may perhaps be seen as *lex specialis* vis-à-vis the domestic jurisdiction clause of Article 2(7) of the UN Charter, which states, 'Nothing contained in the present Charter shall authorise the United Nations to intervene in matters which are essentially within the domestic jurisdiction of any State or shall require the Members to submit such matters to settlement under the present Charter; but this principle shall not prejudice the application of enforcement measures under Chapter VII.'

[34] See Raphaëlle Maison, 'Article 14', in Cot *et al.* (eds.), *La Charte des Nations Unies*, pp. 747–8. Terming the 'general welfare' ('bien général') 'une sorte de bizarrerie', but adding that it allows 'en tout état de cause à l'Assemblée générale de réagir à des comportements qui, au sens originel du terme de menace à la paix, c'est-à-dire avant l'élargissement de cette notion, n'étaient pas considérés comme engendrant une telle menace: non-respect des droits de l'homme et du droit des peuples à disposer d'eux-mêmes par exemple' and that 'l'Assemblée est donc autorisée à connaître de situations qui surgissent à l'intérieur même d'un Etat'. Referring to self-determination, human rights, fundamental freedoms in the context of Article 14 of the UN Charter, see Simma *et al.* (eds.), *Charter of the United Nations*, p. 324.

[35] See the UN website for an overview of all relevant resolutions and records of these emergency special sessions at www.un.org/en/ga/sessions/emergency.shtml. The tenth – and last – emergency special session with regard to 'illegal Israeli actions in occupied East Jerusalem and the rest of the Occupied Palestinian Territory' is still ongoing and is

GA recommendation of forcible action and sanctions to address R2P situations

From the above legal–institutional analysis, it follows that the UN Charter gives the General Assembly sufficient leeway to recommend measures to address a R2P situation. Possibly, the GA may even recommend forcible action, although it should be noted that a number of authoritative recent UN documents appear to have disavowed this option on legal grounds.[36] In light of these statements, it is unlikely that the GA will ever authorise, if only on the basis of a recommendation, the use of force, even if such is contemplated by *Uniting for Peace*.[37] By way of comparison, it is pointed out that the Constitutive Act of the African Union explicitly confers the power on its Assembly to decide on the Union's (military) intervention in a Member State 'in respect to grave circumstances, namely: war crimes, genocide, and crimes against humanity', that is, precisely in R2P situations.[38]

The GA is not only precluded from authorising the use of force, but also *a fortiori* from giving *binding effect* to such an authorisation. This inability to give binding effect to GA decisions does apply not only to authorisations to use force, but also to *any* restrictive measures, including diplomatic and economic sanctions. The taking of binding sanctions remains the prerogative of the Security Council in accordance with Chapter VII of the UN Charter (Article 41 in particular). Still, the General Assembly may want to *recommend* sanctions. Given its representative character and the higher legitimacy which its decisions are endowed with (as compared to decisions

periodically resumed. During this session, the GA requested the ICJ 'to urgently render an advisory opinion on the following question: What are the legal consequences arising from the construction of the wall being built by Israel, the occupying Power, in the Occupied Palestinian Territory, including in and around East Jerusalem, as described in the Report of the Secretary-General, considering the rules and principles of international law, including the Fourth Geneva Convention of 1949, and relevant Security Council and General Assembly resolutions?' (UNGA Res. ES-10/14, UN Doc. A/RES/ES-10/14, 12 December 2003).

[36] See nn. 5–7, above.

[37] In fact, only once did the GA authorise coercive action, during the Korea crisis, but it is of note that the relevant resolution does not cite *Uniting for Peace* as its legal basis. UNGA Res. 498 V, UN Doc. A/RES/498(V), 1 February 1951, p. 1; UNGA Res. 500 V, UN Doc. A/RES/500(V), 18 May 1951, p. 2. But see UNGA Res. 498 V, which clearly echoes the *Uniting for Peace* wording, 'Noting that the SC, because of lack of unanimity . . .'.

[38] The right of the Union to intervene in a Member State is listed as one of the purposes of the Union. Constitutive Act of the African Union, adopted 11 July 2000 and entered into force 26 May 2001, 2158 UNTS 3, art. 4(h). For a detailed discussion, see Dersso, Chapter 10 in this book.

of the Security Council),[39] it may choose to assume its responsibility to recommend sanctions if the Security Council fails to live up to its R2P responsibilities in this respect.[40]

General Assembly steps towards the implementation of R2P

Having discussed the political and legal obstacles to GA action to address on its own initiative specific R2P threats, let us now consider the follow-up which the GA has recently given to the SG report with regard to the implementation of the responsibility to protect.[41] This report not only emphasised the potential role of the GA with regard to the protection of peace and security based on the *Uniting for Peace* initiative – a role discussed in the first part of this chapter – but it also urged the GA to take effective steps towards the implementation of R2P by Member States, supported by various international partners. Those steps do not so much relate to forcible action or the taking of sanctions – that is, the subject of the first part of this chapter – but rather to agenda-setting, facilitation of R2P and institutional coordination. The first subsection of this part will consider the GA's response to the SG's call on the GA to develop a strategy for implementation of R2P as laid down in paragraph 71 of the SG report. In the second subsection, the GA's efforts in respect of early warning and assessment, to which the SG specifically referred in paragraph 12 of his 2009 report, will be highlighted.

The proper role for the General Assembly in implementing R2P

In his 2009 report, the SG provided a number of specific suggestions with regard to the role the GA should play in the implementation of R2P. More particularly, he urged the GA to take the following steps:

[39] Gareth Evans, *The Responsibility to Protect: Ending Mass Atrocity Crimes Once and for All* (Washington, DC: Brookings Institution, 2008), p. 136. Evans states, albeit primarily with reference to *military* intervention, that 'if a decision were supported by an over-whelming majority of member states, it would provide a high degree of legitimacy for international intervention'.

[40] Mehrdad Payandeh, 'With Great Power Comes Great Responsibility? The Concept of the Responsibility to Protect within the Process of International Lawmaking', *Yale Journal of International Law*, 35 (2010), 469–516, at 505. Payandeh submits that 'the General Assembly could ... become a forum for the coordination of sanctions by individual member states when the Security Council does not decide upon collective action'.

[41] UNSG, 'Implementing the Responsibility to Protect'.

(1) welcome or take note of the present report;
(2) define its 'continuing consideration' role as mandated in paragraph 139 of the 2005 World Summit Outcome;
(3) address ways to define and develop the partnerships between States and the international community, under pillar two, 'International assistance and capacity-building', of the strategy outlined in the present report;
(4) consider whether and, if so, how to conduct a periodic review of what Member States have done to implement the responsibility to protect; and
(5) determine how best to exercise its oversight of the Secretariat's effort to implement to responsibility to protect.

The SG presented his report on the implementation of R2P to the GA on 21 July 2009. In his speech accompanying the presentation of the report, Ban Ki-moon reminded the GA that the commitment they made by endorsing the responsibility to protect in the 2005 World Summit Outcome Document is universal and irrevocable and that the task is now to 'deliver on this historic pledge to the peoples of the world'.[42] In other words, the task of the GA is not to redefine the concept of R2P, but to ensure its effective implementation.

In the days following the presentation by the SG of his report, the debate asked for by the SG in paragraph 71 of said report took place. While the expectations for participation in the debate were quite low, the turnout proved to be a big surprise. Indeed, while UN experts had initially deemed that three three-hour sessions would be more than enough, ninety-two governments signed up and spoke during the plenary session concerning the implementation and follow-up of the outcome of the Millennium Summit and the debate lasted over two and a half days.[43] The debate was ultimately considered a success by the civil society. The International Coalition for the Responsibility to Protect affirmed that this display of support from governments for the implementation of R2P was a consequence of the hard work and dedication of

---

[42] Secretary-General Ban Ki-moon, 'Remarks to the General Assembly on the Responsibility to Protect (RtoP)', speech delivered to the General Assembly, New York, 21 July 2009, at www.un.org/apps/news/infocus/sgspeeches/statments_full.asp?statID=544.

[43] International Coalition for the Responsibility to Protect, 'Report on the General Assembly Plenary Debate on the Responsibility to Protect', p. 1, available at www.responsibilitytoprotect.org.

different actors: the UN Secretariat, civil society organisations, the ad hoc pro-R2P government grouping called the 'Friends of R2P' co-chaired by the governments of Canada and Rwanda, and some individuals dedicated to the cause such as Desmond Tutu, Gareth Evans, Kofi Annan and many more.[44] With regard to the role of the UN Secretariat, the importance of the work of the SG Special Adviser on R2P matters, Edward Luck, as well as his collaboration with the SG Special Adviser on the Prevention of Genocide, Francis Deng, was especially emphasised as having contributed to the success of this debate.[45] Of course, interest in the debate and high participation are one thing, but concrete achievements of the debate are quite another.

During the sessions, there were a certain number of recurring themes. In general, the delegates started by recognising the importance of the concept of R2P in the fight against gross and systematic violations of human rights, and they mentioned a few examples of situations that could and should have been avoided (such as Rwanda, Srebrenica and so on). Most of the speeches delivered during the plenary session welcomed the SG report on the implementation of R2P. The delegates also emphasised the fact that the objective of the debate was not to discuss again the notion of R2P, since it had already been endorsed by the international community in the 2005 World Summit Outcome Document, but that the focus should be laid on operationalisation and implementation. In other words, it was considered to be time to move from theory to practice. As the delegate of Moldova put it, 'the report at hand is a critical first step towards turning the authoritative and enduring words of the 2005 World Summit Outcome (GA Resolution 60/1) into doctrine, policy and, most importantly, deeds'.[46] With regard to the concept of R2P, as endorsed during the 2005 World Summit, most delegates seemed to agree on a narrow approach focused on the protection against four specific crimes, namely genocide, war crimes, crimes against humanity and ethnic cleansing. It is also the view of the present authors that, indeed, a more narrow and focused approach could help to implement the concept. The important elements that were put forward by Secretary-General Ban Ki-moon during his presentation of the report to the GA, namely the importance of the three pillars structure, the importance of prevention and the importance of capacity-building and improvement of the early warning system were also emphasised by most of the speakers. Finally, it was also recalled that the GA had a role to play in the maintenance of

[44] *Ibid.*, pp. 2–3.   [45] *Ibid.*, p. 2.   [46] *Ibid.*, p. 5.

international peace and security, especially when the SC fails to act. The need for reforming the Security Council was also discussed at length.

We can infer from the discussions in the GA that the Member States at least seem to be embracing the ideas of the SG with regard to implementation. However, if we look at GA Resolution 63/308,[47] which was adopted on the issue a few months later, on 7 October 2009, it is difficult not to be at least somewhat disappointed. Undoubtedly, this resolution is of great symbolic importance, since it is the first resolution adopted by the GA on the responsibility to protect. However, its content is far from satisfactory.

True, the resolution reaffirms the importance of the respect for the principles and purposes of the UN Charter and recalls paragraphs 138 and 139 of the 2005 World Summit Outcome, and 'takes note of the report of the Secretary General and of the timely and productive debate organised by the President of the General Assembly on the responsibility to protect held on 21, 23, 24 and 28 of July 2009, with full participation by Member States'. Thus, note was taken by the GA of the 2009 SG report and the extensive exchange of views among the Member States. Resolution 63/308 also states that the GA will 'continue its consideration of the responsibility to protect', which is in line with was has been set out in paragraph 139 of the 2005 World Summit Outcome, as well as the suggestion of the SG, namely of the need for the General Assembly to continue consideration of the responsibility to protect populations from genocide, war crimes, ethnic cleansing and crimes against humanity and its implications bearing in mind the principles of the Charter and international law.[48]

However, Resolution 63/308 only *partly* meets the second suggestion by the SG in his report: the SG asked the GA to '*define* its "continuing consideration" role as mandated in paragraph 139 of the 2005 World Summit Outcome' (emphasis added). In its Resolution 63/308, the GA only reaffirms that it will *continue* its consideration of R2P, it does not *define* the scope of this consideration. Additionally, the three last suggestions contained in the report, concerning namely the ways to define and develop partnerships between States and the international community, the possible conduct of periodic review of Member States on the implementation of R2P and how to best exercise the oversight of the Secretariat's efforts to implement R2P remained unaddressed.

---

[47] UNGA Res. 63/308, UN Doc. A/RES/63/308, 7 October 2009.
[48] 'World Summit Outcome 2005', para. 139.

Regrettably, even though most of the suggestions put forward by the SG in his report on implementation were extensively discussed in the GA, the GA resolution subsequently adopted on the matter addresses a few points only superficially.

While the extensive debate on R2P that took place in the GA, as well as the adoption of the first GA resolution on the subject are important steps forward, a lot remains to be done to operationalise R2P. It must be recalled that, during his speech on the matter, the president of the GA stated that

> [t]he concept of the responsibility to protect has the potential to evolve further into a full-fledged rule of customary international law. Whether to argue that such a norm already exists is, ultimately, up to this body to decide. I need not remind anyone present in this forum that, in terms of the United Nations Charter, it is the General Assembly that develops international law.[49]

While one may take issue with the law-developing role of the GA, including as regards customary international law formation, it is quite clear that, if the GA wants to realise, even at the political level, what its president hinted to in his speech, there still is a long road ahead.

The role of the General Assembly with regard to early warning and assessment

In paragraph 12 of the report on implementing R2P, the SG not only raised five points for the GA to consider, but also provided some initial ideas on early warning and assessment, which are fleshed out in the annex to the report.[50] Moreover, he committed to later on 'submit to the Assembly modest proposals for implementing improvements in the early warning capability of the Organisation, as called for in paragraph 138 of the Summit Outcome'.[51] Considering that early warning and assessment are crucial in the implementation of R2P, it is important to briefly address this specific issue in addition to the points set out in paragraph 71 of the report. The annex to the report emphasises the need for better cooperation between the different UN organs on the matter, as well as mainstreaming of the principle of R2P within the ongoing work

---

[49] UNGA Verbatim Record, UN Doc. A/63/PV.97, 23 July 2009, p. 2.
[50] UNSG, 'Implementing the Responsibility to Protect', annex, pp. 31–3.
[51] *Ibid.*, para. 12. See also 'World Summit Outcome 2005', para. 138, emphasising the importance of prevention and urging the international community to 'support the United Nations in establishing an early warning capability'.

of the organisation. As noted there, 'For the responsibility to protect . . . teamwork and collaboration must become standard operating procedure, not aspirational goals'.[52]

As far as prevention, early warning and assessment are concerned, the problem does not lie so much in the absence of information on the situation, but in the difficulty of painting a general picture of the situation due to a lack of communication between the different bodies. Such a general picture would allow for better assessment of the risks involved and for earlier reaction, if needed. In his report, the SG especially emphasised the important role of the Special Adviser on R2P matters and the Special Adviser on the Prevention of Genocide in this respect. As these two advisers have distinct yet closely related mandates, and collaboration between them is important, the SG called upon the GA to consider the proposals for the setting up of a small joint office, in which both advisers will share space and support staff.[53] This highlights the potentially important role which the GA can play – also on the basis of its budgetary powers – in setting, or at least considerably influencing, the UN's priorities.

These points were further elaborated upon in an SG report on early warning, assessment and the responsibility to protect released on 14 July 2010.[54] In the introduction, the SG states that the report 'is prepared in order to update Member States on certain aspects of the responsibility to protect, pursuant to General Assembly Resolution 63/308, in which the Assembly confirmed its intention "to continue its consideration of the responsibility to protect" as called for in the 2005 World Summit Outcome'.[55] The report reminds the Member States of the mandate set out in paragraph 138 of the Summit Outcome Document, which urges for an expansion of the UN capabilities for early warning and assessment. Subsequently, it is noted that '[t]he political dialogue on how best to implement the responsibility to protect is off to a good start, although a number of critical implementation issues will require a continuing conversation among the Member States, the United Nations systems and civil society organisations.'[56] Finally, the report announces an informal interactive dialogue to take place during the sixty-fourth session on the early warning and assessments dimensions of the responsibility to

---

[52] UNSG, 'Implementing the Responsibility to Protect', annex, p. 31.   [53] Ibid., p. 33.

[54] UNSG, 'Early Warning, Assessment and the Responsibility to Protect', UN Doc. A/64/864, 14 July 2010.

[55] Ibid., para. 1.   [56] Ibid., para. 14.

protect.[57] In preparation of this informal interactive dialogue, the SG provided the GA with some remarks on the subject.[58] He once again emphasised the need for system-wide coherence, for information and consultation with other UN entities and for mainstreaming responsibility to protect perspectives.[59] He also reiterated his call for the creation of a joint office for the SG special advisers on R2P matters and on Prevention of Genocide.

The issue of early warning was discussed in the GA on 9 August 2010. Forty-two Member States, two representatives from international organisations and two representatives from civil society spoke during that meeting.[60] That showed once again, the close attention paid to R2P by the members of the GA, who warmly welcomed the report.[61] States' representatives generally agreed that the challenge with regard to early warning and assessment laid in the translation of the information at the disposal into analysis and then into action.[62] With regard to the creation of a joint office, the Member States mainly indicated that they were looking forward to hearing concrete proposals on this matter.[63] Once again, while the issues proposed by the SG were thoroughly discussed, no concrete action was taken.

The GA on the role of the regional and sub-regional organisations in implementing the responsibility to protect

In his report on early warning, assessment and the responsibility to protect, the SG stated that it would be useful to also organise an informal interactive dialogue, similar to the ones on R2P in general and on early warning and assessment respectively held in July 2009 and August 2010, on the role of regional and sub-regional organisations in implementing the responsibility to protect. Such an informal interactive dialogue took place on 12 July 2011. In anticipation of the dialogue, on 27 June 2011 the SG released a report on the role of the regional and sub-regional

---

[57] *Ibid.*

[58] Secretary-General Ki-moon, 'Remarks', speech delivered at the General Assembly Informal Interactive Dialogue on Early Warning, Assessment, and the Responsibility to Protect (RtoP), New York, 23 July 2010, available at www.responsibilitytoprotect.org.

[59] *Ibid.*, p. 3.

[60] ICRtoP, 'GA Dialogue on Early Warning, Assessment and the Responsibility to Protect', August 2010, available at www.responsibilitytoprotect.org.

[61] *Ibid.* [62] *Ibid.* [63] *Ibid.*

organisations in implementing the responsibility to protect.[64] In an information note on the matter, the GA President Joseph Deiss stated that the present debate had several purposes: (1) reconfirming that R2P is an evolving principle, on which the continuing input of the Member States is both needed and valued; (2) creating an opportunity for cross-regional exchanges on lessons learned and best practices; and (3) offering a forum for considering new ideas and approaches to enhancing global–regional–sub-regional cooperation on R2P, as well as for reflecting on implementation efforts to date.[65] As it had been the case for the two previous informal interactive dialogues on R2P, there was also great interest for this specific topic among the Member States. The GA platform was once again used to voice support for the norm and provide suggestions for its implementation.[66] Most Member States agreed that, since the concept itself was now relatively clear, the focus should lie on the interpretation and the operationalisation of the different pillars of the concept.[67] While recognising the importance of regional organisations in preventing and reacting to mass atrocities, most of them also pleaded for increased cooperation among regional and sub-regional bodies.[68] The importance of prevention, and more specifically the importance of early warning and the role of the International Criminal Court, was once again emphasised.[69] The importance of the 'joint office' mentioned above was also reiterated. Finally, with regard to the theme of 2012, the proposition of the SG to focus on the third pillar of R2P (timely and decisive response, which should not be limited to the use of force), was echoed by a certain number of Member States and the EU.[70] Most important, the Member States once again agreed that the dialogue was not a platform for renegotiating the concept of R2P, but rather a place to discuss how to move forward with the implementation of the norm.[71]

---

[64] UNSG, 'The Role of Regional and Sub-regional Arrangements in Implementing the Responsibility to Protect', UN Doc. A/65/877–S/2011/393, 27 June 2011.

[65] UNGA Information Note, 'Informal Interactive Dialogue on the Role of Regional and Sub-regional Arrangements in Implementing the Responsibility to Protect', 12 July 2011, available at www.responsibilitytoprotect.org.

[66] For more details, see International Coalition for the Responsibility to Protect, 'Report on the Interactive Dialogue of the UN General Assembly on the Role of Regional and Sub-regional Arrangements in Implementing the Responsibility to Protect', August 2011, p. 1, available at www.responsibilitytoprotect.org.

[67] Ibid., p. 3.   [68] Ibid., p. 4.   [69] Ibid., pp. 4–5.   [70] Ibid., p. 5.   [71] Ibid., p. 8.

Interim evaluation

The GA appears to have carved out a clear role for itself as a platform for R2P policy coordination over the last years. This is in full accordance with the central position bestowed to the GA at the 2005 World Summit as 'the chief deliberative, policymaking and representative organ of the United Nations'.[72] Confronted with the pre-eminence of the Security Council in matters of peace and security, and the Council's reactive mandate under Chapter VII of the Charter in particular, the GA has focused on other R2P dimensions than the use of force or the imposition of sanctions. It has given due consideration to early warning capabilities, assessment of threats and conflict prevention in general. Capacity-building by Member States and regional organisations has rightly been considered as crucial.

This interest and involvement of the GA in R2P matters and more specifically the efforts to define an agenda towards implementation of the concept are necessary in order to forge broad consensus. But, ultimately, whether these efforts are really making a difference is hard to say. Following up on the SG's R2P reports of 2009, 2010 and 2011, the GA has organised several debates in which a considerable number of delegates have taken the floor, but the transition from words to deeds still needs to materialise. While the very debating of the different facets of R2P in the GA is already a step forward, Member States need to engage more concretely on the operationalisation of R2P.

Whether all Member States are truly committed to go further than simply paying lip-service to the lofty concept of R2P remains questionable. Most likely, repressive regimes are not prepared to redesign their institutions, exchange best practices and have the international community assist in, and monitor, their efforts to implement R2P mechanisms. Ultimately, the GA, like other UN organs, can only do what its Member States allow and enable it to do. That is even more so for a politically sensitive field as R2P, which ultimately requires Member States to cede portions of their sovereignty to the international community. If the response to the situations in Syria and Yemen are to be seen as indicative of a general position on R2P, window-dressing strategies and opposition to concrete blueprints for R2P early warning mechanisms is likely going to emanate from various reluctant Member States at the GA.

---

[72] 'World Summit Outcome 2005', para. 149.

Concluding observations

As explained above, there is a legal basis in the UN Charter for GA action in respect of R2P situations. General Assembly powers possibly include recommending forcible military action and sanctions; although no GA-mandated measures can be binding, given the institutional position of the GA within the UN. Irrespective of the legal basis, however, it is open to doubt whether the GA will willingly assume an institutional responsibility to protect under pillar three on 'timely and decisive action' by authorising sanctions in R2P situations. If the GA's past, very scarce and one-sided practice of relying on *Uniting for Peace* to address threats to peace and civilian populations,[73] is to be taken as an indication of future practice in this regard, one can hardly be optimistic. To be fair, in recent times, the GA, in a show of 'Group of 77' solidarity with the Palestinian people, has focused on the specific case of Israel and the Occupied Palestinian Territories. However, GA attention for this case has eventually drawn attention away from other equally, if not more precarious R2P situations as Syria and Myanmar. The 'symbolic politics' in which the GA – and the recently revamped Human Rights Council as its subsidiary organ – appear to occasionally engage in,[74] might potentially undermine the overall UN role in assuming an unbiased responsibility to protect vulnerable civilian populations.[75]

While the GA has held extensive debates on R2P issues since mid-2009, those debates have still to deliver concrete results in terms of developing tools, policies and measures for operationalising R2P in a variety of R2P situations. Terms such as 'mainstreaming', 'system-wide coherence', 'information', 'consultation' and 'the law-making role of the GA' are often tossed around, but so far the GA has failed to take specific measures that could really make a difference on the ground. Those measures would include the development of partnerships between

---

[73] Payandeh notes that the practical significance of *Uniting for Peace* is rather marginal ('With Great Power', 503).

[74] Also observing that the GA mainly uses *Uniting for Peace* 'to take a stand against the increasing dominance of the UN by the Security Council', see Zaum, 'The Security Council, the General Assembly, and War', in Lowe *et al.* (eds.), *Security Council and War*, pp. 173–4.

[75] Compare Simma *et al.* (eds.), *Charter of the United Nations*, p. 296, stating 'There is much disagreement over whether the GA's gain in procedural independence for dealing with specific threats to world peace, which has gone hand in hand with the reduction in scope of Article 12(1), has furthered the overall ability of the UN to maintain international peace and security.'

States and the international community, the conduct of periodic review of Member States on the implementation of R2P, and strong support for the joint office of the SG special advisers on R2P matters and on Prevention of Genocide. It is to be hoped that the GA will soon engage in more concrete steps and truly translate words into deeds.

6

The Secretary-General

NICHOLAS TURNER

At the UN General Assembly in 2005, Member States made a commitment to protect populations from genocide, war crimes, ethnic cleansing and crimes against humanity. This collective responsibility to protect (RtoP) developed in response to the tragic failures of the United Nations in Somalia, Rwanda and Srebrenica, which, together with the controversy over NATO's Kosovo operation, had prompted renewed debate over the legitimacy of intervention for humanitarian purposes. The concept is thus, in many ways, a child of the UN system, and in particular of the UN Secretary-General (SG).[1] RtoP was formulated in response to Kofi Annan's explicit challenge to Member States for consensus on how to respond to such mass atrocities. Annan himself was instrumental in championing the concept, and promoting and crystallising the emerging normative developments concerning the protection of vulnerable peoples which culminated in the 2005 World Summit agreement. The SG is also, as acknowledged by the commission which devised RtoP, 'an obvious starting point when looking for multilateral leadership on questions relating to intervention'.[2] Since the 2005 agreement, the SG has continued to play a prominent role in building consensus on RtoP and driving its conceptual development, most notably through Ban Ki-moon's 2009 report which outlined a strategy for moving the concept from words to deeds. At the same time, both Kofi Annan and Ban Ki-moon have taken initial steps towards the institutionalisation of RtoP within the UN system, and invoked the principle in specific country situations from Darfur to, most recently, Côte d'Ivoire, Libya and Syria.

---

[1] This chapter uses the terms 'principle' and 'concept' to describe RtoP, as it has not yet become a norm with binding legal status.

[2] International Commission on Intervention and State Sovereignty, *The Responsibility to Protect* (Ottawa: International Development Research Centre, 2001).

This chapter explores the role of the SG in the development and implementation of RtoP. It begins by outlining the SG's mandate and the relevant operational, institutional and normative dimensions of his evolving responsibilities. Next, it traces the contributions of Secretaries-General to the development of RtoP, leading to its eventual adoption at the 2005 World Summit. The chapter proceeds to show how the early RtoP cases revealed the extent of the conceptual and political difficulties in implementing the principle, and examines Ban Ki-moon's strategy for resolving these difficulties. It then explores the role of the SG in implementing RtoP under this strategy, and some of the challenges ahead.

The possibilities of an impossible mandate

The role of Secretary-General is widely seen as a thankless task, famously described as 'the most impossible job on this earth' by Dag Hammarskjöld.[3] The SG acts on behalf of the organisation and depends upon the support of all UN members. Yet, he must remain independent of any single State.[4] He assists the UN Security Council (Council) and the General Assembly in making informed decisions, implements their decisions and reports back to them on progress made. The politics of the time both constrains the ability of the SG to perform his role, and shapes the way in which he does so.

Despite his extensive responsibilities, the specific powers of the SG as defined in the UN Charter are surprisingly limited. His authority derives primarily from Article 97, under which he is chief administrative officer of the Secretariat.[5] Article 98 provides for the SG to be tasked with various functions by the General Assembly, the Security Council or the Economic and Social Council. With these principal organs gradually taking on a broader range of tasks, this provision has resulted in the delegation of progressively greater responsibilities to the SG, including command authority for peace operations.

Article 99 of the Charter empowers the SG to 'bring to the attention of the Security Council any matter which in his opinion may threaten the maintenance of international peace and security'. It was described by the

---

[3] Quoted in United Nations press release, 'Statement at a General Meeting of the Staff', UN Doc. SG/299, 1 May 1953.

[4] As there has not yet been a female Secretary-General, this chapter uses masculine pronouns.

[5] See for example Bruno Simma, Andreas Paulus and Eleni Chaitidou (eds.), *The Charter of the United Nations: A Commentary*, 2nd edn (Oxford University Press, 2002).

Preparatory Commission of the United Nations as 'a quite special right which goes beyond any power previously afforded to an international organisation'.[6] Indeed, it is the discretionary language of Article 99 which provides the legal basis for the SG to engage in political activities independent of the Security Council. His right to place 'any matter' on the agenda of the Security Council also has broader scope than the right of Member States under Article 35 to refer 'any dispute or situation'. The SG thus has a particular responsibility to investigate and report 'any developments – for example in the economic or social field – which in his view could have serious political implications remediable only by political action'.[7]

In practice the political role and responsibilities of the SG have expanded considerably, as specific disputes and crises have required incumbents to creatively interpret the limited Charter mandate for the office. The most prominent example of this is the introduction of peace-keeping by Dag Hammarskjöld during the Suez Crisis of 1956, and later its deployment on a massive scale in the Congo operation. The SG's expanded political action has taken various forms, including preventive diplomacy through 'good offices' undertaken by the SG, his envoys or representatives, and fact-finding missions to gather information on evolving situations.

In addition to quiet diplomacy, the SG has a more public role as the spokesperson and moral voice of the international community, using his institutional platform to shape the global agenda and focus attention on particular situations and crises. As head of the Secretariat, under Article 7 the SG has a responsibility to uphold the principles and purposes of the Charter, and can therefore use his office as a 'bully pulpit' from which to promote these principles and expose governments and other actors violating them.

The discretion afforded by the Charter definition of his role allows the SG to engage in what the constructivist literature terms 'norm entrepreneur-ship' – persuading a critical mass of States to adopt a new shared expect-ation of appropriate behaviour.[8] The SG has unique status as a normative actor due to the legitimacy of the world body, and his independence

---

[6] Preparatory Commission of the UN, 'Report of the Preparatory Commission of the United Nations', UN Doc. PC/20, 23 December 1945, ch. 8, section 2, para. 16.

[7] Executive Committee of the Preparatory Commission of the UN, Committee 6, 4th Meeting, UN Doc. PC/EX/SEC/9.

[8] See for example Martha Finnemore and Kathryn Sikkink, 'International Norm Dynamics and Political Change', *International Organization*, 52 (1998), 877–917, at 897.

established in Article 100. He can claim to be impartially applying the principles of the Charter, and thus acting in the collective interest of humanity, to present norms as universal. The SG can apply this normative influence in reports to the main UN organs and speeches, but also in his operational and managerial activities. The ability to institutionalise new norms within the UN system is of particular importance, as the literature on norm socialisation suggests that institutionalisation can make a strong contribution to the consolidation of emerging norms.[9]

To be sure, the success of such efforts depends on the incumbent – arguably only Dag Hammarskjöld and Kofi Annan have had the ambition and personal qualities to bring about significant normative changes, of which RtoP is a prime example. The SG's normative influence is also constrained by politics, as Member States can perceive a strong, activist SG as undermining their interests and respond with opposition – as both Hammarskjöld and Annan experienced.

Addressing mass atrocities after 1945

The imperative for action when faced with humanitarian crises or mass violations of human rights has been keenly felt and often expressed by Secretaries-General. In 1971 U Thant asserted that 'the Secretary-General's obligations under the Charter must include any humanitarian action that he can take to save the lives of large numbers of human beings.'[10] In practice, however, the ability of the United Nations to act in such situations has been severely constrained by political and normative realities, particularly during the Cold War. For most of the twentieth century, collective efforts to address gross violations of human rights were seen as unacceptable violations of the principles of State sovereignty and non-interference which had been enshrined in the UN Charter in the aftermath of the Second World War.

Given these constraints, the international community would often look to the SG to take action through his good offices. In 1979 the General Assembly reaffirmed that 'mass and flagrant violations of human rights are of special concern to the United Nations', and highlighted 'the important role that the Secretary-General can play' in such

---

[9] *Ibid.*, 900.

[10] U Thant, 'The Role of the Secretary-General', *UN Monthly Chronicle*, 9 (October 1971), 178–87.

situations.[11] The SG engaged his good offices in cases such as Chile in 1975 at the request of the General Assembly, and during the Iran–Iraq war in the 1980s, where he also conducted fact-finding concerning chemical weapon usage by Iraq, and then urged the Security Council to adopt Resolution 598 calling for an immediate ceasefire.

With the end of the Cold War the confluence of several trends began to weaken the norm of non-intervention. This saw the SG asserting his normative influence, capturing and furthering these normative shifts through public statements, reports and institutional reforms. With the loosening of constraints on collective UN action, the SG oversaw the development of new activities – such as innovations in peace operations – which in turn expanded the SG's own responsibilities.[12]

The further strengthening and institutionalisation of international human rights norms had brought a gradual acceptance that human rights violations within a State's borders were a matter of international concern. Even more significant was a broadening interpretation by the Security Council of threats to international peace and security, to include massive violations of human rights, with Resolution 688 (April 1991) on Iraq's repression of its Kurdish minority.

Both Javier Pérez de Cuéllar and Boutros Boutros-Ghali recognised and furthered these developments, promoting the view that massive abuses of human rights could question State sovereignty and non-intervention. In his annual report on the work of the UN in 1991, de Cuéllar observed that non-interference 'cannot be regarded as a protective barrier behind which human rights can be massively or systematically violated with impunity'. A year later, in the context of a dramatic expansion of UN peace operations, Boutros-Ghali pronounced in *An Agenda for Peace* that 'The time of absolute and exclusive sovereignty ... has passed; its theory was never matched by reality.'[13] The Department of Political Affairs was established in 1992, providing a support structure for good offices and mediation by the SG and his envoys and representatives.

With its resolutions on Somalia (1992) and Bosnia (1993) the Security Council continued to demonstrate a greater willingness to intervene on

---

[11] UN General Assembly Res. 34/175, UN Doc. A/34/829, 17 December 1979.

[12] On the post-Cold War role of the Secretary-General, see Edward Newman, *The UN Secretary-General from the Cold War to the New Era: A Global Peace and Security Mandate?* (New York: Palgrave Macmillan, 1998).

[13] UN Secretary-General, 'An Agenda for Peace: Preventive Diplomacy, Peacemaking and Peace-keeping', UN Doc. A/47/277–S/24111, 17 June 1992, para. 17.

humanitarian grounds. Boutros-Ghali noted that with Resolution 794 on Somalia the Council had 'established a precedent in the history of the United Nations: it decided for the first time to intervene militarily for strictly humanitarian purposes'.[14] But both missions would ultimately end in failure, with the 1995 Srebrenica massacre in particular leaving a lasting stain on the world body's reputation.

While Iraq, Somalia and Bosnia prompted fresh interest in the doctrine of humanitarian intervention as a right to intervene in the affairs of another sovereign State for humanitarian reasons,[15] it remained fiercely resisted by most developing States, fearing its use by the major powers as a pretext for self-interested action. Moreover, the painful experience of Somalia had severely reduced the political will for intervention, particularly in the US, which was all too evident in the failure to act during the 1994 genocide in Rwanda.

When Kofi Annan became SG in 1997, he commissioned inquiries into the failures to halt the Rwanda genocide,[16] and to prevent the Srebrenica massacre.[17] They highlighted the lack of political will as a key factor, but were also forthright in identifying shortcomings in the actions of the Secretariat. Annan was highly conscious of the UN's failures, and even felt a sense of personal culpability given his position as Assistant Secretary-General for Peacekeeping Operations during both crises. On receiving the report on Rwanda in 1999, he stated that 'Of all my aims as Secretary-General, there is none to which I feel more deeply committed than that of enabling the United Nations never again to fail in protecting a civilian population from genocide or mass slaughter.'[18]

Annan planted conceptual and institutional roots for RtoP by introducing the concept of 'protection of civilians' (PoC) in a 1998 report on Africa,[19] and initiating the development of this protection agenda within the UN

---

[14] UNSG, 'The Work of the Organization', UN Doc. A/48/1, 10 September 1993, para. 431.

[15] The concept of humanitarian intervention has a long history; see for example, Michael Akehurst, 'Humanitarian Intervention', in Hedley Bull (ed.), *Intervention in World Politics* (Oxford: Clarendon Press, 1984), pp. 95–117.

[16] UNSC, 'Report of the Independent Inquiry into the Actions of the United Nations during the 1994 Genocide in Rwanda', UN Doc. S/1999/1257, 16 December 1999.

[17] UNSG, 'Report Pursuant to General Assembly Resolution 53/35: The Fall of Srebrenica', UN Doc. A/54/549, 15 November 1999.

[18] UNSG press release, 'Statement on receiving the Report of the Independent Inquiry into the Actions of the United Nations during the 1994 Genocide in Rwanda', UN Doc. SG/SM/7263, 16 December 1999.

[19] UNSG, 'The Causes of Conflict and the Promotion of Durable Peace and Sustainable Development in Africa', UN Doc. A/52/871–S/1998/318, 13 April 1998.

system. This marked a significant transition towards addressing civilian protection as a distinct thematic issue, rather than on the basis of individual cases. The Security Council began to explicitly include civilian protection in its resolutions, placing the issue at the 'heart of the UN's future agenda'.[20] In 2001 the Council resolved to take action to prevent recurrence of a Rwanda or a Srebrenica, and invited the SG to refer any serious violations of international humanitarian law and international human rights law.[21]

Meanwhile, further humanitarian interventions had been undertaken towards the end of the 1990s, including those in Sierra Leone and in Timor Leste, where Kofi Annan played a prominent role in persuading Indonesia to eventually consent to an Australian-led intervention. Yet, global opinion remained sharply divided, with calls for a 'right to intervene' on one side, and defenders of an absolute notion of State sovereignty on the other.

Developing the responsibility to protect

In the context of continued regrets over inaction in Rwanda and Srebrenica, and controversy over NATO's unauthorised use of force over Kosovo in 1999, Annan continued to keep the issue of intervention high on the global agenda. He was careful to emphasise both the need to take action in the face of massive violations of human rights, and the authority of the Security Council in matters of international peace and security. At the 1999 General Assembly he launched a debate on humanitarian intervention, highlighting the need to 'forge unity behind the principle that massive and systematic violations of human rights – wherever they take place – cannot be allowed to stand'.[22] Despite the moral resonance of his call, articulated in the form of humanitarian intervention it remained unpalatable to many States, particularly in the developing world. At the General Assembly in 2000, Kofi Annan again passionately emphasised the imperative to act when faced with gross violations of human rights, and called for consensus on how to respond to such cases. His *Millennium Report* posed the challenge to the international community: 'if humanitarian intervention is, indeed, an

[20] International Commission on Intervention and State Sovereignty, *The Responsibility to Protect: Research, Bibliography, Background* (Ottawa: International Development Research Centre, 2001), p. 178.

[21] UNSC Res.1366, UN Doc. S/RES/1366, 30 August 2001.

[22] UNSG press release, 'Secretary-General presents his Annual Report to General Assembly', UN Doc. SG/SM/136, 20 September 1999.

unacceptable assault on sovereignty, how should we respond to a Rwanda, to a Srebrenica, to gross and systematic violations of human rights that affect every precept of our common humanity?'[23]

Again this prompted heated reactions from Member States, but it led to the forming of the International Commission on Intervention and State Sovereignty (ICISS) by the government of Canada in direct response to the SG's challenge. The commission articulated the concept of RtoP in a report presented to the SG in December 2001.[24] The report outlined detailed criteria for the use of force, drawing from the just war tradition. Under the ICISS formulation of RtoP, prior Security Council authorisation must be sought for any intervention, but if the Council fails to act, action may be taken through the 'uniting for peace' procedure in the General Assembly,[25] or through regional or sub-regional organisations with subsequent Security Council approval.

The ICISS envisaged a central role for the SG in the implementation of RtoP. Its report highlighted the SG's 'formidable, but hitherto much underutilized' Article 99 authority, and his direct prevention role through his fact-finding missions, good offices and groups of friends.[26] The report emphasised the SG's ability to shape and influence the deliberations of the Security Council, and to mobilise political support and resources for the implementation of peace operations.

The concept was generally well received by commentators and civil society, but there was considerable scepticism among the permanent five members (P5) of the Security Council, and concern in the global South that RtoP could be abused by powerful States – concerns reinforced by the misuse of humanitarian arguments by the US and the UK in attempting to justify the 2003 Iraq war. The timing of the report was also unfortunate – as noted by ICISS co-chair Gareth Evans, RtoP was 'almost suffocated at birth' due to the global preoccupation with terrorism after the attacks of 11 September 2001.[27] But as Kofi Annan, the ICISS commissioners and other advocates remained committed to RtoP

---

[23] UNSG, 'We the Peoples: The Role of the United Nations in the 21st Century', UN Doc. A/54/2000, 27 March 2000.

[24] ICISS, *Responsibility to Protect*.

[25] For a more detailed discussion, see Ryngaert and Cuyckens, Chapter 5 in this book.

[26] ICISS, *Responsibility to Protect*, para. 4.31.

[27] Gareth Evans, 'The responsibility to protect: from an idea to an international norm', speech delivered at the Responsibility to Protect: Engaging America, Chicago Council on Global Affairs, Chicago, 15 November 2006, at www.gevans.org/speeches/speech202. html.

and kept it within the focus of the international community, the concept gradually gained momentum.

In September 2003 Annan established a High-Level Panel (HLP) of fifteen experts to recommend reforms in the doctrine and structure of the United Nations. Its report, delivered in December 2004, endorsed RtoP as an 'emerging norm', and adopted several of the ICISS recommendations.[28] In order to assuage the concerns of members over the erosion of State sovereignty, it avoided considering alternatives to the Security Council, focusing instead on how to make the Council work better by proposing guidelines for the use of force and a system of 'indicative voting' to increase the accountability of the veto function.[29] The HLP report formed the basis of Kofi Annan's own report of March 2005, *In Larger Freedom*, in which he called on the international community to embrace and act upon RtoP.[30] Although since Kosovo Annan had expressed the view that action outside the authority of the Security Council could be legitimate in cases of mass atrocities, he adopted the HLP's approach, explicitly acknowledging the need for sensitivity. Annan omitted any appeal to restrict use of the veto, and rather than explicitly proposing criteria for the use of force, he instead recommended that they be formulated by the Council.[31] By skirting such contentious issues, he presented RtoP in a form which was acceptable to Member States, conscious of the need to build consensus prior to the 2005 World Summit.

At the 2005 summit it took intensive negotiations and the determined encouragement of Kofi Annan and Jean Ping, President of the General Assembly, for Member States to eventually agree on the text of paragraphs 138–40 in the Outcome Document.[32] Consensus could only be reached by narrowing the scope of RtoP from 'serious harm' to the four atrocity crimes of genocide, war crimes, ethnic cleansing, and crimes against humanity, and tightening the trigger condition to a State 'manifestly failing' to protect its population, from the original 'unable

---

[28] UNSG, *A More Secure World: Our Shared Responsibility* (New York: United Nations, 2004).

[29] *Ibid.*, para. 257.

[30] UNSG, 'In Larger Freedom: Towards Development, Security and Human Rights for All', UN Doc. A/59/2005, 21 March 2005, para. 135.

[31] *Ibid.*, para. 126.

[32] On the role of Kofi Annan and the secretariat in the negotiation of the Outcome Document, see James Traub, *The Best Intentions: Kofi Annan and the UN in the Era of American World Power* (London: Bloomsbury, 2006).

or unwilling'. The document omitted criteria for the use of force and the ICISS appeal for permanent members to refrain from use of the veto, and even abandoned the HLP's proposed indicative voting reform. As such, in substance the agreement amounted to little more than a commitment to implement existing international law.

This 'RtoP-lite' agreement was criticised by scholars and RtoP advocates for having sacrificed so many of the original ICISS recommendations.[33] Statements by leaders after the adoption of the Outcome Document also revealed lingering divisions, with concern among governments in the global South over the possibility of misuse of RtoP. Nevertheless, it remains a significant achievement for Member States to have made such a commitment to protect populations, and one that owes much to the advocacy of Kofi Annan, along with fellow 'norm entrepreneurs' such as the ICISS commissioners and the Canadian government. It represented one of the few major successes of the ambitious reform agenda promoted by Annan, who in the process had expended much of the considerable political capital accumulated during his first term.

Kofi Annan's engagement in the conceptual and normative development of RtoP reflected his acute sensitivity to what Member States would accept, refined through his extensive experience within the UN system. He was well aware of the controversy surrounding questions of intervention, as well as the limitations placed on his office by the need to maintain the trust of Member States – particularly the US. After repeatedly drawing global attention to the issue of intervention, and calling for a new approach, Annan wisely entrusted the substantive construction of RtoP to an independent commission, in effect boosting the legitimacy of the concept. This in turn allowed him to champion the result of the commission while maintaining his own 'impartial' status. Key to this process was the balanced composition of the ICISS and the HLP, and the former's extensive regional consultations, which enhanced RtoP's universal credentials and helped to further distinguish it from the tainted doctrine of humanitarian intervention. It also reflected Annan's characteristic approach of engaging with actors from outside the UN system, in particular academia and civil society.

Annan's role in the development of RtoP thus demonstrates how, as Ian Johnstone argues, the SG is most effective as a norm entrepreneur

---

[33] For example, Alex Bellamy suggested that it did little to prevent another Rwanda or Kosovo ('Whither the Responsibility to Protect? Humanitarian Intervention and the 2005 World Summit', *Ethics and International Affairs*, 20 (2006), 143–69, at 169).

when he 'joins emerging normative trends ... rather than trying to generate new norms out of whole cloth'.[34] He successfully employed the techniques of norm entrepreneurship, using his organisational platform to draw international attention to an existing problem and promote a solution. In doing so he engaged in 'framing' the issue, and connected RtoP with established principles – in this case the universal values of human rights – to ensure the emerging norm resonated with Member States.

RtoP's troubled childhood

The Outcome Document explicitly bound RtoP to the UN system, with collective responses to be undertaken through the Security Council, and further consideration of the concept tasked to the General Assembly. This set the scene for the SG to continue to drive the implementation of the concept and its further development. The difficulties of implementation soon became apparent, however, even within the Secretariat. The Office for the Coordination of Humanitarian Affairs (OCHA) argued that RtoP should be limited to extreme cases to avoid politicising humanitarian activities, while the Office of the High Commissioner for Human Rights maintained that effective prevention required all cases to be considered.[35]

The application of RtoP to country situations also revealed enduring conceptual and political challenges, with deep-rooted disagreement over when and how the concept should be practically employed. This was evident in the intensive negotiations required for the Security Council to eventually adopt Resolution 1674 in April 2006 explicitly reaffirming RtoP. The Council became increasingly reluctant to invoke RtoP in specific country situations. In the case of Somalia in 2008, despite a strong appeal by the SG's Special Representative to the Council, the resolution adopted contained no mention of RtoP, instead referring to the protection of civilians.

Even when employed, the rhetoric of RtoP in most cases did not translate into decisive action. In the Darfur and Democratic Republic

---

[34] Ian Johnstone, 'The Secretary-General as Norm Entrepreneur', in Simon Chesterman (ed.), *Secretary or General? The UN Secretary-General in World Politics* (Cambridge University Press, 2007), pp. 123–38, at p. 134.

[35] Ekkehard Strauss, *The Emperor's New Clothes? The UN and the Implementation of R2P* (Baden-Baden: Nomos, 2009), p. 63.

of the Congo (DRC) crises, despite broad agreement that the concept was applicable, it failed to generate the political will or resources necessary for an adequate response. In his final year as SG, Kofi Annan repeatedly called on the Security Council to act on Darfur, but to no avail.

Much more successful was the application of RtoP in Kenya during the post-election violence of 2007. Ban Ki-moon referred to RtoP in the context of a specific country situation for the first time, explicitly reminding the government of its responsibility to protect.[36] After successful mediation by the African Union, the UN, former SG Kofi Annan and several influential Member States resulted in the halting of violence, Annan suggested that the 'effective external response proves that the responsibility to protect can work'.[37] It was telling, however, that the mediators consciously refrained from using the language of RtoP during negotiations.

The limits of the concept's applicability were tested in May 2008 when Bernard Kouchner, former French Foreign Minister, attempted to invoke RtoP in the context of Cyclone Nargis, proposing that the Security Council authorise the non-consensual delivery of aid to Myanmar's population. The extension of RtoP to natural disasters was rejected by other permanent members and the Association of Southeast Asian Nations (ASEAN), as well as by most RtoP advocates, including Gareth Evans, who expressed concern that doing so would undermine the consensus on the concept.[38] Although diplomatic engagement by the SG and ASEAN eventually resulted in the regime granting consent for the international relief effort, Ban was widely criticised for failing to publicly condemn the junta.

The issue of RtoP's applicability arose again in August 2008 when Russia employed the concept in an attempt to justify its unilateral intervention to protect its nationals in South Ossetia. Although Russia's arguments were widely rejected, they reawakened lingering concerns over the potential for deliberate misuse of RtoP.

These cases threatened to unravel the hard-fought 2005 agreement, and illustrated the desperate need for conceptual clarity over when and how RtoP should be applied. At the same time, the absence of an

---

[36] UNSG press release, 'Secretary-General troubled by escalating Kenyan tensions, violence', UN Doc. SG/SM/11356, 2 January 2008.

[37] Kofi Annan, 'Opening remarks to the Opening Plenary Session', speech delivered at Kenya National Dialogue: One Year Later, Geneva, 30 March 2009.

[38] Evans, 'Facing up to our responsibilities', The Guardian, 12 May 2008, at www.guardian. co.uk/commentisfree/2008/may/12/facinguptoourresponsbilities.

adequate response to the situations in Darfur and the DRC, and the complete refusal to apply RtoP to the crisis in Somalia, underscored the need to build the political will necessary to authorise decisive action and mobilise the required resources.

Consolidation and implementation

Ban Ki-moon's approach to RtoP has acknowledged these challenges, emphasising the need to move from theory to practice by developing and promoting a strategy for its implementation. Soon after taking office in 2007, he called upon Member States to operationalise the principle.[39] Later that year he informed the Security Council and General Assembly of his intention to appoint a Special Adviser for the Responsibility to Protect (SARtoP), to complement the Special Adviser on the Prevention of Genocide (SAPG). Although the proposal was not received favourably by the General Assembly, Ban eventually appointed Edward Luck in December 2007, tasked with 'conceptual development and consensus-building, to assist the General Assembly to continue consideration of this crucial issue'.[40] Conscious of the initial controversy over his appointment, Luck focused on developing a sensitive approach to implementation in order to maintain the fragile consensus on RtoP, by engaging in broad consultations with Member States and civil society groups.

Under the SG's strategy, as laid out in a July 2008 speech in Berlin, RtoP would be 'narrow but deep' – limited in scope to the four crimes agreed to in 2005, but utilising the 'whole prevention and protection tool kit' of the United Nations, regional organisations, civil society, and Member States.[41] It identified three pillars upon which RtoP rests:

(1) the obligations of States to protect their own populations;
(2) the commitment of the international community to assist States in meeting these obligations; and

---

[39] UNSG press release, 'On anniversary of Rwanda genocide, Secretary-General says current challenge is to make responsibility to protect operational', UN Doc. SG/SM/10934, 5 April 2007.

[40] UNSG press release, 'Secretary-General appoints Special Adviser on the Responsibility to Protect', UN Doc. SG/A/1120, 21 February 2008.

[41] UNSG press release, 'Secretary-General defends, clarifies "responsibility to protect" at Berlin event on "Responsible Sovereignty: International Cooperation for a Changed World"', UN Doc. SG/SM11701, 15 July 2008.

(3) the responsibility of Member States to respond in a timely and decisive manner when a State is manifestly failing to provide protection.

The SG's 2009 report on implementing RtoP detailed this strategy, while strongly accentuating prevention and international assistance (the second pillar) in order to consolidate support for the norm. His approach was endorsed at the General Assembly debate on the report six months later, with the vast majority of States expressing support for the concept and the SG's three-pillar approach. Although supporters of RtoP had been apprehensive about reopening the concept to challenge, and during the debate reservations were apparent concerning the third pillar, the General Assembly adopted a resolution by consensus which acknowledged the SG's report.[42]

The SG's strategy has been successful in building consensus on RtoP. In particular, by providing conceptual clarification on the limits and scope of the principle it has reduced the ability of States to misapply RtoP. The strategy was further developed through follow-up reports in 2010 on early warning and assessment,[43] in 2011 on the role of regional and sub-regional arrangements in implementing RtoP,[44] and in 2012 on timely and decisive response.[45] With persistent advocacy by the SG and the SARtoP through speeches, public statements and consultations, support for the concept was again expressed by the overwhelming majority of States during informal General Assembly debates on these reports.

This has also generated support for the specific measures detailed in the SG's reports for implementing RtoP. Under the SG's strategy, actions are required of Member States, regional and sub-regional organisations, as well as efforts within the UN system, to implement each of the three pillars of RtoP. As well as providing strategic direction for such efforts, the SG also plays a direct role in the implementation of the principle, both in specific crises and through its institutionalisation within the UN system. The next sections consider the SG's role in implementing RtoP under his three-pillar strategy, and some of the challenges ahead.

---

[42] UNGA Res. 63/208, UN Doc. A/RES/63/208, 3 February 2009.
[43] UNSG, 'Early Warning, Assessment and the Responsibility to Protect', UN Doc. A/64/864, 14 July 2010.
[44] UNSG, 'The Role of Regional and Sub-regional Arrangements in Implementing the Responsibility to Protect', UN Doc. A/65/877–S/2011/393, 27 June 2011.
[45] UNSG, 'Responsibility to Protect: Timely and Decisive Response', UN Doc. A/66/874–S/2012/578, 25 July 2012.

International assistance to States and structural prevention

The SG's emphasis on the second pillar sees assisting States in meeting their RtoP obligations as a way of preventing the development of situations that require responses under the third pillar. Under his strategy, ultimately many UN development and capacity-building programmes fall under the umbrella of RtoP. Although specific actors are identified, including the OHCHR and the Peacebuilding Commission, the SG acknowledges that most activities related to good governance can be seen as contributing to RtoP.

This inclusive approach has been criticised for weakening RtoP's focus on extreme situations – which some advocates, notably Gareth Evans, argue is needed to maintain the capacity of the concept to mobilise 'in the cases when it is really needed'.[46] The comprehensiveness of prevention under RtoP represents a key conceptual challenge – whether RtoP should be limited to 'operational' prevention to avert imminent threats, or also encompass 'structural' prevention aimed at building societies better able to avoid or halt mass atrocities.[47] While the SG's strategy has clearly endorsed the 'maximalist' vision, his 2011 report acknowledged the need for conceptual distinction between structural and operational prevention.[48]

A fundamental difficulty confronting efforts to implement RtoP's second pillar is the lack of empirical research and analysis of what strategies and measures are most effective in the prevention of atrocity crimes. The approach taken by the SG – and indeed most policymakers – has been to engage the existing conflict prevention agenda, on the basis that RtoP situations often occur in the context of violent conflict. The SG's Five Point Action Plan to Prevent Genocide, launched in an address by Kofi Annan to the Human Rights Commission marking the tenth anniversary of the Rwandan genocide, includes as its first point preventing armed conflict.[49]

---

[46] Evans, 'The Responsibility to Protect: An Idea Whose Time Has Come ... and Gone?', *International Relations*, 22 (2008), 283–98.

[47] See Barnett Rubin and Bruce Jones, 'Prevention of Violent Conflict: Tasks and Challenges for the United Nations', *Global Governance*, 13 (2007), 391–408; Carnegie Commission on Preventing Deadly Conflict, *Preventing Deadly Conflict: Final Report with Executive Summary* (Washington, DC: Carnegie Corporation of New York, 1997).

[48] UNSG, 'Regional and Sub-regional Arrangements', para. 21.

[49] UNSG press release, '"Risk of genocide remains frighteningly real", Secretary-General tells Human Rights Commission as he launches Action Plan to Prevent Genocide', UN Doc. SG/SM/9245, 7 April 2004.

The SG's initial steps towards institutionalising RtoP's second pillar centred on the creation of the post of Special Adviser for the Prevention of Genocide, announced in the same 2004 speech. Although this pre-dated the World Summit agreement, the SG conceived of the SAPG's mandate as relating 'also to mass murder and other large-scale human rights violations, such as ethnic cleansing.'[50] The SAPG was seen as 'the institutional expression of the responsibility to protect and a focal point for the prevention of genocide and similar crimes within the United Nations system.'[51] The close relationship between the mandate of the SAPG and RtoP was affirmed in the 2005 Outcome Document, which expressed full support for his mission, and the SG's Policy Committee soon decided to institutionalise this relationship by developing a joint office on prevention of genocide and RtoP. With continued concerns on the part of several States, Ban Ki-moon was careful to emphasise the distinct responsibilities of the two Special Advisers when including this proposal in his 2009 and 2010 reports. In 2011, the Fifth Committee of the General Assembly finally endorsed the integration of RtoP into the office of the SAPG, by approving the expansion of his mandate to include all four atrocity crimes.

Broader efforts to institutionalise RtoP's second pillar within the Secretariat, however, have suffered from the lack of a clear framework that could bring coherence to the efforts of the vast range of agencies and agendas encompassed by the SG's strategy, and provide a structured toolbox of measures to be engaged to assist States in specific RtoP situations. Attempts to infuse RtoP into established UN conflict preven-tion and capacity-building agendas have also met with bureaucratic and political resistance.

The SG has explicitly acknowledged the need to gain a better under-standing of what specific institutional capacities are needed for preven-tion and protection assistance, and how to build these capacities. Among the few concrete suggestions in the SG's 2009 report was to draw upon procedures developed recently within the UN system to respond to State requests for building capacity for conflict prevention, including a joint programme by the United Nations Development Programme and the Department of Political Affairs. This report also highlighted the diffi-culty in mobilising police and civilian resources that are often required to

---

[50] *Ibid.*
[51] Payam Akhavan, 'Report on the Work of the Office of the Special Adviser of the United Nations on the Prevention of Genocide', *Human Rights Quarterly*, 28 (2006), 1043–70.

address RtoP crimes, and the need for further development of proposals for standby capacity for rapid deployment.

With the SG's designation of 2012 as the 'year of prevention', there is an opportunity to harness growing interest within the Secretariat and Member States towards conflict prevention, to develop RtoP-specific tools and capacities. One possibility is for the SG to commission an in-depth review of civilian capacities for RtoP, based on the model of the Senior Advisory Group he appointed in March 2010, which focused on post-conflict peacebuilding.

Early warning and assessment

Weaknesses in the UN's capacity for early warning of gross violations of human rights have been particularly prominent, as highlighted in the reports on Rwanda and Srebrenica. Previous efforts to address these weaknesses, however, have often encountered resistance from States considering greater power and resources for the Secretariat in the area of peace and security a threat to their sovereignty. Such concerns blocked Kofi Annan's attempt to establish an Information and Strategic Analysis Secretariat in 2000, and were voiced by several States during the 2005 World Summit debates. But recent years have seen a greater willingness to accept strengthening of Secretariat capacity in this area, with almost unanimous support expressed during the 2009 General Assembly debate. The SG's 2010 report focused on early warning and assessment, and was well received by States in the subsequent General Assembly dialogue.

The SG's efforts to address these gaps within the UN system have centred on the SAPG and the creation of the joint office. In view of Security Council Resolution 1366 (2001), the SAPG is required to keep the Security Council informed, through the SG, of any serious violations of international humanitarian or human rights law which could result in genocide. The SAPG's office has developed its own Analysis Framework identifying specific factors which can increase the risk of genocidal violence, and maintains records of situations based on the framework.[52] Among these factors are inter-group relations (discrimination and human rights violations), the presence of illegal arms and groups, the motivations of leading actors, genocidal acts, evidence of genocidal intent and triggering events.

---

[52] UN Office of the Special Adviser on the Prevention of Genocide, 'Analysis Framework', at www.un.org/en/preventgenocide/adviser/pdf/osapg_analysis_framework.pdf.

The creation of the joint office clearly represents an important step in strengthening capacity for early warning and analysis within the Secretariat, to pursue the closely related mandates of the two special advisers. It provides a much-needed focal point for information and analysis on situations under these mandates, drawn from a wide range of sources including regional and sub-regional organisations and civil society, as well as the UN's substantial existing reporting mechanisms for political, human rights and humanitarian developments. Although the information gathered by each of these UN mechanisms and bodies can be relevant to the prevention of the four RtoP crimes, none of them are designed or mandated to apply an RtoP perspective. The joint office provides an early warning capacity specifically tailored to the exceptional nature of RtoP situations, able to analyse and evaluate this information through the lens of RtoP. In doing so it will utilise the SAPG's Analysis Framework, but this will need to be expanded to account for the wider range of crimes covered by RtoP. It should also engage under-utilised sources of information such as the Special Representative for Children and Armed Conflict, the Special Rapporteur on Violence against Women, and the Committee on the Elimination of Racial Discrimination, whose early warning mechanism issued urgent warnings in the contexts of Yugoslavia and Darfur.

Early warning and analysis are necessary, but not sufficient, for effective 'operational' prevention and timely responses; early warning must also be translated into early action. In order to improve coherent decision-making and the rapid development of policy options when the special advisers provide early warning of a situation, the SG has also developed a new internal procedure whereby the advisers may convene an emergency meeting of Under-Secretaries-General to identify options under Chapters VI and VII, or regional arrangements under Chapter VIII.[53]

Timely and decisive response

The SG's 'narrow, but deep' strategy reflects a conscious decision to reduce the emphasis on military responses under RtoP, instead highlighting the broad range of tools and measures that can contribute to prevention. Proceeding in this cautious manner has been successful in

[53] UNSG, 'Early Warning', para. 18.

building general commitment to the idea of RtoP, but has left important questions unanswered concerning the circumstances and manner in which responses should be implemented. Indeed, the third pillar of RtoP clearly remains its most divisive, as evident in controversies over the responses to recent crises in Côte d'Ivoire, Libya and Syria.

Mindful of the sensitivities over military responses, the SG's strategy has strongly emphasised the role of non-coercive measures, including good offices and crisis diplomacy by the SG and his envoys and representatives, and by regional organisations. Although the Kenya crisis demonstrated the potential of mediation to address rapidly escalating situations, particularly when implemented with regional actors, more capacity and political will are clearly needed, as evident in the case of Zimbabwe. Until recently, however, attempts to strengthen Secretariat capacity even in this area have been resisted by a number of States. The SG's efforts to restructure the Department of Political Affairs – originally called for by the HLP in 2004 – have met with only limited success, with the creation of the Mediation Support Unit in 2006 and the Standby Team of Mediation Experts in 2008, to provide technical assistance and expertise for good offices activities. But in 2009 Ban Ki-moon's report on enhancing mediation capacity was well received by the Security Council,[54] leading to a General Assembly resolution in July 2011,[55] and he is continuing to call for increased political support and more reliable funding for these activities.

The role of the SG's own bully pulpit has been prominent during recent crises, with Ban Ki-moon becoming increasingly outspoken. For the majority of his first term, he was reluctant to raise RtoP in the context of specific country situations, and largely confined his criticism of specific governments to private meetings. Combined with perceptions of his weak leadership and lack of charisma, this led to widespread criticism from human rights advocates. But the 'Arab Spring' has seen a marked transformation in Ban's use of the bully pulpit concerning RtoP, demonstrating a willingness to publicly condemn governments and leaders using force against civilians. This has impressed his critics; for example Ramesh Thakur acknowledged that 'Secretary-General Ban Ki-moon has been impressively firm and consistent on R2P, leading

---

[54] UNSG, 'Enhancing Mediation and Its Support Activities', UN Doc. S/2009/189, 8 April 2009.
[55] UNGA Res. 65/283, UN Doc. A/RES/65/283, 28 July 2011.

from the front'.[56] Ban's strong stance during the Arab Spring has also brought newfound respect within the Secretariat.[57] In his 2012 report the SG noted that it was 'essential that I apply [RtoP] principles consistently in my statements and actions'.[58] There is potential, however, for the SG's robust use of the bully pulpit to compromise his diplomatic role – a tension Ban acknowledged in a January 2012 speech, noting that 'I am also acutely aware of the need to preserve my own diplomatic space for the crucial moment when the UN's good offices may be needed.'[59]

When timely responses under RtoP's third pillar require action by the Security Council, under Chapters VI, VII or VIII, the SG's responsibility to bring matters to its attention under Article 99 is critical, particularly given his more direct access to early warning from the Secretariat, now enhanced with the creation of the joint office. In his 2009 report, the SG emphasised this responsibility, including his obligation – previously noted in the *Brahimi Report* – to tell the Council what it needs to know, not what it wants to hear. In practice, however, the SG has not always been willing to exercise Article 99 – for instance, Ban Ki-moon failed to do so when the Council refused to engage in a formal discussion of the 2009 Sri Lanka crisis despite a clear threat of mass atrocities. In such cases of intransigence on the part of the Council, the SG bears an even greater responsibility to press issues into its attention on behalf of the population at risk.

The SG can also exert a certain degree of influence upon the Council's consideration of specific crises, both directly through his reports and speeches in Council meetings, and indirectly by reminding members – particularly the P5 – of their responsibilities under the third pillar of RtoP. Public statements, early warnings and recommendations can contribute to setting the parameters of debate within the Council; indeed, the consistent use of RtoP language by the SG and Secretariat officials with reference to recent crises has been significant in leading the Security Council to consider these crises in terms of civilian protection.

[56] Ramesh Thakur, 'UN Breathes New Life into "Responsibility to Protect"', *Toronto Star*, 21 March 2011, available at www.thestar.com.
[57] See Richard Gowan, 'Floating down the River of History: Ban Ki-moon and Peacekeeping, 2007–2011', *Global Governance*, 17 (2011), 399–416.
[58] UNSG, 'Timely and Decisive Response', para. 20.
[59] UNSG, 'Address to Stanley Foundation Conference on the Responsibility to Protect', UN News Centre, 18 January 2012, at www.un.org/apps/news/infocus/sgspeeches/search_full.asp?statID=1433.

The institutionalisation of the protection of civilians (PoC) agenda, introduced by Kofi Annan in 1998, has also been an important influence on the Council. Since authorising the United Nations Mission in Sierra Leone (UNAMSIL) in 1999 it has become standard practice for the Security Council to include PoC in the mandates of peace operations, and OCHA has been leading the development of policy. In his fifth report on PoC of November 2005, Annan connected the two concepts,[60] and it was in the context of PoC that RtoP was first referred to by the Security Council in Resolution 1674 (2006). There is a risk, however, that this connection might result in the application of RtoP being restricted to situations of armed conflict. Conversely, advocates of the PoC agenda have been reluctant to associate it with RtoP, fearful that its progress may be impeded by controversies over the latter concept. While the SG's 2012 report recognises that RtoP and PoC 'have separate and distinct prerequisites and objectives',[61] further conceptual clarity on their relationship must be incorporated into his strategies for both concepts.

These normative and institutional efforts by the SG contributed to an increased willingness within the Security Council to authorise the use of force for protection under RtoP, apparent in the unprecedented international response to the crises in Côte d'Ivoire and Libya. The Council explicitly invoked RtoP in specific country situations for the first time. Resolution 1973 on Libya is particularly significant,[62] as it marks the first Council authorisation of non-consensual Chapter VII enforcement action to protect a population – a textbook example of RtoP's third pillar in practice. But the subsequent controversies over implementation of these resolutions revealed the extent to which States remain divided over RtoP's third pillar. In Côte d'Ivoire, critics considered the United Nations Operation in Côte d'Ivoire (UNOCI) action against Laurent Gbagbo's forces to protect civilians as abandoning impartiality by taking the side of Ouattara's Force Républiques de Côte d'Ivoire (RFCI), which had also committed atrocities. In Libya, while NATO's strikes on Gaddafi's forces resulted in the halting of a massacre in Benghazi, it became committed to supporting the rebel forces and ultimately to regime change with the removal of Gaddafi. NATO's expansive interpretation of Resolution 1973 prompted widespread criticism, and with

---

[60] UNSG, 'The Protection of Civilians in Armed Conflict', UN Doc. S/2005/740, 28 November 2005.
[61] UNSG, 'Timely and Decisive Response', para. 16.
[62] UNSC Res. 1973, UN Doc. S/RES/1973, 17 March 2011.

increasing concerns over civilian casualties, there were signs that even Ban Ki-moon's firm support was beginning to waver.[63]

The perception of overreach in Côte d'Ivoire and Libya has reawakened fears over the selective application of RtoP for regime change, directly contributing to the failure of the Council to authorise even non-military coercive measures against the Assad regime in Syria. Clearly evident in the Council's consideration of Syria was a desire on the part of several members to reassert a more impartial stance after Côte d'Ivoire and Libya. Russia and China justified their vetoes with the claim that even sanctions could lead to the illegitimate overthrow of the government, although there were clearly other factors behind their opposition, including strategic interests in the region. Nevertheless, concerns were shared by other States, with India's permanent representative to the UN noting that the Libyan intervention 'has given R2P a bad name'.[64]

These concerns were prominent at the July 2011 informal General Assembly debate on RtoP, but Member States expressed a desire to address them through continued discussion of the third pillar, welcoming the SG's proposal to focus on this aspect of RtoP for the 2012 debate. In his report prior to this debate, the SG reflected on the lessons of Côte d'Ivoire and Libya, noting that although each situation is unique and responses should be tailored to the specific circumstances, consistent application of RtoP is essential. The SG used the report to further underline the mutually supportive relationship between the three pillars of RtoP, and that effective strategies require a combination of preventive and responsive measures.[65]

The key conceptual and political challenge highlighted by recent crises is for States to develop criteria to guide their decisions to use military force. Ensuring that decisions are based on agreed-upon principles would make application of RtoP more consistent, and reduce concerns over the selective use of the concept to justify regime change. There have also been calls to revive the proposal of the ICISS for a 'code of conduct' to encourage the P5 to restrict their use of the veto in RtoP situations.

Côte d'Ivoire and Libya also underlined the urgent operational challenge of finding ways to frame and conduct third-pillar responses that

---

[63] Colum Lynch, 'Did ban just subtly admonish NATO's Libya campaign?', *Foreign Policy*, 12 August 2011, available at www.foreignpolicy.com.

[64] Hardeep Singh Puri, remarks at Responsibility to Protect: An Emerging Principle, International Peace Institute Policy Forum, 28 June 2011, at www.ipacademy.org/images/TEST/ipimeiko.pdf.

[65] UNSG, 'Timely and Decisive Response', para. 20.

can distinguish them from regime change. The UN is no stranger to tensions between mandates and impartiality, however, having learned from the failures of the 1990s that halting atrocities sometimes requires taking sides – as highlighted by Kofi Annan and the *Brahimi Report*. Indeed, SARtoP Edward Luck acknowledged that 'it may be in some cases that the only way to protect populations is to change the regime, but that certainly isn't the goal of the R2P per se'.[66] There is, however, a clear need to address issues of control and accountability, to ensure that the way coercive measures are implemented reflects the intentions of the Council and remains within the boundaries of the authorising resolutions.

The recent 'responsibility while protecting' initiative of Brazil aimed at tackling these challenges has been broadly welcomed by the SG, although certain elements of the proposal do present tensions with his own strategy. Brazil's November 2011 concept note proposed a strict chronological sequencing of the three pillars, criteria for the decision to use force, and a review mechanism to keep Member States informed about implementation of mandates.[67] In his July 2012 report the SG emphatically asserted that 'pillars are not sequenced', and that 'none of the pillars is likely to be effective standing alone',[68] a position later endorsed by the majority of States at the 2012 informal dialogue. During an informal UN meeting on Brazil's initiative in February 2012, SARtoP Edward Luck acknowledged the need for responsibility in all actions under RtoP, but warned against creating any barriers to timely and decisive action, as 'delaying a response does not make it more responsible'.[69] At the 2012 informal dialogue the SG also cautioned against misuse of RtoP, but many States shared his view that 'fears of its possible misuse should not inhibit us in the face of incitement and grave violence'.[70]

---

[66] Edward Luck, 'Will Syria follow Libya?', interview by Bernard Gwerzman, Council on Foreign Relations, 1 September 2011, at www.cfr.org/syria/syria-follow-libya/p25745.

[67] UN, 'Responsibility While Protecting: Elements for the Development and Promotion of a Concept', letter dated 9 November 2011 from the Permanent Representative of Brazil to the United Nations Addressed to the Secretary-General, UN Doc. A/66/551–S/2011/701, 11 November 2011, p. 2.

[68] UNSG, 'Timely and Decisive Response', paras. 13 and 20.

[69] Luck, 'Opening statement', speech delivered at Informal Discussion on the 'Responsibility While Protecting' initiative organised by the Permanent Mission of Brazil, 21 February 2012, available at www.un.org/en/preventgenocide/adviser/pdf/EL%27s%2021%20February%20statement%20-%20English.pdf.

[70] Secretary-General's remarks to General Assembly Informal Interactive Dialogue, available at www.un.org/sg/statements/index.asp?nid=6271.

While progress on addressing these fundamental questions will depend on States reaching agreement, the SG himself can take institutional steps to improve military operations under RtoP's third pillar, given the Secretariat's extensive discretion on the practical implementation of mandates. His 2011 report acknowledged that doctrine for peacekeeping and military operations in RtoP situations remained poorly developed.[71] This is particularly evident in hostile environments such as the DRC, where despite a robust civilian protection mandate the United Nations Organization Stabilization Mission in the Democratic Republic of the Congo (MONUSCO) failed to protect the population. The development of more coherent doctrine appropriate to the specific tasks of preventing and responding to mass atrocities, including coercive protection, should incorporate the lessons and innovations of recent protection operations such as MONUSCO and the United Nations–African Union Mission in Darfur (UNAMID), as well as initiatives by Member States such as the *Mass Atrocity Response Operations* handbook developed for the US military.[72] In particular, recent coercive operations have shown the need to explore ways of better mitigating unintended human, political and economic consequences.

The SG has also continued to play a normative role in further consolidating State commitment to RtoP, by encouraging national governments to adopt strategies for RtoP and, as proposed by the SAPG in 2005, to establish focal points for situations related to RtoP, such as the recently appointed Director for War Crimes and Atrocities within the US National Security Council. These initiatives serve to build political will for responses under RtoP's third pillar, while facilitating timely decision-making and strengthening accountability for inaction in the face of mass atrocities.

Regional and sub-regional organisations

Ban Ki-moon has made collaboration between the UN and regional and sub-regional organisations an important component of his strategy for implementing RtoP, reinforced by focusing on this topic in his 2011

---

[71] For a detailed discussion on peacekeeping operations and RtoP, see Breau, Chapter 3 in this book.

[72] Sarah Sewall, Dwight Raymond and Sally Chin, *Mass Atrocity Response Operations: A Military Planning Handbook* (Cambridge, MA: Carr Center for Human Rights Policy, Harvard Kennedy School, 2010).

report. This acknowledges the potential for regional actors to play a critical role in resolving RtoP crises, such as the African Union (AU) in Kenya, the Organization for Security and Co-operation in Europe's (OSCE) High Commissioner for National Minorities in Kyrgyzstan, the Economic Community of West African States (ECOWAS) in Côte d'Ivoire, the Gulf Cooperation Council in Yemen, and the League of Arab States in Libya. The July 2011 informal dialogue of the General Assembly endorsed the SG's report, and underscored the need for further collaboration among the UN, regional and sub-regional organisations on best practices and early warning, as well as the coordination of prevention strategies and sanctions.

The SG has overseen improvements in operational collaboration with these partners, including the establishment of a stronger regional presence for the Department of Political Affairs in West Africa and Central Asia, providing forward platforms for preventive diplomacy. His joint office is already incorporating information and assessments from regional and sub-regional organisations for early warning, and building commitment and institutional capacity for RtoP at the regional and sub-regional levels. The AU's early warning mechanism has incorporated the SAPG's Analysis Framework, and in the Great Lakes region the SAPG contributed to the founding in September 2010 of the first sub-regional body created specifically to prevent mass atrocity crimes.[73]

From promise to practice

The SG has been a prominent actor in the development and implementation of RtoP, engaging the operational, normative and institutional capabilities of his office. In specific RtoP crises the SG plays an important role both through his private diplomacy and in public, using his bully pulpit to expose abusers. He has the ability to influence the Security Council, both directly through Article 99 and public calls for the Council to act, and indirectly by framing crises in RtoP terms, which contributed to its robust action on Côte d'Ivoire and Libya. The failure of the Council to agree on coercive action in Syria, however, serves as a blunt reminder that responses under RtoP ultimately depend upon sufficient political will among Member States, and in particular of the P5.

---

[73] The Regional Committee for the Prevention and Punishment of the Crime of Genocide, of the International Conference on the Great Lakes Region.

The SG and the SARtoP have strengthened State commitment to RtoP, successfully consolidating the fragile 2005 consensus by clarifying the concept, and the 'narrow, but deep' approach has charted a pragmatic way forward for its implementation. The steps taken by the SG to institutionalise RtoP within the Secretariat have necessarily been incremental, given the inherently slow pace of change in the UN system, as well as enduring political and bureaucratic resistance. His strategy emphasises second-pillar efforts to build State capacity, but the lack of a clear framework for how different actors and agendas can contribute to RtoP continues to hinder its implementation. In striving to reduce the emphasis on the third pillar of RtoP, important questions were left unanswered concerning the circumstances and manner in which force should be used – questions which have now risen to the fore in the context of Côte d'Ivoire, Libya and Syria.

The effectiveness of the SG's ongoing efforts to implement RtoP will be limited by both political constraints, and the personal qualities and priorities of the office holder. Thus far the particular attributes of the two SGs involved have been well suited to the needs of RtoP at each stage of its development. Kofi Annan's moral authority and his political capital with both powerful States and the global South helped him to persuade States to embrace RtoP; and when it came to fleshing out the concept and its implementation, Ban Ki-moon's quiet diplomacy and cautious, pragmatic approach have been reasonably successful. Although Ban's initial reticence on RtoP was disappointing, recently his more vocal, assertive public engagement has offered promising signs for the remainder of his second term.

While RtoP's record has been mixed at best, the concept has undeniably contributed to improving the response of the international community to mass atrocities. With attention now focused on how the principle can be implemented, the unique capabilities of the SG's office will continue to be critical in finding ways to translate the rhetorical commitment of Member States into effective action to prevent, and if necessary, respond, to the next Cambodia, Rwanda or Darfur.

7

The Human Rights Council

LYAL S. SUNGA

Introduction

Developed first by the Canadian-sponsored International Commission on Intervention and State Sovereignty (ICISS), and further elaborated by the United Nation's High-Level Panel on Threats, Challenges and Change and in a number of UN instruments, the 'responsibility to protect' has attracted much attention over the past several years from UN bodies, governments, think-tanks and scholars. This idea seems to offer a fresh perspective on how the State, international collective security frameworks and other actors should prevent, halt and react to genocide, war crimes and crimes against humanity. The concept did not, however, emerge from the settled jurisprudence of courts or tribunals, or from institutional practice. It was articulated mainly by a small group of experts and many of its key elements remain unclear or controversial.[1]

This chapter identifies and evaluates the Human Rights Council's current and possible future role in operationalising the 'responsibility to protect'. Accordingly, the present chapter first considers briefly whether the responsibility to protect adds anything valuable to international law and practice, and if so, what its added value might be. Second, it reviews pertinent Human Rights Council resolutions and

I would like to thank Dr Ilaria Bottigliero, Director of Research and Policy, International Development Law Organization, Rome, for her many valuable comments on drafts of this chapter.
[1] International Commission on Intervention and State Sovereignty, *The Responsibility to Protect* (Ottawa: International Development Research Centre, 2001). This study, commissioned by the government of Canada, was published in response to Secretary-General Kofi Annan's challenge to the General Assembly to reflect upon humanitarian intervention to protect civilians from 'wholesale slaughter'. See UN press release, 'Secretary-General presents his annual report to the General Assembly', UN Doc. SG/SM/7136–GA/9596, 20 September 1999.

reports to check on usages of the term. Third, it explores the Human Rights Council's role in advancing the practical application of the 'responsibility to protect' with regard to specific country situations that seem to involve genocide, war crimes or crimes against humanity. The chapter concludes with some observations and practical recommendations geared towards improving the work of the Human Rights Council concerning the responsibility to protect.

As for terminology, the present chapter refers to the responsibility to protect as an 'idea', 'concept', 'notion', 'perspective' or 'approach', rather than as a fully-fledged 'doctrine', or even less, a 'norm', 'legal norm' or 'principle', because the latter terms might be taken to imply that the idea has achieved some sort of normative status already which, depending on the particular interpretation of the responsibility to protect, might not be correct.

What does the responsibility to protect add to international law?

As a political body established and operating under the authority of the UN General Assembly, the Human Rights Council does not function in isolation. Before exploring the Human Rights Council's present and future role in implementing the responsibility to protect, it is necessary to take account of the wider debate surrounding the concept. In December 2001, ICISS put forward a conceptual framework to view State sovereignty less as a set of rights of the State, and more as the source of the State's responsibility to protect its citizens. The ICISS emphasised that where a State was unwilling or unable to fulfil its own responsibility to halt or avert serious harm in the case of 'internal war, insurgency, repression or state failure', and 'the principle of non-intervention yields to the international responsibility to protect'. This shift in emphasis from a traditional State-centric focus towards a residual general 'international responsibility to protect', which kicks into action once the State fails to fulfil its protection responsibilities, entails a responsibility to prevent, to react, to respond and to rebuild.[2] Moreover, the ICISS contended that, in extreme cases, the responsibility to protect encompassed even a responsibility on the part of States to undertake unilateral or joint military intervention in the territory of another State to protect people from the latter State's inability or unwillingness to halt or prevent mass atrocities.[3] The 2001 report went on to

[2] ICISS, *Responsibility to Protect*, p. xi, synopsis.   [3] *Ibid.*, para. 4.1.

posit a number of precautionary principles to define the conditions under which resort to military intervention for humanitarian ends might be permissible, or even legally obligatory.[4]

Developing the ICISS proposals further, the 2004 report of the Secretary-General's High-Level Panel on Threats, Challenges and Change recommended reform of the UN collective security system to serve better the international responsibility to protect. Part IX of the report endorsed 'the emerging norm that there is a collective international responsibility to protect, exercisable by the Security Council authorizing military intervention as a last resort, in the event of genocide and other large-scale killing, ethnic cleansing or serious violations of international humanitarian law which sovereign Governments have proved powerless or unwilling to prevent'[5] and it spelled out five criteria to guide Security Council intervention.[6] However, the Panel dropped the ICISS report's explicit endorsement of unilateral or joint military intervention beyond Security Council authorisation, bringing the responsibility to protect back squarely within the parameters of the UN Charter.

In mid-September 2005, the historic three-day UN World Summit, attended by 150 Heads of State or Government, embraced the responsibility to protect as laid down in the 'World Summit Outcome Document'.[7] According to this resolution, 'Each individual State has the responsibility to protect its populations from genocide, war crimes, ethnic cleansing[8] and crimes against humanity' including through preventive measures. The

---

[4] The precautionary principles involve: (1) right intention; (2) last resort; (3) proportional means; and (4) reasonable prospects of success (*ibid.*).

[5] UN Secretary-General, *A More Secure World: Our Shared Responsibility* (New York: United Nations, 2004), p. 66, para. 203.

[6] See *ibid.*, part 3, 'Collective Security and the Use of Force'.

[7] '2005 World Summit Outcome', UN Doc. A/RES/60/1, 24 October 2005.

[8] Since its usage in the early 1990s in connection with genocidal policies carried out during the war in the former Yugoslavia (which the *Encyclopaedia Britannica* notes is a translation from the Serbo-Croat term 'etničko čišćenje'), the term 'ethnic cleansing' has been used to refer to the systematic, forcible displacement of a targeted ethnic population from its territorial home, through intimidation, killings, mass rape, summary executions or other serious violations of human rights or humanitarian law. However, it does not appear either in the Rome Statute of the International Criminal Court, nor in multilateral conventions on human rights, humanitarian law or international criminal law. It would be more precise to refer instead to 'genocide', 'war crimes' and 'crimes against humanity' which have been defined in the Rome Statute for the purposes of criminal prosecution and which in any case cover the kinds of acts commonly understood as acts of 'ethnic cleansing'. See *Encyclopaedia Britannica*, 'Ethnic Cleansing', at www.britannica.com/EBchecked/topic/194242/ethnic-cleansing.

Summit declared for good measure that, 'We accept that responsibility and will act in accordance with it' and it invited the international community to 'encourage and help States to exercise this responsibility'.[9] At the same time, the Summit also recognised the international community's responsibility, through the United Nations, to use appropriate diplomatic, humanitarian and other peaceful means, in accordance with Chapters VI and VIII of the Charter, to help to protect populations from genocide, war crimes, ethnic cleansing and crimes against humanity.[10] The Security Council echoed the concept in a number of important resolutions, as for example Resolution 1325 which 'emphasizes the responsibility of all States to put an end to impunity and to prosecute those responsible for genocide, crimes against humanity, and war crimes including those relating to sexual and other violence against women and girls'.[11] Security Council Resolutions 1674 and 1894 on the Protection of Civilians in Armed Conflict also reaffirmed the Outcome Document and the Council's strong opposition to impunity for 'serious violations of human rights and humanitarian law'.[12] In July 2009, the General Assembly held a two-day debate on the responsibility to protect during which more than ninety Member States affirmed their interest in and commitment to the concept. This was followed by the adoption of Resolution 308 on the responsibility to protect in September 2009 in which the Assembly took note of the Secretary-General's report[13] and its own debate, and decided to continue its consideration of the issue.[14]

These auspicious events led a good number of commentators to proclaim the responsibility to protect as a new, or at least emerging, norm of international law.[15] On the other hand, since the responsibility to protect did not arise from one of the recognised sources of international law outlined in

---

[9] '2005 World Summit Outcome', para. 138.   [10] *Ibid.*, para. 139.

[11] UN Security Council Res. 1325, UN Doc. S/RES/1325, 31 October 2000, para. 11.

[12] See respectively the Security Council resolutions on the Protection of Civilians in Armed Conflict. UNSC Res. 1674, UN Doc. S/RES/1674, 28 April 2006, para. 4; *ibid.*, pmbl., para. 3; and UNSC Res. 1894, UN Doc. S/RES/1894, 11 November 2009.

[13] UNSG, 'Implementing the Responsibility to Protect', UN Doc. A/63/677, 12 January 2009.

[14] UN General Assembly Res. 63/308, UN Doc. A/RES/63/308, 7 October 2009.

[15] See for example Louise Arbour, 'The Responsibility to Protect as a Duty of Care in International Law and Practice', *Review of International Studies*, 24 (2008), 445–58; Alex Bellamy, *Responsibility to Protect: The Global Effort to End Mass Atrocities* (Cambridge, UK: Polity Press, 2009); Richard Cooper and Juliette Voïnov Kohler (eds.), *Responsibility to Protect: The Global Moral Compact for the 21st Century* (New York: Palgrave Macmillan, 2009); Cristina Badescu, *Humanitarian Intervention and the Responsibility to Protect: Security and Human Rights* (New York: Routledge, 2010); Frank Chalk, Kyle Mathews and Karla Barqueiro, *Mobilizing the Will to Intervene: Leadership to Prevent Mass Atrocities* (Quebec: McGill-Queen's University Press,

Article 38(1) of the Statute of the International Court of Justice, but rather from the proposals of a small number of experts, others expressed their scepticism over its content and purported legal status.[16] First, despite strong endorsement of the responsibility to protect from 150 governments at the World Summit, serious disagreement persists over its scope and application.[17] UN Member States' support for the responsibility to protect may not be as solid as it appeared to have been at the World Summit, especially with regard to the ICISS 2001 report's consideration of the possible legality of humanitarian intervention outside UN and regional collective security frameworks.[18] Second, the harmful consequences of military invasion very

2010); Sara Davies and Luke Glanville (eds.), *Protecting the Displaced: Deepening the Responsibility to Protect* (Leiden: Martinus Nijhoff, 2010); Thomas Weiss, *Military-Civilian Interactions: Humanitarian Crises and the Responsibility to Protect: Second Edition* (Lanham, MD: Rowman & Littlefield, 2004); Ramesh Thakur, *The United Nations, Peace and Security: From Collective Security to the Responsibility to Protect* (Cambridge University Press, 2006); Thomas Weiss, *Humanitarian Intervention: War and Conflict in the Modern World* (Cambridge, UK: Polity Press, 2007). There is also a journal *Global Responsibility to Protect*, published by Brill, and many articles in scholarly journals on international law, international relations, ethics, political science and other fields, devoted to the responsibility to protect.

[16] Stephanie Carvin, 'A Responsibility to Reality: A Reply to Louise Arbour', *Review of International Studies*, 36 (2010), 47–54; Carsten Stahn, 'Responsibility to Protect: Rhetoric or Emerging Legal Norm?', *American Journal of International Law*, 101 (2007), 99–120; Roberto Belloni, 'The Tragedy of Darfur and the Limits of the "Responsibility to Protect"', *Ethnopolitics*, 5 (2006), 327–46; Alex de Waal, 'Darfur and the Failure of the Responsibility to Protect', *International Affairs*, 83 (2007), 1039–54; Dan Bulley, 'The Politics of Ethical Foreign Policy: A Responsibility to Protect Whom?', *European Journal of International Relations*, 16 (2010), 441–61.

[17] Even Gareth Evans, who co-chaired the ICISS with Mohamed Sahnoun, and has been one of its strongest proponents, conceded that many governments backed away from their earlier expressions of support for the concept. See Evans, 'The Responsibility to Protect: An Idea Whose Time Has Come and Gone?', *International Relations*, 22 (2008), 283–98, at 288.

[18] A plain reading of Article 2(4) of the UN Charter seems to rule out such military adventures and does not seem to admit any lawful exception beyond the customary right of self-defence or Security Council authority under Chapter VII in regard to the threat or breach of international peace and security. Moreover, actual historical practice involving the very few candidates that might reasonably be considered to exemplify humanitarian intervention, namely, Indian intervention in East Pakistan (1971), Tanzanian intervention in Uganda (1979) and Vietnamese intervention in Cambodia (1979), have all involved palpable political and military self-interests on the part of the intervening States. Tellingly, none of these instances which some have claimed to have been humanitarian interventions, were even claimed as such by the intervening States themselves. For a more detailed discussion, see Lyal S. Sunga, 'The Role of Humanitarian Intervention in International Peace and Security: Guarantee or Threat?', in Hans Kochler (ed.), *The Use of Force in International Relations: Challenges to Collective Security* (Vienna: International Progress Organisation, 2006), pp. 41–82.

often seem to be seriously underestimated, at least by the intervening State or States such that the costs of humanitarian intervention, particularly to the local population, are often ignored. Third, as Belloni has argued, the responsibility to protect might actually encourage a greater incidence of political violence because certain rebel leaders may conclude that it is worth raising the level of violence in order to attract international support, including military intervention from other States.[19] Fourth, it is not clear, where the Security Council remains deadlocked in the face of ongoing atrocities, whether the responsibility should then devolve to a regional peace and security organisation such as NATO or the African Union,[20] or further to a group of States, or even to a single State. Fifth, if one takes the High-Level Panel vision of the responsibility to protect which dropped the ICISS idea that humanitarian intervention could legitimately be undertaken without Security Council authorisation, then we are brought right back to the classical notion of sovereignty as responsibility dating back to the time of Grotius and the rise of modern Westphalian international law itself. In that case, one has to wonder whether the High-Level Panel's version of the responsibility to protect really adds anything at all to international law. Sixth, the notion of legal responsibility implies legal liability to be sanctioned for breach of that responsibility, as well as a duty to make reparation, but as Stahn has pointed out, 'it is difficult to imagine what legal consequences noncompliance by a political body like the Security Council should entail.'[21]

In sum, the ICISS's formulation of the responsibility to protect remains unclear as regards content and legal status. On the other hand, responsibility to protect, in its diluted variants as expressed in the High-Level Panel report and paragraphs 138 and 139 of the World Summit Outcome Document are far less controversial, but seem to add little to existing international law. Thus, depending on which version one is talking about, the responsibility to protect seems either too vague on key points, or devoid of added value to the existing corpus of international law.

---

[19] See Belloni, 'The Tragedy of Darfur'.

[20] The constituent instrument of the African Union authorises humanitarian intervention to halt or prevent genocide, war crimes or crimes against humanity: see Constitutive Act of the African Union, adopted 11 July 2000 and entered into force 26 May 2001, 2158 UNTS 3. For a comprehensive and in-depth study on the scope and limits of Article 4(h) of the AU Constitutive Act, see Dan Kuwali, *The Responsibility to Protect: Implementation of Article 4(h) Intervention* (Leiden: Martinus Nijhoff, 2011) and Dersso, Chapter 10 in this book.

[21] Stahn, 'Responsibility to Protect', 118.

The concept's currently weak claim to the status of a principle or rule of international law does not mean that it could not acquire prescriptive force in the future. The responsibility to protect could eventually acquire legally binding force if:

(1) its content eventually becomes articulated in sufficiently clear and precise terms as to prescribe specific acts either on a mandatory or permissive basis;

(2) legal consequences can be shown to accrue from a breach of the responsibility to protect (such as the duty to make reparations to the injured party or parties or to restore the status quo ante the breach); and

(3) it becomes validated through one of the recognised sources of international law as enunciated in Article 38(1) of the Statute of the International Court of Justice.

Even if the responsibility to protect were never to become recognised as an international legal norm or principle, it could still play a useful role in international relations.

This ongoing debate probably has limited the extent to which the Human Rights Council has called upon the responsibility to protect in explicit terms to respond to situations involving serious violations of international human rights and humanitarian law. As argued in the next section, however, the practice of the Human Rights Council seems to offer greater promise than either the Security Council or the General Assembly as regards the international responsibility to protect in relation to situations involving genocide, war crimes or crimes against humanity.

Scattered Human Rights Commission/Council references to the responsibility to protect

For the sake of completeness, it is useful to note that the phrase 'responsibility to protect' has percolated up here and there in various studies and reports of the Human Rights Commission, and its successor, the Human Rights Council. Vladimir Kartashkin's 2006 working paper entitled 'Human Rights and State Sovereignty' for the Sub-Commission on the Promotion and Protection of Human Rights for example touches on issues relating to the use of force for humanitarian purposes in relation to State sovereignty.[22] The 2006 report of the High Commissioner for

---

[22] See Vladimir Kartashkin, 'Administration of Justice, Rule of Law and Democracy: Human Rights and State Sovereignty', working paper, UN Commission on Human

Human Rights on systematic rape, sexual slavery and slavery-like practices during armed conflict underlined the need for victims of violence to obtain justice, and the international community's duty to take measures in that regard. The report considered that the World Summit Outcome constituted 'a real breakthrough' in this connection, but without elaborating the point further.[23]

During the transition phase from Commission to Council, the Human Rights Council considered the possible contribution of special procedures to the practical implementation of the responsibility to protect in 2006. Certain States expressed their view that special procedures country mandates should be abolished altogether. Other States insisted that the Council must be in a position to investigate situations urgently on a country basis, particularly since thematic mandates, which were mandated to look into the situation in any country, were often stretched too thin to study, monitor and report on particular situations in depth or to accord them sufficient attention or follow up over time. The Human Rights Council did eventually agree to retain country mandates, and this has allowed it to focus on the situations involving issues of genocide, war crimes or crimes against humanity, discussed below.[24] When these issues were still under discussion, a Group of Experts met in May 2007 to discuss current issues and challenges facing the UN human rights special procedures system and the institution of UN human rights mandate-holders. The group adopted the 'Lund Statement to the United Nations Human Rights Council on the Human Rights Special Procedures' which was transmitted to the President of the UN Human Rights Council and ultimately tabled before the Council as document HRC/5/18 of 13 June 2007. The Lund Statement on the Human Rights Council's Special Procedures, underlined the role of special procedures 'as an early warning mechanism' which formed 'an intrinsic part of the efforts of the UN and the international community to give effect to the responsibility to protect human rights and to maintain a global watch over human security' and that 'the General Assembly and the Security Council's

---

Rights, UN Doc. E/CN.4/Sub.2/2006/7, 5 May 2006, paras. 31–5, which discuss the responsibility to protect.

[23] UN High Commissioner for Human Rights, 'Systematic Rape, Sexual Slavery and Slavery-like Practices during Armed Conflicts', UN Doc. A/HRC/Sub.1/58/23, 11 July 2006, para. 47.

[24] UN Human Rights Council, 'Intersessional Open-ended Intergovernmental Working Group on the Implementation of Operative Paragraph 6 of General Assembly Resolution 60/251: Preliminary Conclusions, by the Facilitator on the Review of Mandates, Mr Tomas Husak', UN Doc. A/HRC/3/4, 30 November 2006, para. 14.

commitment to act on the responsibility to protect, particularly as regards genocide, war crimes and crimes against humanity, needs to be noted in this regard'.[25]

A number of Commission on Human Rights/Human Rights Council special rapporteurs have referred pointedly in relation to their mandates to a particular government's responsibility to protect. In her report on her Mission to the Sudan (1–13 June 2004), the Special Rapporteur on Extrajudicial, Summary or Arbitrary Executions, Asma Jahangir reminded the government of the Sudan that it had 'a responsibility to protect the lives of the internally displaced persons as well as others affected by the conflict and will ultimately be responsible for their deaths'.[26] The Special Representative of the Secretary-General on the Situation of Human Rights Defenders, Hina Jilani, in her 2008 Indonesia Mission report, welcomed the adoption of a new law accepting the government's responsibility to protect all human rights and reminded the government of its responsibility to protect citizens against the harmful activities of non-State actors as well.[27] Similarly, the Special Rapporteur on Adequate Housing referred to the government's responsibility to protect all human rights and to 'establish appropriate legal and procedural framework to guarantee that private entities, including sponsors . . . do not infringe upon the right to adequate housing of the local population'.[28] The report of the Working Group on Mercenaries also referred to the responsibility to protect the right to life.[29] In his

---

[25] See UNHRC, 'Letter Dated 18 May 2007 Addressed by the Rector of the United Nations University to the President of the Human Rights Council', UN Doc. A/HRC/5/18, 13 June 2007, annex, para. 34. See further Lyal S. Sunga, 'Introduction to the "Lund Statement to the United Nations Human Rights Council on the Human Rights Special Procedures"', *Nordic Journal of International Law*, 76 (2007), 281–300.

[26] UNHCR, 'Extrajudicial, Summary or Arbitrary Executions: Report of the Special Rapporteur, Ms. Asma Jahangir, Addendum, Mission to the Sudan', UN Doc. E/CN.4/2005/7/Add.2, 6 August 2004, para. 3.

[27] UNHRC, 'Report of the Special Representative of the Secretary-General on the Situation of Human Rights Defenders, Ms. Hina Jilani, Addendum, Mission to Indonesia', UN Doc. A/HRC/7/28/Add.2, 28 January 2008, paras. 7 and 67.

[28] UNHRC, 'Report of the Special Rapporteur on Adequate Housing as a Component of the Right to an Adequate Standard of Living, and on the Right to Non-Discrimination in this Context, Raquel Rolnik', UN Doc. A/HRC/13/20, 18 December 2009, paras. 66–7.

[29] UNHRC, 'Report of the Working Group on the Use of Mercenaries as a Means of Violating Human Rights and Impeding the Exercise of the Right of Peoples to Self-Determination, Addendum, Regional Consultation for Africa on the Activities of Mercenaries and Private Military and Security Companies: Regulation and Monitoring 3–4 March 2010', UN Doc. A/HRC/15/25/Add.5, 2 June 2005, para. 25, mentioned a government's responsibility to protect the right to life.

report of February 2008, the Special Rapporteur on the situation of human rights in the Democratic People's Republic of Korea, Vitit Muntarbhorn, underlined 'the need to assist all victims of the human rights situation in the country in a sustained and comprehensive manner, bearing in mind the physical, psychological and other damage incurred, and to offer redress based upon the responsibility to protect people from human rights violations, bolstered by international solidarity to ensure such responsibility'.[30] More explicit reference to the responsibility to protect in relation to genocide, war crimes and crimes against humanity is found in the March 2010 report of the Special Rapporteur on Racism, Githu Muigai, which identifies racism as a trigger for the outbreak of violence under certain circumstances.[31] The Council also referred generally to the primary responsibility of governments to protect their citizens in relation to inter-ethnic violence that took place in Kyrgyzstan and Afghanistan in 2010.[32] The 2010 report of the Independent Expert on Minority Issues recalled the World Summit Outcome formulation of the responsibility to protect to emphasise a need to develop the UN's early warning capacity with regard to threats to the rights of minorities.[33] While many of these references to the responsibility to protect did not relate directly to genocide, war crimes, ethnic cleansing or crimes against humanity, they emphasise the importance of the Human Rights Council's role in drawing the international community's attention to situations that appeared to be seriously degrading.

Using the responsibility to protect to spearhead investigations into serious violations of human rights and humanitarian law

The Human Rights Council has made more deliberate use of the concept of the responsibility to protect to spearhead investigations into serious violations of human rights and humanitarian law in Darfur (Sudan),

---

[30] UNHRC, 'Report of the Special Rapporteur on the Situation of Human Rights in the Democratic People's Republic of Korea, Vitit Muntarbhorn', UN Doc. A/HRC/7/20, 15 February 2008, para. 69.

[31] UNHRC, 'Report of the Special Rapporteur on Contemporary Forms of Racism, Racial Discrimination, Xenophobia and Related Intolerance, Githu Muigai', UN Doc. A/HRC/14/43, 30 March 2010, paras. 2 and 63–4.

[32] See respectively UNHRC Res. 14/14, UN Doc. A/HRC/RES/14/14, 23 June 2010 and UNHRC Res. 14/15, UN Doc. A/HRC/RES/14/15, 23 June 2010.

[33] UNHRC, 'Report of the Independent Expert on Minority Issues, Gay McDougall', UN Doc. A/HRC/16/45, 16 December 2010, para. 68.

Israeli Occupied Palestinian Territories, Côte d'Ivoire, Libya and Syria. In these instances, the Council has invoked the concept to signal to the government, territorial authorities and international community at large, the existence of reasonable grounds to infer that:

- serious violations of human rights (and/or humanitarian law) have been or are being committed;
- such violations might qualify as genocide, war crimes or crimes against humanity;
- the government and/or territorial authorities have failed or are failing to fulfil their responsibility to protect people from genocide, war crimes or crimes against humanity; and
- if the government or territorial authority continued to show little or no immediate and credible prospect of meeting their responsibility to protect, then the UN Security Council or competent regional collective security arrangement could take concrete action through the range of available multilateral institutions. Such action would seek to address the root causes of the conflict, prevent and react to violations, even through the use of coercive measures such as sanctions and international criminal prosecutions, and to assist recovery, reconstruction and reconciliation.

These instances, which are explored in more detail below, seem to point the way for the more concrete operationalisation of the responsibility to protect through the Human Rights Council.

Darfur

A major step to halt and prevent genocide, war crimes and crimes against humanity in Darfur was taken by the Security Council in adopting Resolution 1564 under Chapter VII of the UN Charter, on 18 September 2004. Resolution 1564 reminded the government of the Sudan of its primary responsibility to abide by its international human rights and humanitarian law obligations. This resolution also established an International Commission of Inquiry on Darfur to determine whether or not acts of genocide had been perpetrated and to identify the perpetrators. In December 2006, the Secretary-General's Special Adviser on the Prevention of Genocide addressed a letter to the Human Rights Council urging it to take measures to protect civilians in Darfur and to support the work of the International Criminal Court (ICC).[34]

The High-Level Mission's report of 9 March 2007 is heavily based on the responsibility to protect. The report devotes four pages first to discussing the concept and then goes on to analyse the main political obstacles to peace in Part II entitled 'The Darfur Peace Agreement, the Ensuing Violence and the Responsibility to Protect'. Part III is entitled 'Sudan's Action regarding the Responsibility to Protect' and Chapter V is 'The International Community's Responsibility to Protect'.[35] Part C of Chapter V considers 'The Responsibility of the International Community to Protect the People of Darfur: Current Status'. The Mission found that the 'justice system as a whole was unable or unwilling to pursue justice or prevent attacks'. This statement pertained directly to a key element relating to the complementary operation of the ICC as foreseen in Article 17 of the Rome Statute: the ICC can only exercise jurisdiction over a situation where the territorial government is itself unwilling or unable to prosecute genocide, war crimes or crimes against humanity perpetrated in its territory or by its nationals. The Mission recommended that the Human Rights Council express its regret over the 'Government's manifest failure in its responsibility to protect civilians, condemn the continuing violations, and call for effective protection for civilians, accountability for perpetrators (including through action by the ICC) and compensation and redress for victims'.[36] Unfortunately, the government of the Sudan stalled the High-Level Mission's access to the Sudan including Darfur, effectively preventing the Mission from carrying out any first-hand human rights fact-finding and investigation.

The experience of the High-Level Mission offers some important lessons. First, whether the High-Level Mission had any effect on the human rights situation in Darfur remains doubtful. Invoking the responsibility to protect is no magic wand. Merely calling on the notion did not secure the government's cooperation to allow fact-finding and investigation. On the other hand, the Mission evidently felt that the responsibility to protect was a valuable rallying cry for action on the human rights situation in Darfur. Perhaps more important, the Mission's report

[34] UNHRC, 'Letter Dated 8 December 2006 from Mr Juan E. Méndez, Special Adviser to the Secretary-General on the Prevention of Genocide, addressed to the President of the Human Rights Council', UN Doc. A/HRC/S-4/3, 11 December 2006.

[35] UNHRC, 'Report of the High-Level Mission on the Situation of Human Rights in Darfur Pursuant to Human Rights Council Decision S-4/101', UN Doc. A/HRC/4/80, 9 March 2007.

[36] Ibid.

provides a schema for the Human Rights Council to apply the responsibility to protect more practically to situations that seem to involve genocide, war crimes or crimes against humanity. In other words, Human Rights Council commissions of inquiry and other human rights investigators could find the concept to be a useful way of structuring their reports and recommendations more coherently in terms of the linkage between serious violations of human rights or humanitarian law and criminal responsibility for genocide, war crimes or crimes against humanity. This in itself would represent an advance over classical human rights monitoring and investigation which tend to paint a general picture of the human rights situation and States' responsibility for violations in broad strokes, without sufficient detail or precision as to implicate specific individuals in international criminal responsibility.[37]

Israeli Occupied Palestinian Territories

Fact-finding missions into Israeli abuses in Palestinian territories have cited the failure to fulfil the responsibility to protect. In Resolution S-3/1 of 15 November 2006, the Human Rights Council expressed its concern that Israeli military incursions carried out in Beit Hanoun, Gaza on 8 November 2006 constituted a form of 'collective punishment of the civilians therein and exacerbate[d] the severe humanitarian crisis in the Occupied Palestinian Territory'. The resolution called 'for immediate protection of the Palestinian civilians in the Occupied Palestinian Territory in compliance with human rights law and international humanitarian law' and the urgent dispatch of a high-level fact-finding mission – to be appointed by the Council's president – to Beit Hanoun in order to assess the situation of victims, the needs of survivors and to recommend ways and means to protect Palestinian civilians against any further Israeli assaults.[38] After several failed attempts to obtain Israel's cooperation to facilitate safe transit through Israel, the fact-finding mission finally was able to visit Beit Hanoun in May 2008. The Mission's fact-finding report underlines the government of Israel's responsibility to protect Palestinian civilians in territories

---

[37] For a comparison of human rights and criminal law investigation procedures, see Sunga, 'How Can UN Human Rights Special Procedures Sharpen ICC Fact-Finding?', *International Journal of Human Rights*, 15 (2011), 187–204.

[38] UNHRC Res. S-3/1, UN Doc. A/HRC/RES/S-3/1, pmbl., paras. 5 and 7.

under its effective control in line with established international human rights law.[39]

On 27 December 2008, Israel launched a large-scale aerial and naval offensive in the Gaza Strip code-named 'Operation Cast Lead'. This was followed by a major ground offensive on 3 January 2009 with coordinated air and naval attacks that culminated in Israeli ground forces entering Beit Hanoun in the early hours of 4 January 2009. Israel stated that it was responding to the firing of rockets into Israel by Palestinian militants. On 20 January, Israeli forces withdrew their troops from the Gaza Strip. The Secretary-General underlined that:

> While States have a primary responsibility to protect all persons under their jurisdiction or control from war crimes, crimes against humanity, genocide and ethnic cleansing, under the doctrine reaffirmed in the 2005 World Summit Outcome, the international community in its entirety shares the responsibility for protecting civilians, in particular where and when the authorities concerned are unable or unwilling to do so.

The Secretary-General's report went on to remind the international community of the various options available to ensure accountability.[40] In his 2010 report, Professor Richard Falk reiterated that Israel's blockade of Gaza was 'a continuing and massive form of collective punishment' and that it represented 'a fundamental violation of Israel's responsibility to protect the civilian population of the occupied Gaza Strip'.[41]

On 3 April 2009, the President of the Human Rights Council established the Fact Finding Mission on the Gaza Conflict with a mandate 'to investigate all violations of international human rights law and international humanitarian law that might have been committed at any time in the context of the military operations that were conducted in Gaza during the period from 27 December 2008 and 18 January 2009, whether before, during or after'.[42] In its report, the Mission urged the Palestinian

---

[39] UNHRC, 'Report of the High-Level Fact-Finding Mission to Beit Hanoun Established under Council Resolution S-3/1', UN Doc. A/HRC/9/26, 1 September 2008, para. 12.

[40] UNHRC, 'Follow-up on the Implementation of the Recommendations Contained in the Report of the High-Level Fact-Finding Mission to Beit Hanoun Established under Human Rights Council Resolution S-3/1', UN Doc. A/HRC/10/27, 6 March 2009, para. 18.

[41] UNHRC, 'Report of the Special Rapporteur, on the Situation of Human Rights in the Palestinian Territories Occupied since 1967, Richard Falk', UN Doc. A/HRC/13/53/Rev.1, 7 June 2010, para. 32.

[42] UNHRC, 'Report of the United Nations Fact Finding Mission on the Gaza Conflict', UN Doc. A/HRC/12/48, 15 September 2009, para. 1.

Authority (PA) to take effective measures to ensure meaningful account-ability for perpetrators of serious violations of international law and 'that the responsibility to protect the rights of the people inherent in the authority assumed by the PA must be fulfilled with greater commit-ment'.[43] The fact-finding mission further underlined both the interna-tional community's and the State of Israel's responsibility to protect victims of violations[44] and referred to the responsibility to protect, including the World Summit Outcome Document.[45] The report other-wise makes scant mention of the responsibility to protect, and only indirectly, for example, to point out that the Secretary-General's report, 'Implementing the Responsibility to Protect' indicated that the concept did not diminish the legal obligations arising from international human-itarian law, international human rights law, refugee law and interna-tional criminal law.

Côte d'Ivoire

The Human Rights Council's reaction to the post-election violence in Côte d'Ivoire arising from incumbent President Laurent Gbagbo's refusal to recognise the democratic electoral victory of Alassane Dramane Ouattara embraced the main elements of the responsibility-to-protect notion, but without employing the exact phrase. Human Rights Council Resolution S-14/1 of 28 December 2010 on the situation in Côte d'Ivoire urged defence and security forces to refrain from violence, respect human rights and 'assume their responsibilities for the protection of the civilian population'.[46] This resolution also called upon UN Member States to assist the country to build up its capacity and underlined 'that the legitimate Government of Côte d'Ivoire has the primary responsibility to make every effort to strengthen the protection of the civilian population and to investigate and bring to justice perpe-trators of violations of human rights and of international humanitarian law'. Further, the resolution called upon the international community to support the government's efforts to stabilise the situation in the country. The resolution also requested the High Commissioner for Human Rights to report to the Council on violations in relation to the election.[47] The

---

[43] *Ibid.*, para. 126.   [44] *Ibid.*, para. 1672.   [45] *Ibid.*, para. 1710.
[46] UNHRC Res. S-14/1, UN Doc. A/HRC/RES/S-14/1, 23 December 2010. para. 3. The resolution was adopted without a vote.
[47] *Ibid.*, para. 12.

High Commissioner's report of February 2011 reminded Gbagbo that his military and law enforcement officials had an ongoing responsibility to protect civilians and to prevent serious human rights violations committed by security forces as well as to prosecute perpetrators of such violations.[48]

The Human Rights Council then initiated more concrete action to assist in the enforcement of individual responsibility for crimes under international law with the adoption of Resolution 16/25 which reaffirmed the 'responsibility of Côte d'Ivoire to promote and protect all human rights and fundamental freedoms, to investigate alleged violations of human rights and international law and to bring to justice the perpetrators of such acts, who are answerable for their deeds before the judicial process'.[49] In Resolution 16/25, the Human Rights Council also decided to send an independent, international commission of inquiry to investigate serious human rights violations committed in Côte d'Ivoire following the election, to identify individuals responsible for such acts with a view to bringing them to justice, and to report back to the Council at its next session.[50] In its report of June 2011, the Commission of Inquiry laid the blame for the serious violations of human rights and humanitarian law squarely on Gbagbo's rejection of the election results, and it indicated that some of the violations might amount to war crimes and crimes against humanity.[51]

Libya

On 25 February 2011, the Human Rights Council strongly condemned gross and systematic human rights violations being committed in Libya that included indiscriminate armed attacks against civilians, extrajudicial killings, arbitrary arrests, detention and torture of peaceful demonstrators and it indicated that these violations could amount to crimes against humanity. It strongly called upon 'the Government of Libya to meet its responsibility to protect its population, to immediately put an end to all human rights violations, to stop any attacks against civilians,

---

[48] UNHRC, 'Report of the United Nations High Commissioner for Human Rights on the Situation of Human Rights in Côte d'Ivoire', UN Doc. A/HRC/16/79, 25 February 2011, para. 42.

[49] UNHRC Res. 16/25, UN Doc. A/HRC/RES/16/25, 13 April 2011, pmbl., para. 9.

[50] Ibid., para. 10.

[51] UNHRC, 'Rapport de la Commission d'Enquête Internationale Indépendante sur la Côte d'Ivoire', UN Doc. A/HRC/17/48, 14 June 2011, para. 91.

and to fully respect all human rights and fundamental freedoms, including freedom of expression and freedom of assembly'.[52] In the same resolution, the Human Rights Council decided to establish an international commission of inquiry to investigate the violations, to make recommendations on accountability measures and to report back to the Council at its next session.[53]

The same day, a cross-regional group of governments calling itself the 'Group of Friends on Responsibility to Protect on the Situation in the Libyan Arab Jamahiriya' issued a statement referring to paragraphs 138 and 139 of the World Summit Outcome Document and expressing its concern over the violations as possible crimes against humanity. The statement called upon the government of Libya 'to meet its Responsibility to Protect its population and put an immediate end to all human rights violations and ensure the full respect of human rights and fundamental freedoms'. It also called upon 'all the relevant bodies of the United Nations to take urgent and appropriate measures to put into practice the commitment of the international community to the Responsibility to Protect'.[54]

The following day, the Security Council adopted Resolution 1970 reiterating the Libyan government's 'responsibility to protect its population'.[55] Strikingly, Resolution 1970 referred the situation to the International Criminal Court,[56] enforced an arms embargo upon all UN Member States on direct or indirect supply of arms to Libya,[57] put in place a travel ban on sixteen members of the Gaddafi family and persons close to the regime[58] as well as an assets freeze on six Gaddafi family members.[59] It also established a Sanctions Committee as well as criteria for designating individuals involved or complicit in ordering, controlling or otherwise directing, the commission of serious human rights abuses.[60] It called upon all UN Member States to facilitate humanitarian assistance and indicated the Council's decision to remain seized of the matter.

---

[52] UNHRC Res. S-15/1, UN Doc. A/HRC/RES/S-15/1, 3 March 2011, paras. 1 and 2.
[53] *Ibid.*, para. 11.
[54] See Group of Friends on Responsibility to Protect, 'Statement of the Group of Friends on Responsibility to Protect on the Situation in the Libyan Arab Jamahiriya', 1 March 2011, available at www.missionfnnewyork.um.dk.
[55] UN Security Council Res. 1970, UN Doc. S/RES/1970, 26 February 2011, pmbl., para. 10.
[56] *Ibid.*, paras. 4–8.   [57] *Ibid.*, paras. 9–14.
[58] *Ibid.*, paras. 15–6. See also *ibid.*, annex I.
[59] *Ibid.*, paras. 17–21. See also *ibid.*, annex II.   [60] *Ibid.*, paras. 22–5.

Syria

By 1 October 2011, the Human Rights Council had held a second special session on the human rights situation in Syria and adopted a resolution in which the Council referred to the government's responsibility to protect its population. By late August 2011, the Human Rights Council had decided to dispatch an international commission of inquiry to investigate serious human rights violations being perpetrated in Syria.[61] Addressing the opening of the 18th regular session of the Human Rights Council on 12 September 2011, Navi Pillay, the High Commissioner for Human Rights, stated that more than 2,600 people had been killed in Syria since the outbreak of violence in mid-March of 2011.[62] In October 2011, China and Russia vetoed a draft Security Council resolution to place sanctions on Bashar al-Assad's regime.[63] In a press statement on 14 October 2011, the High Commissioner revised the number killed to 3,000, noted that the government of Syria had 'manifestly failed to protect its population' and failed to cooperate with international investigations.[64] Around 187 children were reported to have been killed since the start of the violence and more than 100 people killed in the period 4–14 October 2011 alone.

On 23 February 2012, former UN Secretary-General Kofi Annan was appointed as a joint envoy of the UN and League of Arab States and on 16 March 2012, he unveiled a 'six point plan' to reduce hostilities and encourage the opposing parties to enter into a process of political dialogue. On 12 April 2012, a ceasefire was announced and the UN Supervision Mission in Syria (UNSMIS) was established.

The Chair of the Commission of Inquiry on Syria was permitted by the government to visit Damascus from 23–25 June 2012 to explain the Commission's mandate and methods to government officials. In an Oral Update to the Human Rights Council, the Commission of Inquiry

---

[61] See OHCHR press release, 'Human Rights Council decides to dispatch a commission of inquiry to investigate human rights violations in the Syrian Arab Republic', 23 August 2011, available at www.ohchr.org.

[62] See UN High Commissioner for Human Rights, Navi Pillay, 'Opening statement', speech delivered at 18th Session of the Human Rights Council, Geneva, 12 September 2011, available at www.ohchr.org.

[63] See Jonathan Marcus, 'Why China and Russia rebuffed the West on Syria', BBC, 5 October 2011, at www.bbc.co.uk/news/world-middle-east-15180732.

[64] See OHCHR press release, 'Pillay urges United International action to protect Syrians', 14 October 2011, available at www.ohchr.org.

reported that the government had informed it that by the end of April 2012, around 6,143 Syrian citizens had been killed which included:

> 3211 civilians, 478 public order officers, 2088 military personnel, 204 women and 56 children. Another 106 people were assassinated according to the Government. The Syrian Government supplemented these figures, according to which 804 persons were killed (both armed forces and civilians) in the period between 7 May and 4 June 2012.[65]

The Commission's report noted that reports from certain other entities, mainly non-governmental organisations, reckoned that the total number of persons killed since the onset of hostilities had reached somewhere between 13,000 and 17,000, but the Commission cautioned that it could not confirm these figures.[66]

Discernible shift from rhetoric to action in Human Rights Council practice on the responsibility to protect

On 23 March 2011, the government of Australia made a statement on behalf of 56 countries on the responsibility to protect which reaffirmed paragraphs 138 and 139 of the 2005 World Summit Outcome and resolved how the Human Rights Council should operationalise the responsibility to protect:

> We must work with the High Commissioner [for Human Rights], to support long-term measures that help states exercise their responsibility to protect, such as institution building, strengthening the rule of law, and technical cooperation to promote respect for human rights and to prevent and address human rights violations. The Council also has a role in working with states to help build capacities and share best practices that reduce social tensions and contribute to conflict prevention.[67]

---

[65] See UNHRC, 'Oral Update of the Independent International Commission of Inquiry on the Syrian Arab Republic', UN Doc. A/HRC/20/CRP.1, 26 June 2012, para. 21.

[66] *Ibid.*, para. 22.

[67] 'Joint Statement on the Responsibility to Protect, Human Rights Council 16th Session', 23 March 2011, at www.geneva.mission.gov.au/gene/Statement189.html. The fifty-six countries were: Albania, Armenia, Australia, Austria, Belgium, Bulgaria, Canada, Colombia, Costa Rica, Cote d'Ivoire, Croatia, Cyprus, Czech Republic, Denmark, Estonia, Finland, France, Georgia, Germany, Greece, Honduras, Hungary, Iceland, Ireland, Israel, Italy, Latvia, Liechtenstein, Lithuania, Luxembourg, Malta, Mexico, Monaco, Montenegro, the Netherlands, New Zealand, Nigeria, Norway, Panama, Poland, Portugal, Republic of Korea, Republic of Moldova, Romania, Slovakia, Slovenia, Somalia, Spain, Sweden, Switzerland, Tanzania, Thailand, United Kingdom of Great Britain and Northern Ireland, Ukraine, United States of America and Zambia.

While short on conceptual content, the government of Australia's statement above signifies a discernible shift in the Human Rights Council from rhetoric to more practical action, because it garnered the support of fifty-six UN Member States in:

- identifying the Human Rights Council as an important institutional actor to operationalise the responsibility to protect;
- indicating how the responsibility to protect can be mainstreamed and operationalised within the UN human rights programme; and
- charting a way for the Human Rights Council to use the responsibility to protect to orient its investigations into serious violations of human rights and humanitarian law towards eventual international criminal law enforcement.

With these elements in mind, it is useful next to consider the outlook for future Human Rights Council implementation of the responsibility to protect.

Prospects for the Human Rights Council's future role in operationalising the responsibility to protect

If the international community at large fully supported the responsibility to protect, then arguably we should have seen the phrase employed more systematically in recent Human Rights Council resolutions and reports, and many more than 56 of the 193 UN Member States support the government of Australia's statement with regard to serious violations. Many African and Asian countries remain wary that the responsibility to protect is little more than a ploy for more powerful countries to cover their unwarranted military interventions in other States. The Human Rights Council's practice over the next few years could indicate whether the responsibility to protect perspective will revert to its more rhetorical role, or whether it will figure more as a prescriptive norm, if not of legal import, perhaps as useful guidance for more systematic implementation of a more coherent UN system-wide response to complex situations involving genocide, war crimes and crimes against humanity.

Indeed, sustained political support for the responsibility to protect in the Human Rights Council to address urgent situations involving serious human rights and humanitarian law violations in terms of the responsibility to protect, together with the involvement and support of the Security Council, the General Assembly, the International Criminal Court and other bodies, brightens prospects for the Human Rights

Council's future role in operationalising the responsibility to protect. The fact that practice has been galloping ahead even before the responsibility to protect has been fully defined, shows that many governments and the UN consider that the concept serves an important purpose.

Human Rights Council action has drawn heavily on the responsibility-to-protect perspective to address the situations in Darfur, the Israeli Occupied Palestinian Territories, Côte d'Ivoire, Libya and Syria, because this concept helps to:

- identify clearly human rights violations as a threat to international peace and security;
- remind the State concerned of its responsibility to protect people under its jurisdiction, particularly in time of severe political instability and armed conflict; and
- encourage a 'One UN' approach to address genocide, war crimes and crimes against humanity by mainstreaming international criminal law solutions as part of broader efforts to counter impunity with regard to serious violations of human rights and humanitarian law.

Because the Human Rights Council has been mandated first and foremost to address urgent situations involving the risk or actual occurrence of genocide, war crimes or crimes against humanity, it is the natural institutional home for the 'responsibility to protect' to mature and develop with the support of the Security Council, the General Assembly and other UN organs, as well as of regional peace and security organisations and governments.

Recommendations for operationalising the 'responsibility to protect'

The above discussion implies that the Human Rights Council should adopt or maintain certain policies with regard to: investigations and early warning; capacity-building; and the generation and sharing of knowledge on the responsibility to protect within the UN system. These policy recommendations are set forth below.

With regard to investigations and early warning, the Human Rights Council should continue fielding missions of inquiry to investigate situations at risk from imminent or actual serious violations of international human rights or humanitarian law. Where the government or territorial authority fails to cooperate adequately with the Human Rights Council or its investigative mission, the Council should remind the government or territorial authority of the possibility of a Security Council referral of the situation to the International Criminal Court, and/or of other possible action such as blockades, or military action through UN Charter Chapter VII authority. Second, the Human Rights Council should maintain full support for the work of UN human rights special procedures mechanisms and mandate-holders to enhance their early warning capacity. Third, the Council should also stay alert to emerging patterns of gross and systematic violations of human rights and consider possible preventive measures to be taken at an early stage. Fourth, the Human Rights Council should make full use of the Universal Periodic Review process to bring to light worrying trends in countries under review, specifically with an eye to detection and prevention of serious human rights and humanitarian law violations. Fifth, the Human Rights Council should support OHCHR's Rapid Response Unit to strengthen the UN Secretariat's capacity to undertake timely human rights assessment missions in the field and to take other appropriate measures.

With regard to capacity-building elsewhere within the UN and regional organisations, the Human Rights Council should support the training of peacekeepers, peace operations officials, military observers, military police and UN civilian police, to assist them to recognise serious violations of human rights and humanitarian law and to channel information on their occurrence confidentially to the appropriate human rights mechanism and OHCHR. Second, the Council should also help to mainstream human rights more systematically throughout peacekeeping operations and contribute to ensuring a coordinated 'One UN' response to conflict situations, for example, through the placing of experienced human rights officers in peacekeeping operations who are trained in the fundamentals of human rights, humanitarian law and international criminal law. Third, the Council should support the training of UN humanitarian personnel to identify vulnerable groups at particular risk of genocide, war crimes or crimes against humanity. Fourth, it should work in closer cooperation with regional and sub-regional collective security frameworks to coordinate preventive, diplomatic and reactive action in case situations degrade, or appear likely to degrade, to the point of widespread, serious or systematic violations of human rights and humanitarian law.

With regard to generation and sharing of knowledge on the practical implementation of the 'responsibility to protect', the Human Rights Council should distil best practices from its recent actions relating to the 'responsibility to protect', for example, on Darfur, the Israeli Occupied Palestinian Territories, Côte d'Ivoire, Libya, Syria and other situations as they may arise. This could help to identify key operational elements of the concept of the 'responsibility to protect' and support its place in international law and practice, as well as the Council's role in implementing it.

8

The International Law Commission

ARNOLD N. PRONTO

Introduction

The concept of responsibility to protect (R2P) has been the subject of limited consideration by the International Law Commission (Commission). This is not to say that it has not been raised in the debates held in the Commission, nor that the Commission's work-product is without relevance to at least some of precepts underlying the idea of a responsibility on the international community to protect populations from mass atrocities. Nonetheless, it is clear that the Commission has not been a significant actor in the development of the concept. There are several possible reasons for this.

The most obvious is that the Commission's working methods are such that it proceeds on the basis of a fixed work programme of topics which are deemed suitable for codification or progressive development.[1] With one exception, the Commission has not had a topic related to R2P since the 2005 World Summit Outcome Document.[2] Nor does it usually consider issues in international law on an ad hoc basis, which would typically occur following a request from the United Nations General Assembly to do so. Since no such request has been made (nor realistically contemplated), the Commission's interaction with the R2P concept, as presently conceived, has been fleeting at best.

It is also not entirely clear how the topic could be framed for consideration by the Commission, or what contribution it might make. The Commission is a subsidiary organ of the United Nations General

---

The views expressed herein do not necessarily reflect those of the United Nations, including the International Law Commission.

[1] See Statute of the International Law Commission, adopted by United Nations General Assembly Resolution 174 (II), 21 November 1947, arts. 16 and 18.

[2] '2005 World Summit Outcome', UN Doc. A/RES/60/1, 24 October 2005.

Assembly and has traditionally been reluctant to enter (or has at least proceeded with caution) into matters concerning questions of peace and security which more appropriately come under the mandate of the Security Council. To the extent, therefore, that R2P, as conceived of in 2005, pertains to the authority of the Security Council to act under Chapter VII of the Charter of the United Nations, it is doubtful that the Commission would consider including the topic (or one related thereto) within its work programme. The position might be different when coming to the aspect of the World Summit Outcome Document dealing with the activities of the General Assembly,[3] but this has thus far not been the primary focus of activity in the context of assertions of R2P, particularly in recent times.

A further, more diffuse, and accordingly more tentatively advanced, reason pertains to the idea that the Commission is, or views itself as, the guardian of traditional international law, developed over centuries of practice and contemplation. A law that is at its core State centric and rooted, even in its contemporary form, in notions of sovereignty of States and its corollary of non-intervention in domestic affairs. This is not to say that the Commission has not gone a long way to embrace modern ideas of restricted sovereignty or sovereignty as responsibility. Nonetheless, this continues to be done within the confines of what is referred to as 'general international law'. From this perspective, the concept of R2P is a relative newcomer, which has not emerged from the traditional process of lawmaking: General Assembly resolutions, other than those adopting soft law texts such as declarations or hard law treaties, are typically not a source of law even if they may constitute evidence of the existence elsewhere of a norm of international law. It is on these points that views in the Commission seem to part ways. While there certainly have been members who have voiced support for R2P, there remains an undertow of scepticism concerning the legal content of the concept or lack thereof, that is, whether it imposes a legal – as opposed to political – obligation on States implying legal consequences for failure to perform. This may also be linked to a certain weariness based on a sanguine world-view that has seen its fair share of assertions of the lawfulness of humanitarian intervention, of which R2P may be simply the latest manifestation – old wine in new bottles.

---

[3] *Ibid.*, para. 139 also contemplates 'the need for the General Assembly to continue consideration of the responsibility to protect populations from genocide, war crimes, ethnic cleansing and crimes against humanity and its implications, bearing in mind the principles of the Charter and international law'.

Regardless of the veracity of these latter considerations (which is not the subject of consideration here), what is clear is that at a stage in its work when the Commission, upon concluding a number of major topics, has been casting around for new subjects of international law to consider, no serious proposal pertaining to R2P has been contemplated. What is more, and as will be discussed below, the few times the Commission has debated, even if tangentially, the concept of R2P, primarily in the context of its work on the protection of persons in the event of disasters, it was by way of arriving at the decision – which was taken relatively easily – to exclude it from the scope of consideration.[4] All of this seems to point in the direction that the Commission's contribution to the development of the concept of R2P will remain minor into the foreseeable future as well.

Having said so, it might be worthwhile to consider the (limited) things the Commission has said about R2P. Furthermore, the Commission has, in its prior work, covered issues implicated in some of the components of R2P. For example, the version of R2P encapsulated in the World Summit Outcome Document restricts the scope *ratione materiae* of the concept, *inter alia*, to the 'core crimes' of international law, namely genocide, war crimes and crimes against humanity. These have most recently been codified in the Rome Statute of the International Criminal Court,[5] adopted in 1998, which was based in part on the work undertaken by the Commission on and off over a period of forty years, both in the context of developing a draft statute for the ICC[6] and of the draft

---

[4] The concept of R2P was also referred to in the work on the topic of responsibility of international organisations, if only by way of making sure that it was excluded from the scope *ratione materiae*. In 2006, the Chairman of the Drafting Committee explained, in the context of the provision on distress – at the time, draft article 21 – that the Committee had declined to consider the question of United Nations forces present in one area being in a position to prevent the loss of civilian lives in an adjacent area because 'the question involved much larger issues of the responsibility to protect and humanitarian intervention, which could not be dealt with under the current topic'. See International Law Commission, 'Provisional Summary Record of the 2884th Meeting', UN Doc. A/CN.4/SR.2884, 18 July 2006, p. 6. Similarly, in 2008, the Drafting Committee decided to replace, in what was draft article 52 – on the invocation of responsibility by non-injured States or international organisations – the word 'protecting' with 'safeguarding' so as to 'avoid any confusion with the recent principle of the "responsibility to protect"'. See ILC, 'Provisional Summary Record of the 2971st Meeting', UN Doc. A/CN.4/SR.2971, 6 February 2009, p. 22.

[5] Rome Statute of the International Criminal Court, adopted 17 July 1998 and entered into force 1 July 2002, 2187 UNTS 90.

[6] ILC, 'Report of the International Law Commission on the Work of Its Forty-Sixth Session (2 May–22 July 1994)', UN Doc. A/49/10, p. 26.

code of crimes against the peace and security of mankind, which the Commission finalised in 1996.[7] Furthermore, the concept of the international community as a whole[8] as a legal notion, an idea also espoused by the International Court of Justice,[9] features in several ways in the Commission's work on State responsibility, which culminated in the adoption of the 2001 articles on the responsibility of States for internationally wrongful acts (the '2001 articles on State responsibility').[10] Of particular relevance is the Commission's work on the possibility of so-called 'collective countermeasures' involving non-injured States taking lawful measures to ensure the cessation of a breach of collective international legal obligations.

R2P and the protection of persons in the event of disasters

The protection of persons in the event of disasters is the only topic on the work programme of the Commission in which R2P has been referred

---

[7] *Ibid.*, p. 17. The Commission is presently considering two further issues related to individual criminal responsibility which may be of consequential interest to the R2P project, namely the question of the nature and extent of the obligation to extradite or prosecute (*aut dedere aut judicare*) under international law, as well as the existence (and extent) at the international level of the immunity of State officials, including heads of State, from foreign criminal jurisdiction. See ILC, 'Report of the International Law Commission: Sixty-Third Session (26 April–3 June and 4 July–12 August 2011)', UN Doc. A/66/10, chs. X and VII, respectively. Furthermore, the question of the survival (or not) of treaties between belligerents – and those between belligerents and third parties – in the context of armed conflict – whether international or non-international in character – which may also be of relevance to the R2P concept, was the subject of consideration in the draft articles on the effects of armed conflicts on treaties, adopted by the Commission in 2011. Humanitarian law treaties and treaties for the international protection of human rights are included in those draft articles among the categories of treaties which are considered, by implication from their subject matter, to continue in operation, in whole or in part, during armed conflict. See *ibid.*, p. 174, art. 7; and *ibid.*, p. 176, annex.

[8] '2005 World Summit Outcome', para. 139, refers to 'the international community'.

[9] See *Barcelona Traction, Light and Power Company, Limited (Belgium* v. *Spain), Second Phase, Judgment*, ICJ Reports 1970, p. 32: '[A]n essential distinction should be drawn between the obligations of a State towards the international community as a whole, and those arising *vis-à-vis* another State . . . By their very nature the former are the concern of all States. In view of the importance of the rights involved, all States can be held to have a legal interest in their protection; they are obligations *erga omnes*' (para. 33).

[10] ILC, 'Report of the International Law Commission on the Work of Its Fifty-Third Session (23 April–1 June and 2 July–10 August 2001)', UN Doc. A/56/10, p. 26. See also Arnold Pronto and Michael Wood, *The International Law Commission 1999–2009, Volume IV: Treaties, Final Draft Articles, and Other Materials* (Oxford University Press, 2011), pp. 79ff.

to in any significant way. In fact, the reference to R2P was made right from the very beginning, but has, to date, not substantially proceeded beyond the question of its applicability in the context of the disasters topic. Nonetheless, echoes of the R2P debate can be identified in the Commission's substantive work on the disasters topic.

That topic was included on the work programme of the Commission at the suggestion of its Secretariat which, in a supporting memorandum, indicated, *inter alia*, that it was to be 'viewed as located within contemporary reflection on an emerging principle entailing the responsibility to protect, which, although couched primarily in the context of conflict, may also be of relevance to that of disasters'.[11] This was done out of recognition that the topic had strong parallels with the subject matter of R2P in that they both consider questions of humanitarian assistance to protect victims of calamity (even if of different sorts). In fact, the Commission, upon deciding to include it within its work programme, purposefully reoriented the topic closer to a protection-centred approach by deciding to give it the title 'protection of persons in the event of disasters' as opposed to 'international disaster relief law' which had been proposed by the Secretariat, but which was more neutral on the question of protection.

The R2P concept was first referred to in the substantive discussions of the Commission on the disasters topic during the debate on the preliminary report[12] of the Special Rapporteur, Eduardo Valencia-Ospina, in 2008. At the time, the Special Rapporteur had proposed a cautious approach to the relevance of R2P to the topic even though the 'concept entails the responsibility to prevent, react and rebuild, corresponding, respectively, to the three phases of a disaster situation'.[13] To his mind, even if R2P were to be recognised in the context of the protection of persons in the event of disasters

> its implication would be unclear. For example, to what extent would the responsibility create rights for third parties? What would the content of those rights be? What would trigger those rights? Would those rights be singular or collective?[14]

---

[11] ILC, 'Report of the International Law Commission: Fifty-Eighth Session (1 May–9 June and 3 July–11 August 2006)', UN Doc. A/61/10, annex C, para. 9 (fn. omitted).

[12] ILC, 'Preliminary Report on the Protection of Persons in the Event of Disasters by Mr Eduardo Valencia-Ospina, Special Rapporteur', UN Doc. A/CN.4/598, 5 May 2008.

[13] *Ibid.*, para. 55.　[14] *Ibid.*

The Commission was of two minds on the issue. Some members considered a treatment of R2P as being inevitable and suggested that the Special Rapporteur discuss the matter further in a future report.[15] Others 'doubted the existence of a responsibility to protect, particularly in the context of disasters' and felt that '[i]ts emergence as a principle was confined to extreme circumstances, namely situations of persistent and gross violations of human rights and could not be easily transferable to disaster relief without State support'.[16] This difference of opinion was largely echoed by the governments in the Sixth Committee of the General Assembly, upon considering the report of the Commission later that year.[17]

---

[15] ILC, 'Report of the International Law Commission: Sixtieth Session (5 May–6 June and 7 July–8 August 2008)', UN Doc. A/63/10, para. 247.

[16] *Ibid.*, para. 248. Some ILC members were also of the view that R2P had 'a bearing on humanitarian intervention' and that it 'was still primarily a political and a moral concept the legal parameters of which were yet to be developed and did not change the law relating to the use of force', and accordingly that the 'Commission should ... be cautious in its approach' (*ibid.*, para. 249).

[17] Those that favoured the consideration of R2P as an aspect of the disasters topic included the Nordic countries, who 'considered R2P to be "central" to the topic' (UNGA Official Records, UN Doc. A/C.6/63/SR.22, para. 55); Poland, '[the] emerging concept of responsibility to protect was closely connected to the changing understanding of the principle of sovereignty, as encompassing not only rights but also responsibilities towards all persons under the State's jurisdiction to ensure that they were free from fear and want, and not only from acts of aggression by other States ... [there was] no compelling reason why the responsibility to protect could not be extended to disaster situations' (UNGA Official Records, UN Doc. A/C.6/63/SR.24, para. 51); Portugal, '[t]he concept of "responsibility to protect" must also be taken into account' (UNGA Official Records, UN Doc. A/C.6/63/SR.25, para. 6). A number of States doubted the relevance of R2P in the context of disasters, including India, 'the concept "Responsibility to protect" was not relevant to the topic, as the State concerned bore primary responsibility for the protection of persons in its territory or within its jurisdiction' (UNGA Official Records, UN Doc. A/C.6/63/SR.23, para. 20); China, '"Responsibility to protect" was a new concept, surrounded by uncertainty ... [i]t would not be helpful to introduce that concept into the area of disaster relief' (*ibid.*, para. 31); Japan, '[t]he emerging concept of responsibility to protect was confined to extreme circumstances, for example, where there were persistent and gross violations of human rights, such as genocide, and it should not automatically be applied to the topic of disaster relief' (*ibid.*, para. 42); Malaysia, 'the concept ... related to the responsibility to protect populations from genocide, war crimes, ethnic cleansing and crimes against humanity' (*ibid.*, para. 80); the United States, '[had] objections to incorporating the concept of the responsibility to protect' (*ibid.*, para. 86); Iran, 'the concept of the responsibility to protect was designed to secure the protection of the civilian population from genocide, war crimes and crimes against humanity, and was therefore a completely different topic' (UN Doc. A/C.6/63/SR.24, para. 42); Russian Federation, '[t]he concept of a "responsibility to protect" had

This difference of position was largely settled in 2009 in the direction of *excluding* R2P from the scope of the disasters topic following the issuance that year of the report of the Secretary-General of the United Nations on implementing the responsibility to protect, which maintained that:

> The responsibility to protect applies, until Member States decide otherwise, only to the four specified crimes and violations: genocide, war crimes, ethnic cleansing and crimes against humanity. To try to extend it to cover other calamities, such as HIV/AIDS, climate change or *the response to natural disasters*, would undermine the 2005 consensus and stretch the concept beyond recognition or operational utility.[18]

The Commission agreed with the conclusion of the Special Rapporteur that the position taken by the Secretary-General had confirmed the non-applicability of the R2P concept to the disasters topic, albeit without prejudice to its possible relevance in the future.[19] That decision was generally endorsed by the governments in the Sixth Committee later that year.[20] The relevance of the R2P concept was raised again in the Commission in 2011, during the debate on the fourth report of the

no place in the topic' (UN Doc. A/C.6/63/SR.25, para. 5). Austria maintained that a State's duty not to reject an offer of help arbitrarily and to allow access to victims 'could be deduced from human rights law, irrespective of any responsibility to protect' (UN Doc. A/C.6/63/SR.23, para. 10).

[18] UN Secretary-General, 'Implementing the Responsibility to Protect', UN Doc. A/63/677, para. 14(c) (emphasis added). See also the position taken by the Secretariat of the Commission, 'the concept of the "responsibility to protect", as formulated in the 2005 World Summit Outcome, was not conceived to apply in the context of disasters', in ILC, 'Protection of Persons in the Event of Disasters', UN Doc. A/CN.4/590, 11 December 2007, para. 250 (fn. omitted).

[19] ILC, 'Report of the International Law Commission: Sixty-First Session (5 May–6 June and 7 July–8 August 2008)', UN Doc. A/64/10, para. 164.

[20] The decision of the Commission was supported by China (UNGA Official Records, UN Doc. A/C.6/64/SR.20, para. 22), United Kingdom (*ibid.*, para. 39), Czech Republic (*ibid.*, para. 43), Russian Federation (*ibid.*, para. 46), Spain (*ibid.*, para. 48), Cuba (UNGA Official Records, UN Doc. A/C.6/64/SR.21, para. 10), Thailand (*ibid.*, para. 16), Venezuela (*ibid.*, para. 41), Sri Lanka (*ibid.*, para. 54), Ghana (UNGA Official Records, UN Doc. A/C.6/64/SR.22, 8 February 2010, para. 12), Ireland (*ibid.*, para. 14), Iran (*ibid.*, para. 82; and UNGA Official Records, UN Doc. A/C.6/65/SR.24, 1 December 2010, para. 36) and Israel (UN Doc. A/C.6/64/SR.22, para. 40). Only Poland (UN Doc. A/C.6/64/SR.21, para. 76; and UNGA Official Records, UN Doc. A/C.6/65/SR.23, para. 101) took a contrary view. The following year Hungary expressed the view that 'the widely accepted principle of the responsibility to protect, should be kept in mind' (UNGA Official Records, UN Doc. A/C.6/65/SR.21, para. 33), and Austria noted that '[a]lthough the Commission had discarded the concept of responsibility to protect, international law might evolve' (UN Doc. A/C.6/65/SR.23, para. 39).

Special Rapporteur,[21] in the context of the discussion of the possible duty of the affected State not to arbitrarily withhold its consent to external assistance, but was not pursued owing to the decision taken in 2009.[22]

Nonetheless, some of the considerations underlying the R2P concept have found their parallel in the Commission's work on disasters, particularly as relating to the above-mentioned issue of whether an absolute regime of State consent was to be recognised, or whether, in exceptional circumstances, a State affected by a disaster was under an international obligation to accept humanitarian assistance from abroad. The Secretariat, in its study on the topic,[23] took the latter view, albeit cautiously without reference to a broader *'droit d'ingérence'* which is an equivalent to R2P in the literature on humanitarian assistance.[24] It chose to focus on the mechanism of requesting and offering assistance and identified a trend in favour of 'greater recognition of a positive duty on affected States to request assistance, at least where the domestic response capacity is overwhelmed by a disaster ... which would constrain [an affected State's] ability to decline offers of assistance, and would suggest that consent should not be arbitrarily withheld'.[25]

The Special Rapporteur took a similar view in his fourth report in which he posited a dual duty on the affected State to 'seek assistance from among third States, the United Nations, other competent intergovernmental organisations and relevant non-governmental organisations if the disaster exceeds its national response capacity' and a duty not to withhold consent arbitrarily 'if the affected State is unable or unwilling to provide the assistance required'.[26] The latter scenario of an affected State being 'unwilling' to provide assistance in the context of a calamity, thereby triggering the right of the international community to intervene, is perhaps the closest parallel to the R2P concept. However, it is instructive to consider the Commission's response to that part of the Special Rapporteur's proposal, by way of illustrating the difficulty that arises

---

[21] ILC, 'Fourth Report on the Protection of Persons in the Event of Disasters by Eduardo Valencia-Ospina, Special Rapporteur', UN Doc. A/CN.4/643, 11 May 2011; and the corresponding corrigendum, UN Doc. A/CN.4/643/Corr.1, 8 July 2011.

[22] ILC, 'Sixty-Third Session', para. 286.

[23] UN Doc. A/CN.4/590; and the corresponding addenda, UN Doc. A/CN.4/590/Add.1, 26 February 2008; UN Doc. A/CN.4/590/Add.2, 31 March 2008; and UN Doc. A/CN.4/590/ Add.3, 19 June 2008.

[24] See, for a discussion on the *'devoir d'ingérence'*, UN Doc. A/CN.4/590, fn. 756.

[25] *Ibid.*, paras. 57 and 65.

[26] UN Doc. A/CN.4/643, para. 44, draft art. 10; *ibid.*, para. 77, draft art. 11; UN Doc. A/CN.4/643/Corr.1.

when trying to convert a political concept into legal terms. The Commission established, in draft article 9, a positive duty on the affected State 'to ensure the protection of persons and provision of disaster relief and assistance on its territory'.[27] When coming to the Special Rapporteur's proposal concerning affected States being 'unwilling' to provide assistance to their people, some members took exception for the technical reason that, as a matter of drafting, it would be unusual to be, in effect, expressly anticipating the violation of draft article 9.[28]

The Commission subsequently adopted, in 2011, two draft articles recognising the duty of the affected State to seek assistance when a disaster exceeds its national response capacity (draft article 10) as well as not to withhold consent to external assistance arbitrarily (draft article 11).[29] Neither provision, however, seeks to pronounce on the legal consequences that arise for failure to perform either of those obligations, including, in particular, the consequential rights (or even obligations) of third States or the international community as a whole that may flow from such non-performance (which would more fully track the contours of the R2P project). While the Commission has largely stayed away from such issues in the disasters topic, they were considered, in a more general way, in its earlier work on State responsibility.

'Collective countermeasures' in the regime on State responsibility

One of the components of the R2P concept is the idea that, presented with a manifest failure by a State to protect its population from genocide, war crimes, ethnic cleansing and crimes against humanity, the Member States of the United Nations are 'prepared to take collective action ... through the Security Council, in accordance with the Charter, including

---

[27] See ILC, 'Sixty-Third Session', para. 288.

[28] See for example, the view expressed by Prof. Alain Pellet, 'opposé au fait de mettre sur le même pied, dans le paragraphe 1 du projet d'article 11, la situation dans laquelle l'État n'a pas la capacité de faire face et celle dans laquelle il n'en a pas la volonté. L'État peut évidemment manquer de moyens, ce que l'on ne saurait lui reprocher, mais il n'a pas le droit de manquer de volonté: il doit vouloir aider ses populations affectées. Or, si l'on accepte ... on semblera admettre que l'État peut se décharger sur la communauté internationale ou sur d'autres États de sa responsabilité de protéger, ce qui serait incompatible avec le paragraphe 1 du projet d'article 9' (ILC, 'Provisional Summary Record of the 3102nd Meeting', UN Doc. A/CN.4/SR.3102, 25 January 2012).

[29] See *ibid.*, para. 288. The related issue of the right of the international community to offer assistance was left over to the following session.

Chapter VII ... should peaceful means be inadequate'.[30] The notion of action taken by third States in response to a breach of international law is not a new one. Under the contemporary international arrangement most such action, particularly that involving the collective use of force, has been reserved to the domain of the Security Council. Yet, there exists within the accepted body of international law some recognition of the practice, however embryonic, of action, whether collective or not, being taken, outside of the context of the Security Council, in response to violations of obligations owed to a group of States or to the international community as a whole.

One such possibility is recognised in the 2001 articles on State responsibility, adopted by the International Law Commission, which includes article 54 on 'measures taken by states other than an injured state'. It is admitted upfront that any similarity with the R2P project implied herein is only partial, and the example of article 54 is being advanced only tentatively. The differences between the two are important and should be borne in mind: in particular, the concept developed by the Commission, contrary to R2P, refers to action by States taken *outside* of existing institutional arrangements, such as the Charter of the United Nations.[31] The regime established by the 2001 articles on State responsibility is being referred to here by way of illustration of the fact that, notwithstanding its position taken thus far on the R2P project, the Commission actually did consider, in the past, an arrangement with a similar objective to R2P.

A less-known fact about its work on State responsibility is that the Commission completed the draft articles over what amounted to three, as opposed to the usual two, readings. A complete set was finalised in 2000 and attached to the report of the Commission of that year and sent to the governments for comment.[32] On the basis of the comments

---

[30] '2005 World Summit Outcome', para. 139.

[31] ILC, 'Fifty-Third Session', p. 350, art. 54, commentary, para. 2. Nonetheless, only 'lawful' measures are envisaged, in the sense that they themselves have to conform with international law including the rules constraining the resort to the use of force existing under the Charter of the United Nations: 'non-forcible countermeasures must be clearly distinguished from reactions involving the use of force. Measures involving the use of force in international relations, or otherwise covered by article 2(4) of the Charter, are regulated by the relevant primary rules, and do not fall within the scope of the secondary obligations covered by the draft articles [on the responsibility of states for internationally wrongful acts]' (ILC, 'Third Report on State Responsibility by Mr James Crawford, Special Rapporteur: Addendum', UN Doc. A/CN.4/507/Add.4, 4 August 2000, para. 389).

[32] ILC, 'Report of the International Law Commission on the Work of Its Fifty-Second Session (1 May–9 June and 10 July–18 August 2000)', UN Doc. A/55/10, p. 65, ch. 4, annex.

communicated in the Sixth Committee that year, the Commission set about finalising a revised version which it adopted in 2001. One of the major changes made between the 2000 and 2001 versions pertained to draft article 54. The version adopted in 2000 read as follows:

Article 54. Countermeasures by States other than the injured State

1. Any State entitled under article 49, paragraph 1, to invoke the responsibility of a State may take countermeasures at the request and on behalf of any State injured by the breach, to the extent that that State may itself take countermeasures under this chapter.
2. In the cases referred to in article 41, any State may take countermeasures, in accordance with the present chapter in the interest of the beneficiaries of the obligation breached.
3. Where more than one State takes countermeasures, the States concerned shall cooperate in order to ensure that the conditions laid down by this chapter for the taking of countermeasures are fulfilled.

The provision was based on an earlier proposal by the Special Rapporteur, James Crawford, for what he called 'collective countermeasures', by which he meant responses to violations of *collective* obligations, namely those owed to more than one State (in the case of a multilateral treaty), or those owed *erga omnes*, that is, to the international community as a whole.[33] The other sense of the word 'collective', namely countermeasures taken *jointly* by States, was implicit, as evident in paragraph 3. Accordingly, those third States entitled to invoke the responsibility of a wrongdoing State (by virtue of the fact that the wrongful actions of that State violated an obligation owed to them or to the international community as a whole) would also be entitled to take countermeasures in order to induce the State to comply with its obligations. Such right was subject to several restrictions on the nature and duration of the countermeasures as well as on the types of obligations which may be the subject of countermeasures.[34]

Of particular interest here is paragraph 2 referring to then draft article 41 which, in the 2000 version, covered serious breaches of *erga omnes* obligations, that is, those 'owed to the international community as a whole and essential for the protection of its fundamental interests'.[35]

---

[33] UN Doc. A/CN.4/507/Add.4, para. 386.
[34] ILC, 'Fifty-Second Session', p. 70, draft arts. 50–3.
[35] See *Barcelona Traction*. See also *Case Concerning East Timor (Portugal v. Australia), Judgment*, ICJ Reports 1995, p. 102, para. 29, '[i]n the Court's view, Portugal's assertion that the right of peoples to self-determination, as it evolved from the Charter and from United Nations practice, has an *erga omnes* character, is irreproachable.' And *Case Concerning the Application of the Convention on the Prevention and Punishment of the*

That draft article was also narrowed down in the shift from the 2000 to the 2001 texts, so as to eventually refer to 'an obligation arising under a peremptory norm of general international law'.[36] While peremptory norms (*jus cogens*) give rise to obligations having an *erga omnes* effect, not all *erga omnes* obligations enjoy a peremptory status.[37] It is the view of the present writer that the crimes referred to in the World Summit Outcome (to the extent codified in Rome Statute) *also* enjoy a peremptory status under international law, even if such designation is not particularly necessary for their classification as 'international crimes'. To maintain otherwise would be to recognise that there may be situations where non-compliance could be lawful,[38] which is hard to conceive of, for example, in the way the crime of genocide is defined. Nor would it accord with the status of 'crimes' under international law.

The net effect of this, therefore, is that, to the extent that the crimes referred to in the R2P project give rise to obligations (of the State in question) owed *erga omnes*,[39] such as to prevent the occurrence of

Crime of Genocide (Bosnia and Herzegovina v. *Serbia and Montenegro), Preliminary Objections, Judgment*, ICJ Reports 1996, p. 595, para. 31.

[36] ILC, 'Fifty-Third Session', p. 282, art. 40. *Ibid.*, art. 41, further recognises specific consequences arising from a serious breach of a peremptory norm – in addition to the consequences flowing from a breach of a regular international obligation – namely the legal requirement to cooperate to bring to an end through lawful means the serious breach; as well as the requirement of non-recognition of the lawfulness of the situation created by the breach, and prohibits providing aid or assistance in maintaining such situation.

[37] Peremptory norms are defined in Article 53 of the Vienna Convention on the Law of Treaties, '[f]or the purposes of the present Convention, a peremptory norm of general international law is a norm accepted and recognized by the international community of States as a whole as a norm from which no derogation is permitted and which can be modified only by a subsequent norm of general international law having the same character' (Vienna Convention on the Law of Treaties, adopted 22 May 1969 and entered into force 27 January 1980, 1155 UNTS 331, art. 53).

[38] Situations of non-compliance being nonetheless lawful – excused through the preclusion of wrongfulness – are to be distinguished from those where allegations of criminal activity were not proved, for example, by means of the successful assertion of available criminal defences or procedural protections.

[39] See *Barcelona Traction*, para. 34, '[s]uch [*erga omnes*] obligations derive, for example, in contemporary international law, from the outlawing of acts of aggression, and of genocide, as also from the principles and rules concerning the basic rights of the human person, including protection from slavery and racial discrimination.' The importance of such designation pertains also to the range of possibilities for the invocation of international responsibility. Under the scheme of the 2001 articles, a State may be considered injured (and thereby entitled to invoke responsibility) by an act (or omission) committed by another State in breach of an obligation owed to a group of States, including that State (*erga omnes partes*), or owed to the international community as a whole (*erga omnes*), if the injured State is, among other things, specially affected by the breach. See

genocide and to protect civilians in times of armed conflict, then, under the 2000 version of draft article 54, any State, whether acting singularly or jointly with other States, having invoked the responsibility of the wrongdoing State, would be entitled to 'take countermeasures ... in the interest of the beneficiaries of the obligation breached'. The significance of the latter reference was that, in addition to the traditional position of a third State taking countermeasures in support of an injured State (covered by paragraph 1), the draft provision went further and anticipated third States taking countermeasures on behalf of 'beneficiaries of the obligation breached', which would certainly include victims of gross violations of human rights obligations such as those envisaged in the crimes covered by the R2P.

Such possibility of third State action on behalf of rights-holders was posited as a right ('may') as opposed to an obligation ('shall'), which left it to the discretion of the third State or States, and, accordingly implied no legal consequences if no action was taken. This is perhaps another difference with the R2P concept which employs the more ambiguous term 'responsibility', suggesting an obligation to act even if not necessarily legal in nature – that is, it is not clear what the *legal* consequences of failure to exercise such responsibility would be.

In proposing the inclusion of a specific draft article[40] on such 'collective countermeasures', the Special Rapporteur cited a number of examples of State practice where States had reacted – individually or jointly – in response to violations of collective obligations, even though they could not themselves claim to have been directly injured by those violations.[41]

ILC, 'Fifty-Third Session', p. 294, art. 42. In addition, third States – i.e., States other than the injured State – are entitled to invoke the responsibility of the wrongdoing State if the obligation breached is owed, among others, to the international community as a whole (*ibid.*, p. 319, art. 48(1)(b)). It should be noted that the Commission – perhaps differently from R2P as conceptualized in 2005 – did not limit the possibility of invocation in the context of breaches of *erga omnes* obligations to legally interested States: in its 2011 draft articles on the responsibility of international organisations, the Commission expressly recognised the possibility that international organisations may also enjoy the right to invoke the responsibility of other international organisations – not States – for such breaches either directly as injured international organisations (ILC, 'Sixty-Third Session', p. 134, art. 43) or indirectly for breaches of *erga omnes* obligations (*ibid.*, p. 143, art. 49).

[40] While no equivalent provision had been proposed, the idea of countermeasures taken by non-injured States was implicit in the first reading text, adopted in 1996. See UN Doc. A/CN.4/507/Add.4, para. 389.

[41] Those examples of State practice found their way into the commentary to the final version of Article 54. See ILC, 'Fifty-Third Session', pp. 351–3, art. 54, commentary, para. 3.

Some of those responses amounted to countermeasures, as envisaged by the draft articles, because they were themselves prima facie wrongful acts, but were justified by the fact that they were being taken in response to a prior breach.[42] He drew the conclusion that '[t]his seems to suggest that a right to resort to countermeasures cannot be restricted to the victims of the breach in question, but can also derive from violations of collective obligations'.[43] At the same time, he qualified the conclusions as being 'necessarily tentative', with the practice being sparse and involving a limited number of States.[44] Yet:

> [a]s a matter of policy, the constraints and inhibitions against collective countermeasures – in particular, concern about due process for the allegedly responsible State, the problem of intervention in and possible exacerbation of an individual dispute – are substantially reduced where the breach concerned is gross, well-attested, systematic and continuing. To disallow collective countermeasures in such cases does not seem appropriate. Indeed to do so may place further pressure on States to intervene in other, perhaps less desirable ways. It is not the function of the Commission to examine in the present context the lawfulness of humanitarian intervention in response to gross breaches of community obligations. But at least it can be said that international law should offer to States with a legitimate interest in compliance with such obligations, some means of securing compliance which does not involve the use of force.[45]

Although the Commission, in 2000, approved the version of draft article 54 reproduced above, it was not without controversy. Concerns were expressed, for example, that it amounted to a 'system of multilateral public order' and that '[p]remature efforts to create rules about collective countermeasures could damage both the draft articles and the gradual development of the new notions that had been referred to'.[46] It was maintained that 'support for collective countermeasures was only possible in the context of the action of competent international organisations, whether regional or universal'.[47]

---

[42] 'Unfriendly acts', such as retorsions, and even non-recognition, regardless of the nature of the obligation in reaction to the violation they are taken, are prima facie lawful and therefore would not need to be covered by a regime of countermeasures.

[43] UN Doc. A/CN.4/507/Add.4, para. 395.   [44] *Ibid.*, para. 401 (fn. omitted).

[45] *Ibid.*, para. 405.   [46] ILC, 'Fifty-Second Session', p. 60, para. 365.

[47] *Ibid.*, para. 366. The draft articles on the responsibility of international organisations, adopted by the Commission in 2011, do not cover the taking of countermeasures by international organisations against responsible States. Accordingly, the equivalent provision (draft article 57) to Article 54 of the 2001 articles on State responsibility, only envisages non-injured States or international organisations taking countermeasures, in

The reaction of the Sixth Committee later that year was equally luke-warm, with concerns being expressed by a significant number of States (United Kingdom,[48] China,[49] Germany,[50] Israel,[51] Botswana,[52] Australia,[53] Austria,[54] Jordan,[55] Poland[56] and Cuba[57]). Only Spain,[58] Italy,[59] Chile[60] and Costa Rica[61] expressed support. Some governments such as Mexico[62]

[48] 'Even accepting the proposition, on the basis of the *Barcelona Traction* case, that States at large had a legal interest in respect of violations of certain obligations, it did not necessarily follow that all States could vindicate those interests in the same way as directly injured States' (UNGA Official Records, UN Doc. A/C.6/55/SR.14, para. 31).

the collective interest, against a responsible international organisation, which at present no examples of practice seem to exist. See ILC, 'Sixty-Third Session', p. 52, para. 87.

[49] '[Draft art. 54] would ... run counter to the basic principle that countermeasures should and could be taken only by a country injured by an internationally wrongful act' (*ibid.*, para. 40).

[50] '[T]here was a danger that disproportional unilateral acts, which in reality were not justified by the interest they sought to protect, might be disguised countermeasures. That would threaten the credibility of the concept' (*ibid.*, para. 54).

[51] '[S]uch [provision] would have a destabilizing effect by creating a parallel mechanism for responding to serious breaches which lacked the coordinated, balanced and collective features of existing mechanisms' (UNGA Official Records, UN Doc. A/C.6/55/SR.15, para. 25).

[52] '[T]he scope of draft article 54 was too wide' (*ibid.*, para. 63).

[53] 'The [phrase] "in the interest of the beneficiaries" ... ought to be clarified in order to elucidate the scope of ... draft article 54' (UNGA Official Records, UN Doc. A/C.6/55/SR.16, para. 41).

[54] 'The provision was confusing' (UNGA Official Records, UN Doc. A/C.6/55/SR.17, para. 77).

[55] '[T]he issue of whether to authorize "any" State to take countermeasures against the author of a serious breach of the essential obligations owed to the international community needed to be studied further. It was hard to envisage how the principle of proportionality could be respected if "any" State was authorized to take countermeasures, as it deemed appropriate' (UNGA Official Records, UN Doc. A/C.6/55/SR.18, para. 17).

[56] '[H]ad serious doubts about the formulation used in article 54, paragraph 2 ... Although there was a trend in that direction, it hardly reflected the general practice of States' (*ibid.*, para. 48).

[57] '[C]ountermeasures in the interest of the beneficiaries of the obligation breached went well beyond the progressive development of international law' (*ibid.*, para. 59).

[58] '[C]ould accept ... the proposal contained in article 54, paragraph 2' (UN Doc. A/C.6/55/SR.16, para. 13).

[59] *Ibid.*, para. 28.   [60] UN Doc. A/C.6/55/SR.17, para. 48.

[61] 'In principle, the consequences stipulated in ... draft article 54, paragraph 2, were acceptable' (*ibid.*, para. 63).

[62] 'It was not appropriate to alter the principles of the Charter by allowing for collective countermeasures, undertaken unilaterally, without the involvement of the central body of the international community, leaving it up to the individual State to decide whether there had been a serious breach, what sort of countermeasure should be applied and under what circumstances they should be lifted. The latitude fostered by such a system was incompatible with the institutional system that had been created in 1945' (UNGA Official Records, UN Doc. A/C.6/55/SR.20, para. 36).

and Cameroon[63] expressed concern as to the possible effect on the Charter system, and Iran[64] and Greece[65] insisted that the only avenue open was that envisaged in the Charter of the United Nations.

One can presumably ascribe some of the negative views to the reluctance of Member States of the United Nations to endorse actions taken outside the organisation (a complication which does not arise in the R2P context). Nonetheless, it was particularly striking that governments drew the opposite inference, from that drawn five years later in the World Summit Outcome Document, as to the advisability – as a matter of policy – of action taken by third States, in the words of the Commission, 'in the interest of the beneficiaries of the obligation breached'. Many chose to focus on the possibility of abuse,[66] as opposed to the potential for ensuring the protection of victims. While the purpose here is not to speculate on the political context in which the various positions were taken, it is worth pointing out that the recent 'humanitarian intervention' in Kosovo was fresh in the minds of many delegations at the time.[67]

---

[63] '[C]oncerned that draft article 54, which had not been included in the text adopted on first reading, might lead to the taking of multilateral or collective countermeasures simultaneously with other measures taken by the competent United Nations bodies; the draft articles must not be allowed to create overlapping legal regimes that could weaken the Organization as a whole or marginalize the Security Council ... The situations envisaged in draft article 54 were adequately dealt with under Articles 39 to 41 of the Charter of the United Nations, which was the best expression of the will of the community of States' (UNGA Official Records, UN Doc. A/C.6/55/SR.24, para. 64).

[64] '[W]here there had been a serious breach of an essential obligation owed to the international community as a whole, countermeasures must be coordinated by the United Nations' (UN Doc. A/C.6/55/SR.15, para. 17).

[65] '[C]ountermeasures should not be taken unilaterally by any State if the organized international community was seized of the matter through the Security Council' (UN Doc. A/C.6/55/SR.17, para. 85).

[66] See for example, the statements of the United Kingdom, '[a]s they stood, the proposals were potentially highly destabilizing of treaty relations' (UN Doc. A/C.6/55/SR.14, para. 31); China, '[m]ore ominously, "collective countermeasures" could provide a further pretext for power politics in international relations. The reality was that only powerful States and blocs were in a position to take countermeasures, usually against weaker nations' (ibid., para. 40); Botswana, '[i]t was open to abuse by powerful States against a weaker State that they might particularly dislike for other reasons. The role of the one international policeman State should be controlled. A situation in which a State was both judge and jury should be avoided' (UN Doc. A/C.6/55/SR.15, para. 63); Jordan, 'such countermeasures could well provoke an escalation, instead of restoring legality' (UN Doc. A/C.6/55/SR.18, para. 17).

[67] It was alluded to in the statement of Cameroon, 'in the light of the recent and disturbing tendency of some States to take action, including armed intervention, without the [Security] Council's consent' (UN Doc. A/C.6/55/SR.24, para. 64).

As a consequence of this, the following year the Commission decided that, in light of the controversy that draft article 54 and, in particular, paragraph 2, had generated, it was advisable to take a more cautious approach, albeit not simply to delete the draft article, since doing so would:

> [C]arry the implication that countermeasures could only be taken by injured States, narrowly defined. The state of international law on measures taken in the general or common interest [was] no doubt uncertain. But [it could not] be the case ... that countermeasures in aid of compliance with international law [were] limited to breaches affecting the individual interests of powerful States or their allies. Obligations towards the international community, or otherwise in the collective interest, [were] not 'second-class' obligations by comparison with obligations under bilateral treaties. While it [could] be hoped that international organizations [would] be able to resolve the humanitarian or other crises that often arise from serious breaches of international law, States have not abdicated their powers of individual action.[68]

Article 54 was instead adopted as part of the final draft articles in 2001 in the form of a saving clause, which reads as follows:

> This chapter does not prejudice the right of any State, entitled under article 48, paragraph 1, to invoke the responsibility of another State, to take lawful measures against that State to ensure cessation of the breach and reparation in the interest of the injured State or of the beneficiaries of the obligation breached.

The commentary to the provision confirms, in cautionary terms, the final view of the Commission that '[a]t present, there appears to be no clearly recognized entitlement of [legally interested] States ... to take countermeasures in the collective interest. Consequently, it is not appropriate to include in the present articles a provision concerning the question whether other States ... are permitted to take countermeasures in order to induce a responsible State to comply with its obligations.'[69] This latter point was, instead, expressly reserved leaving 'the resolution of the matter to the further development of international law'.[70]

Conclusion

As a political statement of common will, it is increasingly evident that the assertion by States, in 2005, of a joint responsibility to protect victims

---

[68] ILC, 'Fourth Report on State Responsibility by Mr James Crawford, Special Rapporteur', UN Doc. A/CN.4/517, 2 April 2001, para. 74.

[69] ILC, 'Fifty-Third Session', p. 355, art. 54 commentary, para. 6.   [70] *Ibid.*

of gross and systematic violations of human rights and humanitarian law such as genocide, war crimes, ethnic cleansing and crimes against humanity, was a seminal event in the history of the United Nations (and perhaps in that of the fight against impunity more broadly). What is less clear is the effect R2P has had on the existing corpus of international law. From the perspective of the International Law Commission, the concept has thus far had limited impact on its work. Nor does it seem likely that this will change anytime soon. Such a state of affairs is due in part to the fact that the issue has still to be placed squarely before the Commission for its consideration. It might also be a function of a more cautious approach taken in the wake of the Commission's recent experience with proposing its own arrangement for the protection of collective obligations.

PART III

Regional and security organisations

9

The European Union

DANIEL FIOTT AND MARIE VINCENT

Introduction

In its own right and as a partner in the international division of labour, the European Union (EU or Union) has widely been recognised as an actor with a key role to play in upholding and implementing the responsibility to protect (RtoP). Commentators have pointed to the special legacy of the EU as the embodiment of a unique model of cooperation which, in the aftermath of the Second World War, was successful in substituting force with the rule of law through the gradual and voluntary transfer of national sovereignty – first in the economic sphere and increasingly in the political one. Passing the test of successive enlargements, the European integration process proved its 'transformative power', securing an extended area of peace and prosperity through the use of strict membership conditionality in areas such as democracy, the rule of law, respect for human rights, respect for and protection of minorities and the market economy.[1] Consolidating a Union of more than 500 million citizens from twenty-seven Member States previously torn by war and political division in what has become the world's largest economy, the European project has been hailed as 'possibly the world's most successful conflict prevention model',[2] allegedly earning by its very nature positive authority to engage in the defence and promotion of RtoP.

In its ambition to assert itself as a relevant global actor, the EU has established a clear link between its internal values and the objectives of its external action. Article 21 of the Lisbon Treaty (2009), which innovates in setting general provisions on the EU's external action, thus reads:

[1] The Copenhagen Criteria were established by the European Council in 1993 in view of the accession of Member States from Eastern Europe.
[2] Gareth Evans, *The Responsibility to Protect: Ending Mass Atrocity Crimes Once and for All* (Washington, DC: Brookings Institution Press, 2008), p. 183.

> The Union's action on the international scene shall be guided by the
> principles that have inspired its own creation, development and enlarge-
> ment, and which it seeks to advance in the wider world: democracy,
> the rule of law, the universality and indivisibility of human rights and
> fundamental freedoms, respect for human dignity, the principles of
> equality and solidarity, and respect for the principles of the United
> Nations and international law.[3]

In line with its commitment to 'effective multilateralism', the EU also
reasserts that it shall seek to develop relations with international partners
and 'promote multilateral solutions to common problems, in particular
in the framework of the United Nations (UN)'.[4]

More specifically, and of direct relevance to RtoP, the EU sees conflict
prevention and peacebuilding as key objectives of its external action
and a core part of its Common Foreign and Security Policy (CFSP),
while increasing its crisis management capabilities under the Common
Security and Defence Policy (CSDP). With the adoption of the Göteborg
Programme for the Prevention of Violent Conflicts (2001), the EU
pledged to take action at four levels: in setting clear political priorities
for preventive actions; in improving its early warning, action and policy
coherence; in enhancing its instruments for long- and short-term prevention; and in building effective partnerships for prevention.[5]

The EU has since worked to integrate preventive strategies in its many
policy areas, developing a broad range of distinctive economic, political
and civilian–military tools that have been seen to complement the work
of organisations such as the UN, the North Atlantic Treaty Organization
(NATO), the Organization for Security and Co-operation in Europe
(OSCE) and the African Union (AU).[6] In accordance with conceptual
developments at the UN level and in line with the discourse on human
security,[7] the EU has adopted a comprehensive approach, linking

---

[3] Consolidated version of the Treaty on European Union, 2010 OJ C 83/13, art. 21, para. 1.
[4] The notion of effective multilateralism was officially introduced in the European Security
Strategy. European Council, *A Secure Europe in a Better World: European Security
Strategy*, 12 December 2003.
[5] European Council, 'EU Programme for the Prevention of Violent Conflicts', EU Council
Doc. 9537/1/01 REV 1, 7 June 2001, p. 1.
[6] See respectively Prescott, Chapter 15; Sandole, Chapter 14; and Dersso, Chapter 10 in this
book.
[7] The human security approach has influenced a number of UN documents since the
United Nations Development Programme's 1994 Human Development Report, which
relates international security to the need to ensure individuals' 'freedom from want' and
'freedom from fear' (UNDP, *1994 Human Development Report* (New York: Oxford
University Press, 1994)).

security to development and human rights considerations. Accordingly, it has made use of 'positive' measures – such as financial assistance (including development and humanitarian aid), membership conditionality, election observation missions, political dialogue and mediation – but also of 'negative' measures, including sanctions such as the suspension of aid, asset freezing, travel bans and arms embargoes. Moreover, since the creation of CSDP, the EU has become increasingly competent in the deployment of civilian missions, developing expertise in policing, justice and the rule of law, while also developing military capabilities, partly in coordination with NATO.

And, yet, for all its potential added value, experience has seen the EU often failing to live up to its foreign policy commitments. With operations often politically and materially under-resourced, the civilian and military 'capabilities–expectations gap' continues to impact on the Union's international credibility.[8] Furthermore, the EU has come under increased scrutiny for its lack of consistency and double standards in its approach to human rights and good governance in third countries, with events in North Africa exposing the ambiguous founding principles of the European Neighbourhood Policy – seemingly more concerned with issues such as the control of migration rather than the promotion of genuine democratic values. The specific crisis in Libya has also exposed the EU's continued difficulties in achieving consensus on the use of force. It is likely that as long as the Member States retain their foreign policy prerogatives, the EU will often only be able to articulate positions reflecting the lowest common denominator, at the expense of its own response. Hopes have been raised that the European External Action Service (EEAS) under the guidance of the High Representative for Foreign Affairs and Security Policy, also Vice-President of the European Commission (HR/VP), will develop a diplomatic culture of its own through the fusion of staff from the European Commission, the Council of the EU and national diplomatic institutions. However, in view of the economic crisis the EU is confronted with, it is likely that economic reform issues will continue to dominate the EU agenda for some time to come, at the likely expense of advancing its external action.

This chapter aims to provide an overview of the EU's RtoP efforts. It seeks to analyse the difference between the EU's words and deeds on RtoP by giving a balanced appraisal of the individual and common

---

[8] Christopher Hill, 'The Capability–Expectations Gap, or Conceptualising Europe's International Role', *Journal of Common Market Studies*, 31 (1993), 305–28.

responses of both the EU institutions and the Member States in terms of their political, economic and military resources. The chapter begins by looking at the EU's stated support of and approaches to RtoP. The chapter then provides a survey and analysis of the EU's institutional organisation, and outlines the constellation of individuals and bodies involved in the EU's work on RtoP. Finally, the chapter considers the EU's track record in responding to certain crises since 2005 that have seen the invocation of RtoP, before concluding with recommendations.

The EU's stated commitment to RtoP

The EU's declared support for RtoP is well documented.[9] In its 2008 follow-up report on the European Security Strategy, there is acknowledgement of the 'shared responsibility to protect populations from genocide, war crimes, ethnic cleansing and crimes against humanity'.[10] The current High Representative has also referred to RtoP in a number of official statements, for example on 1 August 2011 when reminding the Syrian authorities to stop its 'brutal violence' against its population,[11] as had her predecessor. The European Consensus on Development (2005) and European Consensus on Humanitarian Aid (2007)[12] also refer to RtoP, with the former reading, '[t]he EU strongly supports the responsibility to protect'.[13] Additionally, the European Parliament has underlined this commitment through a number of non-binding resolutions invoking RtoP. Throughout its public statements, the EU has consistently argued that RtoP should be upheld within the UN framework, under the authority of the UN Security Council (UNSC), and that its primary focus should be on prevention. This has been supported by EU Member States through such initiatives as the informal and cross-regional[14] 'Group of Friends on RtoP',

---

[9] It is noteworthy that 'RtoP' does not appear in the EEAS's 'A to Z' directory of issues, available at www.eeas.europa.eu/a_to_z/a_to_z_en.htm.

[10] European Council, 'Report on the Implementation of the European Security Strategy', EU Council Doc. 17104/08, 10 December 2008, p. 3.

[11] European Council press release, 'Statement of the High Representative on the Extension of Restrictive Measures against Syrian Individuals Responsible for and Associated with Repression', 1 August 2011, available at www.consilium.europa.eu/documents.

[12] European Council, 'The European Consensus on Humanitarian Aid', EU Council Doc. 15099/07, 20 November 2007, para. 4.

[13] European Council, 'The European Consensus on Development', EU Council Doc. 14820/05, 22 November 2005, para. 37.

[14] It is difficult to ascertain which EU Member States are signed up to the initiative, given the lack of transparency over its membership.

which seeks to advance RtoP within the UN system and in regional fora through the release of joint press statements on relevant RtoP crises; the publication of non-papers on issues such as UN capability gaps; and providing financial support for civil society organisations.

The EU's interpretation of RtoP closely follows the wording of the 2005 World Summit Outcome Document, and the 'three-pillar' approach subsequently developed in Ban Ki-moon's 2009 report to the UN General Assembly (UNGA). This approach being defined as: (pillar one) the responsibility of the State to protect its own population from genocide, war crimes, ethnic cleansing and crimes against humanity; (pillar two) the responsibility of the international community to provide assistance and capacity-building to States to protect their own population against the four crimes; and (pillar three) the responsibility of the international community to respond collectively in a timely and decisive manner when a State is unable or unwilling to protect its own population.[15] As reiterated in the Secretary-General's 2011 report on the role of regional and sub-regional organisations in implementing RtoP, the 'three-pillar' approach is indispensable in emphasising the preventive and non-coercive elements of the principle.[16]

In a declaration at the UNGA in support of the 'three-pillar' approach, the 2009 Swedish presidency of the EU specified what relevant instruments might be required of the EU to operationalise RtoP: 'capacity building in areas of conflict prevention, development and human rights, good governance, rule of law and judicial and security sector reform'.[17] Yet again, at the Interactive Dialogue on RtoP – held at the General Assembly on 12 July 2011 – the EU reaffirmed its strong support for the operationalisation of RtoP. The Union also emerged as an advocate for greater dialogue between regional organisations on the 'pillar three' approach, with the EU seeking to move the debate beyond talk of military intervention to include non-military political and economic tools.[18]

---

[15] UNSG, 'Implementing the Responsibility to Protect', UN Doc. A/63/677, 12 January 2009.

[16] UNSG, 'The Role of Regional and Sub-regional Arrangements in Implementing the Responsibility to Protect', UN Doc. A/65/877–S/2011/393, 27 June 2011.

[17] Anders Lidén, Ambassador of Sweden, 'Statement on behalf of the EU', speech delivered at the UN General Assembly Debate on the Responsibility to Protect, New York, 23 July 2009, at www.responsibilitytoprotect.org/EU_Sweden_ENG.pdf.

[18] Pedro Serrano, Former Head of EU Delegation, 'Intervention on behalf of the EU', speech delivered at the Role of Regional and Sub-regional Organisations in Implementing the Responsibility to Protect, New York, 12 July 2011, at www.responsibilitytoprotect.org/EU%20Stmt.pdf.

Within the scope of their national foreign policies, EU Member States have also expressed their commitment to RtoP, but the nuances in each State's treatment of the principle are insightful. Interestingly, some of the Member States, as well as the European Parliament, have sometimes favoured a broader interpretation than the UN 'three-pillar' approach.

France has been a vocal proponent of RtoP, especially during Bernard Kouchner's – the famous advocate of *le droit d'ingérence* – tenure as French Foreign Minister. France has spoken in the past of the 'daily effort' needed for the principle's implementation.[19] Its most vigorous commitment to the RtoP principle can, however, be found in its *White Papers on Defence and National Security* and *on Foreign and European Policy*, both released in 2008. The *White Paper* on defence notably holds the right for France to use military intervention in RtoP situations, should prior examination of all other possible measures give strong reasons to think that they would fail.[20] The *White Paper* on foreign policy, on the other hand, places RtoP in the context of French action on human rights, recalling its triple dimension: 'the responsibility to protect, the responsibility to intervene, if need be through military force, and the responsibility to rebuild'.[21] France has often been an advocate of a broad conceptual interpretation of RtoP, standing against the UN in affirming that the principle should apply to the protection of populations in the aftermath of natural disasters, such as in the case of Cyclone Nargis in Burma.

In contrast, the British 2010 *Human Rights and Democracy*'s emphasis is on strengthening regional early warning structures, especially on the African continent. Accordingly, the government supported the establishment of the Joint Office of the Special Advisers and made financial contributions to the Special Adviser for the Prevention of Genocide's early warning 'conflict pool'.[22] While there exists an Advisory Group on Human Rights (established in 2010), none of its experts include one

---

[19] Jean-Pierre Lacroix, Ambassador of France, 'Statement by Mr Jean-Pierre Lacroix, Deputy Permanent Representative of France to the United Nations', unofficial translation, speech delivered at UNGA Debate on the Responsibility to Protect, New York, 23 July 2009, at www.franceonu.org/spip.php?article4072.

[20] French Ministry of Foreign Affairs, *Le Livre Blanc: Défense et Sécurité Nationale* (Paris: Odile Jacob, 2008), p. 76.

[21] French MFA, 'Le Livre Blanc sur la Politique Étrangère et Européenne de la France 2008–2020 – La France et l'Europe dans le Monde', White Paper, 2008, p. 48.

[22] United Kingdom Foreign and Commonwealth Office, *Human Rights and Democracy: The 2010 Foreign and Commonwealth Office Report* (Norwich, UK: The Stationery Office, 2011), pp. 64–5.

specifically dedicated to RtoP. In 2008, the security review published by the Labour government placed RtoP within its efforts to reform the international system including the need to build 'a better rules-based framework for intervention' so as to act when necessary.[23] In contrast, the present Conservative–Liberal coalition government's 2010 national security review pays no formal attention to RtoP.[24] However, beyond official declarations, experience in Libya has shown that it is ready to act upon the principle, including through military intervention. Finally, the British House of Commons has an All-Party Parliamentary Group on Genocide Prevention, which scrutinises government on its prevention activities.

Germany places RtoP within the Federal Foreign Office's human rights work, although its commitment is weak in its written statements. Indeed, the 2010 human rights report does make mention to RtoP as a 'new' concept, but this treatment is antiquated given the present international emphasis on operationalisation.[25] This is confirmed by the absence of RtoP under the German Commissioner for Human Rights Policy and Humanitarian Aid's portfolio. Furthermore, Germany's *White Paper on German Security Policy and the Future of the Bundeswehr* (2006) treats RtoP as a matter for international law and emphasises the principle's relative infancy, but it does recognise that '[e]ven if the states that have adopted this doctrine are probably still not in the majority, the debate about the Responsibility to Protect is increasingly impacting on the ways of thinking in western countries.'[26]

The Dutch *Human Rights Strategy* (2007), by contrast, reiterates the Netherlands' commitment to operationalising RtoP, and a 2011 Memorandum to the Strategy states that 'the future of [RtoP] lies to a large degree at the regional level'.[27] The Dutch government had also invoked RtoP over the post-Cyclone Nargis crisis in Burma, stating that: '[e]ach individual state has the responsibility to protect its populations.

---

[23] UK Cabinet Office, *The National Security Strategy of the United Kingdom: Security in an Interdependent World* (Norwich, UK: The Stationery Office, 2008), p. 48.

[24] UK Cabinet Office, *Securing Britain in an Age of Uncertainty: The Strategic Defence and Security Review* (Norwich, UK: The Stationery Office, 2010), p. 49.

[25] German Federal Foreign Office, *9. Bericht der Bundesregierung über ihre Menschenrechtspolitik: Berichtszeitraum: 1. März 2008 bis 28* (Berlin: Federal Foreign Office, 2010), p. 75.

[26] German Federal Ministry of Defence, *German White Paper on German Security Policy and the Future of the Bundeswehr* (Berlin: Federal Ministry of Defence, 2006), p. 44.

[27] Netherlands Ministry of Foreign Affairs Memorandum, 'Responsible for Freedom: Human Rights in Foreign Policy', 7 August 2011, p. 21, at www.government.nl/issues/human-rights/human-rights-in-dutch-foreign-policy.

Gross negligence and woefully inadequate responses to threats may actually lead to even greater humanitarian suffering . . . thus forming a ground for action.'[28] The Netherlands also currently co-chairs the 'Group of Friends' on RtoP. It has shown great commitment to the fight against impunity, playing a pivotal role at the EU level to maintain the conditionality of Serbia's membership bid to its full cooperation with the International Criminal Tribunal for the former Yugoslavia (ICTY).

Like the Netherlands, Denmark has placed importance on promoting a regional approach to RtoP.[29] The Danish government's work on RtoP is outlined in its *Strategy for Danish Humanitarian Action, 2010–15* (2009), rather than its strategy on democratisation and human rights (2009),[30] and is one of the few to have appointed a national RtoP focal point in the personage of the Human Rights Ambassador. Denmark, along with Costa Rica and Ghana, held its first meeting of national focal points in New York on 17–18 May 2011. Denmark leads the way on RtoP focal points within the Union, even though the Czech Republic and Spain let it be known at the July 2011 UNGA Interactive Dialogue that they would be appointing national focal points within their respective foreign ministries. But whether these will be formal or informal positions remains unclear.

As one of the leading advocates of the conflict prevention approach in the EU, Sweden had recognised RtoP long before the 2005 World Summit, with a declaration in 2003 stating that the responsibility to protect individuals and their human rights rested principally with governments.[31] RtoP was also mentioned in the outcome declaration of the 2004 Stockholm international forum entitled Preventing Genocide: Threats and Responsibilities organised under the initiative of the Swedish Prime Minister and attended by fifty-five governmental representatives.[32] Sweden treats RtoP as an

[28] Netherlands MFA press release, 'Verhagen puts pressure on Burma in Security Council', 22 May 2008, available at www.government.nl.

[29] Ministry of Foreign Affairs of Denmark, *Strategy for Danish Humanitarian Action 2010–15: Addressing Vulnerability, Climate Change and Protection Challenges* (Copenhagen: Ministry of Foreign Affairs of Denmark, 2009), p. 23.

[30] Ministry of Foreign Affairs of Denmark, *Democratisation and Human Rights for the Benefit of the People: Strategic Priorities for Danish Support for Good Governance* (Copenhagen: Ministry of Foreign Affairs of Denmark, 2009).

[31] Ministry of Foreign Affairs of Sweden, 'Government Communication to Parliament: Human Rights in Swedish Foreign Policy', 30 October 2003, p. 5.

[32] 'Declaration of the Stockholm International Forum on Preventing Genocide: Threats and Responsibilities', in *The Stockholm International Forum Conferences (2000–2004)* (Värnamo, Sweden: Fälth & Hässler, 2006), p. 26, at www.sweden.gov.se/content/1/c6/06/66/96/52af23bc.pdf.

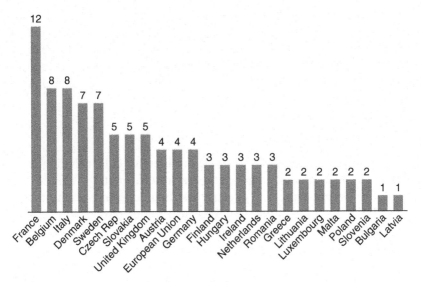

Figure 1 EU statements at the UN (2005–11)

Note: Voting records have been collated from the International Coalition for RtoP's website www.responsibilitytoprotect.org.

aspect of international humanitarian law, but it does not appear among the government's eight human rights in foreign policy priorities.[33] Furthermore, the Göteborg Programme (2001), which was pioneered by Sweden, places an emphasis on the need for the EU to put in place conflict prevention capacities. Sweden has also been among those Member States who recognise that it is time for the EU to seek methods of operationalising the concept.[34]

Many other EU Member States have stated their commitment to RtoP. As Figure 1 highlights, a number of RtoP specific statements have been made at the UNSC, UNGA and the UN Human Rights Council (UNHRC) respectively. Statements were made in the UNSC Open Debates on the Protection of Civilians in Armed Conflict which took place from 2005–10. The statements made by the EU and Member States in the UNGA took place in the regular sessions of the Assembly occurring every September

[33] Swedish Ministry for Foreign Affairs, 'Human Rights in Swedish Foreign Policy', 17 March 2009, at www.regeringen.se/content/1/c6/04/10/01/76de1ece.pdf.
[34] Gunilla Carlsson, Swedish Minister for International Development Cooperation, 'The responsibility to protect in Africa', speech, 3 June 2007, at www.sweden.gov.se/sb/d/8812/a/83504.

since 2006 except the extraordinary meetings in July 2009, which saw RtoP as the specific focus of debate, and March 2011, which met to confirm Libya's suspension from the UNHRC. Finally, statements were made in the UNHRC at the 2011 Fifteenth Special Session on Human Rights in Libya and the Sixteenth Session. Cyprus, Estonia, Portugal and Spain did not make statements in these meetings.

The EU's capacities for RtoP

Each RtoP pillar requires a multitude of different tools including polit-ical, economic, diplomatic and, as a last resort, military. The EU can claim, in varying degrees of effectiveness and coherence, each of these tools. However, pinpointing the exact institutions responsible for RtoP within the EU is a difficult task. In keeping with Ban Ki-moon's com-ment that RtoP should not 'add a new layer of bureaucracy',[35] and given the External Action Services' relative youth, the EU has not as yet nominated a high-level RtoP 'focal point'. It indeed remains to be seen whether the EU will continue its approach of horizontal integration of the issue across its human rights, conflict prevention, security and development work, whether an individual at the high level will take active charge of the RtoP portfolio, or whether both will prevail.[36] Nevertheless, there are a number of EU institutions, departments and individuals that engage with RtoP.

As head of the approximately 3,700 strong EEAS, the High Representative coordinates much of the EU's policy work on RtoP. Two Deputy Secretary-Generals with oversight for political affairs, mul-tilateral issues and crisis management, plus ensuring cohesion among the geographical and thematic departments of the EEAS, support the High Representative with the monitoring of RtoP situations. The High Representative is further supported by eleven individual EU Special Representatives conducting regional and country-specific reporting on conflict-sensitive issues; the 135 EEAS delegations and Member State embassies which feed crisis information back to Brussels; and a number of adjunct policy advisers specialising in security-related issues. The Directorates-General for Human Rights and Democracy and for Conflict Prevention and Security Policy, located in the Department for

---

[35] UN press release, 'Secretary-General defends, clarifies "responsibility to protect" at Berlin Event "Responsible Sovereignty: International Cooperation for a Changed World"', 15 June 2008, at www.un.org/News/Press/docs/2008/sgsm11701.doc.htm.
[36] Two EEAS staff members, interview by author, Brussels, 21 January 2011.

Global and Multilateral Affairs within the EEAS, are the EU's principle policy coordinators on RtoP especially when it comes to the EU's work on conflict prevention. Supporting the work of the HR/VP and these Directorates-General are the Working Parties on the UN, Human Rights and Africa – working committees which bring together Member State and EU officials – through the provision of policy support on development, economic, social and humanitarian issues.

A major element of the EU's conflict prevention capacities is its early warning capacities. Timely, substantive and continuous monitoring of fragile States and situations through early warning tools such as satellite imagery and field-based reporting is critical for identifying and responding to each of the RtoP pillars. To this end, the High Representative is aided by early warning and monitoring tools provided by the Joint Situation Centre and the EU Situation Room – which brings together the Commission's Crisis Room and the Council of the EU's Watch-Keeping Capability – each pooling classified and open-source intelligence on ongoing crises and conflicts from the EU Member States. The EU Satellite Centre based in Torrejon, Spain, also provides geospatial intelligence for crisis management tasks to the Council of the EU and External Action Service. The European Commission's Joint Research Centre also assists in the EU's early warning work through the production of statistical and cartographical information related to fragile areas.

The High Representative can also make use of the EU's civilian capabilities, which are potentially of use when the Union is called upon to provide capacity-building assistance in fragile countries. These civilian capabilities can also be potentially utilised by the EU for 'pillar three' actions. The EU's civilian assets range from customs training officials to judicial experts, deployable for civilian tasks to oversee security sector reform and rule-of-law operations. The High Representative draws on the Crisis Management Planning Directorate, the Civilian Planning and Conduct Capability and the policy input of the Committee for Civilian Aspects of Crisis Management to ensure the planning and conduct of the EU's crisis response and peacekeeping operations. These crisis and civilian bodies also play an advisory role to the Political and Security Committee (PSC) – a permanent politico-military structure that forms and monitors the EU's civil–military operations[37] – the Council of the EU and the Commission on all areas of civilian operations.

---

[37] Consolidated Version of the TEU, 2010, OJ C 83/36, art. 38.

Furthermore, there are a range of military tools which the High Representative can draw on in fulfilment of the 'Petersberg Tasks'.[38] These tasks mandate the EU to use civilian and military means for 'joint disarmament operations, humanitarian and rescue tasks, military advice and assistance tasks, conflict prevention and peace-keeping tasks, tasks of combat forces in crisis management, including peace-making and post-conflict stabilisation'.[39] To this end, the EU can draw on battalions labelled EU Battle Groups, which have never been deployed by the Union. The Battle Groups consist of 1,500 troops put on standby for a six-month rotating period, deployable within fifteen days after a request for support and sustainable in the field for up to 120 days in the event of a 'pillar-three' crisis in a third country. Additionally, the High Representative is able to draw on cooperative mechanisms such as the 'Berlin-Plus' Arrangement (2002), which makes it possible for the EU to draw on NATO's military, operational and intelligence capabilities for its operations – e.g. Operations Concordia and Artemis.[40] To coordinate the EU's military efforts, the High Representative relies on the EU Military Committee and the EU Military Staff. Both these military bodies are composed of Member State military officials responsible for feeding operational analysis into the Political and Security Committee.

The European Commission also plays a role in the High Representative's work on RtoP. This supranational body is engaged with RtoP through development aid, as managed and distributed by EuropeAid Development and Cooperation. Development aid plays a crucial role in conflict prevention and in bolstering third-countries' obligation under RtoP's 'first pillar' by emphasising socio-economic development. Additionally, the Commission's Foreign Policy Instrument Service, which directly feeds into the work of the High Representative and the EEAS, is geared to supporting crisis situations through election observation missions and management of the Instrument for Stability – the Instrument refers to the Commission's funded projects for crisis response – e.g. rule of

---

[38] Consolidated Version of the TEU, 2010, OJ C 83/38, arts. 42–6.

[39] Consolidated Version of the TEU, 2010, OJ C 83/39, art. 43(1).

[40] Operation Concordia (2003) was an EU-led military mission to the former Yugoslav Republic of Macedonia which aimed at providing security and stability during the implementation of the Ohrid Framework Agreement; and Operation Artemis (2003) was an EU-led military operation to the region of Bunia, Democratic Republic of Congo in order to protect civilians in towns and in refugee camps affected by attacks from Ituri Region-based militia groups.

law, mediation and the Peacebuilding Partnership.[41] The work of Directorate-General Humanitarian Aid and Civil Protection plays a role through the delivery of food and medication to conflict and disaster-affected civilian populations. Being a member of the Commission, the HR/VP can also draw on the support of relevant fellow Commissioners – e.g. the Commissioner for International Cooperation, Humanitarian Aid and Crisis Response. That said, trade and agriculture, which are among the Commission's main policy prerogatives, have so far been relatively neglected as part of the EU's overall conflict prevention and RtoP efforts.

The intergovernmental Council of the EU also plays a crucial role, for it is the institution that brings together the EU Member States to decide on political, economic and military action related to norms such as RtoP. International issues are dealt with in the Committee of Permanent Representatives (COREPER II), which is attended by the heads of the Member States' Permanent Representations to the EU in Brussels each week. If, for example, the EU wishes to impose restrictive measures on a particular State for human rights abuses it occurs through the formation of a Common Position in COREPER II, before being published in the EU's Official Journal and implemented by the relevant Member State authorities.[42] COREPER II, fed with analysis from the Political and Security Committee, lays the foundations for the monthly meeting of the Foreign Affairs Council – which assembles Member States' Foreign, Defence and Development Ministers under the HR/VP's chairmanship – and the biannual meeting of Heads of Government under the European Council. The Foreign Affairs Council discusses and votes on action, first through unanimity, if it can be achieved, or else, if agreed on, through qualified majority voting (QMV)[43] which requires a two-thirds majority, representing at least 62 per cent of the EU population.

---

[41] Launched in 2008, the Partnership seeks to channel the work of international, regional and civil society organisations into the EU's conflict prevention and crisis response policies.
[42] European Commission, 'Restrictive Measures (Sanctions) in Force', 18 June 2012, at www.eeas.europa.eu/cfsp/sanctions/docs/measures_en.pdf.
[43] As prefigured by the Lisbon Treaty, after October 2014 the voting system switches to double majority voting (DMV), which requires a 55 per cent majority of Member States, representing 65 per cent of the population if the Council works on a proposal put forward by the HR/VP and Commission – if the Council acts alone, 72 per cent of Member States, representing 65 per cent of the population are required. From November 2014 to March 2017 any Member State may request QMV to be used instead of DMV.

The European Parliament plays an important RtoP function. The Parliament has budgetary influence over the Common Foreign and Security Policy, given its role in setting the Union's overall budget, and the budget lines for civilian missions conducted under the CSDP, given that non-military and defence-related operations are charged to the CFSP budget. Furthermore, the HR/VP is supposed to 'regularly consult' with the Parliament on major foreign, security and defence decisions.[44] The Parliament's most valuable role in supporting RtoP, however, is in mobilising public opinion and raising awareness. This it does through the publication of non-binding resolutions drafted in the Committees for Foreign Affairs and Development, and the two Foreign Affairs sub-Committees on security and defence and Human Rights.

Finally, the EU makes an important point about cooperating with the UN on RtoP, and it does this mainly through the EU Delegation to the UN in New York. The Delegation forms a conduit between the High Representative, EEAS and Commission and UN bodies such as the Department of Political Affairs, the Office of the Coordination of Humanitarian Affairs, the Office of the High Commissioner on Human Rights, the Human Rights Council and the Peacebuilding Commission. Where conflict prevention and crisis management is concerned there are EU–UN 'desk-to-desk' dialogues, which encourage joint early warning and conflict prevention work. Where the UN Joint Office of the Special Advisers on the Prevention of Genocide and RtoP is concerned, however, no formal EU interlocutor on RtoP exists and joint work is conducted on an ad hoc basis. That said, there is a direct link between the Office and the EU Situation Centre for the purposes of early warning.[45] Furthermore, while unable to vote on the Security Council and the General Assembly the EU is able to present its views to the latter through its own and through the Member States' representatives.[46] EU statements are formulated through the Delegation in tandem with the High Representative, Commission and the Member States. The High Representative may also present the EU's position in the UNSC, if permitted by France and the UK.

[44] Consolidated Version of the TEU, 2010, OJ C 83/35, art. 36.
[45] UN staff member, e-mail message to author, 18 May 2011.
[46] On 3 May 2011 the EU was granted special observer status at the UNGA. This allows the EU to present common positions to the Assembly, the right to intervene during UNGA sessions, the right to present proposals and amendments agreed by EU Member States and the right of reply concerning positions on the EU. The EU will still not have the right to vote or to put forward candidates to the Assembly for key posts.

The EU's implementation of RtoP

Having looked at the EU's stated commitment to and its capacities for supporting RtoP, these elements now need comparing with the EU's concrete reaction to crisis situations which have triggered – rightly or wrongly – an invocation of RtoP since 2005. It will be important to see what political, economic and military tools the EU made collective and individual use of in its response under each of the pillars of RtoP. The following selection of examples will also allow one to gauge the level of coherence and effectiveness of the EU's response.

Since 2006 the European Parliament had released a number of resolutions[47] invoking RtoP and calling on the EU to end the atrocities against civilians in Darfur, Sudan. However, the EU and other major international players have not heeded the Parliament's calls or international sentiment by acting to stop the atrocities. Indeed, the EU's first response was to apply economic sanctions on key individuals. This was due in part to the Sudanese government's refusal to allow UN peacekeeping forces from deploying in the region. Nevertheless, the EU did act through the use of force, belatedly and indirectly – under French influence – in 2008 under a UN mandate in neighbouring Chad and the Central African Republic. EUFOR Chad/CAR is to date the EU's largest military deployment under CSDP, and played a role in protecting refugees and aid workers from cross-border attacks perpetrated by militia groups. While the operation[48] was undermined by logistical weaknesses and a narrow mandate from the UNSC, it showed the EU's willingness to deploy militarily, if indirectly, where RtoP obligations had not been respected.

Aside from the military response, however, was the EU's role in supporting the International Criminal Court's (ICC) arrest warrants for Sudan's President Omar al-Bashir for the crimes of genocide, crimes against humanity and war crimes. In response to the first arrest warrant issued on 4 March 2009,[49] which did not refer to the crime of genocide,

---

[47] For example, the European Parliament Resolution on the Situation in Darfur, called on 'the Member States, the Council and the Commission to assume their responsibilities and make every possible effort to provide effective protection for the people of Darfur from a humanitarian disaster' (European Parliament, *European Parliament Resolution on the Situation in Darfur*, EP Doc. P6_TA-PROV(2007)0342, 12 July 2007).

[48] The force was assembled on an ad hoc basis and not from the EU Battle Groups.

[49] ICC, Pre-Trial Chamber I, 'Warrant of Arrest for Omar Hassan Ahmad Al Bashir', ICC Doc. ICC-02/05-01/09, March 2009, at www2.icc-cpi.int/iccdocs/doc/doc639078.pdf.

the EU issued a declaration 'taking note' of the warrant,[50] and it supported the second arrest warrant of 12 July 2010,[51] which did indict al-Bashir for the crime of genocide. That said, with its focus on enforcing the Comprehensive Peace Agreement (2005), which obligated the EU to deal with al-Bashir directly, it was put in the uncomfortable position of being 'ready to engage with the Government of Sudan on the issue of the voluntary return of' internally displaced persons in the knowledge that its leader was an ICC indictee.[52]

If the EU's response to Darfur was a case of 'too little too late', its response to the humanitarian crisis in Burma/Myanmar following Cyclone Nargis in October 2008 was one of confusion. Indeed, after the Burmese regime's decision to obstruct international efforts to deliver humanitarian aid to victims, it was the then French Foreign Minister, Bernard Kouchner, who invoked RtoP only two days after he had called for the unobstructed delivery of aid. He was supported by David Miliband, then British Foreign Secretary, who had contradicted his own Prime Minister to acknowledge that aid obstruction could trigger RtoP, even if he realised that intervention was difficult, given the regime's '400,000 troops'.[53] France had made efforts to encourage the EU to also invoke RtoP over the crisis, but the former High Representative Javier Solana and the bulk of EU development ministers resisted and instead called for the use of 'all means' under the UN Charter to deliver the aid.[54]

Clearly, individuals such as Kouchner pursued a wider application of RtoP which would deal with 'human suffering' more broadly than the four crimes. This was not the view of the then UN Secretary-General's Special Adviser, Edward Luck, who saw the invocation as a 'misapplication of the doctrine' because natural disasters and aid obstruction did not

---

[50] European Council press release, 'Declaration by the presidency on behalf of the European Union following the ICC decision concerning the arrest warrant for President Al-Bashir', 6 March 2009, available at www.consilium.europa.eu/documents.

[51] ICC, Pre-Trial Chamber I, 'Second Warrant of Arrest for Omar Hassan Ahmad Al Bashir', ICC Doc. ICC-02/05-01/09, 12 July 2010, at www.icc-cpi.int/iccdocs/doc/doc907140.pdf.

[52] European Council press release, 'Council conclusions on Sudan', 13 December 2010, available at www.consilium.europa.eu/documents.

[53] 'The UN and humanitarian intervention: to protect sovereignty, or to protect lives?', *The Economist*, 15 May 2008, at www.economist.com/node/11376531.

[54] European Council press release, 'Remarks by Javier Solana, EU High Representative for the CFSP, on the latest developments in Burma/Myanmar', 13 May 2008, available at www.consilium.europa.eu/documents.

give the UNSC grounds to act.[55] On this basis, the language used by those from the EU who had invoked RtoP added to the general confusion, with expressions stressing the need to intervene 'under all circumstances'[56] hinting at military intervention and undermining the principle's emphasis on responsibility. However, the real problem to emerge, given the adequate humanitarian aid action by the EU, was whether political dialogue or military intervention was the best tool to force aid deliveries. After aid had started to trickle into Burma/Myanmar in July 2008, the more fruitful approach appeared to be the UN Secretary-General's political dialogue with Burmese General Than Shwe,[57] rather than the EU's 'megaphone diplomacy'.

The EU's tone changed markedly during the 2008 crisis in Guinea, which saw the 28 September massacring of 157 protesting civilians at a sports stadium in Conakry. While Kouchner had harshly denounced the crimes, he did not invoke RtoP and instead took a more legalistic tone calling for an international criminal investigation, even though the chances of further civilian attacks and a moderate risk of genocide occurring remained.[58] The EU again responded with the imposition of restrictive measures, including an arms embargo and a withdrawal of economic agreements related to fishing, but it was the Economic Community of West African States (ECOWAS) which mediated in the post-crisis period between the opposition and the junta leader Captain Moussa Dadis Camara. Ultimately, this more cautious approach, of de-emphasising military intervention and not immediately invoking RtoP, may have done more good than harm for the acceptance of the principle.

However, by the time tensions broke out in June 2010 in southern Kyrgyzstan, the EU was slow to act, despite the opportunities – its early warning mechanisms should have been triggered following the riots of April. On 15 June 2010, the UN Secretary-General's then Special

---

[55] Jonathan Marcus, 'World wrestles with Burma aid issues', BBC, 9 May 2008, at http://news.bbc.co.uk/2/hi/asia-pacific/7392662.stm.

[56] French Embassy in the United Kingdom press release, 'Burma – joint communiqué issued by the Ministry of Foreign and European Affairs and Ministry of Defence', 25 May 2008, at www.ambafrance-uk.org/Bernard-Kouchner-on-Burma-disaster.html.

[57] International Crisis Group, *Burma/Myanmar after Nargis: Time to Normalise Aid Relations – Asia Report No. 161* (Yangon, Burma; Brussels: International Crisis Group, 2008), p. 8.

[58] Office of the Special Adviser on the Prevention of Genocide, 'Report of the Special Adviser to the Secretary-General on the Prevention of Genocide on his Mission to Guinea from 7 to 22 March 2010', available at www.un.org/en/preventgenocide/adviser/documents.shtml.

Advisers, Francis Deng and Edward Luck, issued a call to operationalise RtoP in order to stop ethnic violence from spreading further, and stated that international actors should do 'everything in their power' to stop the violence.[59] But by this time the EU's €5 million worth of humanitarian aid did little to stem the potential for further violence, and its support for an understaffed OSCE peacekeeping mission was underwhelming. That said, given the strategic sensitivity towards Kyrgyzstan – which is home to an American military presence – it is fair to say that humanitarian motives played a minimal role in the international response.[60] Again, the EU's main reaction in support of RtoP took the form of trade and development assistance through the 'Central Asia DCI Indicative Programme' (2007),[61] although even this strategy has been criticised for privileging energy security and counter-terrorism over human rights.[62]

Some of the EU Member States undertook a far more belligerent response, however, after Colonel Gaddafi's attacks on civilians in February 2011, which led not only to the invocation of RtoP by the UNSC, but also to the establishment of a no-fly zone over Libya under Resolution 1973.[63] While the EU made it clear long before Resolution 1973 that the Libyan regime was not living up to its RtoP duties,[64] it did not directly intervene,[65] even if some of its Member States chose to. Indeed, while there was EU consensus on the need for Gaddafi to

---

[59] UN press release, 'UN Special Advisers of the Secretary-General on the prevention of genocide and on the responsibility to protect on the situation in Kyrgyzstan', 15 June 2010, available at www.responsibilitytoprotect.org.

[60] Clifford Levy, 'In Kyrgyzstan, failure to act adds to crisis', *New York Times*, 17 June 2010, at www.nytimes.com/2010/06/18/world/asia/18kyrgyz.html.

[61] European Commission, 'Central Asia DCI Indicative Programme 2011–2013', pp. 36–41, at www.eeas.europa.eu/central_asia/docs/2010_ca_mtr_en.pdf.

[62] One EU official stated that 'it is unrealistic to expect these countries [Kazakhstan, Uzbekistan, Turkmenistan, Tajikistan and Kyrgyzstan] to become like Europe' (Philippa Runner, 'Human rights take back seat at EU–Central Asia talks', EUobserver, 19 September 2008, at www.euobserver.com/9/26778).

[63] UNSC press release, 'Security Council press statement on Libya', 22 February 2011, at www.un.org/News/Press/docs/2011/sc10180.doc.htm.

[64] EU, 'Situation of Human Rights in the Libyan Arab Jamahiriya' (15th Special Session of the UN Human Rights Council), 25 February 2011.

[65] The EU has a standby military force ('EUFOR Libya') that will be deployed to deliver humanitarian assistance should the UN give authorisation. European Council press release, 'Council decides on EU military operation in support of humanitarian assistance operations in Libya', 1 April 2011, available at www.consilium.europa.eu/documents.

'relinquish power immediately',[66] and support for referral of the crisis to the Prosecutor of the ICC, there was disagreement between the Member States over the means to ensure Gaddafi saw to his responsibility, with Germany abstaining on the Security Council vote for military intervention. In contrast, and following debates about NATO's Libya intervention and the operational and strategic differences, the current crisis in Syria has seen the EU agree on the non-use of force to alleviate President Bashar al-Assad's attacks on civilians. The EU has once again responded through the application of targeted sanctions against the regime, but interestingly it has been the UN which has taken the lead in trying to defuse the crisis through mediation and the deployment of UN peacekeepers.

If RtoP is about a continuous process of engagement with third countries to ensure the protection of civilians, even when there is no immediate risk of violence, the case of Libya highlights that the EU fared poorly. The Commission, for example, was part of a rapprochement with Gaddafi that began in 2004 and continued with its *Strategy Paper* (2011–13) for Libya, which stressed free trade and investment without ever directly and explicitly criticising Gaddafi's government for human rights abuses.[67] To a certain degree the same is true of Bashar al-Assad and Syria. Furthermore, since 2005 France and Italy had reportedly made respective transfers of anti-tank missiles and helicopters to the Gaddafi regime.[68] Given the colonial past, migration fears and oil interests, Italy had long courted Gaddafi; the Italian government pledged $US 5 billion over twenty years in 'colonial reparations' in 2008. Tony Blair also favoured Libya for his last destination as British Prime Minister where he had stated that the country had been 'completely transformed', which not only paved the way for defence and counter-terrorism talks but also the return of British energy companies after a thirty-year absence in the country.[69]

Conclusion

Any assessment of the EU's support for RtoP should appreciate some important dynamics, which, while not an excuse to defend inaction,

---

[66] EU press release, 'Statement by the High Representative following the London conference on Libya', 29 March 2011, available at www.consilium.europa.eu/documents.

[67] European Commission, 'Libya Strategy Paper and Indicative Programme 2011–2013', at www.ec.europa.eu/world/enp/pdf/country/2011_enpi_csp_nip_libya_en.pdf.

[68] Stockholm International Peace Research Institute, 'Arms Trade Database', at http://armstrade.sipri.org/armstrade/page/trade_register.php.

[69] 'Blair hails positive Libya talks', BBC, 29 May 2007, at http://news.bbc.co.uk/2/hi/uk_news/politics/6699447.stm.

presently impact on the EU's effectiveness. First, RtoP is still an emerging international norm. This implies insufficient international and European understanding over the principle's applicability and operability, in turn leading to confusion over the required response. Second, the EU is itself an emerging international actor. This implies some imperfections in the EU's own understanding of and response to RtoP, and also in the degree to which the current stage of integration – i.e. a diplomatic culture in the making and no unified military – gives the EU the tools to play a meaningful role. Finally, there are divergent attitudes to the use of force. There is still difficulty in securing EU and international consensus on the use and aims of force because of each State's sensitivity to troop casualties, mission creep and operational spill-overs, public opinion and domestic interests – e.g. upcoming elections – among other things. Arguments over the proportionality and the unintended consequences of armed intervention also impact on the EU's response under RtoP's 'third pillar', namely 'timely and decisive response'.

Nevertheless, there is much the EU can do to improve its capacities in supporting RtoP. Indeed, the overarching conclusion that emerges from the analysis above is that if the EU is to better react to RtoP it must first work towards a unified notion of what RtoP means, when it applies and how it should be operationalised. Unity in this sense would aid in promoting an EU approach to RtoP situations, similar to the one it is committed to pursuing in the field of conflict prevention. Such an approach would reduce a confused and mixed EU message from emerging and increase its credibility, legitimacy and coherence. This drive for a more unified EU approach should be led by the HR/VP, but the Member States will also have to facilitate this by bringing greater coherence and consistency to their professed commitment by limiting the degree of 'double standards' in their individual foreign policies. This could be encouraged by introducing national focal points for RtoP, which would work with a dedicated high-level EU 'special adviser' and in tandem with the UN Secretary-General's own special adviser. This would also promote a more coherent international response to RtoP.

While the EU has a range of institutional capabilities, an emphasis needs to be placed on promoting an adaptable EU response to RtoP. Some situations will require intensive diplomacy, whereas others may require a more belligerent response. Other times it will be best for the EU not to get involved. Each situation will call for a flexible approach, and the available tools will have to be tailored to this end. Accordingly, officials across all the EEAS's departments, as well as Member States' diplomatic and military structures, should be trained in what RtoP implies, when it applies and what tools will be required to support it over the short and long term. Increasing the connectivity and complementarity between EEAS officials and departments, plus promoting an environment of greater RtoP sensitivity, will allow the EU to tailor approaches to RtoP situations on a case-by-case basis. It is hoped that these suggestions will also mean that the EU will in future move in step with RtoP efforts, rather than it running to keep up with the need to see it implemented.

10

The African Union

SOLOMON A. DERSSO

Introduction

The recent military interventions in Côte d'Ivoire and Libya have heightened the debate about the responsibility to protect (RtoP) and importantly its application with respect to Africa. Together with the earlier experience in Darfur, Sudan and the notable normative and institutional developments at the level of the African Union (AU), these interventions highlighted the urgent need to assess the role and application of RtoP in Africa. Accordingly, this chapter has two purposes. First, it discusses how RtoP is given institutional expression in the AU peace and security architecture. To this end, I will discuss and analyse the AU's normative commitment to RtoP and how this is given institutional expression. Second, I will try to discern the AU's approach towards the RtoP principle and its application. This discussion will reflect how the AU has applied this norm in practice and the nuances, ambivalence and dilemmas in the AU's approach, as illustrated in the crises particularly in Darfur and Libya.

The application of RtoP is a shared responsibility. The primary responsibility is that of the individual sovereign State. It is when the State is unable or manifestly fails to protect its population from mass atrocities that the responsibility shifts from the State to the members of the international community. As far as Africa is concerned, there are two possibilities. One possibility is for African countries acting through the AU to take the lead role in assuming the responsibility in accordance with Article 4(h) of the Constitutive Act of the AU. Issues that arise in such an instance include the role of the international community within the framework of the UN Charter and of the decisions at the 2005 World Summit. The second

The author would like to thank Dr Jide Okeke for critical comments on an earlier draft of this chapter.

possibility is when the international community acting through the UN decides to take the lead in assuming the responsibility to protect as in Libya and Côte d'Ivoire. In this instance, an important issue that arises is the processes for UN decisions and the role of the AU. A discussion on these issues thus forms part of the analysis.

The normative commitment of the African Union to the responsibility to protect

The new world order established under the 1945 UN Charter was premised on two principles that have shaped the politics and laws of the international system since then. The first involves the State-centred principle of sovereignty set out in Articles 2(1), 2(4) and 2(7) of the UN Charter. The second involves the new commitment to the promotion and protection of human rights enunciated, among others, in the preamble and Article 1(3) of the UN Charter. During the subsequent decades, although international human rights norms have been institutionalised through various conventions and declarations, States generally resisted that these norms trample upon the principle of State sovereignty. There was little consensus at the international level that human rights norms mandate Member States of the international community to forcibly intervene, through or outside the UN, in a Member State to prevent or halt human rights violations and atrocities that State authorities perpetrate, or fail to prevent, against individuals or communities within their jurisdiction. One of the most contentious issues within the international system has therefore been the legality of the concept of humanitarian intervention.[1]

The post-Cold War period saw the rise of violent conflicts in Africa, as in many other parts of the world. As opposed to the inter-State conflicts common during the Cold War, most of these conflicts have been intra-State in nature, pitting one section of society against another, or against the State. One of the characteristics of these conflicts has been that they involve grave violations of international human rights and humanitarian law including genocide and ethnic cleansing. In the context of this changing

---

[1] See James Pattison, *Humanitarian Intervention and the Responsibility to Protect: Who Should Intervene?* (Oxford University Press, 2010), ch. 2; Ryan Goodman, 'Humanitarian Intervention and Pretexts for War', *American Journal of International Law*, 100 (2006), 107–41. See also the discussion of the relationship between humanitarian intervention and RtoP, Gill, Chapter 4 in this book.

dynamics of conflicts and in the aftermath of the horrific events in Rwanda and the NATO intervention in Kosovo, the wholesale rejection of military intervention for human protection purposes proved to be unsustainable.

In his *Millennium Report*, entitled *We the People*, former UN Secretary-General Kofi Annan formulated the long-standing controversy around humanitarian intervention involving the dilemma of how to reconcile the tension between the principle of sovereignty and the need to protect people from grave violations. Against the background of the changing nature of conflicts and the failure of the international community in Rwanda and Bosnia, Annan urged Member States of the UN to take steps towards overcoming this dilemma.[2] In setting in motion the process for formulating a framework that reconciles the two principles with the result of permitting the international community to act against mass atrocities, he argued that:

> Surely no legal principle – not even sovereignty – can ever shield crimes against humanity. Where such crimes occur and peaceful attempts to halt them have been exhausted, the Security Council has *a moral duty* to act on behalf of the international community. The fact that we cannot protect people everywhere is no reason for doing nothing when we can. Armed intervention must always remain the option of last resort, but in the face of mass murder it is an option that cannot be relinquished.[3]

For Africa, apart from the change in the nature of conflicts, another important factor has also been the increasing inability or unwillingness of the international community to deploy its response mechanisms to prevent or stop the atrocities attendant to such conflicts. For many, the occurrence of the 1994 genocide in the presence of a UN mission in the country as a result of the inaction of the UN Security Council (UNSC) was both inexplicable and inexcusable. The sense that emerged on the continent was that the international community acting within the frame-work of the UN could not always be relied upon to protect people on the continent from mass atrocity crimes.[4] Therefore, it was felt that Africa

---

[2] UNSG, 'We the Peoples: The Role of the United Nations in the 21st Century', UN Doc. A/54/2000, 27 March 2000, p. 35, para. 217.

[3] *Ibid.*, p. 35, para. 219 (emphasis added).

[4] See, among others, Ben Kioko, 'The Right of Intervention under the African Union's Constitutive Act: From Non-Interference to Non-intervention', *International Review of the Red Cross*, 85 (2003), 807–25, at 821. Kioko points out that the Constitutive Act of the AU is a manifestation of Africa's 'frustration with the slow pace of reform of the international order, and with instances in which the international community tended to focus attention on other parts of the world at the expense of more pressing problems in Africa'.

had to find its own mechanisms for addressing such conflicts and protecting its people from such atrocities.[5] The opportunity for examining the fundamental issues of the acceptable limits on the principle of State sovereignty and the circumstances in which the regional organisation comes to assume an obligation to forcibly intervene against a Member State in case of RtoP crimes, however, came some time before both the ICISS report and the 2005 World Summit. That was in the context of the transformation of the Organization of African Unity (OAU) into the African Union (AU).

Against the background of changing security dynamics on the continent and the reluctance of the international community to act, African States introduced, as part of the OAU's transformation, substantive normative changes that marked a sweeping departure from the norms and practices of the OAU. A prominent example of these normative changes is best encapsulated in the now famous Article 4(h) of the Constitutive Act of the African Union.[6] The pertinent parts of this article provides for 'the right of the [AU] to intervene in a Member State pursuant to a decision of the Assembly in respect of grave circumstances, namely: war crimes, genocide and crimes against humanity'. This principle is meant to ensure that the AU would not be indifferent in the face of the occurrence or threat of mass atrocity crimes in any country on the continent. It also represents a more tailored and legally binding AU formulation of the internationally evolving norm of RtoP.

Despite its formulation as a right, Article 4(h) not only creates the legal basis for intervention, but also imposes an obligation on the AU to intervene to prevent or stop the perpetration of such heinous international crimes anywhere on the continent. Given that the purpose of the provision is to protect people from such atrocities, it is not a matter of discretion for the AU to intervene; it is rather a legal obligation.[7] If the

---

[5] In adopting the Protocol Relating to the Establishment of the Peace and Security Council, Member States expressed that the establishment of the African Peace and Security Architecture was an expression of their determination 'to enhance (our) capacity to address the scourge of conflicts on the continent and to ensure that Africa, through the African Union, plays a central role in bringing about peace, security and stability on the continent' (AU, Protocol Relating to the Establishment of the Peace and Security Council of the AU (PSC Protocol), adopted 9 July 2002 and entered into force on 26 December 2003, pmbl., para. 16).

[6] For a detailed analysis on Article 4(h), see Girmachew Aneme, *A Study of the African Union's Right of Intervention against Genocide, Crimes against Humanity and War Crimes* (Oisterwijk, the Netherlands: Wolf, 2011).

[7] Kioko, 'The Right of Intervention', 807.

provision is not understood as entailing such legal obligation, it cannot be considered as establishing adequate protection from the crimes it seeks to address.

Additionally, the AU reaffirmed its commitment to RtoP when it adopted the Ezulwini Consensus in March 2005.[8] This Consensus representing the Common African Position on the Reform of the UN endorsed the inclusion of the 'responsibility to protect' in the report of the Secretary-General's High Panel on Threats, Challenges and Change. In particular, the Consensus provided that 'authorization for the use of force by the Security Council should be in line with the conditions and criteria proposed by the Panel, but this condition should not undermine the responsibility of the international community to protect.'[9]

The African Union institutional dimension of the responsibility to protect

For its operationalisation, RtoP requires and assumes the existence of decision-making institutions and intervention mechanisms. Some of the issues to be examined from an institutional perspective include the structures and processes for identifying and analysing threats in the form of early warning mechanisms, as well as the responsible institutions and approaches for responding to such threats and the capabilities required to carry out these tasks. This brings us to analysing the institutional and operational dimensions of RtoP in Africa. The most important of these components include the AU Assembly and the African Peace and Security Architecture (APSA).

The African Union Assembly

The AU Assembly is the supreme decision-making organ of the Union.[10] It is composed of the Heads of State and Government of all Member States of the African Union or their accredited representatives. The Assembly meets at least once a year in an ordinary session and convenes for extraordinary meetings at the request of a Member State and at the

---

[8] AU, 'The Common African Position on the Proposed Reform of the United Nations: "The Ezulwini Consensus"', AU Doc. Ext/Assembly/AU/Dec.1 (IV), 7–8 March 2005.

[9] *Ibid.*

[10] More information on the African Union Assembly is available at www.au.int/en/organs/assembly.

approval of a two-thirds majority of Member States. In its 2004 summit the AU Assembly decided to meet twice a year in ordinary session, citing its increasing responsibilities in the face of the many challenges of the continent.

As the supreme organ of the Union, the Assembly determines the policies of the Union. It monitors the implementation of policies and decisions by its organs and takes decisions on reports and recommendations from its organs, such as a recommendation for intervention in Member States from the Peace and Security Council (PSC). In particular, the Assembly directs the Executive Council, the Peace and Security Council and the Commission on management of conflicts, acts of terrorism and emergency situations. The Assembly is mandated to impose sanctions on Member States for violation of the principles enshrined in the Constitutive Act.

According to the Constitutive Act of the AU, the ultimate authority to decide on intervention under Article 4(h) lies with the Assembly. The Assembly decides on intervention under Article 4(h) either by consensus, or, if that is not possible, by a two-thirds majority of the fifty-four members of the Union.[11] The process for such a decision commences following a proposal submitted to the Assembly from the Peace and Security Council after the latter has determined pursuant to Article 7(1)(e) of the PSC Protocol that grave circumstances envisaged under Article 4(h) of the AU Act have arisen, or there is an imminent threat of such circumstances arising in a Member State warranting intervention.

As it will be discussed in more detail below, the practice thus far has been to avoid both the direct citation of Article 4(h) and the determination of the existence of alleged situations of genocide or similar 'grave circumstances'. This practice first emerged in relation to the crisis in Darfur. When allegations of genocide and other grave circumstances drew the attention of the UN, the media and international civil society organisations in 2004, the Assembly opted not 'to wait to investigate reports of genocide', but took a 'proactive role in convincing the Sudanese Government to accept African Union mediation'.[12] Since then, this has become a standard approach of the Assembly.

---

[11] Constitutive Act of the African Union, adopted 11 July 2000 and entered into force 26 May 2001, 2158 UNTS 3, art. 7.

[12] AU, 'Report of the Pan-African Parliament Fact Finding Mission on Darfur, the Sudan', AU Doc. AU/PAP/PRT/CIRC.CTTEE, 23 February 2005, para. 1.5.

The African Peace and Security Architecture

At the institutional level, one of the outcomes of the transformation of the OAU to the AU was the establishment of a comprehensive normative and institutional regime for maintaining peace and security on the continent. This is known as the African Peace and Security Architecture. The APSA was established to serve as the 'operational structure for the effective implementation of the decisions taken in the areas of conflict prevention, peacemaking, peace support operations and *intervention*, as well as peace-building and post-conflict reconstruction'.[13] Central to the APSA is the Peace and Security Council.[14] According to Article 2 of the Protocol Relating to the Establishment of the Peace and Security Council of the African Union (PSC Protocol, or Protocol), the PSC is 'a standing decision-making organ for the prevention, management and resolution of conflicts' which operates as 'a collective security and early warning arrangement to facilitate timely and efficient response to conflict and crisis situations in Africa'. The mandate of the PSC as stipulated under Article 7 of the Protocol includes the following competences:

(1) anticipate and prevent disputes and conflicts, as well as policies that may lead to genocide and crimes against humanity;
(2) undertake peacemaking and peacebuilding functions in order to resolve conflicts where they have occurred;
(3) authorise the mounting and deployment of peace-support missions;
(4) *recommend to the Assembly intervention in a Member State in respect of grave circumstances as provided for in Article 4(h) of the Constitutive Act* (emphasis added); and
(5) support and facilitate humanitarian action in situations of armed conflicts or major natural disasters.

The PSC's decisions are generally guided by the principle of consensus. However, in case of failure to reach a consensus, decisions on procedural matters are taken by a simple majority and on substantive matters by a two-thirds majority of members eligible to vote.[15] The PSC is the strategic decision-making body of the APSA that conceptualises or designs

---

[13] See AU, PSC Protocol, pmbl (emphasis added).
[14] More information on the Peace and Security Council is available at www.au.int/en/organs/psc.
[15] AU, PSC Protocol, art. 8(13); Rule 28 of the Rules of Procedure of the Peace and Security Council on the African Union.

and oversees the implementation of initiatives relating to RtoP cases envisaged under Article 4(h). On the basis of Article 6 of the PSC Protocol, the modalities for the PSC to exercise its powers include early warning and preventive diplomacy, peacemaking, including the use of good offices, mediation, conciliation and enquiry and peace-support operations and intervention, pursuant to Article 4(h) of the Constitutive Act.

With respect to the operationalisation of its responsibilities relating to Article 4(h) of the Constitutive Act, there are a number of issues that the PSC needs to address. These issues include:

(1) elaborating both the process for determining when a crisis has reached the threshold of the grave circumstances envisaged under Article 4(h) of the Constitutive Act and the threshold of those circumstances, the nature and gravity of which would trigger intervention;

(2) establishing the spectrum of measures that could be applied and the point at which a decision is to be made to move from mediation, peacemaking and sanctions to the deployment of a military intervention force;

(3) determining the principles (such as right intention, proportional means, the application of force only for the intended purpose of halting mass atrocity crimes) that should be complied with when intervening by military force;

(4) elaborating the division of labour and mechanisms for coordination between itself and sub-regional mechanisms for peace and security; and

(5) identifying mechanisms for consultation with and getting authorisation for the use of force from the UN Security Council.

For discharging its mandate including with respect to Article 4(h) of the Constitutive Act, the PSC is supported by other structures that form part of the APSA. According to Article 2 of the PSC Protocol, the other parts of the APSA that support the PSC include the AU Commission, a Panel of the Wise, a Continental Early Warning System (CEWS), an African Standby Force (ASF) and a Special Fund.

The African Union Commission implements AU policies, prepares its strategic plans and coordinates the body's activities and meetings. In the area of peace and security, the AU Commission, particularly the Chairperson acting through the Commissioner for Peace and Security also has a more substantive role. Article 10, paragraph 1, of the Protocol states that 'the Chairperson of the Commission shall, under the authority of the Peace and Security Council, and in consultation with all parties involved in a conflict, deploy efforts and take all initiatives deemed appropriate to prevent, manage and resolve conflicts.'[16] According to the PSC Protocol, the Chairperson of the Commission also has the prerogative to bring to the attention of the PSC issues which may threaten peace, security and stability in the continent.[17] As most members of the PSC lack the requisite technical capacity and in-house expertise, they rely for taking decisions with respect to situations envisaged under Article 4(h) of the Constitutive Act on the information and analysis that they receive from the AU Commission, either through the Chairperson or through the Commissioner for Peace and Security.

Apart from providing the information and analysis required for enabling the PSC to execute its mandate with respect to Article 4(h) of the Constitutive Act, the Commission is also assigned the responsibility of ensuring 'the implementation and follow-up of the decisions taken by the AU Assembly in conformity with Article 4(h) of the Constitutive Act'.[18] This may range from launching an investigation, deploying a preventive force, facilitating talks for negotiating a ceasefire and a final political settlement, to suspending the target State from participating in the activities of the Union, to deploying an intervention force into the affected country. It clearly emerges from this that the AU Commission plays a key role in initiating actions for applying Article 4(h) of the Constitutive Act, and in mobilising the political will of Member States for ensuring that prompt decisions are taken and that such decisions are implemented.

For purposes of providing the PSC with relevant data and analysis the AU Commission, in principle, depends on the Continental Early Warning System (CEWS), another component of the APSA. The CEWS is tasked with the responsibility of collecting, analysing and assessing emerging threats to peace and security in Africa. Accordingly, the purpose of the CEWS is the provision of timely advice, otherwise known as early warning, by availing information and analysis to the Chairperson of the AU Commission on potential conflicts and threats to peace and security. That information would enable the Chairperson or the Commissioner for Peace and Security to draw the attention of the PSC and ultimately develop appropriate and timely

---

[16] AU, PSC Protocol, art. 10(2)(c).   [17] Ibid., art. 10(2)(a).   [18] Ibid., art. 10(3)(b).

response to prevent or resolve conflicts or crisis situations in Africa including those envisaged under Article 4(h).

The PSC Protocol provides that the CEWS undertakes its functions in collecting, analysing and transmitting data on potential conflicts or crisis situations based on the development by the system of 'an early warning module based on clearly defined and accepted political, economic, social, military and humanitarian indicators'.[19] Structurally, the CEWS is linked, through appropriate communication channels, to the observation and monitoring units of the regional mechanisms, which feed the data they collected and processed to the Situation Room, based at the AU Headquarters in Addis Ababa, Ethiopia.[20] Given that the AU does not have field offices in all African countries, it does not have means of collecting information directly from the field. It only has about a dozen liaison offices that serve as a primary source of data.[21]

Although significant progress has been made towards operationalising the CEWS, a lot remains to be done for its full operationalisation. In this regard, issues that require further attention include developing or recruiting the necessary technical expertise; the deployment of the necessary tools or indicators for data collection and analysis and revising them periodically; institutionalising a standardised early warning system at the Regional Economic Communities (RECs) level and establishing the necessary legal and political framework for institutionalised relations with RECs. Prevention of or responding to RtoP situations needs to receive special consideration given the gravity of the situations envisaged. In terms of enabling the CEWS to play the role also of effectively addressing the specificities of RtoP, it is thus imperative that its tools and analysis frameworks are also adequately tailored to encompass RtoP situations.

The major initiatives that the AU deploys in cases of the eruption of violent crisis including those involving RtoP cases include the launching of an investigation mission and series of diplomatic efforts including mediation processes. Once seized of an early warning on the emergence of a violent crisis involving an RtoP situation, the AU Commission through the Chairperson issues a press statement expressing concern and urging for an end to violence, sometimes even condemning those perpetrating violence. This is followed by a debate at the PSC on the

---

[19] *Ibid.*, art. 12(4).   [20] *Ibid.*, art. 12(2)(*b*).

[21] Discussion with Shewit Hailu, coordinator, Situation Room of the Continental Early Warning System at the AU Headquarters in Addis Ababa on 8 March 2012.

situation and the course of action that the AU should pursue. Often the PSC outlines a framework for a political resolution of the crisis. On the basis of such a framework, the AU Commission launches a mediation mission through a special representative of the Chairperson of the Commission or through a high-level ad hoc committee.

Failing such investigative and mediation efforts and when the PSC decides to deploy an intervention force, the PSC Protocol envisages a resort to the African Standby Force, another component of the APSA. As provided for under Article 13 of the PSC Protocol, 'In order to enable the Peace and Security Council to perform its responsibilities with respect to the deployment of peace support missions and intervention pursuant to article 4(h) and (j) of the Constitutive Act, an African Standby Force shall be established.' Clearly, the ASF is one of the most critical elements of the APSA that will enable the AU to deliver on its promise of intervention to protect people against grave violations and of prompt and robust response to manage and resolve any serious humanitarian crisis in Africa. The ASF's mission is to enable the PSC to:

(1) prevent and manage conflicts by containing their spread or escalation, through preventive deployment;
(2) support its peace processes where the AU or Regional Economic Communities/Regional Mechanisms separately or jointly with other organisations such as the UN are involved in negotiating with warring parties for reaching a peaceful settlement, as a peace support mission as in the case of the African Union Mission in Sudan (AMIS); and
(3) enforce PSC's decisions for intervention in cases of grave violations of human rights and humanitarian law.

As envisaged in the PSC Protocol, the ASF is to be prepared for rapid deployment for a range of operations, including:

(1) observation and monitoring missions;
(2) other types of peace-support missions;
(3) intervention in accordance with Arts. 4(h) and (j) of the Constitutive Act;
(4) preventive deployment in order to prevent a conflict from escalating, or an ongoing conflict from spreading to neighbouring areas or states, or the resurgence of violence after peace agreements are achieved;

(5) peacebuilding, including post-conflict disarmament and demobilisation; and

(6) humanitarian assistance in situations of conflicts and major natural
disasters.[22]

At the moment, the ASF is in the process of being institutionalised both
at the level of the AU Commission and at the level of the five sub-regions.
After the October 2010 Command Post Exercise, known as Exercise
AMANI Africa, that sought to determine the initial operational readiness of the ASF, it was acknowledged that the ASF would not be operationally ready before 2015. Moreover, it is not clear whether the
operational readiness of the ASF would ever allow the AU to enforce
military intervention, particularly in respect to a reasonably strong and
resisting State. In terms of AU's ability to operationalise Article 4(h) of
the Constitutive Act, what one can reasonably expect is for the ASF to
enable the AU to deploy more quickly and at the required force level with
the required strategic-level management capacity.

From Darfur to Libya: diplomatic intervention, interim measures and the AU's comparative advantage

The Darfur conflict is one of Africa's most complex and deadly conflicts.
It is estimated that over 200,000 people have lost their lives and more
than two million others fled from their homes either as internally displaced persons (IDPs) or refugees. As Tim Murithi insightfully observed,
'[t]he Darfur situation has become the AU's most significant test to date
and defies simplistic analysis.'[23] The Darfur crisis happened at a time
when the AU was still busy with putting in place its ambitious peace and
security architecture. Despite the bad timing, the AU was involved from
the very beginning in the search for a negotiated settlement. This started
with the assistance that it gave Chad in organising the initial round of
negotiations to resolve the Darfur conflict. This resulted in the 8 April
2004 N'djamena Ceasefire Agreement signed between the government of
Sudan, the Sudan Liberation Army (SLA) and the Justice and Equality
Movement (JEM). In the subsequent agreement on modalities signed in

---

[22] AU, PSC Protocol, art. 13(3).
[23] Tim Murithi, 'The African Union's Evolving Role in Peace Operations: The African
Union Mission in Burundi, the African Union Mission in Sudan and the African Union
Mission in Somalia', *African Security Review*, 17 (2008), 70–82, at 76.

Addis Ababa on 28 May 2004, the AU was assigned the role of being the lead international body in Darfur.

In the meantime, the PSC has made Darfur a regular agenda item for discussion. Over the last eight years, the PSC has issued over twenty communiqués on the situation in Darfur. Some of the notable initiatives of the PSC from these communiqués include the negotiation and signing of the 2004 Ceasefire Agreement, the 2005 Comprehensive Peace Agreement and the subsequent Darfur Peace Agreement, which was hoped to herald the beginning of peace in Darfur. At the time that the Darfur Peace Agreement was signed in May 2005, the PSC stated that it:

> Considers that the Darfur Peace Agreement, which was the culmination of intensive deliberations and negotiations, conducted by the AU Mediation with the support of the facilitators and international partners, represents a fair and comprehensive solution to the conflict in Darfur, addresses the legitimate demands of the Movements, and meets the aspirations of the people of Darfur. The Council, therefore, is of the view that there are no legitimate grounds for any group in Darfur to use military means to achieve its goals.[24]

Although the level of violence has substantially decreased, these peace agreements have not, however, led to the desired result of ending the conflict and the violence Darfuris continue to endure.

AU's mediation and peacemaking efforts demonstrate that an area where the AU has a comparative advantage over other stakeholders is its ability to garner the trust of parties to a violent conflict, particularly of governments, which generally object to outside interference. The AU has been able to use this trust to convince the parties, as in the Darfur situation, to agree on negotiations and to secure compromise. Alongside peacemaking efforts, the PSC has been appropriately resorted to developing the instrument of interim measures, which, if properly formulated and implemented, can contribute in particular to reducing violence against civilians. At its meeting of 4 July 2004, for example, the PSC urged 'the Sudanese authorities to assess the extent of the destruction related to the conflict in Darfur and to consider the ways and means of compensating the affected populations'.[25] Most importantly, in 2006 the PSC demanded that the parties cease all acts of violence and atrocities

---

[24] AU Peace and Security Council, 'Communiqué of the 51st Meeting of the PSC', AU Doc. PSC/MIN/1(LI), 15 May 2006, para. 8.

[25] AUPSC, 'Communiqué of the 12th Meeting of the PSC', AU Doc. PSC/MIN/Comm (XII), 4 July 2004, para. 5.

on the ground, particularly those committed against the civilian population, humanitarian workers and AMIS personnel.[26] It also demanded that the government of Sudan refrain from conducting hostile military flights in and over Darfur, and to expeditiously implement its stated commitment to neutralise and disarm the armed Janjaweed militias.

In expressing its support for the affected population, in many of its communiqués the PSC has also called for providing that population with humanitarian assistance. Accordingly, in the communiqué it issued at its Fifth Session, the PSC urged 'the international community to provide, as a matter of priority, humanitarian assistance to the population of Darfur, particularly internally displaced persons and the refugees in neighbouring Chad'.[27] For this, as the cooperation of the warring parties was necessary, the PSC also urged 'the Parties, particularly the Government, to facilitate the delivery of humanitarian assistance and to cooperate fully with humanitarian agencies'.[28]

While symbolically important, almost all of the measures that the PSC indicated suffered from at least two problems. The first is the failure to define suitable mechanisms to ensure that the measures indicated by the PSC were implemented, particularly by the relevant governments. The other deficiency is the lack of provisions identifying the mechanisms for follow-up and for ensuring compliance.

An incremental approach to deploying an intervention force: the Darfur case

The AU Chairperson, Alpha Omar Konare, reiterated that the AU was duty-bound to play a leading role in resolving the crisis and rightly noted that Darfur is the first major challenge for the newly established PSC. Indeed, the Darfur crisis was the first occasion to test the application of the AU norms, most particularly the right of intervention in case of 'grave circumstances' as provided for under Article 4(h) of AU's Constitutive Act. Following the signing of the Humanitarian Ceasefire Agreement of April 2004, the PSC decided to send a mission to Darfur. The first step was the deployment of military observers for monitoring,

[26] AUPSC, 'Communiqué of the 46th Meeting of the PSC', AU Doc. PSC/MIN/2(XLVI), 10 March 2006, para. 13.
[27] AUPSC, 'Communiqué of the 5th Meeting of the PSC', AU Doc. PSC/PR/Comm(V), 15 May 2006.
[28] Ibid.

verifying, investigating and reporting transgressions of the ceasefire agreement, known as the African Union Mission in Sudan (AMIS) I.[29] Subsequently, the AU deployed a fully-fledged mission to Darfur, known as AMIS II.[30]

When AMIS I was first introduced, its mandate was limited to monitoring the observance of the ceasefire agreement. In the light of the magnitude of the crisis in Darfur, particularly in terms of the humanitarian dimension, clearly this mandate was extremely inadequate and so was the nature of the mission. AMIS I provided for the protection of observers and not of civilians under attack.[31] The lack of such a mandate meant that AMIS could not have extended its help to civilians, even if it were possible for it to do so. Additionally, the human and logistic capacities made available to AMIS I were not enough to even enable it to fulfil that very limited mandate. Only around sixty military observers were tasked to monitor an area the size of France.[32]

When AMIS II was deployed, the PSC expanded both the mandate and the size of the mission.[33] The revised mandate of AMIS included the following functions:

(1) monitoring and observing compliance with the Humanitarian Ceasefire Agreement of 8 April 2004 and all such agreements in the future;
(2) assisting in the process of confidence building; and
(3) contributing to a secure environment for the delivery of humanitarian relief and, beyond that, the return of IDPs and refugees to their homes, in order to assist in increasing the level of compliance of all Parties with the Humanitarian Ceasefire Agreement of 8 April 2004 and the improvement of the security situation throughout Darfur.[34]

---

[29] For more on AMIS, see Seth Appiah-Mensah, 'AU's Critical Assignment in Darfur: Challenges and Constraints', *African Security Review*, 14 (2005), 7–21.

[30] AUPSC, 'Communiqué of the 17th Meeting of the PSC', AU Doc. PSC/PR/Comm (XVII), 20 October 2004.

[31] Peter Kagwanja and Patrick Mutahi, 'Protection of Civilians in African Peace Missions: The Case of the African Union Mission in Sudan, Darfur', occasional paper 139, Institute for Security Studies, May 2007, p. 6, at www.issafrica.org/uploads/PAPER139.PDF.

[32] Arvid Ekengard, 'The African Union Mission in Sudan (AMIS): Experiences and Lessons Learned', occasional paper, Swedish Defence Research Agency, 2008, p. 25.

[33] See AUPSC, '17th Meeting', AU Doc. PSC/PR/Comm(XVII), 20 October 2004.

[34] *Ibid.*, para. 4.

The tasks assigned by the PSC to AMIS II included:

(1) protecting civilians whom it encounters under imminent threat and in the immediate vicinity, within resources and capability, it being understood that the protection of the civilian population is the responsibility of the government of Sudan; and

(2) protecting both static and mobile humanitarian operations under imminent threat and in the immediate vicinity, within capabilities.[35]

AMIS signified 'the most concrete manifestation of the AU response to Darfur'.[36] Despite its various limitations, AMIS was the only international military presence in Darfur for a considerable period of time. As the only line of defence between the notorious Janjaweed militia and Darfur civilians, in those areas under its military presence AMIS, at the very least prevented the armed groups from causing more destruction.[37] In his report to the Security Council in 2005, former Secretary-General Kofi Annan observed that 'in the areas where AMIS had deployed, it was doing an outstanding job under very difficult circumstances, greatly contributing to an improved security situation'.[38]

As the experience in Darfur shows, the ability of the AU to deploy an intervention force in a relatively short period of time or in situations where the UN is unable or unwilling to deploy can prove to be of invaluable importance in RtoP situations. Admittedly, the inadequate force strength, the poorly formulated mandate, the lack of required equipment and dependence on external funding proved AMIS to be an inadequate response to the crisis, particularly in the eyes of Western countries that sought a more robust presence in Darfur.[39] In the context

---

[35] *Ibid.*, para. 6.

[36] Cristina Badescu and Linnea Bergholm, 'The African Union', in David Black and Paul Williams (eds.), *The International Politics of Mass Atrocities: The Case of Darfur* (Abingdon, UK; New York: Routledge, 2010), pp. 100–18.

[37] According to Appiah-Mensah, AMIS 'has acted as an interposition force to protect the vulnerable, especially, internally displaced persons (IDPs), during imminent attacks. The rapid and timely deployment of AMIS to Zalingei, following a tense situation after the kidnapping of civilians by SLM/A, helped to prevent retaliation against IDPs; also the deployment of AMIS to Muhajeriya stopped the advance of Government of Sudan forces into this town and thus averted a probable displacement of some 40,000 IDPs' ('AU's Critical Assignment in Darfur', 8). See also International Crisis Group, Africa Briefing No. 28, pp. 4–6.

[38] UNSG, 'United Nations Assistance to the African Union Mission in the Sudan', UN Doc. S/2005/285, 3 May 2005, para. 5.

[39] Mahmood Mamdani, *Saviors and Survivors: Darfur, Politics and the War on Terror* (New York: Pantheon, 2009), pp. 39–47.

of the signing of the Abuja Peace Agreement in 2006, the Security Council of the UN adopted Resolution 1706 (2006) proposing the replacement of AMIS with a UN force. In the face of consistent rejection of this proposal by the government of Sudan and the reluctance of the international community to intervene forcibly, the role of the AU was found to be critical to secure a compromise from Khartoum. The outcome of this joint effort on the part of the AU and the UN was the agreement of Khartoum for deployment in 2007 of a joint AU–UN force, known as the United Nations and African Union Hybrid Mission in Darfur (UNAMID).

The politics of naming: the case of Libya

One area of controversy with respect to RtoP is what I call the 'politics of naming'. Since the application of the measures for enforcing RtoP depends on determination of existence of RtoP situations, questions of who decides, how, when and who intervenes (defining elements of the politics of naming) are crucial. The case of Libya exemplifies how this politics have seriously affected the role that the AU sought to play for resolving the crisis in Libya.

The crisis in Libya began on 15 February 2011 in Libya's second largest city, Benghazi, when residents of the city staged the first demonstration against the government, protesting against the arrest of a human rights campaigner. Initially, police and paramilitary forces employed brutal but non-lethal tactics, relying on rubber bullets and tear gas to disperse protestors on 15 and 16 February. This response was short-lived though. From 17 February, the Libyan government security forces started to use live ammunition, reportedly killing more than 150 people over the next three days. As the protests spread to many parts of Libya and the government security forces continued to use violence for repressing protestors, the situation descended into an armed conflict. Although considerably weaker, the opposition forces managed to push government security forces out of many parts of eastern Libya. On 23 February 2011, Gaddafi vowed to 'cleanse Libya house by house' until he had crushed the armed opposition, whom he sometimes labelled as 'cockroaches' and 'traitors' who were 'drug-fuelled, drunken and duped'.[40]

---

[40] 'Defiant Gaddafi vows to fight on', Al Jazeera, 23 February 2011, at www.aljazeera.com/news/africa/2011/02/201122216458913596.html

In response to the crisis, the PSC issued a number of communiqués and press statements. In the initial communiqué, the PSC was largely limited to expressing its 'deep concern' and condemning 'the indiscriminate and excessive use of force and lethal weapons against peaceful protestors'.[41] Lacking in this response is the failure of the PSC to go beyond condemning the 'indiscriminate attacks and use of lethal weapons against peaceful protestors'. Additionally, the nature of the violence required investigation. Significantly, however, the PSC underscored the legitimacy of the aspirations of the Libyan people for democracy, political reform, justice, peace and security, as well as for socio-economic development.

Soon, the situation that started as a peaceful protest descended into a fully-fledged civil war. This development necessitated an approach different from the approach pursued until that point. Accordingly, at its 265th meeting held on 10 March 2011 at the level of Head of State and Government, the PSC adopted a major new initiative tailored to the changed nature of the crisis.

Apart from reiterating its condemnation of indiscriminate attacks and the legitimacy of the demand of the people of Libya for reforms and the need to ensure that they are achieved through peaceful and democratic means, the PSC outlined a four-point framework tailored to address the evolving situation in Libya. The suggested measures were (1) the immediate cessation of all hostilities; (2) the cooperation of the competent Libyan authorities to facilitate the timely delivery of humanitarian assistance to the needy populations; (3) the protection of foreign nationals, including the African migrants living in Libya; and (4) the adoption and implementation of the political reforms necessary for the elimination of the causes of the current crisis.[42] In the same communiqué, the PSC rejected military intervention as a solution to the crisis. This was against the background of what the PSC called 'the transformation of pacific demonstration into an armed rebellion'. Subsequently, the four-point framework was developed into the AU Roadmap for the political resolution of the crisis in Libya.

Following its policy emphasis on negotiated settlement as the best means of resolving crisis and the priority of a political solution, the AU insisted that its roadmap offered a comprehensive framework to politically resolve the crisis in Libya. Its rejection of military intervention was

---

[41] AUPSC, 'Communiqué of the 265th Meeting of the PSC', AU Doc. PSC/PR/COMM (CCLXI), 23 February 2011.

[42] AUPSC, 'Communiqué of the 265th Meeting of the PSC', AU Doc. PSC/PR/COMM.2 (CCLXV), 10 March 2011, para. 7.

also in line with the policy position in the international political arena that the use of force should be a last resort measure. In a media release that lent support to the AU Roadmap and position on military intervention, the International Crisis Group underscored that ceasefire and negotiated transition were the right way to resolve the Libyan crisis.[43]

While the AU outlined its Roadmap and established a high level ad hoc committee for pursuing the implementation of the Roadmap, the conditions on the ground were changing fast. Most notably, two developments in the civil war created the conditions that were opportune for UN Security Council to assume leadership and adopt Resolution 1973.[44] The first of the two crucial developments was the successful offensive that government forces launched in early March for retaking the towns they lost to the armed opposition. At the initial stages of the civil war, the armed opposition assumed control over not only Benghazi, but also many other particularly eastern towns and cities. By the end of February and early March 2011, rebel forces had made huge gains and assumed control of several coastal cities, including Ajdabiya, Ras Lanuf, Brega and Misrata in eastern Libya and the towns of Zuwara, Yefren, Zenten and Jadu in the west. In early March, Gaddafi's forces launched an offensive against the rebels in an effort to retake the coastal towns and strategic locations under the control of the opposition. In mid-March, the balance of power changed in favour of Gaddafi forces. After a sweeping victory over the rebel forces, government forces threatened to crush the opposition in its stronghold city of Benghazi.

The other crucial development was unsubstantiated reports of use of artillery, snipers and even air power, which were reportedly used indiscriminately against civilians, which, according to human rights advocates, amounted to crimes against humanity. This was accompanied by Gaddafi's unhelpful and very threatening rhetoric. In his televised address on 11 March 2011, Gaddafi urged his supporters to 'show no mercy' and go 'house to house' in Benghazi.[45]

---

[43] ICG, 'A Ceasefire and Negotiations the Right Way to Resolve the Libya Crisis', 10 March 2011, at www.crisisgroup.org/en/publication-type/media-releases/2011/a-ceasefire-and-negotiations-the-right-way-to-resolve-the-libya-crisis.aspx.

[44] UNSC Res. 1973, UN Doc. S/RES/1973, 17 March 2011. The resolution imposed a no-fly zone and authorised Member States 'to take all necessary measures' in order 'to protect civilians and civilian populated areas under threat of attack'.

[45] Douglas Stanglin, 'Gadhafi vows to attack Benghazi and show "no mercy"', *USA Today*, 17 March 2011, at http://content.usatoday.com/communities/ondeadline/post/2011/03/gadhafi-vows-to-retake-benghazi-and-show-no-mercy/1.

As in the case of Darfur, in adopting its roadmap, the PSC avoided determining the existence or threat of 'grave circumstances' in Libya. When first seized of the situation soon after the beginning of the uprising, the AU opted for sending an investigation team. As the AU lacked the means to immediately implement this course of action, its decision was taken over by events as the protests soon descended into civil war. The AU did not adequately and powerfully communicate to, and promote, its roadmap among members of the international community. During the ministerial meeting of the 275th session of the PSC, Rwanda's Minister of Foreign Affairs thus lamented:

> We are all in agreement that Africa should not condone a Head of State who holds his own people in contempt. And that we shall never tolerate a Head of State that intentionally takes lives of its own people. Despite all this, why has the African Union not responded timely and taken a leadership role to put in place practical steps to stop this?[46]

This suggests that at some level the AU was very ineffective in communicating with and mobilising effectively the totality of AU Member States on the subject. As a result, its proposed approach did not gain the attention of public opinion both within and outside the continent. This was further compounded by the disconnect between the PSC and African States that serve as non-permanent members of the Security Council. Therefore, its roadmap was very easily overshadowed and marginalised, particularly following the adoption of Resolution 1973 by the UN Security Council.

After NATO started its aerial military operation, whatever space was available for the implementation of AU's Roadmap was altogether lost. Although it started off as an intervention meant to spare civilians, particularly those in Benghazi, from threats of violence from government forces, NATO's operation quickly morphed from the protection of civilians into direct, military assistance to an armed group fighting to overthrow Gaddafi's government. The leading intervening NATO countries openly declared that the objective of the intervention included removing Gaddafi's government from power. In an open letter dated 15 April 2011, the US President Barack Obama, French President Nicolas Sarkozy, and UK Prime Minister David Cameron, while emphasising that their duty and mandate under Resolution

---

[46] Hon. Louise Mushikiwabo, Minister for Foreign Affairs and Cooperation of the Republic of Rwanda, 'The new threats to peace and security in Africa: lessons learned from North Africa crisis and Cote d'Ivoire', speech delivered at the 275th Ministerial Session of the PSC, Addis Ababa, 26 April 2011, available at www.au.int.

1973 was not to remove Gaddafi by force, stated that 'it is impossible to imagine a future for Libya with Qaddafi in power' and that it is 'unthinkable that someone who has tried to massacre his own people can play a part in their future government'.[47] As Professor Falk has observed, 'the NATO operation quickly lost sight of the mission as authorised, and almost immediately acted ... to make non-negotiable the dismantling of the Gaddafi regime without much attention to the protection of Libyan civilians.'[48] Using Resolution 1973, these countries sought to achieve unauthorised ends. While acknowledging that they were not mandated to remove Gaddafi by force, the intention was that the pressure on the regime through military means would be maintained until he was no longer in power.[49]

With the objective of regime change quickly supplanting the rationale of establishing a no-fly zone and protecting civilians, NATO countries were determined to use military means as the only solution to the crisis in Libya. NATO's intervention was therefore not sufficiently flexible to give enough opportunity for AU's push for a negotiated settlement. Thus, the opportunities that arose when the Libyan government declared its willingness for ceasefire and negotiated settlement were not adequately explored. Instead, the government's declarations of ceasefire and willingness for negotiation were dismissed as a deliberate ploy by Gaddafi to buy time to shield himself from the escalating military assault targeting him and his government. By May 2011, the AU even managed to secure Gaddafi's commitment that he would not be part of the negotiation for the formation of a new government and of the government to be formed. It was intriguing that many expected a ceasefire to exist where Gaddafi forces unilaterally silenced their guns, while the armed rebel groups continued to use their fire-power. On 12 January 2012, South Africa's President Jacob Zuma, during an address to the UN Security Council stated that 'the AU's plan was completely ignored in favour of bombing Libya by NATO forces.'[50]

---

[47] Barack Obama, David Cameron and Nicolas Sarkozy, 'Libya's pathway to peace', editorial, *International Herald Tribune*, 15 April 2011.

[48] Richard Falk, 'Chapter VII: a loophole for imperialists?', Al Jazeera, 6 September 2011, at www.aljazeera.com/indepth/opinion/2011/09/2011958322588815.html.

[49] Christian Henderson, 'International Measures for the Protection of Civilians in Libya and Côte d'Ivoire', *International and Comparative Law Quarterly*, 60 (2011), 767–78, at 777.

[50] Jacob Zuma, President of South Africa, 'Statement on the occasion of the UN Security Summit Debate', speech delivered at UN Security Summit Debate, New York, 12 January 2012, at www.thepresidency.gov.za/pebble.asp?relid=5564&t=79.

Despite its Charter-based legal authority to determine the existence of threats to international peace and security, as a club whose veto-holding membership is limited to very few and mostly powerful Western powers, the UNSC is seen as an institution lacking in global legitimacy and democratic credentials. It is in this context that the power of 'naming' when assumed by the UNSC makes fundamentally important the question of what the acceptable processes for using such power are and how to determine the existence of an RtoP situation warranting intervention. As James Pattison has rightly pointed out, the 'Security Council's representativeness (especially the veto powers of the permanent members) are morally problematic, and this means that it is far from obvious that interveners authorised by the Security Council are legitimate.'[51]

The process accompanying the military intervention in Libya clearly underscores the imperative of having an inclusive and adequate consultative process for determining the existence or threat of an RtoP situation warranting intervention. However, this process has to be accompanied by interim measures that ensure that intervention does not come too late. Otherwise, an unduly prolonged process will stifle timely action and thereby defeat the very purpose of RtoP, although evidently the rubric of timely action includes more options than military action.

It is granted that the subsequent aerial military campaign, initially by the coalition of three of the permanent members of the UNSC and a few Gulf States and later by NATO, was necessary. Given the genuinely perceived risks of mass atrocities at the time, the intervention might have frustrated Gaddafi's threats of unleashing violence, particularly against the residents of Benghazi. Despite its initial legitimacy, the Libyan intervention reinforced the concerns of many, particularly in the Global South and most notably Africa, that the responsibility to protect entails the risk of giving the pretext for powerful States to intervene in the internal affairs of weaker States and effect regime change.

The collection of the countries that led the intervention, their history and current status as global powers further compounded the problem. Notwithstanding the fact that the military intervention was sanctioned through a global multilateral forum, namely the UNSC as envisaged in the 2005 World Summit Outcome, the neo-imperialist appearance of the intervention was reinforced by the fact that the interveners were mainly from the Global North and the target country was part of the Global

---

[51] Pattison, *Humanitarian Intervention*, p. 6.

South. Equally important, the main countries to intervene militarily included the three permanent members of the UN Security Council, the body that authorised the intervention.

The way that Resolution 1973 (2011) of the SC was executed further heightened the concerns that the protection of civilians was just a pretext for effecting regime change. Although little doubt exists as to the genuineness of the civilian protection mandate, this mandate was also made to serve additional ends, more specifically regime change to the liking of the intervening old global powers.

The problem with pursuing regime change, in addition to the central mission of protection of civilians, is not simply that it entails the risk of undermining the authorised end.[52] It also deprives RtoP of its palatability for acceptance in the Global South compared to the controversial doctrine of humanitarian intervention. Admittedly, one of the advantages of RtoP over humanitarian intervention is that its objective is strictly confined to halting the occurrence of specifically identified mass atrocity crimes. It is the focus on the needs of victims that earned acceptability for RtoP, even among those who continue to hold reservations about the principle.

In the context of the apparent determination of NATO countries to rely solely on force to resolve the crisis in Libya, the AU could have made a meaningful contribution, if it adjusted its approach to focus on mobilising members of the Union and others in the international community to ensure that the ends and limits of the authorisation were strictly adhered to. First, the AU could have called on the UNSC to closely monitor the situation and to ensure that the NATO aerial military campaign was strictly limited to the protection of civilians. Moreover, by coordinating and leading the actions of its Member States in the UN Security Council, the AU could have ensured that its voice and concerns were properly taken into account. In doing so, the AU could have served both the protection of civilians and respect for international legality. Finally, instead of its protracted refusal to recognise the National Transitional Council, the AU could also have emphasised the need for an inclusive transitional process and respect for the rights of migrant African workers.

---

[52] As Henderson has rightly pointed out, while UNSC authorisation provides a pre facto determination that force is necessary, questions remain over whether the actions taken in Libya 'have been proportional to the aim of the protection of civilians' ('Civilians in Libya and Côte d'Ivoire', 769).

A delicate balancing act: applying RtoP to a crisis situation while respecting sovereignty

In terms of the operationalisation of Article 4(h) of the Constitutive Act of the AU, the Darfur crisis and PSC's efforts to deploy an intervention force there revealed that the AU faces significant gaps and dilemmas in applying RtoP in practice. First of all, in the context of allegations of the existence of the grave circumstances including genocide referred to in Article 4(h) and warranting intervention, the PSC has been reluctant to directly invoke the principle both for political and institutional reasons. Politically, the AU seems to fear that invoking that provision will antagonise the target government and undermine its efforts for meaningfully engaging the parties to end the violence. Institutionally, there is no established mechanism for determining the emergence or imminence of the grave circumstances envisaged under Article 4(h). Accordingly, the PSC held, without receiving or undertaking due analysis of the situation, that 'even though the crisis in Darfur is grave, with the attendant loss of lives, human suffering and destructions of homes and infrastructure, the situation cannot be defined as a genocide.'[53] This finding was made without a clearly established process, duly considering and analysing the situation. Moreover, it left unanswered the issue of whether the situation, which it characterised as grave, revealed the commission of any of the crimes other than genocide falling under RtoP, namely war crimes and crimes against humanity.

Most significantly, the AU's approach revealed that the application of RtoP in the African context is fraught with serious dilemmas. In light of its limited capacity to enforce decisions, particularly against a resisting government, the AU has chosen to strike a delicate balance between its duty to protect people at risk of mass atrocities and the sensitivities of African governments for sovereignty. The experience in Darfur was a clear illustration of this balancing act. When the PSC was considering the deployment of AMIS II with expanded mandate and force size, Sudan invoked its sovereignty in resisting the plan.[54] The result was the insertion into the protection of civilian mandate of the controversial qualification that 'the protection of the civilian population is the responsibility of the GoS (Government of Sudan)'.[55] Indeed, this controversial qualification to the protection mandate of AMIS inserted into the PSC

[53] AUSPC, '12th Meeting', AU Doc. PSC/MIN/Comm.(XII), 4 July 2004, para. 2.
[54] See Kagwanja and Mutahi, 'Protection of Civilians in African Peace Missions', pp. 6–7.
[55] See AUPSC, '17th Meeting', AU Doc. PSC/PR/Comm.(XVII), 20 October 2004, para. 4.

communiqué that mandated the deployment of AMIS II was included as a result of the insistence of the government of Sudan on the basis of respect for its sovereignty.[56]

Apart from being a pragmatic framework for negotiating the application of Article 4(h) and respect for State sovereignty, the Libyan experience reveals that there is some policy conviction on the part of the AU that Article 4(h) or RtoP should not close options for negotiated settlement of crises by members of the affected society.[57] This in part reflects the belief that external intervention should be very limited in its objectives, means and effects. Intervention should also be pursued without compromising and having due regard to the fundamental rights of people to self-determination. This suggests that the occurrence or imminence of RtoP situations does not result in the wholesale suspension of the principle of sovereignty. To put it differently, in assuming the responsibility to protect, the international community does not have a blank authorisation to take the place of the national society in determining the course and shape of the politics of that country such as through regime change.

Conclusion

The AU has developed rich normative and institutional frameworks that express clear commitment to RtoP. Article 4(h) of the Constitutive Act of the AU authorises the Union to intervene in cases of 'grave circumstances', involving genocide, war crimes and crimes against humanity. The institutions and processes for enforcing this provision are also duly established. Notwithstanding these and the dynamic involvement of the PSC in various situations, there are significant limitations as far as the actual operationalisation of these normative and institutional frameworks is concerned.

Major challenges for the AU in this regard include its limited operational and institutional capacities. The AU lacks the funds,

---

[56] See Solomon Dersso, 'The Role and Place of Human Rights in the Mandate and Works of the PSC of the AU: An Appraisal', *Netherlands International Law Review*, 58 (2011), 77–101, at 98–9.

[57] For a discussion on how to negotiate the tension between RtoP and protection of national sovereignty, see Alex de Waal, 'The Tension between the Responsibility to Protect and the Protection of Sovereignty', in *Inter-Africa Group Proceedings of Conference on the Implications of North Africa Uprisings for Sub-Saharan Africa* (Addis Ababa: Universal Printing Press, July 2012), pp. 218–33.

infrastructure, the management capabilities and well-equipped, well-trained and interoperable troops.[58] Another challenge for the AU is its lack of the required carrots and sticks for enforcing its decisions. The ongoing situation in Darfur has shown that the AU lacks the necessary clout for enforcing its decisions against resisting and intransigent governments. For the time being, the AU's main instruments for enforcing RtoP under the framework of Article 4(h) of its Constitutive Act are limited to its diplomatic influence and the general acceptance by African States of its decisions. On its own, the AU lacks the requisite enforcement capabilities, particularly where the use of military force against a reasonably strong resisting government is needed for enforcing Article 4(h). Related to this are also issues surrounding achieving consensus among Member States and creating the required political will for pursuing the objectives of Article 4(h).

These conditions under which the AU operates have given rise to questions about how the AU negotiates the tension between Article 4(h) and the principle of State sovereignty.[59] Where an intervention force is to be deployed to discharge its responsibilities of protection, the AU has to first negotiate with and secure the consent of the target government without invoking Article 4(h) and hence without questioning the authority of the State concerned. For this approach to work, the AU needs to avoid determining expressly the existence of 'grave circumstances' in the target country. Both the cases of Darfur and Libya have established that this approach seems to better serve the AU in pursuing the objectives of Article 4(h), while avoiding the complications that arise with the target country from making express reference to Article 4(h).

The case of Libya illustrated the impossibility for the AU of pursuing a course of action it has outlined for addressing RtoP situations, where others in the international community decide to pursue a different course. This is particularly aggravated by lack of clarity on the interpretation and scope of Security Council authorisation. There is no effective regulatory framework within the UN system to ensure that intervening powers implement resolutions of the Security Council within established legal bounds. Confusing the protection of civilians with support for rebel forces and pursuing regime change raised concerns within the AU about

---

[58] See Dersso, 'The Role and Place of the African Standby Force within the African Peace and Security Architecture', occasional paper 209, Institute for Security Studies, January 2010, at www.iss.co.za/uploads/209.pdf.

[59] See Dersso, 'Role and Place of Human Rights', 99–100.

the manipulation of RtoP to pursue imperialist agendas. Apart from the need for clarifying how the PSC and the UNSC can achieve synergy in pursuing the application of RtoP in Africa, the situation highlighted the importance of coherence within the AU, especially between the AU and the African States that are non-permanent members of the UNSC. Significantly, the crisis in Libya also highlighted that intervention should be pursued in a manner that encourages (rather than inhibits) a negotiated settlement of the crises that necessitated the intervention.

11

The Association of Southeast Asian Nations

NOEL M. MORADA

Introduction

Norm-building has been one of the main preoccupations of the Association of Southeast Asian Nations (ASEAN) since its creation in 1967.[1] Since its formative years, Member States have held sacred its traditional norms – i.e. protection of State sovereignty and territorial integrity, as well as the principle of non-interference. However, in the aftermath of the Asian financial crisis of 1997, which led to democratic transition in Indonesia and calls for political reforms in other parts of the region, the idea of a people-centred ASEAN emerged as key to transforming this regional organisation. In 2003, the Bali Concord II – also known as the ASEAN Community Framework – incorporated principles that give importance to the promotion of democracy, good governance and the rule of law among its Member States. Subsequently, the adoption and ratification of the ASEAN Charter and the creation of a regional human rights body in 2008 and 2009, respectively, became part of the process of norm-building within ASEAN.

This chapter identifies the institutional frameworks of ASEAN that could be linked to the norm of Responsibility to Protect (RtoP) and attempts to examine the process and dynamics of norm-building and practice of human rights and civilian protection in the region. It argues that although ASEAN has not formally adopted the language of RtoP in its institutional frameworks and documents, it has nonetheless incorporated certain elements of the norm, particularly in the areas of human rights promotion, international humanitarian law, as well as principles

---

[1] The ten Member States of ASEAN are Indonesia, Malaysia, the Philippines, Singapore, Thailand, Brunei Darussalam, Vietnam, Lao PDR, Myanmar and Cambodia. More information on ASEAN is available at www.aseansec.org.

related to conflict prevention and post-conflict rebuilding. ASEAN members have also 'practised' some elements of RtoP albeit unconsciously, as demonstrated in the case of Cyclone Nargis in 2008 and participation of some of its members in UN peacekeeping operations within and outside the region. This regional organisation clearly has a long way to go as far as capacity-building of its Member States in the preventive aspect of RtoP is concerned. Even so, ASEAN and the larger security framework of the ASEAN Regional Forum (ARF) have a significant role to play in strengthening and implementing the norm in this part of the world.

The next section of this chapter provides an overview of RtoP in the context of ASEAN. Specifically, it identifies the issues and challenges related to promoting RtoP in South-East Asia.

ASEAN and RtoP: an overview

The responsibility to protect remains a difficult norm to promote and gain acceptance in South-East Asia, primarily because it appears to go against the very traditional norms of sovereignty and non-interference that are still valued by Member States of the ASEAN. Their discomfort towards the idea springs from a number of factors, namely: (1) a shared colonial history; (2) the importance attached to territorial integrity; (3) their bitter experience with external big powers, particularly during the Cold War period when they tried to undermine the political stability of States and directly intervene in their domestic affairs; and (4) the continuing challenge they face in nation-State building in the context of their multi-ethnic societies.[2]

Member States of ASEAN basically expressed support to RtoP based on the 2005 World Summit Outcome Document, even though some of its members also expressed their reservations or concerns about how this norm would be implemented. Quite surprisingly, in fact, even Myanmar in the 2009 UNGA debate argued that there was already a consensus about RtoP and supported the Secretary-General's appeal to move the debate towards implementing the 2005 agreement. Even so, ASEAN

---

[2] See Noel Morada, 'R2P Roadmap in Southeast Asia: Challenges and Prospects', Discussion Paper No. 11, Research Unit on International Security and Cooperation, Complutense University of Madrid, May 2006, at www.ucm.es/info/unisci/revistas/UNISCI11Morada.pdf.

members have stated that RtoP upholds State sovereignty as they have underscored the importance of adhering to the UN Charter and international law if, and when, the international community has to respond to humanitarian crisis situations.[3]

That RtoP to some extent also resonates in South-East Asia is not surprising, despite the persistence of traditional norms in ASEAN for a number of reasons. For one, the region experienced its worst mass atrocity in contemporary history during the Khmer Rouge rule of Cambodia from 1975 to 1978, also known as the 'Killing Fields' period. Other conflict-related atrocities – for example East Timor in the 1990s, the ongoing violence in southern Thailand, the problem of ethnic minorities in Burma/Myanmar (including the Rohingyas), and the Maguindanao massacre in 2009 – have yet to be resolved. The need for addressing these conflicts and their root causes makes RtoP even more relevant for the region in the long run, especially in the context of building capacities of ASEAN States in preventing the four crimes covered by this norm.

In an effort to generate further consensus in the region on this norm, a Track II-initiated study on RtoP was undertaken in 2010 by the Council for Security Cooperation in the Asia Pacific (CSCAP). A series of consultation meetings held in Indonesia, the Philippines and Cambodia generated some ideas on how to promote the norm and what existing institutional framework in the region could play a role in its promotion and implementation. Some of the important points of consensus that emerged from these meetings of the CSCAP Study Group on RtoP in 2010 were as follows:

- the nature and scope of RtoP is set out in paragraphs 138–140 of the World Summit Outcome Document and the primary RtoP obligations rest with the State;
- RtoP is consistent with existing international law and especially with the UN Charter;
- regional arrangements, including those in the Asia-Pacific region, have a role to play in implementing RtoP;

---

[3] For a more detailed discussion of the nuances in positions of ASEAN Member States in the 2009 UN General Assembly debate on Responsibility to Protect, see Asia Pacific Centre for the Responsibility to Protect, *Implementing the Responsibility to Protect: Asia Pacific in the General Assembly Dialogue* (Brisbane: Asia Pacific Centre for the Responsibility to Protect, 2009).

- the ASEAN Regional Forum should play a role in implementing RtoP;
- devising effective and appropriate early warning and assessment mechanisms and empowering regional actors to act upon these warnings;
- developing more regularised and defined channels of UN–regional dialogue around RtoP-related matters;
- recognising the importance of the first pillar of RtoP (the State's primary responsibility to protect) and highlighting the steps that some regional States are taking to strengthen their capacities in this regard;
- combining forces with the UN Peacebuilding Commission (PBC) to ensure that post-conflict environments do not become breeding grounds for the four RtoP crimes; and
- reviewing regional organisations' existing definitions of preventive diplomacy and examining ways of making them consistent with a more proactive RtoP role.

The final report of the CSCAP Study Group on RtoP is discussed in a separate section of this chapter, focusing mainly on a set of recommendations at the national, regional and global levels on how to operationalise the norm. Specifically, the report identified a number of recommendations on what role the ASEAN Regional Forum could take in implementing RtoP in the region.

The next section of this chapter examines the various ASEAN frameworks in promoting human rights and civilian protection, which are essential elements of RtoP. That part identifies and deals with the specific provisions of the ASEAN Charter, the mandate and role of the ASEAN Intergovernmental Commission on Human Rights (AICHR), the importance of the ASEAN Political Security Community (APSC) Blueprint, as well as the role of the ASEAN Regional Forum.

ASEAN frameworks for human rights and civilian protection

ASEAN has not formally adopted the language of RtoP in its institutional framework. However, a number of norms and principles related to RtoP have been incorporated in its Charter, which was ratified in 2008, and other pertinent documents of the organisation. Specifically, the promotion and protection of human rights, international humanitarian law and other relevant international laws and conventions are clearly embodied in the ASEAN Charter's purposes and principles, to wit:

(1) 'To strengthen democracy, enhance good governance and the rule of law, and *to promote and protect human rights* and fundamental freedoms, with due regard to the rights and *responsibilities* of the Member States of ASEAN';[4]

(2) 'adherence to the rule of law, good governance, the principles of democracy and constitutional government';[5]

(3) 'respect for fundamental freedoms, the *promotion and protection of human rights*, and the promotion of social justice';[6] and

(4) 'upholding the United Nations Charter and international law, including *international humanitarian law*, subscribed to by ASEAN Member States'.[7]

Article 14 of the ASEAN Charter paved the way for the creation in 2009 of a regional human rights body called the ASEAN Intergovernmental Commission on Human Rights.

ASEAN Intergovernmental Commission on Human Rights

The AICHR's terms of reference include, among others, the following as part of its mandate: (1) develop strategies for the promotion and protection of human rights and fundamental freedoms to complement the building of the ASEAN Community; (2) develop an ASEAN Human Rights Declaration with a view to establishing a framework for human rights cooperation through various ASEAN conventions and other instruments dealing with human rights; (3) enhance public awareness of human rights among the peoples of ASEAN through education, research and dissemination of information; (4) promote capacity-building for the effective implementation of international human rights treaty obligations undertaken by ASEAN Member States; (5) *encourage ASEAN Member States to consider acceding to and ratifying international human rights instruments*; (6) consult, as may be appropriate, with other national, regional and international institutions and entities concerned with the promotion and protection of human rights; and (7) develop

---

[4] Charter of the Association of Southeast Asian Nations, adopted 20 November 2007 and entered into force on 15 December 2008, ch. 1, art. 1(7) (emphasis added).

[5] *Ibid.*, ch. 1, art. 2(2)(h).   [6] *Ibid.*, ch. 1, art. 2(2)(i) (emphasis added).

[7] *Ibid.*, ch. 1, art. 2(2)(j) (emphasis added).

common approaches and positions on human rights matters of interest to ASEAN.[8]

The regional human rights body is also governed by a set of principles, which include, among others: (1) respect for international human rights principles, including universality, indivisibility, interdependence and interrelatedness of all human rights and fundamental freedoms, as well as impartiality, objectivity, non-selectivity, non-discrimination, and avoidance of double standards and politicisation; (2) recognition that the *primary responsibility to promote and protect human rights and fundamental freedoms rests with each Member State*; (3) pursuance of a constructive and non-confrontational approach and cooperation to enhance promotion and protection of human rights; and (4) adoption of an evolutionary approach that would contribute to the development of human rights norms and standards in ASEAN.[9]

Although AICHR is considered an integral part of the regional organisation's structure, it is essentially an intergovernmental and consultative body that is not autonomous.[10] Currently, it is in the process of working on the ASEAN Declaration on Human Rights in consultation with various sectors, including civil society groups and human rights advocates in the region. A drafting group on the declaration was set up in April 2011 and the declaration is expected to be adopted by ASEAN in the course of 2012.[11] AICHR is also undertaking discussions about the key elements of a five-year work plan for the period 2012–16 and thematic studies related to migration.[12] Given its intergovernmental character and limited mandate, a number of civil society groups in the region remain cynical about the effectiveness of AICHR in promoting the protection of human rights in South-East Asia. To start with, this body does not have monitoring and sanctioning powers against erring members, nor does it entertain complaints about human rights violations in Member States. More importantly, only five of the ten ASEAN members have their respective national human rights commission, with

---

[8] ASEAN Intergovernmental Commission on Human Rights, 'Terms of Reference', October 2009, paras. 4.1–4.5, 4.9 and 4.11 (emphasis added), at www.asean.org/Doc-TOR-AHRB.pdf.

[9] *Ibid.*, paras. 2.2–2.5 (emphasis added).   [10] *Ibid.*

[11] For more information on the work of the AICHR, see www.aseansec.org/22769.htm. More information on the Working Group for an ASEAN Human Rights Mechanism efforts towards establishing an intergovernmental human rights commission for ASEAN is available at www.aseanhrmech.org.

[12] ASEAN press release, 'Fifth AICHR meeting', 25–29 April 2011, at www.asean.org/26208.htm.

varying degrees of autonomy.[13] In early September 2011, Burma/ Myanmar launched its national human rights body composed of 15 retired civil servants, which came on the heels of an earlier visit by a special human rights envoy of the United Nations.[14] Cambodia has yet to set up its own national human rights body with a number of civil society groups pushing for adoption of domestic law for its creation.[15] Apparently, for various political reasons, the rest of the ASEAN members do not seem to give priority to setting up their respective national human rights institutions.

ASEAN Political Security Community[16]

Apart from the ASEAN Charter and AICHR, another important institutional framework for the promotion of human rights and protection of civilians is also the ASEAN Political Security Community. In 2004, the ASEAN Security Community (ASC) Plan of Action was adopted and the major areas for security community building were identified as political development, *shaping and sharing of norms, conflict prevention, conflict resolution and post-conflict peace building*. Among the specific activities under the political development are:

- strengthening democratic institutions and popular participation;
- promoting understanding and appreciation of the political system, the culture, and the history of ASEAN member countries;
- strengthening the rule of law and judiciary systems, legal infrastructure and capacity-building;
- promoting free flow of information among and within ASEAN member countries;
- enhancing good governance in public and private sectors;

---

[13] The five members with national human rights bodies are Indonesia, Malaysia, Myanmar, the Philippines and Thailand.

[14] See UN Human Rights Council, 'Report of the Special Rapporteur on the Situation of Human Rights in Myanmar, Tomás Ojea Quintana', UN Doc. A/HRC/19/67, 7 March 2012, especially paras. 17–19. A similar body was set up in 2000 composed of government officials, which apparently was not effective in protecting human rights in the country.

[15] Working Group for an ASEAN Human Rights Mechanism, 'Cambodian Civil Society Continues to Push for National Human Rights Institution', at www.aseanhrmech.org/news/cambodian-civil-societies-continues.html.

[16] This section is based on the author's chapter, 'Asia and the Pacific', in Jared Genser and Irwin Cotler (eds.), *Responsibility to Protect: The Promise of Stopping Mass Atrocities in Our Time* (Oxford University Press, 2012).

- establishing a network among existing human rights mechanisms;
- protecting vulnerable groups including women, children, people with disabilities and migrant workers; and
- promoting education and public awareness on human rights.[17]

In the area of conflict prevention, the ASC Plan of Action identified specific activities that include:

- strengthening confidence-building measures (e.g. utilising civilian and military personnel in disaster relief operations);
- strengthening preventive measures (e.g. developing an ASEAN early warning system based on existing mechanisms to prevent occurrence and escalation of conflict); and
- strengthening ASEAN Regional Forum process in support of the ASC (e.g. moving the ARF to the preventive diplomacy stage and beyond).

The Action Plan also identified activities under conflict resolution, such as:

- developing regional cooperation for maintenance of peace and stability, such as:
  - promoting technical cooperation with the UN and relevant regional organisations;
  - establishing/assigning national focal points for regional cooperation for maintenance of peace and stability; and
  - utilisation of national peacekeeping centres to establish regional arrangement for maintenance of peace and stability; and
- developing or supporting initiatives such as:
  - promoting exchange and cooperation among ASEAN centres of excellence on peace, and conflict management and resolution studies; and
  - considering the establishment of an ASEAN Institute for Peace and Reconciliation.[18]

Finally, in the area of post-conflict peacebuilding, some of the activities identified in the Plan of Action include:

- strengthening ASEAN humanitarian assistance through:
  - providing safe havens in conflict areas;
  - ensuring delivery of basic services or assistance to victims of conflict;

---

[17] ASEAN, *Declaration of ASEAN Concord (Bali Concord II)*, ASEAN Knowledge Kit (Jakarta: ASEAN Secretariat, 2006), pp. 41–2.
[18] *Ibid.*, pp. 44–8.

- orderly repatriation of refugees/displaced persons and resettlement of internally displaced persons;
- ensuring the safety of humanitarian assistance workers;
- promoting humanitarian relief assistance organisations;
- considering the establishment of an ASEAN humanitarian assistance centre; and
- intensifying cooperation with the UN and other regional organisations/donor countries;
- developing cooperation in post-conflict reconstruction and rehabilitation in affected areas, such as:
  - undertaking human resources development and capacity-building;
  - assisting in institutional-building and promoting popular participation;
  - reducing intercommunal tensions through education exchanges and curriculum reform; and
  - increasing cooperation in reconciliation and promotion of a culture of peace; and
- establishing a mechanism to mobilise necessary resources to facilitate post-conflict peacebuilding (e.g. a stability fund), including through cooperation with donor countries and international institutions.[19]

In 2009, the ASEAN Political Security Community Blueprint was adopted by Member States, which built on the previous ASC Plan of Action. Specifically, the Blueprint stated that the principal characteristics and elements of the APSC include:

- promotion of political development 'in adherence to the principles of democracy, rule of law and good governance, *respect for and promotion and protection of human rights and fundamental freedoms*';
- promotion of '*a people-oriented ASEAN* in which all sectors of society, regardless of gender, race, religion, language, or social and cultural background, are encouraged to participate in, and benefit from, the process of ASEAN integration and community building';
- that in the implementation of the Blueprint, ASEAN should 'strive towards promoting and supporting gender-mainstreaming, *tolerance, respect for diversity*, equality and mutual understanding'; and
- that the APSC 'subscribes to a *comprehensive approach to security*, which acknowledges the interwoven relationships of political, economic, social–cultural and environmental dimensions of development'.[20]

---

[19] *Ibid.*, pp. 49–50.
[20] ASEAN, *Political-Security Community Blueprint* (Jakarta: ASEAN Secretariat, 2009), pp. 1–2, at www.aseansec.org/5187-18.pdf (emphasis added).

Based on the above, the APSC Blueprint could serve as the main framework in promoting and strengthening RtoP norm internalisation in the region. Although these ASEAN documents are of a general nature and do not use the language of RtoP, the essential elements of APSC are clearly related to the responsibility to protect norm, particularly in regard to human rights protection, conflict prevention and resolution and post-conflict peacebuilding. To some extent, RtoP could even enhance the APSC Blueprint if this norm could be incorporated into the framework, especially in developing the capacity of ASEAN States to prevent genocide and mass atrocities. In a region that is made up of multi-ethnic societies and governed by States with a variety of political systems and culture, the language used in the APSC documents that are undoubtedly linked to RtoP include 'people-oriented ASEAN', 'promoting tolerance, respect for diversity, and equality' and 'comprehensive security'. Given that ASEAN members have adopted the APSC Blueprint, this document could then serve as a useful benchmark for measuring progress in the areas of political development, norm-building and conflict prevention. Non-State actors and civil society groups that advocate human rights protection, RtoP, and participatory regionalism could also exert pressure on governments to implement the APSC Blueprint and make substantial progress in realising the goals of this particular pillar of the ASEAN community.

Since the adoption of the APSC Blueprint in early 2009, a number of activities related to the promotion of human rights protection in the region have been undertaken, such as the adoption of the terms of reference of both AICHR and the ASEAN Commission on the Promotion and Protection of Women and Children (ACWC). The ASEAN Secretary-General's report also noted the activities and proposals for strengthening conflict prevention, peace and conflict management and regional cooperation in maintaining peace and stability. These include joint studies, seminars and dialogues in conflict reduction and resolution with Track II institutions; the adoption of a three-year work programme (2008–10) by the ASEAN defence ministers meeting (ADMM) that aims to take stock of existing peacekeeping capabilities of ASEAN Member States and the establishment of ASEAN peacekeeping centres to conduct joint planning, training and sharing of experiences aimed at establishing an ASEAN arrangement for the maintenance of peace and stability; and strengthening ASEAN humanitarian assistance through the promotion of civil–military dialogue and coordination in human-itarian relief efforts.[21]

One could argue that the focus of the ASEAN Political Security Community Blueprint in relation to RtoP is the prevention of mass atrocities by upholding universal principles related to protection of human rights, respect and tolerance for diversity, as well as underscoring the concept of comprehensive security. That members of the regional organisation are expected to adhere to these principles also presupposes that States are cognisant of the fact that they have the primary obligation or responsibility to implement these principles at home. Comprehensive security is also useful in preventing mass atrocities in the region because it includes not just the security of the State but, more importantly, human security which covers protection of peoples from violence. Even so, a number of challenges and constraints remain as far as implementing these principles are concerned. With regard to protection of human rights, for example, not all Member States have set up their respective national human rights bodies and the mandate of AICHR for now remains quite limited, especially in the area of monitoring human rights violations and sanctioning erring members. The diversity of political systems in the region, together with current institutional constraints in ASEAN, also contributes to difficulties in implementing these principles uniformly across all Member States. Specifically, the less democratic members of ASEAN are more cautious, if not necessarily unwilling to recognise the important role of non-State actors or civil society groups in promoting human rights protection in the region.

ASEAN Regional Forum[22]

The ARF remains the most important security dialogue framework in the Asia-Pacific region since its creation in 1994. Composed of

---

[21] Laos DPR Public Administration and Civil Service Authority, 'Status of the Implementation of the ASEAN Political Security Community (APSC) Blueprint (March–September 2009)', available at www.pacsa.gov.la/accsm/common.html. See also ASEAN, *Annual Report 2009/2010: Bridging Markets Connecting Peoples* (Jakarta: ASEAN Secretariat, July 2010), at www.aseansec.org/publications/AR0910.pdf.

[22] This section of the chapter is drawn from the author's short article, 'The Role of Regional and Sub-regional Arrangements in Strengthening RtoP: ASEAN and the ARF', in Stanley Foundation, *The Role of Regional and Sub-regional Arrangements in Strengthening RtoP* (New York: The Stanley Foundation, 2011), pp. 19–29, at pp. 25–6.

twenty-seven participating States and organisations from various regions,[23] over the last eighteen years the ARF has covered a range of traditional and non-traditional security issues. As a forum for security dialogue, ASEAN envisioned the ARF to evolve into three stages: confidence-building, preventive diplomacy and conflict resolution (later modified to approaches to conflict resolution). Discussions on preventive diplomacy, although a sensitive issue to many in the region, because of being perceived as undermining the norm of non-interference and respect for State sovereignty, have moved into some identification of medium and long-term measures, such as the creation of a risk reduction centre.[24] The core principles of preventive diplomacy, however, have underscored the following points: (1) that preventive diplomacy is about the employment of diplomatic and peaceful means to resolve conflicts; (2) preventive diplomacy *is non-coercive* and does not include military action or use of force; and 3) preventive diplomacy applies to *conflict between and among States.*[25] The ASEAN Regional Forum has also adopted as one of its concrete preventive diplomacy approaches the development of an early warning system for conflict prevention.[26] It is not clear, however, whether such an early warning system would include monitoring intra-State conflicts given the sensitivities of some ARF States to external involvement and supervision. In 2008, the ARF Experts and Eminent Persons meeting in Beijing agreed that preventive diplomacy discussions should focus on non-traditional security issues,

[23] Participating States in the ARF include the ten members of ASEAN and East Timor, four North-East Asian States (China, Japan, South Korea and North Korea), Mongolia, two North American States (the US and Canada), four South Asian States (India, Pakistan, Sri Lanka and Bangladesh), as well as Australia, New Zealand, Papua New Guinea, Russian Federation and the European Union (EU).

[24] Morada, 'ARF: Origins and Evolution', in Jurgen Haacke and Noel Morada (eds.), *Cooperative Security in the Asia Pacific: The ASEAN Regional Forum* (Abingdon, UK: Routledge, 2010), p. 28.

[25] ASEAN Regional Forum, 'Concepts and Principles of Preventive Diplomacy', 25 July 2001, available at www.aseanregionalforum.org. For an elaborate discussion of the debates about preventive diplomacy in the ARF, see Takeshi Yuzawa, 'The Evolution of Preventive Diplomacy in ASEAN: Problems and Prospects', *Asian Survey*, 46 (2006), pp. 785–804.

[26] ARF Working Group on Preventive Diplomacy, 'Chairman's Statement', delivered at ASEAN Regional Forum Seminar on Preventive Diplomacy, the Institute Français des Relations Internationales and the Centre for Strategic and International Studies, Paris, 7–8 November 1996, at www.aseansec.org/arf4xh.htm.

such as disaster management, nuclear proliferation and terrorism.[27] This meeting also stressed that preventive diplomacy should be based on non-interference, trust and consent.

In the seventeenth ARF Ministerial Meeting in Hanoi in July 2010, the ASEAN Regional Forum adopted a Plan of Action that includes, among others, reaching the following goals by 2020:

- further enhancement of regional capacity and readiness for peace-keeping activities, including through necessary training measures;
- integration of defence track and personnel in the ARF process;
- consolidation of confidence-building measures while implementing a number of Preventive Diplomacy measures;
- development and implementation of the ARF Preventive Diplomacy Work Plan as mandated by the sixteenth ARF Ministerial Meeting; and
- expansion and enhancement of the ARF's institutional effectiveness in implementing the ARF Plan of Action, which includes the promotion of the role of the ARF Chair with the assistance of the ASEAN Secretary General as point of contact in cases of emergency or crisis.[28]

The important role of the ARF in strengthening and implementing RtoP in the larger context of the Asia Pacific has been identified in the final report of the Council for Security Cooperation in the Asia Pacific in June 2011. Specifically, the list of recommendations pertaining to enhancing the role of the ARF includes: (1) establishing a Risk Reduction Centre to conduct early warning and assessment of the risk of genocide, war crimes, ethnic cleansing and crimes against humanity, and to cooperate with the UN; (2) strengthening ARF's capacity to employ diplomacy to mediate and resolve crises before they escalate; (3) establishing a stand-ing regional capacity to prevent genocide, war crimes, ethnic cleansing and crimes against humanity and respond to them in a timely and decisive manner; (4) ARF participants should consider providing volun-tary background briefings; (5) establishing an Inter-Sessional Meeting on Small Arms and Light Weapons; (6) creating a consultative

[27] ARF, 'Co-Chair's Summary Report of the Third Meeting of the ASEAN Regional Forum Experts and Eminent Persons, Beijing, 13–15 November 2008', available at http://aseanregionalforum.asean.org/library/arf-chairmans-statements-and-reports.html.

[28] ARF, 'Hanoi Plan of Action to Implement the ARF Vision Statement', July 2009, available at http://aseanregionalforum.asean.org/library/arf-chairmans-statements-and-reports.html. More information on the Hanoi Plan of Action is available at www.aseansec.org/8754.htm.

mechanism to monitor and advise the UN Peacebuilding Commission and support national capacity-building to prevent the four RtoP crimes; and (7) strengthening the Experts and Eminent Persons Group, so that it may play a role in implementing RtoP.[29] It was also recommended that the role of the ARF is to be complemented by capacity-building of States that specifically involve the appointment of national focal points for RtoP, raising awareness about the norm among States and societies in the region, and the use of education as an important tool to promote skills and values that would help resolve conflicts in a peaceful manner.[30] At the global level, the CSCAP report recommended the need for the UN and the region to have an 'anticipatory' relationship that could assist in their partnership towards preventing the four crimes under RtoP and adopting effective responses, as well as engaging in region-to-region and intra-regional dialogue on best practices and lessons learned in implementing the norm.[31]

The recommendations of the CSCAP in implementing RtoP may be selectively and incrementally adopted by the ARF participating States and a number of factors could influence such decision. For one, a number of ASEAN and non-ASEAN participants in the ARF remain conservative with regard to the issue of sovereignty and non-interference. The Libyan crisis may have caused some backlash for advocating RtoP in Southeast Asia, as some States in the region perceived the actions of NATO to have overstepped the mandate given under the UN Security Council Resolutions 1970 and 1973. From an institutional context, given that the ARF remains an ASEAN-centred process, it is faced with a number of constraints and challenges in implementing its peacebuilding objectives and projects. For example, contributions to the budget of the ARF under the ARF Fund remain voluntary among participating States. The ARF Unit within the ASEAN Secretariat is also limited in terms of human resources to effectively coordinate and implement many of the ARF activities and projects. More importantly, decisions made in the ARF – because it is primarily a post-ministerial meeting held annually – are not necessarily binding on all participating States without the political support of heads of States or

---

[29] Council for Security Cooperation in the Asia Pacific, Study Group on Responsibility to Protect, 'Final Report', p. 4, at www.r2pasiapacific.org/cscap-study-group-on-rtop-final-report-june-2011. More information on the work of the Study Group on the Responsibility to Protect is available at www.cscap.org/index.php?page=responsibility-to-protect.

[30] *Ibid.*   [31] *Ibid.*

governments back home. While there have been proposals to elevate the ARF into summit meetings, so far this idea has not been met with positive response from ASEAN leaders.[32]

Overall, ASEAN and the ARF evidently provide the institutional and normative framework for promotion of human rights and the protection of civilians in the region based on their existing operating principles and mechanisms. While the language of RtoP has not been formally adopted by ASEAN and the ARF, they have nonetheless incorporated key elements of the norm in a number of formal documents and agreements. The next section of this chapter provides a discussion of how ASEAN and some of its members have in a way 'practised' the principle of RtoP in certain situations.

ASEAN and the 'practice' of RtoP

To some extent, ASEAN has also practised some aspects of RtoP – without necessarily calling it as such or consciously being aware of it – through the use of diplomacy in preventing the escalation of conflicts at the regional level as well as the appropriate responses of some Member States to internal conflicts that could potentially become RtoP crisis situations. A few examples are discussed in this section, including the Maguindanao massacre in the Philippines in November 2009.

Cyclone Nargis in Burma/Myanmar[33]

ASEAN's experience in dealing with Burma/Myanmar after Cyclone Nargis in 2008 may prove to be instructive in general, as far as managing humanitarian crisis situations in the region are concerned, and, in particular, with regard to practising to some extent some aspects of 'non-coercive' RtoP. Although RtoP per se does not cover natural disasters, it could still be argued that the ensuing humanitarian crisis situations could potentially lead to mass atrocities, especially if there is a deliberate policy on the part of the State to withhold assistance to populations or certain ethnic groups. In fact, the International Commission on Intervention and State Sovereignty (ICISS) that produced *The Responsibility to Protect* report in 2001 included

---

[32] Morada, 'ASEAN and the ARF', pp. 25–6.
[33] This section is based on the author's chapter, 'Asia and the Pacific', in Genser and Cotler (eds.), *Responsibility to Protect*; and Morada, 'ASEAN and the ARF'.

environmental and natural disasters as situations where the principle could apply, whereas the 2005 UN World Summit Outcome Document did not include them.[34] Thus, one could eventually consider natural disasters a precipitating or antecedent cause of mass atrocities.

Clearly, neither the outrage of the international community, nor the proposals put forward by supporters of intervention under an RtoP banner convinced the military junta in Myanmar to open its doors to international humanitarian assistance. Instead, it was ASEAN's quiet back-door diplomacy that ultimately proved to be more effective. Much of this could be attributed to the fact that no member of ASEAN overtly condemned the military junta for not responding to humanitarian assistance being offered by Western countries led by the US and France. Instead, there was only sympathy and understanding for the constraints faced by the government in Burma. That ASEAN had to secure the consent and cooperation of the military junta to allow international humanitarian assistance to come in is another important lesson, as it demonstrates the importance of respecting sovereignty and territorial integrity of a Member State even in a crisis situation. More importantly, the role of ASEAN as the main vehicle for coordinating international humanitarian assistance cannot be overemphasised. Apparently, the military junta in Burma trusted ASEAN, given its adherence to traditional norms more than Western countries, that were viewed with much suspicion, if not absolute paranoia.

As expected, some civil society groups in the region expressed extreme disappointment with ASEAN's soft approach towards the Myanmar military junta during the crisis. Moreover, some strong RtoP interventionist advocates went as far as invoking the principle based on contrived legal arguments, alleging for example that the ruling junta was guilty of committing a 'sin of omission' when it initially refused to accept international humanitarian assistance.[35] However, they failed to acknowledge

---

[34] Jayshree Bajoria, 'The Dilemma of Humanitarian Intervention', *Council on Foreign Relations*, 24 March 2011, at www.cfr.org/human-rights/dilemma-humanitarian-intervention/p16524.

[35] Certain international law experts used this argument during an international conference on RtoP organised by the Amsterdam Centre for International Law, University of Linkoping, and the Global Center for Responsibility to Protect in Linkoping, Sweden in June 2010. For an examination of the various arguments invoking RtoP in the aftermath of Cyclone Nargis, see Asia Pacific Centre for the Responsibility to Protect, *Cyclone Nargis and the Responsibility to Protect: Myanmar/Burma Briefing No. 2* (Brisbane: Asia Pacific Centre for the Responsibility to Protect, 2008), at www.r2pasia pacific.org/documents/Burma_Brief2.pdf.

that, first, the humanitarian crisis situation was mitigated when the military junta eventually backtracked from its initial intransigent position after ASEAN mediation; and, second, RtoP cannot be invoked under the circumstances, given its limited scope and difficulties in showing that the Myanmar junta committed any of the four mass atrocity crimes when it initially declined to accept international humanitarian assistance.

ASEAN's efforts in helping Myanmar deal with the humanitarian crisis in 2008 after Cyclone Nargis served as an important lesson for the organisation to enhance further cooperation in disaster relief among Member States. Indeed, were it not for the intervention of ASEAN, Myanmar could have faced mounting international pressures that included the risk of some members of the international community invoking RtoP in responding to the crisis situation in the country.[36] ASEAN essentially presented to the military junta three options in resolving the impasse at the time, namely: (1) for the Myanmar government and the UN to lead the relief efforts; (2) for a tripartite ASEAN–Myanmar–UN coordination; and (3) for the Myanmar government and the rest of the world to deal with the issue. In the end, the second option was chosen by the military junta, which led to the creation of the Tripartite Core Group and the ASEAN Humanitarian Task Force.[37]

There is no question that the post-Nargis experience has led to enhanced cooperation between ASEAN and the UN. For example, the Third ASEAN–UN Summit held in Hanoi in October 2010, saw the launching of the Post Nargis Recovery and Preparedness Plan, as well as the adoption of the Joint ASEAN–UN Collaboration on Disaster Management. It was also agreed that the two organisations would prepare and implement the 'ASEAN–UN Strategic Plan of Action on Disaster Management 2011–2015' in coordination with the relevant ASEAN bodies and established UN mechanisms.[38]

East Timor

Through its peacekeeping operations, de facto ASEAN has practised RtoP in the region. Notwithstanding initial difficulties in dealing with

---

[36] ASEAN Post Nargis Knowledge Management Portal, 'ASEAN-led Mechanism', at www.aseanpostnargiskm.org/response-to-nargis/asean-led-mechanism.

[37] *Ibid.*

[38] ARF, 'Co-Chair's statement, delivered at Third ASEAN-UN Summit', Hanoi, 29 October 2010, at www.aseansec.org/25496.htm.

the crisis in East Timor in 1999–2000 prior to that country's independence, some ASEAN Member States contributed a significant number of troops to the UN International Force on East Timor (INTERFET) and later the UN Transitional Authority in East Timor (UNTAET) as part of peacekeeping operations. To some extent, the participation of ASEAN members were encouraged by Indonesia, largely because it wanted to diminish Australia's influence in East Timor, given that country had contributed about one-third of the close to 10,000-strong peacekeeping troops. Thailand, the Philippines and Singapore contributed about 2,500 troops to INTERFET/UNTAET. It must be noted, however, that the participation of these individual members in peacekeeping operations in East Timor was not carried out under the banner of ASEAN. Following a referendum organised by the UN, East Timor became an independent State in May 2002.

Even prior to the crisis in East Timor, some of the original ASEAN members have also participated in the peacekeeping mission in Cambodia following the Paris Peace Agreement in 1991 that ended the civil war in that country and paved the way for the UN Transitional Authority in Cambodia (UNTAC) to administer its first general elections. Indonesia, Malaysia, the Philippines and Singapore sent peacekeeping troops to the country under UNTAC. Subsequently, some ASEAN members have also actively contributed peacekeeping troops in other parts of the world as part of their efforts in assisting the UN in its peace missions. To some extent, this experience also enabled ASEAN to entertain the idea of creating a regional peacekeeping centre as one of the important tools for promoting preventive diplomacy in South-East Asia. In May 2011, for example, during the fifth meeting of the ASEAN Defence Ministers in Jakarta, members agreed to establish an ASEAN Peacekeeping Centres Network to facilitate peacekeeping planning, training and exchange of experiences.[39]

Maguindanao massacre

It is noteworthy to look into the practice of RtoP of some ASEAN Member States at the domestic level. It is in this regard that the example of the Philippines may be instructive in understanding the challenges and constraints faced by States in terms of their capacity to prevent mass

---

[39] ASEAN press release, 'ASEAN defense cooperation enters higher gear', 20 May 2011, at www.asean.org/26308.htm.

atrocities or respond to developments that could become serious RtoP crisis situations. In the Philippines, public outrage following the Maguindanao massacre in November 2009 that killed close to sixty civilians – which included some thirty journalists – exerted tremendous pressure on the government of former President Gloria Arroyo to arrest her former close political ally belonging to the Ampatuan clan. The whole province was placed under martial law for a limited period and three weeks following the incident, Arroyo signed the first domestic law (RA 9851) against genocide and crimes against humanity, which interestingly was already passed by the Philippine Congress approximately five months before the heinous crime happened. The law, however, did not take effect until it was published in two major dailies in March 2010. To date, the trial of some members of the Ampatuan clan, along with some 157 other people charged in the Maguindanao massacre, is yet to commence. Nonetheless, the government of President Benigno Aquino III promised that it would give priority to bringing justice to the victims of the massacre.

Although the Arroyo government evidently practised its responsibility to respond swiftly to the situation and avoided its escalation into a crisis situation, there is no question that the heinous crime could have been prevented if an early warning system was in place and the national government had the political will to disarm political warlords in the area especially in the run-up to the general elections in 2010. Following the incident, President Arroyo created a commission that was given broad investigative powers and tasked to make recommendations on dismantling private armies all over the country. The commission, whose members were appointed in early January 2010, was mandated to finish its task within four months, or a month before the elections in May.[40] It is estimated that there are some 800,000 loose firearms all over the country that are in the hands of private armies.[41] To date, it is not clear whether the successor government of President Aquino III has any plans to abolish private armies, which undeniably contribute to political violence and the risk of mass atrocities being committed in the country.[42]

---

[40] T. J. Burgonio, 'Six named to panel vs private armies', *Philippine Daily Inquirer*, 1 January 2010, at www.inquirer.net/specialreports/inquirerpolitics/view.php?db=1&article=20100101-245098.

[41] *Ibid.*

[42] See for example Sidney Jones, 'Philippines: is Aquino prepared to take on private armies?', *South China Morning Post*, 18 May 2010.

Overall, this particular example demonstrates that even in a demo-cratic country like the Philippines, the risk of mass atrocities being committed is quite high because the State remains institutionally weak in protecting civilians from local political warlords who rule with impunity, particularly in the conflict areas of Mindanao. Obviously, State capability-building in the context of pillar one of RtoP based on the 2005 UN World Summit Outcome Document would only be possible if the State has the political will to promote the rule of law, good governance and the protection of human rights.

Conclusion

This chapter examined existing frameworks in ASEAN that deal with areas which are relevant to RtoP, such as human security and the protection of civilians from mass atrocities. From the foregoing discus-sion, it is evident that while ASEAN has not yet formally adopted the language of RtoP in its Charter and institutional frameworks like the African Union, it has nonetheless incorporated the protection of human rights, international humanitarian law and other principles of interna-tional law and conventions among its core purposes and principles. A major challenge in the operationalisation of these principles, however, is the existing procedure of consensus decision-making in ASEAN (as well as in the ARF), which essentially forces the organisation to adopt an incremental and evolutionary approach to human rights promotion and protection in the region. Another problem concerns the competing priorities in the regional organisation's community-building pillars. Some members, in particular Indonesia and the Philippines, are more focused on political security and socio-cultural aspects of the ASEAN community, respectively, while Singapore pushes hard on the economic pillar. Related to this is the revolving chairmanship of the organisation, which allows a leading member to set and shape the priority agenda of ASEAN. Indeed, the implementation of various plans of action in all three pillars of the ASEAN community is dependent on these con-straints, including the limited resources of the organisation. In the last ASEAN Foreign Ministers Meeting in Jakarta in July 2011, Member States had agreed to set up a regional Institute for Peace and Reconciliation, but the details of which has not yet been disclosed to the public. While this is one clear step in the direction of preventing mass atrocities in the region, it remains to be seen whether it would be an effective mechanism in advancing the elements related to RtoP.

The diversity of political systems and differences in priorities of Member States to some extent has also limited ASEAN's capability to respond to crisis situations more effectively. To be fair, however, the ASEAN's experience and limited 'practice' in peacekeeping operations within and outside the region had made some of its members to become more open to conflict prevention strategies and preventive diplomacy approaches, without being too sensitive about sovereignty and non-interference. Over the long term, the bigger challenge to the promotion and implementation of RtoP in the region is not posed by ASEAN's limitations in its capability as a regional organisation, but more by its Member States' political willingness and commitment to abide by international norms related to promotion and protection of human rights and protection of civilians. In the end, ASEAN's normative values and principles will only be meaningful if members take seriously their rights and, more importantly, their *responsibilities* as *protectors* of their own people.

12

The Organization of American States

PAULO DE TARSO LUGON ARANTES

Introduction

The Organization of American States (OAS) has not been endowed with a peace-enforcement mechanism, such as that provided under Chapter VII of the United Nations Charter. However, as a regional organisation, the OAS can play an important role in preventing and addressing violations triggering the responsibility to protect (RtoP) framework, by helping the United Nations discharge one of its most fundamental functions.[1]

A marked characteristic of the OAS is the enormous political and economic asymmetry among the Member States. The Americas, cut by the equator line, also face socio-economic, cultural and ideological contrasts. This vertically oriented positioning of the region's geography has led to the incorporation of the global North–South debate into the OAS's political agenda. Members of the OAS include some of the world's largest economies, such as the United States of America and Canada, as well as some of the poorest, such as Haiti and Bolivia. The appearance of emerging economies, with growing global and regional influence, such as Brazil, Mexico and Argentina has brought about some power balance within the OAS.

These differences have a direct impact on the discussion about RtoP within the OAS. Although there is general agreement among the States in the region concerning the upholding of human rights and a State's responsibility to protect individuals under its jurisdiction against genocide, war crimes, crimes against humanity and ethnic cleansing,

---

[1] For a general discussion of the role of regional organisations, see Kristin Haugevik, 'Regionalizing the Responsibility to Protect: Possibilities, Capabilities and Actualities', *Global Responsibility to Protect*, 1 (2009) 346–63, at 350. See also in this book: Fiott and Vincent, Chapter 9; Dersso, Chapter 10; Morada, Chapter 11; Aljaghoub, Aljazy and Bydoon, Chapter 13.

differences appear in their respective approaches to RtoP in action. The RtoP concept entails issues of human security, humanitarian law and human rights. The debates about these issues are considerably contrasted in the region. The trend perceived is that of a preference for RtoP as a political avenue, rather than as a legal commitment. Interestingly, countries that are the strongest advocates of RtoP have the weakest records of treaty ratification in relevant areas.

This chapter aims at analysing the inception, evolution and future importance of RtoP within the framework of the OAS. The positions of several members and nuances of the different political and legal positions will be espoused in more detail in the following sections of this chapter.

Human rights in the Organization of American States

The OAS has a well-established system of human rights protection, consisting of the Inter-American Commission on Human Rights (IACHR, or Commission) and the Inter-American Court of Human Rights (IACtHR, or Court). Both Court and Commission have adjudicated contentious cases concerning State responsibility for human rights violations, frequently involving the core international crimes triggering RtoP.[2] The Commission, as an organ established under the OAS Charter, has jurisdiction over all OAS members. The Court, for its part, has jurisdiction over the States that have ratified the American Convention of Human Rights and have expressly accepted its contentious jurisdiction.

A number of human rights treaties have been adopted within the framework of the OAS. The American Convention on Human Rights,[3] as a general instrument, entered into force on 18 July 1978 and to date has been ratified by twenty-five of the thirty-five OAS members.[4] A clear cultural and language line can be traced between the ratifying and the non-ratifying States. Thus, States that have ratified the American Convention generally come from a Latin American culture, whereas all the non-ratifying States are of an Anglo-Saxon background. One of the

---

[2] See Hilaire Sobers, Chapter 20 in this book, for a detailed discussion on the responsibility to protect and the Inter-American human rights system.

[3] American Convention on Human Rights, adopted 22 November 1969 and entered into force 18 July 1978, OAS Treaty Series No. 36, 1144 UNTS 123.

[4] Organization of American States (OAS) countries that have not ratified the American Convention on Human Rights include Antigua and Barbuda, Bahamas, Belize, Canada, Guyana, Saint Kitts and Nevis, Saint Lucia, San Vicente and Grenadines and the United States of America.

explanations for this might be the difference between the domestic legal regimes (continental as opposed to common law systems), which might influence the culture of treaty ratification. However, a remarkable absence is the lack of Canada and the United States of America as parties to the American Convention. This is in remarkable contrast with the latter country's well-known defence of human rights in the OAS and other fora, as well as its most outspoken rhetoric on RtoP, both regionally and internationally. As regards Canada, although it accepts the jurisdiction of several UN treaty bodies, the lack of ratification of the American Convention leaves out of the Inter-American Court's jurisdiction a major country that plays a notable role in human rights worldwide.

Sovereignty

Sovereignty and non-intervention in internal affairs is a recurring issue surrounding the concept of RtoP. The perception whereby the region's North is more prone to justified intervention, whereas the region's South is hesitant to such intervention, deserves some attention. The issue of sovereignty within the Americas is rather nuanced than well defined. A balanced analysis is still missing on the relations between sovereignty and the acceptance of the concept of RtoP.

A number of recent writings have in fact revealed the variegated set of opinions among the Latin American States on the issue.[5] In any case, in order to understand this hesitance towards military intervention, it is important to understand the reasons why most of the region's countries strongly uphold the principle of non-intervention. Substantial asymmetry in economic, political and military powers among the Member States, particularly at the time of the OAS establishment in 1948, and continuing during the Cold War, has justified the desire of weaker nations, to seek a strict legal and diplomatic approach which would compensate for such asymmetry. Attempts to move towards more socialist regimes were severely suppressed by national forces, aided in different degrees by the United States, including the sponsoring by the latter (or at least sympathy for) of a number of military dictatorships during the 1970s and 1980s.

---

[5] See for instance, Andrés Serbin and Gilberto Rodrigues, 'The Relevance of the Responsibility to Protect for Latin America and the Caribbean Region: Prevention and the Role of Civil Society', *Global Responsibility to Protect*, 3 (2011), 266–85, at 267; and Ricardo Arredondo, 'La Responsabilidad de Proteger: Una Visión desde el Sur', *Agenda Internacional*, 19 (2009), 24–39.

Paradoxically, military elites in Latin America, trained by the School of Americas to suppress any attempts in the region to shift to the left, were the strongest defenders of sovereignty during and in the aftermath of the falling of several dictatorships. This trend endured even in the following decades. Redemocratisation of the South in the Americas was multi-burdened by the open wounds of mass atrocities, extreme poverty and inequality, economic stagnation,[6] wrecking of State institutions in terms of both resources and personnel and a history of internal security forces that worked to 'capture the internal enemy' instead of serving the citizens' real security concerns.

During the 1990s, one of the main commitments of the Americas' emerging democracies to the international community was the ratification of the OAS and global human rights treaties, with many of the Latin American States acceding to important international instruments such as the Statute of the International Criminal Court. Moreover, another trend in the last decades was the establishment of various truth and reconciliation commissions to account for the atrocities committed during the rule of military juntas.

A first reaction of these countries, as a repositioning measure in the international arena, was the call for greater sovereignty. Eduardo Stein contends that, under the Latin American perspective, it became clear that the fundamental concerns of those States who criticised the concept of humanitarian interventions were not due to any philosophic objection to the idea of helping populations in danger, but the fear that the relevant humanitarian principle would be abused by a few States to the benefit of the their own agendas.[7] However, the process of being more exposed to international human rights mechanisms has had the effect of necessitating a review of a number of traditional conceptions on sovereignty and intervention.

The security and democracy agenda in the Organization of American States

The OAS does not have a peace-enforcement mandate, despite the fact that the OAS Charter's Article 1 determines that its main objective is to 'achieve an order of peace and justice, to promote their solidarity, to

---

[6] The 1980s is known as 'the lost decade' for Latin America.
[7] Eduardo Stein, 'Democracia, Elecciones y Carta Democrática: Algunos Elementos de Reflexión sobre Práctica Democrática Compartida', *Revista Costarricense de Política Exterior*, 2 (2001), 6–22, at 13.

strengthen their collaboration, and to defend their sovereignty, their territorial integrity, and their independence'. Articles 19 and 21 of the OAS Charter expressly prohibit intervention in a Member States' affairs and ensure territorial inviolability. The OAS Charter text is inspired by the desire of rebuilding a peaceful world after the Second World War, based on the idea of sovereign States. Nevertheless, Article 23 provides that measures adopted for the maintenance of peace and security in accordance with existing treaties do not constitute a violation of the principles set forth in Articles 19 and 21, namely the principles of sovereignty and territorial integrity. The OAS Charter also provides for a security system based on solidarity and commonalities. Article 28 declares that an act of aggression against a given American State is deemed an act of aggression against all other counterparts.

After a relatively peaceful period during the last decades, the entire region and especially Latin American States have shifted their security concerns to other areas closely linked to development and social justice. In fact, the OAS has enshrined in Article 30 of its Charter the concept of integral development, as a key element to peace and security. Regional solidarity is expressed in the 1945 Conference of Chapultepec, which adopted an Act bearing the same name, whereby the central idea was that an attack on a signatory State is deemed as an attack on all States. Solidarity was also present in the Inter-American Treaty of Reciprocal Assistance (Rio Treaty), adopted in 19 February 1947, which reflects the normative framework on security issue of the region, under Article 3(1) of the treaty.[8]

After the Cold War, the OAS adapted its security agenda to the region's needs when a remarkable redemocratisation process took place. The OAS then gradually embraced the notion known today as human security, as opposed to State security. However, democracy, development and healing from the atrocities committed in the past had to be consolidated to a more refined debate on human security. Resolution 1080 (1991), entitled

---

[8] OAS, Inter-American Treaty of Mutual Assistance, adopted 2 September 1947 and entered into force 3 December 1948, OASTS Nos. 8 and 61, 21 UNTS 92. A current list of signatories to the Inter-American Treaty of Mutual Assistance (Rio Treaty) is available at www.oas.org/juridico/english/sigs/b-29.html. Interestingly, except Canada, only small States of the region have not ratified the treaty. Article 3(1) of the Rio Treaty provides that: 'The High Contracting Parties agree that an armed attack by any State against an American State shall be considered as an attack against all the American States and, consequently, each one of the said Contracting Parties undertakes to assist in meeting the attack in the exercise of the inherent right of individual or collective self-defense recognized by Article 51 of the Charter of the United Nations.'

'Representative Democracy', adopted by the OAS twenty-first General Assembly, established an automatic convening procedure among foreign ministers in the event of a *coup d'état* or any disturbance to a legitimately elected government.[9]

The following year, the OAS Charter was amended, giving powers to the OAS General Assembly to suspend membership of a government that overthrows a democratic regime.[10] At the same time, through the 'Santiago Commitment to Democracy and Renewal of the Inter-American System' the OAS Ministers of Foreign Affairs decided to start a process of consultations to review the current state of affairs of the issue of hemispheric security.[11] In 1993, the Managua Declaration established that the mission of the OAS is not only to restore democracy, but also to prevent and anticipate the causes of the problems that work against democratic rule. During the Second Summit of the Americas, held in Santiago, in 1998, Member States adopted a wide-ranging Plan of Action, which included security issues. On the occasion, the Committee on Hemisphere Security was requested to 'analyze the meaning, scope and implication of international security concepts in the Hemisphere', as well as to 'pinpoint ways to revitalize and strengthen' the regional system on issues relating to hemispheric security.

At the Third Summit of the Americas held in Quebec in April 2001, the Plan of Action was adopted, reaffirming the commitment of OAS members to combat genocide, crimes against humanity and war crimes,

---

[9] OAS General Assembly Res. 1080, OAS Doc. AG/RES. 1080 (XXI-0/91), 5 June 1991. Resolution 1080 decided: 'To instruct the Secretary General to call for the immediate convocation of a meeting of the Permanent Council in the event of any occurrences giving rise to the sudden or irregular interruption of the democratic political institutional process or of the legitimate exercise of power by the democratically elected government in any of the Organization's Member States, in order, within the framework of the Charter, to examine the situation, decide on and convene an ad hoc meeting of the Ministers of Foreign Affairs, or a special session of the General Assembly, all of which must take place within a ten-day period.'

[10] OAS, Protocol of Amendments to the Charter of the Organization of American States (A-56) 'Protocol of Washington', adopted 14 December 1992 and entered into force 25 September 1997.

[11] OAS, Santiago Commitment to Democracy and the Renewal of the Inter-American System, adopted 4 June 1991. The decision of the Minister of Foreign Affairs was to initiate a process of consultation on hemispheric security in light of the new conditions in the region and the world, from an updated and comprehensive perspective of security and disarmament, including the subject of all forms of proliferation of weapons and instruments of mass destruction, so that the largest possible volume of resources may be devoted to the economic and social development of the Member States; and an appeal was made to other competent organisations to join in the efforts of the OAS.

and calling on Member States to adhere to the Rome Statute of the International Criminal Court.[12] In this summit, Canada requested the OAS Committee on Hemispheric Security to review all issues related to common approaches to international security in the hemisphere, as a preparation for the Special Conference on Security the following year.

In 2001, the Inter-American Democratic Charter was adopted during the General Assembly Special Session in Lima, Peru.[13] Its Article 3 considers respect for human rights and fundamental freedoms as an essential element for representative democracy. Moreover, under Article 21, the Declaration renewed the suspension mechanism of the 1991 Santiago Commitment and gave effectiveness to the democratic clause proposed by Canada at the Quebec Summit.

In 2002, the OAS General Assembly endorsed the multidimensional concept of security, as a result of a meeting with heads of delegations at its thirty-second regular session. According to the heads of delegations gathered on that occasion, the region faced security threats, which were of a multidimensional scope and of diverse nature. For them, the traditional concept and approach of security was to be expanded to embrace the so-called 'new and non-traditional security threats' that included political, economic, social, health and environmental aspects.[14] As a means of materialising this common ideal, the Declaration of Bridgetown was adopted on 4 June 2002. This instrument paved the

---

[12] See OAS, Québec Plan of Action, adopted April 2001, p. 5. The relevant part reads, 'Combat, in accordance with international law, genocide, crimes against humanity and war crimes wherever they might occur, and in particular, call upon all States to consider ratifying or acceding to, as the case may be, the *Rome Statute of the International Criminal Court.*' More information on the Third Summit of the Americas and the documents adopted at this event are available at www.summit-americas.org/iii_summit.html.

[13] OAS, Inter-American Democratic Charter, adopted 11 September 2001. More information on the Inter-American Democratic Charter is available at www.oas.org/en/democratic-charter.

[14] OAS, Declaration of Bridgetown: The Multidimensional Approach to Hemispheric Security, adopted 4 June 2002, OAS Doc. AG/DEC. 27 (XXXII-O/02). The relevant part reads, 'The Ministers of Foreign Affairs and Heads of Delegation, assembled in Bridgetown, Barbados, on the occasion of the Thirty-Second Regular Session of the General Assembly of the Organization of American States, considering the topic "The Multidimensional Approach to Hemispheric Security" ... DECLARE that the security of the Hemisphere encompasses political, economic, social, health, and environmental factors [and] DECIDE to include the multidimensional approach to hemispheric security raised by the Ministers of Foreign Affairs at the Thirty-Second Regular Session of the General Assembly as a topic on the agenda of the Special Conference on Security, and to use the compendium of views expressed by the Ministers as a base document for the consideration of the item.'

way for the first Special Conference on Security, in Mexico City. The debates in Bridgetown were also dominated by the issues of weapons of mass destruction and terrorism in the region, having regard naturally to the attacks on the Twin Towers in New York on 11 September 2001. It was for that reason that the American Convention on Terrorism, unique in its kind, was adopted during the OAS General Assembly meeting in Bridgetown.[15]

During the debates of the Special Conference on Security in the Americas, RtoP was approached in different forms. While a number of countries were hesitant to support it (mostly the Latin American countries), the Anglo-Saxon countries defended this concept openly. For instance the Canadian Deputy-Minister of Foreign Affairs, Peter Harder, gave a statement defending the International Commission on Intervention and State Sovereignty (ICISS) document entitled *Responsibility to Protect*. He provided an overview of recent events worldwide, focusing on the shift from international to internal conflicts and terrorism. Harder also declared that 'the threats became asymmetrical, and terrorists – sometimes finding safe haven in failed States – developed networks capable of devastating attacks far from their homes'.[16]

In contrast with Harder's statement, the Brazilian Minister of Foreign Affairs, Celso Amorim, made clear his objection to a wide acceptance of RtoP in the OAS agenda, while at the same time recognising the contemporary global threats. Amorim mainly expressed concern about the new roles some military alliances self-attributed and the doctrines that mislead in a dangerous way established notions of self-defence, sovereignty, territorial integrity and the authority of the UN Security Council.[17]

The Mexican representative, General Clemente Ricardo Vega García, Defence Secretary, underscored that security priorities were combating extreme poverty and social exclusion, fighting against organised crime,

---

[15] OAS, Inter-American Convention on Terrorism, adopted 3 June 2002, OAS Doc. AG/RES. 1840 (XXXII-O/02).

[16] Peter Harder, Deputy Minister of Foreign Affairs of Canada, 'Statement by Mr Peter Harder', speech delivered at OAS Special Conference on Security, Mexico City, OAS Doc. OEA/Ser.K/XXXVIII CES/INF. 7/03 rev. 1, 28 October 2003.

[17] Celso Amorim, Ambassador and Minister of Foreign Affairs of Brazil, 'Statement by Ambassador Celso Amorim', speech delivered at OAS Special Conference on Security, Mexico City, OAS Doc. OEA/Ser.K/XXXVIII CES/INF. 12/03, 28 October 2003 (author's translation).

the world problem of drugs, the illicit traffic of weapons, the laundering of criminal activity proceeds, the prevention and mitigation of natural and human-made disasters as well as environmental preservation.[18] The Peruvian Chancellor, Ambassador Allan Wagner Tizón, for his part, emphasised that, in terms of security, poverty is the most important structural risk faced by the American countries.[19]

The Declaration on Security in the Americas, adopted at that Conference, reaffirmed the principle of multidimensional security and enumerated a large list of new threats, such as terrorism, corruption, extreme poverty, natural and human-made disasters, HIV/AIDS, maritime pollution, trafficking in persons and weapons of mass destruction.[20] It should be noted that the declaration was the result of a compromise between the interests of the developing countries, by bringing in the development agenda, and the interests of the developed North, by bringing in issues related to terrorism and weapons of mass destruction.

The 2009 IACHR's *Report on Citizen Security and Human Rights* is the most comprehensive OAS document on the issue of a State's obligation to protect individuals from atrocities triggering RtoP.[21] Building upon the hemisphere's own experience, the report tackles only crimes against

---

[18] General Gerardo Clemente Ricardo Vega García, Defence Secretary of Mexico, 'Statement by General Gerardo Clemente Ricardo Vega García', speech delivered at OAS Special Conference on Security, Mexico City, OAS Doc. OEA/Ser.K/XXXVIII CES/INF. 26/03, 28 October 2003 (author's translation).

[19] Allan Wagner Tizón, Ambassador and Minister of Foreign Affairs of Mexico, 'Statement by Ambassador Allan Wagner Tizón', speech delivered at OAS Special Conference on Security, Mexico City, OAS Doc. OEA/Ser.K/XXXVIII CES/INF. 32/03, 28 October 2003 (author's translation).

[20] OAS, Declaration on Security in the Americas, adopted 28 October 2003, OAS Doc. OEA/Ser.K/XXXVIII CES/DEC.1/03 rev.1, 28 October 2003. The operative paragraph 4(m) reads: 'terrorism, transnational organized crime, the global drug problem, corruption, asset laundering, illicit trafficking in weapons, and the connections among them; extreme poverty and social exclusion of broad sectors of the population, which also affect stability and democracy. Extreme poverty erodes social cohesion and undermines the security of states; natural and man-made disasters, HIV/AIDS and other diseases, other health risks, and environmental degradation; trafficking in persons; attacks to cyber security; the potential for damage to arise in the event of an accident or incident during the maritime transport of potentially hazardous materials, including petroleum and radioactive materials and toxic waste; and the possibility of access, possession, and use of weapons of mass destruction and their means of delivery by terrorists.'

[21] Inter-American Commission on Human Rights, 'Report on Citizen Security and Human Rights', OAS Doc. OEA/Ser.L/V/II. Doc. 57, 31 December 2009, at www.oas.org/en/iachr/docs/pdf/CitizenSec.pdf.

humanity, in the context of impunity. Nevertheless, the report makes the necessary link between this crime and rights enshrined in the American Convention, as it underscores that 'crimes against humanity give rise to the violation of a series of non-derogable rights that are recognised by the American Convention.'[22] On the issue of impunity, the report replicates the well-known *due diligence* doctrine that is a cornerstone of the Inter-American human rights system, requiring States to act in time to prevent acts of violence or to pursue the perpetrators.[23] Moreover, the report tackles the still unsolved issue of amnesty laws by stating that they are overtly incompatible with the wording and the spirit of the American Convention.[24]

Much from the 2009 Citizen Security report inspired the San Salvador Declaration on Citizen Security, adopted in 2011.[25] This declaration recognised both States' individual responsibility for protection of human rights[26] and the collective responsibility of the international community to provide humanitarian assistance.[27] However, the language on responsibility is considerably soft and no reference is made to the four crimes triggering RtoP.

In sum, the security agenda of the OAS is largely based on regional solidarity and on addressing social and other root causes of insecurity, as per the agreed multidimensional concept of security.

Different views among OAS members

Three different groups can be identified among OAS members when comparing their views on RtoP doctrine. The group which favours RtoP is composed of North American States and a few Latin American States, namely Chile and Mexico. Canada is the country that has advocated this doctrine the most in both regional and universal fora. It sponsored the

---

[22] Report on Citizen Security and Human Rights, p. 18, para. 46.

[23] Due diligence is referred to *ibid.*, paras. 47, 49, 63, 110, 124 and 136.

[24] *Ibid.*, para. 46.

[25] OAS, Declaration of San Salvador on Citizen Security in the Americas, adopted 7 June 2011, OAS Doc. AG/DEC. 66 (XLI-O/11).

[26] *Ibid.* The relevant part of this declaration reads: 'The obligation of states to develop and implement public policies in the area of public security in the framework of a democratic order, the rule of law, and observance of human rights, geared towards providing security and strengthening peaceful coexistence in their communities.'

[27] *Ibid.*, para. 19: 'Reaffirming that states have a duty and responsibility to provide the humanitarian assistance necessary to protect the life, integrity, and dignity of their inhabitants in natural or man-made disasters.'

initial study on the issue, carried out by the ICISS. This initiative was also supported by the United States.

The group holding the opposite views is composed of some South American countries, namely Bolivia, Venezuela and Nicaragua. These countries consistently reject the doctrine, as they perceive it as a justification for military intervention.

A third group of Latin American countries which includes Argentina, Costa Rica and Guatemala has increasingly accepted the concept of RtoP, but doubts and reservations on certain issues remain. More specifically, Brazil, the Caribbean Community (CARICOM) members and States forming the Rio Group have demonstrated their dissatisfaction with the lack of criteria and ambiguity surrounding this emerging principle.[28]

Among this latter group, there seems to be a wide acceptance of RtoP's first pillar, on States' primary responsibility, and of the second pillar, on provision of cooperation and assistance. However, as regards the third pillar, on timely and decisive action, there are concerns about interventions carried out without a proper UN Security Council mandate, about the misuse of the mandate favouring hidden agendas and also about the overstretching of the mandate to conduct activities not included therein. There is a recent and ongoing debate on the harm reduction of the interventions, when authorised by the UN Security Council.

There is a common understanding in Latin America that the UN General Assembly, due to its universal composition, is the appropriate venue par excellence to establish and codify the criteria for the exercise of RtoP.[29] The dissatisfaction with the lack of consistency and ambiguity surrounding the enforcement of RtoP obligations has led some members of this latter group, particularly Brazil, to abstain in a number of resolutions on human rights issues and military intervention adopted by the General Assembly and the Security Council.[30] Rather than defending unjustifiable State sovereignty, this behaviour, according to recent writings reflects a call for non-selectivity and coherence in the international debate.[31] As a soft-power player, it calls for a greater

---

[28] Serbin and Rodrigues, 'Prevention and the Role of Civil Society', 276.

[29] Juan Manuel Gómez-Robledo, Ambassador of Mexico, 'Statement by Ambassador Juan Manuel Gómez-Robledo', speech delivered at Cluster III: Liberty to Live in Dignity, New York, 20 April 2005, available at www.un.int/mexico/2005/interv_042005.htm.

[30] For example, on UNSC Resolution 1973 (2011), on the situation in Libya.

[31] 'Brazilians use the abstention to express frustration with unsystematic treatment of issues, often raising, for example, the contradiction of the international community's

democratisation of multilateral arrangements and more consistent actions by the international community. An illustration of this approach is the preference for thematic discussions (instead of country situations), as a means to have a horizontal and universal perspective on human rights and security issues.

A review of voting and statements at both the OAS and the UN demonstrates that these moderate countries are prepared to analyse military intervention on a case-by-case basis, instead of giving a blanket authorisation. Clear examples in this regard are Brazil and Argentina. For instance, these countries were non-permanent members of the UN Security Council in 1999 when the NATO-led Allied Force operation took place in Kosovo. Together with Western countries, Argentina and Brazil voted against the draft resolution tabled by Russia, Belarus and India that sought to condemn use of force outside the Security Council.[32] In its explanation of its vote, Argentina, which took part in a peace-keeping mission in the Balkans, expressed the urgent need to take action. The speech reveals the dissatisfaction with the absence of references to previous UN Security Council resolutions, which disregarded the history of previous actions and thus misrepresented the process. The Argentine delegate, however, expressed the concern of carrying out the intervention within the framework of the UN Charter and international law.[33] Uruguay – more discretely than its South American peers – has also called for the need to conduct military interventions within the framework of the UN Charter.[34]

In the same year, during the meeting of the Rio Group, in Santiago, Chile, the respective State delegates of the OAS were invited to participate in the roundtable of the ICISS. On that occasion, Colombia invited its regional counterparts for a reflection meeting. One of the representatives rejected any action outside the UN Charter as a means to deal with

---

censuring of Iran but not of Saudi Arabia. In Brazilian foreign policy, explanations accompanying abstentions are a way to express concern while upholding insistence on universality.' Council on Foreign Relations, *Independent Task Force Report 66: Global Brazil and US–Brazil Relations* (New York: Council on Foreign Relations, 2011), p. 49.

[32] UNSC Draft Resolution S/1999/328 was rejected by a count of 3 votes for and 12 against. *In favour:* China, Namibia and the Russian Federation; *Against:* Argentina, Bahrain, Brazil, Canada, France, Gabon, Gambia, Malaysia, Netherlands, Slovenia, United Kingdom of Great Britain and Northern Ireland and United States of America. UNSC Verbatim Record, UN Doc. S/PV.3989, 26 March 1999.

[33] *Ibid.*, pp. 7–8.

[34] See Benítez Sáenz, Ambassador of Uruguay, UNGA Verbatim Record, 11 October 1999, UN Doc. A/54/PV.33, p. 5.

emergency situations.[35] The strict adherence to the UN Charter as a precondition for military intervention was also emphasised during the Third EU–Latin American and Caribbean Summit, in May 2004, when multilateralism was discussed. The common perception was that there was a need to take joint action to prevent humanitarian crises, but at the same time it was necessary to adopt clear guidelines in order to avoid particular interpretations. Moreover, the Latin American countries have expressed their preference for actions within the multilateral system over ad hoc coalitions of countries, in case of conflicts.[36]

In general, Latin American States supported the principle of RtoP in the text of the 2005 World Summit Outcome, including paragraphs 138 and 139, specifically in cases where States are unwilling or unable to protect their own civilian populations from massive violations of human rights and international humanitarian law. Chile and Mexico, together with Japan, elaborated and circulated a *non-paper*, proposing the inclusion of prevention and international assistance measures, and the need to address the root causes of the atrocities, including racial hatred and inequalities.[37] This group has accepted the idea of RtoP, according to the letter and spirit of the UN Charter. Therefore, military intervention – which would be a measure of last resort – should take place in accordance with Chapter VII of the UN Charter.[38] The statement of the Brazilian representative, Ambassador Celso Amorim, during the sixtieth session of the General Assembly, seemed to represent the regional trend on the issue. He did not reject RtoP, in principle, but imparted that the root causes of human atrocities deserve a holistic approach, besides military actions. While agreeing on the merits of this doctrine, he emphasised that 'it is an illusion to believe that we can combat the dysfunctional politics at the root of grave human rights violations

---

[35] 'We consider inadmissible any action outside the framework of the Charter of the United Nations to deal with emergency situations, in conformity with the principles on humanitarian assistance agreed by the General Assembly' (OAS, Declaration of Cartagena de Indias: Un Compromiso para el Milenio, OAS Doc. GRIO/SPT-00/PDT1/03, para. 19 (author's translation)).

[36] 'We share a core belief in the multilateral system of collective security enshrined in the Charter of the United Nations. We stress our strong support for UN organs in the exercise of their full responsibilities, functions and powers, in accordance with Charter' (Declaration of Guadalajara, Third EU, Latin America and Caribbean Summit, 28 May 2004, para. 10, at eeas.europa.eu/lac/guadalajara/decl_polit_final_en.pdf).

[37] Herldo Muñoz, 'La Responsabilidad de Proteger: Tres Pilares y Cuatro Crímenes', *Foreign Affairs Latinoamérica*, 10 (2010), 101–9.

[38] Arredondo, 'Una Visión desde el Sur', 32.

by military means alone', before having exhausted diplomacy and persuasion.[39]

Chile, for its part, has shown a more straightforward and unrestricted approach, by declaring 'we believe that the international community has a responsibility to protect all human beings against war crimes, crimes against humanity, genocide and ethnic cleansing'.[40] Argentina, demonstrating the region's vocation for preventive diplomacy, during the Security Council Open Debate on the Protection of Civilians in Armed Conflict on 28 June 2006, called for the implementation of paragraph 138 of the 2005 World Summit Outcome Document, and supported the creation of an early warning mechanism, arguing that this could be an initial step regarding the implementation of paragraph 138 of the 2005 World Summit Outcome Document.[41] During the January 2007 UN Security Council debate on threats to international peace and security, the Peruvian delegate openly supported military intervention, while adding the careful caveat of 'unwilling or unable', suggesting a criterial assessment on a case-by-case basis.[42]

Two years later, a regional meeting was hosted by Mexico and the Global Centre for the Responsibility to Protect. On that occasion, the divide between countries in favour of the RtoP doctrine (especially of Chile and Mexico) and the remaining countries objected to it was clear. The side opposed to RtoP demonstrated preoccupation about the risks that the adoption of such a concept might entail.[43] In June 2009, during the UN General Assembly debates on the implementation of RtoP, Venezuela emphasised that RtoP represented a licence to unilateral intervention for the powerful countries. In contrast, Chile argued that misuse of the principle does not invalidate it. Mexico called for strengthened mediation efforts, while Colombia called for increased

---

[39] Statement by Celso Amorim, Ambassador of Brazil, UNGA Verbatim Record, UN Doc. A/60/PV.9, 17 September 2005, p. 5. For Brazil and like-minded countries, the debates on responsibility to protect cannot be properly addressed without a major institutional reform at the UN, particularly regarding the enlargement of the permanent and temporary memberships of the UN Security Council. See also Arredondo, 'Una Visión desde el Sur', 33.

[40] Statement by Alejandro Foxley, Minister of Foreign Affairs of Chile, 'Visión Estratégica de la Inserción de Chile en el Mundo', presentation delivered at National Congress, 4 April 2006.

[41] World Federalist Movement – Institute for Global Policy, 'Government Statements on Responsibility to Protect – Latin-America Region – 2005–2007', available at www.responsibilitytoprotect.org.

[42] *Ibid.*, p. 3.   [43] Arredondo, 'Una Visión desde el Sur', 33.

capacity-building. Brazil had shown scepticism during the preceding months, but adopted a positive language, arguing, as Argentina had, that RtoP was not a new legal norm, but a powerful political call for States to comply with their legal obligations set forth in the UN Charter and human rights and humanitarian treaties.[44] Moreover, the occupation of Iraq was recalled by Brazil as a 'painful experience', during the discussions regarding Iraq at the Security Council in 2010. Brazil stressed again the importance of upholding the UN Charter when military action and resort to Chapter VII measures are being contemplated.[45]

As regards the action in Libya, both Brazil and Colombia, temporary members of the UN Security Council, initially lent their support to Resolution 1970, which imposed targeted sanctions.[46] By the time of the adoption of UN Security Council Resolution 1973, however, Colombia voted in favour, whereas Brazil, together with India, Russia, China and Germany, abstained.[47] Despite having voted differently, the relevant explanations of each vote by both countries reveal caution on the issue. Brazil argued that it was not convinced that the use of force would lead to the end of violence and protection of civilians. Brazil was also concerned at the collateral damages of the intervention, but also implicitly at the allegedly hidden agenda behind this action.[48] Colombia, for its part, tried to make clear that its support for the resolution had the sole purpose of protecting the Libyan civilians, excluding territorial occupation.[49]

In sum, it can be said that a minority among the Latin American countries of the OAS is opposed to RtoP. Although some other countries demonstrate scepticism on the issue of RtoP, they have recently demonstrated more flexibility and brought new elements to the discussion. What is notable from the positions expressed by different OAS Member States over the years is that many of these countries do not oppose military intervention in all cases; rather, they ask for a strict

---

[44] Global Centre for the Responsibility to Protect, 'Implementing the Responsibility to Protect: The 2009 General Assembly Debate', at globalr2p.org/media/pdf/ GCR2P_General_Assembly_Debate_Assessment.pdf.

[45] UNSC Verbatim Record, UN Doc. S/PV.6450, 15 December 2010, p. 16.

[46] Brazil expressed its reservation to the relevant Article 6, which, according to its understanding, exempted some individuals from the International Criminal Court's jurisdiction. UNSC Verbatim Record, UN Doc. S/PV.6491, 26 February 2011, p. 7.

[47] *In favour*: Bosnia-Herzegovina, Colombia, France, Gabon, Lebanon, Nigeria, Portugal, South Africa, United Kingdom of Great Britain and Northern Ireland, United States of America; *against*: none; *abstaining*: Brazil, China, Germany, India, Russian Federation. UNSC Verbatim Record, UN Doc. S/PV.6498, 17 March 2011, p. 6.

[48] *Ibid.*, p. 6.   [49] *Ibid.*, p. 7.

analysis on a case-by-case basis. This general agreement among the Latin American States has the potential of promoting further debates on RtoP within the framework of the OAS.

Alternative and new approaches

Within the OAS members, in particular the Latin American ones, the discourse on RtoP has undergone a visible refinement, demonstrating, to a certain extent, flexibility on the principle of sovereignty to which the relevant countries were strongly attached a few decades ago. Some alternatives have been brought forward through statements and papers on the part of these States.

Non-indifference

A common discourse, by both Brazil and Argentina has been the principle of non-indifference with regard to RtoP crimes, similar to the African Union practice. As early as 2000, Argentine President Fernando de La Rúa, during the Security Council Summit, made a statement explaining the complementarity between the principles of non-intervention and non-indifference. He argued that countries have a wide range of actions at their disposal, other than, and before resorting to military intervention. He also argued that non-indifference does not mean international impunity, citing the examples of the various international criminal tribunals as important deterrent tools.[50]

Likewise, the non-indifference approach was the flair of the Brazilian President Luiz Inácio Lula da Silva's foreign policy in 2003–10. Brazilian Minister of Foreign Affairs Celso Amorim, during the OAS General Assembly in 2006 affirmed:

> It is very important that we are all capable of practicing the non-indifference, i.e., an engagement in aiding, whenever requested, for the democratic consolidation of the countries. But, at the same time, it is also important that we abstain from interfering in internal affairs.[51]

[50] Fernando de la Rúa, President of Argentina, 'Statement by the President of the Argentine Republic', speech delivered at Millennium Summit, New York, 7 September 2000, at www.un.org.

[51] Statement by the Brazilian Minister of Foreign Affairs, Ambassador Celso Amorim, at the 38th OAS General Assembly in Santo Domingo, 5 June 2006, available at www.itamaraty.gov.br/ sala-de-imprensa/discursos-artigos-entrevistas-e-outras-comunicacoes/ministro-estado-relacoes-exteriores.

According to Ricardo Seitenfus, member of the Inter-American Juridical Committee, although the approach of non-indifference has not been consolidated as a regional principle yet, the practice of the OAS members in several actions, including towards Haiti, is characterised by the application of integral development, as enshrined in the OAS Charter. He contends that this is part of the so-called solidarity diplomacy, whereby a great number of countries of the Americas, acting collectively, search to address beyond the cold *raison d'état* the challenges of human beings.[52]

The practice of non-indifference at the OAS has, in fact, demonstrated the ability to mobilise regional diplomacy, by means of persuasion and dialogue. It has also the advantage of going into the root causes of the violations that trigger RtoP. It opens a window of opportunity for preventive action, provided that the State in question has the willingness to engage in the process. However, it cannot exclude criminal responsibility of both State agents and private parties involved in the violations being addressed.

Responsibility while protecting

Brazil has proposed the concept of *'responsibility while protecting'*.[53] This concept does not exclude military intervention, but requires exhaustion of all peaceful diplomatic channels and express authorisation of any such military intervention by the UN Security Council. More importantly, this initiative represents the first significant mandate-oriented concept, in that it seeks a strict abidance to the relevant UN Security Council mandate in a given military intervention. It also adds a content of accountability in the conduct of military interventions mandated under Chapter VII.[54] This new idea might represent a bridging element among the opposing nations, in that while it allows military intervention as a measure of last resort, it calls for a greater care in the discharging of the relevant mandate.

The concept seems to be a reflection of the experience in past actions, with negative impacts on the civilian population in the mid and long terms, including new cycles of violence. The concept note, elaborated by Brazil, is quite emphatic:

---

[52] Statement of Mr Ricardo Seitenfus at the Special Session on the Principles of International Law contained in the OAS Charter, 22 March 2007, Washington, DC.

[53] UN, 'Responsibility While Protecting: Elements for the Development and Promotion of a Concept', letter dated 9 November 2011 from the Permanent Representative of Brazil to the United Nations Addressed to the Secretary-General, UN Doc. A/66/551–S/2011/701, 11 November 2011.

[54] *Ibid.*, para. 11(i).

Yet attention must also be paid to the fact that the world today suffers the painful consequences of interventions that have aggravated existing conflicts, allowed terrorism to penetrate into places where it previously did not exist, given rise to new cycles of violence and increased the vulnerability of civilian populations.[55]

The concept note brought a clear message on the possible abuse of RtoP to seek regime change, one of the concerns usually raised by the opponents of military intervention.[56] Furthermore, it put forward nine parameters and procedures to be considered, including preventive diplomacy, exhaustion of all peaceful means to protect civilians under threat and use of force authorised by the UN Security Council, under Chapter VII's framework. As an operational requirement, use of force under *responsibility while protecting* should be judicious, proportionate and limited to the objectives established by the Security Council.[57] Notable among the parameters is also the limitation of legal, operational and temporal elements and scope of the action.[58] Another important requirement put forward is that use of force must produce as little violence and instability as possible and 'under no circumstance can it generate more harm than it was authorized to prevent'.[59] The concept paper also calls for enhanced procedures at the Security Council to monitor and evaluate the implementation of the military actions taken by the international community.[60]

This concept is likely to permeate the following OAS debates, although this regional institution does not have powers to decide on military intervention. This doctrine, combining elements of accepting military intervention as a last resort and strict mandate and abidance to the UN Charter, has the potential of gathering greater consensus among the OAS members.

Conclusions and the way forward

The OAS has strong components on democracy and human rights, which are related to RtoP. The strong feelings for sovereignty, especially from the Latin American and Caribbean countries, have been replaced by a considerable degree of flexibility when RtoP issues are concerned, whether by accepting supranational human rights supervision or by

---

[55] *Ibid.*, para. 9.
[56] *Ibid.*, para. 10: 'There is a growing perception that the concept of the responsibility to protect might be misused for purposes other than protecting civilians, such as regime change. This perception may make it even more difficult to attain the protection objectives pursued by the international community.'
[57] *Ibid.*, para. 11(f).   [58] *Ibid.*, para. 11(d).   [59] *Ibid.*, para. 11(e).   [60] *Ibid.*, para. 11(h).

having steadily recognised the concept of RtoP. Important countries in the region, which were quite sceptical on humanitarian intervention, like Brazil, have explained their reasons for such hesitation. Moreover, Brazil has proposed the *responsibility while protecting* alternative, which is also likely to be introduced in future OAS debates.

Admittedly, in the last decades, the region has not witnessed mass atrocities on the scale of other regions. However, crimes against humanity remain unpunished in a number of instances. The case law of the Inter-American Court of Human Rights reveals problems relating to national amnesty laws, passed in order to shield perpetrators of murder, torture, forced disappearances and other crimes from domestic prosecution. To name the few most recent, this Court has ruled in *Moiwana Community* v. *Suriname* that the Surinamese amnesty law left a vague interpretation of crimes against humanity, leading to dangerous interpretation on the content of these crimes and to a potential denial of justice for the African descendant community.[61] In *Almonacid Arellano et al.* v. *Chile*, the Court ruled that the Chilean amnesty law was not compatible with the American Convention, since the victim, having suffered a crime against humanity, could not be granted proper justice and reparations.[62] The Court's judgment in *Gomes Lund et al.* v. *Brazil* invalidated Brazil's amnesty law of 1979 that left unpunished crimes affecting thousands of victims of the military regime from 1964 to 1985.[63] In *Gelman* v. *Uruguay*, the Court took a similar approach.[64]

Although gross and systematic violations of human rights are currently a low risk in the Americas, it is the duty of all stakeholders, including regional organisations, to prevent and address by various means war crimes, crimes against humanity, ethnic cleansing and genocide. It should be noted that recent gross human rights violations in the region, while involving a reduced number of victims, have targeted the

---

[61] *Case of the Moiwana Community* v. *Suriname, Judgment*, IACtHR, Series C, No. 124, 15 June 2005, paras. 165–7.

[62] *Case of Almonacid Arellano et al.* v. *Chile, Judgment*, IACtHR, Series C, No. 154, 26 September 2006, para. 119.

[63] *Case of Gomes-Lund et al. (Guerrilha do Araguaia)* v. *Brazil, Judgment*, IACtHR, Series C, No. 219, 24 November 2010, para. 325(3). The Brazilian Supreme Court, in opposite direction, has ruled for the validity of the amnesty law, in a judgment in May 2010, on an injunction (153/DF) filed by the Brazilian Bar Association. The implementation of IACtHR's judgment faces serious implementation challenges due to the Supreme Court ruling.

[64] *Case of Gelman* v. *Uruguay, Judgment*, IACtHR, Series C, No. 221, 24 February 2011, para. 229.

most vulnerable groups, such as indigenous peoples and former slave communities. While the OAS does not have a peace-enforcement mandate, that fact does not discharge the OAS from its duty to be prepared to respond promptly to atrocities that might take place in the region.

Besides its political mechanisms, the OAS is endowed with a system of human rights protection composed of a Court and a Commission, as well as a growing number of Rapporteurships.[65] While these mechanisms have been fundamental to set regional standards and to create important precedents that are applied in a number of jurisdictions, most of their work focuses on the aftermath of the violations committed. Both the Court and the Commission are granted powers to decide on provisional or interim measures of protection and such measures in the case of categories of crimes falling under RtoP deserve greater attention.

Ramcharan has proposed the creation of a Rapporteurship on Responsibility to Protect.[66] Alternatively, a member of the Inter-American Commission on Human Rights could be appointed to monitor State compliance with RtoP obligations.[67] If this suggestion were to be implemented by the OAS, the respective Rapporteur could oversee among others the implementation of precautionary measures aimed at preventing crimes falling under RtoP. They could be an essential link between the expertise of the Court and Commission and the political structure of the OAS. The Rapporteur could assume the role of an early warning mechanism, which could trigger action by the political and other organs of the OAS.

The OAS has the successful experience of the Santiago Commitment and the Democratic Charter, which include an urgent mechanism of consultation in case of democratic rupture of a country in the region, with the possibility of suspending membership until the rule of law is restored. Based on and profiting from the region's great vocation for preventive diplomacy,[68] a similar mechanism with a focus on RtoP could be adopted through a resolution. This mechanism would have the nature

---

[65] See Chapter 20 of this book for a detailed discussion of the Inter-American system of human rights and RtoP.

[66] Bertrand Ramcharan, 'Enhancing the Responsibility to Protect in Latin America and the Caribbean', in Stanley Foundation, The Role of Regional and Subregional Arrangements in Strengthening the Responsibility to Protect (New York: Stanley Foundation, 2011), pp. 38–42, at p. 40.

[67] In any case, a report of the Inter-American Commission on Human Rights on the responsibility to protect, including current law applicable, past violations and current threats, best practices and recommendations would be quite useful.

[68] The second pillar of RtoP has not been a contentious issue in the region.

of early warning for preventing serious crimes in the OAS area. It could call, for instance, urgent meetings of foreign ministers, ministers of defence or permanent representatives to the OAS in Washington to agree on a timely and decisive course of diplomatic action.[69] The issue, with coordination among the OAS members sitting in the UN Security Council at the time, could be reported *incontinenti* to the UN Security Council and the UN General Assembly. This urgent meeting would be considerably productive if a final document is adopted, indicating the actions taken and further steps envisaged.

An effective mechanism must necessarily have a mix of expert and political components. The Rapporteur on RtoP could have the mandate to request an urgent meeting of the OAS in case of an RtoP situation, but this could also be open to an OAS Member State. Reasons to request such a high-level meeting could be a given precautionary measure issued by the Court or Commission or credible and reliable information brought to the Rapporteur. Possibilities of action would have to involve urgent *in loco* visits by the Rapporteur, facilitated by ministers who would receive an interim report of such visits after a few days. The Rapporteur could receive assistance from a commission of specialists on RtoP and on the country in question, appointed from a previously established roster.

Evidently, from a more structural perspective, universal ratification of the American Convention on Human Rights, and acceptance of the Court's contentious jurisdiction, should be attained. This achievement would allow equal treatment among the OAS Member States, especially if monitoring of precautionary measures is envisaged.[70] A commitment to universalise the ratification of the Rome Statute of the International Criminal Court can also be put in place among the regional peers.[71] That would ensure that a permanent international court such as the ICC could get involved if crimes such as genocide, war crimes, crimes against humanity or ethnic cleansing were imminent or were already being committed.

---

[69] Given the urgency of the issues at stake, these meetings could be virtual when necessary.

[70] OAS Member States, in particular the Latin American and Caribbean Group (GRULAC) countries, have used the Universal Periodic Review mechanism, of the UN Human Rights Council, to recommend their regional counterparts to ratify the American Convention and the Rome Statute, among other important human rights treaties.

[71] Periodic resolutions of the OAS General Assembly already call upon States to ratify this treaty. For a detailed discussion of the ICC and RtoP, see Contarino and Negrón-Gonzales, Chapter 18 in this book.

13

The Arab League

MAHASEN M. ALJAGHOUB, IBRAHIM M. ALJAZY
AND MAYSA S. BYDOON

Introduction

The Arab League was established at the end of the Second World War, as a regional political organisation, with a desire to foster Arab independence and unity.[1] However, in its almost sixty-six-year history, the Arab League was not able to fulfil its expectations. Its effectiveness has been hampered by divisions among its Member States. Consequently, the League proved unwilling or unable to solve recurring regional problems.

The recent 'Arab Spring', as it has come to be known, has brought down a number of authoritarian regimes and has accelerated necessary political reforms in many Arab countries. The grave humanitarian situation in Libya, Yemen, Bahrain and Syria has offered an opportunity to test the doctrine of the responsibility to protect (RtoP). However, only in the Libyan case, the Security Council, with the support of the Arab League, adopted Resolution 1973 (2011) which expressly referred to RtoP in imposing a no-fly zone over Libya and in authorising a military intervention to protect civilians. The Arab League might be accused of double standards because, as explained below, it has taken an active stand on the crises in Libya and Syria, but it has failed to respond to human rights abuses in Yemen and Bahrain following the government forces' crackdowns on peaceful protests in those countries. To avoid that, the Arab League should apply consistent standards in responding to human rights violations in the region. This chapter argues that the Arab League should play a key role in implementing RtoP measures, because,

---

[1] For more information on the League of Arab States, see Ahmed Gomaa, *The Foundation of the League of Arab States: Wartime Diplomacy and Inter-Arab Politics* (London: Longman, 1977).

as a regional organisation, it understands better the causes and nature of problems affecting the region.

The chapter is divided into three sections. The first section examines the origin, structure, objectives and institutional limitations of the Arab League. Some consideration is also given to the human rights system of this regional organisation. The mechanism of the League's Charter and the Arab Charter for Human Rights needs improvements and modifications. One of these improvements and modifications should be the creation of an Arab Court of Human Rights. It is also suggested that the League's members should take necessary steps to improve the League's institutional and legal architecture which would eventually allow the League to offer assistance to States that encounter problems which might lead to RtoP situations based on fulfilling the second pillar of RtoP, namely international assistance and capacity-building.

Section two of the chapter focuses on the role of the Arab League in supporting Security Council Resolution 1973 (2011), which authorised the taking of all necessary measures with the only purpose of protecting civilians in Libya. It is argued that although the Arab League supported this resolution, it did not, however, approve NATO's way of carrying out the Security Council mandate and not-so-implicit pursuance of the aim of regime change, which arguably was not the aim of RtoP.

In analysing the crisis in Syria, section three argues that the high number of unarmed civilians killed by government forces should make a stronger case for RtoP. However, RtoP was not invoked and not even seriously contemplated in this situation. The section analyses the reasons behind the League's reluctance of using the Libyan-style international intervention in Syria. Indeed, the perceived overstepping of the UN mandate by NATO has led to an increased reluctance on the part of the Arab League to set the stage for applying RtoP in Syria. The stance of the Arab League, until now, is based on not allowing any international intervention in Syria, because such intervention will not be devoid of foreign ambitions. Therefore, the Arab League is called upon to create mechanisms and solutions within the Arab circle, outside the agendas and interests of international players. Lastly, the section analyses the Arab League's successive resolutions, most importantly Resolution 7438 (12 November 2011) to suspend Syria's membership and Resolution 7442 (27 November 2011) to impose economic sanctions on Syria.

The military intervention in Libya largely confirmed the pre-existing doubts that its main objective was to protect the self-interest of some intervening States, rather than to protect civilians. Therefore, it is suggested that the organised Arab community should maintain its control over the situation in Syria in order to prevent the chaotic situation created by the external intervention in Libya. However, if the Arab League is incapable of saving endangered civilians, then any international military intervention has to be carried out under the necessary restrictions, agreed beforehand.

The Arab League: origin, objectives, structure and limitations

Following the adoption of the Alexandria Protocol in 1944,[2] the Arab League was founded in Cairo as a regional organisation on 22 March 1945. The League was established by seven countries: Iraq, Egypt, Syria, Lebanon, Jordan, Saudi Arabia and Yemen, to respond to the contemporary challenges at that time. The Charter of the Arab League consists of a Preamble, twenty Articles, and three Appendices.[3] Article 2 of the Arab Charter affirms the commitment of the founding members to strengthen the relationships among Member States and to safeguard their independence and sovereignty. The original thought behind establishing the Arab League was the desire of the British to unite the Arab nations against the Axis powers. Mr Anthony Eden, British Secretary of State for Foreign Affairs, in his declaration at the Mansion House on 29 May 1941 stated that:

> The Arab world has made great strides since the settlement reached at the end of the last War, and many Arab thinkers desire for the Arab peoples a greater degree of unity than they now enjoy. In reaching out towards this unity they hope for support. No such appeal from our friends should go unanswered. It seems to me both natural and right that the cultural and economic ties, too, should be strengthened. His Majesty's Government for their part will give their full support to any scheme that commands general approval.[4]

The establishment of an Arab union was also an aspiration of Arab nationalists. Although Arabs fought on the side of the Allies in the First World War to achieve their freedom from Ottoman rule, the League was not formed until the final months of the Second World War.

[2] For further details, see the Arab Unity Declaration: Minutes Regarding the Discussions and Ratification of Alexandria Protocol, reprinted in *Journal of Arab Affairs*, 43 (1985), 283–313; Gomaa, *The Foundation of the League of Arab States*.

[3] Charter of the League of Arab States, adopted 22 March 1945, 70 UNTS 237.

[4] Majid Khaddari, 'International Affairs, Towards an Arab Union: The League of Arab States', *American Political Science Review*, 40 (1946), 90–100.

The Arab League is organised into a Council, Special Committees and a Permanent Secretariat.[5] The League's highest body is the Council, which has one representative from each Member State with one vote and no veto mechanism.[6] The voting procedures in the Arab League's Charter provide that unanimity shall be the general rule. Decisions taken by unanimous votes bind all Member States, whereas decisions taken by majority bind only the members that have accepted them.[7] Contrary to the United Nations system, the Charter of the Arab League leaves resolutions to be independently adopted and enforced by Member States. Regrettably, the Arab League has no effective mechanisms to enforce its own resolutions.

The League's Charter grants the Council several competences which include accepting new members, expelling members from the League, appointing the Secretary General, amending the Charter, and mediating in disputes that arise between members or between members and non-members. The Council, moreover, promotes the realisation of the objectives of the League.[8]

As for the General Secretariat, which has its headquarters in Cairo, it consists of a Secretary-General, Assistant Secretaries and an appropriate number of officials. Article 12 of the Arab Charter provides that the Secretary-General is appointed by the League's Council, by a majority of two-thirds of Member States. The Secretary-General oversees the work of the Secretariat which acts as the executive body of specialised ministerial councils. As for the Committees, Article 4 of the League's Charter provides that the main task of the Committees is to expand the cooperation between Member States, and to draft international agreements for discussion and approval by the League's Council.[9]

According to Article 1 of the Charter, membership to the Arab League is open to independent Arab States. The League currently has twenty-two members: all of them members of the United Nations, except for Palestine

---

[5] There are other organs in the League which were created under the Treaty of Joint Defence and Economic Cooperation. These organs include the Joint Defence Council (JDC); Consultative Military Organisation (CMO); the Permanent Military Commission (PMC); the Arab Unified Command (AUC) and the Economic Council (EC).

[6] Charter of the League of Arab States, arts. 3(1) and 7.   [7] Ibid., art. 7.   [8] Ibid., art. 5.

[9] The Committees meet at the permanent seat of the League in Cairo, Egypt, however, it is possible with the approval of the Secretary-General, to meet in another Member State. See League of African States, Internal Regulations of the Committees of the League of Arab States, adopted 13 October 1951, arts. 5, 7 and 9. There are eleven Committees created in accordance with Articles 2 and 4 of the Charter.

whose request is currently pending.[10] The Charter of the Arab League has granted its members the right to withdraw from the League, if their respective interests demand such withdrawal.[11] Moreover, in accordance with Article 18(2), the Council has the right to expel any member that fails to fulfil its obligations under the Charter.[12] The decision does not take effect, unless adopted by unanimity vote, not counting the vote of the member concerned. The Council has never used this competence.

Initially, the League's Charter did not provide for the suspension of membership in any of its articles. Nevertheless, the Council suspended Egypt's membership in 1979, subsequent to Egypt's signature of the peace treaty with Israel.[13] In applying its RtoP measures, Libya became the second member in the League's history to be suspended on 22 February 2011, since the Libyan government kept using military force against civilians. Although the Arab Parliament recommended the suspension of Syria and Yemen on 20 September 2011 over several reports of disproportionate violence against civilians during the Arab Spring, the decision was taken on 12 November 2011 to suspend only Syria.[14]

Regrettably, the Charter of the Arab League does not include any reference to human rights. The Arab Charter on Human Rights (ACHR) was first drafted in 1971 and was adopted by the Council of the Arab League in 1994, however, it never came into force. An updated version of the Charter was introduced in 2004, and this final version has been in force since 15 March 2008. The 2004 version of the Charter came as part of an effort to 'modernise' the League of Arab States.[15]

---

[10] Although Palestine has not yet achieved independence, it has been a member of the Arab League since 1976.

[11] 'If a member state contemplates withdrawal from the League, it shall inform the Council of its intention one year before such withdrawal is to go into effect' (Charter of the League of Arab States, art. 18(1)).

[12] 'The Council of the League may consider any state which fails to fulfil its obligations under the Charter as separated from the League, this to go into effect upon a unanimous decision of the states, not counting the state concerned' (*ibid.*, art. 18(2)).

[13] This decision was taken by a resolution adopted during the Conference of the Arab Ministers of Foreign Affairs held in Iraq. In addition to the membership suspension of Egypt, political and economic measures were taken against Egypt such as the discontinuation of economic contributions, and the removal of the League's permanent headquarters from Cairo to Tunisia. For more details about this treaty and other related documents, see 'Egypt–Israel–United States: Camp David Agreements', *International Legal Materials*, 17 (1978), 1463–74; 'Egypt–Israel: Treaty of Peace', *International Legal Materials*, 18 (1979), 362–93.

[14] Syria, Lebanon and Yemen voted against the decision, while Iraq abstained.

[15] League of Arab States, Arab Charter on Human Rights, adopted 22 May 2004 and entered into force 15 March 2008.

The Charter affirms the universality and indivisibility of human rights and recognises the right to health, education, fair trial, and freedom from torture, the independence of the judiciary, and many other rights. The preamble accepts the principles of the Islamic Shari'a, and those of other divine religions, regarding fraternity and equality among people. It also stresses the total rejection of discrimination and Zionism, both of which are viewed as constituting a violation of human rights and a threat to world peace. In addition, the preamble also contains a strong emphasis on the principles of the United Nations Charter, the Universal Declaration of Human Rights, the provision of the two United Nations International Covenants and the 1990 Cairo Declaration on Human Rights in Islam.

It is argued that the continued unrest in the Arab world demonstrates the ineffectiveness of the ACHR, which, although demands Member States to respect basic human rights, does not create sufficient enforcement mechanisms. The expert Committee remains the only system for monitoring State compliance.[16] The Committee, which comprises seven members, receives periodic reports from States Parties. After that, the Committee examines the periodic reports and issue recommendations on the necessary action to be taken to improve compliance.[17] There is no mechanism for petitions from individuals to this Committee for violations of the ACHR. However, the ACHR allows for the adoption of additional protocols for amendments of the instrument in its Articles 50 and 52, which opens the door for future additional rights and, it is hoped, for establishing efficient enforcement mechanisms.[18] Needless to say, the supervisory mechanism of the ACHR needs improvement. One of these potential improvements should be the creation of an Arab Court of Human Rights and an Arab Court of Justice.[19] It should be mentioned

---

[16] The Arab Human Rights Committee was established in March 2009 as an expert treaty body of seven members to supervise the implementation of the Arab Charter on Human Rights.

[17] Article 48 of the Charter provides that States Parties undertake to submit reports to the Secretary General of the League of Arab States on the measures they have taken to give effect to the rights and freedoms recognised in this Charter and on the progress made towards the enjoyment thereof. The Secretary General shall transmit these reports to the Committee for its consideration. The Committee will submit an annual report to the Secretary General of the Arab League, with its recommendations and reports entering the public domain.

[18] Mervat Rishmawi, 'The Revised Arab Charter on Human Rights: A Step Forward', *Human Rights Law Review*, 50 (2005), 361–76.

[19] It should be noted that there were many proposal for creating an Arab court on human rights. One of them was the 'Draft Charter on Human and People's Rights in the Arab World 1978' prepared by the International Institute of Higher Studies in Criminal

that, since the inception of the League, several attempts have been made to create an Arab court of justice, similar to the International Court of Justice (ICJ). However, these efforts have so far been unsuccessful.

The Libyan crisis: background and regional and international response

RtoP as a principle was adopted by the majority of the world's leaders in the 2005 World Summit Outcome. Paragraphs 138–9 of the relevant document lay down that sovereign States have a responsibility to protect their own population, but when they are unwilling or unable to do so, that responsibility must be borne by the international community which is to 'take collective action, in a timely and decisive manner'.[20] The Arab League has supported the enforcement of RtoP obligations in Libya, among others, by lending legitimacy to NATO's intervention. Undeniably, the Arab League's involvement and support for the intervention in Libya sent a strong, clear and unprecedented message that RtoP is a vital doctrine that has to apply when the lives of civilians are at risk.

Protests against Muammar Gaddafi's regime seeking governmental reform began in Libya's second city, Benghazi, in mid-February 2011. Gaddafi responded forcefully, trying to end the protests by using military force. Moreover, in his speech on 22 February 2011, Gaddafi called on his people to capture the protesters and bring them 'to justice', and to attack and 'cleanse Libya house by house' until the protesters surrendered.[21] The tragic humanitarian situation in Libya during the uprising was noted in many UN statements.[22] Many refugees fled to Egypt or flocked

Sciences in Syracuse, Italy. See Mohammed A. Al-Midani, 'The Enforcement Mechanisms of the Arab Charter on Human Rights and the Need for an Arab Court of Human Rights', Arab Centre for International Humanitarian Law and Human Rights Education, at www.acihl.org/articles.htm?article_id=22.

[20] '2005 World Summit Outcome', UN Doc. A/RES/60/1, 24 October 2005.

[21] For news reports on Gaddafi's threatening statements, see, among others, www.responsibilitytoprotect.org/index.php/crises/crisis-in-libya; and 'Libyan Leader Muammar Gaddafi Appears on State TV', BBC, 22 February 2011, at www.bbc.co.uk/news/world-africa-12533069.

[22] See among others the statement by the Special Advisers on the Prevention of Genocide and RtoP, condemning the widespread and systematic attacks against civilian populations. UN press release, 'UN Secretary-General Special Adviser on the Prevention of Genocide, Francis Deng, and Special Adviser on the Responsibility to Protect, Edward Luck, on the situation in Libya', 22 February 2011, at www.un.org/en/preventgenocide/adviser/statements.shtml; UN Security Council press release, 'Security Council press statement on Libya', UN Doc. SC/10180, 22 February 2011, recalling Libya's responsibility to protect its population; UN Office of the High Commissioner for Human Rights

to neighbouring States' borders, especially on the Tunisia–Libya border, thereby creating a serious humanitarian crisis. The UN High Commissioner for Refugees (UNHCR) estimated that about 243,000 Libyans were internally displaced because of the fighting.[23] In its June 2011 report to the Human Rights Council, the High Commissioner for Human Rights noted among others that the Working Group on Enforced or Involuntary Disappearances had expressed deep concern about allegations, according to which hundreds of enforced disappearances had been committed over the last few months in Libya, and referring to the fact that these may amount to crimes against humanity.[24]

Many States, international organisations and NGOs voiced their strong condemnation of the excessive use of force against civilians in Libya and declared that such situation represented a violation of international law and human rights. The General Secretariat of the Organization of the Islamic Conference (OIC) considered the ongoing coercion and oppression in Libya 'a humanitarian catastrophe which goes against Islamic and human values'.[25] In the same vein, the OIC called on Libyan authorities to stop immediately their acts of violence against innocent Libyans, and emphasised the need to address their claims peacefully, through serious dialogue instead of assassination and bloodshed.[26]

The representative of Lebanon introduced the draft resolution on suspension of the membership of Libya from the Human Rights Council.[27] He also stated that 'time was of the essence, as evidenced by the violence and killing endured by the Libyan people in the last few weeks'.[28] He underlined that the measure to suspend Libya's membership was 'exceptional and

---

press release, 'Pillay calls for international inquiry into Libyan violence and justice for victims', 22 February 2011, at www.ohchr.org; and UN High Commissioner for Refugees, 'UNHCR Fears for the Safety of Refugees Caught in Libya's Violence', 22 February 2011, at www.unhcr.org/print/4d6393e06.html.

[23] More information on civilian displacement in Libya and the work of the UNHCR is available at www.unhcr.org/pages/49e485f36.html.

[24] See UN Human Rights Council, 'Report of the High Commissioner under Human Rights Council Resolution S-15/1', UN Doc. A/HRC/17/45, 7 June 2011, pp. 8–9, para. 31.

[25] Organisation of the Islamic Conference press release, 'OIC General Secretariat condemns strongly the excessive use of force against civilians in the Libyan Jamahiriya', 22 February 2011, available at www.oic-oci.org. See also OIC press release, 'Statement of Professor Ekmeleddin Ihsanoglu, OIC Secretary General to the Meeting of the Permanent Representatives on the Situation in the Libyan Jamahiriya', 8 March 2011, available at www.oic-oci.org.

[26] Ibid.

[27] UN General Assembly Res. 65/L.60, UN Doc. A/65/L.60, 25 February 2011.   [28] Ibid.

temporary'.[29] Consequently, in March 2011, the UN General Assembly considered the situation in Libya, and adopted by consensus a resolution suspending Libya from 'the rights of the membership' on the Human Rights Council.[30] This was the first time a Member State has been suspended from the Human Rights Council.

The role of the Arab League in supporting Security Council Resolution 1973

Both the Arab League and the Security Council referred to RtoP obligations on the part of the State in the case of Libya. It is undeniable that the Arab League, as a regional organisation, played a critical role in providing to the Security Council accurate and relevant information from a regional perspective. The relationship between the UN and regional organisations is regulated in Chapter VIII of the UN Charter. Article 53(1) of the UN Charter does not permit any enforcement action without the authorisation of the Security Council. The stance of the Arab League in suspending the membership of Libya and Syria is encouraging in terms of accountability, and it could be potentially helpful in encouraging such countries to meet at least basic human rights standards.[31] The continuing cooperation between the UN and the Arab League is manifested also in the efforts of the Joint Special Envoy for the United Nations and the Arab League aimed at bringing an immediate end to all human rights violations in Syria. Although these last efforts were neither decisive nor timely, such efforts support the second pillar of RtoP in terms of assisting States in meeting their obligations. It should be noted that such non-coercive measures are the first to be employed to respond to a situation through the RtoP framework.[32]

The intervention in Libya raises the issue of the relationship between the Arab League and the Security Council in terms of the proper role of

---

[29] UN press release, 'General Assembly suspends Libya from Human Rights Council', UN Doc. GA/11050, 1 March 2011.

[30] UNGA Res. 65/265, UN Doc. A/RES/65/265, 3 March 2011.

[31] See UN Secretary-General, 'The Role of Regional and Sub-regional Arrangements in Implementing the Responsibility to Protect', UN Doc. A/65/877–S/2011/393, 27 June 2011, paras. 34 and 40.

[32] The Security Council gave full support to efforts of joint special envoy of UN and the Arab League to end violence in Syria. See UNSC press release, 'In presidential statement, Security Council gives full support to efforts of Joint Special Envoy of United Nations, Arab League to end violence in Syria', UN Doc. SC/10583, 21 March 2012.

regional organisations in supporting the use of the RtoP doctrine. The UN Secretary-General has affirmed that:

> The responsibility to protect relies on the whole range of policy instruments addressed in Chapters VI, VII, and VIII of the Charter. Since there may be cases where less coercive policy tools are insufficient to protect populations, then no broad strategy for implementing RtoP could be completed without some reference to Chapter VII.[33]

That leaves regional organisations in a somewhat peculiar position, since they cannot take enforcement action without prior authorisation by the Security Council.[34]

Military intervention and the threat or use of force are prohibited and are considered against the spirit and purposes of the United Nations. Article 2(4) of the UN Charter provides that States should refrain from acts which are against the sovereignty of other States. Such a prohibition is reinforced further by UN resolutions and declarations,[35] and through the practice of the International Court of Justice.[36] Paragraph 139 of the 2005 World Summit Outcome Document requires that collective action should be taken 'through the Security Council, in accordance with the

---

[33] UNSG, 'Regional and Sub-regional Arrangements', para. 30.

[34] According to Article 53 of the UN Charter, the Security Council shall, where appropriate, utilise such regional arrangements or agencies for enforcement action under its authority, but no enforcement action shall be taken under regional arrangements or by regional agencies without the authorisation of the Security Council.

[35] The Declaration on the Inadmissibility of Intervention in the Domestic Affairs of States and the Protection of their Independence and Sovereignty was adopted on 21 December 1965, by a vote of 109 in favour to none against, with one abstention. UNGA Res. 2131 (XX), UN Doc. A/RES/2131(XX), 21 December 1965. In the preamble and opening paragraph, this resolution cites the 'gravity of the international situation and the increasing threat to universal peace due to armed intervention and other direct or indirect forms of interference threatening the sovereign personality and the political independence of States.' See also the Declaration on Principles of International Law Concerning Friendly Relations and Co-operation among States in Accordance with the Charter of the United Nations adopted in UNGA Res. 2625 (XXV), UN Doc. A/RES/2625(XXV), October 1970.

[36] In the *Nicaragua* case, the ICJ concluded that non-intervention 'forbids all States or group of States to intervene directly or indirectly in internal or external affairs of other States'. The ICJ defined prohibited intervention through the use of various methods of coercion, including the use of force. See Military and Paramilitary Activities in and against Nicaragua (Nicaragua *v.* United States of America), Merits, Judgment, ICJ Reports, 1986, p. 14. See also Ramesh Thakur, *The Responsibility to Protect: Norms, Laws and the Use of Force in International Politics* (New York: Routledge, 2010), pp. 86–111; and Zyberi, Chapter 16 in this book.

Charter'. In other words, the collective nature of RtoP requires authorisation from the UN Security Council.

The involvement of the Security Council in authorising coercive measures or approving military intervention is generally seen as a measure of last resort. In the case of Libya, as discussed below, the Arab League suspended Libya's membership for its repeated attacks on the civilian population before the enforcement action taken by the Security Council.[37]

Support for the no-fly zone over Libya and democratic transition

The Arab League took a strong stand against the violence on Libyan civilians. On 22 February 2011, the Arab League condemned serious violations of human rights and international humanitarian law that were being committed in Libya. Consequently, the League suspended Libya's membership therein. The Arab League Secretary-General at the time, Amr Moussa, announced that the organisation has decided to halt the participation of the Libyan delegations from all Arab League sessions. That decision made Libya the second country in the League's history to have its membership suspended.

In Resolution 7360 adopted by consensus on 12 March 2011, the Arab League's Council requested the UN Security Council 'to bear its responsibilities towards the deteriorating situation in Libya, and to take the necessary measures to impose immediately a no-fly zone on Libyan military aviation, and to establish safe areas in places exposed to shelling as a precautionary measure that allows the protection of the Libyan people and foreign nationals residing in Libya, while respecting the sovereignty and territorial integrity of neighbouring States.'[38] Moreover, in paragraph 3 of the same resolution, the Arab League called on Member States, friendly countries, international organisations and Arab and international civil society to provide support and urgent humanitarian assistance to the Libyan people during this critical period of their history through various channels.

In its Resolution 1970, the UN Security Council condemned the use of force against civilians and deplored the gross systematic violations of

---

[37] UNSG, 'Regional and Sub-regional Arrangements', para. 34.
[38] See UNSG, 'Letter dated 14 March 2011 from the Permanent Observer of the League of Arab States to the United Nations addressed to the President of the Security Council', UN Doc. S/2011/137, 15 March 2011.

human rights in Libya.[39] Furthermore, acting under Chapter VII of the UN Charter and taking measures under its Article 41, the Security Council demanded an immediate end to the violence, decided to refer the situation to the International Criminal Court (ICC), and imposed an arms embargo, travel ban and asset freeze for a number of named individuals.[40] Because of the continuation of massive human rights violations and the Libyan disregard of Resolution 1970, on 17 March 2011 the Security Council adopted Resolution 1973. This resolution was adopted by a vote of ten in favour and five abstentions.[41] Among others, the resolution reiterated the responsibility of the Libyan authorities to protect the Libyan population and reaffirmed that parties to an armed conflict bear the primary responsibility to take all feasible steps to ensure the protection of civilians. Lebanon, as a non-permanent member of the Security Council, supported the resolution and maintained that 'Libya was suffering heavily, with hundreds of victims dying and thousands displaced. Faced with those risks and the great danger of those crimes, the United Nations had acted earlier, but Colonel Gaddafi had not heeded those actions.'[42] Resolution 1973 strengthened the measures already adopted in Resolution 1970, and authorised 'Member States that have notified the Secretary-General, acting nationally or through regional organisations or arrangements, and acting in cooperation with the Secretary-General, to take all necessary measures' to protect civilians.[43] Moreover, this resolution also established a ban on all flights in the airspace of Libya in order to protect civilians.[44]

With regard to the provisions of Resolution 1973, some of the abstaining countries raised many debatable questions concerning how and by whom the measures would be enforced and what the limits of the engagement would be. For example, the representatives of China and the Russian Federation explained their abstentions by the necessity to exhaust all peaceful means, as an initial measure to resolve the conflict. The delegations of India, Germany and Brazil equally stressed 'the need

[39] UNSC Res. 1970, UN Doc. S/RES/1970, 26 February 2011.
[40] UNSC Res. 1973, UN Doc. S/RES/1973, 17 March 2011.
[41] The five States abstaining were Brazil, China, Germany, India and the Russian Federation.
[42] UNSC press release, 'Security Council approves "no-fly zone" over Libya, authorizing "all necessary measures" to protect civilians, by vote of 10 in favour with 5 abstentions', UN Doc. SC/10200, 17 March 2011.
[43] UNSC Res. 1973, para. 4.   [44] Ibid., paras. 6 and 7.

for peaceful resolution of the conflict and warned against unintended consequences of armed intervention'.[45]

The ambiguity of Resolution 1973 has raised many problematic issues, especially concerning whether it included the possibility of regime change. According to this resolution, the Security Council authorised the taking of all necessary measures to protect civilians, without providing any assurances that the authorised entities were not to exceed the scope of authorisation. Paragraph 4 of Resolution 1973 imposed limitations on the scope of 'all necessary measures' that must be directed 'to protect civilians and civilian populated areas under threat of attack in the Libyan Arab Jamahiriya'. The US Defense Secretary, Robert Gates, voiced a restrictive view in the terms of Resolution 1973. He maintained that 'the one thing that there is agreement on are the terms set forth in the Security Council resolution', adding that, 'If we start adding additional objectives then I think we create a problem in that respect.'[46] Akande has argued that paragraph 4 of Resolution 1973 did not prohibit the targeting of Gaddafi and authorised it where this were deemed necessary to protect civilians.[47] Shaw has maintained that 'Anything that supports Libyan jets – including the military command structure, airfields and anti-aircraft batteries – would be legitimate.'[48] In the same vein, Sands believed that 'The authorisation of "all necessary measures" is broad and appears to allow the targeting of Gaddafi and others who act to put civilians "under threat of attack", words that go beyond the need to establish a connection with actual attacks.'[49]

---

[45] UNSC press release, 'Security Council approves "no-fly zone"'. On 19 March 2011, a multi-State coalition began a military intervention in Libya to implement UN Security Council Resolution 1973, which was taken in response to events during the 2011 Libyan civil war. On 19 March, military operations began, with US and British forces firing over 110 Tomahawk cruise missiles and the French Air Force and British Royal Air Force undertaking sorties across Libya, as well as the implementation of a naval blockade by the Royal Navy. The official names for the interventions by the coalition members are Operation Harmattan (France), Operation Ellamy (United Kingdom), Operation Mobile (Canada) and Operation Odyssey Dawn (United States of America).

[46] Patrick Wintour and Owen Bowcott, 'Libya: the legal case for deployment', *The Guardian*, 21 March 2011, at www.guardian.co.uk/world/2011/mar/21/libya-arab-and-middle-east-protests.

[47] Dapo Akande, 'What Does UN Security Council Resolution 1973 Permit?', *EJIL:Talk*, 23 March 2011, at www.ejiltalk.org/what-does-un-security-council-resolution-1973-permit.

[48] Wintour and Bowcott, 'Case for Deployment'.

[49] Philippe Sands, 'UN's Libya Resolution 1973 is better late than never', *The Guardian*, 18 March 2011, at www.guardian.co.uk/law/2011/mar/18/libya-un-resolution-1973.

Actually, a textual reading of Resolution 1973 reveals that its objective was to protect civilians at risk, not to change the regime. Even if ultimately the protection of civilians required the change of the Gaddafi regime, this should have been done with more caution. In this regard, Shaw argues that blowing up the Finance Ministry in Tripoli was not authorised.[50] Piotrowicz, also maintains that:

> The [attorney general's] note fails to clarify the extent to which force might be used to protect civilians. Targeted attacks on senior Libyan officials might be justified if this is the only way to stop attacks on civilians. That would include an attack on Colonel Gaddafi himself. The government is acting prudently in not clarifying this now because to do so might limit its freedom of action later, or reveal just how far it is prepared to go.[51]

At the London Conference on the Libyan crisis held on 29 March 2011, a Contact Group on Libya was set up to find a solution to the crisis.[52] The Arab League and other participants[53] in this conference reaffirmed their support through military, logistical, financial or humanitarian contributions, and pledges in support of the people of Libya.[54] Moreover, the participants agreed that only the Libyan people can choose the government of Libya, as they must be free to determine their own future. Participants recognised in terms of supporting democracy the need for all Libyans to come together to begin an inclusive political process, consistent with the relevant UN Security Council resolutions, through which they can choose their own future.[55]

The support of the Arab League lent legitimacy to all the measures taken by the Security Council. Moreover, Qatar, one the League's Member States, offered to cooperate with other Member States in

---

[50] Wintour and Bowcott, 'Case for Deployment'.   [51] *Ibid.*

[52] The Contact Group held its three previous meetings respectively in Doha, Rome and Abu Dhabi. The Libya Contact Group met for the fourth time in Istanbul on 15 July 2011 under the co-chairmanship of the Republic of Turkey and the United Arab Emirates. The Contact Group held its sixth and final meeting on 1 September 2011 in Paris. At the meeting, the Contact Group was dissolved and replaced with a new international meeting group called the Friends of Libya.

[53] Participants included the Foreign Ministers and representatives from the United Nations, the League of Arab States, Organisation of the Islamic Conference, the European Union and NATO.

[54] Conference Chair William Hague, UK Foreign Secretary, 'Chair's Statement', following London Conference on Libya, at www.fco.gov.uk/en/news/latest-news/statements1/.

[55] *Ibid.*

implementing the no-fly zone.[56] The active Arab partnership with the international community was expressed not only in the measures that would be taken, but also in the financial support for such measures. Qatar for example became the first Arab state to contribute to no-fly-zone patrols over Libya. Qatar deployed six Mirage fighter aircraft and two C-17A aircraft for the no-fly zone and relief operations. The United Arab Emirates pledged six F-16 and six Mirage fighter aircraft for the no-fly-zone operation. Qatar was also the first country in the region to grant recognition to the National Transitional Council (NTC).[57]

With respect to the Jordanian role in addressing the Libya crisis, Abdel-Elah Mohamed Al-Khatib, former Minister for Foreign Affairs of Jordan, was appointed as the UN Special Envoy to Libya, and played an important role in trying to end the violence, ensuring accountability and facilitating humanitarian assistance.[58] Jordan called for intensifying international efforts over the Libyan crisis and took a leading role in supporting the political development and social and humanitarian development of Libya.[59] During the Paris conference, King Abdullah II of Jordan called on the international community to support the Libyan people to draw up their democratic and political future on their own.[60] King Abdullah II stated that 'this requires a comprehensive political

---

[56] The initial coalition of Belgium, Canada, Denmark, France, Italy, Norway, Qatar, Spain, UK and US has expanded to nineteen States, with newer States mostly enforcing the no-fly zone and naval blockade or providing military logistical assistance. For more information, see www.itar-tass.com/en/c53/186440.html.

[57] From 17 February 2011 to 13 June 2011, thirteen nations recognised the National Transitional Council (NTC) following Australia, Britain, France, Gambia, Italy, Jordan, Malta, Qatar, Senegal, Spain, the United Arab Emirates and the United States. See 'Germany Recognizes Rebel Leadership in Libya', at www.dw-world.de/dw/article/0,,15150852,00.html.

[58] See UNSG, 'Letter Dated 10 March 2011 from the Secretary-General to the President of the Security Council', UN Doc. S/2011/126, 11 March 2011; UNSC, 'Letter Dated 11 March 2011 from the President of the Security Council to the Secretary-General', UN Doc. S/2011/127, 11 March 2011.

[59] Minister of Foreign Affairs Nasser Judeh called for intensifying international efforts to arrive at a political solution in Libya. During his participation in the fourth meeting of the Libya Contact Group in Istanbul, Judeh stressed the need for a ceasefire, in accordance with the UN Security Council Resolution 1973, which authorises all measures to protect Libyan civilians. See Royal Hashemite Court Media and Communications Directorate press release, 'King takes part in Paris conference on Libya rebuilding', 1 September 2011, at www.kingabdullah.jo/index.php/en_US/news/view/id/9469/videoDisplay/1.html.

[60] The conference held on 1 September 2011 in Paris was co-hosted by French President Nicolas Sarkozy and British Prime Minister David Cameron. It was attended by head of the Libyan National Transitional Council Mustafa Abdul Jalil, executive head of the

process based on tolerance, reconciliation, justice and the role of law under the leadership of the National Transitional Council to consolidate the unity of the Libyan people, guarantee their sovereignty and enable them to restore security and achieve development.'[61]

On 25 August 2011, the Contact Group reaffirmed that the Gaddafi regime no longer had any legitimate authority in Libya. Henceforth and until an interim authority was in place, participants agreed to deal with the National Transitional Council as the legitimate governing authority in Libya.[62] On 27 August 2011, the Arab League recognised the NTC. The National Transitional Council is internationally accepted as the governing body of Libya.

Although the Arab League supported Security Council Resolution 1973, it did not approve of NATO's way of carrying out that mandate and not-so-implicit pursuance of the aim of regime change. In fact, the Arab League questioned the collateral bombing of civilians, when Amr Moussa, the then-Arab League Secretary General, declared that 'What has happened in Libya differs from the goal of imposing a no-fly zone and what we want is the protection of civilians and not bombing other civilians.'[63] Moreover, he underscored that:

> The goal should be to protect Libyan civilians. Why did I say so? There were reports that civilian casualties started to appear as a result of the attacks by the coalition. As a result, I said that all civilian casualties and attacks that would affect the civilians are our concern – and that is why we needed to establish a no-fly zone and safe areas in the first place. We are committed to the Security Council goals, letter and spirit according to what the resolution determines.[64]

Consequently, as Amr Moussa stated, from the Arab League's perspective, the purpose of military operations and Resolution 1973 was 'not to give the

NTC Mahmoud Jibril, UN Secretary-General Ban Ki-moon, Bahraini King Hamad Ben Isa Al Khalifa, Qatari Emir Sheikh Hamad Ben Khalifa Al Thani, German Chancellor Angela Merkel and US Secretary of State Hillary Clinton, among others. For more information, see, among others, Jamey Keaton, 'World Conference on Libya urges new UN resolution', *The Guardian*, 1 September 2011, at www.guardian.co.uk/world/feedarticle/9826008.

[61] Royal Hashemite Court, 'Paris Conference'.

[62] Turkish Ministry of Foreign Affairs, 'Fourth Meeting of the Libya Contact Group Chair's Statement', 15 July 2011, available at www.mfa.gov.tr.

[63] Martin Beckford, 'Libya attacks criticised by Arab League, China, Russia and India', *The Telegraph*, 21 March 2011, at www.telegraph.co.uk.

[64] Raghida Dergham, 'The goal in Libya is not regime change', interview with Amr Moussa, *New York Times*, 23 March 2011, at www.nytimes.com/2011/03/24/opinion/24iht-edmoussa24.html.

rebels support. It is not a question of supporting a regime, a government or a council. It is to save the situation from further, bloody deterioration.'[65] However, according to the resolution's wording, the only obligation on Member States in implementing Resolution 1973 was to inform the UN Secretary-General of the measures they took. The resolution did not specify any kind of legal or political control over military operations by the Security Council. In addition, there was no specification in the resolution of any guidelines affecting rules of engagement. Based on the experience in Libya, it is debatable whether or not the Arab League will be able to take similar decisions in the coming period regarding Syria.

From Libya to Syria: can RtoP survive?

Since mid-March 2011, major human rights violations have taken place in Syria.[66] Thus, the Syrian government's response to the anti-regime protests amounts to a clear and grave violation of human rights obligations. The Security Council condemned the violence against civilians and the widespread human rights violations, and called upon the Syrian government to respect, and to alleviate the humanitarian situation in crisis areas by ceasing the use of force against affected towns.[67] The UN Human Rights Council also condemned the continued grave and systematic human rights violations committed by the Syrian authorities and called upon them to fully comply with their obligations.

Unlike the Libyan case, the Security Council's draft resolution concerning Syria was vetoed by Russia and China. The opposing countries stressed the importance of finding a peaceful settlement through dialogue and reiterated the importance of Syrian territorial integrity. The negative experience in Libya and other relevant considerations complicated the possibility to use the RtoP doctrine in this case. Russia, among others, supported the use of peaceful means and non-military intervention.[68] South Africa also referred to the 'hidden agendas' by NATO's

---

[65] *Ibid.*

[66] For details on the sequence of events and human rights violations since March 2011, see UNHRC, 'Report of the Independent International Commission of Inquiry on the Syrian Arab Republic', UN Doc. A/HRC/S 17/2/Add.1, 23 November 2011.

[67] Only Lebanon, one of the non-permanent members of the Security Council, disassociated itself from the consensual statement. UNSC Verbatim Record, UN Doc. S/PV.6598, 3 August 2011.

[68] In this regard, Vitaly Churkin, Ambassador of Russia, maintained that, 'The situation could not be considered apart from the Libyan experience'. He also stated that 'compliance with Security Council resolutions in Libya had been considered a model for

regime change operation and asserted that the UN Mandate in Libya 'had been abused and implementation had gone far beyond mandates' and that the Security Council 'should not be part of any hidden agenda for regime change'.[69]

The role of the Arab League in Syria

As noted above, faced with the Libyan crisis, the Arab League asked the Security Council to establish a 'no-fly' zone over Libya. However, in the case of Syria, RtoP was not invoked and not even seriously contemplated by the Arab League. This approach might be interpreted as being informed by a fear on the part of the League that such measures could eventually lead to regime change in Damascus. The then-Secretary General of the League, Amr Moussa, declared that what has happened in Libya differs from the goal of imposing a no-fly zone.[70] Indeed, the overstepping of the UN mandate by NATO has made it much harder for the Arab League to set the stage for applying the RtoP in Syria. If this happens again, the region might enter into a new period of instability, as any external intervention in Syria will be even more complicated than Libya.

Syria has a strategic position and influence in the Middle East. It shares borders with Israel, Lebanon, Jordan, Turkey and Iraq. Moreover, Syria has a strong alliance with Iran and Hezbollah. Therefore, many countries in the region fear that the United States' recent withdrawal from Iraq might leave the country more beholden to Iran, which would give Iran a large sphere of influence stretching from western Afghanistan to the Mediterranean Sea.[71] Even the thought of such a possibility is discomforting for most of the Middle Eastern States, Israel and the US. The potential consequences of military action are some of the factors that animate the complex situation and that make Syria a linchpin to many American foreign policy goals in the Middle East.

---

future actions by the North Atlantic Treaty Organization (NATO). It was important to see how that model had been implemented. The demand for a ceasefire had turned into a civil war, the humanitarian, social and military consequences of which had spilled beyond Libya. The arms embargo had turned into a naval blockade on west Libya. Such models should be excluded from global practice' (UNSC Verbatim Record, UN Doc. S/PV.6627, 4 October 2011, p. 4).

[69] *Ibid.*   [70] Beckford, 'Libya attacks criticised'.

[71] George Friedman, 'Syria, Iran and the balance of power in the Middle East', *Stratfor*, 22 November 2011, at www.stratfor.com/weekly/20111121-syria-iran-and-balance-powermiddle-east.

The division in Syrian society in terms of religious sectarianism, ethnicity and ideology is considered to be challenging when it comes to contemplating potential ways to deal with the Syrian regime. This division has hampered the formation of an organised Syrian opposition, which is much needed to speak on behalf of the people it represents and to coordinate subsequent pressure by the international community and to strengthen its resolve for change.

The Arab League's sanctions on Syria

In view of the previous experience in Libya, it seems that the Arab States are planning to maintain their control over the situation in Syria in order to avoid the chaotic situation created by external intervention in Libya. The League took a remarkably firm line by suspending Syria's membership on 12 November 2011 pursuant to its Resolution 7438.[72] This resolution called on Arab States which still maintain ambassadors in Damascus to withdraw them and announce economic and other unspecified political sanctions. Eighteen out of twenty-two Member States of the Arab League approved this decision.[73] On 23 November 2011, the League delivered a three-day ultimatum to Syria to stop its murderous repression. Subsequently, by Resolution 7442 of 27 November 2011, the League decided to enforce economic sanctions against Syria.[74] The measures imposed by the League include cutting off transactions with the Syrian central bank, a travel ban on senior Syrian government officials travelling to other Arab countries, a freeze on assets of the Assad government and an embargo on investments into the country. The decision was endorsed by nineteen members with Iraq, Lebanon and Algeria abstaining.[75]

The Arab League's Protocol for Syria

The Syrian government has signed the Arab League initiative to end the violence in the country. Under the plan it must allow Arab League

---

[72] For a discussion of this action taken by the Arab League, see, among others, Neil MacFarquhar, 'Arab League votes to suspend Syria over crackdown', *New York Times*, 12 November 2011, at www.nytimes.com.

[73] Lebanon and Yemen voted against, while Iraq abstained.

[74] See, 'Full Text of Arab League Resolution Against Syria', *Open Briefing*, 8 November 2011, at www.openbriefing.org/regionaldesks/middleeast/resolution7442.

[75] *Ibid.*

monitors into the country, withdraw the army from towns, release political prisoners and start a dialogue with the opposition. The Syrian Foreign Affairs' Minister Walid al-Moallem declared that 'The signing of the protocol is the beginning of cooperation between us and the Arab League and we will welcome the Arab League observers.'[76] Al-Moallem also stated that Syria will be coordinating 'on daily basis' with present Arab League Secretary General, Nabil Elaraby.[77]

The Arab Parliament, an Arab advisory body, urged the Arab League to terminate the monitors' mission in Syria, saying the mission had failed to end the bloodshed in the country. After admitting 'mistakes' in the League's Syria monitoring mission, the League turned to the United Nations for help. The head of an Arab League task force on Syria asked the UN Secretary-General for technical help by stating, 'We are coming here for technical help and to see the experience the UN has, because this is the first time the Arab League is involved in sending monitors, and there are some mistakes.'[78] On 22 January 2012, at the League's meeting of Foreign Affairs Ministers in Cairo, Saudi Arabia pulled out of the Arab League monitoring mission, criticising Damascus for failing to act to stop violence against protesters and because the Syrian government had not followed an Arab peace plan it agreed to, before the monitors were sent.[79]

In this meeting, the League's Foreign Affairs Ministers declared the new Arab League plan which contains the formation of a national unity government under the auspices of Syria's vice-president. According to this plan, the Syrian opposition would begin a dialogue with the government under the auspices of the Arab League and that Syria's vice-president would be tasked with forming a new government within two months. The plan also calls for parliamentary and presidential elections to be held in the coming months. In this regard, the Secretary-General of the Arab League stressed that the Arab League seeks a peaceful solution similar to what happened in Yemen and

---

[76] Bassem Mroue, 'Syria signs Arab League deal to allow observers', *The Guardian*, 19 December 2011, at www.guardian.co.uk/world/feedarticle/10002558.

[77] *Ibid.*

[78] 'Arab League admits "mistakes" on Syria mission', France 24, 5 January 2012, at www.france24.com.

[79] 'Syria unrest: Saudis pull out of Arab League mission', BBC, 22 January 2012, at www.bbc.co.uk/news/world-middle-east-16670007.

opposes a Libyan-style international intervention.[80] On 23 January 2012, the Arab League Secretary General, Nabil Elaraby, sent a letter to the UN Secretary-General, Ban Ki-moon, asking for a joint meeting between them in the UN headquarters to inform the Security Council about developments and obtain the support of the Council for this plan. Damascus, on its part, rejected the League's proposals, calling them an 'attack' on its national sovereignty and a 'flagrant interference' in its internal affairs.[81]

The future of RtoP in Syria

The crisis in Syria has reached a critical point with several thousand persons killed from Syrian government forces. The regime has stood firm against the popular uprising and has not hesitated to shell unarmed civilians. The role of the League in Syria is particularly important, as the chances of international action, such as the one in Libya, are unlikely since Russia and China have already cast their vetoes to block a Security Council resolution in Syria. The question remains whether Russia and China will come under more pressure to go along with other members of the UN's Security Council and whether they will agree to authorise an intervention in Syria?

The Security Council is not the only organ of the UN that carries the responsibility to maintain international peace and security, although the UN Charter vests it with broad powers and primary responsibility in this respect. Also the General Assembly carries certain responsibility for maintaining international peace and security, especially when the Security Council is deadlocked.[82] In the *Certain Expenses* Advisory Opinion, the International Court of Justice has examined the powers of the General Assembly and the Security Council in maintaining international peace and security and has concluded that the powers of the Security Council in such matters are primary, but not exclusive.[83]

---

[80] 'Arab League extends Syria observer mission amid serious divisions', *Voice of America*, 21 January 2012, at www.voanews.com.

[81] Alistair Lyon, 'Arab League turns to UN as Gulf observers quit Syria', Reuters, 24 January 2012, at www.reuters.com.

[82] Maysa Bydoon, 'The Amendment of the United Nations Charter without using Article 108 of the UN Charter', *European Journal of Social Sciences*, 16 (2010), 167–74, at 172–3.

[83] The Court stated that 'The functions and powers conferred by the Charter on the General Assembly are not confined to discussion, considerations, the initiation of studies and the making of recommendations; they are not merely hortatory' (*Certain Expenses of the United Nations, Advisory Opinion*, ICJ Reports 1962, p. 163).

One theoretically possible way to provide a legal justification for intervention in Syria without a UN Security Council resolution is for the General Assembly to invoke the 'Uniting for Peace' resolution. However, an authorisation of the use of force in Syria by the General Assembly is unlikely to pass without support from the majority of the General Assembly's members. Thus, for such an initiative to be successful lobbying from the Arab League and the Organisation of the Islamic Cooperation, which has fifty-seven Member States drawn from the Muslim majority and Arab countries, is necessary.

Concluding remarks

Over the course of 2011 and 2012 a number of Arab countries, have been witnessing a critical wave of popular uprisings, which have resulted in the re-evaluation of the relationship between the ruling system of each of these countries and their citizens. More specifically, the amount of State violence against civilians in the uprising in both Libya and Syria highlighted an essential tension within the international community regarding the RtoP doctrine. This tension might be related to the fact that under the current international legal system framework the application of the third pillar of the RtoP doctrine, namely that of timely and decisive response, is largely associated with the Security Council. NATO's intervention in Libya with the support of the Arab League has become a controversial issue within the Arab world, raising the question of why the Security Council decided to intervene in Libya, but stayed out of the crisis in Syria. Consequently, the Arab League's position towards Syria seems to take into consideration its negative experience with regard to Libya. Indeed, the perceived overstepping of the UN mandate by NATO has led to an increased reluctance on the part of the Arab League to set the stage for applying RtoP in Syria.

On the other hand, the Security Council has not been able to adopt a satisfactory resolution regarding Syria, due to disagreements among its permanent members. The question remains why, short of authorising intervention in Syria, the Security Council is not referring the Syrian case to the International Criminal Court, or not imposing any meaningful sanctions? The reasons behind this state of affairs might be that certain members of the Security Council think that there is nothing to be gained from adopting such measures and there is not enough support from the Arab League. As discussed above, it seems that Arab States are planning to supervise themselves the situation in Syria, in order to avoid another

Libya. In any event, the League has taken a remarkably firm line by suspending Syria's membership pursuant to Resolution 7438 and by enforcing economic sanctions against Syria pursuant to Resolution 7442.

Regrettably, the inconsistent responses of the international community to similar situations as those of Libya and Syria underpin the claims about international community's double standards. This inconsistency puts the efficiency of the doctrine of RtoP at risk. The moral purpose for the military intervention in Libya, of stopping all forms of violence, was rather agreeable; however, the main political purpose therein remains questionable. Accordingly, the strong reaction and military intervention in Libya seems to confirm doubts on the part of developing States that the main objective was to protect self-interest of some of the intervening States rather than to, *solely* and *primarily*, protect civilians. For the Arab League, the experiences of Libya and Syria might mean that in order to have an objective application of the RtoP doctrine and to justify the interference in a State's domestic jurisdiction, the scope of RtoP has to be interpreted quite narrowly.

14

The Organization for Security and Co-operation in Europe

DENNIS J. D. SANDOLE

Introduction

The objective of this chapter is to examine the Organization for Security and Co-operation in Europe (OSCE), the world's largest and most comprehensive, regional 'soft' security organisation,[1] and its conceptual and empirical fit with a recent contribution to international law agreed to at the UN World Summit in 2005, the 'Responsibility to Protect' (RtoP).

Developed as a reaction to the failure of the international community *to prevent genocide, war crimes, ethnic cleansing and crimes against humanity* in, among others, Rwanda during April–July 1994 and one year later in Srebrenica, Bosnia-Herzegovina during 12–18 July 1995, the responsibility to protect is meant to prevent such atrocities in the future by calling upon members of the international community to protect populations at risk, *especially from their own governments,* by taking appropriate collective action, including the use of military force, within the context of the United Nations.

This chapter will first articulate a conceptual device, the '3 Pillar Framework' (3PF), to facilitate discussion of the various facets of RtoP. It will then present a detailed narrative on the OSCE and its predecessor, the Conference on Security and Cooperation in Europe (CSCE), and the evolving organisation's convergence with the various elements of RtoP. This will be followed by a summary that highlights the nexus between the CSCE/OSCE and RtoP. We will then examine the results of interviews I conducted with CSCE/OSCE heads of delegation in Vienna over an eleven-year period that provide complimentary text on where the

The author gratefully acknowledges Dr Ingrid Sandole-Staroste and Dr Gentian Zyberi who have read and commented on earlier drafts of this chapter.
[1] See Joseph Nye, Jr, *Soft Power: The Means to Success in World Politics* (New York: Public Affairs, 2004).

CSCE/OSCE has been heading with regard to RtoP. We conclude with a discussion of what the OSCE should/could be doing in the future to maximise the fit between it and RtoP.

Setting the stage for discussion of the CSCE/OSCE-RtoP nexus: the 3 Pillar Framework (3PF)

To facilitate the discussion of the nexus between the CSCE/OSCE and RtoP, I have located it within the Comprehensive Mapping of Conflict and Conflict Resolution: A Three Pillar Approach, or simply the '3 Pillar Framework'. I developed the 3PF originally to integrate the vast amount of multidisciplinary information on the field of conflict analysis and resolution, but soon realised that the 3PF was also useful for mapping any particular conflict situation as a basis for exploring what, if anything, could be done about it.[2] Graphically, the 3PF appears as depicted in Table 1.

The working hypothesis of the 3PF is that, in order to deal with any given conflict situation, we must first understand it. We need to know what its essential elements are (Pillar 1), such as the parties involved, the issues over which they are in conflict, the objectives they hope to achieve, the means they are employing, their preferred conflict-handling orientations, and the overall environment within which their conflict is playing out. Then, we must ascertain what the underlying causes and conditions of the conflict are (Pillar 2); for example, factors operative at the individual, societal, international, and global/ecological levels that drive the conflict. Once we have mapped Pillars 1 and 2, we are then ready to assume the daunting task of attempting to design an appropriate intervention into the conflict (Pillar 3).

Pillar 3, on conflict intervention, is subdivided into two related dimensions: 'third-party objectives' and 'third-party means for achieving goals'. Among 'third-party objectives', potential interveners can choose either to prevent a house from catching on fire (*violent conflict prevention*, often known as *preventive diplomacy*), prevent an existing fire from spreading (*conflict management* or *peacekeeping*), suppress an existing

---

[2] See Dennis Sandole, 'A Comprehensive Mapping of Conflict and Conflict Resolution: A Three Pillar Approach', *Peace and Conflict Studies*, 5 (1998), 1–30; Sandole, 'Typology', in Sandra Cheldelin, Daniel Druckman and Larissa Fast (eds.), *Conflict: From Analysis to Intervention* (London; New York: Continuum International, 2003), pp. 39–54; Sandole, *Peace and Security in the Postmodern World: The OSCE and Conflict Resolution* (London; New York: Routledge, 2007), ch. 2; and Sandole, *Peacebuilding: Preventing Violent Conflict in a Complex World* (Cambridge, UK; Malden, MA: Polity Press, 2010), ch. 2.

Table 1 *A comprehensive mapping of conflict and conflict resolution:*
a three pillar approach (3PF)

Pillar 2: Conflict causes and conditions	Pillar 1: Conflict elements	Pillar 3: Conflict intervention
Individual	Parties	*Third-party objectives*
Societal	Issues	[Violent] Conflict prevention
International	Objectives	Conflict management
Global/ecological	Means	Conflict settlement
	Preferred conflict-handling orientations	Conflict resolution
	Conflict environment	Conflict transformation
		Third-party means for achieving goals
		Confrontational and/or collaborative means
		Negative peace and/or positive peace orientations
		Track 1 and/or multi-track actors and processes

fire (*conflict settlement* or *coercive peacemaking*), deal with the underlying causes and conditions of a recent fire (*conflict resolution* or *non-coercive peacemaking*), and/or work with the survivors of a recent fire to build new mechanisms that, had they been in place earlier, could have prevented the fire in the first place (*conflict transformation* or *peacebuilding*).[3]

Under 'third-party means for achieving goals', interveners can choose between confrontational and/or collaborative means, 'negative peace' (no hostilities) and/or 'positive peace' (elimination of underlying causes and conditions),[4] and 'track 1', governmental actors and/or 'multi-track'

---

[3] For further discussion of 'preventive diplomacy', 'peacekeeping', 'peacemaking' and 'peacebuilding', see United Nations Secretary-General, 'An Agenda for Peace: Preventive Diplomacy, Peacemaking and Peace-keeping', UN Doc. A/47/277–S/24111, 17 June 1992.

[4] See Johan Galtung, 'Violence, Peace and Peace Research', *Journal of Peace Research*, 6 (1969), 167–91.

actors from NGO, business, educational/research, philanthropic, religious, media and other sectors as well as from government.[5]

RtoP is a creature of Pillar 3, where, as part of 'third-party objectives', it comprises three facets:

(1) *responsibility to prevent* (before the crisis);
(2) *responsibility to react* (during the crisis); and
(3) *responsibility to rebuild* (after the crisis).[6]

While the 'responsibility to prevent' includes violent conflict prevention (or preventive diplomacy), the 'responsibility to react' includes conflict management (or peacekeeping), conflict settlement (or coercive peacemaking) and conflict resolution (or non-coercive peacemaking) and the 'responsibility to rebuild' includes conflict transformation (or peacebuilding).

In terms of 'third party means for achieving goals', all three facets of RtoP can involve confrontational and/or collaborative means, 'negative peace' and/or 'positive peace' orientations, and track-1 and/or multi-track actors and processes. A major example of the application of all of these with regard to 'responsibility to prevent' is the United Nations' first and only preventive deployment which successfully prevented the genocidal warfare in Bosnia-Herzegovina from spilling over into neighbouring Macedonia: the United Nations Preventive Deployment Force (UNPREDEP).[7]

The CSCE/OSCE: a major institutional representation of Pillar 3

Comprising fifty-six participating States from North America, Europe and Central Asia, the Organization for Security and Co-operation in Europe (OSCE) is the world's largest and most comprehensive regional security organisation (RSO). The membership includes all of the North

---

[5] See Louise Diamond and John McDonald, Jr, *Multi-Track Diplomacy: A Systems Approach to Peace*, 3rd edn (West Hartford, CT: Kumarian Press, 1996).
[6] See International Commission on Intervention and State Sovereignty, *The Responsibility to Protect* (Ottawa: International Development Research Centre, 2001), p. xi. For a detailed discussion, see Alex Bellamy, *Responsibility to Protect: The Global Effort to End Mass Atrocity* (Cambridge, UK; Malden, MA: Polity Press, 2009); Gareth Evans, *The Responsibility to Protect: Ending Mass Atrocity Crimes Once and For All* (Washington, DC: Brookings Institution Press, 2008).
[7] See Henryk Sokalski, *An Ounce of Prevention: Macedonia and the UN Experience in Preventive Diplomacy* (Washington, DC: United States Institute of Peace Press, 2003).

Atlantic Treaty Organization (NATO), the former Warsaw Treaty Organization and the neutral and non-aligned States of Europe.[8]

The CSCE: basic institutional structure

The OSCE was launched during the Cold War in the early 1970s as the Conference on Security and Cooperation in Europe to manage relations between the two competing, nuclear superpowers and their respective alliance systems; on the one hand, the United States and NATO and, on the other hand, the Soviet Union and the Warsaw Pact. The initial product of CSCE efforts to prevent a major war in Europe between NATO and the Warsaw Pact was the Helsinki Final Act,[9] which established parameters for relations between the potentially hostile adversaries based on three elements of institutional structure: the (1) security; (2) economic and environmental; and (3) humanitarian 'baskets'.

Preceding the three baskets in the Final Act was the 'Declaration on Principles Guiding Relations between Participating States' – the so-called 'Decalogue' – which comprises ten principles, the seventh of which is '[r]espect for human rights and fundamental freedoms including the freedom of thought, conscience, religion or belief':[10]

> The inclusion of the principle on the respect for human rights was a major achievement. Together with the third basket recommendations contained in the *Act*, it represented the first acknowledgement in an international document of the direct link between human rights and security.[11]

Thus, from the outset, the CSCE started on a path that made an eventual commitment to the 'responsibility to protect' more likely. Indeed, 'The mere fact that human rights, a long-standing taboo in East–West relations, had become a legitimate subject of dialogue represented progress.'[12]

Human rights: the human dimension

By the time Mikhail Gorbachev became general secretary of the Communist party of the USSR in the mid-1980s, with his emphasis on

---

[8] For a listing of the fifty-six participating States, see 'Participating States', Organization for Security and Co-operation in Europe, at www.osce.org/who/83.

[9] OSCE, 'Conference on Security and Cooperation in Europe: Final Act', 1 August 1975.

[10] *Ibid.* See also OSCE, *OSCE Handbook* (Vienna: OSCE Press and Public Information Section, 2007), p. 3.

[11] OSCE, *Handbook*, p. 3.   [12] *Ibid.*, p. 5.

glasnost (openness) and *perestroika* (restructuring),[13] the international climate in which the CSCE found itself had become more conducive to constructive dialogue and problem-solving. So, by the time of the third follow-up meeting, convened in Vienna on 4 November 1986, eleven years after the signing of the Helsinki Final Act, the most substantial commitments agreed to deal with human rights, including a commitment to convene a Conference on the Human Dimension of the CSCE. This conference, held in three successive sessions in Paris in 1989, Copenhagen in 1990 and Moscow in 1991, generated significant agreements on 'free elections, freedom of the media, *the protection of persons belonging to national minorities*, the right to peaceful assembly and *the rights of children*'.[14]

The term, 'Human Dimension' – which has special relevance for the responsibility to protect – was employed for the first time during the Vienna follow-up conference. 'Dimension' eventually replaced 'basket' as the CSCE reframed security as a comprehensive concept comprised (1) political–military, (2) economic and environmental and (3) humanitarian and human rights *dimensions*: 'Baskets had served to sort issues during long discussions in which participating States strove to agree on common recommendations. Dimensions gave structure to the operational measures that began to be developed for them to be realized.'[15]

Ending the Cold War: the Paris Summit

The implications of the new leadership in Moscow for further constructive dialogue within the CSCE were enhanced by paradigm-shattering changes in the international system, including 'the demise of Communism at the end of the 1980s, the dissolution of the Warsaw Pact, the unification of Germany and the disintegration of the Soviet Union'.[16] Indeed, the Cold War and the bipolar confrontation between the two nuclear superpowers that was its signature process had come to a definitive end – a development in which the CSCE had played no small part!

CSCE participating States celebrated the ending of the Cold War with a special summit in Paris from 19–21 November 1990. Underlying the Paris summit was 'the vision of a new role for the CSCE as the main

---

[13] Mikhail Gorbachev, *Perestroika: New Thinking for Our Country and the World* (London: HarperCollins, 1987).

[14] OSCE, *Handbook*, pp. 5–6 (emphasis added). [15] *Ibid.*, p. 6. [16] *Ibid.*

guarantor of security in a new Europe free of dividing lines'.[17] The most important development associated with the Paris CSCE summit was the Charter of Paris for a New Europe which, for all the (then thirty-four) CSCE participating States, formally brought the Cold War to an end: *'The era of confrontation and division of Europe [had] ended. We declare that henceforth our relations will be founded on respect and co-operation.'*[18]

The Charter also took initial steps to institutionalise the CSCE which, until the Paris summit, had been a process with no fixed address, secretariat or regularly scheduled meetings. The new measures included:

(1) A CSCE Secretariat in Prague (which subsequently was relocated to Vienna, but with an office remaining in Prague);
(2) An Office for Free Elections in Warsaw (later renamed the Office for Democratic Institutions and Human Rights [ODIHR]); and
(3) A Conflict Prevention Centre (CPC) in Vienna.[19]

The Conflict Prevention Centre (CPC)

The Conflict Prevention Centre (CPC) initially had responsibility to provide support for the implementation of a number of newly created confidence and security-building mechanisms (CSBMs), i.e.:

(1) annual exchange of military information;
(2) consultation and cooperation regarding unusual military activities;
(3) communications network;
(4) cooperation regarding hazardous incidents of a military nature; and
(5) the annual implementation assessment meetings.

What was not clear was whether the Centre would also provide a forum for dispute settlement. The Charter had affirmed the commitment of the participating States, not only to *prevent* (violent) conflicts, but to define and seek 'appropriate mechanisms for the *resolution* of any disputes which may arise'.[20] It mentioned the opportunity provided by the

---

[17] *Ibid.* The discussion in this and the following section reflects and builds upon parts of Sandole, *Peace and Security*, ch. 4, specifically pp. 65–74.
[18] Charter of Paris for a New Europe, 21 November 1990, p. 13 (emphasis added).
[19] A Commission on Security and Cooperation in Europe Parliamentary Assembly was established later, in April 1991, with a Secretariat in Copenhagen. See 'CSCE Parliament Established at Madrid Meeting', *CSCE Digest*, 14 (1991), 3.
[20] Charter of Paris, p. 18 (emphasis added).

CSCE experts-meeting scheduled to convene in Valletta, Malta, from 15 January to 8 February 1991, whose purpose was to create a mechanism for the peaceful settlement of disputes.

The Valletta meeting took place and established the 'CSCE Procedure for Peaceful Settlement of Disputes'.[21] It did not, however, assign the Procedure to the Conflict Prevention Centre. That task was left to the first meeting of the Council of Ministers for Foreign Affairs, which took place in Berlin, 19–20 June 1991.

Among other decisions, including accepting Albania into the CSCE and adopting the Berlin Mechanism for consultation and cooperation regarding emergency situations, the Council of Ministers for Foreign Affairs designated the Conflict Prevention Centre as the 'nominating institution' for the CSCE Procedure (the Valletta Mechanism); i.e. for any given dispute, the Centre director could preside over the creation, but not the functioning, of a 'CSCE Dispute Settlement Mechanism'. The Berlin meeting of the Council, therefore, provided the CPC with a conflict resolution supplement to its original crisis-prevention/management function.

Contributing further to the eventual creation of a 'responsibility to protect' orientation among CSCE/OSCE members, the Charter also affirmed, 'that the ethnic, cultural, linguistic and religious *identity* of national minorities will be *protected* and that persons belonging to national minorities have the right freely to express, preserve and develop that *identity* without any discrimination and in full equality before the law'.[22] The signatories expressed their 'determination to combat all forms of racial and ethnic hatred, anti-Semitism, xenophobia and discrimination against anyone as well as persecution on religious and ideological grounds'.[23] This concern was based, in large part, on right-wing extremist developments in Austria, France, Germany and elsewhere,[24] which led to the CSCE Experts Meeting on National Minorities in Geneva, 1–19 July 1991. The purpose of this meeting

---

[21] CSCE, 'Report of the CSCE Meeting of Experts on Peaceful Settlement of Disputes', Valletta, 8 February 1991.

[22] Charter of Paris, p. 14 (emphasis added).   [23] *Ibid.*, p. 17.

[24] See, for example, Herbert Kitschelt and Anthony McGann, *The Radical Right in Western Europe: A Comparative Analysis* (Ann Arbor: University of Michigan Press, 1995); Peter Merkl and Leonard Weinberg, *The Revival of Right-wing Extremism in the Nineties* (Newbury Park, CA: Sage, 1997); Evens Foundation, *Europe's New Racism: Causes, Manifestations, and Solutions* (Oxford; New York: Berghahn Books, 2002); Nora Langenbacher and Britta Schellenberg (eds.), *Is Europe on the 'Right' Path: Right-Wing Extremism and Right-Wing Populism in Europe* (Berlin: Friedrich-Ebert Stiftung, 2011).

was, 'to hold a thorough discussion on the issue of national minorities and of the rights of persons belonging to them'.[25]

Mandatory OSCE rapporteur missions and consensus-minus-one decision-making

Shortly after the failed coup attempt against Soviet President Mikhail Gorbachev of 19–21 August 1991, the Moscow Meeting of the Conference on the Human Dimension of the CSCE took place during 10 September–4 October 1991. This contributed further to the development of the evolving Human Dimension Mechanism (the Moscow Mechanism), including conditions under which '[a] state may ... be *forced* to receive a rapporteur mission ... for fact-finding'.[26]

Also, during 30–31 January 1992, the CSCE Council of Foreign Ministers met in Prague. One of its decisions was to establish the possibility of *consensus-minus-one* decision-making in cases of flagrant violations of CSCE principles and commitments.[27] Specifically, in cases of 'clear, gross and uncorrected violations' of CSCE commitments, the CSCE Council of Foreign Ministers or Committee of Senior Officials (CSO) could take 'appropriate action', even, if necessary, '*in the absence of the consent of the State concerned.*' But this particular encroachment on the principles of consensus and national sovereignty went only so far: 'Such actions would consist of political declarations or other political steps to apply *outside* the territory of the State concerned.'[28] Nevertheless, this move contributed further to the development of an environment conducive to the CSCE/OSCE embracing of the 'responsibility to protect'.

---

[25] Charter of Paris, p. 22; and CSCE, 'Report of the CSCE Meeting of Experts on National Minorities', Geneva, 19 July 1991.

[26] CSCE, *The Conference on Security and Cooperation in Europe: An Overview of the CSCE Process, Recent Meetings and Institutional Developments* (Washington, DC: CSCE, 1992), p. 27 (emphasis added).

[27] *Ibid.*, p. 22.

[28] CSCE, '*Prague Meeting of the CSCE Council*', Prague, CSCE Doc. 2PRAG92.e, 30–31 January 1992, para. 16 (emphasis added). The 'consensus-minus-one' procedure was used by the Committee of Senior Officials (CSO) at the end of the fourth CSCE review conference in Helsinki, on 8 July 1992, to 'suspend the presence' of Yugoslavia (then comprising only Serbia and Montenegro) at the CSCE Summit, held 9–10 July, 'and [at] all CSCE meetings'. The suspension lasted until November 2000, when, following the removal from power of Slobodan Milošević, the Federal Republic of Yugoslavia (FRY) was invited to return to full OSCE participation.

The pièce de résistance of the CSCE/OSCE: the High Commissioner on National Minorities (HCNM)

The Helsinki CSCE review conference, which met during 24 March–8 July 1992, concluded with a two-day summit during 9–10 July and a declaration which reflected the recommendation of the 1991 NATO Rome summit to improve CSCE conflict prevention and crisis management mechanisms.[29] Accordingly, the Helsinki CSCE created a High Commissioner on National Minorities (HCNM) which, using the resources of the Warsaw-based Office for Democratic Institutions and Human Rights (ODIHR), would have two functions: (1) *early warning*; and (2) *early action.*

At the 'early warning' stage, the HCNM could collect and assess information concerning minority issues 'from any source, including the media and non-governmental organizations'.[30] Also at this stage, the HCNM could visit any CSCE State and 'communicate in person . . . with parties directly concerned to obtain first-hand information about the situation', e.g. the 'role of the parties directly concerned, the nature of the tensions and recent developments . . . and . . . the potential consequences for peace and stability within the CSCE area'.[31] If the HCNM were to determine 'that there [was] a *prima facie* risk of potential conflict . . . he/she [could then] issue an early warning, which [would] be communicated promptly . . . to the CSO'.[32]

Part of the HCNM's 'early action' function could be 'to enter into further contact and closer consultation with the parties concerned with a view to possible solutions, according to a mandate to be decided by the CSO'.[33] The HCNM could consult up to three persons 'with relevant expertise in specific matters'.[34] Such persons would 'be selected by the High Commissioner with the assistance of the ODIHR from the resource list established at the ODIHR as laid down in the Document of the Moscow Meeting'.[35]

As soon as it received an early warning from the HCNM or any other appropriate source – e.g. other CSCE offices, or a State directly involved

---

[29] NATO, *Rome Declaration on Peace and Cooperation* (Brussels: NATO Office of Information and Press, 1991).

[30] *Ibid.*, p. 11.

[31] CSCE, 'Helsinki Document 1992: The Challenges of Change', ch. II, pp. 9–12, at www.osce.org/mc/39530.

[32] *Ibid.*, p. 10, para. 13.   [33] *Ibid.*, para. 16.   [34] *Ibid.*, p. 11, para. 31.

[35] *Ibid.*, p. 12, para. 35.

in a dispute – the CSO could also 'seek independent advice and counsel from relevant experts [as well as from] institutions, and international organizations'.[36] Thereafter, the CSO, acting on behalf of the Council of Foreign Ministers, would have 'overall CSCE responsibility for managing [any] crisis with a view to its resolution':

> It may, *inter alia*, decide to set up a framework for a negotiated settlement, or to dispatch a rapporteur or fact-finding mission. The CSO may also initiate or promote the exercise of good offices, mediation or conciliation.[37]

The Code of Conduct on Politico-Military Aspects of Security

Decisions taken at the Budapest CSCE summit, on 5–6 December 1994, included, among others:

(1) The *CSCE becoming the body of first resort for dealing with conflicts*: 'a primary instrument for early warning, conflict prevention and crisis management in the region';

(2) Agreement on a Code of Conduct on Politico-Military Aspects of Security, setting forth guidelines for the 'role of armed forces in democratic societies';

(3) Agreement on the 'political will to provide, with an appropriate resolution from the [UN] Security Council, a multinational peace-keeping force [for Nagorno-Karabakh] following agreement among the parties [i.e. Armenia and Azerbaijan] for cessation of the armed conflict'; and

(4) As of 1 January 1995, 'the CSCE [would be] known as the *Organization for Security and Co-operation in Europe* (OSCE)'.[38]

---

[36] *Ibid.*, ch. III, p. 13, para. 7.

[37] *Ibid.*, p. 13, para. 8. The Three Pillar Framework (3PF), discussed earlier, could be used as a conceptual basis for framing early warnings and exploring early and subsequent actions.

[38] CSCE, 'Budapest Document 1994: Towards a Genuine Partnership in a New Era', CSCE Doc. DOC.RC/1/95, 6 December 1994, chs. I–II and IV (emphasis added). Other name changes included: (1) the CSCE Council of Ministers became the Ministerial Council, the OSCE's 'central decision-making and governing body [to] meet, as a rule, towards the end of every [one-year] term of chairmanship at the level of Foreign Ministers'; (2) the Committee of Senior Officials (CSO) became the Senior Council, to 'meet in Prague twice a year, at the minimum [to] discuss and set forth policy and broad budgetary guidelines'; and (3) the Permanent Committee became the Permanent Council (PC), 'the regular body for political consultation and decision-making [which meets weekly and] can also be convened for emergency purposes'. The PC comprises the permanent representatives of the participating States and hence, meets in Vienna. CSCE, 'Budapest Document 1994', ch. I.

The platform for cooperative security and the Rapid Expert Assistance and Co-operation Teams (REACT)

One noteworthy result of the OSCE summit at Lisbon during December 1996 was the Lisbon Declaration on a Common and Comprehensive Security Model for Europe for the Twenty-first Century. Once finalised, the model would comprise, among other things, a Platform for Co-operative Security, defining 'modalities for cooperation between the OSCE and other security organizations', and a Charter on European Security.[39] The Platform and Charter were among the results of the OSCE summit at Istanbul during November 1999. These measures enhanced the capabilities of the OSCE to respond more effectively to Yugoslav-type conflicts. Another consequence of Istanbul was the decision to create Rapid Expert Assistance and Co-operation Teams (REACT) which would enable the OSCE to respond quickly to demands for assistance and for large civilian field operations. The Istanbul summit recognised that the ability to deploy rapidly civilian and police expertise is essential to effective conflict prevention, crisis management and post-conflict rehabilitation. The Implementation of the REACT initiative would give the OSCE 'the ability to address problems before they become crises and to deploy quickly the civilian component of a peace-keeping operation when needed'.[40] REACT was clearly relevant to the OSCE's development of an RtoP capability.

The Russian challenge: reforming the OSCE

As the OSCE entered the twenty-first century, it was characterised by 'an impressive set of assets, none of which had existed in 1990'.[41] In

---

[39] See OSCE, 'Lisbon Document 1996', OSCE Doc. DOC.S/1/96, 3 December 1996; CSCE, *The OSCE After the Lisbon Summit* (Washington, DC: Commission on Security and Cooperation in Europe, 1997).

[40] OSCE Secretary General, 'Annual Report 2000 on OSCE Activities (1 November 1999–31 October 2000)', OSCE Doc. SEC.DOC/5/00, 24 November 2000, pp. 110–11. For assessments of REACT and OSCE field missions in general, see P. Terrence Hopmann, 'Building Security in Post-Cold War Eurasia: The OSCE and US Foreign Policy', working paper no. 31, United States Institute of Peace, September 1999, at www.usip.org/files/resources/pwks31.pdf; Hopmann, 'The Organization for Security and Co-operation in Europe: Its Contribution to Conflict Prevention and Resolution', in Paul Stern and Daniel Druckman (eds.), *International Conflict Resolution After the Cold War* (Washington, DC: National Academy Press, 2000), pp. 569–616; Hopmann, 'The OSCE Response to 9/11', in Ian Cuthbertson and Heinz Gärtner (eds.), *European Security after September 11 and the War in Iraq* (Basingstoke, UK: Palgrave Macmillan, 2005), pp. 199–214.

[41] OSCE, *Handbook*, p. 10.

addition, the OSCE continued to help participating States, recovering from violent conflict and war, to build democratic institutions, ensure the rule of law and to advance economic development. In this regard, the OSCE responded to State requests to provide 'expertise, assistance and training to civil servants, judges, journalists, small- and medium-sized enterprises and civil society groups'.[42]

However, as the OSCE began to shift from emergency interventions to long-term projects, especially in Eastern and Central Europe and the former Soviet Union, some delegations (the Russian Federation in particular) began to be critical of the OSCE's 'geographical one-sidedness' and 'overemphasis on the human dimension'.[43] One result of this critique was the OSCE Strategy to Address Threats to Security and Stability in the Twenty-First Century, which was adopted by the 2003 Maastricht Ministerial Council:

> Threats to security and stability in the OSCE region are today more likely to arise as negative, destabilizing consequences of developments that cut across the politico-military, economic and environmental and human dimensions than from any major armed conflict.[44]

Given the OSCE's comprehensive reformulation of security to include all three 'baskets' (or 'dimensions'), plus its status as the world's largest regional security organisation, the Strategy maintained that the OSCE was well equipped to deal with these new security challenges – including terrorism and human trafficking – which, reflective of their increasing complexity, cut across the three dimensions.

Extending its reach and influence beyond the borders of its membership, the OSCE, like the European Union's Neighbourhood Policy, has Partners for Co-operation in the Mediterranean (Algeria, Egypt, Israel, Jordan, Morocco and Tunisia) and Asia (Afghanistan, Korea, Japan, Mongolia and Thailand). The objective is to deal with common, cross-border problems by applying OSCE norms, processes and comprehensive framing of security beyond the original Vancouver-to-Vladivostok region.

In recent years, the OSCE has sought, through various reforms, to enhance its effectiveness and relevance.[45] One potential impact of such reforms is that the OSCE will become even more likely to continue to be relevant to the operationalisation of the 'responsibility to protect'. Following some interim observations on the discussion thus far, we will discuss one means for achieving this goal through an application

---

[42] *Ibid.*   [43] *Ibid.*, p. 11.   [44] *Ibid.*   [45] *Ibid.*, p. 12.

of Pillar 3 of the 3 Pillar Framework to conflict intervention: the 'New European Peace and Security System' or NEPSS.[46]

The CSCE/OSCE–RtoP nexus: interim observations

Given the foregoing discussion, the three core components of RtoP are compatible with a number of dimensions and mechanisms of the CSCE/OSCE, including the Human Dimension, Office for Democratic Institutions and Human Rights (ODIHR), High Commissioner on National Minorities (HCNM), mandatory OSCE rapporteur missions and consensus-minus-one decision-making, Centre for Conflict Prevention (CPC), field missions, Code of Conduct and REACT. Given the priority of the Human Dimension and the basically soft-power orientation of the OSCE, this organisation is especially relevant to the 'responsibility to prevent' and the 'responsibility to rebuild'. While discussing the responsibility to prevent, Gareth Evans, former Australian foreign minister, who played a major role in developing the RtoP concept, praises the 'heroic efforts' of the High Commissioner on National Minorities over many years, particularly during the volatile early post-Cold War period when Max van der Stoel held the post, to quietly stop as many as a dozen major ethnic and language-based conflicts from breaking out across Central and Eastern Europe, from the Baltics to Romania.[47]

The UN Secretary-General not only agrees with this sanguine assessment, but also argues that the HCNM can be a model for similar mechanisms in other regions:

> One of the longest-standing and most quietly effective instruments for preventing atrocity crimes has been the office of the [OSCE's] High Commissioner on National Minorities ... Other regions could establish similar posts for undertaking early warning and quiet diplomacy to ease tensions among groups within societies.[48]

The HCNM's major efforts occurred in the Baltic States (Estonia, Latvia and Lithuania) shortly after independence, when grievances on the part

---

[46] See Sandole, *Peace and Security*, ch. 3.

[47] Evans, *Responsibility to Protect*, p. 90. See also Walter Kemp, *Quiet Diplomacy in Action: The OSCE High Commissioner on National Minorities* (The Hague: Kluwer Law International, 2001).

[48] UNSG, 'The Role of Regional and Sub-regional Arrangements in Implementing the Responsibility to Protect', UN Doc. A/65/877–S/2011/393, 27 June 2011, p. 6, para. 18.

of Russian-speaking minorities ran high with regard to their exclusion from citizenship status. Despite some issues that render the CSCE/OSCE likely to 'make more often than not for lowest common denominator decision-making and less than vibrant operational impact', Evans concludes that, 'in the RtoP-related areas in which it has performed well – above all, the protection of national minorities – it has performed very well indeed.'[49]

In addition to the HCNM's noteworthy efforts to prevent violent conflict, the activities of 'the OSCE's preventive missions in the Baltics, Balkans, Caucasus and Central Asia' have been helpful.[50] Operating under the direction of the Centre for the Prevention of Conflict, these missions, like the HCNM, have employed early warning as well as early action.[51] According to Evans:

> The OSCE's Conflict Prevention Center maintains an early warning situation room and focuses operationally on confidence-building measures (particularly involving military transparency), helping states with border security and small arms stockpile management, and supporting multiple field missions – nineteen currently, engaging over 2,800 staff members – working mainly on post-conflict capacity building.[52]

Bellamy has noted that the OSCE's early warning mechanism is the most advanced of all the systems in place at regional organisations. The OSCE system comprises 'field missions which provide ongoing reporting on current potential crises to the organization's permanent council and scrutinize[s] the members' compliance with human rights standards'.[53] In addition to the efforts of the HCNM, 'OSCE field missions have been credited with helping several former Soviet states, especially Estonia, Latvia and Ukraine to avoid potential ethnic conflict between the majority nationalities and significant Russian minorities.'[54]

We now turn to the New European Peace and Security System (NEPSS), which could enhance the OSCE's trajectory towards embracing RtoP.

The new European peace and security system (NEPSS)

The New European Peace and Security System (NEPSS) concept was originally developed by this author, by applying Pillar 3 of the 3 Pillar Framework to post-Cold War Europe – specifically, post-Yugoslavia

---

[49] Evans, *Responsibility to Protect*, p. 194.   [50] Bellamy, *Global Effort*, p. 103.
[51] *Ibid.*, p. 107.   [52] Evans, *Responsibility to Protect*, p. 194.
[53] Bellamy, *Global Effort*, p. 108.   [54] *Ibid.*

Table 2 *The structure of NEPSS*

	Track 1	Track 2	Track 3	Track 4	Track 5	Track 6	Track 7	Track 8	Track 9
Local	—	—	—	—	—	—	—	—	—
Societal	—	—	—	—	—	—	—	—	—
Sub-regional	—	—	—	—	—	—	—	—	—
Regional	—	—	—	—	—	—	—	—	—
Global	—	—	—	—	—	—	—	—	—

Europe – as part of an overall effort by many to ensure that the genocidal conflict that led to the unravelling of the former Yugoslavia throughout the last decade of the twentieth century never happened again. Despite this original European bias of NEPSS, the design can be employed to shape interventions in any part of the world. NEPSS incorporates the 'multi-track' framework designed by Ambassador John McDonald and Dr Louise Diamond for identifying and coordinating the simultaneous and/or sequenced activities of multi-sectoral, multi-task actors in any given intervention.[55] Graphically, the nine tracks of the multi-track framework represent the horizontal axis of NEPSS, while local, societal, sub-regional, regional and global levels of analysis constitute the vertical axis, as shown in Table 2.

With regard to the need to prevent the resumption of violent conflict, which remains a major concern since conflict recurrence is common,[56]

---

[55] See Diamond and McDonald, Jr, *Multi-Track Diplomacy*. The nine 'tracks' are: (1) Government; (2) NGOs and Professional Conflict Resolution; (3) Business; (4) Private Citizens; (5) Research, Training, and Education; (6) Peace Activism; (7) Religion; (8) Funding; and (9) Media, Communications and Public Opinion.

[56] According to the World Bank, in 44 per cent of all post-conflict situations, war recurs during the first five years following the cessation of violence. See World Bank, *The Role of the World Bank in Conflict and Development: An Evolving Agenda* (Washington, DC: World Bank, 2004), p. 8. Paul Collier argues that approximately 50 per cent of post-conflict countries go back to war during the first ten years of peace. See Paul Collier *et al.*, *Breaking the Conflict Trap: Civil War and Development Policy* (Washington, DC: World Bank, 2003), p. 7. Both are cited in Gerd Junne and Willemijn Verkoren (eds.), *Postconflict Development: Meeting New Challenges* (Boulder, CO; London: Lynne Rienner, 2005). Further, 'of the 39 different conflicts that became active in the last 10 years, 31 were conflict recurrences – instances of resurgent, armed violence in societies where conflict had largely been dormant for at least a year. Only eight were entirely new conflicts between new antagonists involving new issues and interests.' See J. Joseph Hewitt, Jonathan Wilkenfeld and Ted Robert Gurr (eds.), *Peace and Conflict 2010* (Boulder, CO; London: Paradigm Publishers, 2010), p. 1. The reason for conflict recurrence offered by Hewitt *et al.* is 'that the internationally brokered settlement or

an assumption underlying NEPSS is that, 'all conflicts are *local*'. Accordingly, 'once some early warning system registers that a conflict is developing in a certain village, city or any other location in a certain country at any point in time, track 1–9 resources from the local–global levels would be brought to bear on the event, if not at the same time then certainly in sequence.'[57]

While the nine tracks would be integrated horizontally in converging on the locus of conflict, resources at the societal, sub-regional, regional and global levels would be integrated vertically in converging on the conflict. If diplomatic and development-oriented measures were undermined by a government's actual use of violence, then, under the clear criteria for using forceful measures under RtoP,[58] 'force could be used to pull an attacker off of a besieged population'.[59] This use of coercion by the international community would be a necessary (but *not* a sufficient) condition to achieve *negative peace* – i.e. the elimination of hostilities – as a basis for moving eventually to *positive peace* 'where the conditions for *structural, cultural* and *physical violence* would be managed if not eliminated'.[60] More efforts are necessary for achieving what John Burton calls '*provention*', namely the elimination of the deep-rooted, underlying causes and conditions of fractured relationships that give rise to violent conflict and subsequent establishment of positive relations among the former adversaries.[61]

By achieving 'provention', the OSCE could coordinate its activities with other actors embedded in the Platform for Co-operative Security, perhaps in a NEPSS-like configuration, to maximise the potential of the interplay of the three components of RtoP – *prevention, reaction* and *rebuilding* – to guarantee the protection of minorities in any given situation. Given the degree of convergence between the mechanisms of the world's largest and most comprehensive regional security organisation and RtoP, this author was curious to find out to what extent it would also be revealed in discussions with the heads of delegation to the CSCE/OSCE in Vienna.

---

containment of many armed conflicts since the early 1990s did not deal effectively with root causes' (*ibid.*, p. 4). This finding only reinforces the importance of the *need to rebuild*.

[57] Sandole, *Peacebuilding*, p. 168.

[58] The criteria are: (1) Seriousness of Harm; (2) Proper Purpose; (3) Last Resort; (4) Proportional Means; and (5) Balance of Consequences. See Evans, *Responsibility to Protect*, p. 141.

[59] Sandole, *Peacebuilding*, p. 169.

[60] See Johan Galtung, *Peace by Peaceful Means: Peace and Conflict, Development and Civilization* (London; Thousand Oaks, CA: Sage, 1996).

[61] *Ibid.*; John Burton, *Conflict: Resolution and Provention* (New York: St. Martin's Press, 1990).

The wisdom of CSCE/OSCE practitioners as predictors of things to come

This author conducted a series of interviews, primarily with heads of delegations to the CSCE/OSCE in Vienna in 1993, 1997, 1999 and 2004.[62] These interviews were helpful in exploring to what extent the perceptions of members of the delegations mirrored the official reports and other documents discussed above, especially given the prominence of early warning and early action either spelled out or implicit in the CSCE/OSCE's developing mechanisms. These four interview surveys comprised basically the same closed-ended[63] and open-ended questions,[64] with some revision to take into account developments related to each of the four data points. In each case, it was attempted to interview as many of the heads of delegation as possible.[65] One of the open-ended questions concerned the lessons of the wars in the former Yugoslavia. Among the most common responses, revealed by analysis of the content of responses to the question, was the need for early warning and early action, which is clearly relevant to the responsibility to *prevent* as well as the responsibility to *rebuild*.

The 1993 CSCE survey

In the 1993 survey, for example, the need for early warning and early action was the dominant lesson learned, reflecting the responses of 45 per cent of the thirty-one delegations interviewed.[66] The other responses for 1993, in descending order, were:

(1) The likelihood that the wars in the former Yugoslavia would serve as a model for others elsewhere (ranked second for 29 per cent of thirty-one).
(2) The need to focus attention on complex, identity-based ethnic-type conflicts in the OSCE region (ranked third for 23 per cent of thirty-one).
(3) The need for forceful action in such situations (ranked fourth for 16 per cent of thirty-one).

---

[62] See Sandole, *Peace and Security.*   [63] See *ibid.*, chs. 5 and 9.

[64] *Ibid.*, chs. 6–9. The difference between *closed-ended* and *open-ended* questions is that the former are accompanied by pre-set responses among which the interviewee chooses – e.g. 'Male/Female', 'Yes/No', 'Strongly Agree, Agree, Mixed Feelings, Disagree, Strongly Disagree'. Open-ended questions, by contrast, are not accompanied by such predetermined response schema; hence, the researcher must analyse the content of responses to each question to ascertain common and dissimilar themes and patterns.

[65] For further details on the research design which guided this study, see *ibid.*, ch. 4.

[66] *Ibid.*, p. 113.

(4) The need for complementarity and coordination among the various actors involved in dealing with such situations (ranked fifth for 13 per cent of thirty-one).[67]

These other lessons also have RtoP relevance – i.e. the need for forceful action captures the 'need to react' aspect of RtoP – while the wars in the former Yugoslavia constituting a model for wars elsewhere in the OSCE region, the need to focus on ethnic-type conflicts and the need for complementarity and coordination cover all three aspects of RtoP.

The 1997 OSCE survey

The 1997 survey also revealed the need for early warning and early action as the dominant lesson learned, for 50 per cent of the fifty-two delegations interviewed.[68] The remaining lessons for 1997, in descending order, were:

- The need for complementarity and coordination among the various actors involved in dealing with such situations (ranked second for 44 per cent of fifty-two).
- The need to focus attention on complex, identity-based ethnic-type conflicts in the OSCE region (ranked third for 33 per cent of fifty-two).
- The need for forceful action in such situations (ranked fourth for 17 per cent of fifty-two).
- The need for US leadership in such situations (ranked fifth for 13.5 per cent of fifty-two).[69]

Three of the remaining lessons for 1997 corresponded to three of those for 1993, with two of them, the need to focus on ethnic-type conflicts and the need for forceful action, again occupying third and fourth place, respectively. Meanwhile, the need for coordination moved from fifth to second place. One new lesson, in fifth place, was the need for US leadership in responding to ethnic-type conflicts, which is relevant to all three aspects of RtoP.

The 1999 OSCE survey

Remarkably, the 1999 survey again revealed the need for early warning and early action as the dominant lesson learned, for 60 per cent of the

---

[67] *Ibid.*   [68] *Ibid.*, p. 114.   [69] *Ibid.*

forty-five delegations interviewed.[70] Interestingly, the proportion of the delegations calling for early warning and early action increased from 1993 (45 per cent) to 1997 (50 per cent) and then to 1999 (60 per cent). The remaining lessons for 1999 included basically the same themes, but with some changes in ranking, i.e.:

- The need for complementarity and coordination among the various actors involved in dealing with such situations (ranked second for 44 per cent of forty-five).
- The need for forceful action in such situations (ranked third for 29 per cent of forty-five).
- The need to focus attention on complex, identity-based ethnic-type conflicts in the OSCE region (ranked fourth for 20 per cent of forty-five).
- It was illusory for the international community to trust Serbian leader Slobodan Milošević (ranked fifth for 18 per cent of forty-five).[71]

The 2004 OSCE survey

Perhaps incredibly – given that these themes were derived from content analyses of responses to open-ended questions – the dominance of early warning and early action persisted for the 2004 survey at 63 per cent for a sample of nineteen delegations.[72] In addition, the remaining lessons for 2004 again included basically the same themes, with one exception, i.e.:

- The need to focus attention on complex, identity-based ethnic-type conflicts in the OSCE region (ranked second for 37 per cent of nineteen).
- The need for complementarity and coordination among the various actors involved in dealing with such situations (ranked third for 26 per cent of nineteen).
- The need for forceful action in such situations (tied for third place for 26 per cent of nineteen).
- Members of the international community could use soft power as well as hard power in dealing with the sources of developing ethnic-type conflicts (ranked fifth for 21 per cent of nineteen).[73] This lesson reflects the full range of RtoP which, as we have noted, is not only about 'the apparent choice between doing nothing and sending in the Marines'.[74]

---

[70] *Ibid.*, p. 115.   [71] *Ibid.*   [72] *Ibid.*, p. 162.   [73] *Ibid.*
[74] See Bellamy, *Global Effort*, p. 3.

Comparisons across the four surveys

In addition to early warning and early action increasing in proportion of total sample size from 1993 (45 per cent), to 1997 (50 per cent), to 1999 (60 per cent) and 2004 (63 per cent), there were interesting patterns among the remaining lessons. For instance, the need to pay attention to ethnic-type conflicts increased from 1993 (23 per cent) to 1997 (33 per cent), then decreased for 1999 (20 per cent), but increased overall by 2004 (37 per cent). The need for coordination increased from 1993 (13 per cent) to 1997 (44.2 per cent), and increased again, but barely for 1999 (44.4 per cent), and then decreased by 2004 (26 per cent). Finally, the need for the use of force increased from 1993 (16 per cent), to 1997 (17 per cent), to 1999 (29 per cent), but then decreased somewhat by 2004 (26 per cent), where it was followed by the lesson that soft power as well as hard power could be employed to deal with ethnic-type conflicts (21 per cent).

Across the eleven-year period when interviews were conducted, some of the most important results, among the lessons learned were:

(1) Steady growth in support of the *need for early warning and early action*, perhaps due in part to a growing consciousness among members of the CSCE/OSCE that preventive diplomacy was exceedingly difficult to conduct.[75]

(2) Uneven growth in support of the *need to pay attention to complex, identity-based, ethnic conflicts*; perhaps due in part to the 'new' terrorism of 11 September 2001 competing with ethnic conflict as a source of threats to international peace and security.

(3) Fundamentally a steady increase in support of the *need for coordination* of interventions into such conflicts, which decreased after 9/11, perhaps because, after 9/11, the 'new' terrorism competed with ethnic conflicts for strategic concern, plus the new threat had galvanised the West in its response – as symbolised in part by NATO's mission in Afghanistan – thereby reducing the need for further efforts toward coordination.[76]

---

[75] See Michael Lund, *Preventing Violent Conflicts: A Strategy for Preventive Diplomacy* (Washington, DC: United States Institute of Peace Press, 1996).

[76] Article V of the North Atlantic Treaty specifies that an attack on any one of its members shall be construed as an attack on all. It was invoked for the first time in response to the terrorist attacks of 11 September 2001. This led to the deployment of NATO's collective defence mission, the International Security Assistance Force (ISAF), to combat terrorism in Afghanistan, the source of the attacks on 11 September 2001. See 'NATO and the

(4) Basically the same pattern for the *use of force* in such conflicts, with, after 9/11, the reduction in the need for force being complemented by the addition of a new lesson: the *need for soft power as well as hard power (force)* in interventions into ethnic conflicts. The US decision to launch a 'shock-and-awe' invasion and occupation of Iraq in March 2003 before the results of UN WMD inspectors were definitive, may have made fellow members of the international community reluctant to depend on force alone as a basis for influencing global affairs.

The need for hard power to be complemented by soft power was reinforced by responses to another open-ended question: 'If you could design the ideal peace and security system for Europe, what would it look like?' The objective here was to elicit CSCE/OSCE practitioners' wisdom on how to prevent future Yugoslav-type conflicts in Europe. Responses for 1993, 1997, 1999 and 2004 are summarised as follows:

> Overall findings ... reinforced the hypothesized emergence of [a] paradigm where military force (*Realpolitik*) and *soft power* (*Idealpolitik*) were conceptually integrated in coordinated international interventions to prevent and otherwise deal with complex ethnic and other conflicts involving multiple issues.[77]

Across the four surveys, the OSCE remained consistently in first place, while NATO tended to eclipse the EU by one or two rankings, as components of an *ideal* peace and security system for postmodern Europe.[78]

In addition, the perceptions of the CSCE/OSCE ambassadors and others in the four samples moved progressively closer over time to a NEPSS type of security architecture, comprising:

> Coordinated 'contingency' and multitrack approaches to conflict prevention, management, settlement, resolution, and transformation, where 'hard power' may sometimes be necessary but only as part of a larger, integrative framework inclusive of 'soft power' – *e.g.* civil society – elements with a regional focus to 'capture the complexity' of complex conflicts such as those that led to the genocidal warfare in former Yugoslavia.[79]

This tilting of the interview findings toward NEPSS, is reinforced by the response by one NATO head of delegation in the 2004 survey to the 'ideal peace and security' question:

Scourge of Terrorism: What Is Article V?', NATO, 18 February 2005, at www.nato.int/terrorism/five.htm.
[77] Sandole, *Peace and Security*, p. 174 (emphasis in original).   [78] *Ibid.*   [79] *Ibid.*, p. 144.

> [E]ach actor must do what it does best: (1) NATO is for 'hard security'; (2) the Council of Europe (CoE) is for the legal aspects of the Human Dimension; and (3) the OSCE is for 'soft security,' conflict prevention and post-conflict rehabilitation, and it is politically binding.
>
> The biggest question is: Where does the European Union (EU) fit in here? The EU is trying to do everything [and it] does not have a policy vis-à-vis the OSCE with regard to common security.[80]

According to the heads and other high-level members of CSCE/OSCE delegations that were interviewed in 1993, 1997, 1999 and 2004, therefore, there is a 'theory of practice', with a bias toward a NEPSS-type of security architecture that should characterise responses by the international community to Yugoslav-type conflicts. This theory, comprising early warning and coordinated early action in ethnic conflicts where diplomacy as well as military force can be applied, converges with the essential elements of RtoP, as articulated in paragraphs 138 and 139 of the 2005 World Summit Outcome Document that established RtoP.[81]

Accordingly, it is clear that the CSCE/OSCE practitioners in the four surveys became more 'friendly' to RtoP-type thinking and action over time, during the period when the Balkan Wars started up (1991), continued and terminated (1999). Gratifyingly, these results from one-on-one interviews correspond with the impressions gained earlier from the CSCE/OSCE documents that have been cited, covering the same period.[82]

Conclusion

The CSCE/OSCE has clearly been receptive to developing a consciousness among its members that would allow an RtoP orientation to take hold, especially regarding *the need to prevent* and the *need to*

---

[80] *Ibid.*, p. 164.

[81] Paragraph 138 of the World Summit Outcome Document (2005) outlines each State's responsibility to protect its own population, and the international community's commitment to assisting States in ensuring RtoP and the United Nations in establishing an early warning system. When any given State fails to protect its population in accordance with paragraph 138, then paragraph 139 applies, specifying the obligation of the international community to take the necessary collective action to enforce RtoP in the State concerned. Such action should be implemented, on a peaceful–coercive gradient, through the UN Security Council and in cooperation with appropriate regional organisations.

[82] To avoid a 'party line' type response from my interviewees, when the issue arose, I always stressed that I preferred their personal views.

rebuild. Through its various mechanisms, the OSCE can intervene in any participating State to work toward conflict prevention, crisis management, or post-conflict rehabilitation. The OSCE can help potential, actual or former adversaries, for instance, to deal with arms control, confidence building, counterterrorism, post-conflict capacity-building, human rights, protection of minorities – e.g. the Roma and Sinti – elections, democratisation, policing and the environment.[83]

As part of the Platform for Co-operative Security, the OSCE can continue, including within a NEPSS-type arrangement, to work with NATO, the European Union, Council of Europe as well as other international organisations, including NGOs, thus allowing it to be relevant to the need to *react* as well as to *prevent* and *rebuild.* Hence, the OSCE remains in Bosnia-Herzegovina and Kosovo, plus, in 2004, even sent an election support team to one of its Asian Partners for Co-operation, Afghanistan, 'the first of its kind to be sent to a non-participating State'.[84] Presumably, the OSCE could do the same in post-Gaddafi Libya by participating in the rebuilding of the country after the intervention.

In time, perhaps the OSCE could do the same in a post-Assad Syria, although at the time of this writing – some fourteen months after the Arab Spring-related uprising against the government in Damascus began, with 10,000 fatalities attributable by UN estimates to military action by the government and Assad-friendly militia – RtoP has not served the citizens of Syria well.[85]

At least on the European continent, RtoP allows, at minimum, the OSCE to do what RtoP architect Gareth Evans claims for the organisation: 'the OSCE now has both the need, and the opportunity through the

---

[83] Evans, *Responsibility to Protect*, p. 194. [84] OSCE, *Handbook*, p. 12.

[85] Factors accounting for the continued deterioration of the conflict in Syria include the absence of US leadership, Russia's continuing support for the Assad regime and blocking of action in the UN Security Council, and the preoccupation of European members of NATO with financial and political crises threatening the future integrity of the European Union. See for example 'NATO's blind spot: a summit in Chicago ignores the thousands dying in Syria', *Washington Post*, 22 May 2012, p. A14; Michael Birnbaum, 'European leaders cautious on Syria: unlike in Libya crisis, NATO nations distracted by own troubles', *Washington Post*, 1 June 2012, p. A10; 'What to do in Syria: US action far short of invasion could help prevent a regional conflagration', *Washington Post*, 1 June 2012, p. A20; 'Russia's shame: Moscow's support for Assad is damaging to its interests', *Financial Times*, 1 June 2012, p. 8.

office of the HCNM in particular, to become a major institutional player in the operationalisation of the [RtoP] concept.'[86]

The OSCE also represents the best opportunity to enhance RtoP in a way that no other regional security organisation could, especially in dealing with issues that still exist after the establishment of RtoP at the World Summit in 2005. According to the UN Secretary-General's own report:

> We should note that the worst human tragedies of the past century were not confined to any particular part of the world. They occurred in the North and in the South, in poor, medium-income and relatively affluent countries. Sometimes they were linked to ongoing conflicts but quite often – including in some of the worst cases – they were not. *In retrospect, three factors stand out. First, in each case there were warning signs . . . Second, the signals of trouble ahead were, time and again, ignored . . . Third, at times the United Nations – its intergovernmental organs and its secretariat – failed to do its part. . . .* Nine years after . . . sobering reports [on Rwanda and Srebrenica] . . . *The United Nations and its Member States remain underprepared to meet their most fundamental prevention and protection responsibilities.* We can, and must, do better. Humanity expects it and history demands it.[87]

Through its various mechanisms and other organisations within the Platform for Co-operative Security, perhaps in NEPSS-type configurations,[88] and its weekly meetings in Vienna of the Permanent Council, when participating States are called upon to respond to queries concerning violations of human rights within their own borders, the OSCE is

---

[86] Evans, 'European politics after the Russia–Georgia war', speech delivered at the OSCE in an Open World: Trade, Security and Migration, Toronto, 18 September 2008, at www.gevans.org/speeches/speech305.html.

[87] UNSG, 'Implementing the Responsibility to Protect', UN Doc. A/63/677, 12 January 2009, p. 6 (emphasis added).

[88] One example of OSCE–EU collaboration is the Dvani/Ergneti Incident Prevention and Response Mechanism (IPRM) established in February 2009, following the termination of hostilities between Georgia and south Ossetia in 2008. To date, there have been eight regular meetings of the IPRM, co-facilitated by the OSCE and European Union Monitoring Mission (EUMM), 'to discuss, among other issues: identification of potential risks, follow-up on incidents and exchange information, as well as problems affecting the communities on a daily basis. Regular meetings of the mechanism broke down in October 2009 and resumed in October 2010.' See OSCE Chairmanship press release, 'Incident prevention and response mechanism meeting takes place in Ergneti', 10 December 2010, at www.osce.org/cio/74549; and OSCE Chairmanship press release, 'OSCE chairman welcomes resumption of the Dvani/Ergneti IPRM', 28 October 2010, at www.osce.org/cio/74072.

especially well poised to take on the historical imperative of nudging the United Nations system and international community in general toward full operationalisation of RtoP. As the UN Secretary-General has correctly put it, 'Humanity expects it and history demands it.' Including in Syria![89]

---

[89] The longer that the bloodshed in Syria continues, the more that it is being compared to the genocidal implosion of the former Yugoslavia, such as the genocidal atrocities committed at Srebrenica in July 1995, one of the developments that spawned RtoP. See Michael Dobbs, 'Houla: shadows of Srebrenica', *Washington Post*, 3 June 2012, p. A10. The more that such comparisons are made, the more likely calls for military intervention, citing RtoP in the process, will be made. See Roula Khalaf, 'It is time to consider the military options in Syria', *Financial Times*, 6 June 2012, p. 9.

15

The North Atlantic Treaty Organization

JODY M. PRESCOTT

Introduction

In March 1999, without authorisation by the United Nations Security Council, North Atlantic Treaty Organization (NATO) forces began air strikes against Serbian targets in response to Yugoslavia's refusal to comply with NATO's demands to cease its attacks on Kosovar Albanians. During its air campaign NATO refined and expanded its objectives to include 'a verifiable stop to all military action and the immediate ending of violence and repression' and 'the unconditional and safe return of all refugees and displaced persons and unhindered access to them by humanitarian aid organisations'.[1] Although the legality of NATO's military intervention in response to the humanitarian crisis engulfing the Kosovar Albanian people has been debated,[2] its reality marked a milestone in State practice regarding the use of force on this basis, and fostered greater consideration in the international and academic communities as to the conditions under which such an intervention would be proper, and the development of the concept of responsibility to protect (R2P). Twelve years later, with UN Security Council backing, and consistent with the principles of R2P, NATO air assets began attacking Libyan government forces to prevent them from attacking dissident Libyan populations.[3] This intervention, although successful in providing the Libyan rebels the military capabilities they needed to

---

[1] NATO, 'NATO's Role in Relation to the Conflict in Kosovo', at www.nato.int/kosovo/history.htm.

[2] See for example Julie Mertus, 'Special Project: Humanitarian Intervention and Kosovo: Reconsidering the Legality of Humanitarian Intervention: Lessons from Kosovo', *William and Mary Law Review*, 41 (2000), 1743–87, at 1748–50.

[3] David Kirkpatrick, Steven Erlanger and Elisabeth Bumiller, 'Allies Open Air Assault on Qaddafi's Forces', 19 May 2011, at www.nytimes.com/2011/03/20/world/africa/20libya.html.

eventually defeat the Libyan government forces, has raised new legal, political and ethical issues regarding the use of force in humanitarian intervention.

The concept of R2P and the use of different measures by the international community to ensure that States protect their citizens from serious human rights violations were comprehensively addressed in the seminal report of the International Commission on Intervention and State Sovereignty (ICISS) in 2001. In particular, the report focused on the use of military intervention to protect human rights from the complementary perspectives of when such intervention could be appropriate and what military intervention in an operational context might look like.[4] During the decade since the report's release, a general consensus has developed that at least with regard to the use of non-military measures such as diplomacy and economic sanctions, R2P marked an appropriate evolution in the understanding of State sovereignty in both international relations and international law.[5] As to the propriety of military intervention to protect human rights, however, the consensus is not so clear. In the Outcome Document of the 2005 World Summit, the world's leaders agreed that:

> We are prepared to take collective action in a timely and decisive manner, through the Security Council, in accordance with the Charter, including Chapter VII, on a case-by-case basis and in cooperation with relevant regional authorities as appropriate, should peaceful means be inadequate ... We also intend to commit ourselves, as necessary and appropriate, to helping States build capacity to protect their populations from genocide, war crimes, ethnic cleansing and crimes against humanity and to assisting those which are under stress before crises and conflicts break out.[6]

The 2009 UN General Assembly debate on R2P generally confirmed the 2005 Outcome Document's list of those human rights violations that were considered so serious that they constituted threats against international peace and security; namely, genocide, war crimes, ethnic cleansing and crimes against humanity,[7] and therefore trumped the general

---

[4] International Commission on Intervention and State Sovereignty, *The Responsibility to Protect* (Ottawa: International Development Research Centre, 2001), pp. 1–2, 29–37 and 57–8.

[5] See Global Centre for the Responsibility to Protect, 'Implementing the Responsibility to Protect: The 2009 General Assembly Debate', pp. 4–5, available at www.globalr2p.org.

[6] '2005 World Summit Outcome', UN Doc. A/RES/60/1, 24 October 2005, para. 139.

[7] GCR2P, '2009 General Assembly Debate', pp. 5–6.

principle of non-intervention by the UN. However, the debate revealed serious concerns held by some countries as to whether military intervention was proper, and, if so, under what conditions it could be authorised. In the end, the General Assembly resolved only to study the issue of military intervention further.[8] These concerns have likewise been identified in research on this topic, which has suggested a general unwillingness among the international community to conduct military intervention on humanitarian grounds.[9]

In light of the controversy regarding its use, military intervention is perhaps the most important implementation mechanism to examine in the NATO context. The issue of military intervention is composed of two parts: questions of whether and when intervention is legitimate and appropriate; and if those questions are resolved in favour of intervention, concerns as to the means by which the military intervention is to be executed. This second half of the military intervention issue, implementation, is very important in terms of keeping the conduct of the mission consistent with its purpose, but it seems to have been left to the side in most of the discussions following the ICISS report. In addressing both halves of the military intervention issue, this chapter will first briefly describe NATO's structure and its function. Second, NATO's strategic concept and its policies with regard to human rights will be explored to better understand the limited conditions under which it might find itself intervening militarily to protect human rights and stop mass atrocity crimes. Third, the mode of military engagement set out in the ICISS report and subsequent scholarship by R2P advocates will be reviewed, and their assumptions with regard to the actual use of military force analysed in detail. Finally, this chapter will look at the way in which NATO military operations are actually conducted, and identify areas in which best practices might be identified and used not just to effectively promote the observance of international humanitarian law (IHL) and international human rights law (IHRL) by NATO forces if a military intervention were to occur, but also to set out examples and standards by which similar capacities could be fostered in crisis States' forces as well.

---

[8] UN General Assembly Res. 63/308, UN Doc. A/63/308, 7 October 2009.
[9] Victoria Holt and Tobias Berkman, *The Impossible Mandate? Military Preparedness, the Responsibility to Protect and Modern Peacekeeping Operations* (Washington, DC: Henry L. Stimson Center, 2006).

NATO structure and function

NATO was formed in 1949 under the North Atlantic Treaty, often called the Washington Treaty. Parties to the treaty committed themselves to international action consistent with the UN Charter in the areas of international relations, dispute resolution and economic interaction. To effect these aims, the parties agreed to 'maintain and develop their individual and collective capacity to resist armed attack', and to consult with each other in the event any believed that 'the territorial integrity, political independence or security of any of the Parties' was threatened. Were any parties to suffer armed attack against their territory or armed forces in Europe, North America or the Atlantic Ocean north of the Tropic of Cancer, and later, Turkey, this would 'be considered an attack against them all'. Such an attack would trigger the parties' responsibilities to take action individually and collectively to assist those whom had been attacked, including the use of armed force if 'deem[ed] necessary'. To ensure timely response by the Alliance, the North Atlantic Council (NAC) was created as an executive body, and it was given the authority to set up the subsidiary organs necessary to implement the treaty.[10]

As 'NATO's most important decision-making body', the NAC 'brings together representatives of all the Allies at the level of ambassadors, ministers or heads of State and government'. Decisions are all made on the basis of consensus, with each member having an equal say. NATO itself has no operational forces; instead it relies upon its members to assign forces to it, and upon force contributions from non-NATO partners.[11] NATO Headquarters is located in Brussels. NATO has one operational command, Allied Command Operations (ACO), located in Mons, Belgium, and still commonly known by its former title, SHAPE (Supreme Headquarters Allied Powers Europe); and one functional command, Allied Command Transformation (ACT), located in Norfolk, Virginia, in the US. Whereas SHAPE commands subordinate operational headquarters located in Italy, the Netherlands, and Portugal, and the forces assigned to those

---

[10] North Atlantic Treaty, adopted 4 April 1949 and entered into force 24 August 1949, 34 UNTS 243, arts. 1–6 and 9; see also NATO, *NATO Handbook* (Brussels: NATO Public Diplomacy Division, 2006), p. 9.

[11] NATO, *Handbook*, p. 15. An exception is the aircraft and crews of the NATO early warning unit, which fly under Luxembourger registration but are NATO assets with multinational crews. NATO, 'NATO Airborne Early Warning and Control Force: E3A Component', at www.e3a.nato.int/eng/html/organizations/history.htm.

headquarters,[12] ACT commands training, research and educational facilities across Europe and North America.[13]

To guide its actions in achieving its fundamental purpose of safeguarding 'the freedom and security of all its members by political and military means', NATO relies upon its published Strategic Concept. The Strategic Concept describes the Alliance's fundamental security tasks, and serves as 'the authoritative statement of the Alliance's objectives and provides the highest level guidance on the political and military means to be used in achieving them'. To implement the political and military guidance set out in the Strategic Concept, NATO engages in a number of relationships with non-NATO countries and international organisations. Perhaps the largest and most successful political and military engagement of NATO with non-NATO countries has been the Partnership for Peace (PfP) programme, through which many countries have moved to full NATO membership status. NATO has sought to improve its relationship with nations in Mediterranean Africa and the Middle East through its Mediterranean Dialogue (MD) and Istanbul Cooperative Initiative (ICI) programmes, but these programmes do not appear to have truly moved beyond the dialogue stage towards true partnership. Further, NATO maintains a number of formalised political consultative bodies and relationships with individual non-NATO members, such as the NATO–Russia Council and its engagement with Ukraine and Georgia. Finally, NATO maintains coordinating and liaison relationships with many international organisations, most particularly with the EU and to a lesser degree with the UN.[14]

NATO is not a regional organisation, which is why some of the more significant reports by the UN Secretary-General on the implementation of R2P and the role of regional organisations do not mention it, despite its significant experience in humanitarian intervention.[15] NATO is a

---

[12] NATO Allied Command Operations, 'ACO Organisation', at www.aco.nato.int/struc ture.aspx. For example, the International Security Assistance Force (ISAF) in Afghanistan is subordinate to Joint Force Command Brunssum, in the Netherlands (*ibid.*).

[13] NATO Allied Command Transformation, 'ACT Organisation', at www.act.nato.int/ organisation/141-structure. NATO is currently reorganising its headquarters structure from 13,000 personnel to 8,800 to streamline its operations. NATO, 'Background on NATO Command Structure Review', June 2011, at www.nato.int/nato_static/assets/pdf/ pdf_2011_06/20110609-Backgrounder_Command_Structure.pdf.

[14] NATO, *Handbook*, pp. 18, 27–8, 185–9, 197–200 and 229–35.

[15] UN Secretary-General, 'The Role of Regional and Sub-regional Arrangements in Implementing the Responsibility to Protect', UN Doc. A/65/877–S/2011/393, 27 June

collective defence organisation, and although it has significant political and diplomatic means at its disposal, its primary strength lies in its military capabilities. As demonstrated by the work done by the NATO Training Missions in Iraq (NTM-I)[16] and Afghanistan (NTM-A),[17] for example, NATO has shown that it can use its military capabilities in conjunction with civilian resources to build capacity in crisis States to promote the protection of human rights writ broadly without having to first intervene to protect those rights in a military operation. For NTM-I, specific examples of capacity-building in this regard include such events as the Italian Carabinieri conducting training for the Iraqi Federal Police which included instruction on professional police ethics,[18] and Norway hosting twice-yearly training sessions for senior Iraqi officers from the Ministries of Defence and Interior which included instruction on and discussion of human rights and the standard of professionalism consistent with a democratic society.[19] For NTM-A, examples of capacity-building particularly tailored to the situation in Afghanistan include literacy training for members of the Afghan National Security Forces,[20] and seminars on gender and domestic violence issues to students studying to become Afghan National Police trainers.[21] NATO has, therefore, deemed the use of its military capabilities to build capacity in crisis States to be in keeping with the organisation's collective defence mission.

NATO strategy and policy

NATO periodically reviews and revises its strategy, and it takes a holistic approach in assessing its role and what, as a manifestation of the shared intent of its members, it should seek to accomplish through its military,

---

2011; UNSG, 'Implementing the Responsibility to Protect', UN Doc. A/63/677, 12 January 2009.

[16] NATO, 'NATO's Assistance to Iraq', at www.nato.int/cps/en/natolive/topics_51978. htm.

[17] NATO Training Mission Afghanistan, 'NTM-A Mission Statement', available at www. ntm-a.com.

[18] NATO, 'Assistance to Iraq'.

[19] Inci Kucukaksoy, 'Joint Warfare Centre Conducted IKLT 13', 31 October 2010, at www. jwc.nato.int/jwc-news/joint-warfare-centre-conducted-iklt-13.

[20] Fraidoon Hoshang, 'Literacy summit at Camp Eggers – Dari version', video file, NTM-A Public Affairs Office, 7 February 2011, at www.youtube.com/watch?v=tFxgoZL72Yo &feature=youtube_gdata.

[21] John Herrera, 'Afghan National Police gender seminar', video file, at www.youtube.com/ watch?v=n2T0XpaMfB0.

political and diplomatic capabilities.[22] Prior to the most recent strategy review in 2010, NATO Secretary General Anders Fogh Rasmussen convened a diverse group of experts chaired by former US Secretary of State Madeleine Albright to research and analyse what NATO's goals and means to accomplish these goals should be.[23] Over a period of eight months, the group of experts conducted numerous conferences, seminars and consultations with NATO's senior civilian leadership and the NAC; senior NATO military leaders; partners from the Mediterranean Dialogue, the Istanbul Cooperative Initiative and the Euro-Atlantic Political Council; Organization for Security and Co-operation in Europe; NATO and European Union parliamentarians; individual NATO governments; and representatives of Russia, Ukraine and Georgia. In their final report, the group of experts confirmed that NATO's primary purpose was to provide collective defence for its members. In addition to the tasks contained in the existing strategy, the group of experts also recommended that NATO focus on ballistic missile defence and reacting to terrorist and cyber-attacks, and its efforts to better partner with other organisations such as the EU and the UN.[24] Specifically with regard to NATO's relationship with the UN, the group of experts made a number of recommendations that are pertinent to R2P, and one which is most significant regarding the issue of military intervention:

> Coordination between the UN and NATO can prove crucial in the event of genocide, other massive violations of human rights, or humanitarian emergency. The Strategic Concept should make clear that NATO is willing to consider requests from the UN to take appropriate action in such circumstances (possibly in support of other regional organisations), provided the NAC agrees to the mission and resources are available to carry it out.[25]

---

[22] NATO, *Handbook*, p. 18.

[23] NATO, *NATO 2020: Assured Security; Dynamic Engagement* (Brussels: NATO Public Diplomacy Division, 2010), p. 4. Presumably, NATO was well aware of its potential role in R2P generally given its role in Kosovo, and specifically in light of the article of Mr Gareth Evans, the ICISS co-chair, in *NATO Review*. Gareth Evans, 'The Responsibility to Protect', *NATO Review*, 4 (2002), 31–5. As well as Mr Evans's presentation to the Shadow NATO Summit in 2009 in which he urged NATO to devote its military resources and political will towards making R2P an operational reality. Evans, 'NATO and the responsibility to protect', presentation to NATO Shadow Summit, Options for NATO: Pressing the Re-Set Button on the Strategic Concept, Brussels, 31 March 2009, at www.gevans.org/speeches/speech313.html.

[24] NATO, *NATO 2020*, pp. 8–9, 11, 17, 22–3 and 49–50.   [25] *Ibid.*, p. 24.

The group of experts further recommended that NATO should establish guidelines for the use of force beyond the Alliance area, and importantly, it addressed the tension between a strict interpretation of collective defence versus the political reality of national agendas that might militate toward a more expansive view of the need to act on the basis of R2P:

> Because of its visibility and power, NATO may well be called upon to respond to challenges that do not directly affect its security but that still matter to its citizens and that will contribute to the Alliance's international standing. These challenges could include the humanitarian consequences of a failed State, the devastation caused by a natural disaster, or the dangers posed by genocide or other massive violations of human rights.[26]

In the approved strategic concept[27] unveiled at the Lisbon Summit in November 2010, NATO accepted several of the group of experts' recommendations, such as increased partnering to leverage the Alliance's political and diplomatic capabilities.[28] This is consistent with the evolving use by NATO of the Comprehensive Approach and its military sub-methodology of the Effects Based Approach to Operations (EBAO). The impetus for the Comprehensive Approach was the successful Danish experience within its national contingent with statutorily mandated civil-military cooperation in its overseas missions.[29] NATO endorsed this concept at the 2006 Riga Summit, and the NAC was directed to propose 'pragmatic measures to improve coherent application of NATO's own crisis management instruments', and to 'enhance the interface of civilian and military efforts with organizations such as the UN, non-governmental organizations, and local actors'.[30] EBAO is perhaps best described as the Comprehensive Approach's implementation

---

[26] *Ibid.*, pp. 9, 15 and 32.

[27] NATO, 'Active Engagement, Modern Defence: Strategic Concept for the Defence and Security of the Members of the North Atlantic Treaty Organization', 19 November 2010, at www.nato.int/lisbon2010/strategic-concept-2010-eng.pdf.

[28] *Ibid.*, pp. 1–3 and 5–10.

[29] Kristian Fischer and Jan Top Christensen, 'Improving Civil–Military Cooperation the Danish Way', *NATO Review*, summer 2005, at www.nato.int/docu/review/2005/issue2/english/special.html.

[30] Jody Prescott, 'The Development of NATO EBAO Doctrine: Clausewitz's Theories and the Role of Law in an Evolving Approach to Operations', *Penn State Law Review*, 27 (2008), 126–68, at 126–7, quoting Tim Williams (ed.), 'The Road to Riga and the Path Ahead: NATO's Transformation Agenda before and after the Riga Summit', Royal United Services Institute for Defence and Security Studies, at www.rusi.org/downloads/assets/The_Road_to_Riga_and_the_Path_Ahead.pdf.

in a military context to create a more holistic picture of the operational environment, which should allow for the better use of limited resources and better cooperation between NATO and national and international organisations.[31] In this sense, 'effects' are the changes in perceptions, behaviours and capabilities that must be achieved among the actors in an operational environment to accomplish NATO's objectives.[32]

In large part, however, the new Strategic Concept did not incorporate the group of experts' recommendations that would have more clearly fostered military intervention on the basis of R2P becoming a more common operational reality for the Alliance. For example, the new Strategic Concept neither includes explicit guidelines as to when the use of force is appropriate, nor does it address the topic of crises that might be of interest to individual NATO members but are not really critical to NATO's collective defence mission. The new Strategic Concept identifies three tasks considered essential for safeguarding members of the Alliance: collective defence, crisis management and cooperative security.[33] Of the three, only crisis management was defined in terms that suggested the Alliance might play a role in R2P, but not necessarily through the use of its primary military capability:

> NATO has a unique and robust set of political and military capabilities to address the full spectrum of crises – before, during and after conflicts. NATO will actively employ a mix of those political and military tools to help manage developing crises that have the potential to affect Alliance security, before they escalate into conflicts; to stop ongoing conflicts where they affect Alliance security; and to help consolidate stability in post conflict situations where that contributes to Euro-Atlantic security.[34]

The section of the Strategic Concept that explains the meaning of 'Security through Crisis Management' recognises that '[c]rises and conflicts beyond NATO's borders can pose a direct threat to the security of Alliance territory and populations'. In response, 'NATO will therefore engage, where possible and when necessary, to prevent crises, manage crises, stabilize post-conflict situations and support reconstruction.' Where crises devolve into conflict, the Strategic Concept recognises

---

[31] Prescott, 'NATO EBAO Doctrine', 127.
[32] NATO, *Bi-Strategic Command Pre-Doctrinal Handbook (Effects Based Approach to Operations)* (Stavanger, Norway: Joint Warfare Centre, 2007), paras. 1-1–1-3.
[33] NATO, 'Active Engagement, Modern Defence', para. 4.   [34] *Ibid.*, para. 4(b).

that 'management' 'includ[es] the unparalleled capability to deploy and sustain robust military forces in the field'. In its assessment of the security environment facing NATO, the Strategic Concept appears to have further refined its crisis management task, noting that 'Instability or conflict beyond NATO borders can directly threaten Alliance security, including by fostering extremism, terrorism, and trans-national illegal activities such as trafficking in arms, narcotics and people.'[35] In this context, it is useful to compare NATO's intervention in Kosovo with its actions in Afghanistan to gain a better appreciation of how direct the threat must be to NATO before it would engage in humanitarian intervention. Kosovo bordered Albania and Macedonia, two States which were already PfP members, and whose stability was directly threatened by events in Kosovo. The persecution of Kosovar Albanians was being conducted by the forces of the former Republic of Yugoslavia (composed of Serbia and Montenegro), which bordered on two other PfP countries, Bulgaria and Romania, and a NATO member, Hungary. NATO already had forces in two other countries bordering the former Republic of Yugoslavia, namely Bosnia-Herzegovina and Croatia, forces which were there in large part because of the role Serbia had played in ethnic persecution of non-Serbs in those countries during the violent break-up of Yugoslavia. From a feasibility standpoint, the proximity of overwhelming NATO land, sea and air forces, coupled with secure logistical facilities and short lines of communication, made a military intervention quite practicable. NATO's evolving engagement in Afghanistan, on the other hand, although quite a distance from the Alliance area, was based upon an actual attack on one of its members which triggered Article 5 of the Washington Treaty,[36] and has been regularly reapproved by the UN Security Council.[37] In sum, although the strategic concept recognises out-of-area crisis management can include military deployment, military intervention on humanitarian grounds is only likely when Alliance security is directly threatened by events on or near its borders, or when the humanitarian crisis, wherever it occurs, may lead to conditions of extremism or terrorism which could project a direct threat to the Alliance area. Further, the logistical situation must be favourable for sustained support of operations.

---

[35] *Ibid.*, paras. 11, 20 and 23.   [36] NATO, *Handbook*, p. 20.
[37] See for example UN Security Council Res. 1943, UN Doc. S/RES/1943, 13 October 2010.

The mode of military action

In advocating for the use of military intervention as a last resort to avert serious violations of human rights, the ICISS report arguably posits a scenario in which the legal aspects of the actual implementation of the intervention are borne out neither by the principles of IHL, nor by operational experience. First, the report distinguishes between 'traditional warfighting' and humanitarian intervention, noting that:

> While military intervention operations require the use of as much force as is necessary, which may be on occasion a great deal, to protect the population at risk, their basic objective is always to achieve quick success with as little cost as possible in civilian lives and inflicting as little damage as possible so as to enhance recovery prospects in the post-conflict phase. In warfighting, by contrast, the neutralization of an opponent's military or industrial capabilities is often the instrument to force surrender.[38]

Accordingly, the report argues that as to the rules applicable to the conduct of the military intervention operations, 'even higher standards should apply in these cases'. Apparently, these higher standards are to be found in the rules of engagement (ROE), which 'must reflect a stringent observance of international law, and international humanitarian law in particular'. Interestingly, the report also notes that although military intervention forces will not have the benefit of surprise, they should be restricted in their desire to compensate for this operational disadvantage by concentrating their combat power, because this would cause them to lose the 'hearts and minds' of those whom the intervening force attacks as it seeks to prevent them from committing further serious human rights violations. In light of all these factors, the report recommended that the UN create a new 'doctrine for human protection operations', which would reflect that the purpose of such missions would be to 'enforce compliance with human rights and the rule of law', and principles such as the incremental and gradual use of force, strict adherence to IHL, and recognition that 'force protection for the intervening force must never have priority over the resolve to accomplish the mission'.[39] A potential example of what such higher standards might look like is perhaps found in a recent book in which the author advocates the use of only limited force against combatants opposing an intervention, and the

---

[38] ICISS, *The Responsibility to Protect*, para. 7.1.

[39] *Ibid.*, paras. 4.40, 7.28, 7.31, 7.50 and 7.51. The report correctly and succinctly defines rules of engagement (ROE) as 'the directions guiding the application of the use of force by soldiers in the theatre of operations' (*ibid.*, para. 7.26).

separation of combatants into two categories; those who are morally responsible because they are voluntarily fighting an unjust war, and those who are morally innocent because they have been conscripted, for example.[40] Against the morally innocent, the author argues that interveners should only use limited force against them as long as it 'is a last resort, and providing that they attempt to minimise the harm to these combatants by accepting risk themselves'.[41] Further, a principle of proportionality which requires the use of the least amount of force possible should be used, and 'foreseeable civilian casualties are also impermissible, even if unintended'.[42]

As a practical matter, agreeing to a military intervention under these conditions would likely be very difficult for a NATO nation, because they reflect a lack of understanding of how dangerous and complex even well-intentioned military operations can be. First, if military intervention is being used as a last resort, it necessarily means other means did not work, and the situation is potentially grim. An intervening force may therefore find itself engaged in intense combat simply because of the timing of its use. Second, although evidence from the field suggests that immediate demonstrations of overwhelming military force and the willingness to use it may persuade less disciplined human-rights violators to not challenge the intervening forces,[43] the opposition always gets a vote. Although the intent of the military intervention is to succeed quickly with as little damage as possible so that its actions are conceptually consistent with its reasons for being there, the opposition forces in the invaded State will likely neither respect the intervening force's laudable intentions nor wish to cooperate with it in achieving its mission. Third, military action occurs along a spectrum, and setting 'traditional war-fighting' (presumably the clash of large, mechanised military units in an extensive theatre of operations) as the alternative to humanitarian military intervention sets out a false choice not reflected in reality. Fourth, handicapping commanders by not permitting them to use all the forces at their disposal as allowed by IHL to accomplish the protection mission, especially if the purpose of such limitations is to win the affection and appreciation of those engaged in serious human rights violations, flies in

---

[40] James Pattison, *Humanitarian Intervention and the Responsibility to Protect* (Oxford University Press, 2010), pp. 108–9.
[41] *Ibid.*   [42] *Ibid.*
[43] Victoria Holt and Joshua Smith, *Halting Widespread or Systematic Attacks on Civilians: Military Strategies and Operational Concepts*, Report from an International Experts Workshop (Washington, DC: Henry L. Stimson Center, 2008), pp. 12 and 22.

the face of common sense. Fifth, separating out the morally innocent combatants from those who are morally responsible for atrocities is at best unworkable. There is no internationally recognised symbol for identifying such personnel, nor are there any standards for determining which personnel would be entitled to wear it. Sixth, IHL already requires the strict application of distinction and proportionality in all international armed conflicts, which a military intervention into a sovereign State would always be. As the Libyan air operation shows, even when the intervener chooses to apply very restrictive ROE, avoid ground combat, and apply the latest technology and doctrine, it is impossible to keep errors from occurring which cost civilian lives. Seventh, all soldiers and units have an inherent right to self-defence when engaged in operations, and their rules on self-defence and ROE might allow them to respond with lethal force to manifestations of hostile intent, or to hostile acts short of an imminent attack. Asking a nation to agree to contribute its forces under the condition that they will have their rights to self-defence trumped by the need to accomplish the mission is neither militarily sound, nor politically feasible. To analogise them to a domestic police force accepting risks in protecting its own society is, at best, flawed. Few soldiers volunteer to serve in their respective country's militaries so that they may deploy abroad and die without the means to protect themselves in the service of other peoples' crumbling societies. Finally, the use of the least amount of force is not likely to lead to a quick victory, which means that more civilians suffer and more property is damaged in the long run. In Libya, for example, although the very limiting ROE under which NATO operated meant that very few civilians were unintentionally killed, the conflict lasted seven months before the Libyan rebels captured Tripoli, the capital. During this time, perhaps as many as 25,000 civilians were killed, and the regime was given the opportunity to commit mass atrocities against protected persons.[44]

A more productive approach to sorting through the use of force issues in a military humanitarian intervention may be to contrast them with the conduct of peacekeeping operations. Whereas peacekeeping operations tend to have long-term security and stability as their goal, military interventions may need to shift to a coercive protection posture, where an immediate goal is physical protection and may require the use of force, either to defend civilians or to compel belligerents to no longer

---

[44] 'Turkey's Erdogan pays tribute to "martyrs" against Gaddafi', Trend, 20 September 2011, at http://en.trend.az/regions/met/turkey/1934494.html.

threaten a population.[45] Simulation research suggests that unless the mandate to intervene is backed by sufficiently numerous, well-resourced, well-trained and well-equipped soldiers, operating under ROE that allow them to engage in dynamic (offensive) protection by going after human rights violators, commanders may be forced to resort to static (defensive) measures that prove less effective in actually protecting the threatened population, and thereby threaten mission accomplishment.[46] NATO's air operation in Libya confirms this – the limitations inherent in conducting a purely defensive operation become quickly manifest in the face of a determined and adaptive opponent. Focusing only on the actual combat, though, ignores the fact that successful operations are much more than just fighting, especially in an R2P intervention situation. In this context, it is useful to look at certain methods NATO currently uses in preparing for and conducting its operations which meet the spirit of R2P and human rights protection in general. These methods potentially have a synergistic positive effect on the observation of human rights by NATO forces when deployed, and have great value as a demonstration of best practices to be used in standardising capacity within the national contingents of the NATO and non-NATO forces. More importantly, in keeping with paragraph 139 of the 2005 World Summit Outcome Document, these field-tested methodologies could be used effectively to help build capacity within States that are under stress before the outbreak of crisis and conflict.

Best practices in NATO operations

Training

States have the primary responsibility for ensuring that their armed forces are properly trained in IHL. NATO, as a multinational collective defence organisation, cannot be party to the different IHL treaties, and some question whether such an organisation could be legally bound by customary IHL. This uncertainty is perhaps even more pronounced when an established organisation such as NATO forms the core of a temporary headquarters, such as the International Security Assistance Force (ISAF). Importantly, however, all the NATO countries have ratified the 1949 Geneva Conventions, and all but two have ratified

---

[45] Holt and Smith, 'Attacks on Civilians', p. 8.
[46] *Ibid.*, pp. 19–20; see also *ibid.*, pp. 38–9. Srebrenica perhaps represents a commander's worst nightmare in this sense.

Additional Protocols I and II. All of the ISAF Troop Contributing Nations (TCNs) have likewise ratified the 1949 Geneva Conventions, and they are of course all bound by customary IHL. Furthermore, many TCNs choose to implement IHL to some degree in all of their military operations as a matter of domestic law or policy, irrespective of the sort of operation.[47]

Because training is a national obligation, each State implements its training strategy to meet national requirements. Therefore, even forces that habitually train and operate together may have received their IHL training differently, and may therefore have different perspectives on IHL implementation in the field. To help to regularise IHL training within the Alliance where possible, NATO has promulgated Standardisation Agreement (STANAG) 2449, *Training in the Law of Armed Conflict*. STANAG 2449 recognises NATO Member States' obligations to train their own units and personnel in IHL, even those units and personnel that are part of multinational headquarters units. It also recognises that pursuant to NATO policy, NATO forces will follow the spirit and principles of IHL even in operations outside of armed conflicts.[48]

STANAG 2449 establishes broad training principles, such as the need for regular IHL training prior to deployments and even during operations, and the need for IHL to be incorporated into training exercises. Upon these principles, the STANAG establishes training objectives intended to ensure conformance with IHL in actual operations, through such measures as the incorporation of conflict situations in exercises, and having commanders and staffs take IHL factors into consideration during both the planning and the execution of operations. The STANAG further provides outlines for the different kinds of IHL training that should be given to different personnel based upon their ranks and levels of command responsibility, and identifies certain areas that are highly relevant in modern multinational force operations, such as working with ROE and civil military affairs. Many of the NATO members that have ratified the STANAG have done so with reservations, but these tend to be fairly minor and deal with technical matters. Some, such as Norway, have used the STANAG to revamp their IHL training programmes. NATO encourages PfP nations to adopt STANAGs to enhance

---

[47] Jody M. Prescott, 'Training in the Law of Armed Conflict – A NATO Perspective', *Journal of Military Ethics*, 7 (2008), 66–75, at 66–8.

[48] *Ibid.*, 67–9.

interoperability, and in fact many of the non-NATO TCNs in ISAF are PfP countries.[49] This high degree of utilisation not only suggests that this STANAG is a very good candidate for a best practice in this area, it also suggests that the STANAG mechanism would be an effective way to develop flexible doctrine in other areas that could help build capacity to both detect impending crisis situations and to plan how to conduct military operations geared towards defusing these situations. For example, President Obama recently ordered the US government to begin planning for the conduct of Mass Atrocity Response Operations, based in large part upon the pioneering work of the Carr Center for Human Rights Policy at Harvard and the US Army Peacekeeping and Stability Operations Institute.[50] Using the STANAG development process, a national doctrinal work could be appropriately 'internationalised' to make it more accessible and acceptable to the international community.

Rules of engagement

When deployed, NATO forces operate under ROE approved by the NAC. Within NATO, ROE are defined as 'directives to military forces (including individuals) that define the circumstances, conditions, degree, and manner in which force, or actions which might be construed as provocative, may be applied'.[51] ROE are formulated in accordance with a NATO Military Committee document, MC 362/1, which provides both interpretive guidance and a menu of potential, specific ROE from which the actual rules may be selected or modified.[52] Many States will issue so-called 'caveats' to these rules, which will reflect specific national understandings as to implementation of the rules, consistent

---

[49] *Ibid.*, 68–72.
[50] Sarah Sewall, Dwight Raymond and Sally Chin, *Mass Atrocity Response Operations: A Military Planning Handbook* (Boston: Carr Center, 2010). See White House press release, 'Fact sheet: a comprehensive strategy and new tools to prevent and respond to atrocities', 23 April 2012, at www.whitehouse.gov/the-press-office/2012/04/23/fact-sheet-comprehensive-strategy-and-new-tools-prevent-and-respond-atro.
[51] NATO Military Committee, *NATO Rules of Engagement*, MC 362/1 (Brussels: NATO HQ, 2003), p. 2 (copy on file with author). The Military Committee is a subordinate organ of the North Atlantic Council. NATO, *Handbook*, p. 85.
[52] See Osman Aytaç, 'Laws and Rules for Soldiers in Armed Conflicts, Crises and Counter-Terrorism', *Legal Aspects of Combating Terrorism*, 47 (2008), 77–90, at 85–8.

with domestic and international legal obligations and political considerations.[53]

Although ROE are ordinarily considered in relation to the use of armed force in combat, the broad definition of NATO ROE allows for potential flexibility to implement a theatre commander's guidance to subordinate forces to act and react in defined ways which could promote the observance of human rights in an operation, even though it is not likely that the effected ROE would actually state that explicitly. For example, ROE 184, which allows the use of specified force to detain designated vessels and their personnel in designated circumstances,[54] could be implemented as, 'Use of minimum force is authorised to detain vessels and their personnel that are reasonably believed to be engaging in human trafficking.' Were NATO to conduct a humanitarian intervention, the most significant rules are likely to be ROE 423 (hostile intent) and ROE 424 (hostile act).[55] These ROE allow NATO forces to respond to demonstrations of hostile intent or hostile acts short of imminent attack to protect Persons with Designated Special Status (PDSS).[56] Victims of human rights violations could be affirmatively protected in this manner with up to lethal force if necessary.

ROE are promulgated to NATO forces outside of the actual NAC approved rules as well, as best shown by the continuing efforts by successive ISAF commanders to find ways to minimise civilian casualties and damage to civilian property while engaging Taliban and other anti-government forces in Afghanistan.[57] These 'tactical directives' by the most senior NATO commander in Afghanistan, directed down to the most junior soldier, contain specific guidance on calling in air strikes and disengaging from the enemy when non-combatants are present.[58] Statistics regarding civilian casualties in Afghanistan suggest that these directives have had a positive impact in reducing civilian deaths and injuries, although the tempo of combat has increased significantly over

---

[53] 'Germany's non-combat caveats to be reviewed by NATO', *Deutsche Welle*, 28 November 2006, at www.dw.de/dw/article/0,,2250071,00.html?maca=en-rss-en-all-1573-rdf.

[54] NATO MC, *Rules of Engagement*, annex A, series 18, A-8.   [55] *Ibid.*, series 42, A-19.

[56] *Ibid.*, app. 1, annex A, A-1-1 and 2.

[57] ISAF Headquarters press release, 'General Petraeus issues updated tactical directive: emphasizes "disciplined use of force"', 4 August 2010, at http://smallwarsjournal.com/documents/isafnewsrelease2.pdf; ISAF HQ Memorandum, 'Subject: Tactical Directive', 6 July 2009, at www.nato.int/isaf/docu/official_texts/Tactical_Directive_090706.pdf; ISAF HQ Memorandum, 'Subject: Tactical Directive', 30 December 2008, at www.nato.int/isaf/docu/official_texts/Tactical_Directive_090114.pdf.

[58] *Ibid.*

the time during which they have been in effect.[59] ROE can also be found in the standard operating procedures (SOPs) promulgated to soldiers guiding escalation in the use of force at vehicle checkpoints, for example.[60] Reducing civilian casualties from incidents at checkpoints has proved challenging,[61] but ensuring that all forces regardless of nationality follow the same procedures should reduce the uncertainty among Afghan civilians in approaching the checkpoints in terms of how their actions would likely be interpreted, thereby assisting them in transiting checkpoints safely.

NATO air operations in Libya, however, have shown how difficult it can be to execute an R2P military intervention with strict ROE that call for no civilian casualties as collateral damage. First, otherwise valid military targets that are contributing to the attacks on the civilian population cannot be prosecuted.[62] Second, even with sophisticated targeting technology and methods, targeteers cannot know for an absolute certainty that there are not protected civilians present,[63] an unfortunate lesson long since learned in Afghanistan.[64] Third, military organisations and soldiers are adaptive and reasoning beings. Libyan forces loyal to Colonel Gaddafi quickly learned to avoid using obvious military equipment and formations and to don civilian clothing to make it harder for NATO aircraft to target them,[65] and in some cases Libyan rebels had taken over captured government equipment.[66] This may have in part been responsible for NATO airstrikes that actually targeted rebel

---

[59] Jason Motlagh, 'Petraeus toughens Afghan rules of engagement', *Time*, 6 August 2010, at www.time.com/time/printout/0,8816,2008863,00.html.

[60] Prescott, 'Fall 2008 – ISAF LEGAD and Targeting Conference', *NATO Legal Gazette*, 17 (2008), 7–9.

[61] Richard Oppel, Jr, 'Tighter rules fail to stem deaths of innocent Afghans at checkpoints', *New York Times*, 26 March 2010, at www.nytimes.com/2010/03/27/world/asia/27afghan.html.

[62] 'Canadian pilots abort bombing over risk to civilians', CTV News, 19 May 2011, at www.ctv.ca/CTVNews//20110322/canadian-cf-18s-operation-odyssey-dawn-libya-110322.

[63] Lin Noueihed, 'Gaddafi's son buried as NATO air-strike support continues', *The Scotsman*, 2 May 2011, at www.news.scotsman.com/libya/Gaddafi39s-son-buried-as-Nato.6761458.jp.

[64] David Cloud, 'Predator drones: high-tech tools and human errors', *Stars and Stripes*, 11 April 2011, at www.stripes.com/news/predator-drones-high-tech-tools-and-human-errors-1.140744.

[65] Ben Farmer, 'Libya: Gaddafi forces "disguised as civilians"', *The Telegraph*, 31 March 2011, at www.telegraph.co.uk/news/worldnews/africaandindianocean/libya/8419832/Libya-Gaddafi-forces-disguised-as-civilians.html.

[66] David Wood, 'Libya air war: pilots struggle to avoid civilian casualties', 25 May 2011, at www.huffingtonpost.com/2011/03/21/libya-air-war-pilots-civilians_n_838733.html.

forces by mistake, ironically killing a number of people they were seeking to protect.[67]

Claims

As a result of NATO missions following the breakup of Yugoslavia, different claims regimes were created to settle claims resulting from injuries to civilians and damage to their property by NATO forces and personnel. Because of Bosnia-Herzegovina's and Croatia's unhappy experiences with the UN claims system during the existence of the UN Protection Force, in 1995 NATO's first significant out-of-area operation found itself working under a complicated and untried system involving host-nation participation in claims settlement and appeals. The NATO-led Implementation Force (IFOR) quickly recognised that these claims procedures agreed to in the General Framework Agreement for Peace were impractical, so separate agreements between IFOR and these two receiving States were negotiated which made the IFOR TCNs primarily responsible for collecting, investigating and adjudicating claims. IFOR claims offices handled claims resulting from the operations of the IFOR headquarters units, and sought to mediate disagreements on claims between TCNs and claimants prior to appeals to claims commissions composed of host country, IFOR and third party members.[68] Over time, the IFOR mission evolved in large part to an EU mission, and the foreign troop presence in both Bosnia-Herzegovina and Croatia was reduced. As of late 2007, however, the claims operations had received approximately 13,200 claims from receiving State citizens for injuries and damages, and had made payments of approximately €11,700,000.[69] Although the NATO-led Kosovo Force (KFOR) units were originally not held liable for any claims,[70] they eventually fell under a claims regime similar to that used in Croatia and Bosnia-Herzegovina.[71]

---

[67] Hadeed Al-Shalchi, 'Heavy clashes in Libya's rebel-held Misrata', *San Diego Union-Tribune*, 8 April 2011, at www.utsandiego.com/news/2011/apr/08/heavy-clashes-in-libyas-rebel-held-misrata.

[68] Prescott, 'Claims', in Dieter Fleck (ed.), *Handbook of the Law of Visiting Forces* (Oxford University Press, 2001), pp. 159–86 and 172–6.

[69] Jody M. Prescott, 'EBAO and Operational Claims', *The Three Swords*, 10 (2007) (copies available upon request to the Joint Warfare Centre Public Affairs Office, at pao@jwc.nato.int).

[70] See NATO, 'Military Technical Agreement between the International Security Force ("KFOR") and the Governments of the Federal Republic of Yugoslavia and the Republic of Serbia', 2 August 1999, app. B, para. 3.

[71] Prescott, 'Operational Claims', 7.

Similar to the situation in Kosovo, NATO-led forces which were part of ISAF were not liable for claims for injuries to civilians and damages to their property under the agreement setting out the status of NATO forces in Afghanistan.[72] However, just as KFOR had, the ISAF command quickly realised that paying meritorious claims for such damages helped foster the rule of law in its war-torn receiving State. A claims policy has evolved over successive rotations of the ISAF command whereby TCNs are responsible for administering their own claims programmes to settle claims. The ISAF claims office will settle meritorious claims if the proper TCN cannot be identified, but it will not accept claims for contractual issues, combat damage or those which result from operational necessity.[73] As the ISAF mission grew to cover all of Afghanistan and the Taliban and other anti-government forces began re-establishing their presence in the countryside, ISAF forces have increasingly engaged in heavy combat. This has resulted in an increase in the numbers of injured and killed Afghans and the amount of damaged civilian property, which have generated many more claims than were likely contemplated when ISAF was restricted to patrolling in Kabul.[74] Recognising the negative impact upon the mission and the inequity of being unable to reimburse innocent Afghans for the losses they suffered because of combat, certain ISAF TCNs have created and contributed toward a Post-Operations Emergency Relief Fund (POERF).[75] As of October 2009, this fund had been used to provide €2,369,791 worth of 'quick humanitarian assistance, such as the supply of food, water and shelter, or the repair of buildings or key infrastructure, immediately following sizable ISAF military operations'.[76] Recently, demonstrating the importance this issue has to the Alliance, the NATO members agreed on a set of

---

[72] ISAF, 'Military Technical Agreement between the International Security Assistance Force (ISAF) and the Interim Administration of Afghanistan', 5 March 2003, annex A, para. 10.

[73] Prescott, 'Operational Claims', 8.

[74] *Ibid.* The Afghan presidential commission estimated combat damages in Kandahar area over six months to be over $US 100 million, although this amount was disputed by the civilian governor and the ISAF military commander. Taimoor Shah and Rod Nordland, 'Afghan panel and US dispute war's toll on property', *New York Times*, 14 January 2011, at www.nytimes.com/2011/01/14/world/asia/14afghan.html.

[75] Originally called the Post-Operations Humanitarian Relief Fund (Prescott, 'Operational Claims', 8).

[76] NATO Public Diplomacy Division, 'Fact Sheet, NATO–ISAF Post-Operations Emergency Relief Fund (POERF)', October 2009, available at www.nato.int/cps/en/SID-6196C618-0EDCE907/natolive/official_texts.htm.

guidelines to bring more uniformity to the way in which humanitarian aid is provided to non-combatants who suffer losses from combat operations.[77] These measures, as well as adjudicating and paying for non-combat damages through claims processes, demonstrate respect for the rule of law and human rights, and set a standard of accountability that is a very important best practice in a crisis-torn State.

Planning and staff processes

An area that ordinarily does not receive much attention in terms of fostering observance of human rights is that of military planning and staff processes, generally documented in the form of SOPs.[78] With regard to planning, NATO has directed its units to integrate UN Security Council Resolution 1325 regarding the role of women in peace in security into their educational curricula and their operational planning.[79] These measures are supported in practice by the establishment of NATO Standards of Behaviour which proscribe illegal acts 'of unnecessary violence or threat to anyone in custody', 'result in physical, sexual or psychological harm of suffering, especially related to women and children', and the participation 'in activities which support human trafficking including prostitution'.[80] These standards are enforced by reporting requirements to NATO command chains and TCN disciplinary authorities in the event of breach by NATO personnel.[81]

Another example of a staff process which not only impacts upon the observance of human rights, but also serves as a best practice in terms of accountability, is the procedure by which ISAF tracks civilian casualties. At the NAC level, guidance was recently issued to better standardise the methods by which civilian casualties are tracked and counted.[82] ISAF has set up a Civilian Casualty Tracking Cell, which both oversees investigations into civilian casualty incidents and liaisons with human rights

---

[77] NATO, 'NATO Nations Approve Civilian Casualty Guidelines', 6 August 2010, at www. nato.int/cps/en/SID-9D9D8832-42250361/natolive/official_texts_65114.htm.

[78] See Jody M. Prescott, 'Training EBAO and Humanitarian Considerations in Operations: Blue Force Looks within', *The Three Swords*, 8 (April 2007), 25–9.

[79] NATO, 'Integrating UNSCR 1325 and Gender Perspectives in the NATO Command Structure including Measures for Protection during Armed Conflict', Bi-SC Directive 40–1, September 2009.

[80] *Ibid.*, paras. 2-1, 2-2 and 2-5.   [81] *Ibid.*, paras. 3-4 and 3-2.

[82] NATO press release, 'NATO nations approve civilian casualty guidelines', 6 August 2010, at www.nato.int/cps/en/SID-9D9D8832-42250361/natolive/official_texts_65114. htm.

groups engaged in protection of the civilian population.[83] Determining who and how many non-combatants have been injured or killed is fundamental to assessing whether forces are acting in compliance with IHL, but is likewise as important to the broader question of human rights because of the ripple effects of such losses among a civilian population.[84] Arriving at an accurate count is difficult in a theatre such as Afghanistan, and requires not just reconciliation of facts but of the counting methodologies as well.[85] More important in the long term than just accurate counting is the ability to analyse incidents in which civilian casualties have occurred and determine in a systematic fashion whether modifications to tactics used by NATO forces might result in fewer incidental losses among non-combatants. Such a system[86] was used in 2010 by a subordinate ISAF headquarters in Kandahar, and was apparently successful not just in identifying beneficial changes in tactics, but also in increasing the transparency of the process by including the UN, the International Committee of the Red Cross and human rights groups as participants.[87]

Conclusion

NATO's role and legal status as a collective defence organisation and its current strategy suggest that humanitarian intervention by NATO forces in accordance with R2P will be ordinarily unlikely. Viewed against the backdrop of the group of experts' recommendations, a conservative interpretation of the new Strategic Concept would argue that NATO should primarily use its diplomatic and political capabilities in seeking to defuse out-of-area crises that could potentially affect Alliance security. Further, while its military capabilities have been shown to be effective in building capacity, military intervention into out-of-area conflicts is only

---

[83] See ISAF press release, 'Ask ISAF: civilian casualty tracking cell manager answers your questions', 24 May 2009, at www.nato.int/isaf/docu/mediaadvisory/2009/05-may/ma090524-035.html.

[84] Prescott, 'Humanitarian Considerations', 29.

[85] See UN Assistance Mission in Afghanistan, *Annual Report on Protection of Civilians in Armed Conflict, 2009* (Kabul, Afghanistan: UNAMA, 2010), pp. 6–7.

[86] Ewan Cameron, Michael Spagat and Madelyn Hicks, 'Tracking Civilian Casualties in Combat Zones Using Civilian Battle Damage Assessment Ratios', *British Army Review*, 147 (2009), 87–93.

[87] Bruce Spencer, interview with Ewan Cameron, Health Care Adviser, Regional Command South, audio file, Association of Military Surgeons of the United States, at www.amsus.org/index.php/podcast-list.

likely when there is a direct threat to Alliance security. 'Direct threats' would appear to be further qualified to mean those conflicts or activities whose effects register transnationally, that is, upon the NATO Member States themselves, or on or near their borders. Finally, unless an out-of-area military intervention were 'possible' (operationally and logistically feasible) and 'necessary' (a last resort for Alliance security), NATO will not likely engage militarily in such a conflict. Arguably under this view, if genocide occurred in a country a great distance outside the NATO area, and its effects registered in the NATO area but posed no direct threat to the security of NATO members, NATO would likely not intervene with armed forces even if it were the only organisation capable of doing so. To define the limits on NATO military intervention more finely, proximity to the NATO area is probably the most important strategic criterion to determine whether NATO should intervene with armed forces – the closer to the NATO area, the more feasible an intervention becomes, and the more likely the effects of the conflict are to represent a direct threat to NATO security. NATO's operations in and around Libya illustrate the applicability of this criterion very well. By way of contrast, however, even though the Syrian government's violent crackdown on political dissidents has led to precisely the same sorts of atrocities against civilians that the NATO operation in Libya was launched to prevent, NATO has shown little official interest in military intervention, despite the fact that Syria borders a NATO country. Unlike Libya, Syria appears to enjoy the continued political support of powerful members of the international community, and its military is large, well-trained and well-equipped. Further, intervention in Syria could potentially draw Israel and Iran into the conflict.

Regardless, the means and modes by which NATO conducts its operations establish a useful set of potential best practices which not only enjoy wide international acceptance, but have been implemented in the field, and are therefore worthy of consideration in building capacity to avert crises and conflicts, as well as employment in any R2P military intervention. Further, as shown by the recent deployment of US Special Forces to Africa to assist in the hunt for Joseph Kony, the indicted commander of the murderous Lord's Resistance Army,[88] individual NATO members, and potentially, ad hoc functional coalitions of NATO members, might choose to act outside of NATO's formal

---

[88] Jake Tapper, 'President Obama talks about Joseph Kony', ABC News, 8 March 2012, at www.abcnews.go.com/blogs/politics/2012/03/president-obama-talks-about-joseph-kony.

command structure to engage in R2P missions. Even if NATO itself is not conducting these operations, the methods by which it does so are still likely to be employed to a significant degree. These focused, smaller-scale deployments might in fact prove to have a disproportionately positive effect on building protection capacity at the small unit level in pre-crisis States, and might also prove more affordable for the cash-strapped NATO nations.

PART IV

International courts and tribunals

16

The International Court of Justice

GENTIAN ZYBERI

Introduction

In spite of considerable literature on different aspects of the responsibility to protect and related institutions, little attention has been paid to the important role that a key international judicial institution such as the International Court of Justice (ICJ, or the Court) can play in interpreting and developing the scope of State and non-State actors' obligations under the responsibility to protect (RtoP), as well as enforcing those obligations in cases brought before it. This chapter examines the contribution of the ICJ to interpreting and developing legal obligations incumbent upon States which fall under RtoP. At the same time, an effort is made to expose also the possibilities and limitations of the Court in implementing RtoP. To that aim, the relevance of the ICJ's jurisdiction with regard to ensuring international responsibility for violations of legal obligations arising under the responsibility to protect is dealt with first. In turn, the chapter provides a detailed analysis of relevant findings of the ICJ with regard to the different components of RtoP which interpret and develop their legal basis. Among those notions are the duty to prevent genocide and other serious international crimes, the duty to cooperate with international tribunals established to prosecute the alleged perpetrators and making reparations for gross violations of human rights and serious violations of the law of armed conflict.

The beginning of the third millennium witnessed the emergence, refinement and adoption of the notion of 'responsibility to protect',

This chapter draws heavily and expands on a previous shorter article entitled 'The Responsibility to Protect through the International Court of Justice', in André Nollkaemper and Julia Hoffmann (eds.), *Responsibility to Protect: From Principle to Practice* (Amsterdam University Press, 2012), pp. 305–17. I would like to thank Professors Bruno Simma, André Nollkaemper and Terry Gill for their comments on a previous draft. Any possible mistakes are my own.

originally based on three components, namely the duty to prevent, the duty to react and the duty to rebuild.[1] That initial approach has been replaced by the three pillar strategy adopted in the 2009 report of the Secretary-General on implementing RtoP, where pillar one focuses on the protection responsibilities of the State, pillar two on international assistance and capacity-building and pillar three on timely and decisive response.[2] The responsibility to protect, as a doctrine of collective human security and mass atrocity prevention, is founded on the premise that, at a minimum, every State must protect its population from genocide, war crimes, ethnic cleansing and crimes against humanity. In case a State fails, that responsibility must be borne by the broader organised community of States. Founded on the legal interest of the whole international community in protecting basic human rights and fundamental freedoms, this overarching principle raises a whole range of questions – moral, legal, political and operational on the scope and character of incumbent obligations and the proper means and manner of their implementation.

In addition to framing and endorsing it as a generally agreed concept, the 2005 World Summit Outcome Document (WSOD) entrusted the UN General Assembly with continuing consideration of the responsibility to protect populations from genocide, war crimes, ethnic cleansing and crimes against humanity and its implications, bearing in mind the principles of the Charter and international law.[3] As a result, this important issue, intrinsically related to global human security and protection of basic human rights, was finally placed in the agenda of the most representative international forum, the UN's General Assembly.[4] In 2006, the Security Council reaffirmed the provisions of paragraphs 138 and 139 of the WSOD regarding the responsibility to protect populations from genocide, war crimes, ethnic cleansing and crimes against humanity.[5]

---

[1] International Commission on Intervention and State Sovereignty, *The Responsibility to Protect* (Ottawa: International Research Centre, 2001).

[2] United Nations Secretary-General, 'Implementing the Responsibility to Protect', UN Doc. A/63/677, 12 January 2009.

[3] '2005 World Summit Outcome', UN Doc. A/RES/60/1, 24 October 2005, para. 139.

[4] For a detailed discussion of the General Assembly and RtoP, see Ryngaert and Cuyckens, Chapter 5 in this book.

[5] UNSC Res. 1674, UN Doc. S/RES/1674, 28 April 2006, para. 4. For a detailed discussion of the Security Council and RtoP, see Gill, Chapter 4 in this book.

As an important and binding component of the international legal order, the ICJ can provide necessary guidance in clarifying the legal scope of RtoP and relevant obligations incumbent upon States and other relevant stakeholders. The UN Charter provides that the ICJ is one of the main organs of the organisation and its principal judicial organ. Entrusted with settling inter-State disputes and advising the main UN organs and specialised agencies on legal matters, the ICJ can assist in providing more clarity on RtoP through interpreting and developing the rationale behind, and the incumbent legal duties upon States, while offering the necessary legal venue for enforcing obligations arising under RtoP. Such legal guidance is even more necessary, in view of the fact that the scope and character of this overarching principle remain highly contentious and are vigorously debated in key international political forums as the UN General Assembly.

In emphasising the responsibility of the international community to prevent mass atrocities and in embracing the concept of sovereignty as responsibility, Judge Weeramantry has eloquently stated:

> Human rights violations on this scale are such as to throw upon the world community a grave responsibility to intervene for their prevention and it is well-established legal doctrine that such gross denials of human rights anywhere are everyone's concern everywhere. The concept of sovereignty is no protection against action by the world community to prevent such violations if they be of the scale and nature alleged.[6]

The prohibition and the punishment of the internationally recognised crimes falling under the responsibility to protect represent commonly shared global values, which have become crucial to UN's *raison d'être* and an important part of its core activities. Yet, as the UN Secretary-General has rightly pointed out, operationalising RtoP remains one of the cardinal challenges of our time.[7]

The ICJ's jurisdiction and the law of international responsibility

An important aspect of State obligations arising under RtoP is that of international legal responsibility attached to their breaches through acts or omissions. Both the contentious and the advisory function of the ICJ

---

[6] *Legality of Use of Force (Serbia and Montenegro v. Belgium), Request for the Indication of Provisional Measures, Dissenting Opinion of Vice-President Weeramantry*, ICJ Reports 1999, p. 183.
[7] UNSG, 'Implementing the Responsibility to Protect'.

are relevant in this regard.[8] An advisory opinion by the ICJ could assist the General Assembly in its deliberations regarding the scope and character of RtoP and in clarifying pertinent legal obligations on the part of States and relevant international and regional organisations and security arrangement mechanisms. Also the Security Council could profit from the Court's legal guidance, especially regarding the establishment of certain criteria for the use of its wide powers under Chapter VII of the UN Charter, as well as on the sensitive issue of the use of veto from its permanent members, in RtoP situations.

Inter-State disputes concerning breaches of obligations arising under RtoP could be resolved through the Court's contentious jurisdiction. However, establishing the contentious jurisdiction of the Court is anything but simple. Only six of the major international human rights treaties have a compromissory clause bestowing jurisdiction on the Court.[9] And, a number of States have entered reservations excluding or limiting the jurisdiction of the Court. Regrettably, the compulsory jurisdiction of the Court under Article 36(2) of its Statute is accepted by only 67 States out of the 193 members of the UN.[10] Different jurisdictional barriers have prevented the Court from dealing with the merits of the cases brought before it, which could be considered as RtoP situations.[11]

---

[8] There have been several proposals to widen the jurisdiction of the Court and access to that jurisdiction. Recently, it has been argued that the General Assembly of the UN should give the ICJ 'referral jurisdiction'. This new form of jurisdiction would allow States to secure advisory judgments in their disputes with fellow States, regardless of whether those States had consented to the Court's jurisdiction. For a detailed discussion, see Andrew Strauss, 'Cutting the Gordian Knot: How and Why the United Nations Should Vest the International Court of Justice with Referral Jurisdiction', *Cornell International Law Journal*, 44 (2011), 603–58.

[9] Namely Article IX of the Convention on the Prevention and Punishment of the Crime of Genocide; Article 22 of the International Convention on the Elimination of All Forms of Racial Discrimination; Article 29 of the Convention on the Elimination of All Forms of Discrimination against Women; Article 30 of the Convention against Torture and Other Cruel, Inhuman or Degrading Treatment or Punishment; Article 92 of the International Convention on the Protection of the Rights of All Migrant Workers and Members of Their Families; Article 42 of International Convention for the Protection of All Persons from Enforced Disappearance. The main instruments of international humanitarian law, namely the Geneva Conventions of 1949 and their Additional Protocols do not include compromissory clauses bestowing jurisdiction on the ICJ.

[10] For more details, see www.icj-cij.org/presscom/en/inotice.pdf.

[11] See the *Legality of Use of Force* cases brought by the former Yugoslavia against ten NATO countries in April 1999. Those cases were brought before the Court in response to the military operation Allied Force launched by NATO to stop the campaign of ethnic

Simply put, RtoP situations are those where mass atrocities against a population are either impending or ongoing and the State which holds the duty to protect that endangered population is either unable or unwilling to stop the atrocities, or otherwise complicit in them.

Under Article 93(1) of the UN Charter all UN Member States are *ipso facto* members of the Statute of the ICJ. Thus, in principle any of them can eventually seize the Court of a dispute involving serious violations of international law obligations arising in the context of an RtoP situation. Moreover, under Article 48(1)(b) of the Articles on State Responsibility for Internationally Wrongful Acts adopted by the International Law Commission (ILC) in 2001, any State, other than an injured State, is entitled to invoke the responsibility of another State when the obligation breached is owed to the international community as a whole.[12] Most recently, in the case of *Belgium* v. *Senegal*, the Court found that Belgium as a State party to the 1984 Convention against Torture had standing to invoke the responsibility of Senegal for the alleged breaches of its obligations under Articles 6(2) and 7(1) of the Convention to make an immediate preliminary inquiry into the facts and prosecute or extradite Mr Hissène Habré, former President of Chad, for large-scale violations of human rights.[13] According to the Court, Belgium's standing was based on the entitlement of each State party to the Convention against Torture to make a claim concerning the cessation of an alleged breach by another State party.[14] Making use of the legal procedures available before the ICJ, nevertheless, remains at the discretion of the States concerned. Arguably, invoking that responsibility could involve bringing a case before the ICJ

cleansing carried out by Serb forces against Kosovar Albanians in Kosovo. In June 1999, the Court dismissed the cases brought by the former Yugoslavia (Serbia and Montenegro) against the United States and Spain. On 15 December 2004, the Court found it did not have jurisdiction in the cases brought against Belgium, Canada, France, Germany, Italy, the Netherlands, Portugal and the United Kingdom. See also *Case Concerning Armed Activities on the Territory of the Congo (New Application: 2002) (Democratic Republic of the Congo* v. *Rwanda), Jurisdiction of the Court and Admissibility of the Application*, ICJ Report 2006; *Case Concerning Application of the International Convention on the Elimination of All Forms of Racial Discrimination (Georgia* v. *Russian Federation), Preliminary Objections, Judgment*, ICJ Report 2011.

[12] International Law Commission, 'Draft Articles on Responsibility of States for Internationally Wrongful Acts', in 'Report of the International Law Commission on the Work of Its Fifty-Third Session (23 April–1 June and 2 July–10 August 2001)', UN Doc. A/56/10, art. 48(1)(b).

[13] For a summary of the facts of the case, see *Questions Relating to the Obligation to Prosecute or Extradite (Belgium* v. *Senegal), Judgment*, 20 July 2012, paras. 15–41, at www.icj-cij.org/docket/files/144/17064.pdf.

[14] *Ibid.*, paras. 67–70.

when the obligation breached concerns the prohibition of genocide. Besides the crime of genocide, a potential case could also be based on widespread and systematic violations of basic human rights. Indeed, the subject-matter jurisdiction of the Court is quite broad and covers also the other categories of crimes falling under RtoP, namely war crimes and crimes against humanity. Ethnic cleansing is not a stand-alone category of crimes under international law, but can be easily subsumed under war crimes and crimes against humanity.

It has been noted elsewhere that the notion of responsibility has been drastically modified as a result of a tripartite evolution, which reflects that of international law itself, to the extent that it is no longer reserved only to States and has become an attribution of the international legal personality of other subjects of international law; it has lost its conceptual unity as a result of the elimination of damage as a condition for the engagement of responsibility for breach; and the common point of departure which it shared with liability for acts not involving a breach of international law has disappeared.[15] There is also a diversification of actors that might be held responsible, since failure to comply with obligations arising under RtoP can give rise to State responsibility, responsibility of international organisations and individual criminal responsibility. Several international criminal courts and tribunals have been established in the last two decades to prosecute individuals responsible for certain internationally recognised crimes falling under RtoP.[16] Taken together, these judicial bodies provide the enforcement arm of international law obligations concerned with the protection of populations from genocide, war crimes, ethnic cleansing and crimes against humanity. Because of statutory limitations based on Article 34 of its Statute which allows standing only to States, the function of the ICJ is primarily central to issues of State responsibility.

---

[15] Allain Pellet, 'The Definition of Responsibility in International Law', in James Crawford, Allain Pellet and Simon Olleson (eds.), *The Law of International Responsibility* (Oxford University Press, 2010), pp. 3–16, at p. 6.

[16] See Frencken and Sluiter, Chapter 17 and Contarino and Negrón-Gonzales, Chapter 18 in this book, respectively on the two ad hoc UN tribunals for Yugoslavia and Rwanda and the International Criminal Court. See also Michael Contarino and Selena Lucent, 'Stopping the Killing: The International Criminal Court and Juridical Determination of the Responsibility to Protect', *Global Responsibility to Protect*, 1 (2009), 560–83; Héctor Olásolo, *Essays on International Criminal Justice* (Oxford: Hart Publishing, 2012), pp. 1–19.

The ICJ and the responsibility to protect

As already stated above, the role of the ICJ in ensuring State compliance with RtoP obligations is potentially quite significant. Two interrelated, though still separate, aspects of that role can be easily discerned, namely the preventive aspect and that of adjudication of inter-State disputes, which includes also awarding reparations to the injured party. The Court's preventive function is mainly discharged through the indication of provisional measures to one or both parties to a dispute, which are aimed at stopping or averting harm to populations at risk of mass atrocities. Besides this procedural mechanism, the very existence of the Court as a forum for the settlement of international disputes can potentially dissuade a State from engaging in wrongful conduct prohibited under international law. Having been seized on several occasions with requests for provisional measures in a situation of armed conflict, the ICJ has indicated such measures in a number of cases.[17] That said, the record of compliance with the Court's provisional measures in these cases is far from acceptable.

The ICJ could also guard against cases of potential abuse of RtoP. Thus, even before RtoP was adopted the Court rejected the unilateral use of force as an appropriate method to ensure respect for human rights in the *Nicaragua* case.[18] The Court clarified that while a State can form its own view with respect to the situation of human rights in a country, the use of force could not be the appropriate method to monitor or ensure such respect. This finding fits well with paragraph 139 of the WSOD, which notes the responsibility of the international community, through the United Nations, to use appropriate diplomatic, humanitarian and other peaceful means, in accordance with Chapters VI and VIII of the Charter, to help to protect populations from genocide, war crimes, ethnic cleansing and crimes against humanity. Only when peaceful measures prove inadequate, the international community needs to take collective action, in a timely and decisive manner, through the Security Council, in accordance with the Charter, including Chapter VII.

---

[17] See, among others Gentian Zyberi, 'Provisional Measures of the International Court of Justice in Armed Conflict Situations', *Leiden Journal of International Law*, 23 (2010), 571–84, at 584; Eva Rieter, *Preventing Irreparable Harm: Provisional Measures in International Human Rights Adjudication* (Cambridge, UK: Intersentia, 2010), pp. 67–71.

[18] *Military and Paramilitary Activities in and against Nicaragua (Nicaragua v. United States of America)*, Merits, Judgment, ICJ Reports 1986, pp. 134–5, para. 268.

In its case law the Court has dealt with several legal issues which are relevant to different aspects of international legal responsibility for the violation of obligations arising under RtoP. The Court's findings relevant to the doctrinal legal foundations of RtoP are dealt with first. Subsequently, the focus shifts to important components of RtoP, namely the duty of States to prevent genocide and their duty to punish perpetrators and to cooperate with international tribunals established to prosecute persons for having committed the crime of genocide. This section ends with a discussion of issues concerning reparations that the Court can indicate for violations of RtoP obligations.

The legal foundations of the responsibility to protect

From its launch as a concept in the 2001 ICISS report, it has been pointed out that RtoP has a strong foundation on specific legal obligations under human rights and human protection declarations, covenants and treaties, international humanitarian law and national law.[19] Indeed, there are a considerable number of international human rights and humanitarian law treaties which impose upon States' legal obligations concerning the protection of populations from genocide, war crimes, crimes against humanity and ethnic cleansing. The ICJ has developed two basic legal principles, namely that of *elementary considerations of humanity* and *erga omnes* obligations, which do highlight respectively the humanitarian value and the nature of obligations arising under RtoP.

The principle of 'elementary considerations of humanity' encapsulates such common global values as respect for human dignity, the prohibition of arbitrary deprivation of life and liberty, and basic principles of justice and due process. Initially, this principle was used to underline the obligation of States not to knowingly allow their territory to be used for causing harm to others, a prerequisite for ensuring friendly relations among States.[20] In practical terms, the principle required States to behave responsibly in the international arena so as not to intentionally endanger human lives and through that international peace and security. The Court gave more substance to the principle of elementary

---

[19] ICISS, *Responsibility to Protect*, p. xi.

[20] See *Corfu Channel Case, Merits, Judgment*, ICJ Reports 1949, p. 22. For a more detailed discussion, see, among others, Zyberi, *The Humanitarian Face of the International Court of Justice: Its Contribution to Interpreting and Developing International Human Rights and Humanitarian Law Rules and Principles* (Cambridge, UK: Intersentia, 2008), pp. 94–5 and 282–3.

considerations of humanity by linking it to fundamental rules and principles of international humanitarian law. Thus, in the *Legality of the Threat or Use of Nuclear Weapons* case the Court stated that 'a great many rules of humanitarian law applicable in armed conflict are so fundamental to the respect of the human person and 'elementary considerations of humanity', and that they are 'to be observed by all States whether or not they have ratified the conventions that contain them, because they constitute intransgressible principles of customary international law'.[21] The purpose of many of these rules is to establish a minimum level of protection for certain categories of persons during an armed conflict, including civilians, and to provide for the investigation and prosecution of persons suspected of having committed serious war crimes.

The Court has considered that 'fundamental general principles of humanitarian law' are an expression of elementary considerations of humanity.[22] Notably, the rules which are part of Common Article 3 to the 1949 Geneva Conventions have been considered by the Court as a minimum yardstick to be applied in both international and non-international armed conflicts, since they reflect elementary considerations of humanity.[23] By affirming that the rules enshrined in Common Article 3 constitute 'a minimum yardstick' to be respected in both non-international and international armed conflict, the Court implicitly accentuates the individual rights of protected persons against extreme acts of violence such as wilful killing, torture or inhuman treatment, or serious injury to body and to health.[24] These findings of the Court serve to emphasise the obligation incumbent upon States to protect their population from war crimes.

The concept of obligations *erga omnes*, introduced by the Court in the famous dictum in the *Barcelona Traction* case, is also quite relevant to RtoP.[25] It can be said that the obligation of a State to protect its

---

[21] *Legality of the Threat or Use of Nuclear Weapons, Advisory Opinion*, ICJ Reports 1996, p. 257, para. 79.

[22] *Nicaragua v. United States of America*, p. 113, para. 218.   [23] *Ibid.*, p. 114, para. 218.

[24] Zyberi, *Humanitarian Face*, p. 287.

[25] *Barcelona Traction, Light and Power Company, Limited (Belgium v. Spain), Second Phase, Judgment*, ICJ Reports 1970, p. 32, para. 34. For a detailed discussion of the concept and the application of *erga omnes* obligations, see, among others, Andre de Hoogh, *Obligations Erga Omnes and International Crimes: A Theoretical Inquiry into the Implementation and Enforcement of the International Responsibility of States* (The Hague; London; Boston: Kluwer Law International, 1996); Christian Tams, *Enforcing Obligations Erga Omnes in International Law* (Cambridge University Press, 2005);

population from the crimes of genocide, war crimes, crimes against humanity and ethnic cleansing is owed to the international community as a whole. Consequently, the compliance of individual States with such obligations is the concern of all States. The relevant international legal obligations include the prohibition of genocide, and a number of principles and rules concerning the protection of basic rights of the human person, as the right to life and bodily integrity. As the Court has clarified, some of the corresponding rights of protection have entered into the body of general international law; others are conferred by international instruments of a universal or quasi-universal character.[26] Taking into account also their humanitarian and civilising purpose vis-à-vis general public international law,[27] the international human rights treaties adopted over the years, can be seen as instruments having a universal or quasi-universal character imposing upon States certain legal obligations relevant to RtoP.

Referring to the principle of elementary considerations of humanity in its Advisory Opinion on the *Wall in the Occupied Palestinian Territory*, the Court declared that, in its view, the rules included in Common Article 3 to the 1949 Geneva Conventions incorporate obligations which are essentially of an *erga omnes* character.[28] Apparently, for the Court not only customary rules of humanitarian law, but also those rules stemming from elementary considerations of humanity impose upon States certain obligations of an *erga omnes* character. The concept of 'obligations *erga omnes*' provides a valid justification for the international monitoring of the situation and the human rights practices of States.

Two notable characteristic features embraced by RtoP are those of *universality* and *solidarity*. Universality consists in that protection of basic human rights for persons under their jurisdiction is an obligation binding on all States without exception. Solidarity, on the other hand, is expressed in that every State is deemed to have a legal interest in ensuring the protection of populations from genocide, war crimes, crimes against

---

Christian Tomuschat and Jean-Marc Thouvenin (eds.), *The Fundamental Rules of the International Legal Order: Jus Cogens and Obligations Erga Omnes* (Leiden: Martinus Nijhoff, 2006); Maurizio Ragazzi, *The Concept of International Obligations Erga Omnes* (Oxford University Press, 2010).

[26] *Barcelona Traction*, p. 32, para. 33.

[27] *Reservations to the Convention on the Prevention and Punishment of the Crime of Genocide, Advisory Opinion*, ICJ Reports 1951, p. 23.

[28] *Legal Consequences of the Construction of a Wall in the Occupied Palestinian Territory, Advisory Opinion*, ICJ Reports 2004, p. 199, para. 157.

humanity and ethnic cleansing and that it employs the means reasonably available to it to assist in preventing or stopping RtoP situations.

Obligations *erga omnes* in the field of human rights reflect common basic legal and moral values in the form of elementary considerations of humanity and elementary considerations of morality which have become an intrinsic part of international law through the necessary political processes. Obligations arising under RtoP impose upon States the duty to cooperate to bring an end to, not to recognise and not to render assistance in the maintenance of a situation involving the commitment of large-scale and systematic violations of human rights by a State against its population. The purpose of the above-mentioned obligations on the part of the international community of States as a whole is to prevent, or otherwise to stop the commitment of genocide, war crimes, crimes against humanity and ethnic cleansing by a State against its own population.

The duties of the State under the 1948 Genocide Convention

A number of salient legal issues related directly to the duty to prevent, often hailed as the most important component of RtoP, have been dealt with by the ICJ. The duty to prevent mass atrocities is part of both the first pillar of RtoP on the protection responsibilities of the State, as well as of pillar three on a timely and decisive response by the international community. Also international assistance and capacity-building offered by individual States or international or regional organisations, which falls under pillar two of RtoP, has a preventive function. Several cases brought before the Court have involved armed conflict situations where populations were either suffering from the negative effects of such a conflict or were exposed to serious risk. In these cases the applicant States requested the Court to indicate provisional measures, that is, to order measures aimed at putting an end to the hostilities or preventing their destructive effects on the civilian population. Rosenne has rightly noted that, as a time-honoured attribute of the judicial mission courts should, within the limits of the judicial function, do what they can to prevent the escalation of the conflict between the litigating parties.[29]

---

[29] Shabtai Rosenne, 'A Role for the International Court of Justice in Crisis Management', in Gerard Kreijen, Marcel Brus, Jorris Duursma, Elizabeth De Vos and John Dugard (eds.), *State, Sovereignty, and International Governance* (Oxford University Press, 2002), pp. 195–214, at p. 181.

While the Court did order provisional measures in four cases involving armed conflict situations,[30] compliance with these orders was problematic, notwithstanding the fact that such orders are considered legally binding. In two of these cases the Court found the States concerned in violation of its provisional measures order.[31] Notwithstanding the present unsatisfactory record of State compliance, in the long term provisional measures indicated by the Court can serve a useful preventive role and potentially strengthen the protection of populations from mass atrocities.

According to the Court, the prohibition of genocide under the 1948 Genocide Convention includes the following legal obligations: the duty to prevent as an obligation of conduct; the duty to prosecute or extradite, also known as the principle of *aut dedere aut judicare* – under Articles IV, V and VI of the Genocide Convention; and, the duty to cooperate with international courts and tribunals under Article VI in so far as it obliges States to cooperate with the 'international penal tribunal'. Findings relating to the duty to prevent genocide and that of States to prosecute and cooperate with international courts and tribunals established to prosecute persons for having committed genocide are separately dealt with below.

The duty to prevent genocide

Reference to RtoP proper before the Court was made for the first time on 7 March 2006 by Counsel for Bosnia-Herzegovina in the course of oral proceedings in the *Application of the Genocide Convention* case.[32] According to Counsel for Bosnia-Herzegovina:

---

[30] Provisional measures were granted in four cases, namely in the *Nicaragua v. United States of America*; *Case Concerning the Application of the Convention on the Prevention and Punishment of the Crime of Genocide (Bosnia and Herzegovina v. Serbia and Montenegro)*; *Case Concerning Armed Activities on the Territory of the Congo (Democratic Republic of the Congo v. Uganda)*; and most recently in *Case Concerning Application of the International Convention on the Elimination of All Forms of Racial Discrimination (Georgia v. Russian Federation)*. For more details, see Zyberi, 'Provisional Measures', 572.

[31] *Case Concerning Armed Activities on the Territory of the Congo (Democratic Republic of the Congo v. Uganda), Judgment*, ICJ Reports 2005, p. 168, paras. 262–5; *Case Concerning the Application of the Convention on the Prevention and Punishment of the Crime of Genocide (Bosnia and Herzegovina v. Serbia and Montenegro), Judgment*, ICJ Reports 2007, pp. 230–1 and 235, paras. 451–8 and 467–9.

[32] A somewhat cursory reference to the responsibility to protect had been made earlier by Portugal in *Legality of Use of Force (Serbia and Montenegro v. Portugal), Preliminary*

[P]revention means that every State must adopt 'appropriate and necessary means' (I would prefer to say: all appropriate and necessary means) to 'protect populations from genocide, war crimes, ethnic cleansing and crimes against humanity': I am using the language in which the World Summit of last September couched what it proclaimed as the 'responsibility to protect'. A responsibility which – as the document I am citing indicates – is borne by each State but also by the 'international community, through the United Nations'. I would point out that, by proclaiming the responsibility to protect, it was intended to provide a solemn response – albeit one which quite clearly was inherently inadequate, though nonetheless significant – to the concerns forcefully expressed by the Secretary-General in his millennium report, regarding the international community's capacity to prevent future grave and massive violations of human rights of the kind committed in Rwanda and Srebrenica.[33]

In the *Application of the Genocide Convention* case the Court dealt extensively with the specific scope of the duty to prevent genocide, albeit it did not address the relevant State obligations under the Genocide Convention as part of RtoP. With regard to the obligations incumbent upon States party to the 1948 Genocide Convention in preventing genocide, the ICJ held that:

> The obligation on each contracting State to prevent genocide is both normative and compelling. It is not merged in the duty to punish, nor can it be regarded as simply a component of that duty. It has its own scope, which extends beyond the particular case envisaged in Article VIII, namely reference to the competent organs of the United Nations, for them to take such action as they deem appropriate.[34]

According to the Court, the obligation on the part of States to prevent genocide has a continuous and distinct character, extending alongside that of the competent organs of the UN:

Objections, Verbatim Record, ICJ Doc. CR 2004/18, 22 April 2004, para. 8. Other references to RtoP key documents to date are included respectively in *Accordance with International Law of the Unilateral Declaration of Independence in Respect of Kosovo (Request for an Advisory Opinion)*, Written Statement of the Czech Republic, April 2009, p. 7, fn. 24, making reference to the 2005 WSOD and the 2009 UN Secretary-General Report on RtoP; and *Case Concerning Jurisdictional Immunities of the State (Germany v. Italy: Greece Intervening)*, Written Statement of the Hellenic Republic, August 2011, para. 32 and fn. 14, making reference to the 2005 WSOD.

[33] *Bosnia and Herzegovina v. Serbia and Montenegro, Merits*, Verbatim Record, ICJ Doc. CR 2006/11, 7 March 2006, para. 3.

[34] *Bosnia and Herzegovina v. Serbia and Montenegro, Judgment*, para. 427.

> Even if and when these organs have been called upon, this does not mean
> that the States parties to the Convention are relieved of the obligation to
> take such action as they can to prevent genocide from occurring, while
> respecting the United Nations Charter and any decisions that may have
> been taken by its competent organs.[35]

From a general perspective, these findings of the Court clarify the separate existence of obligations arising under the first pillar of RtoP on the protection responsibilities of the State and pillar three providing for a timely and decisive response on the part of the international community. Notably, that separate existence of legal obligations incumbent upon both States and international organisations guards against a potential dilution of international responsibility. As expected, the Court adopts a cautious approach in viewing the nature and scale of what States should do as depending on their overall capabilities and being subject to the existing limitations under the UN Charter and relevant international law.

In clarifying the nature of the duty to prevent genocide, the Court stated that the obligation in question is *one of conduct and not one of result*; so, a State cannot be under an obligation to succeed, whatever the circumstances, in preventing the commission of genocide. Consequently, the obligation of States Parties to the Genocide Convention is rather to employ all means reasonably available to them, so as to prevent genocide so far as possible.[36] According to the Court, a State does not incur responsibility simply because the desired result is not achieved; responsibility is however incurred if the State *manifestly* failed to take all measures to prevent genocide which were within its power, and which might have contributed to preventing the acts of genocide.[37] Most probably, the Court's use of the word '*manifestly*' to denote the applicable threshold for incurring responsibility was deliberately intended to reflect the language of the 2005 WSOD which declares a preparedness of the international community to react when national authorities are *manifestly* failing to protect their populations from genocide, war crimes, ethnic cleansing and crimes against humanity.[38] Although the term 'manifestly' seems like a self-explanatory threshold for incurring State responsibility, ascertaining what 'manifestly' means in practice might prove to be a rather elusive task. Moreover, assessing State responsibility on the basis of that threshold is complicated by the

---

[35] *Ibid.*   [36] *Ibid.*, para. 430 (emphasis added).   [37] *Ibid.* (emphasis added).
[38] '2005 World Summit Outcome', para. 139 (emphasis added).

composite nature of State actions and their extension in time. In view of the *jus cogens* character of the prohibition of genocide and the *erga omnes* obligations attached to it, a threshold of 'manifest failure' to take preventive action seems to limit the scope of obligations upon third States to prevent the serious crimes falling under RtoP.

The Court linked the evaluation of measures taken by a State with the notion of *'due diligence'*, which in its view called for an assessment *in concreto*, and was of critical importance.[39] In laying out the 'due diligence' test for assessing a State's measures to comply with the duty to prevent genocide the Court noted that the first aspect, varying greatly from one State to another is, the capacity to influence effectively the action of persons likely to commit, or already committing, genocide. According to the Court, that capacity depends among others on the geographical distance of the State concerned from the scene of the events, and on the strength of the political links, as well as links of all other kinds, between the authorities of that State and the main actors in the events. Additionally to these largely fact-based considerations, the Court stated that a State's efforts had to be assessed also on the basis of legal criteria. Thus, in the Court's view, a State's capacity to influence may vary depending on its particular legal position *vis-à-vis* the situations and persons facing the danger, or the reality, of genocide and the limits permitted by international law.[40] The Court concluded that a State can be held responsible for breaching the obligation to prevent genocide only if genocide was actually committed. That finding establishes damage as a necessary precondition for the existence of State responsibility for failure to prevent genocide.

The duty to ensure accountability for mass atrocity crimes

The Court also addressed in considerable detail the *duty to punish* or *aut dedere aut judicare* – under Articles IV, V and VI and the *duty to cooperate with international courts and tribunals* under Article VI of the Genocide Convention.[41] Since the genocide was not carried out in its territory, the Court concluded that Serbia could not be charged with not having tried before its own courts those accused of having participated in the Srebrenica genocide, either as principal perpetrators or as accomplices, or of having committed one of the other acts mentioned in Article III of the Convention in connection with the Srebrenica genocide.[42]

---

[39] *Bosnia and Herzegovina* v. *Serbia and Montenegro, Judgment*, para. 430.   [40] *Ibid.*
[41] *Ibid.*, paras. 439–50.   [42] *Ibid.*, para. 442.

According to the Court, Article VI of the Genocide Convention only obliges the Contracting Parties to institute and exercise territorial criminal jurisdiction; and, while it certainly does not prohibit States, with respect to genocide, from conferring jurisdiction on their criminal courts based on criteria other than where the crime was committed which are compatible with international law, in particular the nationality of the accused, it does not oblige them to do so.[43] Through this finding the Court emphasised territorial jurisdiction over other forms of jurisdiction, while acknowledging other possible grounds to establish and exercise jurisdiction over the crime of genocide, as chosen by different States.

Turning to the issue of cooperation with international criminal tribunals, the Court held that Article VI obliges the Contracting Parties 'which shall have accepted its jurisdiction' to cooperate with it, which implies that they will arrest persons accused of genocide who are in their territory – even if the crime of which they are accused was committed outside it – and, failing prosecution of them in the parties' own courts, that they will hand them over for trial by the competent international tribunal.[44] The determination of whether a State has fulfilled its obligations in this respect, would then hinge on a two-pronged test, namely whether the court in question constituted an 'international penal tribunal' within the meaning of Article VI and whether the State could be regarded as having 'accepted the jurisdiction' of the tribunal within the meaning of that provision.[45]

The Court found that the notion of an 'international penal tribunal' within the meaning of Article VI must at least cover all international criminal courts created after the adoption of the Genocide Convention of potentially universal scope, and competent to try the perpetrators of genocide or any of the other acts enumerated in Article III.[46] In the Court's view, the nature of the legal instrument by which such a court is established is without importance in this respect. In this case, cooperation with the International Criminal Tribunal for the former Yugoslavia (ICTY) constituted both an obligation stemming from the resolution concerned and from the United Nations Charter, or from another norm of international law obliging Serbia to cooperate, and an obligation arising from its status as a party to the Genocide Convention, this last clearly being the only one of direct relevance in the present case. The way the Court construed the term 'international penal tribunal' within the

---

[43] *Ibid.*, paras. 439–45.   [44] *Ibid.*, para. 443.   [45] *Ibid.*, para. 444.   [46] *Ibid.*, para. 445.

meaning of Article VI of the Genocide Convention would include, among other international courts and tribunals, also the permanent International Criminal Court (ICC).

Reparations for the violation of responsibility to protect obligations

Another important aspect of the activity and competences of the Court is its power to order reparations for violations of international law obliga-tions.[47] Besides the general principle of States being obligated to make reparations for injuries caused by an internationally wrongful act on their part,[48] there is a broad legal basis for reparations for violations of international humanitarian law and human rights laid down in a number of international instruments pertaining to these fields of international law.[49] The issue of providing reparations to individuals for violations of

[47] See, among others, Conor McCarthy, 'Reparation for Gross Violations of Human Rights Law and International Humanitarian Law at the International Court of Justice', in Carla Ferstman, Mariana Goetz and Alan Stephens (eds.), *Reparations for Victims of Genocide, Crimes against Humanity and War Crimes: Systems in Place and Systems in the Making* (Leiden: Martinus Nijhoff, 2009), pp. 283–311; Zyberi, 'The International Court of Justice and Applied Forms of Reparation for International Human Rights and Humanitarian Law Violations', *Utrecht Law Review*, 7 (2011), 204–15.

[48] This principle has been codified in Article 31 of the International Law Commission's Articles on State Responsibility for Internationally Wrongful Acts adopted in 2001. This article reads: '(1) The responsible State is under an obligation to make full reparation for the injury caused by the internationally wrongful act. (2) Injury includes any damage, whether material or moral, caused by the internationally wrongful act of a State.'

[49] Human rights provisions which provide a legal basis for reparations are Article 8 of the 1948 Universal Declaration of Human Rights; Articles 2(3), 9(5) and 14(6) of the 1966 International Covenant on Civil and Political Rights; Article 6 of the International Convention on the Elimination of All Forms of Racial Discrimination; Article 39 of the Convention of the Rights of the Child; and Article 14 of the Convention against Torture and other forms of Cruel, Inhuman and Degrading Treatment. The right to reparations is also found in several regional instruments, such as Articles 5(5), 13 and 41 of the European Convention on Human Rights and Fundamental Freedoms; Articles 25, 68 and 63(1) of the Inter-American Convention on Human Rights; Article 21(2) of the African Charter of Human and Peoples' Rights. Provisions contained in international humanitarian law instruments which provide a legal basis for reparations are Article 3 of the Hague Convention regarding the Laws and Customs of Land Warfare, 1907 Hague Convention IV; Article 51 of Geneva Convention I; Article 52 of Geneva Convention II; Article 131 of Geneva Convention III; Article 148 of Geneva Convention IV; and Article 91 of the 1977 Additional Protocol I. For a detailed discussion, see, among others, Emanuela-Chiara Gillard, 'Reparations for Violations of International Humanitarian Law', *International Review of the Red Cross*, 85 (2003), 529–53; Dinah Shelton, *Remedies in International Human Rights Law* (Oxford University Press, 2001).

their rights has attracted a lot of attention, especially after the adoption of the Statute of the International Criminal Court in 1998.[50] While individuals themselves cannot bring a case before the ICJ, States have brought a number of cases involving RtoP issues.[51] Most of these cases relate to violations of international law during armed conflict situations, whereas others relate to jurisdictional immunities of States or senior State officials accused of crimes falling under RtoP.

In the context of enforcing RtoP obligations, the Court could eventually order reparations when a State is involved in committing genocide, war crimes, ethnic cleansing or crimes against humanity against the population of another State, or even when it fails to take possible steps to prevent or put a stop to ongoing violations in another State. In order to award reparations the Court needs to find a causal link between the wrongful conduct and the harm caused. In the words of the Court, awarding reparations depends on 'whether there is a sufficiently direct and certain causal nexus between the wrongful act, the Respondent's breach of the obligation to prevent genocide, and the injury suffered by the Applicant, consisting of all damage of any type, material or moral, caused by the acts of genocide.'[52] It seems that the Court requires a high

---

[50] Article 75 of this Statute entitled 'Reparations to victims' authorises the International Criminal Court to establish principles relating to reparations to, or in respect of, victims, including restitution, compensation and rehabilitation. On the basis of the Statute the Court may, either upon request or on its own motion in exceptional circumstances, determine the scope and extent of any damage, loss and injury to, or in respect of, victims. Article 79 of the ICC Statute established a Trust Fund for the victims, whose function is twofold: giving reparations in the course of implementing Court-ordered awards against a convicted person and, second, giving general assistance to victims, that is, providing victims and their families in situations where the Court is active with physical rehabilitation, material support, or psychological rehabilitation. For a detailed discussion of the ICC and the responsibility to protect, see Contarino and Negrón-Gonzales, Chapter 18 in this book.

[51] See *Application of the Convention on the Prevention and Punishment of the Crime of Genocide (Bosnia and Herzegovina v. Serbia and Montenegro); Application of the Convention on the Prevention and Punishment of the Crime of Genocide (Croatia v. Serbia); Legality of Use of Force cases (Yugoslavia v. 10 NATO countries); Armed Activities in the Territory of the Congo cases (Democratic Republic of Congo v. Uganda; Democratic Republic of Congo v. Rwanda; and Democratic Republic of Congo v. Burundi); Arrest Warrant of 11 April 2000 (Democratic Republic of the Congo v. Belgium); Certain Criminal Proceedings in France (Republic of the Congo v. France); Application of the International Convention on the Elimination of All Forms of Racial Discrimination (Georgia v. Russian Federation); Jurisdictional Immunities of the State (Germany v. Italy); and Questions relating to the Obligation to Prosecute or Extradite (Belgium v. Senegal).*

[52] *Bosnia and Herzegovina v. Serbia and Montenegro, Judgment*, para. 462.

level of certainty that the wrongful act would not have occurred, if the third State had complied with its duty to prevent.

While the Court requires a direct causal link between the violation and the injury before awarding financial compensation for material and moral damages, the question is whether the threshold set is higher than that necessary or desirable? Indeed, in the case of harm resulting from composite acts carried out through the concurrent, combined or concerted action of two or more States or of a State and non-State actors, it might be extremely difficult, if at all possible, to predict how events would have unfolded had one of the entities involved withdrawn its support.[53] Such cases present a formidable challenge for the Court. The question which arises in such situations is whether a State should be liable to provide compensation when its wrongful conduct amounts to a significant contributing factor to the injuries suffered?[54] While not necessarily to the same degree, the due diligence requirement to prevent genocide, war crimes, ethnic cleansing and crimes against humanity applies not only to the State concerned, but also to third States. Moreover, the elusive threshold of 'sufficient degree of certainty' for crimes of utmost gravity seems to create little incentives for States to engage in preventive action, while at the same time depriving the victims of potential compensation by the wrongdoer. An approach that accommodates the division of reparation between the responsible entities based on their contribution towards the wrongful act seems better suited to further the upholding by States of obligations owed to the international community as a whole, both in terms of preventing serious international crimes and in inducing responsible behaviour on the part of the States concerned.

---

[53] Article 15 of the International Law Commission's Articles on State Responsibility for Internationally Wrongful Acts entitled 'Breach consisting of a composite act' reads: '(1) The breach of an international obligation by a State through a series of actions or omissions defined in aggregate as wrongful occurs when the action or omission occurs which, taken with the other actions or omissions, is sufficient to constitute the wrongful act. (2) In such a case, the breach extends over the entire period starting with the first of the actions or omissions of the series and lasts for as long as these actions or omissions are repeated and remain not in conformity with the international obligation.'

[54] See, among others, Alexander Orakhelashvili, 'Division of Reparation between Responsible Entities', in Crawford et al. (eds.), Law of International Responsibility, pp. 647–65.

Concluding remarks

Millions of civilians around the world have either perished or their lives are under daily threat due to violent conflicts. Thus far, the collective response of the international community of States to crises unfolding in different areas of the world has been far from adequate. Clearly, as Rosenne has noted, the judicial treatment of appropriate elements of the crisis can, although not necessarily will, perform a significant, albeit not exclusive, role in the management of that crisis.[55] International legal procedures can be resorted to in pre-conflict, during the conflict, or in a post-conflict situation to hold accountable those States responsible for violating international law. Evidently, proper use of existing international judicial procedures and relevant institutional mechanisms which are entrusted with upholding commonly agreed global values is necessary to implement RtoP.

Both the advisory function and the dispute settlement function of the ICJ are relevant to interpreting, developing, and enforcing obligations arising under RtoP for States and international organisations, including the UN. As mentioned above, provisional measures indicated by the ICJ could be a useful tool in protecting populations from the risks posed by armed conflict situations. A number of cases decided by the ICJ have helped provide a better understanding of international legal obligations arising under the responsibility to protect.

Despite the progress made, the ongoing situations in Darfur (Sudan), the Democratic Republic of the Congo, Syria and other places around the world illustrate the fact that the level of accountability remains less than adequate, even when States and individuals are responsible for large-scale and systematic violations of human rights. Obviously, the enforcement of obligations arising under RtoP depends upon access to international political and judicial mechanisms, legal and judicial activism, action by the relevant political organs, and civil society awareness and participation. The current debate surrounding the enforcement of RtoP obligations takes place in a legal framework of recently adopted norms of conduct for States, international organisations and individuals, embodied in international and regional treaties, customary international law, and domestic law. Despite the establishment over the last decades of

---

[55] Rosenne, 'ICJ in Crisis Management', in Kreijen *et al.* (eds.), *International Governance*, p. 212.

other adjudication mechanisms, such debate cannot lose sight of more traditional mechanisms of dispute settlement as the ICJ.

Notwithstanding jurisdictional and other obstacles, the important role for the ICJ in developing, interpreting and enforcing human rights standards relevant to RtoP and its contribution in that regard is fairly obvious. A permanent international court as the ICJ, being one of the main organs of the UN and its principal judicial organ, can be instrumental in interpreting and developing further the legal components of RtoP expressed in the obligations of States and other relevant actors. The Court has shed light on relevant legal components of the responsibility to protect populations from genocide, namely on the duty to prevent and the duty of States to punish perpetrators and to cooperate with international courts and tribunals. As Judge Simma has put it, that contribution of the Court can be seen as providing some important stones in the bigger 'responsibility to protect' mosaic.[56]

Ensuring State and non-State actors' compliance with the relevant and legally binding international legal standards remains problematic. Notably, the lack of sufficient clarity regarding specific duties incumbent upon the different international and domestic entities involved in carrying out obligations arising under RtoP raises a number of complex issues. That notwithstanding, the cases already decided and those in the docket of the Court demonstrate its involvement and major importance for societies heavily affected by protracted armed conflicts. Occasionally, the ICJ has provided a last resort forum for populations threatened by genocide, war crimes, ethnic cleansing and crimes against humanity. Working alongside other important international and regional political and judicial organs, the ICJ can provide necessary legal guidance and oversight in the process of clarifying and enforcing international legal obligations arising under the RtoP framework.

---

[56] Bruno Simma, 'Human rights before the International Court of Justice: community interest coming to life?', lecture delivered at Supranational Criminal Law Lecture Series, The Hague, 31 March 2011.

17

The United Nations Criminal Tribunals
for Yugoslavia and Rwanda

NIKI FRENCKEN AND GÖRAN SLUITER

Introduction

Over the last two decades the international community has pledged in various ways to protect the world population against mass atrocities. That promise, encapsulated in the 'responsibility to protect' (R2P) principle has come to occupy a central place in international law and politics. The core element of R2P is the protection of individuals from international crimes such as war crimes, crimes against humanity, ethnic cleansing and genocide.[1] Such protection was also pursued through the establishment of international criminal tribunals having, among others, the objective to put an end to impunity. It is often argued that by ending impunity tribunals contribute to the prevention of international crimes through the assumed deterrent effect of prosecution both in individual cases and more generally. Whether and how international criminal tribunals contribute to the prevention of crimes and thereby R2P remains an under-researched issue, which tends to be approached on the basis of largely unproven assumptions.

As tribunals at the forefront of contemporary international criminal justice, the International Criminal Tribunal for the former Yugoslavia (ICTY) and the International Criminal Tribunal for Rwanda (ICTR) (or Tribunals) provide us with the best experience and results to explore the question of whether and how modern-day international criminal tribunals contribute to R2P. For the purposes of this chapter this question is dealt with from two correlated dimensions. First, we shall examine the contribution of the ICTY and ICTR to R2P in terms of their deterrent

---

[1] 'Each individual State has the responsibility to protect its populations from genocide, war crimes, ethnic cleansing and crimes against humanity' ('2005 World Summit Outcome', UN Doc. A/RES/60/1, 24 October 2005, para. 138).

effect. In other words, whether it is possible to claim that the Tribunals have in fact deterred individuals from committing crimes falling under the R2P. The second dimension of the contribution of the Tribunals to R2P relates to their legal suitability to prevent crimes from being committed. This issue is related to the scope and content of both substantive and procedural law of the Tribunals and the legal tools at their disposal to intervene prior to the execution of mass atrocities and what lessons can be drawn from the (provisional) answer to that question for the functioning of the International Criminal Court (ICC).

Deterrence and the Tribunals

The Tribunals' approach to deterrence is set in a larger paradigm that is framed by the international criminal justice discourse. This discourse envisages international criminal law as having a global constituency that is committed to universal norms. These shared common values are so fundamental that their violation justifies investigation, prosecution and punishment against their transgressors. This paradigm installs the ICTY and ICTR, as well as the ICC, with epic ambitions. By bestowing upon these international judicial mechanisms such an important role and by offering through them open-ended promises of implied protection, the international community leads them to a direct clash with the harsh realities and complexities of contemporary conflicts. Arguably, this approach would set these institutions up for failure from the outset, in terms of achieving their stated goals.

The goal of ending impunity and preventing future mass atrocities is difficult to operationalise and also difficult to measure in an empirically sound manner. Aside from the vagueness of the goal, the incredible complex realities on the ground make it very difficult to objectively measure the deterrent effect of international prosecution as an independent variable. An obvious dependent variable to measure the relation would be a change in (criminal) behaviour before and after the international criminal trials. However, in the context of ongoing conflict, the vast abundance of factors that shape conflict dynamics could easily influence behaviour. The large assortment of interfering variables, thus, makes it close to impossible to single out whether prosecution, as an independent variable, has an effect on behaviour. Even more fundamental is the question of whether a deterrent effect can *ever* be objectively measured. Essentially, deterrence is aimed at preventing recidivism (specific deterrence) or minimising the amount of first time offenders (general deterrence). Thus, deterrence is future-oriented and meant to measure something that has not come into existence. Although it could be claimed that all those not being prosecuted have apparently been deterred, this would be based on faulty reasoning for it need not necessarily be prosecution that motivates individuals to refrain from committing criminal acts.

Acknowledging the measurement difficulties, efforts can nevertheless be undertaken to identify key factors of prosecution that are important for deterring criminal behaviour. In fact, the relationship has been widely theorised about, dating back to renowned scholars such as Jeremy Bentham and has been studied and heavily debated at the national level in established domestic systems.[2] By applying these theories and studies to the international level and the Tribunals, they can help to develop an analytical framework that will facilitate the evaluation of the assumed deterrent effect of international criminal prosecution.

The basis for a framework to analyse international criminal tribunals' contribution to deterrence

According to classical deterrence theory, individuals are rational beings that will be deterred from criminal behaviour if the likelihood of the materialisation of the perceived costs (punishment through prosecution) outweighs the expected benefits of the crime. The theory stipulates that these costs must be sufficiently certain, swift and severe. The *certainty* is dependent on the likelihood of actually being apprehended for the crime. The *swiftness* refers to how quick punishment follows the commission of the crime, and the *severity* is determined by the intensity (nature and level) of the punishment. This all furthermore requires the individual to have *knowledge of the legal norm and the corresponding punishment*; a fourth factor by which punishment is thought to influence criminal behaviour. The latter deterrence factor requires the legislator to formulate the legal norm in a manner that is understandable to the norm

---

[2] Travis Pratt, Francis Cullen, Kristie Blevins, Leah Daigle and Tamara Madensen, 'The Empirical Status of Deterrence Theory: A Meta-Analysis', in Francis Cullen, John Wright and Kristie Blevins (eds.), *Taking Stock: The Status of Criminological Theory* (New Brunswick, NJ: Transaction, 2009), pp. 367–95; Martin Mennecke, 'Punishing Genocidaires: A Deterrent Effect or Not?', *Human Rights Review*, 8 (2007), 319–39; Julian Ku and Jide Nzelibe, 'Do International Criminal Tribunals Deter or Exacerbate Humanitarian Atrocities?', *Washington University Law Review*, 84 (2006), 777–833, at 789.

addressees, as well as to undertake efforts to make the norm known to its addressees. Deterrence is also thought to take effect through indirect experience. This implies that an individual will engage in crime if he knows that someone else has not been punished for it,[3] or otherwise has sufficient opportunity to do so.[4] This adds yet another factor to the equation: *knowledge of consistent rule enforcement*.

A number of national empirical studies of the deterrence theory[5] show a much weaker correlation between criminal prosecution and deterrence than initially theorised. First, the threshold of *credibility*, implying that the *threat of prosecution* must be meaningful to potential criminals, was found to affect the deterrent effect. The individual must be convinced that the threat of prosecution will materialise. Second, it was found that the – what had always been thought to be objective – factors of certainty, swiftness and severity are contested and partly subjectively shaped, since they must also be *perceived* to be convincing enough.[6] This *subjective assessment* depends on the personal characteristics of the individual, such as 'their values, background, personal circumstances, mental capacity, position'[7] and their previous experiences with the law, which all affect their reasoning and behaviour.[8]

It thus appears that ultimately, in order for prosecution to have any kind of deterrent effect, the norm addressees must perceive and accept the entirety of the criminal justice system – the prosecuting entity and its procedures as well as the governing body of law – as authoritative; or *legitimate*. Ultimately, the identified factors all contribute to the legitimacy of prosecution in one way or another and form the basis of an analytical framework with which to assess the contribution of international criminal prosecution to deterrence.

---

[3] Raymond Paternoster and Ronet Bachman (eds.), *Explaining Criminals and Crime* (Los Angeles: Roxbury, 2001), p. 5.

[4] Irvin Piliavin, Rosemary Gartner, Craig Thornton and Ross Matsueda, 'Crime, Deterrence and Rational Choice', *American Sociological Review*, 51 (1986), 101–19, at 103.

[5] See for instance Gibbs (1975) and Nagin (1978) in Paternoster and Bachman (eds.), *Criminals and Crime*, p. 16.

[6] *Ibid.*, p. 17; Major Michael Smidt, 'The International Criminal Court: An Effective Means of Deterrence?', *Military Law Review*, 167 (2001), 156–240; Ku and Nzelibe, 'Deter or Exacerbate'.

[7] Immi Tallgren, 'The Sensibility and Sense of International Criminal Law', *European Journal of International Law*, 13 (2002), 561–95, at 571.

[8] Piliavin, Gartner, Thornton and Matsueda, 'Rational Choice', 115.

Deterrence at an international level: situations of violent conflict and rational actors

The fundamental limits of international criminal prosecution become painfully apparent when applying the above mentioned factors important for deterrence to the international level and situations of violent conflict. The most relevant point of criticism to consider for present purposes is that the rational choice theory largely disregards structural factors, such as the broader social and political contexts[9] and social influences that shape the criminalised behaviour. While leaders plausibly engage in rational calculations, the dynamics of violent conflicts and the immediate needs of warfare, e.g. responding to (potential) losses of life, of strategic battles, of access to mineral-rich areas and potential loss of power and wealth, make it unlikely for the remote costs of prosecution to penetrate or override strategic military and political decisions. Moreover, the volatile and disruptive nature of mass violence gives rise to situations in which morality is reversed and violence is the norm, where the use of force is scattered and opportunities to engage in crime are abundant. These circumstances affect the (moral) choices by individuals to such an extent that they do not resemble 'regular' cost–benefit calculations made by 'ordinary' criminals in national contexts.[10]

Indeed, in situations where individuals perceive and experience criminal activity to be widespread – i.e. conflict situations – they have been found to be more likely to commit crimes themselves[11] and violence has been considered to constitute norm-conforming behaviour.[12] In fact, fighting may become a legitimate way to defend one's group or advance the group's interests and contribute to enhancing the perpetrator's status within the group. It is not uncommon for participants in international crimes to believe in the righteousness, or at least necessity, of their

[9] Ronald Clarke and Derek Cornish, 'Rational Choice', in Paternoster and Bachman (eds.), *Criminals and Crime*, pp. 23–42, at pp. 37–8.

[10] Katharine Marshall, 'Prevention and Complementarity in the International Criminal Court: A Positive Approach', *Human Rights Brief*, 17 (2010), 21–6, at 24–5; Frédéric Mégret, 'Three Dangers for the International Criminal Court: A Critical Look at a Consensual Project', *Finnish Yearbook of International Law*, 12 (2001), 195–247, at 202–3; Tallgren, 'Sensibility and Sense', 571; Mark Drumbl, 'Toward a Criminology of International Crime', *Ohio State Journal on Dispute Resolution*, 19 (2003), 263–82.

[11] Dan Kahan, 'Social Influence, Social Meaning, and Deterrence', *Virginia Law Review*, 2 (1997), 349–95, at 350; Tallgren, 'Sensibility and Sense', 575; Drumbl, 'Criminology', 268.

[12] Robert Sloane, 'The Expressive Capacity of International Punishment: The Limits of the National Law Analogy and the Potential of International Criminal Law', *Stanford Journal of International Law*, 43 (2007), 39–94, at 41 and 60.

violent behaviour, whereby such behaviour becomes justified.[13] Alternatively, those not conforming to violent norms may constitute the minority and even be subjected to violent reprisals or punishment by the State or other armed forces, thus driving them to commit crimes out of fear of their own safety.[14] Behaviour is thus strongly shaped by the context in which the actor finds themselves and highly complex in situations of international conflict. If the goal of international prosecution is to influence decision-making so as to induce a deterrent effect, then it is important to be aware of the contextual complexities and understand what drives people to engage in international criminal acts. All in all, decision-making may be more difficult to influence in conflicts, such as national wars of liberation, where fighting is perceived to be 'just', where the immediate needs of warfare outweigh the possible costs of prosecution, and in situations where prosecution and the tribunals' legitimacy are contested.

Certainty of apprehension and swiftness of punishment

The ICTY and ICTR do not have their own police or military force and thus operate without enforcement forces. This makes the Tribunals highly dependent on State cooperation for executing arrest warrants, access to evidence, relocation of witnesses and enforcement of sentences. This is problematic because – despite their legal obligations – the willingness of States to cooperate is ultimately subject to political considerations and interests. Vivid examples of these difficulties are those encountered in arresting Milošević, Karadzić and Mladić and the fact that many ICTR indictees still remain at large. The Tribunals' institutional dependence on States thereby diminishes the *certainty of apprehension*.

In turn, the low level of certainty of apprehension and delays resulting from lack of cooperation contribute to a low *swiftness of punishment*. If caught, however, the suspect will endure some sort of direct and swift 'punishment' in the form of pre-trial detention. Nevertheless,

---

[13] Alette Smeulers, 'Perpetrators of International Crimes: Towards a Typology', in Alette Smeulers and Roelof Haveman (eds.), *Supranational Criminology: Towards a Criminology of International Crimes* (Antwerp: Intersentia, 2008), pp. 233–66, at p. 236; Samuel Tanner, 'The Mass Crimes in the former Yugoslavia: Participation, Punishment and Prevention', *International Review of the Red Cross*, 90 (2008), 273–87, at 277.

[14] Legally speaking, this could qualify as a situation of duress which would exclude the individual in question of his/her criminal responsibility.

international trials are renowned for their long duration. Although the relevance of the swiftness of punishment for purposes of deterrence is contested, this factor should be considered because it is related to another factor that could be significant for deterrence, namely the importance of the alleged perpetrator sought to be put on trial.

Looking at the length of international criminal trials before the ICTY and ICTR, it becomes evident that they generally require many years. As of September 2012, the ICTR had completed 55 cases, 17 were pending on appeal and 1 case was in progress.[15] At the same time, the ICTY has concluded proceedings for 126 accused and has ongoing proceedings for 35 accused.[16] Looking at these figures in light of the thousands of perpetrators of mass atrocities in the conflicts in the former Yugoslavia and in Rwanda, it can be argued that the Tribunals have prosecuted a very small number of persons over a rather long time span to affect (future) perpetrators' criminal behaviour. However, it should be added that the importance of the alleged perpetrators put on trial may also affect a would-be perpetrator's cost–benefit analysis. Arguably, prosecuting high-level alleged perpetrators will increase the chance of deterring other important perpetrators, which in turn may mitigate the relative small amount of trials.[17] The prosecution of the principal perpetrators is thought to have an amplified effect, considering their leadership positions and – in the case of heads of State and ministers – irrelevance of their immunity from prosecution for breaching the most fundamental norms of international law. The prosecution of these leaders is then thought to attain a symbolic function by expressing the international community's condemnation of the crimes falling under the subject-matter jurisdiction of the Tribunals. Assessing the effectiveness of this expressionist function of international criminal law on deterring criminal behaviour, however, is an issue which goes beyond the scope of this chapter.

---

[15] International Criminal Tribunal for Rwanda, 'Status of Cases', at www.unictr.org/Cases/tabid/204/Default.aspx.

[16] International Criminal Tribunal for the former Yugoslavia, 'Key Figures', at www.icty.org/sections/TheCases/KeyFigures.

[17] James Alexander, 'The International Criminal Court and the Prevention of Atrocities: Predicting the Court's Impact', *Villanova Law Review*, 54 (2009), 1–56, at 10. At this point it must also be noted that international criminal trials are by no means the only manner by which the perpetrators in these conflicts have been held accountable. National and local ('traditional') courts – e.g. the *gacaca* courts in Rwanda – have tried a large number of cases.

Aspects of punishment and legal norms and their potential to deter

Punishment must be experienced as significant in order to have a deterrent effect. The level of suffering is thereby frequently coupled with the severity of the punishment. The severity – or intensity – of the punishment can be determined by the nature of the punishment, in the case of crimes falling under R2P usually a term of imprisonment, as well as the level of punishment, that is the length of imprisonment. The severity of punishment in relation to deterrence as such has been the subject of many debates in national parliaments and criminological circles. By now there seems to be widespread consensus that an increase in the severity of punishment does not enhance compliance with the law. National empirical studies have shown that there is no consistent deterrent effect of perceived severity of formal sanctions[18] and that certainty of punishment is a stronger factor contributing to deterrence than the length of punishment.[19] Moreover, informal sanctions such as shaming have shown to have a stronger effect on preventing deviant behaviour than their formal counterparts.[20] Instead of the threat of formal sanctions by a remote international institution, law-conforming behaviour is apparently enhanced more by individuals' perceptions of others. This idea of criminality as a social construct is that crime is not so much an individual's undertaking, as it is embedded in his or her community.[21] Influencing an individual's behaviour may thus be more effective when done in a manner and by an entity that is meaningful, or at least

---

[18] William Bailey and Ruth Lott, 'Crime, Punishment and Personality: An Examination of the Deterrence Question', *Journal of Criminal Law and Criminology*, 67 (1976), 99–109; Robert Meier and Weldon Johnson, 'Deterrence as Social Control: The Legal and Extralegal Production of Conformity', *American Sociological Review*, 42 (1977), 292–304; Matthew Silberman, 'Toward a Theory of Criminal Deterrence', *American Sociological Review*, 41 (1976), 442–61; Gordon Waldo and Theodore Chiricos, 'Perceived Penal Sanctions and Self-Reported Criminality: A Neglected Approach to Deterrence Research', *Social Problems*, 19 (1972), 522–40; Meier and Johnson (1977) in Piliavin, Gartner, Thornton and Matsueda, 'Rational Choice', 102.

[19] Allison Marston Danner, 'Constructing a Hierarchy of Crimes in International Criminal Law Sentencing', *Virginia Law Review*, 87 (2001), 415–501, at 440; Kahan, 'Social Influence', 382–5.

[20] John Braithwaite, *Crime, Shame and Reintegration* (Cambridge University Press, 1999), p. 69; Ku and Nzelibe, 'Deter or Exacerbate', 793; Kahan, 'Social Influence', 384; Tanner, 'Mass Crimes', 282.

[21] Carrie Gustafson, 'International Criminal Courts: Some Dissident Views on the Continuation of War by Penal Means', *Houston Journal of International Law*, 21 (1998), 51–84, at 62 and 69.

acceptable to, the individual and his or her community. Instead of the severity, the meaning of the form of punishment then becomes an important factor for evaluating the deterrent potential of international prosecution. Thus, by drawing from national debates and studies, it can be concluded that the *severity of punishment* is not a key factor for international deterrence. Instead, the *meaning* of punishment has been found to be of greater importance for deterrence. The same may be true for legal norms.

Legal norms prohibiting certain behaviour are traditionally enshrined in national criminal law, which is supposed to be a reflection of common values of a homogeneous constituency, offering a solution to social problems and regulating the relationship between an authoritative State and the individual. These functions experience significant distortion when transposed to the international level. On an international level, the relationship between the authority of 'the international community', in the form of the Tribunals, and the individual does not receive much attention.[22] Additionally, international social problems are so numerous and complex that they represent a web that even entangles the 'legislator' ('the international community'). As far as common values and constituency are concerned, it should be said that the Tribunals focus on the most serious crimes of concern to the international community as a whole.[23] However, on an international level, the pool of norm addressees not only magnifies, but also diversifies on a number of levels, among which on a cultural level. This challenges the commonality of values, which may give rise to conflicting approaches to justice. The constitutionalist approach towards a global constituency is attractive in theory and on a rhetorical level, but may not always hold in the realities of a pluralistic world order.

The breadth of cultures in the world gives rise to a multitude of diverging – and at times conflicting – conceptions of what is deemed criminal behaviour or the most appropriate form of justice. The application of this factor of the framework to the international level lays bare the Tribunals' Western-based, top-down system of 'bringing justice'.[24] This frequently vented point of critique gives rise to allegations that

---

[22] Tallgren, 'Sensibility and Sense', 566.
[23] See the preambular clauses of UNSC Res. 955, UN Doc. D/RES/955, 8 November 1994, establishing the ICTR and the preambular clauses of UNSC Res. 827, UN Doc. D/RES/ 827, 25 May 1993, establishing the ICTY.
[24] The proposition that this system is justified by State consent expressed by via the UNSC can be countered by the argument that the Council only indirectly reflects the will of the

international criminal judicial bodies, such as the ICC and most notably the ICTY, do not do enough justice to local realities, needs and informal justice systems.[25] In addition, their constitutionalist approach risks solidifying a certain level of rigidity which does not allow for cultural flexibility.[26] This approach contributes not only to a disconnect between what occurs in The Hague and Arusha and what is needed by the society affected by the violence,[27] but also to a disconnect of what may be considered criminal behaviour by the international community and individuals on the ground. An example of this disconnect might be the issue of the illegality of the use of, and the critical age for considering persons as, child soldiers. Quite important for achieving deterrence is that the would-be perpetrator must identify the action as potentially 'wrong' and be aware of the possibility of sanction.[28] As such, the 'internationalisation' of some crimes and approaches to justice may be perceived as alien standards of justice by would-be perpetrators (as well as victims), weakening their legitimacy and thereby the potential of international criminal prosecution to have a deterrent effect on the norm addressees.

UN Member States that do not take seat in the UNSC at the time of the respective resolutions and that States in general need not necessarily reflect the views of their society. Furthermore, State consent does not guarantee a democratic, bottom-up process leading to ratification. See Drumbl, 'Collective Violence and Individual Punishment: The Criminality of Mass Atrocity', Northwestern University Law Review, 99 (2005), 539–610, at 540–1 and 598–9.

[25] See Drumbl, 'Criminology', 274; Mariana Goetz, 'The International Criminal Court and its Relevance to Affected Communities', in Nicholas Waddel and Phil Clark (eds.), Courting Conflict? Justice, Peace and the ICC in Africa (London: Royal African Society, 2008), pp. 65–72.

[26] This does not mean to downplay the horrific nature of the crimes that fall within the tribunals' jurisdiction, nor does this intend to suggest not to hold those responsible accountable. We merely argue here that there are other ways to Rome and that international prosecution may benefit from taking a more legally pluralistic approach which takes into account local and cultural values and needs. Although it goes far beyond the scope of this chapter, it would be interesting to research to what extent, and how, tribunals can attain a multicultural justice system.

[27] Most notably in (positivistic) international criminal law circles, informal justice systems are considered to be 'inferior' to the more 'superior' international formal ones. See, Drumbl, 'Collective Violence', 596–7; Phil Clark, 'Changing the game on the ground: the ICC's impact on party politics, elections, and domestic justice in Africa', summary of speech delivered at Post-Conflict Justice and 'Local Ownership', Leiden University, The Hague, 5 May 2011, pp. 5–6, at www.grotiuscentre.org/resources/1/Conference%20Report-Final.pdf.

[28] Carsten Stahn, 'The Future of International Criminal Justice', The Hague Justice Portal, 2009, at www.haguejusticeportal.net/index.php?id=11106.

Although crimes falling under R2P are considered as serious violations by the majority of people, they may lose their meaning in a
situation of violent conflict when their own survival is at stake. Even
though this may not be a tolerable development, in practice it does
diminish the chance of preventing or stopping atrocities. A study
shows that the three communities in Bosnia-Herzegovina spoke of
their soldiers as defenders who gained a kind of special exemption
from the rules of war.[29] Tanner suggests that in situations of violent
conflict, the law is negotiable and its meaning, through (false) justifications, may be (temporarily) neutralised.[30] Especially in situations where
international crimes are associated with some sort of ideological support,
chances are slim that the perpetrator will be deterred.[31]

The importance of acceptance and meaning is not unique to legal
norms, but must also be present for the corresponding punishment.
International criminal prosecutions are but one of many ways to address
accountability of grave crimes. In some societies, traditional conflict
resolution mechanisms and traditional justice systems based on values
such as 'mercy, shaming, recompense, forgiveness, compassion, and
repentance'[32] may be more suitable to ensure accountability, reconcile
deeply divided societies and deter criminal behaviour; although the latter
is a topic yet to be studied.[33] Societies affected by conflict are inherently
divided and may be best served by forms of justice that do not focus as
much on formal sanctions and imprisonment as the Western-based
model does. In broad terms, a tension exists between criminal adjudication and retributive justice as conducted by Tribunals and restorative
and reconciliatory forms of justice preferred by the local communities, at
times, such as the famous *gacaca* courts in Rwanda.

Aside from norms and approaches of justice being meaningful to the
persons concerned, giving effect to this analytical factor also entails broad
dissemination of information about these legal norms and corresponding
punishment. That activity is generally challenged by the rampant insecurity
in situations of violent conflict. Taking into account the discussion above,
the analytical framework must emphasise the importance of the *meaning* of

---

[29] Greenberg Research, Inc., *The People on War Report* (Geneva: ICRC, 1999), p. 34.
[30] Tanner, 'Mass Crimes', 283.   [31] Stahn, 'International Criminal Justice'.
[32] Gustafson, 'Continuation of War by Penal Means', 83.
[33] Linda Keller, 'The False Dichotomy of Peace versus Justice and the International
Criminal Court', *Hague Justice Journal*, 3 (2008), 12–47, at 41.

norms and corresponding punishment and include *access to information, visibility* and *sensitivity to the local context.*

Knowledge and consistency of rule enforcement and credible threat of prosecution

It is assumed that knowledge of consistent rule enforcement is necessary in order to deter individuals via indirect experience. Eventually, an individual will engage in crime more easily, knowing that someone else has not been punished for it, something which in international legal discourse is often referred to as *impunity.* The Tribunals' dependence on State cooperation significantly undermines the knowledge and consistency of rule enforcement.[34]

For the credibility of the threat of prosecution to be meaningful to potential criminals as a deterrent effect, the norm addressees must be convinced that tribunals intend to carry out its threats of prosecution. Giving effect to such threats first of all requires communicating the threat. In order for the potential violator to believe that the threat is real, it is imperative that the communication of the intent is clear, because any mixed signals may temper the value of the threat.[35] The Tribunals' dependence on the cooperation of States as agents tasked with carrying out the arrest warrants issued by the Prosecutor (or indirectly the Security Council), may further reduce the credibility of the threat because the dependence on States increases the chances of sending mixed messages to (future) leaders, if States allow political interests to trump their legal obligations.

Legitimacy

Legitimacy is a crucial element and overarching factor for international criminal mechanisms such as ad hoc tribunals in attempting to deter crimes falling under R2P. The legitimacy of ad hoc tribunals is based on international laws and accountability procedures rather than local laws, norms and accountability procedures, while the latter are more likely to be meaningful to individuals and thereby have a deterrent effect.

---

[34] Lilian Barria and Steven Roper, 'How Effective Are International Criminal Tribunals? An Analysis of the ICTY and ICTR', *International Journal of Human Rights*, 9 (2005), 349–68.

[35] Smidt, 'Means of Deterrence', 169.

Furthermore, the effectiveness of (the threat of) international prosecution rests on the level of authority and legitimacy that is given to the prosecuting institution by the prosecutorial target: the (future) offender. At the international level, this is not only made difficult by the perceptions that tribunals are to some degree culturally foreign and geographically distant,[36] but also subject to political interests. The dependence on States weakens the certainty of apprehension; swiftness of punishment; knowledge of consistent rule enforcement, and the credibility of the threat of prosecution. The decrease of strength in these factors all contribute to a decrease in legitimacy and the deterrent effect of tribunals.

Interim conclusion

In the absence of credible empirical research, it is impossible to claim that ad hoc tribunals have deterred individuals from committing crimes. The transposition of the deterrence argument from the national level to the international level is problematic for a number of reasons. First of all, that is due to the disputed nature of deterrence even at the national level. Second, the typical functions and characteristics of criminal law that the deterrence theory rests on, namely a body of law reflecting common values of a homogeneous constituency, capable of offering a solution to social problems, and regulating the relationship between an authoritative State and the individual living in it, are not present in the international criminal justice system. The analysis of international prosecution has resulted in a basic analytical framework that consists of a number of key factors that have to be present and which were elaborated upon above. In addition there are a few overarching factors which deeply complicate a rational/theoretical application of the analytical deterrence framework to the prosecution of international crimes.

The following factors in fact weaken the ICTY and ICTR's potential contribution to deterrence. First, the dynamics of violent conflict give rise to a significantly different context characterised and dominated by the immediate needs of warfare where actors behave differently than in national contexts of relative stability. Second, the inseparability of international law and politics creates a context in which political interests take precedence over legal obligations. In this situation, the Tribunals' institutional dependence on States negatively affects perceptions of their

---

[36] Sloane, 'Expressive Capacity', 72.

legitimacy. Third, and finally, the heterogeneity of constituencies and corresponding norms and values at the international level lead to a plurality in concepts of criminal behaviour, concepts of justice, and approaches to accountability. This diversity may amount to conflicts between the international and local level and also undermines the perception of legitimacy of the Tribunals.

Preventing the commission of international crimes: the proactive dimension of the ICTY and ICTR through the use of substantive and procedural criminal law

As a result of the increase in organised crime and grave threats to society in the form of terrorist attacks, one notices an increasing expansion of the applicability of both substantive and procedural criminal law in national criminal justice systems over the past decades. Criminal justice systems are no longer merely reactive to the commission of crimes. They seek, just as well, the prevention of the commission of crimes. In respect of preventing terrorist acts, the UN Office on Drugs and Crimes stated that '[a] preventive criminal justice strategy has far more potential to truly implement the ICCPR, to protect the right to life against arbitrary deprivation, and to improve respect for the rule of law, than does prosecution of the surviving attackers after a tragedy.'[37]

National criminal justice systems seek to prevent commission of grave crimes by two alternative, but in practice generally combined, routes. First, one witnesses the introduction and/or increasing use of modes of liability directed at the preparation of criminal conduct, thus preceding the commission thereof. In their most protective form such modes of liability would not require the subsequent commission of the underlying crime or the commencement of execution at all. In other words, these modes of liability even precede the classic form of attempt to commit a crime. Such modes of liability are referred to as 'inchoate crimes' which contemplate or look toward the commission of concrete crimes, less for their inherent danger than for the danger that they may ripen into substantive crimes.[38] An inchoate offence is described as '[a] step toward

---

[37] UN Office on Drugs and Crime, *Preventing Terrorist Acts: A Criminal Justice Strategy Integrating Rule of Law Standards in Implementation of United Nations Anti-Terrorism Instruments*, working paper (Vienna: Vienna International Centre, July 2006), para. 112.

[38] Richard Hoskins, 'A Comparative Analysis of the Crime of Conspiracy in Germany, France and the United States', *New York University Journal of International Law and Politics*, 6 (1973), 245–70, at 245.

the commission of another crime, the step in itself being serious enough to merit punishment'.[39] One of the rationales for the existence of inchoate crimes, which is also pertinent to R2P, is the fact that such criminalisation permits law enforcement officers and the judiciary to become involved before any harm has occurred, and thus serves to reduce the incidence of harm.[40] The inchoate crimes generally recognised and punished are attempt, solicitation or incitement and conspiracy. We will confine ourselves to some brief observations on these crimes.

Criminal liability for conspiracy to commit a crime is a complex notion. In general it can be described as an agreement among participants to commit a crime. This mere agreement suffices in principle to attach criminal liability and it is irrelevant whether or not the plan materialises in the subsequent commission of the crime.[41] However, certain domestic conspiracy laws require that at least one party to the conspiracy commits an overt act in furtherance of the conspiracy.[42] Conspiracy is an important feature of US criminal law, and it can also be found in other common law jurisdictions, such as England. In civil law jurisdictions, the conspiracy concept may be not known as such, but similar modes of liability tend to be available nonetheless. Punishment of inchoate group acts goes, for example, in the Netherlands through the 'criminal association' rule, rather than the common law 'conspiracy' rule. The Dutch Penal Code, by way of Articles 140 and 140a, focuses on the formation of a criminal gang with the purpose of committing crimes, whereas the conspiracy approach focuses on the common purpose of multiple persons, whether or not they constitute an 'organisation'.[43] Similar to conspiracy, it is irrelevant for establishing liability under Article 140 or 140a of the Dutch Penal Code whether or not the

---

[39] Bryan Garner (ed.), *Black's Law Dictionary*, 7th edn (St Paul, MN: West Group, 1999), p. 1108.

[40] Wibke Kristin Timmermann, 'Incitement in International Criminal Law', *International Review of the Red Cross*, 88 (2006), 823–52, at 827.

[41] It is said that the criminal prohibition against conspiracy has two well recognised foundations. First, there is the danger that an agreement to commit a crime will actually be carried out, and as a result, the substantive crime will occur. Second, there is also the ongoing danger presented by any group or association dedicated to the commission of crimes. See Hoskins, 'Crime of Conspiracy', 247.

[42] *Ibid.*, 251–2.

[43] In legal practice the distinction may be marginal, especially if an organisation is defined on the basis of an agreement among its members. This can be the same agreement that would suffice for conspiracy.

organisation has committed crimes, although the fact of commission can serve as important evidence of the criminal intent.

In addition to conspiracy, one can mention incitement to commit crimes. The incitement liability, or solicitation liability, may vary among criminal jurisdictions. The crucial question from an R2P perspective is whether incitement has to be followed by commission of the crime. With the exception of specifically labelled hate speech, it appears that this is the case. As a result, the crime of incitement under national law does not expand the scope of application of substantive criminal law. Rather, it serves to enlarge the group of criminally liable individuals *after* the commission of the crime. For example, Article 47 of the Dutch Penal Code attaches criminal liability to incitement by certain means – such as promises or abuse of power – but only when incitement has been followed by commission of the crime – or at least an attempt to do so. Interestingly, as we will see below, in respect of incitement to genocide, the liability is detached from further commission of the crime, at least in theory. It is one of the exceptional areas where international criminal justice appears more proactive than its national counterparts. However, certain forms of incitement are embodied by specific crimes of hate speech, in which national approaches significantly differ. For example, in the United States constitutional law regarding hate crimes was shaped by the Supreme Court, in which speech restrictions were only allowed if there was a 'clear and present danger' to society.[44]

Finally, we have to mention the way in which certain national criminal justice systems have sought to expand the criminal liability for attempting to commit a crime. In the Netherlands, for example, preparatory acts to commit crimes are punishable.[45] Such preparatory acts precede the attempt, as no start of execution of the crime is required. The classic example is a group of bank robbers who drive to a bank building in a car with masks and guns. This is not yet sufficient for attempted robbery, but they could – in the Netherlands – be convicted for preparatory acts.

It follows from the above that domestic substantive criminal law encompasses a number of modes of liability which precede the start of the actual commission of the crime. It serves the purposes of preventing such commission, while at the same time still being able to punish those who conspired, incited others or prepared the commission of the crime. Substantive and procedural criminal law are directly linked to one

---

[44] The landmark decision in this regard is *Brandenburg* v. *Ohio*, 395 US 444, 1969.

[45] See Article 46 of the Dutch Penal Code.

another. The powers of criminal investigation – including the use of compulsory investigative powers – in criminal justice systems generally depend on the reasonable suspicion that a crime has been committed. But when reference is made to 'commission', this tends to include all available modes of liability. Hence, powers of investigation also exist in respect of conspiracy, incitement and preparatory acts. The expanding scope of substantive criminal law thus directly entails the expanding scope of investigative powers.

The question which then arises is whether, in addition to this increase in investigative powers triggered by expansion of substantive criminal law, there is an autonomous need for proactive criminal procedure. The idea would be that – especially in respect of serious crimes – there should be certain investigative powers available prior to the commission – also in its very broad sense – of such crimes. The objective is not only to generally improve the information and evidence available to the law enforcement officials, but clearly also the prevention of serious crimes, such as terrorism.

Especially after the terrorist attacks of 11 September 2001, we witness a general trend in attribution of investigative powers already prior to the commission of crimes.[46] Such powers can be exercised when there is – for example – a certain degree of information that serious crimes are being planned or organised. The investigative powers may include such matters as the interception of telecommunication or infiltration methods within organisations. At least, these are certain examples of such steps being allowed under domestic laws.[47] The evidentiary threshold can in case of terrorism be lower than 'reasonable suspicion'; 'indications' that a crime of terrorism is prepared or organised, for which vague, anonymous and shielded information can suffice, is at present the basis in Dutch law for the use of certain investigative powers in respect of terrorism.[48]

It is safe to say that the expansion of investigative powers in respect of special crimes, such as terrorism, has been met with criticism.[49] Especially when individual rights and liberties are at stake – such as is the case with interception of telecommunications – it is indeed a legitimate question

---

[46] For some examples of new criminal laws against terrorism in the US and the UK, see Kent Roach, 'The Criminal Law and Terrorism', in Victor Ramraj, Michael Hor and Kent Roach (eds.), *Global Anti-Terrorism Law and Policy* (Cambridge University Press, 2005), pp. 129–51, at pp. 131–5; and Victor Tadros, 'Justice and Terrorism', *New Criminal Law Review*, 10 (2007), 658–89, at 670–5.

[47] See Articles 126za–126zs of the Dutch Code for Criminal Procedure.   [48] See *ibid*.

[49] See, among many others Tadros, 'Justice', 679–88.

whether infringements on these rights are justified from a human rights perspective, when there is no reasonable suspicion yet of the actual commission of a crime. In defence, it has been claimed that both the relatively limited invasion of proactive powers of investigation on individual rights combined with the serious threat to society of the criminal conduct to which they are applicable, would fully justify these powers.

It is interesting to note that national societies have increasingly used criminal law as a tool to protect society over the past decades. Both substantive and procedural criminal law have moved towards addressing the very early and preparatory phases of criminal/undesirable conduct. At the heart of this development lies the keen desire of national justice systems to not only punish, but also prevent the commission of serious crimes. This is definitely a trend that fits well with the process of domestic operationalisation or internalisation of R2P.

Proactive international criminal law: starting the debate?

It is intriguing that this proactive and R2P-compatible approach which one encounters in national criminal justice systems seems absent in the international criminal justice system. This is all the more puzzling, because the category of criminal conduct that is in greatest need of prevention is the group of 'core crimes'; part of the jurisdiction of various international criminal tribunals. Indeed, one cannot imagine a matter of greater importance or urgency than to protect populations at risk from genocide or crimes against humanity.

A look at the substantive and procedural law of international criminal tribunals shows that only in respect of the crime of genocide a proactive dimension exists. Conspiracy and incitement to commit genocide are modes of liability which could – at least in theory – operate without genocide having to be committed. However, these modes of liability do not apply to crimes against humanity or war crimes. Thus, conspiracy or incitement to either of these categories of crimes is not punishable under international criminal law. It is true that over the last two decades modes of quasi-collective liability, such as joint criminal enterprise, have come into existence, with a view to expand the scope of criminal liability for crimes within the Statutes of the ICTY and ICTR.[50] However, this

---

[50] On 'joint criminal enterprise' (JCE), see the special symposium in the *Journal of International Criminal Justice*, 5 (2007), 69–226, with contributions from Harmen van der Wilt, Kai Hamdorf, Katrina Gustafson, Antonio Cassese, Kai Ambos and Jens Ohlin.

particular form of liability was not concerned with proactive extension of the reach of international criminal law, but with targeting the mid- and high-level political and military leadership after the crimes had been committed. All in all, in substantive international criminal law there is hardly attention for a prevention theory and application of criminal law in a way that contributes to prevention.

The same applies to the law of international criminal procedure. Generally speaking, it can be said that this body of law is still very much underdeveloped, especially when compared to domestic criminal justice systems.[51] The investigative powers attributed to the Prosecutor are all based on the traditional functioning of the criminal justice system, i.e. post facto reaction to the commission of a crime. It appears that no attention was given to the question if and to what extent the Prosecutor should have investigative powers prior to the commission of a crime, during the preparatory work establishing the Tribunals or in their case law. To put it more concretely: in case the Prosecutor has evidence that a high government official is organising or preparing crimes against humanity, should the Prosecutor be empowered to request the interception of telecommunications in respect of that official? From an R2P perspective, the availability of such investigative powers from a very early stage allows for swifter investigation results – and issuance of arrest warrants – once the aforementioned government official starts the commission of crimes against humanity.

But in spite of such possible advantages at the national level, the debate on international criminal procedure by and large ignores this issue. Rather, the focus appears to be on fair and expeditious justice and addressing the problem of lengthy international criminal trials. There are a number of plausible explanations why there is practically no R2P approach within the body of positive international criminal law.

First, the majority of international criminal tribunals to date have been established after commission of the atrocities falling under their respective jurisdictions. That includes the International Military Tribunal of Nuremberg, the International Military Tribunal for the Far

---

[51] See on the state of the law of international criminal procedure, Göran Sluiter, 'Trends in the Development of a Unified Law of International Criminal Procedure', in Carsten Stahn and Larissa van den Herik (eds.), *Future Perspectives on International Criminal Justice* (The Hague: TMC Asser Press, 2010), pp. 585–99. For a comprehensive analysis and stocktaking of international criminal procedure, see Göran Sluiter, Hakan Friman, Suzannah Linton, Salvatore Zappala and Sergey Vasiliev (eds.), *International Criminal Procedure: Principles and Rules* (Oxford University Press, 2012).

East, the ICTR and the Extraordinary Chambers in the Courts of Cambodia. In view of the circumstances and events, these tribunals were established to address crimes already committed; no need was felt to take an R2P preventive approach. This does not, however, negate the fact that these tribunals serve the objective of deterrence too. Their creation carried with it the message that future international crimes could give rise to the creation of similar mechanisms of prosecution. Yet, given the jurisdictional restraints of these tribunals, it was impossible to apply their own substantive and procedural criminal law to crimes committed after their creation.[52] However, this was not excluded for other temporary international criminal tribunals, namely the ICTY and the Special Court for Sierra Leone.[53] Most notably, the ICTY has continued investigations and has indicted individuals for crimes committed even a considerable time after its establishment. Hence, the need and attention for proactive use of substantive and procedural criminal law appears warranted at the ICTY. Nevertheless, it is undeniable that, established as a temporary ad hoc tribunal, the ICTY was often taken by surprise by the turns and twists of armed conflicts in the former Yugoslavia and by and large proved incapable of developing an R2P policy, where necessary by adjusting its applicable law.

Preventive international criminal law and the ICTY and ICTR

The ICTY and ICTR have essentially been established and have functioned as post facto ad hoc tribunals. This makes it in and of itself difficult for them to directly contribute to embedding R2P, except seen from the broad perspective of general deterrence and the international

---

[52] The jurisdiction of the Nuremberg Tribunal was limited – according to Article 1 of its Statute – to 'the just and prompt trial and punishment of the major war criminals of the European Axis'; by necessary implication, this limited the International Military Tribunal's jurisdiction to a number of years, prior to its creation. The Statute of the International Military Tribunal for the Far East of Tokyo contained a similar article, limiting its jurisdiction also in time to the Second World War. The jurisdiction of the ICTR is pursuant to Article 1 of its Statute limited to crimes committed in the year 1994. The jurisdiction of the Extraordinary Chambers of the Courts of Cambodia (ECCC) is pursuant to Article 1 of the Law on the ECCC limited to crimes committed during the period from 17 April 1975 to 6 January 1979.

[53] The ICTY, established in 1993 by UN Security Council Res. 808 and 827, has pursuant to Article 1 of its Statute temporal jurisdiction over crimes committed since 1991; hence, its jurisdiction is ongoing. This is also the case with the Special Court for Sierra Leone, which has jurisdiction over crimes committed since 30 November 1996.

criminalisation of the crimes falling under R2P. Due to their post facto nature no need was felt and no attempt was made to adopt a specific R2P-like agenda. At least, no attempts were made and there was no serious discussion to broaden the scope of substantive and procedural criminal law to include events that contribute to and precede the actual commission of international crimes. While in the case of the ICTR the crimes prosecuted had already been committed, also in respect of crimes that were committed after the tribunal's establishment – for example, the 'Kosovo-crimes' in case of the ICTY – the response was of a rather 'reactive' nature. It seems there was no proper prosecutorial policy in place to prevent these crimes from being committed, except for the overall assumption or hope that the past indictments and future prospect of indictments would persuade political and military leaders to refrain from future criminal conduct. Such policy could consist of closer monitoring of armed conflict situations in the former Yugoslavia where crimes were expected to be committed. The Prosecutor could have made known, as a matter of policy, that it was monitoring the situation and indicate with relative precision the consequences in case crimes were committed.

Although the ICTY was thus, in theory, best placed to adopt an R2P-inspired policy, as a result of its open-ended temporal jurisdiction, the ICTR was most active in prosecuting individuals for the crime that most requires a proactive and R2P perspective on international criminal justice, namely genocide. Convictions of the ICTY on genocide are sporadic and confined to accessory liability, whereas prosecuting individuals on genocide charges is the core business of the ICTR and it has resulted in many convictions. For purposes of prevention of crimes falling under R2P it is important to explore how the ICTR has interpreted and applied the crimes of conspiracy to commit genocide and incitement to genocide. Has the ICTR provided us with an interpretation of these modes of liability, which go beyond the limited mandate of the ICTR and could be the starting point for active investigations and prosecutions before genocide is committed?

It appears that the case law of the ICTR has not advanced much the R2P dimension of the crime of genocide. This is understandable in the sense that genocide had occurred in Rwanda and, as a result, there was not much need to explore the modes of liability of incitement and conspiracy from the perspective of preventing genocide. Both the Prosecutor's indictments and the Chambers' interpretations demonstrate a certain reluctance to invest much time or energy on modes of liability that could be perceived as not really doing justice to the situation in Rwanda, where genocide had in fact occurred. Below follow some observations on incitement to commit genocide and conspiracy to commit genocide.[54]

Initially, conspiracy to commit genocide gave rise to some confusion: should it be possible to convict an accused of both conspiracy and a substantive genocide offence? In *Musema*, the Trial Chamber found that – as is the case in certain civil law jurisdictions – this cannot be the case and ruled that 'no purpose would be served in convicting an accused, who has already been found guilty of genocide, for conspiracy to commit genocide, on the basis of the same acts'.[55] This may seem reasonable, but it also unnecessarily turns conspiracy into an inferior mode of liability, compared to the actual commission of genocide. Moreover, being subsumed by the commission of genocide entails the risk of denying conspiracy its place as an autonomous mode of liability.

While the Trial Chamber's approach in *Musema* has not been followed in subsequent case law, conspiracy to commit genocide has remained fairly problematic in the ICTR case law. For example, in the *Nahimana et al.* Appeals Chamber judgment the accused were acquitted from the conspiracy count because the existence of an agreement to commit genocide could not be proven beyond a reasonable doubt.[56] In the *Bizimungu et al.* case the conspiracy charge was dismissed because the Prosecutor had failed to properly plead it in the indictment.[57] The overall impression of ICTR case law on conspiracy to commit genocide is that both Prosecutor and Chambers have not dedicated significant efforts to the conspiracy charges and that they were easily dismissed in light of other, and arguably more serious, modes of liability for genocide.

It appears that with the landmark case of *Nahimana et al.* the issue of incitement to genocide has received more serious attention at the ICTR. But again, the ICTR was in the 'comfortable' position of ruling on incitement not in the abstract, but rather from the background of a genocide that had taken place. It was thus not compelled to rule on incitement liability without genocide having actually occurred. This is an

---

[54] Criminalised in article 2 (3) (b) and (c) of the ICTR Statute.

[55] *Prosecutor v. Musema, Judgment and Sentence*, Case No. ICTR-96-13-T, 27 January 2000, para. 198.

[56] *Prosecutor v. Nahimana, Barayagwiza and Ngeze, Judgment*, ICTR, Case No. ICTR-99-52-A, 28 November 2007, para. 912.

[57] *Prosecutor v. Bizimungu et al., Judgment and Sentence*, Case No. ICTR-99-50-T, 30 September 2011, para. 1971.

important consideration, because the law on incitement may be more lenient in States which attach great importance to free speech, than it may be under the 1948 Genocide Convention. For instance, under US law incitement is defined by the likelihood that it will provoke an immediate response.[58] Although the ICTR Chambers have struggled with the issue to what degree acts of incitement of indicted individuals have provoked an immediate response, it is undeniable that the Rwanda genocide took place and that the respective Chambers could thus easily link the acts of incitement to sudden and precipitous violence, as is required by, for example, US law.[59]

The ICTR's case law on incitement to commit genocide took off with a conviction in the *Ruggiu* case and an acquittal on that charge in the *Akayesu* case.[60] However, it is the case of *Nahimana et al.* which particularly focused on incitement and can be said to really embody the ICTR's views on incitement to commit genocide. By the Appeals Chamber in *Nahimana et al.* the ICTR underlined that 'the crime of direct and public incitement to commit genocide is an inchoate offence, punishable even if no act of genocide has resulted therefrom'.[61] But also the ICTR Appeals Chamber could not – and did not – assess the incitement charges in isolation of the fact that genocide was committed in Rwanda. It held that 'in some circumstances, the fact that a speech leads to acts of genocide could be an indication that in that particular context the speech was understood to be an incitement to commit genocide and that this was indeed the intent of the author of the speech.'[62] Does a reasoning *a contrario*, imply that the fact that the speech did not lead to (acts of) genocide is an indication that the author of the speech did not possess the required genocidal intent underlying the incitement? Although the Appeals Chamber confirmed the proactive and R2P dimension concerning the incitement to genocide – by confirming its punishability even if no act of genocide resulted – the question still remains unanswered whether the genocidal intent required for incitement can be proven without the commission of genocidal acts provoked by the incitement. As a result, with regard to the crime of incitement to commit genocide, the ICTR case law has done fairly little to contribute to an R2P interpretation of this mode of liability.

---

[58] *Brandenburg v. Ohio.*   [59] *Ibid.*

[60] *Prosecutor v. Ruggiu, Judgment and Sentence,* Case No. ICTR-97-32-I, 1 June 2000, paras. 16ff., and *Prosecutor v. Akayesu, Judgment,* Case No. ICTR-96-4-T, 2 September 1998, para. 557.

[61] *Prosecutor v. Nahimana et al., Appeals Judgment,* para. 678.   [62] *Ibid.,* para. 709.

Conclusion

The ICTY and ICTR are widely regarded as the first laboratories of contemporary international criminal justice. And rightly so, since their functioning over the past decade and a half has assisted us significantly in reaching a better understanding of the dynamics and underlying assumptions of international criminal justice. One of these assumptions is that international criminal tribunals are vital tools and mechanisms in ensuring the States and international community's responsibility to protect. This chapter analysed and evaluated the contribution of the Tribunals to R2P from two angles. First, it critically analysed the assumption that the Tribunals can contribute to a climate of deterrence in respect of international crimes. Second, it explored the R2P elements in the Tribunals' substantive and procedural criminal law and addressed the question whether the Tribunals have paid particular attention to interpreting, applying and developing their substantive and procedural criminal law from an R2P perspective.

In conclusion, it can be said that the ICTY and ICTR's contribution to deterring (future) perpetrators is significantly weakened by a number of complicating factors:

(1) the dynamics of violent conflict and immediate needs of warfare;
(2) the inseparability of law and politics and the Tribunals' institutional dependence on States;
(3) the heterogeneity of constituencies and corresponding norms and values that generate a plurality of concepts of criminal behaviour, concepts of justice and approaches to accountability.

These factors seem to undermine the perceived impartiality and legitimacy of the tribunals and their contribution to deterrence.

Furthermore, in spite of the many contributions the ICTY and ICTR have made to the development of international criminal justice, an R2P agenda was not present or pursued by either of them. Several factors explain the lack of attention given to R2P in the ICTY and ICTR context, as well as their very traditional and reactive approach to crime. Certainly the limited temporal jurisdiction in the case of the ICTR and the urgency and focus on having them address crimes committed, resulted in a diminished R2P perspective. Probably even more important is that R2P as an important notion of international law and policy was accepted more than a decade after the creation of the Tribunals.

The experiences of the Tribunals have taught us two important lessons in respect of R2P and international criminal justice. First, the assumptions underlying the expectation of deterrence are by and large under-developed and also painfully unproven. A suitable framework needs to be put in place to test such expectations and – more broadly – assess the effects and effectiveness of international criminal justice mechanisms. Second, it is unfortunate that mechanisms of international criminal justice remain extremely conservative in comparison to their domestic counterparts when it comes to preventive steps. To put it simply, whereas at the national level there is a clear trend to trigger the intervention of criminal justice mechanisms prior to the actual commission of crimes, such trend is largely missing at the international level. The ICTY and ICTR, being very much ad hoc and reactive responses of the international community to grave violations of human rights and humanitarian law, have little to offer in terms of legacy to the International Criminal Court in this respect. It is the nature of the ICC as a permanent court that should open the eyes of involved stakeholders as to its enormous potential to not only react to the commission of international crimes, but also to seek their prevention.

18

The International Criminal Court

MICHAEL CONTARINO AND MELINDA
NEGRÓN-GONZALES

Introduction

The International Criminal Court (ICC or Court) and the responsibility to protect (R2P) principle are both recent innovations of the international community.[1] Both are focused on atrocity crimes, and both are in formative stages, during which their legitimacy, viability and reach are being established. R2P obliges governments to prevent and stop genocide, war crimes, crimes against humanity and ethnic cleansing. The ICC's mandate is to punish and deter genocide, war crimes, crimes against humanity and the crime of aggression. Because of this substantially common focus, the ICC and R2P face similar obstacles. To the extent that R2P is consolidated in the years ahead as a robust international norm, this will help strengthen the mandate, and therefore the legitimacy and the power of the ICC. Similarly, a strong and authoritative ICC could become a powerful tool for the enforcement of the R2P norm, and for the continued re-enforcement of R2P as a robust, 'taken-for-granted' part of the international normative architecture.[2]

The ICC already has had some significant successes – 159 countries have signed the Rome Statute, and 122 countries have ratified it. The Court has

---

The authors thank Kevin T. Mason for his invaluable assistance with the preparation of this chapter.

[1] Rome Statute of the International Criminal Court, adopted 17 July 1998 and entered into force 1 July 2002, 2187 UNTS 90; International Commission on Intervention and State Sovereignty, *The Responsibility to Protect* (Ottawa: International Development Research Centre, 2001). See also '2005 World Summit Outcome', UN Doc. A/RES/60/1, 24 October 2005, paras. 138–40; The UN Security Council first reaffirmed R2P as outlined in the World Summit Outcome Document in UNSC Res. 1674, UN Doc. S/RES/1674, 28 April 2006.

[2] A seminal work on how international norms become 'taken for granted' is Martha Finnemore and Kathryn Sikkink, 'International Norm Dynamics and Political Change', *International Organization*, 52 (1998), 887–917.

also intervened in several situations, establishing its presence and demonstrating its ability to act when the requisite political support is forthcoming. But the ICC also continues to meet with resistance and even hostility, and several important countries have yet to join, including India, USA, Russia and China.[3] The last three of these are permanent members of the UN Security Council (UNSC, Security Council or Council). Recent failure of the Council to refer the Syrian situation to the ICC reveals the limited ability of the ICC to promote R2P in non-States Parties without the support of the powers that dominate the UNSC.

This chapter will consider some potential synergies between R2P and the ICC, as well as some of the legal and political limits to the ICC's ability to promote R2P. We address the following issues: (1) the ICC legal framework's suitability for promoting R2P objectives; (2) the policies and strategies of the ICC Prosecutor; (3) the relationship between the UNSC and the ICC; (4) the ability of the ICC to fulfil the R2P prevention function, including possible tensions between the ICC's pursuit of justice and the goal of peace.

The ICC's legal framework and the responsibility to protect

The important contributions the ICC may make to R2P have been noted often by governments, senior international civil servants, and ICC officers themselves. Most emphasise the role that ICC actions and jurisprudence can play in clarifying the meaning of R2P, and in boosting its enforcement. ICC Chief Prosecutor Luis Moreno-Ocampo, for example, noted in a 2006 keynote address that 'the International Criminal Court could add legitimacy to the Security Council's decision to apply the Responsibility to Protect concept',[4] and he stressed that the common goals of the ICC and R2P mean that they may strengthen one another:

---

[3] See Michael Contarino and Selena Lucent, 'Stopping the Killing: The International Criminal Court and the Responsibility to Protect', *Global Responsibility to Protect*, 1 (2009), 560–83; Megan Fairlie, 'The United States and the International Criminal Court Post-Bush: A Beautiful Courtship but an Unlikely Marriage', *Berkeley Journal of International Law*, 29 (2011), 528–76; Liling Yue, 'Some thoughts on the obstacles to China's accession to the Rome Statute: national sovereignty and human rights', paper prepared for Symposium on the International Criminal Court, Beijing, 3–4 February 2007; Bakhtiyar Tuzmukhamedov, 'The ICC and Russian Constitutional Problems', *Journal of International Criminal Justice*, 3 (2003), 621–6.

[4] Luis Moreno-Ocampo, 'Keynote address', unofficial transcript, speech delivered at the Responsibility to Protect: Engaging America, Chicago, 16 November 2006, at www. R2Pcoalition.org/content/view/61/86. However, the Prosecutorial Policy of 2009–12 and

Let me review the common ground of both ideas, because the scheme envisioned by the Responsibility to Protect where each individual State has the primary responsibility to protect its populations from genocide, war crimes, ethnic cleansing and crimes against humanity, including the prevention of such crimes, and the idea that the international community will only step in when a State is failing to do so is very much the scheme retained in Rome for the International Criminal Court.[5]

At a July 2011 UN General Assembly 'Informal Interactive Dialogue on the Role of Regional and Sub-regional Arrangements in Implementing the Responsibility to Protect' many delegates emphasised the importance of the ICC in promoting R2P. The EU delegate emphasised the *prevention* aspect of R2P:

The EU is determined to put an end to the impunity of perpetrators of mass atrocities. International justice, and in particular the International Criminal Court, can be a powerful tool to prevent the most serious human rights violations.[6]

Many State delegations expressed similar views. For example, the Swedish representative stressed both the role of the ICC in the R2P prevention function and *the need for non-States Parties to join the Court* in order to strengthen its capacity to uphold R2P:

[W]e must acknowledge the link between prevention and accountability, and the closely related role of the International Criminal Court . . . we strongly urge the International Community to ratify the Rome Statute and to co-operate with the ICC.[7]

The Japanese representative expressed similar concerns:

[U]niversalization of the ICC through expanding its membership will play a crucial role for the prevention of the four serious crimes which the concept of the responsibility to protect is supposed to address.[8]

several other documents produced by the ICC's Office of the Prosecutor do not refer to R2P. See ICC OTP, 'Prosecutorial Strategy (2009–2012)', 1 February 2010; ICC OTP, 'Three Year Report', June 2006; and other OTP reports available at www.icc-cpi.int/Menus/ICC/Structure +of+the+Court/Office+of+the+Prosecutor/Policies+and+Strategies.

[5] *Ibid.*

[6] Pedro Serrano, Former Head of EU Delegation, 'Statement as written', speech delivered at the Role of Regional and Sub-regional Arrangements in Implementing the Responsibility to Protect, New York, 12 July 2011, pp. 3–4, at www.responsibilitytoprotect.org/EU%20Stmt.pdf.

[7] Mårten Grunditz, Ambassador of Sweden, 'Statement as written', speech delivered at the Role of Regional and Sub-regional Arrangements in Implementing the Responsibility to Protect, New York, 12 July 2011, at www.responsibilitytoprotect.org/Sweden(3).pdf.

[8] Tsuneo Nishida, Ambassador of Japan, 'Statement as written', the Role of Regional and Sub-regional Arrangements in Implementing the Responsibility to Protect, New York, 12 July 2011, p. 1, at www.responsibilitytoprotect.org/Japan%20stmt.pdf.

Many governments emphasised the importance for R2P of *accountability* for atrocity crimes before the ICC. The Liechtenstein representative (at the time also the President of the Assembly of States Parties of the ICC) noted that this also requires the *UNSC to provide the ICC with robust support*:

> We do believe that having accountability mechanisms in place, in particular the International Criminal Court, can be important in implementing the R2P concept, in particular in relation to situations where a State is not a State party to the Rome Statute; that is where the Security Council can refer a situation to the Court. However, this can only be effective if the Council is also determined to take follow-up action on a referral and to enforce cooperation with action taken by the ICC.[9]

The Swiss representative stressed the *link between prevention and accountability* before ICC:

> [T]he fight against impunity goes hand in hand with prevention. If the preventive impact of international justice is to be strengthened, a set of instruments must be developed that enable impunity to be combated more systematically. Recently, the international community has for example repeatedly used investigation committees and fact-finding commissions. It is important from the outset that the mandates of such commissions are formulated in unambiguous terms, that their procedures are well designed and that the nature of any links they may have to judicial bodies, such as the International Criminal Court, is clearly defined.[10]

That governments see a major role for the Court in the implementation of R2P principles was made concrete with the 2011 UNSC Resolution 1970, which referred the situation in Libya to the ICC. While the UNSC had embraced R2P in earlier resolutions, the Security Council resolutions on Libya were the first time the Council took coercive action against a government based on its failure to fulfil its responsibility to protect. It is notable that it was in this context that the ICC was engaged by the UNSC as a central mechanism to punish perpetrators.

---

[9] Christian Wenaweser, Ambassador of Liechtenstein, 'Statement as written', the Role of Regional and Sub-regional Arrangements in Implementing the Responsibility to Protect, New York, 12 July 2011, p. 3, at www.responsibilitytoprotect.org/Liechtenstein.pdf.

[10] Paul Seger, Ambassador of Switzerland, 'Statement as written', unofficial translation, the Role of Regional and Sub-regional Arrangements in Implementing the Responsibility to Protect, 12 July 2011, pp. 3–4, at www.responsibilitytoprotect.org/Switzerland%20Stmt(1).pdf.

The ability of the ICC to respond swiftly was impressive: the Court completed its preliminary examination and decided to open an investigation in only five days. Arrest warrants for Gaddafi, his son and spy chief were speedily issued. Proponents of intervention claimed that the UNSC referral sent a clear signal to tyrants that their crimes would not go unpunished and that the ICC was the legitimate arbiter of justice. This action was potentially an important step toward demonstrating that the Court can be an effective instrument of R2P enforcement.

ICC jurisprudence may over time strengthen R2P in another way: by helping to clarify what acts constitute specific atrocity crimes.[11] For example, in the Darfur situation, the ICC had to determine whether or not the specific acts taking place there constituted genocide. In May 2004, the US State Department defined ethnically targeted killings, rape and displacement as 'genocide', when it brought the situation to the UNSC. The Security Council established the International Commission of Inquiry into Darfur, but its report concluded that the Sudanese government was guilty of crimes against humanity, not genocide. Several weeks after the Darfur Commission released its report, the UNSC referred the situation to the ICC. In 2005, Prosecutor Moreno-Ocampo reported to the UNSC that he found evidence of mass killing, rape and other gender violence in Darfur, and in 2008 he requested the issuance of an arrest warrant for President al-Bashir, for three counts of genocide. The following year, ICC judges found that the Prosecutor had failed to provide sufficient *indicia* that the Sudanese government acted with specific intent to destroy the groups. Accordingly, they issued a warrant of arrest for crimes against humanity and war crimes. The Prosecutor appealed, arguing that the judges' standard for issuing a

---

[11] Patricia Wald, 'Genocide and Crimes against Humanity', *Washington University Global Studies Law Review*, 6 (2007), 621–33. Lack of consensus regarding the distinction between genocide and crimes against humanity was evident in opinions of International Criminal Tribunal for the former Yugoslavia (ICTY) judges. William Schabas explains, 'judgments of different trial chambers of the ICTY have taken the [genocide] law in opposite directions'. For example, one ruling concludes that 'forcible transfer of a population' can constitute genocide, while another ruling states that only physical and biological destruction constitute genocide. See Schabas, 'Has Genocide Been Committed in Darfur? The State Plan or Policy Element in the Crime of Genocide', in Ralph Henham and Paul Behrens (eds.), *The Criminal Law of Genocide: International, Comparative and Contextual Aspects* (Aldershot, UK; Burlington, VT: Ashgate, 2007), pp. 39–48. See also Schabas, 'Genocide, Crimes against Humanity and Darfur: The Commission of Inquiry's Findings on Genocide', *Cardozo Law Review*, 27 (2006), 1703–21.

warrant for genocide was too high, and in 2010 ICC judges issued a second arrest warrant for al-Bashir, including three counts of genocide. ICC proceedings have not yet defined the dividing line between genocide and crimes against humanity, but the nature of the Court's activities virtually compels the institution to address such issues, and the Court also has demonstrated that it is able and willing to do so. It is reasonable to expect that the ICC will continue to play an important role in clarifying issues relating to individual criminal responsibility for atrocity crimes.

However, the ICC's legal framework also limits the Court's ability to prevent and adjudicate atrocity crimes. First, while the ICC's mandate is to prosecute substantially the same crimes cited in the 2005 UNGA World Summit Outcome, the Court's jurisdiction is limited to States Parties – absent a UNSC referral or self-referral by a non-State Party. Furthermore, Article 16 of the Rome Statute allows the UNSC to temporarily suspend ICC proceedings and to renew such suspensions. In short, while R2P is a principle of general application, the Court is not legally empowered to act globally. If the Security Council does not act, the Court may be powerless, even in the face of grave atrocity crimes taking place in non-States Parties.

Compared to the ad hoc tribunals for the former Yugoslavia (ICTY) and Rwanda (ICTR), the ICC has relatively weak enforcement capacity. The ICC's ability to engage national governments as surrogate enforcers has been limited by the unwillingness of some non-States Parties to cooperate,[12] as was evidenced in June 2011, when the Chinese government provided a red-carpet welcome to Sudanese President al-Bashir, who was subject to an ICC arrest warrant.[13] The ad hoc tribunals have

---

[12] See Victor Peskin, 'The International Criminal Court, the Security Council, and the Politics of Impunity in Darfur', *Genocide Studies and Prevention*, 4 (2009), 304–28.

[13] When the UNSC referred the Darfur and Libya situations to the ICC, it obliged governments to 'cooperate fully', while also recognising that non-States Parties 'have no obligation under the Rome Statute'. '*Decides* that the Government of Sudan and all other parties to the conflict in Darfur shall cooperate fully with and provide any necessary assistance to the Court and the Prosecutor pursuant to this resolution and, while recognizing that States not party to the Rome Statute have no obligation under the Statute, urges all States and concerned regional and other international organizations to cooperate fully' (UNSC Res. 1593, UN Doc. S/RES/1593, 31 March 2005, para. 2); '*Decides* that the Libyan authorities shall cooperate fully with and provide any necessary assistance to the Court and the Prosecutor pursuant to this resolution and, while recognizing that States not party to the Rome Statute have no obligation under the Statute, urges all States and concerned regional and other international organizations to

mandates from the UNSC and jurisdictional primacy – enabling prosecutors to be forceful and to get the cooperation even of reluctant States. The Rome Statute, by contrast, lays the foundation for a more 'consensual' relationship between the Court and States. Victor Peskin explains:

> Whereas the Security Council established the *ad hoc* ICTY and ICTR, the ICC was created by a multilateral treaty to which states have to consent in order to join. And whereas the ICTY and ICTR have enjoyed primacy *vis-à-vis* states and the legal authority to usurp domestic judiciaries, the ICC is more deferential because it is only authorized to prosecute when a state is either unwilling or unable to do so itself.[14]

Peskin here is referring, of course, to the principle of complementarity, which has complex implications for the Court's efficacy regarding R2P. Clearly, complementarity restricts the ICC, by limiting its jurisdiction. But complementarity also enables the ICC to promote accountability indirectly, by assigning R2P responsibility to governments, and pressuring them to hold trials if they wish to avoid ICC intervention. As Prosecutor Moreno-Ocampo put it in 2003:

> As a consequence of complementarity, the number of cases that reach the Court should not be a measure of its efficiency. On the contrary, the absence of trials before this Court, as a consequence of the regular functioning of national institutions, would be a major success.[15]

Colombia's legal reform shows how complementarity may enable the ICC to directly assist governments seeking to meet R2P goals. The ICC had a clear impact on Colombia's Justice and Peace Law, the country's primary framework for transitional justice,[16] and Colombian Supreme Court judges have referred to the ICC in their definitions of crimes against humanity, and in their decision to prosecute, rather than extradite drug-traffickers.[17] Héctor Olásolo has noted the critical importance of the ICC to national authorities:

> Despite the international cooperation of other stakeholders the national authorities of receptive states appear to have a strong preference to receive advice and guidance directly from ICC officials. As national

cooperate fully with the Court and the Prosecutor' (UNSC Res. 1970, UN Doc. S/RES/ 1970, 26 February 2011, para. 5).

[14] Peskin, 'International Criminal Court', 312–13.

[15] ICC OTP, 'Informal Expert Paper: The Principle of Complementarity in Practice', ICC Doc. ICC-01/04-01/07-1008-AnxA, 30 March 2003, p. 3.

[16] Alejandro Chetman, *The ICC and Its Normative Impact on Colombia's Legal System* (Reykjavik: DOMAC, 2011), p. 5.

[17] *Ibid.*, p. 32.

authorities are aware that their efforts to adjudicate atrocity crimes will be reviewed by the ICC, the ICC's advice and guidance is considered of the utmost importance to ensure the success of such efforts. As a result, the potential of the ICC to strengthen through timely intervention the rule of law and improve good governance in receptive states is major.[18]

Complementarity may also strengthen the ICC's ability to support R2P in yet another, somewhat paradoxical way. Complementarity, like R2P, is based on a State's primary responsibility to protect its population. The ICC is a court of last resort, and will not intervene if States enforce R2P themselves. Thus complementarity makes the ICC less threatening to States, by minimising the Court's intrusion into traditional State pre-rogatives. Over time, an ICC that is careful and prudent may impact positively how international actors come to accept or reject the ideas and attitudes that undergird R2P.

Complementarity requires that the ICC defer to domestic investigations and prosecutions, but this means that the Court must ascertain whether a bona fide investigation or prosecution is taking place. The ICC may determine that a case should come before it under the complementarity principle if national proceedings were initiated to shield alleged criminals, or were not conducted independently or impartially. Darfur tested the principle, because Sudan had created special tribunals to try individuals suspected of war crimes, but had failed to actually prosecute the alleged criminals of concern to the ICC. In the ICC case against Thomas Lubanga Dyilo, who was accused of war crimes in the Democratic Republic of Congo – for which he has since been convicted – the Court had determined that national proceedings must 'encompass both the person and the conduct which is the subject of the case before the Court'.[19] Although the special Sudanese tribunals tried some low-level suspects, they failed to prosecute Ahmad Muhammad Harun and Ali Muhammad Ali Abd-Al-Rahman (Ali Kushayb), whose ICC arrest warrants for war crimes and crimes against humanity had been issued in May 2007. Because the Sudanese courts were not trying the suspects

---

[18] Héctor Olásolo, 'The role of the International Criminal Court in preventing atrocity crimes through timely intervention', inaugural lecture as Chair of International Criminal Law and International Criminal Procedure at the University of Utrecht, 18 October 2010, available at http://vkc.library.uu.nl.

[19] Christopher Totten and Nicholas Tyler, 'Arguing for an Integrated Approach to Resolving the Crisis in Darfur: The Challenges of Complementarity, Enforcement, and Related Issues in the International Criminal Court', *Journal of Criminal Law and Criminology*, 98 (2008), 1069–118, at 1095.

cited by the ICC, nor were they addressing the specific crimes cited in the ICC's case, the Court determined that it could move forward with these cases without violating the principle of complementarity.[20] The care which the Court has shown to justify when it may prosecute could mitigate fears of those concerned that the Court might adopt an excessively broad conception of complementarity.

The issue of complementarity is again evident as actors decide how to proceed against Saif al-Islam Gaddafi and Abdullah al-Sanousi for alleged crimes against humanity in Libya during 2011. The Libya situation is particularly important because it was the first time the UNSC simultaneously referred a situation to the Court while explicitly invoking R2P, and thereby directly linking the ICC and R2P. In 'R2P, the ICC and the Libyan arrests',[21] Carsten Stahn examined a variety of legal issues pertaining to the ICC prerogatives. He noted that ICC action mandated by the UNSC referral 'makes the Court an agent of peace-maintenance. The Pre-Trial Chamber has issued warrants of arrest. An international "case" exists, and judicial proceedings have started.' Stahn argues that this means that even if prosecution proceeds at the national level, ICC involvement will continue regarding the situation in Libya.[22]

Such involvement has been encouraged even by some influential Libyans. In an interview with the International Center for Transitional Justice, Tarik El Tumi, programme director for Libyan NGO Lawyers for Justice stated: 'The role of the ICC is to assess the willingness and ability of the Libyan judiciary to prosecute Saif [al-Islam Gaddafi] and Abdullah Senussi. The willingness is undoubtedly there. In the instance that there is a lack of ability, the ICC's role could very well be to mobilise on the

---

[20] *Ibid.*, citing ICC OTP, 'Fifth Report of the Prosecutor of the International Criminal Court to the UN Security Council', 7 June 2007, at www.amicc.org/docs/OTP_ReportUNSC5-Darfur_English.pdf.

[21] Carsten Stahn, 'R2P, the ICC and the Libyan Arrests', *The Hague Justice Portal*, 24 November 2011, at www.haguejusticeportal.net/index.php?id=12998.

[22] Stahn considers options ranging from a UNSC request not to proceed to ICC deferral to domestic authorities, to domestic authorities requesting the ICC Prosecutor to withdraw or amend charges. He also considers the problem posed by the fact that the ICC Statute does not include the death penalty, noting that 'it is controversial to what extent potential human rights violations to the detriment of the defendant should be taken into account in the determination of admissibility assessments under the Statute since they concern primarily jurisdictional issues *per se*.' Stahn concludes that 'a deferral of proceedings to Libyan authorities following the issuance of warrants of arrest, and in the absence of prior international custody over defendants, would mark a novelty in international criminal justice' (*ibid.*).

ground to support the Libyan judiciary's ability to prosecute.'[23] El Tumi also envisions an active role for the ICC, among other international institutions, in the rebuilding of Libya: 'With the right technical assistance and the right initiatives for capacity building from the international community – from the ICC, the UN, and the international development community – as well as from Libyan lawyers from the diaspora, we can help them develop their capacity in such a way as to meet the challenges of post-revolutionary Libya.'[24]

At the time of writing, the ICC has ordered Libya to surrender Saif Gaddafi to the Court's custody, but the Libyan authorities have asserted that he will be tried in Libya. Libya is obligated, under UNSC Resolution 1970, to cooperate with the Court, and Article 87(7) of the Rome Statute allows the ICC to refer non-cooperation to the UNSC for further action.[25] But the Libyans have held him for months, and intend to continue to hold him and eventually try him. The risk for the ICC is that even if Libya were found to be in non-compliance, the UNSC might again fail to assist in enforcing the arrest warrants, revealing again how reliant the ICC is upon the UNSC.

The ICC prosecutorial policy and the responsibility to protect

Within the legal parameters of the Rome Statute, the decisions made by the Office of the Prosecutor (OTP) guide the juridical processes and outcomes of ICC investigations and trials.[26] The Prosecutor enjoys considerable discretionary power within the Court, but he or she is also accountable to States Parties, which can either facilitate or undermine the Court's investigations and trials. Former Prosecutor Moreno-Ocampo faced the daunting task of trying to accomplish two somewhat contradictory objectives: to demonstrate the Court's impartiality in the pursuit of justice, and to satisfy the expectations of important State actors, including States Parties and powerful non-States Parties, such as the US.

---

[23] 'El Tumi: Libyans Want to See Justice Done in Libyan Courts', International Center for Transnational Justice, 3 January 2012, at www.ictj.org/news/el-tumi-libyans-want-see-justice-done-libyan-courts#.

[24] *Ibid.*   [25] Rome Statute, art. 87(7).

[26] See Matthew Brubacher, 'Prosecutorial Discretion within the International Criminal Court', *Journal of International Criminal Justice*, 2 (2004), 71–95; Schabas, 'Prosecutorial Discretion v. Judicial Activism at the International Criminal Court,' *Journal of International Criminal Justice*, 6 (2008), 731–61; David Kaye, 'Who's Afraid of the International Criminal Court?', *Foreign Affairs*, May/June 2011.

An examination of the Court's first decade suggests that former Prosecutor Moreno-Ocampo was always careful not to alienate powerful States (for example, by deciding not to move forward on communications regarding US actions in Iraq),[27] suggesting sensitivity to political realities. Moreno-Ocampo was both praised and criticised for this deference to State actors. Supporters applauded his political realism, but critics argued that he was too submissive, did not employ his *proprio motu* powers enough, and targeted rebel groups more than government officials.[28]

Moreno-Ocampo rarely discussed the link between the ICC and R2P. Exceptions to this rule include his statements made in his 2006 keynote address on 'The Responsibility to Protect – Engaging America'.[29] He also stated that the ICC and the R2P principle have the potential to strengthen one another given their common objectives.[30] But with the exceptions of these and a few other public remarks, Moreno-Ocampo avoided framing the work of the Court in R2P terms, and various OTP reports, including the Prosecutorial Strategy for 2009–12 failed to even mention R2P.[31]

Former Prosecutor Moreno-Ocampo's choice not to embrace R2P too frequently reflected his generally cautious approach. Aware of political constraints, he was careful in the use of his discretionary powers. He followed a policy of encouraging referrals from States Parties, rather than acting on his own,[32] and did not use Article 15 *proprio motu* powers until the 2009 independent referral on Kenya,[33] even though Article 15 would have allowed him to initiate investigations.

However, the Prosecutor did begin shifting to a more assertive strategy in 2007.[34] In Uganda, peace talks between the government and the Lord's

---

[27] ICC OTP, 'Letter from the Office of the Prosecutor Re: Iraq', 9 February 2009, at www.iccnow.org/documents/OTP_letter_to_senders_re_Iraq_9_February_2006.pdf.

[28] See Phil Clark, 'State impunity in Central Africa', *New York Times*, 1 April 2012, at www.nytimes.com/2012/04/02/opinion/02iht-edclark.html?_r=1; Clark, 'Law, Politics and Pragmatism: The ICC and Case Selection in the Democratic Republic of Congo and Uganda', in Nicholas Waddell and Phil Clark (eds.), *Courting Conflict? Justice, Peace and the ICC in Africa* (London: Royal African Society, 2008), pp. 37–46, at pp. 42–4; and Angelo Izama, 'Accomplice to Impunity? Rethinking the Political Strategy of the International Criminal Court in Central Africa', *School of Advanced International Studies Review*, 29 (2009), 51–60.

[29] Moreno-Ocampo, 'Keynote address'. [30] *Ibid.*

[31] See the OTP reports at n. 4, above. [32] Peskin, 'Impunity in Darfur'.

[33] ICC Pre-Trial Chamber II, 'Decision Pursuant to Article 15 of the Rome Statute on the Authorization of an Investigation into the Situation in the Republic of Kenya', ICC Doc. ICC-01/09-19, 31 March 2010.

[34] See Peskin, 'Caution and Confrontation in the International Criminal Court's Pursuit of Accountability in Uganda and Sudan', *Human Rights Quarterly*, 31 (2009), 655–91.

Resistance Army (LRA) led to domestic and international pressure on Moreno-Ocampo to drop his bid for arrest warrants of five LRA leaders – but he refused to back down. Peskin argues that 'Moreno-Ocampo's shift to an adversarial stance' was strategic, based upon 'the diminishing prospects of cooperation'.[35]

Prosecutorial assertiveness in recent years has not always worked, however, as can be seen in Sudanese President al-Bashir's defiance of the Court. Moreno-Ocampo even angered African leaders generally supportive of both the ICC and R2P. The African Union (AU) has embraced the International Criminal Court and the concept of R2P, including the 'third pillar' (international intervention), but has expressed discomfort with former-colonial powers intervening in African affairs, and has emphasised a regional conception of how to enforce compliance with R2P.[36] The AU has objected to what it sees as an excessive ICC focus on Africa, and even directed its members not to cooperate with ICC arrest warrants for al-Bashir[37] and Gaddafi.[38] On 14 July 2010, AU Commission Chairman Jean Ping criticised Moreno-Ocampo's requesting arrest warrants: 'This charge does not solve the problem in Darfur. In fact, it is the contrary . . . We have no problem with the ICC and we are against impunity. But the way Prosecutor Ocampo is rendering justice is the issue.'[39] Prosecutor Moreno-Ocampo's successor,

---

[35] *Ibid.*, 663.

[36] Article 4 of the AU Constitutive Act affirms: 'the right of the Union to intervene in a Member State pursuant to a decision of the assembly in respect of grave circumstances, namely: war crimes, genocide and crimes against humanity' and 'the right of Member States to request intervention from the Union in order to restore peace and security' (Constitutive Act of the African Union, adopted 11 July 2000 and entered into force 26 May 2001, 2158 UNTS 3, art. 4(h) and (j)). Africans have embraced the idea of regional responsibility through the Economic Community of West African States (ECOWAS), as early as the (pre-ICISS) humanitarian interventions into Liberia and Sierra Leone in the 1990s.

[37] African Union, 'Decision on the Meeting of African Parties to the Rome Statute of the International Criminal Court (ICC)', AU Doc. Assembly/AU/Dec.245(XIII) Rev.1, 3 July 2009. In paragraph 10 of this document the AU decided the AU Member States shall not cooperate pursuant to the provisions of Article 98 of the Rome Statute of the ICC relating to immunities, for the arrest and surrender of President Omar al-Bashir of the Sudan.

[38] Associated Press, 'African Union opposes warrant for Qaddafi', *New York Times*, 4 July 2011, at www.nytimes.com/2011/07/03/world/africa/03african.html.

[39] 'AU: Bashir charges won't help Darfur', *Washington Times*, 14 July 2010, at www.washingtontimes.com/news/2010/jul/14/briefly-93-15958/?page=1. Regarding the 2008 ICC arrest warrant for Bashir, Ping stated, 'While we are trying to extinguish the fire here without troops, we don't understand very well that they chose that moment to put more oil on the fire by taking the decision' ('AU stands against Bashir arrest', BBC, 4 August 2008, at http://news.bbc.co.uk/2/hi/africa/7541488.stm).

Fatou Bensouda, is an African lawyer endorsed by the AU.[40] Her term will test whether an African Prosecutor will be able to mitigate tensions between the AU and the ICC.

Another criticism launched against Moreno-Ocampo is that he focused too much on rebel groups rather than on State perpetrators and patrons. For example, the ICC pursued LRA rebel leaders, but not LRA's sponsor, Sudan.[41] Likewise, the Court did not hold the Ugandan government responsible for its support of Sudan People's Liberation Army. Izama notes:

> [T]he fact that the Ugandan government hasn't been investigated by the court for its own participation in the atrocities inflicted on the population of northern Uganda (caused during a brutal counterinsurgency campaign), makes the strategy of the ICC look piecemeal, at best, targeting impunity in certain corners but not in others, and thus not thinking holistically about the court's own potential involvement in the prevention of future flare-ups between these different actors.[42]

The former Prosecutor's choices in the Great Lakes region faced criticism even from Human Rights Watch (HRW), an ICC supporter. A 2011 HRW report questioned the decision to target Mr Lubanga, of the Hema tribe, but not enemies in the Lendu tribe.[43] Almost eighteen months after Lubanga's 2006 arrest, in an attempt to correct perceived bias, arrest warrants were issued for two Lendu leaders, Germain Katanga in 2007 and Mathieu Ngudjolo in 2008. But the charges brought against them were more extensive than those brought against Mr Lubanga, who was accused only of recruiting minors. Locals were once again angered at the perceived disparity.[44]

In the latter years of his tenure, the former Prosecutor has sought to be more attentive to local political realities, and to deliberately target leaders from both sides of conflicts. In Kenya, the ICC indicted an equal number from the two groups and promised to make a single announcement

---

[40] Bensouda was officially endorsed during the AU Executive Council Nineteenth Ordinary Session. AU, 'Decision on African Candidatures for Posts within the International System', AU Doc. EX.CL/Dec.664(XIX), 23–28 June 2011.

[41] Al-Bashir was indicted on charges of atrocity crimes in Sudan, but not for his sponsorship of the Lord's Resistance Army.

[42] Izama, 'Accomplice to Impunity', 54.

[43] *Unfinished Business: Closing Gaps in the Selection of ICC Cases* (New York: Human Rights Watch, 2011).

[44] 'Cosy club or sword of righteousness?', *The Economist*, 26 November 2011, at www.economist.com/node/21540230.

regarding the trial process. On 23 January 2012, the Court announced decisions on all six indictments; four of the individuals indicted, two from each tribe, had their charges confirmed by Pre-Trial Chamber II.[45] However, perceived disparities remain, and some have criticised the Court for targeting the Kalenjins and Kikuyus but not the Luo.[46]

After nearly a decade in operation, the ICC has completed only one trial,[47] and many of its arrest warrants remain unenforced. Perpetrators continue to go unpunished. To some extent, these shortcomings are the result of resource constraints – ICC lacks the resources and personnel to analyse and understand many local situations, and to pursue more perpetrators. But more resources alone would not overcome the Court's inherent enforcement weaknesses and the political constraints it faces. While some attribute the Court's failures to the Prosecutor, clearly the Court is encumbered by political constraints that make its task exceedingly challenging.

The UN Security Council and the International Criminal Court: implications for the responsibility to protect

Atrocity crimes are referable to the Court by the UN Security Council, even when they occur in non-States Parties. The Rome Statute preamble also notes that the crimes falling under ICC jurisdiction 'threaten the peace, security and well-being of the world'. During the ICC's first decade, the UNSC has frequently found itself involved in situations concerning the Rome Statute's four crimes.[48] The relationship between the ICC and the UNSC is direct, important, and complex. In some instances, the relationship between the two bodies is complementary. The UNSC may use the ICC effectively when it refers an R2P situation to the Court, as it did in the Libyan situation. Or it may use the Court somewhat less effectively, as it did in the Sudan situation. The UNSC also may halt ICC action through Article 16, which enables the UNSC to suspend ICC cases for renewable one-year periods, if those cases are determined to pose a threat to international peace and security. And, of course, the ICC is generally powerless in the face of atrocity crimes in

---

[45] Solomon Moore, 'Hague court charges Kenyan leaders', *Wall Street Journal*, 24 January 2012, available at http://online.wsj.com.

[46] 'Cosy club'.

[47] Thomas Lubanga Dyilo was found guilty of war crimes on 4 March 2012.

[48] Kristen Boon, 'Regime Conflicts and the UN Security Council: Applying the Law of Responsibility', *George Washington International Law Review*, 42 (2010), 787–834, at 820.

non-States Parties, unless referred by the UNSC, and – as the al-Bashir case shows – the Court may be unable to ensure cooperation with its orders in the absence of Security Council willingness to back up a referral with meaningful enforcement.

The proximity of their powers requires that the ICC and the UNSC cooperate, and both institutions may be strengthened when they do so, as in the Libyan situation. But tensions between the two bodies also may arise. For example, the UNSC has engaged issues that the Court has concerned itself with, such as the exploitation of children in armed conflict, and the protection of civilians in armed conflict.[49] Boon notes that this may create conflicts between States Parties' obligations to the Court, and their responsibilities as UN members. The Security Council may impose sanctions under Article 41 of the UN Charter and may limit international contact with States where there is evidence of international crimes. It could, therefore, legally prohibit payments or assistance to States whose leaders are under investigation by the ICC, which might interfere with States Parties' ability to cooperate with the Court.[50]

While UNSC resolutions are legally binding on all UN Member States, they are not technically binding upon the ICC, with the exception of referrals made under Article 16. But, Boon notes that while the Court is not directly bound by UNSC Chapter VII resolutions, 'independent responsibility for non-compliance with a Security Council resolution will fall on member States unless excused – under Article 103. These disputes place States in a double bind: should States give precedence to Security Council Chapter VII resolutions, or must they honor competing obligations owed to other institutions?'[51]

In short, a UNSC resolution could require States Parties not to fulfil their obligations to the Court. Faced with the choice between fulfilling its obligations to the Court and its obligations to the UNSC, a State probably will choose to comply with the stronger authority, the UNSC. To date, the Council has not placed the Court in such a situation, and ICC supporters in the UNSC – including veto-wielding UK and France – would likely seek to avoid such a confrontation. But some members of the Council are sceptical or even hostile to the ICC, and could potentially use the threat of confrontation to limit the Court's activities. Delay and

---

[49] *Ibid.*, 821. See UNSC Res. 1882, UN Doc. S/RES/1882, 4 August 2009; UNSC Res. 1612, UN Doc. S/RES/1612, 26 July 2005; UNSC Res. 1539, UN Doc. S/RES/1539, 22 April 2004; UNSC Res. 1674.

[50] Boon, 'Regime Conflict', 822.   [51] *Ibid.*, 804.

obstruction tactics by some Council members regarding the enforcement of arrest warrants in the Darfur situation, as well as resistance by Russia and China to addressing the situation in Syria, exemplify the capacity for the UNSC to prevent the ICC from acting, even in the case of highly-visible mass crimes in non-States Parties.

As a standing court, the ICC seeks to promote the R2P objective of replacing ad hoc enforcement of international criminal law with a more permanent, and less politicised process. But the ICC, like R2P, must rely upon enforcement mechanisms which are beyond its control and hardly insulated from politics. To the extent that the UNSC refers atrocity crimes selectively – e.g. Libya, but not Syria – both the Court and the R2P norm are undermined. Given the veto power of each of the permanent members of the UNSC (the P-5), the ICC's ability to strengthen and enforce the R2P norm will require that the Court work effectively with the UNSC, coaxing the Council over time into using the Court more routinely, and in a less politicised way. Needless to say, gaining routine access to the power of the UNSC without compromising the consistent and impartial application of international law will be a massively difficult political challenge for the Court.

Some scholars maintain that it is Article 16 that assures the Court's subordinate legal position to UNSC.[52] But UNSC has other ways to limit the ICC, even without Article 16.[53] What the ICC gains from Article 16 is the potential backing of a Council whose ultimate authority is clearly recognised. Similarly, the dependency of the ICC upon the Council for enforcement makes ICC defiance of the Council unthinkable. And to the extent that even non-States Parties know they may be held accountable

---

[52] See Morten Bergsmo and Jelena Pejić, 'Article 16: Deferral of Investigation or Prosecution', in Otto Triffterer (ed.), *Commentary on the Rome Statute of the International Criminal Court: Observers' Notes, Article by Article* (Munich, Germany; Oxford, UK: CH Beck, 2008), pp. 595–604, at p. 603, para. 23. For a different perspective, see Luigi Condorelli and Santiago Villalpando, 'Can the Security Council Extend the ICC's Jurisdiction?', in Antonio Cassese, Paola Gaeta and John Jones (eds.), *The Rome Statute of the International Criminal Court: A Commentary* (Oxford University Press, 2002), pp. 571–82, at p. 574; Condorelli and Villalpando, 'Referral and Deferral by the Security Council', in Cassese *et al.*, *Rome Statute*, pp. 627–55, at p. 650; Olásolo, *The Triggering Procedure of the International Criminal Court* (Leiden; Boston: Martinus Nijhoff, 2005), p. 178.

[53] '[Deferral] was a power that was probably never really [the Court's] to recognize since the Council could have exercise[d] it anyhow, but the gesture at least serves to project a vision of the ICC dealing with the Council at arm's length' (Frédéric Mégret, 'ICC, R2P and the International Community's Evolving Interventionist Toolkit', working paper 24, 23 December 2010, at http://papers.ssrn.com/sol3/papers.cfm?abstract_id=1933111).

by the ICC via UNSC referral, the ability of the ICC to advance R2P worldwide is potentially enhanced.

The Security Council's ability to refer R2P situations in non-States Parties became real with Sudan and Libya. While the UNSC failed to back up the Sudan referral with effective efforts to bring the perpetrators before the Court, the referral nevertheless legitimated the ICC's role in addressing such situations, while extending the Court's reach and elevating its profile. The second referral to the Court came in February 2011, regarding Libya. The subsequent Council resolution outlining the intervention in Libya also represented a watershed, as it was the first time the UNSC made reference to R2P as justification for intervention. While the Council had formally embraced R2P in earlier resolutions, UNSC Resolution 1973 was the first time the Council authorised the use of coercive action against a government based on its failure to fulfil its responsibility to protect its population.[54] It was in this context that the Court was engaged by the UNSC as a central mechanism to punish perpetrators of atrocity crimes, and as such it was a very significant moment for both the ICC and for R2P enforcement. The Court promptly issued arrest warrants, setting a precedent for its future use for R2P-related actions.

However, whatever power the Court has derived through its association with the UNSC has come at a cost. The ICC's dependency upon the UNSC regarding non-States Parties reveals the weakness of the link between, as Frédéric Mégret puts it, the 'ICC's aspiration to international criminal justice and R2P's aspiration to the absoluteness of the humanitarian imperative'.[55] Although both Security Council referrals strengthened the Court's legitimacy, the relationship between the Security Council and the Prosecutor has also been strained due to the perceived lack of support by the Council after it authorised ICC involvement. In the words of David Kaye:

> The Security Council, the very body that referred the Sudan situation to the ICC, has not stood firmly behind the arrest warrant against Bashir; it could have increased the cost of doing business with Bashir by imposing sanctions on fugitive Sudanese officials and governments that flout the arrest warrant. The Security Council may deserve credit for making the referral, but it appears uninterested in giving the court the kind of support it needs.[56]

---

[54] UNSC Res. 1973, UN Doc. S/RES/1973, 17 March 2011.
[55] Mégret, 'Interventionist Toolkit', 25.   [56] Kaye, 'Who's Afraid'.

The Security Council's unwillingness to take strong follow-up actions was at least partially because of the Prosecutor's decision to target a sitting head of State, President al-Bashir. This controversial decision[57] according to Kaye, placed the Court's credibility at risk, because the Prosecutor's ambitions exceeded his power. Indeed, even the ICC's strongest backers at the Security Council, the UK and France, have been uncharacteristically reserved in their statements, despite years of blatant non-compliance by al-Bashir and his government.

In short, while the UNSC referral was initially a boost to the Court and its prospects to support R2P in non-States Parties, the Court's failure to bring al-Bashir to justice has exposed the ICC's limitations in this very regard. For advocates of R2P who argue that the Court is a means to end the culture of impunity that exists in much of the developing world, and in Africa specifically, this has been a setback.

While the UNSC did not follow through with robust support in Sudan, the Council also did not invoke Article 16, despite al-Bashir's attempt in 2008 to strike a deal for the suspension of his case. In return for trying the two other suspects, Harun and Kushayb, al-Bashir requested his case be suspended by the Council, and initially even France and the UK were reportedly open to this idea. The plan failed due to al-Bashir's refusal to allow the ICC to perform a judicial review beforehand.[58] Even the Bush administration – which had a history of hostility to the ICC before its decision to bring Darfur to the ICC through the UNSC – also opposed invoking Article 16.[59]

So far, the Libyan situation has shown better coordination between the ICC and the UNSC than was evident regarding Sudan. The Libyan example shows that the ICC may indeed play an effective role in advancing R2P when it works in concert with the UNSC. But, to date, political deadlock in the Council has prevented similar success from taking place in Syria, showing again the ICC's subordination.

In order to advance a more consistent and universal R2P policy, the ICC likely will take any opportunity given to it by the Council, despite the appearance this creates of the Court being a tool of the UNSC. Conceivably, over time this dependency upon the UNSC might lessen,

[57] See Alex de Waal and Gregory Stanton, 'Should President al-Bashir of Sudan Be Charged and Arrested by the International Criminal Court? An Exchange of Views', *Genocide Studies and Prevention*, 4 (2009), 329–53.

[58] 'French official offers Sudan a deal to settle ICC row', *Sudan Tribune*, 4 September 2008, at www.sudantribune.com/French-official-offers-Sudan-a,28511.

[59] Peskin, 'Impunity in Darfur', 319.

if the ICC proves to be both useful and non-threatening to the governments that dominate the Council. By pursuing competently situations extended to it by the Security Council, and by being both proactive and politically astute in asking the Council for referrals and in initiating cases *proprio motu*, a more independent ICC conceivably might someday emerge. It is even possible, though not likely any time soon, that P-5 members might agree to refrain from using the veto in matters pertaining to ICC actions to support R2P.[60] But unless and until that happens, the ICC will remain subordinate to a politicised UNSC, with all the limitations this means for universal use of the Court to pursue the goals of R2P.

The International Criminal Court and prevention

The Rome Statute preamble stresses that the ICC's purpose is not just to punish, but also to prevent atrocity crimes. States Parties, it says, are '[d]etermined to put an end to impunity for the perpetrators of these crimes and thus to contribute to the prevention of such crimes'.[61] Court supporters argue that the possibility of prosecution before an international tribunal may reasonably be expected to affect the calculations of potential perpetrators of atrocity crimes: accountability, they argue, promotes restraint. As Aryeh Neier put it, the Court seeks 'that some future counterparts of Pinochet, Milošević, Pol Pot or Foday Sankoh will have to bear in mind the possibility that [international law] may eventually catch up with them'.[62]

Olásolo has noted that the ICC may help prevent atrocity crimes in various ways: like ad hoc tribunals, the ICC is capable of both 'positive general prevention' and 'negative general prevention'. He defines positive general intervention as 'upholding the application of international criminal law and reinforcing the core societal values protected therein'. Negative general prevention is the deterrence effect of holding atrocity criminals accountable. Unlike ad hoc tribunals, however, the ICC also is capable of 'timely interventions into situations where there are tangible

---

[60] See Ariela Blätter and Paul Williams, 'The Responsibility Not to Veto', *Global Responsibility to Protect*, 3 (2011), 301–22; Daniel Levine, 'Some Concerns about "The Responsibility Not to Veto"', *Global Responsibility to Protect*, 3 (2011), 323–45; Blätter and Williams, 'A Reply to Levine', *Global Responsibility to Protect*, 3 (2011), 346–51.

[61] Rome Statute, pmbl.

[62] Aryeh Neier, 'Will the International Criminal Court Make a Difference?', *Helsinki Monitor*, 12 (2001), 163–4.

threats of future atrocity crimes or where atrocity crimes are already taking place'.[63]

Of course, assessing preventive effects is exceedingly difficult, since it entails examination not of events that happened, but rather of events that did not happen. Former Prosecutor Moreno-Ocampo has cited some specific examples where he perceived the positive impact of the threat of prosecution, either directly by the ICC or through domestic courts acting in a complementary manner:

> [T]he beneficial impact of the ICC and the value of the law to prevent recurring violence is clear. Deterrence has started to show its effect as in the case of Côte d'Ivoire, where the prospect of prosecution of those using hate speech is deemed to have kept the main actors under some level of control. In Colombia, legislation and proceedings against paramilitary were influenced by the Rome provisions, and there are examples of military officials incorporating the constraints of the Rome Statute in their operational planning. In Uganda arrest warrants have contributed to bringing the LRA to the negotiating table, focused national debates on accountability and reducing crimes, and exposed the criminals and their horrendous crimes, all of which has contributed to weakening the support they were enjoying, to de-legitimizing them and their practices such as conscription of children.[64]

Critics of the ICC, however, cite literature on deterrence that shows a limited impact of the threat of punishment on much criminal behaviour.[65] They argue that rarely will perpetrators see potential prosecution by a far-away international court as a sufficient threat to alter their behaviour. Some critics also emphasise that even when the threat of punishment is real, deterrence works on rational actors calculating their odds, and such rationality is unlikely in contexts of lawlessness, social

---

[63] Olásolo, 'Timely intervention'.

[64] Moreno-Ocampo, 'The Role of the International Community in Assisting the International Criminal Court to Secure Justice and Accountability', in René Provost and Payam Akhavan (eds.), *Ius Gentium: Comparative Perspectives on Law and Justice, Confronting Genocide* (New York: Springer, 2011), vol. VII, pp. 279–90, at p. 288.

[65] Studies suggest a general deterrent effect from criminal law, but only when there is a high likelihood of punishment. Paul Robinson and John Darley, 'The Role of Deterrence in the Formulation of Criminal Law Rules: At Its Worst When Doing Its Best', *Georgetown Law Journal*, 91 (2003), 949–1002. James Alexander argues that the Court does not present a sufficient threat to be much of a deterrent ('The International Criminal Court and the Prevention of Atrocities: Predicting the Court's Impact', *Villanova Law Review*, 54 (2009), 1–56).

upheaval and armed conflict, i.e. precisely where atrocity crimes tend to take place.[66]

It should be noted, however, that deterrence studies have examined the impact of law enforcement mainly in domestic contexts. Such studies are not necessarily applicable to the ICC. The ICC is the world's first standing international criminal court, and is still in a formative stage. Its reach is still not universal, given that any one of the P-5 can veto a referral, and non-States Parties have shown themselves capable of defying the Court. Accordingly, it is too soon to directly assess the ICC's potential as an instrument of deterrence. Furthermore, the fact that the threat of punishment fails to deter much crime in many domestic situations, does not necessarily mean that accountability before the ICC may not impact the calculations of the high-level political leaders that the ICC focuses on, who may be more calculating and rational, and removed from the chaos on the ground, than other criminals.

There is evidence that ICC's potential to prevent atrocity crimes may go beyond the possible deterrent effect of ICC investigations and prosecutions, and extend to the more general preventive effects that Olásolo has discussed. While the prosecution of prominent international criminals before the ICC may have great symbolic and even normative value, it is likely that the Court's greatest preventive impact results from its interactions with and impact upon national legal systems. Complementarity, which initially arose out the need to balance international justice with State sovereignty,[67] has evolved into a relationship between the ICC and national courts that is generally cooperative, rather than competitive.[68]

Were the ICC to adopt a highly proactive approach to complementarity, by actively encouraging national capacity-building, it could potentially strengthen deterrence while enhancing the R2P idea that States have the primary responsibility to prevent mass atrocity crimes

---

[66] Katharine Marshall, 'Prevention and Complementarity in the International Criminal Court: A Positive Approach', *Human Rights Brief*, 17 (2010), 21–6, at 24–5. As Mark Drumbl puts it, 'the assumption of perpetrator rationality in the chaos of massive violence, incendiary propaganda, and upended social order' is dubious ('Collective Violence and Individual Punishment: The Criminality of Mass Atrocity', *Northwestern University Law Review*, 99 (2005), 539–610, at 590).

[67] 'At its inception, the idea of complementarity was meant to balance the competing interests of those who sought a court with universal jurisdiction and those who placed a priority on state sovereignty' (Marshall, 'Prevention and Complementarity', 22).

[68] Mahnoush Arsanjani and W. Michael Reisman, 'The Law in Action of the International Criminal Court', *American Journal of International Law*, 99 (2005), 385–403, at 387.

and to prosecute those who carry them out.[69] National proceedings tend to be cheaper and more accessible to local populations,[70] and the ICC Prosecutor has stressed the superior potential of national courts to promote accountability. An OTP policy paper found that, '[n]ational investigations and prosecutions, where they can properly be undertaken, will normally be the most effective and efficient means of bringing offenders to justice; states themselves will normally have the best access to evidence and witnesses.'[71] Christine Chung also notes that:

> The spread of the domestic enactment of ICC standards also strengthens state enforcement. In the United Kingdom, the International Criminal Court Act of 2001, which was enacted in connection with the ratification of the Rome Statute, became the basis for military charges brought in 2005 against soldiers in the British Army for allegedly committing war crimes against civilian prisoners in Iraq.[72]

As noted earlier, the ICC has helped develop international jurisprudence regarding what constitutes specific international crimes, and has clarified and reaffirmed shared definitions. Indeed, by its very existence, the Court has promoted a common understanding of genocide, as laid out in the Genocide Convention and the Rome Statute. Twenty-five countries, that never ratified the Genocide Convention, have ratified the Rome Statute, and by so doing they have embraced the definition of genocide in the Genocide Convention.[73]

Of course, the ICC's limited jurisdiction and the reliance on States and the UNSC for enforcement limit the Court's ability to prevent atrocity

---

[69] In Marshall's words, 'By encouraging national courts to establish systems by which to try international crimes as defined in the Rome Statute, the ICC is making an essential contribution to the prevention of atrocities. Positive complementarity encourages states to build and strengthen their domestic judicial systems. A state with strong judicial institutions and respect for the rule of law is arguably less likely to reach the level of societal upheaval in which international crimes are most often committed' ('Prevention and Complementarity', 24).

[70] William Burke-White, 'Proactive Complementarity: The International Criminal Court and National Courts in the Rome System of International Justice', Harvard International Law Review, 49 (2008), 53–108, at 69.

[71] ICC OTP, 'Paper on Some Policy Issues before the Office of the Prosecutor', September 2003, p. 2, at www.amicc.org/docs/OcampoPolicyPaper9_03.pdf.

[72] Christine Chung, 'The Punishment and Prevention of Genocide: The International Criminal Court as a Benchmark of Progress and Need', Case Western Reserve Journal of International Law, 40 (2007–8), 227–42, at 230. For an account of the guilty plea, see 'UK soldier jailed over Iraq abuse', BBC, 30 April 2007, at http://news.bbc.co.Uk/l/hi/uk/6609237.stm.

[73] Ibid., 229.

crimes. Furthermore, as also noted above, inadequate funding limits the Court. In fiscal year 2005, for example, the ICC's budget was less than a quarter of that of the ICTY, despite the ICC's far broader jurisdiction.[74] And while today the annual budgets of both courts are comparable, the ICC's mandate is far broader. Even today when the ICTY is close to completing its mandate, it employs 173 persons more than the ICC, 869 and 696 respectively,[75] and budgetary constraints restrict the number of investigations and cases the ICC can take on.[76]

Critics of the ICC have argued that the pursuit of international justice, through domestic or international mechanisms, may impede peace and reconciliation because peace agreements may require the possibility of amnesties or exile.[77] Proponents of the ICC counter that justice is a vehicle for peace,[78] and that ICC intervention can alter the political calculus of key actors in a way that provides an incentive to negotiate peace.

The crisis in Libya and the UNSC referral to the ICC provided fodder to both sides in the peace versus justice debate. Some critics of the Court argued that Resolution 1970 may have impeded a political solution, claiming that the ICC arrest warrant might have prevented Gaddafi from seeking safe haven in another State.[79] But proponents of the Court counter these claims, by citing that the Obama administration was aware of the need to provide Gaddafi with a way out, and had told Russian President Medvedev that if Gaddafi voluntarily left Libya, his

---

[74] Burke-White, 'Proactive Complementarity', 66.

[75] International Criminal Tribunal for the former Yugoslavia, 'The Cost of Justice', at www.icty.org/sid/325; ICC Assembly of States Parties, 'Report on the Activities of the Court', ICC Doc. ICC-ASP/10/39, 18 November 2011, p. 14.

[76] UN Department of Public Information, 'Press Conference on Annual Assembly of States Parties to International Criminal Court', 16 December 2011, available at www.un.org; William Pace, Convenor of the Coalition for the International Criminal Court, 'Public Letter to States Parties', 6 July 2012, available at www.coalitionfortheicc.org.

[77] See for example Brett Schafer, 'International Criminal Court complicates conflict resolution in Libya', web memo, *Heritage Foundation*, 9 June 2011, available at www.heritage.org; James Lindsay, 'International Arrest Warrant Could Spur Gadhafi to Fight to the Death', *Council on Foreign Relations*, 17 May 2011, available at www.cfr.org; Deborah Jerome, 'Will the ICC Help Defeat Qaddafi?', *Council on Foreign Relations*, 28 June 2011, available at www.cfr.org.

[78] See Graeme Simpson, 'One Among Many: The ICC as a Tool of Justice During Transition', in Waddell and Clark (eds.), *Courting Conflict?*, pp. 73–9.

[79] Robert Booth, 'Muammar Gaddafi's exit hindered by UN resolution, law experts warn', *The Guardian*, 29 March 2011, at www.guardian.co.uk/world/2011/mar/29/muammar-gaddafi-exit-un-resolution.

safe passage would be guaranteed.[80] This debate regarding Gaddafi remains unsettled, and is likely to remain so. The period between the ICC referral and the resolution authorising military intervention was so short that it is impossible to discern the impact of the referral on the course of events. Indeed, the North Atlantic Treaty Organization intervention was already underway when arrest warrants were issued. While Gaddafi continued to engage in violence despite the ICC warrant, there is no evidence that he continued ordering violence because of the issuance of the warrant. Moreover, there is no evidence that the ICC referral or warrants caused Gaddafi or his son to reject peace talks.[81]

The ICC is still a young institution, and ICC interventions to date are too limited to come to any firm conclusions regarding the peace versus justice debate. Of course, should analysts eventually uncover patterns of ICC effects on peacebuilding, and should judicial intervention be shown to be obstructive, this would suggest that ICC intervention should be used only with great caution and careful timing. However, to date, the evidence supporting any such conclusions is inadequate. Concerns that ICC actions might impede peace efforts have not been substantiated by clear evidence. Therefore, it is simply too soon to tell.

Conclusions

The futures of the ICC and R2P are linked at many levels. The ICC's legal framework enables it to promote R2P objectives – but the Court is limited by jurisdictional and political factors beyond its control, as well as by the skill and choices of the Prosecutor. The Libyan situation demonstrated that the ICC can be an effective instrument of R2P even during an ongoing conflict but both Libya and Sudan – and now Syria – show the dependency of the Court on the UN Security Council and the P-5. The ICC's contributions to international criminal jurisprudence and its unique role as a permanent court have altered the international political landscape, and therefore also the calculations of those who

---

[80] Schafer, 'Conflict resolution in Libya'.

[81] Even if it were shown that ICC action in one case blocked progress toward peace, it would not be logical to generalise that ICC intervention would always be counterproductive. Only if intervention consistently had such an impact, in a variety of contexts, would there be reason to conclude that ICC intervention was generally obstructive of peace efforts. Moreover, the Rome Statute foresaw this potential dilemma and included a safety valve: temporary suspension through Article 16.

might commit mass atrocity crimes. The Court's long-term effectiveness, however, will be determined by how it is perceived – as a viable or as a failed institution. This is by no means entirely within the Court's control. The UN Security Council, and the governments of the P-5, arguably will have the greatest impact on the effectiveness of the ICC as a promoter of R2P.

PART V

Regional human rights protection mechanisms

19

The European system of human rights

RHONA SMITH AND CONALL MALLORY

Introduction

The Council of Europe concluded its European Convention on Human Rights (the Convention, formally the Convention on the Protection of Human Rights and Fundamental Freedoms) some sixty years ago. This instrument remains the foundation of the European human rights system and, accordingly, the focal point of this chapter. Commenting on the scope of the Convention, the European Court of Human Rights (the Court) stated that 'the object and purpose of the Convention as an instrument for the protection of individual human beings requires that its provisions be interpreted and applied so as to make its safeguards practical and effective'.[1] To what extent, however, can action in furtherance of the emerging 'responsibility to protect' doctrine be inferred into the provisions of the Convention and recognised before the European Court of Human Rights?

Naturally, the Convention does not exist in a legal or jurisdictional vacuum. Within Europe, the work of several other organisations may impinge on responsibility to protect, although primary responsibility for supervising State compliance with fundamental human rights and freedoms lies with the Council of Europe (the Council).[2] Its Court of Human Rights has jurisdiction to receive individuals' complaints against its forty-seven Member States, its European Social Committee (and other bodies) monitors compliance with social rights and minority rights, the European Committee on the Prevention of Torture visits detention centres, and the European Commission against Racism and Intolerance

---

[1] *Loizidou* v. *Turkey, Preliminary Objections*, ECtHR, Application No. 15318/89, 23 February 1995, para. 72.

[2] See respectively Fiott and Vincent, Chapters 9 (EU); Sandole, 14 (OSCE); and Prescott, 15 (NATO) in this book.

monitors discrimination and related intolerance throughout the region. Inevitably, there is evidence of joint activities between the various European (and international) bodies aimed at promoting and protecting rights, albeit this stops short of responsibility to protect-based military interventions.

Outlining the general role of the Council of Europe and salient interaction with regional and international organisations, this chapter will highlight the undoubted success of the European regional human rights system in redressing violations of human rights. Potential invocation of the Convention when Member States act in exercise of responsibility to protect will be considered while noting the inherent limitations in the European system in this respect. This chapter will also explore the possibilities of using the existing European human rights framework in a more proactive way, evaluating the positive obligation to protect civilians, revisiting the extraterritorial effect of the European Convention on Human Rights and considering the potential for additional interim measures to be adopted by the Court strengthening the possible obligations incumbent on States. As will be explained, although primarily operating *ex post facto*, nevertheless, the European human rights system contributes towards the international responsibility to protect.

The Council of Europe: its origin and role

The Council of Europe was founded in 1949, in the aftermath of the Second World War and shortly after the early members of the United Nations had adopted the Universal Declaration of Human Rights. Its constituent act, the Statute of the Council of Europe, makes clear that:

(1) The aim of the Council of Europe is to achieve a greater unity between its members for the purpose of safeguarding and realising the ideals and principles which are their common heritage and facilitating their economic and social progress.

(2) This aim shall be pursued through the organs of the Council by discussion of questions of common concern and by agreements and common action in economic, social, cultural, scientific, legal and administrative matters and in the maintenance and further realisation of human rights and fundamental freedoms.[3]

---

[3] Statute of the Council of Europe, adopted on 5 May 1949 and entered into force 3 August 1949, 87 UNTS 103, art. 1(a) and (b).

In comparison with contemporaneous texts, even the UN Charter,[4] this is a visionary statute with acknowledgement of the central role of human rights within the organisation. However, it was adopted in a Europe which had been decimated by wars and still was adjusting to the aftermath of peace: transfers of populations were ongoing; displaced people were returning home; economies were in disarray. There was thus considerable support for an underpinning of rights and freedoms in society. Indeed the peace treaties and post-war constitutions, for example of Germany, made reference to certain rights. Entrenching respect for human rights and fundamental freedoms in national laws and conscience should thwart changes in policy and practice likely to foster atrocity crimes.

Central powers in Europe were founding members of the Council: Belgium, Denmark, France, Ireland, Italy, Luxembourg, the Netherlands, Norway, Sweden and the United Kingdom. Today the Council of Europe has some forty-seven States Parties covering territory from the Sea of Japan in the north-western Pacific Ocean (east) to the Atlantic Ocean (west) and from the Arctic Ocean (north) to the Mediterranean and Black Sea (south).

One of the first substantial measures adopted by the Council was its famous Convention on the Protection of Human Rights and Fundamental Freedoms.[5] This was adopted in 1950[6] and draws in part on the Universal Declaration of Human Rights, indeed there is some overlap in the drafters of both instruments with Council of Europe Member States having participated in the UN Commission on Human Rights' drafting process. However, while the Universal Declaration was an instrument encapsulating the aspirations of the new world

---

[4] The UN Charter's references to rights are 'scattered, terse, even cryptic'. Philip Alston and Ryan Goodman, *International Human Rights* (Oxford University Press, 2013), p. 140.

[5] European Convention for the Protection of Human Rights and Fundamental Freedoms, adopted 4 November 1950 and entered into force 3 September 1953, ETS 005. There are a number of detailed books on the Convention and its jurisprudence. See for example Robin White and Clare Ovey, *Jacobs, White and Ovey: The European Convention on Human Rights*, 5th edn (Oxford University Press, 2009); Pieter van Dijk, Fried van Hoof, Arjen van Rijn and Leo Zwaak (eds.), *Theory and Practice of the European Convention on Human Rights*, 4th edn (Antwerp; Oxford: Intersentia, 2006); David Harris, Michael O'Boyle, Colin Warbrick, Edward Bates and Carla Buckley, *Law of the European Convention on Human Rights*, 2nd edn (Oxford University Press, 2009); Mark Janis, Richard Kay and Anthony Bradley, *European Human Rights Law: Text and Materials*, 3rd edn (Oxford University Press, 2008).

[6] By 1950, Turkey and Greece had joined the Council, bringing membership to twelve.

organisation, and not intended to be legally binding in itself,[7] the European Convention was intended to create binding obligations on States and 'take the first steps for the collective enforcement of certain of the rights stated in the Universal Declaration'.[8] In this respect, it predates the International Covenants (which sought to give binding effect to the Universal Declaration at the UN level) by sixteen years for adoption, and had been operational for almost a quarter of a century before the International Covenants entered into force. Indeed by 1976, when the Covenants entered into force, the European Court of Human Rights had given judgment in some fourteen cases,[9] the European Commission on Human Rights (Commission) considerably more. Nevertheless, the European Convention reflects one crucial aspect of the tenor of early international human rights instruments – it retains a strong element of respect for the sovereignty of States. Previous writers have considered the limitation this can pose on those seeking to exercise the responsibility to protect in respect of internal disputes.[10] Within the Council of Europe human rights system, this manifests itself as a clear direction that the Court supervises States in their implementation of protected human rights and freedoms.[11] Indeed, initially individuals had no *locus standi* before the Court: only States themselves or the Commission on Human Rights could bring cases on behalf of individual complainants,[12] and the Commission's power in this regard was itself dependent on the State accepting explicitly the competence of the Commission to receive individual petitions.[13] State sovereignty was

---

[7] For more on this, see UNGA Res. 217 (III), Universal Declaration of Human Rights, adopted 10 December 1948, UN Doc. A/RES/217(III), p. 71, pmbl. For analysis see Johannes Morsink, *The Universal Declaration of Human Rights: Origins, Drafting, and Intent* (University of Pennsylvania Press, 2000); Gudmundur Alfredsson and Asbjørn Eide (eds.), *The Universal Declaration of Human Rights: A Common Standard of Achievement* (Leiden: Martinus Nijhoff, 1999).

[8] European Convention on Human Rights, pmbl; see also *ibid.*, art. 1.

[9] Judgments delivered before February 1976, statistics from ECtHR, *Survey: Forty Years of Activity 1959-1998* (Strasbourg: Council of Europe, 1998).

[10] See also Thomas Weiss, 'The Sunset of Humanitarian Interventions? Responsibility to Protect in a Unipolar Order', *Security Dialogue*, 35 (2004), 135–53.

[11] European Convention on Human Rights, art. 32. The States themselves must give effect to the judgment, albeit the Committee of Ministers supervises such execution (*ibid.*, art. 46).

[12] See *ibid.*, original art. 44.

[13] *Ibid.*, original art. 25(1) provides that: 'The Commission may receive petitions addressed to the Secretary-General of the Council of Europe from any person, non-governmental organisation or group of individuals claiming to be the victim of a violation by one of the High Contracting Parties of the rights set forth in this Convention, provided that the

thus respected and individuals were not treated as actors in international law. The position was only changed in 1998 when Protocol 11 secured its final ratification and entered into force, thereby abolishing the Commission and instituting a single tier process for complaints under the Convention, with individuals automatically (subject to admissibility criteria) entitled to bring complaints directly to the Court.[14] This proved a catalyst for an unparalleled explosion in the number of individual complaints brought before the new permanent Court. As of 31 March 2013, there were 126,850 applications pending before judicial formations of the European Court.[15] Notwithstanding the impact of this enormous case backlog, the Court maintains its 'supervisory' role over compliance by States with the articles of the treaty.[16] It has virtually no punitive powers, bar award of costs and pecuniary damages though such awards are fairly small when compared to a similar system as the Inter-American one.

Judgments of the Court have strong moral force and are, to a large extent, complied with. They are referred to the Committee of Ministers to monitor implementation. A quick perusal of the last few meetings' minutes of the Committee's deputies reveals some cases have been awaiting legislative changes, or other State responses, for years. States self-report on compliance. State reports are the mode of choice for monitoring compliance with other Council of Europe treaties and agreements: the European Social Charter,[17] the European Charter for Regional and Minority Languages,[18] the Framework Convention for the Protection of National Minorities[19] and even the newer (2011) Convention on Preventing and Combating Violence Against Women

---

High Contracting Party against which the complaint has been lodged has declared that it recognizes the competence of the Commission to receive such petitions.'

[14] Protocol 11 to the European Convention for the Protection of Human Rights and Fundamental Freedoms: Restructuring the Control Machinery Established Thereby, adopted 11 May 1994 and entered into force 1 November 1998, ETS 155.

[15] Statistics of the European Court of Human Rights are available at www.echr.coe.int.

[16] For example *Handyside* v. *United Kingdom, Judgment*, ECtHR, Application No. 5493/72, 7 December 1976; *Otto-Preminger Institute* v. *Germany, Judgment*, ECtHR, Application No. 13470/87, 20 September 1994.

[17] European Social Charter, adopted 18 October 1961 and entered into force 26 February 1965, ETS 35, arts. 21–2; European Social Charter (Revised), adopted 3 May 1996 and entry into force 1 July 1999, ETS 163, art. C.

[18] European Charter for Regional or Minority Languages, adopted 4 November 1992 and entered into force 1 March 1998, ETS 148, art. 15.

[19] Framework Convention for the Protection of National Minorities, adopted 1 February 1995 and entered into force 1 February 1998, ETS 157, art. 25.

and Domestic Abuse.[20] Respect for State sovereignty thus retains pre-eminence and, unlike the European Union (EU), the Council remains an intergovernmental, inter-national rather than supra-national, organisation.

Previous chapters have discussed Europe's other regional organisations, namely the European Union and the Organization for Security and Co-operation in Europe (OSCE).[21] Of course, Europe is also home to the North Atlantic Treaty Organization (NATO) with its inherent protection mandate and consequential potential to deploy military force to protect any Member State. There is potential overlap between the various entities as previous chapters illustrate; a situation the likely future accession of the European Union to the Council of Europe's principal human rights treaty compounds.[22] Naturally, such accession could open potential avenues for the responsibility to protect should the documentation so provide, and the States agree.

This chapter focuses simply on the Council of Europe under the auspices of which operates Europe's principal human rights system. The question is thus the extent to which the present European human rights system can, and perhaps could, contribute towards the responsibility to protect agenda.

Extent of Council of Europe's responsibility to protect

It is uncontroversial that a major role of the Council of Europe is to protect individuals from abuse of power by the State. That is indeed the ethos of its human rights system; Europe had witnessed devastating abuses of State power during two multi-partite wars within the lifetime of the organisation's founders. The core rights enshrined in the European Convention, i.e. infringements of which can be brought before

---

[20] Convention on Preventing and Combating Violence against Women and Domestic Violence, adopted 11 May 2011, CETS 210, art. 68.

[21] These organisations have more experience in exerting influence against atrocity crimes (OSCE) and in coordinating military action (EU). See respectively Sandol, Chapter 14 and Fiott and Vincent, Chapter 9 in this book; UNSG, 'The Role of Regional and Sub-regional Arrangements in Implementing the Responsibility to Protect', UN Doc. A/65/877–S/2011/393, 27 June 2011.

[22] Protocol 14 to the Council of Europe's European Convention on Human Rights (ECHR) inserted new Article 59(2) to the Convention and Article 6(2) Treaty on European Union, Protocol 8 to the Treaty on the Foundation of the European Union (amended by the Treaty of Lisbon) opens the possibility of the European Union acceding to the European Convention, the modalities of which are still being discussed.

the Court, reflect the prevailing international and pertaining political standards of the period – they are essentially civil and political rights[23] including the right to respect for life,[24] the prohibition on torture, inhuman or degrading treatment or punishment[25] and the prohibition on arbitrary deprivation of liberty.[26] Discrimination on grounds including race, language, religion, national origin or even association with national minorities is prohibited[27] – a prohibition strengthened by a subsequent optional protocol.[28] Flagrant and systematic violation of such rights within a State can give rise to a responsibility to protect on the part of third States. Their infringement during conflict and other hostilities may indicate violations of international humanitarian law – there have been a number of allegations of such infringements in the Balkans and the Black Sea region raised before the European Court.[29] However, much of the work of the Court concerns alleged violations of individuals' rights, rather than the sustained systematic grave infringements capable of giving rise to a responsibility to protect.

Under the provisions of the European Convention, however, complaints concerning violations should be lodged before the European Court of Human Rights,[30] following exhaustion of available domestic remedies if brought by an individual.[31] Accordingly, the work of the Court is 'passive' – consideration of facts *ex post facto* brought before it by individual victims of human rights infringements or, very occasionally, by other States.[32] The role of the Court is one of overviewing and supervising national compliance with the terms of the Convention rather than responding to State actions of its own volition in furtherance of a responsibility to protect. The Court has no investigatory power at its own initiation but then, as it has no power to enforce judgments or intervene in national affairs, an *ab initio* investigatory power *ipso facto* would be of

---

[23] The Council of Europe's economic, social and cultural rights appear primarily in separate instruments reviewed by committees.

[24] European Convention on Human Rights, art. 2.   [25] *Ibid.*, art. 3.   [26] *Ibid.*, art. 5.

[27] *Ibid.*, art. 14. Note that this article can only be raised in conjunction with another article of the Convention.

[28] *Ibid.*, Protocol 12.

[29] For example *Ilaşcu and Others* v. *Moldova and Russia, Judgment*, ECtHR, Application No. 48787/99, 8 July 2004; *Isayeva, Yusupova and Bazayeva* v. *Russia, Judgment*, ECtHR, Application Nos. 57947/00, 57948/00 and 57949/00, 24 February 2005.

[30] European Convention on Human Rights, art. 34.   [31] *Ibid.*, art. 35(1).

[32] *Ibid.*, art. 33. For example *Cyprus* v. *Turkey, Judgment*, ECtHR, Application No. 25781/94, 10 May 2001; *Ireland* v. *United Kingdom, Judgment*, ECtHR, Application No. 5310/71, 18 January 1978.

limited use. Nevertheless, the Court can elect to consider a case even if the applicant wishes to withdraw the complaint, disappears or even dies,[33] the emphasis being on ensuring respect for the principles and securing those standards enshrined in the Convention rather than simply addressing any individual's complaint.[34] After all, the State will already have been afforded an opportunity to remedy the alleged Convention infringement during domestic proceedings prior to the European Court's involvement.

The Council of Europe's Commissioner on Human Rights, on the other hand, does have a general power to comment and, as the diplomatic figurehead of the organisation, has the potential to draw attention to situations of concern and institute protection proceedings in other forums. This, however, is merely a power of comment and while publicity has a role, it falls considerably short of positive action in furtherance of the responsibility to protect. The Secretary-General of the Council may also respond to current events with statements – for example, in August 2011 he condemned the outbreaks of violence in England, the United Kingdom.[35] Similarly, the Council of Europe can and does offer assistance to countries experiencing turmoil – as Tunisia in spring 2011 – however, this refers primarily to technical assistance and/or discussions, rather than military support or interventions.

As the foregoing suggests, the European Convention on Human Rights and the emerging responsibility to protect do not make a natural partnership; the European Court of Human Rights is a judicial-based body which acts *ex post facto* and largely considers (individual) human rights violations retrospectively, while the primary focus of the responsibility to protect is on the prevention of future violations.[36] What will follow, therefore, are discussions of how the Council of Europe and the responsibility to protect norm are likely to interact in the future and some imaginative interpretations of how current provisions can be adapted to accommodate the responsibility to protect.

---

[33] Many complaints concerning torture, disappearances and State officials are considered after the death of the victim. For example *Khambulatova* v. *Russia, Judgment*, ECtHR, Application No. 33488/04, 3 March 2011.

[34] See European Convention on Human Rights, art. 37, on striking-out cases. Note also the Brighton Declaration 2012 on monitoring this aspect of Protocol 14.

[35] Comments available at www.coe.int/web/coe-portal/press/pressreleases.

[36] Arguably the prohibition on discrimination has potential to prevent atrocity crimes if rigorously implemented in States and upheld by the Court. See also UNSG, 'Regional and Sub-regional Arrangements'.

The application of the European Convention on Human Rights to States exercising the responsibility to protect

Perhaps the most likely scenario in which the European Convention on Human Rights and the responsibility to protect will coexist is where a Council of Europe Member State conducts military action in furtherance of responsibility to protect obligations. In this scenario the jurisdiction of the European Court of Human Rights could be engaged to comment on the action of the Member State(s) involved. For example, if Sweden were to use the responsibility to protect as a basis for military intervention in Mongolia, it would be the Swedish forces whose actions would be evaluated to consider whether they were compliant with the European Convention on Human Rights. Mongolia is not a party to the Convention and thus has no obligations thereunder.[37] Regardless of the underlying purpose for military action, Judge Giovanni Bonello stated his belief in *Al-Skeini and Others* v. *United Kingdom* that 'those who export war ought to see to the parallel export of guarantees against the atrocities of war'.[38]

Identifying what falls within a State's jurisdiction in terms of the Convention has proven to be a difficult task. Essentially, it is possible for an individual to bring a claim for the breach of a Convention right should that violation occur when they are within a Member State's jurisdiction and the violation is attributable to that State.[39] The Strasbourg bodies have been prepared to find that Council of Europe Member States can only exercise jurisdiction outside their territorial borders in exceptional circumstances. In relation to military operations the jurisprudence of the Court (and Commission)[40] suggests that Member States do not extend their jurisdiction when conducting aerial strikes on declared targets,[41] but may extend their jurisdiction when conducting ground operations where individuals fall within the 'authority and control' of the forces of a Member State.[42]

---

[37] Note, however, that the European Court has, to date, primarily been concerned with civilians rather than combatants.

[38] *Al-Skeini and Others* v. *United Kingdom, Judgment, Concurring Opinion of Judge Giovanni Bonello*, ECtHR, Application No. 55721/07, 7 July 2011, para. 38.

[39] The Convention does not in itself have horizontal effect between private parties.

[40] Until the entry into force of Protocol 11 to the European Convention, there was a two tier system of a Commission and Court of Human Rights.

[41] *Banković and Others* v. *Belgium and Others, Decision (Admissibility)*, ECtHR, Application No. 52207/99, 12 December 2001.

[42] *Öcalan* v. *Turkey, Judgment*, ECtHR, Application No. 46221/99, 12 May 2005; *Issa and Others* v. *Turkey, Judgment*, ECtHR, Application No. 31821/96, 16 November 2004; *Mansur Pad and Others* v. *Turkey, Decision (Admissibility)*, ECtHR, Application No. 60167/00, 28 June 2007.

Through assessing compliance with the Convention, the European Court of Human Rights seeks to ensure that the actions of Council of Europe members are not in violation of their human rights obligations. Although the case law of the Court has predominantly focused on instances where an individual's rights have been violated by their own government in that State, in recent years increasing military operations have given rise to a growing body of case law arising when Council of Europe Member States violate the human rights of individuals living *outside* their territory. This is particularly pertinent in relation to the responsibility to protect norm for the twenty-six Council of Europe Member States who concurrently hold membership of NATO.[43] Thus, if an individual of a State subjected to responsibility to protect action has his or her rights violated in the course of a military intervention conducted by a Council of Europe Member State, that individual may be able to seek recourse for the violation through the European Court of Human Rights. Using the hypothetical example above, in exceptional circumstances a Mongolian resident could thus raise an action against Sweden should they suffer from an infringement of rights and freedoms through Sweden's military incursions into Mongolia in pursuance of responsibility to protect obligations.

The gateway to such recourse is Article 1 of the Convention: 'The High Contracting Parties shall secure to everyone within their jurisdiction the rights and freedoms defined in Section I of [the] Convention.' Where an applicant cannot prove that they were within the jurisdiction of a Contracting Party at the time of the alleged violation the Court will not consider their application and they may be left without a remedy. Consequently, the circumstances which define when an individual is within the jurisdiction of a Contracting Party are pivotal to an applicant's claim.[44]

Establishing 'jurisdiction' under the Convention

Through reference to principles of general international law the Court and Commission have deemed jurisdiction under the Convention to be

---

[43] Of NATO's twenty-eight members only Canada and the United States of America are not signatories of the ECHR. For information on NATO members, see www.nato.int. For a detailed discussion of NATO's role with regard to R2P, see Prescott, Chapter 15 in this book.

[44] This issue has also been debated by the Human Rights Council during universal periodic review, for example, of the United Kingdom. UN Human Rights Council, 'Report of the Working Group on the Universal Periodic Review United Kingdom and Northern Ireland', UN Doc. A/HRC/8/25, 23 May 2008, paras. 41 and 48.

essentially territorial,[45] even in situations where a State does not exercise total control or authority over its own territory.[46] However, the Court has also recognised a number of exceptional circumstances where extra-territorial jurisdiction can exist. The most recent exposition of these 'exceptional circumstances' was provided by the Court in *Al-Skeini and Others* v. *United Kingdom*. In this case a unanimous Grand Chamber found that, through its soldiers engaged in security operations in Basra, Iraq, following the US/UK-led military action in 2003 onwards, the United Kingdom had exercised such authority and control over six individuals killed by British forces as to establish a jurisdictional link between the victims and the United Kingdom.[47] In presenting its decision the Court described two forms of exception to the principle of territoriality: State agent authority and control and effective control of an area.[48]

The 'State agent authority' exception involves situations where the actions of a Contracting Party produce effects outside its own territory. In *Al-Skeini* the Court referred to three examples of such a relationship: acts of diplomatic and consular agents where they exert authority and control over others;[49] situations where the Contracting Party, through the consent, invitation or acquiescence of the government of that territory, exercises all or some of the public powers normally to be exercised by that government[50] and finally occasions when they use force to bring an individual under their control.[51] The Court also found that where Member States exercise such jurisdiction outside their national territory they are bound to comply with the European Convention on Human

---

[45] *Banković and Others* v. *Belgium and Others*, paras. 59–61 and 80.

[46] *Ilaşcu and Others* v. *Moldova and Russia*. The Court found that although Moldova did not have full authority and control over one of its regions, it was still required to fulfil aspects of its positive obligations under the Convention.

[47] *Al-Skeini and Others* v. *United Kingdom*, para. 149. See also Conall Mallory, 'European Court of Human Rights *Al-Skeini and Others* v *United Kingdom* (Application No. 55721/07) Judgment of 7 July 2011', *International and Comparative Law Quarterly*, 61 (2012), 301–12.

[48] *Al-Skeini and Others* v. *United Kingdom*, paras. 134–9; *ibid.*

[49] *X* v. *Federal Republic of Germany, Decision*, ECommHR, Application No. 1611/62, 25 September 1965; *WM* v. *Denmark, Decision*, ECommHR, Application No. 17392/90, 14 October 1992.

[50] *Drozd and Janousek* v. *France and Spain, Judgment*, ECtHR, Application No. 12747/87, 26 June 1992.

[51] *Öcalan* v. *Turkey; Issa and Others* v. *Turkey; Al-Saadoon and Mufdhi* v. *United Kingdom, Decision (Admissibility)*, ECtHR, Application No. 61498/08, 30 June 2009; *Medvedyev and Others* v. *France, Judgment*, ECtHR, Application No. 3394/03, 29 March 2010.

Rights and as such the rights relevant to the particular situation become extraterritorial obligations.[52]

The Court also found that jurisdiction could exist through the 'effective control of an area' when, as a consequence of lawful or unlawful military action, a Contracting State exercised control of an area outside its national territory.[53] This jurisdiction derives from the factual existence of control and occurs whether it is exercised directly or through the support of a local subordinate administration.[54] The existence of jurisdiction through the effective control of an area exception is a question of fact which the Court will decide with reference to such factors as the strength of the State's military presence in the area and the extent of its military, economic or political support of a subordinate regime.[55]

For States who seek to undertake military activity under the responsibility to protect, these extraterritorial obligations should form real practical limitations to the manner in which their operations are conducted. Thus far the Court, and previously the Commission, has appeared willing to find jurisdictional links in applications involving cross-border seizures,[56] military occupation[57] and arrest and detention.[58] Controversially, the Court failed to find a jurisdictional link between seventeen Council of Europe States and the victims of an aerial attack on a Belgrade radio station during hostilities in the Balkans.[59] Therefore, the Convention jurisprudence on jurisdiction remains unsettled with decisions made on the unique factual circumstances of each case. Should the United Nations authorise the military action,[60] the situation may be even more complex as, inevitably, obligations imposed by UN Security Council resolutions should be discharged.[61] The potential for further responsibility to protect actions by Council of Europe

---

[52] *Al-Skeini and Others* v. *United Kingdom*, para. 137.
[53] *Cyprus* v. *Turkey (Admissibility)*, ECommHR, 1 January 1997; *Ilaşcu and Others* v. *Moldova and Russia*.
[54] *Loizidou* v. *Turkey*.   [55] *Al-Skeini and Others* v. *United Kingdom*, para. 139.
[56] *Mansur Pad and Others* v. *Turkey*. Note that in this case as Turkey accepted fire from its helicopters had killed the applicants' relatives, the Court chose not to consider when the victims came within Turkish jurisdiction.
[57] *Al-Skeini and Others* v. *United Kingdom*; *Al-Jedda* v. *United Kingdom*, *Judgment*, ECtHR, Application No. 27021/08, 7 July 2011.
[58] *Hess* v. *United Kingdom*, *Decision*, ECommHR, Application No. 6231/73, 28 May 1975; and *Öcalan* v. *Turkey*.
[59] *Banković and Others* v. *Belgium and Others*.
[60] For example Charter of the United Nations, adopted 24 October 1945, 1 UNTS XVI, art. 7.
[61] *Ibid.*, art. 25. See e.g. *Behrami* v. *France*, *Judgment*, ECtHR, Application No. 71412/01, 78 166/01, 2 May 2007.

Member States adds weight to calls[62] for the Court to fully clarify the jurisdictional question.

Although these judgments would indicate that military forces operating in third States under responsibility to protect could perpetrate infringements of the European Convention, there is considerably less evidence supporting the inference of a positive obligation stemming from the Convention on States to act to protect civilians elsewhere beyond the legal space (*espace juridique*) of the Contracting States.

Is there a positive responsibility to protect embedded in the Convention?

The European Court of Human Rights has frequently extended the pre-existing human rights framework in a proactive way, further advancing protection of human rights.[63] One possibility would thus be for the Court to develop the responsibility to protect as a positive obligation under the Convention. At present, the European Convention imposes a positive obligation on States to protect life (Article 2) and prevent torture, inhuman and degrading treatment or punishment (Article 3) of those within its territory, whether the threat to wellbeing comes from State interventions[64] or at the hands of private individuals.[65] This can include the obligation to investigate unexplained deaths,[66] to prosecute

---

[62] Lord Rodger of Earlsferry of the United Kingdom's House of Lords conveyed his dissatisfaction stating that 'the judgments and decisions of the European court do not speak with one voice' when concerning jurisdiction (*Al-Skeini and Others* v. *Secretary of State for Defence, Consolidated Appeals*, United Kingdom House of Lords Judicial Committee, 13 June 2007, para. 67).

[63] For example closing the State's margin of appreciation in the recognition of post-operative transsexuals, see *Cossey* v. *United Kingdom, Judgment*, ECtHR, Application No. 10843/84, 27 September 1990; cf. *Goodwin* v. *United Kingdom, Judgment*, ECtHR, Application No. 17488/90, 27 March 1996.

[64] Heightened duty of care to those detained by the State or subject to its control. *Salman* v. *Turkey, Judgment*, ECtHR, Application No. 21986/93, 27 June 2000; *Tais* v. *France, Judgment*, ECtHR, Application No. 39922/03, 1 September 2006; *Paul and Audrey Edwards* v. *United Kingdom, Judgment*, ECtHR, Application No. 46477/99, 14 June 2002; *Renolde* v. *France, Judgment*, ECtHR, Application No. 5608/05, 16 October 2008. For a more expansive indication of where the positive duty ends, cf. *Trubnikov* v. *Russia, Judgment*, ECtHR, Application No. 49790/99, 5 July 2005.

[65] *Osman* v. *United Kingdom, Judgment*, ECtHR, Application No. 23452/94, 28 October 1998.

[66] For example *Akkoç* v. *Turkey, Judgment*, ECtHR, Application Nos. 22947/93 and 22948/93, 10 October 2000.

individuals whose actions engage substantive rights,[67] and even to enact legislation.[68] This positive obligation can restrict State action in respect of infringements which would occur at the hands of another (third) State, as in *Soering* v. *United Kingdom*.[69]

This device has enabled the Court to consider, and find infringements of the treaty in respect of, unexplained disappearances during conflict situations.[70] In *Cyprus* v. *Turkey*, the Grand Chamber of the European Court of Human Rights found a violation of the right to life given the lack of substantive investigation into the missing persons and a violation of the prohibition on inhuman treatment given the silence of the Turkish Cypriot authorities as regards the missing persons.[71] The length of time lapsed since hostilities was clearly a determinative factor in the *Cyprus* case, however, it could be deduced that Member States are required to ensure that they take positive steps to ensure respect for human rights including the possibility of precise, confined and targeted military action if such is the only practicable means of ensuring the life and well-being of people within its territory. When discussing such an extension of positive obligations it is possible to use the decision in the *Ilascu* case as evidence that the Court is moving towards a more progressive model of rights protection.[72] In this case Moldova was found to have been in breach of its positive obligations under the Convention even though the violations complained of took place in a separatist region over which Moldova did not exercise effective control. In arriving at such an interpretation, the Court found that 'Moldova still has a positive obligation under Article 1 of the Convention to take the diplomatic, economic, judicial or other measures that it is in its power to take and are in accordance with international law to secure to the applicants the rights guaranteed by the Convention.'[73] These positive obligations are inferred

---

[67] For example *A. and Others* v. *United Kingdom*, *Judgment*, ECtHR, Application No. 3455/05, 19 February 2009, regarding criminal law provisions in England permitting a defence to assault charges of 'reasonable chastisement' for a stepfather accused of beating his stepson; *Okkali* v. *Turkey*, *Judgment*, ECtHR, Application No. 52067/99, 17 October 2006, concerned a 12-year-old beaten by police – no criminal law exercised the relevant and necessary deterrent factor.

[68] For example *Öneryıldız* v. *Turkey*, *Judgment*, ECtHR, Application No. 48939/99, 30 November 2004.

[69] *Soering* v. *The United Kingdom*, *Judgment*, ECtHR, Application No. 14038/88, 7 July 1989.

[70] *Cyprus* v. *Turkey*.

[71] This is similar to *Velásquez Rodríguez* v. *Honduras*, *Judgment*, Inter-American Court of Human Rights, Series C, No. 4, 29 July 1988.

[72] *Ilascu and Others* v. *Moldova and Russia*.   [73] *Ibid.*, para. 331.

from the principal substantive articles and Article 1, the general jurisdiction clause.[74] Similarly in *LCB* v. *United Kingdom*,[75] the positive steps necessary to protect the population were elaborated on by the Court when considering the plight of a woman with leukaemia which conceivably (though not definitively provable) could be linked to the Christmas Island nuclear tests her father was present at during the 1950s.

There would appear to be a ground for arguing that military action within the Council of Europe's geographical jurisdiction in furtherance of the responsibility to protect would be compatible with the European Convention on Human Rights. Obviously such cases will turn on the specific facts and circumstances established; the respondent State will be required to meet a high threshold to justify its actions, demonstrating the absolute necessity thereof and lack of viable alternatives.[76] The State within whose jurisdiction action occurred could well be a co-respondent.

Tangentially, the European Court of Human Rights has frequently reiterated the investigative obligations on States when an individual suffers harm, particularly harm which may engage Articles 2 or 3 of the European Convention on Human Rights.[77] This could result in identification of potential threats to civilian populations which could give rise to a positive obligation to protect. One option to resolve this, and indeed to seek clarification on the relationship (if any) between the responsibility to protect doctrine and the European Convention, would be to seek an advisory opinion thereon from the Court.[78] This possibility is very rarely used, but offers the potential for judicial resolution of tricky legal issues.

The influence the European Convention on Human Rights has on domestic legal systems is such that it creates an environment based on the rule of law and respect for human rights. Moreover it charges States with considering consequences of their action or inaction. It is not too far a stretch to imply protection therein for those within their

---

[74] See also *Assanidze* v. *Georgia*, *Judgment*, ECtHR, Application No. 71503/01, 8 April 2004.

[75] *LCB* v. *The United Kingdom*, *Judgment*, ECtHR, Application No. 23413/94, 9 June 1998.

[76] *McCann, Farrell and Savage* v. *United Kingdom*, *Judgment*, ECtHR, Application No. 18984/91, 27 September 1995.

[77] *Hugh Jordan* v. *United Kingdom*, *Judgment*, ECtHR, Application No. 24746/94, 4 May 2001; *Finucane* v. *United Kingdom*, *Judgment*, ECtHR, Application No. 29178/95, 1 July 2003.

[78] European Convention on Human Rights, art. 47.

geographical territory. Although encouraging, there is no basis for arguing an advancement of this to a general responsibility to protect requiring positive action by States outside their territory, the Court being involved *ex post facto*. Moreover, it would still be essential that a European nexus existed between the State where the responsibility to protect is concerned and the Council of Europe Member State(s); the link between the Convention and the situation would thus need to be clear. It would be much more difficult to find such a link when the situation requiring the responsibility to protect occurred outside the European legal space, and impossible if the situation did not concern a Contracting Party to the Convention.

Extending the responsibility to protect beyond Europe?

Article 56 (formerly Article 63) of the European Convention is one method whereby the Convention could be extended outside European legal space, however this extension is only to any territory for whose international relations a Council of Europe Member State is responsible. In this scenario, if an emergency were to arise in any colony or trust territory of a Council of Europe State that Member State could extend the application of the Convention to that territory and theoretically the positive obligation of the responsibility to protect. Given the extent of French metropolitan territory, for example, the responsibility to protect could arise outwith the prima facie European legal space, albeit requiring a response by one particular Member State only.[79]

If the European Convention on Human Rights were to include the responsibility to protect as an obligation for Member States, it is more likely that the development would arise in the form of official acceptance of an optional protocol by Council of Europe Member States, rather than through the development of a positive obligation by the Court. However, as there is little basis for implying a positive duty to act to protect civilian populations into the terms of the Statute of the Council of Europe as an obligation, this is unlikely.

---

[79] Obviously the nature of the independence/autonomy/external relations agreement or treaty between the Council of Europe Member State and the overseas territory may specify a solution.

The role of interim measures

Like the other regional human rights systems[80] and indeed the European Court of Justice,[81] the European Court of Human Rights can order interim measures. Rule 39 of the Rules of Court states:[82]

(1) The Chamber or, where appropriate, its President may, at the request of a party or of any other person concerned, or of its own motion, indicate to the parties any interim measure which it considers should be adopted in the interests of the parties or of the proper conduct of the proceedings before it.
(2) Notice of these measures shall be given to the Committee of Ministers.
(3) The Chamber may request information from the parties on any matter connected with the implementation of any interim measure it has indicated.

This provision has been increasingly deployed as a final 'appeal' option for those faced with extradition, or deportation.[83] In *Al-Saadoon and Mufdhi v. United Kingdom*[84] the European Court of Human Rights stated that:

> Interim measures under Rule 39 of the Rules of Court are indicated only in limited spheres. In practice, the Court will make such an indication only if there is an imminent risk of irreparable damage. While there is no specific provision in the Convention concerning the domains in which Rule 39 will apply, requests for its application usually concern the right to life (Article 2), the right not to be subjected to torture or inhuman treatment (Article 3) and, exceptionally, the right to respect for private and family life (Article 8) or other rights guaranteed by the Convention.[85]

---

[80] American Convention on Human Rights, adopted 22 November 1969 and entered into force 18 July 1978, OAS TS No. 36, 1144 UNTS 123, art. 63(2); African Charter on Human and Peoples' Rights, adopted 27 June 1981 and entered into force 21 October 1986, OAU Doc. CAB/LEG/67/3 rev. 5, 1520 UNTS 217, art. 27(2).

[81] Consolidated Version of the Treaty on the Functioning of the European Union, adopted 13 December 2007 and entered into force 1 December 2009, Official Journal of the European Union 2008/C 115/01, art. 279.

[82] ECtHR, 'Rules of Court', 1 September 2012, p. 21, rule 39.

[83] See statement accompanying Practice Direction issued by the President of the Court on 16 October 2009 concerning interim measures in immigration and asylum case, as amended 7 July 2011: 112 requests in 2006; 4,786 in 2010 (including almost 2,000 against Sweden and over 2,000 against the United Kingdom).

[84] *Al-Saadoon and Mufdhi v. United Kingdom, Judgment*, 2 March 2010.

[85] *Ibid.*, para. 160.

In an expanding range of cases, however, interim measures are requested in other circumstances,[86] both against the State[87] and against individuals.[88] Interim measures are generally regarded as binding on States, non-respect for which infringes the Convention.[89] Thus in *Al-Saadoon and Mufdhi* the Court found the Convention infringed after two Iraqi prisoners had been transferred to Iraqi authorities despite the Court requesting that they remain within UK custody.[90]

Conclusions

Possibly the principal problem when attempting to reconcile the responsibility to protect with the work of the Council of Europe is that the Council of Europe, by its very nature, responds to events. The human rights system has no comprehensive 'early warning system' and little prospect of rolling out 'interim interdicts', 'injunctions', 'stays' or similar measures forcing a State to cease and desist actions of concern as identified by the Court, rather than through the existing victim-driven process. The length of time a complaint can take from alleged violation, through the national courts and tribunals to exhaust domestic remedies, then to the European Court for a final decision, is inexorably measured in years though certain cases can be expedited.[91] This is a major limitation with regard to urgent responsibility to protect situations.

---

[86] For discussion thereon, see Catharina Harby, 'The Changing Nature of Interim Measures Before the European Court of Human Rights', *European Human Rights Law Review*, 1 (2010), 73–84.

[87] For example *Aleksanyan v. Russia, Judgment*, ECtHR, Application No. 46468/06, 22 December 2008, applicant in pre-trial detention requiring medical evaluation; *Evans v. United Kingdom, Judgment*, Application No. 6339/05, 10 April 2007, regarding the preservation of embryos pending a decision of the Court on the human rights issues.

[88] For example *Rodic and Others v. Bosnia and Herzegovina, Judgment*, ECtHR, Application No. 22893/05, 27 May 2008, in which the applicants themselves were on hunger strike.

[89] See, for example, Yves Haeck, Clara Burbano Herrera and Leo Zwaak, 'Non-compliance with a Provisional Measure Automatically Leads to a Violation of the Right of Individual Application . . . or Doesn't It?', *European Constitutional Law Review*, 4 (2008), 41–63.

[90] *Al-Saadoon and Mufdhi v. United Kingdom*, 2 March 2010.

[91] *Pretty v. United Kingdom, Judgment*, ECtHR, Application No. 2346/02, 29 April 2002, case on the right to life (and death) of a terminally ill woman.

With the Treaty of Lisbon[92] and Protocol 14 to the Convention for the Protection of Human Rights and Fundamental Freedoms,[93] the once theoretically implausible accession of the EU to the European Convention on Human Rights is currently being discussed to determine the modalities and implication of accession. This raises a tantalising futuristic development for interim measures – the European Court could conceivably consider interim measures which are operationalised by the European Union and, as discussed earlier in this book, the EU has more power as a supranational governmental organisation to take coercive, even military measures. However, given the jurisdictional issues, it would seem most likely that this will be restricted to crimes falling under the responsibility to protect, namely genocide, war crimes or crimes against humanity taking place within rather than outside Europe.

To return to the principal question addressed in this chapter: does the European human rights system give rise to a responsibility to protect? The answer appears unequivocally to be 'no'. Neither the Statute of the Council of Europe, nor the European Convention on Human Rights and its associated Rules of Court provide a power for the Council's organs or associated bodies to authorise military action, or otherwise act in furtherance of the responsibility to protect. On the secondary question of could there be a responsibility to protect within the system – possibly yes, though care must be taken to ensure no clash of jurisdictions, given that members of the Council may also be members of the EU, OSCE, NATO and, of course, the UN. Indeed it is this overlap of jurisdictions which presents the strongest argument against the Council of Europe pursuing a responsibility to protect agenda. Given all members of the Council of Europe are also members of the United Nations and over half are members of the European Union, eventually the responsibility to protect can be pursued and realised in other forums. Indeed as the Parliamentary Assembly of the Council of Europe noted:

> [T]he Council of Europe must remain the preferred place for dialogue between the authorities and between peoples at European level as well as an important pan-European forum for analysis and anticipation of destabilising tendencies which jeopardise the cohesion of society, for

[92] Treaty of Lisbon Amending the Treaty on European Union and the Treaty Establishing the European Community, adopted 13 December 2007 and entered into force 1 December 2009, OJEU 2007/C 306/01.
[93] European Convention on Human Rights, Protocol 14.

the sharing of national experience, for the establishment of standards, for enhancing universal values, for the dissemination of good practices and for the search for common answers to the problems which concern Europe as a whole.[94]

It is thus the will of the Member States that the Council of Europe will remain a non-militarised entity, pursuing the discussions of questions of common concern, promulgating economic, social, cultural, legal and administrative matters in furtherance of human rights and fundamental freedoms as the Statute of the organisation suggests. It is unlikely that the Council will evolve the political will and legal capacity to take positive interventionist action in furtherance of the responsibility to protect. Nevertheless, it will continue to fulfil its role as protector of those individuals within the jurisdiction of its Member States who find their rights engaged by the action or inaction of those States. In pursuance thereof, the Council of Europe's Court of Human Rights has unparalleled experience and considerable success. It is in discharging a responsibility to protect individuals from States infringing those rights enshrined in the European Convention that the true value of the Council of Europe becomes clear.

---

[94] COE Parliamentary Assembly Res. 1783, COE Doc. 12458, 4 January 2011, p. 10.

20

The Inter-American system of human rights

O. HILAIRE SOBERS

Introduction

The Inter-American Human Rights System (IAHRS), one of the world's oldest regional systems of human rights protection, emerged in 1948 with the creation of the Organization of American States (OAS), and the simultaneous adoption of the American Declaration on the Rights and Duties of Man by the founding States of the OAS. The OAS is the world's oldest regional organisation, having an institutional ancestry that goes back to the nineteenth century.[1] The IAHRS is thus part of a broader network of institutions, processes, and international legal instruments that are collectively known as the Inter-American System. Institutionally, the IAHRS is expressed through the Inter-American Commission on Human Rights (IACHR), established in 1959, and the Inter-American Court established twenty years later.

The UN Secretary-General has recognised that 'the Inter-American Court of Human Rights and the Inter-American Commission on Human Rights, along with the good offices of the Organization of American States, have made cardinal contributions to efforts to address serious human rights situations and to prevent mass atrocities'.[2] While it may be true that the IAHRS has contributed to advancing Responsibility to

---

The opinions expressed in this chapter are in the author's personal capacity and are not to be attributed to the Inter-American Commission on Human Rights (IACHR), the General Secretariat of the Organization of American States (OAS), or to the OAS.

[1] The OAS dates back to the First International Conference of American States, held in Washington, DC, from October 1889 to April 1890. The OAS Charter was formally adopted in 1948. Charter of the Organization of American States, adopted 30 April 1948 and entered into force 13 December 1951, 119 UNTS 3.

[2] UN Secretary-General, 'The Role of Regional and Sub-regional Arrangements in Implementing the Responsibility to Protect', UN Doc. A/65/877–S/2011/393, 27 June 2011, para. 20.

Protect (RtoP), I wish to advance the following arguments in this chapter:

(1) the contributions of the IAHRS have been largely confined to the first pillar[3] of RtoP, primarily in the form of early warning of (possible) mass atrocities, jurisprudence, and judicial protection of victims of mass atrocities;
(2) the IAHRS's capacity to contribute is limited, and continues to be limited by an institutional framework that does not expressly incorporate the principles of RtoP;
(3) there are measures that can be taken to better integrate RtoP into the existing Inter-American institutional framework, including the establishment of a Special Rapporteur on RtoP.

Background and context

Broadly, the Member States of the OAS share a history of overcoming colonialism in the cause of freedom and self-determination. It is therefore not surprising that the OAS itself is solidly built on, and around, the traditional principles of sovereignty and non-intervention. This is reflected in multiple provisions of the OAS Charter.[4] The Charter contains no express provisions for collective action where an individual Member State is failing, or has failed to protect its population from mass atrocities.

RtoP establishes a twofold obligation: a primary one on States and a complementary one on the international community to protect individuals from mass atrocity crimes. RtoP emphasises prevention above all, which ultimately may mean that traditional principles of sovereignty and non-intervention may have to yield to collective action aimed at protecting populations at risk of mass atrocity crimes. It is this tension between State sovereignty and human rights protection that RtoP seeks to address, when the State concerned has failed to protect its population.

While the 2005 World Summit Outcome Document signalled broad international endorsement of the RtoP doctrine, some States – including some from the Americas – have expressed reservations, if not outright opposition, to RtoP as possibly representing a tool of Western or US

---

[3] RtoP is built on three pillars: pillar one is the enduring responsibility of the State to protect its populations, whether nationals or not, from genocide, war crimes, ethnic cleansing and crimes against humanity, and from their incitement.

[4] See, for example, Charter of the OAS, arts. 1 and 19–23.

hegemony. Following UN-sanctioned interventions in Côte d'Ivoire and Libya in 2011, States like Nicaragua and Venezuela 'used particularly blunt language to criticise what they saw as the UN's complicity in neo-imperialist interventionism dressed up in humanitarian garb'.[5]

Bellamy points to the suspicion on the part of members of the international community that the RtoP doctrine might be subverted to pursue 'regime change', something that is outside the UN's mandate.[6] However, as Bellamy further points out, neither intervention in Cote d'Ivoire or Libya contravened the letter of the 2005 consensus on RtoP as a tool of preventing genocide, war crimes, ethnic cleansing and crimes against humanity or of protecting populations from ongoing atrocities.[7] In both cases, the use of force as authorised by the Security Council did result in regime change, though this was not the express aim of the Security Council. Bellamy acknowledges that though regime change and RtoP are distinct concepts,[8] he identifies a fundamental dilemma: in situations

---

[5] See Alex Bellamy, 'The Responsibility to Protect and the Problem of Regime Change', *e-International Relations*, 27 September 2011, at www.e-ir.info/?p=14350. Bellamy notes that Nicaragua complained: 'Once again we have witnessed the shameful manipulation of the slogan "protection of civilians" for dishonourable political purposes, seeking unequivocally and blatantly to impose regime change, attacking the sovereignty of a State Member of the United Nations [Libya] and violating the Organization's Charter.' Bellamy also mentions Brazil's position: 'The protection of civilians is a humanitarian imperative. It is a distinct concept that must not be confused or conflated with threats to international peace and security, as described in the Charter, or with the responsibility to protect. We must avoid excessively broad interpretations of the protection of civilians, which could link it to the exacerbation of conflict, compromise the impartiality of the United Nations or create the perception that it is being used as a smokescreen for intervention or regime change. To that end, we must ensure that all efforts to protect civilians be strictly in keeping with the Charter and based on a rigorous and non-selective application of international humanitarian law.'

[6] In this regard, Bellamy observes that, 'The relationship between RtoP and regime change has long been an uncomfortable one. The principal objections to the 2001 report of the International Commission on Intervention and State Sovereignty which coined the phrase Responsibility to Protect came from States and commentators worried about the widened potential for abuse that may accompany any relaxing of the general prohibition on force contained in Article 2(4) of the Charter. David Chandler, for instance, described the report as an argument for law-making and enforcement by the West. Amongst states, this view was most clearly expressed by Venezuela, which argued that the responsibility to protect would merely serve the interests of the powerful by granting them more freedom to intervene in the affairs of the weak without necessarily increasing global cooperation in response to humanitarian emergencies' ('Problem of Regime Change').

[7] *Ibid.*

[8] In this respect, Bellamy cites Edward Luck, the UN Secretary-General's Special Adviser on RtoP. Luck, in responding to questions about the link between RtoP and regime change stated, 'I should say that it isn't the goal of the responsibility to protect to change

where a State is responsible for committing genocide, war crimes, ethnic cleansing and/or crimes against humanity, how can the international community exercise its responsibility to protect populations without imposing regime change?

The challenge of integrating RtoP into the Inter-American System requires change, not only at the political and institutional level, but at the conceptual and doctrinal level as well. As the Secretary-General of the UN (UNSG) has pointed out, the concept of sovereignty has been undergoing refinement to make it more centred on 'responsibility'.[9] In this framework, apart from 'international privileges', sovereignty entails enduring obligations towards one's people, whereby the State, 'by fulfilling fundamental protection obligations and respecting core human rights, would have far less reason to be concerned about unwelcome intervention from abroad'.[10] Given the history of the Americas, a fear of 'unwelcome intervention' may manifest itself in continued tension between RtoP and the Inter-American System, if not outright resistance. Resistance may be one feature of the relationship between RtoP and the Inter-American System. However, as discussed below, so too is ambivalence.

The Inter-American System: a history of ambivalence

The history of the Americas reflects multiple instances or periods of mass atrocity crimes including slavery, genocide, and other crimes against humanity. Up until the 1990s, military dictatorships in Latin America routinely committed mass atrocities as a means of 'fighting communism' or maintaining 'national security'.[11] Chile's Pinochet, Paraguay's Stroessner and Nicaragua's Somoza are but a few of the personalities in this well-documented history.

---

regimes. The goal is to protect populations. It may be in some cases that the only way to protect populations is to change the regime, but that certainly is not the goal of the R2P per se' (Bernard Gwertzman, 'Will Syria Follow Libya?', *Council on Foreign Relations*, 1 September 2011, at www.cfr.org/syria/syria-follow-libya/p25745).

[9] UNSG, 'Implementing the Responsibility to Protect: Report of the Secretary General', UN Doc. A/63/677, 12 January 2009, para. 7.

[10] *Ibid.*

[11] See, generally, Martín Lozada, 'Law's response to crimes against humanity: some lessons from Argentina', speech delivered at inaugural address as Visiting Professor to the UNESCO Chair in Education for Peace, Human Rights and Democracy 2008, Utrecht University, 19 September 2008.

Despite the intergovernmental nature of the OAS and its emphasis on sovereignty and non-intervention, it was largely seen as a hostage of US foreign policy during the Cold War era.[12] Former Commissioner of the IACHR, Robert Goldman, offers this stark critique:

> Certainly, some of the [IACHR's] early priorities and activities were shaped in part by the realities of the Cold War and by the agenda that the United States was pushing within the political organs of the OAS, which the United States effectively dominated at the time. With the advent of the Cold War, US Latin American policy underwent significant transformation. The Roosevelt administration's Good Neighbor Policy was replaced in the 1950s by a policy that sought to contain the spread of communism in the hemisphere. Accordingly, the United States began providing a variety of support to numerous authoritarian regimes with questionable human rights practices on the ground that they were bulwarks against communist expansion. Thus, despite its formal espousal of non-intervention and support for human rights, the United States began to intervene, militarily and otherwise, in the domestic affairs of those Latin American states it deemed sympathetic to communist ideologies.[13]

The IAHRS took shape and carried out its activity in this political context. The IAHRS began with the adoption of the American Declaration of the Rights and Duties of Man in Bogotá, Colombia in April of 1948. The American Declaration was the first international human rights instrument of a general nature. For a decade following the adoption of the American Declaration, OAS Member States took no steps to establish any mechanisms to protect the rights enshrined in the American Declaration. The OAS was content with a declaratory regime of human rights until a regional crisis, involving the Dominican Republic, Venezuela and the USA prompted the creation of the Inter-American Commission on Human Rights in 1959.

As Forsythe explains, in 1959, Venezuela accused the Trujillo government in the Dominican Republic of fomenting unrest in Venezuela, and it sought OAS action. Cuba made similar complaints. These charges were couched not only in terms of Trujillo's violations of national sovereignty,

---

[12] See José Insulza, 'Secretary General's speech', speech delivered at Inter-American Bar Association 70th Anniversary Dinner, 15 May 2010, at www.oas.org/en/about/speech_secretary_general.asp?sCodigo=10-0033.

[13] Robert Goldman, 'History and Action: The Inter-American Human Rights System and the Role of the Inter-American Commission on Human Rights', *Human Rights Quarterly*, 31 (2009), 856–87, at 869.

territorial integrity, and non-intervention in domestic jurisdiction, but also in terms of violations of human rights by Trujillo at home.[14]

At the same time, growing concerns by some OAS members including the United States about political developments in Cuba translated into an incipient willingness (by some OAS States) to look into human rights issues within other countries. This represented a break from the traditional view of sovereignty that held that human rights fell within the exclusive province of nation States. The powerful Eisenhower administration, with an eye on Cuba as well, supported regional action on human rights in the Dominican Republic. However, most OAS members remained faithful to the traditional view of sovereignty and human rights, and thus rejected such regional action. Ultimately, to resolve this impasse, the OAS agreed on a compromise to promote human rights, one part of which was the creation of the Inter-American Commission on Human Rights.

The IACHR was initially given a restricted mandate to protect and promote human rights, primarily through the preparation of studies and reports and *in loco* visits to Member States. The IACHR's Statute formally incorporated the American Declaration as the human rights standard by which Member States would be evaluated.

In 1965, the IACHR was expressly authorized by the OAS to receive and decide individual complaints of human rights violations from persons throughout the hemisphere. The IACHR was established as a principal organ of the OAS with the adoption of the Protocol of Buenos Aires, signed in 1967. In 1969, the OAS adopted the American Convention on Human Rights (ACHR), which came into effect in 1978. Apart from prescribing more detailed rights and obligations, the ACHR marked an important institutional development, whereby the IACHR was joined by the Inter-American Court of Human Rights (IACtHR or Court), to establish a two-tier system of human rights protection. By virtue of the OAS Charter and the Commission's Statute, the IACHR continued to have competence to consider alleged violations of the American Declaration by OAS Member States that are not yet parties to the American Convention. The Court's first judges were elected on 22 May 1979 at the seventh special session of the OAS General Assembly. The Court's first hearing was held on 29 and 30 June 1979 at the OAS's seat in Washington, DC.

---

[14] David Forsythe, 'Human Rights, the United States and the Organization of American States', *Human Rights Quarterly*, 13 (1991), 66–98, at 81–3.

Arguably, the evolution of the IAHRS has been shaped by political impulses that have been at times contradictory or ambivalent. For example, in 1948, while all founding OAS States embraced the American Declaration as a normative expression of human rights standards, only six of them wanted the American Declaration to be part of the OAS Charter and hence binding international law. Only eight of the original OAS Member States wanted a binding convention on human rights, while the United States successfully opposed the creation of any OAS agency specifically charged with human rights action.[15] As already noted, sovereignty and non-intervention in domestic affairs was a major preoccupation of OAS States. Forsythe points out that the emphasis on sovereignty was partially shaped by 'repeated United States interventions in the internal affairs of hemispheric states',[16] as a result of which 'national sovereignty [was] thrown up as a barrier not only against the United States, but against the [human rights] regime itself'.[17] This dynamic harmonised well with the traditional view that human rights were a domestic matter – despite what the principles of the Charter and American Declaration might otherwise imply.[18]

At the time, anything beyond a declaratory regime of human rights would have been framed as impinging on sovereignty, given that for much of the hemisphere the practice of human rights at the domestic level was largely at variance with the very same standards set out in the Charter and Declaration. For example, segregation still existed as a matter of law in the United States for almost two decades after the adoption of the Charter and Declaration. In other parts of the hemisphere, systematic human rights abuse was well entrenched, particularly against minorities, and indigenous peoples.

A largely democratic hemisphere

The end of Cold War signalled the decline of anti-communism as the main US foreign policy concern in the Americas, and coincided with the 'third wave' of democratisation in Latin America, when the region's dictatorships largely gave way to newly democratically elected governments. At its 1991 General Assembly (in Santiago, Chile), the OAS could celebrate for the first time that the governments of all its Member States, except Cuba, resulted from democratic elections. The mass atrocities and systematic human rights violations that were associated with the Cold War era declined significantly

---

[15] See Forsythe, 'Human Rights', 77.   [16] *Ibid.*, 74.   [17] *Ibid.*   [18] *Ibid.*, 82.

as democratically elected governments assumed primacy in the Americas. It is this decline in mass atrocities and systematic human rights violations that have led some to question why RtoP is relevant in Latin America and the Caribbean. To illustrate, as recently as July 2011, the Secretary of the Secretariat for Political Affairs of OAS, Victor Rico Frontaura, a senior official, expressed the rather circular view that:

> The OAS has few existing mechanisms and mandates that specifically address and prevent the threats expressed in the narrow definition of RtoP. This situation reflects the positive fact that the region did not face those types of atrocities, except for specific periods when specific regions and countries experienced systematic human rights violations – including torture, forced disappearances of persons, massacres of indigenous peoples and peasants – were committed.[19]

By contrast, Ramcharan observes:

> Based on past experience, one could say that there are risks of genocide, ethnic cleansing, crimes against humanity, and war crimes in Latin America and the Caribbean. However, there are few existing instrumentalities that are specifically mandated to act preventively in response to such threats.[20]

The development of the IAHRS, and its capacity to embrace RtoP, has arguably been shaped by the contradictory political impulses that have shaped the OAS. While the IAHRS has matured from a declaratory regime into a protective regime, its institutional design and capacity continue to militate against a full embrace of RtoP. In this respect, Baranyi notes a 'striking gap in the official inter-American discourse at the interface of human rights and conflict prevention is its silence on the responsibility to protect'.[21]

The human rights bodies of the OAS have been described as 'more classical human rights bodies',[22] in so far as they typically focus more on

---

[19] See Victor Frontaura, 'Transcript from webcast', speech delivered at Informal Interactive Dialogue of the UN General Assembly on the Role of Regional and Sub-regional Arrangements in Implementing the Responsibility to Protect, 12 July 2011, available at www.responsibilitytoprotect.org.

[20] Bertrand Ramcharan, 'Enhancing the Responsibility to Protect in Latin America and the Caribbean', in Stanley Foundation, *The Role of Regional and Subregional Arrangements in Strengthening the Responsibility to Protect* (New York: Stanley Foundation, 2011), pp. 38–42, at p. 40.

[21] Stephen Baranyi, 'Inter-American Institutions and Conflict Prevention', policy paper FPP-05-04, Canadian Foundation for the Americas, March 2005, p. 6.

[22] Ramcharan, 'Enhancing the Responsibility to Protect', in Stanley Foundation, *Regional and Subregional Arrangements*, p. 40.

dispensation of justice after the fact. The very design of these bodies inhibits their capacity to react quickly to the risk or threat of mass atrocities being committed in the hemisphere and, as such, as Ramcharan concludes, 'one cannot say that alone, they can rise fully to the challenge of R2P'.[23] While these organs may indeed have limited capacity to react, this does not mean they lack any capacity to contribute to, or to reinforce the prevention element of RtoP, which arguably is the most important element of the doctrine.

The Inter-American human rights system: the Commission and the Court

The IAHRS is institutionally expressed through the Inter-American Commission and the Inter-American Court, both of which are autonomous organs of the OAS. Generally speaking, the Court exercises a purely judicial role in protecting human rights, while the IACHR plays a broader role that encompasses both protection and promotion of human rights. The Court, unlike the IACHR, is constituted purely by the American Convention, which came into effect in 1978. The IACHR, the older body, while recognised by the American Convention, is not constituted by it. From a juridical standpoint, this means that the Court's contentious jurisdiction is limited to States that not only have ratified the American Convention, but also have subscribed to its compulsory jurisdiction. A case cannot be submitted to the Court until and unless it has been first processed by the Commission in accordance with Articles 48–50 of the American Convention. In discharging its mandate, the Court exercises not only compulsory, but also advisory jurisdiction. Under Article 64 of the American Convention, any OAS Member State 'may consult the Court regarding the interpretation of the Convention or of other treaties concerning the protection of Human Rights in the American States'. States may also request the Court to provide opinions regarding the compatibility of any of their domestic laws with these international instruments. Apart from States, other organs of the OAS, principally the IACHR, may also solicit advisory opinions from the Court.

Given its broader juridical base, the IACHR exercises jurisdiction over all OAS States, whether or not they are signatories to the American Convention. The IACHR plays a mix of quasi-judicial, investigative, fact-finding and promotional roles in the field of human rights. For individuals, the IACHR is the first point of entry into the IAHRS, as

---

[23] *Ibid.*

the Court has no jurisdiction to entertain complaints coming directly from individuals. The different tasks assigned to the IACHR are reflected in the multiplicity of tools at its disposal, including adjudication of individual petitions, issuing precautionary measures, monitoring human rights in OAS States and promoting human rights awareness. The IACHR's mandate is supported by eight thematic rapporteurships,[24] seven of which are headed by IACHR Commissioners. In the first three decades, the IACHR relied substantially on country reports and on-site visits to advance its mandate.[25] While the IACHR continues to employ these mechanisms, the bulk of the IACHR's work is now the processing and adjudicating of individual petitions and cases.

For States that are not signatories to the American Convention, the IACHR generally applies the American Declaration, a standard that is binding on all OAS States. Both bodies have the power to issue interim measures of protection: precautionary measures in the case of the IACHR and provisional measures in the case of the Court.

The Inter-American human rights system and the responsibility to protect

Despite regional resistance and ambivalence towards RtoP, the IAHRS has supported and continues to support pillar one of RtoP by deploying its institutional machinery (1) to warn of possible risk of mass human rights abuses; and (2) to establish juridical precedents that entrench the values of RtoP. The mechanisms of early warning and juridical precedent work in tandem to protect actual or threatened victims of mass atrocities, to hold States accountable for preventing or redressing mass atrocities and to establish standards aimed at shaping domestic laws and practices in individual States.

---

[24] Special Rapporteurship for Freedom of Expression; Rapporteurship on the Rights of Women; Rapporteurship on the Rights of Migrant Workers and Their Families; Rapporteurship on the Rights of the Child; Rapporteurship on the Rights of Human Rights Defenders; Rapporteurship on the Rights of Indigenous Peoples; Rapporteurship on the Rights of Persons Deprived of Liberty; and the Rapporteurship on the Rights of Afro-Descendants and against Racial Discrimination. For information on each rapporteurship, see IACHR, 'Thematic Rapporteurship and Units', at www.oas.org/en/iachr/mandate/rapporteurships.asp.

[25] See Felipe González, 'The Experience of the Inter-American Human Rights System', *Victoria University of Wellington Law Review*, 40 (2009), 103–25, at 105.

As a strategy of preventing mass atrocities, 'early warning' is the centrepiece of the UN Secretary-General's 2010 RtoP report.[26] In that report, the Secretary-General notes that 'early warning does not always produce early action', but that 'it is also true that early action is highly unlikely without early warning'.[27] In this vein, the Secretary-General previously observed that 'in a rapidly unfolding emergency situation, the United Nations, regional, sub-regional and national decision makers must remain focused on saving lives through "timely and decisive" action ... not on following arbitrary, sequential or graduated policy ladders that prize procedure over substance and process over results.'[28]

In his 2009 RtoP report, the UNSG, in recounting the history of some of the major incidents of mass atrocity in the twentieth century, points out that:

> *First, in each case there were warning signs.* Violence of this magnitude takes planning and preparation, as well as a contributing political, social and economic context. *Second, the signals of trouble ahead were, time and again, ignored, set aside or minimized by high-level national and international decision makers with competing political agendas.* Third, at times the United Nations – its intergovernmental organs and its Secretariat – failed to do its part.[29]

The value of juridical precedent is captured by the UN Secretary-General's recognition that:

(1) The ultimate goal is to have States institutionalize and societies internalize these principles in a purposeful and sustainable manner. The more progress that States make towards including these principles in their legislation, policies, practices, attitudes, and institutions, the less recourse will there be to the third pillar (response).[30]

(2) Responsibility requires accountability ... International justice is a fall back option when domestic judicial processes prove inadequate to the task, as accountability should begin at home.[31]

---

[26] UNSG, 'Early Warning, Assessment and the Responsibility to Protect', UN Doc. A/64/864, 14 July 2010.

[27] *Ibid.*, para. 19.

[28] UNSG, 'Implementing the Responsibility to Protect', UN Doc. A/63/677, 12 January 2009, para. 50.

[29] *Ibid.*, para. 6 (emphasis added).

[30] UNSG, 'Regional and Sub-regional Arrangements', para. 11.   [31] *Ibid.*, para. 19.

Against this background, I now turn to the specific contributions made by the IAHRS in supporting pillar one of RtoP by way of early warning and juridical precedent.

Early warning

The former Executive Secretary of the IACHR, Santiago Canton, observes that:

> The IACHR's mandate to receive complaints of human rights violations has enabled it not only to take up individual cases but also to acquire a detailed understanding of situations involving large-scale human rights abuses. It can then take swift action to alert the international community about these situations. Known as 'early warning', this is perhaps the most important function of the IACHR, as it provides an avenue for timely intervention by the international community to prevent the continuation of massive violations of human rights.[32]

Baranyi echoes this view, suggesting that the Commission's 'watching briefs' on countries where there are patterns of systemic human rights violations are an authoritative source of early warning and awareness.[33] This capacity for early warning is arguably supported by the IACHR's tools of investigation and fact-finding, particularly in the form of on-site visits and country reports.

The IACHR's visit to Argentina in 1979 is perhaps one of the most striking examples of this capacity to expose systematic human rights abuses in the region. Until the IACHR's visit, Argentina's dictatorship had consistently denied the practices of clandestine detentions and forced disappearances. After the IACHR delegation arrived in Argentina, it received information that several dozen persons were being held in clandestine detention in an isolated area of an otherwise public prison. Before visiting the prison, the IACHR obtained the names of some of these detainees. During its visit to the prison, the delegation asked for and received a prisoner list that did not include any of the names they had been given. With great reluctance, the prison authorities allowed the delegation full access to the prison. At some point in the

---

[32] Santiago Canton, 'Amnesty Laws', in Katya Salazar and Thomas Antkowiak (eds.), *Victims Unsilenced: The Inter-American Human Rights System and Transitional Justice in Latin America* (Washington, DC: Due Process of Law Foundation, 2007), pp. 167–90, at p. 178.

[33] Baranyi, 'Conflict Prevention', p. 5.

delegation's inspection they heard people screaming from behind a wall *'Estamos aquí, estamos aquí!'* (We are here, we are here!). Confronted by this, the prison authorities were compelled to allow the IACHR delegation access to thirty hidden prisoners, who might otherwise have joined the large numbers of the 'disappeared' persons.[34] The IACHR investigation not only exposed the practice of forced disappearance in Argentina, but also prompted an OAS general resolution condemning the practice, without directly mentioning Argentina. The findings of the IACHR also had an impact at the level of the United Nations, which created a Working Group on Forced Disappearances, whose main initial task was to investigate the situation in Argentina.

The IACHR has also employed its investigative function to expose patterns of mass atrocities in other Latin American States such as Peru, El Salvador, Guatemala, and Nicaragua. In the case of Nicaragua, the IACHR issued a report in 1978 denouncing human rights violations committed by the Somoza regime. Somoza himself is reported as acknowledging that this exposure did contribute to his fall from power.[35]

Precautionary and provisional measures

Another set of potential early warning mechanisms available to the IAHRS are the so-called precautionary measures in the case of the IACHR,[36] and provisional measures in the case of the Court.[37] These measures are generally issued by these bodies when there is a serious risk of irreparable harm to a person if such measures are not indicated. Given its broader jurisdiction, the Commission may request any OAS State to adopt precautionary measures, while the Court can only direct provisional measures to States that have subscribed to the contentious jurisdiction of the Court.

According to Canton, since 1980 the Commission has issued more than 600 such measures. The Commission, in recent years, has received between 250 and 375 requests for precautionary measures annually, but

---

[34] See González, 'Inter-American Human Rights System', 108.   [35] *Ibid.*, 109.

[36] See IACHR, 'Rules of Procedure of the Inter-American Commission on Human Rights', art. 25, at www.oas.org/en/iachr/mandate/Basics/rulesiachr.asp.

[37] See Inter-American Court of Human Rights, 'Rules of Procedure of the Inter-American Court of Human Rights', art. 27, at www.corteidh.or.cr/reglamento/regla_ing.pdf.

grants fewer than 100 of those requests per year.[38] In 2010, the IACHR received 375 requests, but granted only 68 of them.[39]

As a matter of practice, the Commission generally requests provisional measures from the Court only when it finds that a State has failed to, or is reluctant to comply with the precautionary measures issued. According to former IACHR Chair Felipe González, 'Unlike the situation of enforcement of decisions in specific cases, states' record of compliance with the Commission's precautionary measures is very high, particularly regarding the protection of life', and that as regards provisional measures adopted by the Court, 'only in a handful of decisions the states have not obeyed them'.[40]

The power of juridical precedent

As 'classic human rights bodies', the jurisprudence of the Commission and the Court, for the most part, arise only after human rights violations have been established, including mass atrocities of the type that RtoP is designed to address. It might be argued that this *ex post facto* character disqualifies inter-American jurisprudence from being considered as a tool of prevention, particularly with respect to mass atrocity crimes. However, it can equally be argued that jurisprudential precedent can help to establish or clarify the boundaries between acceptable and unacceptable State behaviour as it relates to their international human rights obligations. In so doing, precedents may serve to generate or reinforce domestic laws, policies, practices and institutions so as to substantially reduce the risk of mass atrocities occurring or, in some cases, recurring in the hemisphere. More fundamentally, precedent-setting can have the effect of reinforcing the rule of law, a vital component of any regime of human rights protection.

One area in which the IAHRS has laid down some clear markers is the area of amnesty laws which emerged in many Latin American countries to immunize military dictatorships from criminal responsibility for mass

---

[38] See Canton, 'The Inter-American Commission on Human Rights: 50 Years of Advances and the New Challenges', *Americas Quarterly* (summer 2009), at www.americasquarterly.org/Inter-American-Commission-Human-Rights.

[39] For a more detailed tabulation of precautionary measures requests received and granted in 2010 and in previous years, see IACHR, 'Annual Report on the Inter-American Commission on Human Rights 2010', OAS Doc. OEA/Ser.L/V/II. Doc. 5, rev. 1, 7 March 2011.

[40] González, 'Inter-American Human Rights System', 123–4.

human rights abuses, including crimes against humanity. A number of Member States passed laws that curtailed the scope for investigations, prosecutions and convictions, as well as for making reparations to the victims. These domestic laws conflicted with international law prohibitions on general amnesties in cases of serious violations of international law, including mass atrocity violations such as genocide and crimes against humanity.

The IACHR played a significant role not only in exposing the human rights crimes of military dictatorships, but also in isolating such criminal regimes from the rest of the international community. With a cluster of cases in 1992, the IACHR issued its first juridical rebuke of amnesty laws. These cases emanated from El Salvador, Argentina, and Uruguay.

In the *Las Hojas* case from El Salvador,[41] the IACHR, while limiting its legal analysis to State responsibility for a massacre of seventy-four persons, nevertheless found that El Salvador's amnesty law 'legally eliminated the possibility of an effective investigation and the prosecution of the responsible parties, as well as proper compensation for the victims and their next-of-kin by reason of the civil liability for the crime committed'.[42] In cases coming from Argentina[43] and from Uruguay,[44] the IACHR explicitly found that the amnesty laws of these States were incompatible with the judicial and due process protections enshrined in Article 8 and 25 of the American Convention. The IACHR also concluded that these amnesty laws were incompatible with the obligation of States to guarantee the full and free exercise of the rights recognised in the Convention.[45] These decisions were perhaps the first by an international human rights body to find that amnesty laws violate international human rights law.

Starting with the case of *Barrios Altos*, the Inter-American Court has been as vehement as the IACHR in rejecting amnesty laws as incompatible with the American Convention. The *Barrios* case, from Peru, involved the execution of fifteen people on 3 November 1991 by an 'elimination squad' known as the Colina Group, made up of members

---

[41] *Masacre Las Hojas* v. *El Salvador*, IACHR, Report No. 26/92, Case 10.287, 24 September 1992.

[42] *Ibid.*, para. 11.

[43] *Consuelo et al.* v. *Argentina*, IACHR, Report No. 28/92, Cases 10.147, 10.181, 10.240, 10.262, 10.309 and 10.311, 2 October 1992.

[44] *Mendoza et al.* v. *Uruguay*, IACHR, Report No. 29/92, Cases 10.029, 10.036, 10.145, 10.305, 10.372 10.373, 10.374 and 10.375, 2 October 1992.

[45] For a more detailed analysis, see Canton, 'Amnesty Laws', pp. 170–87.

of the Peruvian army with ties to military intelligence. Despite ongoing criminal proceedings, on 14 June 1995 the Peruvian Congress secretly approved an amnesty law drafted by the then Fujimori regime without congressional debate. This law exempted military and police forces and civilians from any responsibility for any human rights violations that they may have committed or participated in between 1980 and 1995. On 28 June 1995, the Congress passed a second law that (1) barred any judicial review of the amnesty law; and (2) broadened the scope of the original law by conferring a general amnesty on all military or police officers or civilians who might be subject to prosecution for human rights violations committed between 1980 and 1995, even if they had not yet been accused of a crime – effectively precluding any inquiry into such cases. Based on this new amnesty regime, the Criminal Chamber of the Superior Court of Justice in Lima definitively terminated the criminal proceedings against those indicted for the Barrios Altos massacre.

Six years later, on 14 March 2001, the Inter-American Court unhesitatingly rejected Peru's amnesty laws as lacking legal effect, holding that, *inter alia*, 'Self-amnesty laws lead to the defencelessness of victims and perpetuate impunity; therefore, they are manifestly incompatible with the aims and spirit of the Convention.'[46]

In 2006, the Court expressly invalidated Chile's amnesty law in the case of *Almonacid*, where the Court found that the victim had been subjected to a crime against humanity.[47] In rejecting this amnesty law as incompatible with the American Convention, the Court acknowledged that the Decree Law had not been applied by the Chilean courts in several cases since 1998, but nevertheless emphasised that its very existence as part of Chilean domestic law violated the State's obligations under Article 2 of the American Convention.[48] In the case of *Gomes-Lund*, Brazil became the third OAS State to have its amnesty law

---

[46] *Case of Barrios Altos v. Peru, Judgment*, IACtHR, Series C, No. 75, 14 March 2001, paras. 43–4.

[47] *Case of Almonacid Arellano et al. v. Chile, Judgment*, IACtHR, Series C, No. 154, 26 September 2006.

[48] *Ibid.*, see para. 121, where the Court observes that: 'The fact that such Decree Law has not been applied by the Chilean courts in several cases since 1998 is a significant advance, and the Court appreciates it, but it does not suffice to meet the requirements of Article 2 of the Convention in the instant case. Firstly because, as it has been stated in the preceding paragraphs, Article 2 imposes the legislative obligation to annul all legislation which is in violation of the Convention, and secondly, because the criterion of the domestic courts may change, and they may decide to reinstate the application of a provision which remains in force under the domestic legislation.'

invalidated by the Inter-American Court.[49] In February 2011, the Court similarly repudiated Uruguay's amnesty laws in the case of *Gelman*.[50]

The IACHR has continued to maintain pressure on States to conform to this strong jurisprudence against amnesty regimes that immunise State agents from judicial accountability for systematic human rights abuses. In January 2010 the Commission criticized a Honduras amnesty law containing 'concepts that are confusing or ambiguous',[51] and in January 2011 it reminded Haiti of its international obligations in this respect following former dictator Jean Claude Duvalier's return to Haiti.

The domestic effect of jurisprudence

Admittedly, the IAHRS's jurisprudence on amnesty laws has had mixed results. El Salvador has pointedly refused to repeal its amnesty law, despite follow-up activity by the IACHR.[52] With respect to Argentina and Uruguay, neither State was prompted to repeal their amnesty laws as a result of the IACHR's initial decisions in 1992. However, when Argentina's Supreme Court did finally nullify Argentina's 1987 amnesty law, it relied significantly on the Inter-American Court's decision in *Barrios Altos* to ground its judgment.[53] In May 2011, Uruguay's Congress failed to overturn Uruguay's amnesty law despite the Court's decision in *Gelman*.[54] Peru ultimately complied with the Inter-American

---

[49] *Case of Gomes-Lund et al. (Guerrilha do Araguaia) v. Brazil, Judgment*, IACtHR, Series C, No. 219, 24 November 2010.

[50] *Case of Gelman v. Uruguay, Judgment*, IACtHR, Series C, No. 221, 24 February 2011.

[51] In this regard, the Commission referred to 'the doctrinaire reference made to political crimes, the amnesty for conduct of a terrorist nature, and the inclusion of the concept of abuse of authority with no indication of its scope' (IACHR press release, 'IACHR Expresses Concern About Amnesty Decree in Honduras', 3 February 2010, at www. cidh.oas.org/Comunicados/English/2010/14-10eng.htm).

[52] According to Santiago Canton, 'The Inter-American Commission has held follow-up hearings and the State has refused to modify its position: it refuses to entertain any possibility of complying with the IACHR's recommendations' ('Amnesty Laws', in Salazar and Antkowiak (eds.), *Victims Unsilenced*, p. 176).

[53] David Baluarte and Christian De Vos, *From Judgment to Justice: Implementing International and Regional Human Rights Decisions* (New York: Open Society Foundations, 2010), p. 69.

[54] See Lisl Brunner, 'Is Uruguay Foundering on the Path to Accountability? The Aftermath of the *Gelman* Decision of the Inter-American Court', *Accountability* (summer 2011), at www.asil.org/accountability/summer_2011_3.cfm. See also 'Uruguayan Congress fails to gain a majority to annul amnesty law', *Latin America News Dispatch*, 20 May 2011, at www.latindispatch.com/2011/05/20/uruguayan-congress-fails-to-gain-a-majority-to-annul-amnesty-law.

Court's decision in *Barrios Altos*, but not without first threatening to withdraw from the Court's jurisdiction. Notwithstanding the uneven impact of this jurisprudence, it is arguable that the decisions of both the IACHR and the Court have significantly undermined the culture of impunity that characterised the dictatorships in the Americas, and the amnesty laws that this culture promoted. While this jurisprudence can hardly restore the lives lost or shattered by the mass atrocities that occurred, it certainly has the capacity to strengthen the rule of law in the hemisphere, thus restraining governments from inflicting mass human rights abuses on their respective populations.

Conclusion and recommendations

Despite the general acceptance of the RtoP doctrine at an international level, the history of the Americas generally makes the OAS and the IAHRS reflexively wary of embracing it wholeheartedly, particularly where it may be perceived to infringe on traditional notions of sovereignty, or be used as covert tool for regime change. In the context of inadequate resources and the challenges of State compliance, the IAHRS has demonstrated some capacity for supporting RtoP, through its early warning mechanisms and precedent-setting jurisprudence. Both have generally served to strengthen the rule of law in the Americas. In this regard, the IAHRS has not only demonstrated the capacity to alert the international community to threats to or actual human rights violations, but has firmly established the illegality of amnesty provisions for members of authoritarian regimes guilty of systematic human rights violations. Nevertheless, as the IACHR has observed, impunity for human rights violations continues to be 'one of the major obstacles to the effective rule of law in the region'.[55]

Despite the institutional limitations of the OAS and its IAHRS, it may be possible to renovate its architecture in some respects, to make it more responsive to the imperatives of RtoP. One area of renovation might be universal accession to the American Convention coupled with universal acceptance of the Inter-American Court's compulsory jurisdiction. Presently, nine of the thirty-five OAS States are not parties to the Convention, with only twenty-one of thirty-five OAS States accepting the Court's compulsory jurisdiction. This status quo makes for uneven application and reach of the IAHRS, thus undermining its capacity to

---

[55] IACHR, 'Annual Report 2010', p. 1.

respond to threatened mass atrocities. However, it must be said that most, if not all, of the countries with a history of military dictatorships and systematic human rights violations have acceded to the American Convention and accepted the compulsory jurisdiction of the Court. The countries that remain outside of the ambit of the Convention or the Court are the English-speaking Caribbean, the USA and Canada. While these countries may not share the same contemporary history of mass human rights abuses, their full incorporation into the IAHRS would make for a more unified regional system of human rights protection and enforcement. Naturally, a more unified regional system of human rights will require substantially more fiscal support from the OAS Member States than currently obtains.

Bertrand Ramcharan has proposed (*inter alia*) the idea of an *Inter-American Commissioner on Human Rights and the Responsibility to Protect*, with 'specific mandates to act preventively and to spearhead urgent-action responses'.[56] It is unclear whether Ramcharan conceptualizes such a 'Commissioner' as being (1) a functionary of the IACHR only; or (2) a functionary of the OAS. If the former, the functionary would be a Commissioner of the IACHR or a person designated by the Commissioners to act on their behalf. If the latter, it would be a person appointed directly by the OAS Secretary General, presumably based on a mandate issued by the OAS General Assembly.

By way of background, the IACHR has an existing system of rapporteurships, as prescribed by Article 15 of the IACHR's Rules of Procedure.[57] Generally rapporteurships are assigned to Commissioners, but the IACHR has the power to create *special* rapporteurships headed by persons who are not Commissioners. Currently, the IACHR has a Special Rapporteur on Freedom of Expression. Unlike the Commissioners who operate on a part-time basis, the Special Rapporteur on Freedom of Expression operates on a full-time basis.

For the sake of bureaucratic efficiency, it would appear more feasible to take advantage of the IACHR's existing framework of thematic rapporteurships, than navigating the institutional and legal challenges of establishing a separate (OAS) bureaucracy responsible for RtoP. Therefore, the creation of a full time Special Rapporteur on RtoP would be more preferable. While operating primarily within the walls

---

[56] See Ramcharan, 'Enhancing the Responsibility to Protect', in Stanley Foundation, *Regional and Subregional Arrangements*, p. 42.

[57] See IACHR, 'Rules of Procedure'.

of the IACHR, such a Rapporteur could be given additional authority by the OAS to pursue a broader mandate of institutionalising RtoP in the OAS and the Americas. This would be in keeping not only with the OAS's status as a regional agency of the UN, but also with the special role assigned to regional organisations in advancing the imperatives of RtoP.[58] I would see the Special Rapporteur on RtoP as fulfilling a role similar to that of the Special Adviser of the Secretary-General on the Prevention of Genocide (UN Special Adviser).[59] More specifically, however, I would see the Special Rapporteur on RtoP as discharging two interrelated mandates – protection and institutionalisation.

Under the protection mandate, the Special Rapporteur on RtoP would primarily be concerned with activating and monitoring the IAHRS's early warning mechanisms such as precautionary and provisional measures. In addition, the Special Rapporteur could also act as a mechanism of early warning to the OAS Secretary General and through him to the OAS Permanent Council, by bringing to their attention situations that could potentially result in mass atrocities. In this vein, the Special Rapporteur would also make recommendations to the OAS Secretary General and the OAS Permanent Council to prevent or halt mass atrocities.

Using the UN Special Adviser as a model, the Special Rapporteur could also collect existing information, from within the Inter-American System, on massive and serious violations of human rights and international humanitarian law, which, if not prevented or halted, might lead to mass atrocities. In this respect, the Special Rapporteur could avail him/herself of some of the existing powers of the IACHR, including:

---

[58] See '2005 World Summit Outcome', UN Doc. A/RES/60/1, 24 October 2005, para. 139; UNSG, 'Regional and Sub-regional Arrangements', in particular paras. 2, 3, 9, 17, 20, 23 and 27.

[59] See UNSG, 'Early Warning', para. 6, which sets out the responsibilities of the Special Adviser as follows: (1) to collect existing information, in particular from within the United Nations system, on massive and serious violations of human rights and international humanitarian law of ethnic and racial origin which, if not prevented or halted, might lead to genocide; (2) to act as a mechanism of early warning to the Secretary-General, and through him to the Security Council, by bringing to their attention situations that could potentially result in genocide; (3) to make recommendations to the Security Council, through the Secretary-General, on actions to prevent or halt genocide; (4) to liaise with the United Nations system on activities for the prevention of genocide and to work to enhance the capacity of the United Nations to analyse and manage information regarding genocide or related crimes.

preparation of studies or reports,[60] on-site visits[61] (to at-risk States), making recommendations to States[62] on implementing RtoP and thematic hearings[63] during regular sessions of the IACHR. Additionally, the Special Rapporteur might be tasked with monitoring cases before the IACHR and the Inter-American Court of Human Rights that may have a bearing on advancing the principles of RtoP or in holding States accountable for mass atrocities where they have occurred. By utilising these and other related means, the Special Rapporteur would also have a role to play in developing an awareness of RtoP among the peoples of the Americas.[64] As the UN Secretary-General has noted, the ultimate goal is to have States institutionalise and societies internalise these principles in a purposeful and sustainable manner. The more progress that States make towards including these principles in their legislation, policies, practices, attitudes, and institutions, the less recourse will there be to the third pillar (response).[65]

The Special Rapporteur could also spearhead the institutionalisation of RtoP in the OAS by:

(1) assessing the state of 'RtoP readiness' of the Inter-American System; and thereafter developing and advising on programmes, policies, practices, protocols and instruments that systematically entrench all three pillars of RtoP in the legal and institutional machinery of the OAS as well as that of individual Member States;

(2) developing institutional capacity to support and sustain RtoP principles and practices by establishing synergies between key departments of the OAS General Secretariat, and training key OAS officials on incorporating RtoP principles and practices into existing OAS programmes;

(3) liaising with the Special Adviser of the Secretary-General on the Prevention of Genocide, with a view to promoting institutional convergence between the OAS and the UN on RtoP 'best practices'; and

(4) lobbying for universal ratification of key regional human rights treaties, such as the American Convention on Human Rights, coupled with universal accession to the compulsory jurisdiction of the Inter-American Court.

---

[60] See IACHR, 'Statute of the Inter-American Commission on Human Rights', art. 18(c), at www.oas.org/en/iachr/mandate/Basics/statuteiachr.asp.

[61] *Ibid.*, art. 18(g).   [62] *Ibid.*, art. 18(b).

[63] See IACHR, 'Rules of Procedure', arts. 61–70.   [64] See IACHR, 'Statute', art. 18(a).

[65] UNSG, 'Regional and Sub-regional Arrangements', para. 11.

In discharging both mandates, the Special Rapporteur would be positioning not just the IAHRS, but the Inter-American system as a whole, to realise the vision of the 2005 Outcome Document: to prevent genocide, war crimes, ethnic cleansing and crimes against humanity and their incitement, and to respond in a timely and decisive manner when 'peaceful means [are] inadequate and national authorities are manifestly failing to protect their populations' from these crimes and violations.[66]

As already noted, the international community has broadly bought into the vision of RtoP. Greater embrace of RtoP by the Inter-American System/IAHRS will ultimately depend not on the skill of a Special Rapporteur, but on the collective political will of the region's States.

---

[66] *Ibid.*, para. 3.

21

The African system of human rights

FRANS VILJOEN

Terminological and contextual background

The responsibility to protect (R2P) allows the international community to coercively intervene, as a matter of last resort, in the territory and therefore also into the domestic affairs of a State when that State is manifestly unable or unwilling to ensure the protection of the most basic rights of those under its jurisdiction.[1] The responsibility to protect is premised on the acceptance that a State's national sovereignty is derived from, and conditional upon it respecting and protecting at least the most basic rights of its own nationals.[2] Should the State fail in this foundational obligation, the international community is accorded a complementary role to ensure the protection of affected persons in that particular State.[3] It is generally accepted that only violations giving rise to massive killings in the form of genocide, war crimes, ethnic cleansing and crimes against humanity would suffice to trigger coercive intervention under R2P.[4] However, R2P does not manifest itself only as coercive intervention, but may also – and more frequently – be invoked with

---

[1] See '2005 World Summit Outcome', UN Doc. A/RES/60/1, 24 October 2005, para. 139.

[2] In human rights terms, the responsibility to protect is derived from and linked to the notion that 'the primary responsibility for the promotion and protection of human rights lies with the state'. Organization of African Unity, Grand Bay (Mauritius) Declaration and Plan of Action, adopted 16 April 1999, AU Doc. CONF/HRA/DECL (I), para. 15; see also African Union, Kigali Declaration, adopted 8 May 2003, AU Doc. MIN/CONF/HRA/Decl.1 (I), para. 27.

[3] International Commission on Intervention and State Sovereignty, *The Responsibility to Protect* (Ottawa: International Development Research Centre, 2001), para. 2.32.

[4] While both '2005 World Summit Outcome', para. 139 and United Nations Secretary-General, 'Implementing the Responsibility to Protect', UN Doc. A/63/677, 12 January 2009, para. 10(b) mention 'ethnic cleansing', as a legal category this aspect is arguably adequately covered by 'genocide' (if the cleansing is done with the requisite intent), 'war crimes' or 'crimes against humanity'. See also Rome Statute of the International Criminal Court, adopted 17 July 1998 and entered into force 1 July 2002, 2187 UNTS 90, arts. 6–8.

reference to imminent or threatening violations *before* they result in R2P-type situations ('prevention'), the circumstances that led up to and gave rise to these situations ('reaction'), and addressing the consequences of the violations ('rebuilding').[5]

Judicial and quasi-judicial human rights bodies are not themselves engaged directly in the most controversial aspect of R2P, namely coercive intervention. At most, they may play an indirect role by providing relevant information to the political organs in order to inform political decisions to intervene, or to initiate discussions about possible intervention. It is more likely that human rights institutions would be called upon to prevent situations from reaching the tipping point at which R2P could be invoked; and to hold States accountable for transgressions, albeit retrospectively.

This chapter focuses on the role of the African regional human rights system in the context of R2P, and not on the political organs of the African Union (AU) and the mandate under Article 4(h) of the AU Constitutive Act.[6] Under 'African regional human rights system' is understood the African Commission on Human and Peoples' Rights (African Commission, or the Commission) and the African Court on Human and Peoples' Rights (African Human Rights Court, African Court, or the Court). The Commission is designed as an impotent quasi-judicial institution and both the Commission and the Court are charged with monitoring the main normative pillar of the African regional human rights system, as laid out in the African Charter on Human and Peoples' Rights (African Charter or Charter). The Charter was adopted under the auspices of the Organisation of African Unity (now the African Union). In addition, some reference is made to the African Committee of Experts on the Rights of the Child (African Children's Committee), the monitoring body of the African Charter on the Rights and Welfare of the Child (African Children's Charter). The AU also adopted further norms of relevance in the context of R2P, in particular the AU Convention for the Protection and Assistance of Internally Displaced Persons in Africa (Kampala Convention), under which States bear the 'primary duty and *responsibility for providing protection* of and humanitarian assistance to internally displaced persons

---

[5] ICISS, *The Responsibility to Protect*, para. 2.32.

[6] See for example Dan Kuwali, *The Responsibility to Protect: Implementation of Article 4(h) Intervention* (Leiden; Boston: Martinus Nijhoff, 2011); and Dersso, Chapter 10 in this book.

within their territory or jurisdiction without discrimination of any kind'.[7] Internal displacement often results from mass scale violations and calls for State action to ameliorate the effects of these violations on its own population. Failure to do so may easily see the escalation of human rights violations, and may result in widespread insecurity. As an AU instrument without its own monitoring body, the promotion and protection of the rights in the Kampala Convention is also the responsibility of the Commission and the Court.[8]

The responsibility to protect should not be equated with the general obligation on States under human rights law to 'protect' the human rights of those under their jurisdiction against interference or violations by non-State actors. The duty (or 'responsibility') to protect human rights, in this sense, is part of the tripartite obligation of States to *respect*, *protect* and *fulfil* all relevant rights.[9] In this sense, 'protect' is juxtaposed against 'respect' and 'fulfil', which respectively denote non-interference by the State, and the allocation of State resources to the realisation of rights.[10] While the obligation to protect human rights speaks to the obligation of each specific (individual) State, the doctrine of R2P refers to the collective responsibility of the international community, and presumes actions undertaken by actors distinct and separate from the State itself. The duty to protect human rights is part of the State's general obligation, derived from its primary responsibility for the human rights of persons under its jurisdiction. The responsibility to protect is complementary to a State's primary responsibility, and kicks in when a State fails or is unable to respect, protect and fulfil basic human rights. Often, R2P will come into play when the State is unable to protect its nationals or others against non-State actors, such as guerrilla groups in situations of armed civil conflict, or when generalised ethnic violence

---

[7] AU, African Union Convention for the Protection and Assistance of Internally Displaced Persons in Africa (Kampala Convention), adopted 22 October 2009, art. 5(1) (emphasis added).

[8] See AU, Kampala Convention, arts. 14(4) and 20(3). However, the Convention is not yet in force.

[9] Under the African Charter, the main obligation of States Parties is to 'recognise the rights, duties and freedoms' in the Charter and to 'give effect' to them through the adoption of 'legislative and other measures'. Constitutive Act of the African Union, adopted 11 July 2000 and entered into force 26 May 2001, 2158 UNTS 3, art. 1.

[10] The African Commission embraced this terminology in the *Ogoniland* case. *Social and Economic Rights Action Centre (SERAC) and Another v. Nigeria* (2001) AHRLR 60 (ACHPR 2001), paras. 45–6.

takes place.[11] To this extent, there is an overlap between the duty to protect human rights and R2P. However, not every instance of a State's failure to comply with its duty to protect human rights is linked to or will give rise to R2P. It only comes into play when the failure to protect human rights exposes a significant part of the population to threats of or actual violations to their bodily integrity, security and life. Not only the 'protect' element of the obligations-triad potentially justifies an R2P response. A State's obligation to *respect* the rights of those under its jurisdiction is breached if the State unjustifiably interferes into the enjoyment of their rights, most radically, by using government force to deprive them of their lives. As far as the 'fulfilment' obligation is concerned, although this is presently not the case, R2P may in the future also be applicable to situations of natural disasters giving rise to widespread loss of life (such as a famine) due to the State's unwillingness or inability to cope with the situation.[12]

This contribution looks at the potential and actual role of the African regional human rights system in (1) avoiding massive and widespread violations through prevention and early warning strategies; (2) playing an enabling role by providing information to political organs in respect of R2P-type situations; (3) ascribing responsibility and ensuring accountability for large-scale violations; and (4) rebuilding societies after massive violations.

Preventing situations that would necessitate the invocation of R2P

The African Commission and the Court may in a number of ways contribute to prevent circumstances from deteriorating into conditions that potentially justify forcible international intervention. In addition to the instances discussed below, the Commission may also adopt country-specific *resolutions*, but these resolutions are clearly only ad hoc

---

[11] See for example *Commission Nationale des Droits de l'Homme et des Libertés v. Chad* (2000) AHRLR 66 (ACHPR 1995), para. 22. The Commission found that, by failing to 'provide security and stability in the country', Chad allowed 'serious and massive violations of human rights' to take place. See also *Amnesty International and Others v. Sudan* (2000) AHRLR 297 (ACHPR 1999); and *Zimbabwe Human Rights NGO Forum v. Zimbabwe* (2005) AHRLR 128 (ACHPR 2005), para. 151.

[12] ICISS, *The Responsibility to Protect*, para. 4.20. But, see UNSG, 'Implementing the Responsibility to Protect', para. 10(b), which rejects this view on the basis that it would deviate too far from the current consensus on R2P.

recommendatory statements without any tangible follow-up and are consequently lacking in political resonance.[13]

State reporting

States Parties to the African Charter are required to report to the African Commission, sitting as an independent body of experts. States that have accepted the African Peer Review Mechanism (APRM), instituted under the New Partnership for Africa's Development (NEPAD), are also subject to a more politicised system of review by a panel made up of government-instructed representatives. In this respect, the APRM mirrors the UN Universal Periodic Review (UPR). State reporting to both independent expert bodies or under more political review processes is scheduled to take place at more or less regular intervals. If reporting is a continuing process, and is undertaken with rigour, these processes may play an important role in identifying the root causes of potential future human rights violations. Optimal State reporting and political review processes are thus ways of foretelling violations and forestalling their occurrence.

The theory and practice of State reporting under the African Charter are at odds. In theory, State reporting provides an opportunity for constructive dialogue that should identify not only the major obstacles in the way of giving effect to the Charter, but also reveal the major fault lines and smouldering volcanoes that may erupt and lead to serious violations. In practice, however, State reporting under the Charter suffers from numerous deficiencies that limit its role in preventing human rights violations. Some of these deficiencies are: the failure of many States to report at all; irregular and infrequent reporting; the quality of reports, which tend to be overly formulaic and formalistic; delays between the submission of reports and their consideration; and lack of visibility of the reporting process and of the concluding observations.

Today, still, the 1994 Rwandan genocide represents one of the worst failures of a government to exercise its sovereignty responsibly to protect

---

[13] The Commission used 'R2P-language' in one of its resolutions urging the 'parties to the conflicts in north-east DRC, Chad and Central African Republic, to observe their obligations under international human rights law and to ensure that they respect the fundamental human rights of the civilian population, in particular the rights of women, children and internally displaced peoples' (ACHPR Res. 117 (XXXII), AU Doc. ACHPR/Res.117 (XXXXII), 28 November 2007, para. 7).

its own people. In human rights terms, the State failed in its obligation both to respect and protect the rights of its people. Historical reconstructions provide ample evidence that the genocide did not happen overnight, but that many pre-existing factors (such as hate propaganda and discrimination on the basis of ethnicity) contributed to make it possible. It is ironic that Rwanda's initial report was one of the first to be examined by the African Commission, not many years before the genocide erupted, in 1991. Perhaps little should have been expected from its examination, as it was part of the first tentative steps the Commission took in dealing with State reports. Also, the report was only ten pages long, thus limiting the scope and extent of the dialogue with the representatives of the State Party. Even so, the failure of the Commission, at that time, to adopt concluding observations on any of the reports further underlines the potential futility of this exercise. No public record exists of the outcome of this process, apart from a follow-up letter, which the Chair of the Commission wrote to the government, noting that 'some members of the Commission expressed the wish for supplementary information on equality before the law and the prohibition of all forms of discrimination'.[14] While these remarks suggest some sensitivity on the part of the Commissioners for the crucial issue of discrimination on the basis of ethnicity, the lack of rigour and incisiveness rendered the role of this process in addressing the determinants of genocide negligible if not meaningless.[15]

As the Commission placed its reporting procedures on a firmer footing, over time, it started playing a more distinct role in guiding States towards strategies that would contribute to the prevention of serious and widespread human rights violations. One of the strategies it adopted was to encourage human rights education, particularly among police and

---

[14] Astrid Danielsen, *The State Reporting Procedure under the African Charter* (Copenhagen: Danish Centre for Human Rights, 1994), p. 91.

[15] The Commission's role should be contrasted with that of the UN Committee on the Elimination of Racial Discrimination (CERD), which reviewed the country situation in the absence of a State report in March 1994, a few weeks before the crisis started, 'strongly' recommending that 'decisive steps be taken immediately at the international level, through the Secretary-General of the United Nations, and at the regional and national levels, to break the vicious cycle of ethnic violence and atrocities that continues in Rwanda' (UN CERD, 'Report of the Committee on the Elimination of Racial Discrimination', UN Doc. A/49/18, para. 66). The failure within the UN to do anything to prevent the genocide was not due to the lack of identifying the impending disaster by a human rights treaty body, but to the failure of political organs to take action in response to the information provided to them.

other security officials. In its concluding observations, for example, the Commission repeatedly called on States to disseminate and ensure training on the Robben Island Guidelines for the Prohibition of Torture. It also frequently recommended that States should address the underlying causes of human rights violations. In respect of Egypt, for example, the Commission in 2005 called on the government to lift the state of emergency, to engage more with civil society, and to ensure that its measures to curb terrorism are in line with international human rights standards.[16] The Egyptian popular uprising of 2011 attests to the failure of political action in responses to these – and many other – recommendations by the African Commission and other human rights bodies.

So far, 31 African States out of the 54 Member States of the AU have accepted the voluntary review process of the APRM. This review deals with the holistic view of governance and is thus not devoted exclusively to human rights. The APRM differs from the UPR in the voluntary acceptance by States, and the more substantive scope of the review. Although the process is not beyond criticism, its outcome reports and recommendations to States had at least on occasion read like chronicles of massive human rights violations foretold. The APRM *Country Review Report of South Africa* of November 2006, for example, recommended that the government put in place 'better-informed measures in order to combat the growing problem of xenophobia',[17] not long before violent outbreaks of xenophobia in the country in 2008. In similar vein, the 2006 APRM *Country Review Report of Kenya* recommended that steps be taken to 'defuse ethnic tension and promote tolerance',[18] addressing an issue that surged to prominence after the contested presidential elections of late 2007. Timely responses to the pertinent recommendations could have assisted in averting the slide into ethnically based violence, which ultimately led to the prosecution of prominent Kenyans before the ICC.

This discussion underscores that State reporting has significant potential to assist in the early identification and in preventing the intensification of human rights violations to a level where the State becomes unable

---

[16] ACHPR, 'Concluding Observations and Recommendations on the Seventh and Eighth Periodic Report of the Arab Republic of Egypt', 27 April–11 May 2005, paras. 24–37.

[17] African Peer Review Mechanism, 'Country Review Report: South Africa', November 2006, para. 114.

[18] APRM, 'Country Review Report: Kenya', May 2006, para. 3.3.1(iii).

to live up to its primary obligation towards those under its jurisdiction. However, as the discussion also shows, this potential is seriously eroded if the political bodies do not heed these calls and call recalcitrant States to order.

Promotional and protective visits

The Commission conducts two types of visits (or 'missions') to Member States: promotional and protective missions. Each Commissioner is assigned a number of countries to which he or she has to undertake occasional promotional visits. The overall aim of these visits, which present an opportunity to engage with States on their implementation of the Charter, is to help foster a culture of human rights in Member States. Although these visits are therefore more attuned to long-term prevention of all human rights violations, including those that may trigger R2P, the visiting Commissioner should also use this opportunity to obtain information about the potential or actual situations of serious or massive violations. Although the use of 'good offices' and personal persuasion should not be negated, promotional visits should not be viewed primarily as diplomatic courtesy calls, but as valuable opportunities to pre-empt future violations. If relevant information is obtained, it is important that it be channelled to the relevant political channels for consideration. This would require that the Commission excerpts the pertinent information from reports of promotional visits, and specifically draw States' attention thereto in its activity reports.

Protective (on-site or 'fact-finding') missions serve a different purpose. They are usually undertaken when a significant number of complaints had been received against a State Party. Often, the cumulative effect of these communications is that a series of presumably serious or massive human rights violations are occurring. The development of this procedure, which is not explicitly provided for in the African Charter, can be explained as another way of responding to the failure of the AU Assembly to take any action in respect of findings of the Commission related to 'serious or massive' violations.[19] To date, only a limited number of these on-site missions have been undertaken. The major obstacle has been the lack of cooperation by States, which either

---

[19]   As far as it has been made explicit, the legal basis for these visits is located in Article 46 of the Charter, which allows the Commission to resort to 'any appropriate method of investigation'.

expressly refuse permission for a visit, or continue to place obstacles preventing the mission from taking place. For example, the Commission reports that it endeavoured 'from 1990 to 1996' to undertake an on-site visit to Rwanda.[20] Despite its efforts, the Commission never succeeded in sending a mission to Rwanda. The most recent on-site missions were those to Zimbabwe (in 2002) and Sudan (in 2004).

On-site missions play a dual role. On the one hand, the aim of the protective mission is to establish the facts on the ground, which may inform the Commission's finding when it later deals with the communication. In the finding in the *Ogoniland* case, for example, the Commission mentions that it conducted a mission to Nigeria in March 1997, allowing it to witness 'first-hand the deplorable situation in Ogoniland including the environmental degradation'.[21] On the other hand, the mission is also aimed at engaging with the government in an attempt to reach amicable solutions and to improve the situation giving rise to the violations. The report of the mission undertaken to Mauritania in March 1996, for example, clearly indicates that the aim was not to determine right or wrong, but 'above all to listen to all sides with the objective of bringing clarification to the Commission in its contribution to the search for an *equitable solution through dialogue*'.[22] The 'Mission of "Good Offices" to the Casamance Region of Senegal'[23] was undertaken after the Commission had received a complaint from RADDHO about 'grave and massive violations' arising from clashes between the Senegalese army and the Casamance rebel movement, the MFDC.[24] The mission report states that it was undertaken 'with a view to contributing to the resolution of the conflict'.[25] In its recommendations, the Commission called for assistance to refugees and internally displaced persons, the release of political prisoners, and urged the government to fight impunity by prosecuting those responsible for torture and summary executions. The Senegalese and Mauritanian missions are illustrations of how the Commission, as quasi-judicial institution, may be actively involved in resolving tensions amicably.

Despite some accomplishments, the effect of on-site visits has been very limited in the context of R2P. There are many reasons for this

---

[20] *Organisation Mondiale Contre la Torture and Others* v. *Rwanda* (2000) AHRLR 282 (ACHPR 1996), paras. 8 and 9.
[21] *Ibid.*, para. 67.   [22] ACHPR, 'Report of the Mission to Mauritania', 19–27 June 1996.
[23] The mission took place from 1–7 July 1996.
[24] Mouvement des Forces Démocratiques de la Casamance (MFDC).
[25] ACHPR, 'Report of the Mission of Good Offices to Senegal', 1–7 June 1996.

limited impact. To start with, the Commission undertook a very small number of on-site missions. Its practice is to conduct such missions only after receipt of numerous communications against a particular State. Such a requirement leads to an inevitable delay between the occurrence of violations and the conduct of an on-site mission. Once the mission is completed, a mission report is not communicated directly to the OAU/ AU political organs, but is only contained in the next activity report to the Assembly after it has been adopted by the Commission. While this procedure may still be effective in a situation of continuous and protracted violations, it is not suited to situations where immediate action is required.

Visits by special mechanisms

Although special mechanisms are not provided for under the African Charter, the Commission established such mechanisms in the form of Special Rapporteurs, Committees and Working Groups.[26] The 1994 genocide in Rwanda provided the immediate impetus for the establishment of the Commission's first special rapporteur.[27] The Rwanda genocide started on 7 April 1994, the day after the plane of the then sitting Rwandan President Juvénal Habyarimana had been shot down. Meeting for its previously scheduled fifteenth ordinary session, from 18 to 27 April 1994, in Banjul, the Gambia, the Commission's response was ineffective and muted. It adopted a resolution, noting its 'deep concern' about the serious and massive violation of human rights.[28] In this resolution, the Commission placed explicit reliance on the report of the UN Special Rapporteur on Extrajudicial, Arbitrary or Summary Executions, following his visit to the country in 1993, in which the UN Special Rapporteur condemned the violence and called on parties to 'immediately cease hostilities'. The Commission went a bit further in its

---

[26] See however ACHPR, 'Rules of Procedure of the African Commission on Human and Peoples' Rights', 1998, rule 28, which provides for 'committees and working groups' to be established it deems 'necessary for the exercise of its functions'; see ACHPR, 'Rules of Procedure of the African Commission on Human and Peoples' Rights', 12–26 May 2010, rule 23, encompassing also 'Special Rapporteurs'.

[27] It should be noted that the establishment of a special rapporteur dealing with this thematic area was already suggested at the Commission's session in April 1995. See Julia Harrington, 'Special Rapporteurs of the African Commission on Human and Peoples' Rights', *African Human Rights Law Journal*, 1 (2001), 247–67, at 249–54.

[28] ACHPR, 'Resolution on the Situation in Rwanda', Fifteenth Ordinary Session, 18–27 April 1994.

press statement, issued at the end of its fifteenth session, in which it deplored the Security Council's decision to withdraw its forces and urged the UN to send a peacekeeping mission; it also called on the OAU to increase assistance and bring a speedy end to the suffering.[29] However, no political action was taken in response to this call.

In a more promising, but in the end equally ineffectual, move the Commission decided to establish the Special Rapporteur on Extrajudicial, Summary and Arbitrary Executions (SR). One of the serving Commissioners, Commissioner Ben Salem, from Tunisia, was appointed as the first SR. His appointment, and the establishment of this position, created the expectation that the SR would engage with the situation in Rwanda, and report back at the next session, scheduled for late 1994. Instead, when he reported back, his focus was on matters of mandate, procedure, insurance and the intricacies of the terms of reference, which were only finally approved in October 1995. The SR's mandate was conceived as both reactive and preventive.[30] In the end, however, the SR never visited and did very little in respect of the genocide in Rwanda.

Unable to respond effectively not only to the genocide in Rwanda, but also to any of the other major conflict situations on the continent, the SR in 2001 became defunct. With the urgency of Rwanda abating, the Special Rapporteur shifted his focus to other problem spots in Africa. However, also in respect of these countries, his role remained minimal.[31] The SR made some oral reports at various sessions. Countries that received mention included Burundi, Chad, Djibouti, the DRC, Nigeria, Rwanda and Sierra Leone. Over the five years of his mandate, the SR only made one report public, and never undertook an on-site visit to any country in terms of his mandate. Increasingly criticised by both NGOs and other Commissioners, his resignation from the position as SR was announced at the Commission's twenty-ninth session, in April 2001. In October 2001, the Commission expressed its intention to appoint a new Special Rapporteur, but it never did. As the mandate of the Special

---

[29] ACHPR, 'Final Communiqué of the 15th Ordinary Session of the African Commission on Human and Peoples' Rights', 27 April 1994, para. 21.

[30] ACHPR, 'Report on Extra-judicial, Summary or Arbitrary Executions, by Dr Hatem Ben Salem Special Rapporteur', paras. A(1)–(3).

[31] See Harrington, 'Special Rapporteurs'; and also Rachel Murray, 'The Special Rapporteurs in the African System', in Malcolm Evans and Rachel Murray (eds.), *The African Charter on Human and Peoples' Rights: The System in Practice, 1986–2006* (Cambridge University Press, 2008), pp. 344–78, at pp. 346–53.

Rapporteur is for two years at a time, the present position is that the special rapporteurship does not exist. Against this background, the Commission at its 52nd session, in October 2012, expanded the mandate of the Working Group on the Death Penalty in Africa to include monitoring, collecting information, and responding to situations relating to extra-judicial, summary or arbitrary killings. Some of the Commission's other special procedures should also enter the fray. One example is the Special Rapporteur on Human Rights Defenders, which has already shown its potential relevance to the prevention of human rights albeit only in respect of its specific target group.

Decisions on communications and cases not amounting to serious or massive violations

In the exercise of their mandate to decide cases (or 'communications') that fall short of serious or massive violations, the African Commission and the Court may contribute to ensuring that volatile situations are taken up before they escalate into R2P-type conditions. By fostering responsibility for small-scale violations, their potential for becoming large-scale is reduced.

The Court has a clear mandate to consider cases alleging violations on a wide substantive basis. However, by the end of 2012, the Court has not yet decided any case on the merits. With a much less explicit mandate to consider individual communications, the Commission had to forge this competence for itself. As will be discussed more fully below, the drafters of the African Charter seemed to have devised the Commission's protective mandate as mainly dealing with 'serious or massive violations'.[32] The investigation of these violations was made dependent on authorisation by the OAU Assembly. To its credit, however, the Commission developed the practice of dealing with all cases – that is, also less 'serious' cases – under its protective mandate.[33]

---

[32] AU Constitutive Act, art. 58.

[33] *Jawara* v. *The Gambia* (2000) AHRLR 107 (ACHPR 2000), para. 41. The Commission provided two bases for its finding. The first is the text of the Charter itself, which allows for the submission of both inter-state and individual 'communications', and which in addition stipulates admissibility requirements in respect of individual communications. The second leg of the Commission's argument is its own practice of considering communications even if they do not 'reveal a series of serious or massive violations', which it describes as a 'useful exercise' (*ibid.*, para. 42). In a pragmatic way, the Commission held that its practice has established a fait accompli.

In the majority of cases – 'individual communications' involving both individuals and groups ('peoples') – the Commission found violations that did not meet the threshold of 'serious or massive violations'.[34] Viewed together, these findings address many aspects of life such as the marginalisation of minorities, stifling free political expression, incommunicado detention, and the denial of fair trial rights, which relate to the root causes of conflict. By addressing these aspects, further and more widespread violations may, in principle, be avoided. The case of *Gunme et al. v. Cameroon*,[35] in which the Commission held Cameroon in violation of a number of rights of the 'people of Northwest and Southern Cameroon', including the right to non-discrimination on the basis of language, is a good illustration of the Charter being applied to secure minority protection. If the long list of the Commission's recommendations in this case would be implemented, the potential for the escalation of factional conflict in Cameroon may be prevented.

Provisional measures

In most human rights systems, provisional ('precautionary' or 'interim') measures may be issued to prevent irreparable harm to a victim while the case he or she has submitted to the relevant monitoring body is still under consideration. Although they arise in a context in which human rights violations have already occurred, and are therefore 'reactive' in nature, provisional measures also aim to prevent the deterioration of the situation or the specific targeting of 'victims', and arguably fit best in the 'prevention' part of this chapter.

Although the African Charter does not expressly provide for such measures to be adopted, the Commission established this procedure through its Rules of Procedure.[36] The Commission used this measure only on a few occasions, and mostly in respect of the right to life of particular individuals who were awaiting the execution of a death sentence.[37] According to the Commission's report of its on-site visit to

---

[34] The concept of 'massive' violations is only invoked in 28 of the recorded 193 findings of the Commission. See Institute for Human Rights Development in Africa, 'African Human Rights Case Law Analyser', at http://caselaw.ihrda.org.

[35] *Gunme and Others* v. *Cameroon* (2009) AHRLR 9 (ACHPR 2009).

[36] ACHPR, 'Rules of Procedure', 1998, rule 111; ACHPR, 'Rules of Procedure', 2010, rule 98.

[37] *Interights and Others (on behalf of Bosch)* v. *Botswana* (2003) AHRLR 55 (ACHPR 2003); and *International PEN and Others (on behalf of Saro-Wiwa)* v. *Nigeria* (2000)

Darfur, the Chairperson of the Commission requested the Sudanese government to adopt 'urgent provisional measures' in respect of the situation of insecurity, sexual violence, displacement and forced repatriation in Darfur.[38]

Responding to information relating to violations by the Libyan government, submitted to it in early 2011, the Commission for the first time referred a case to the African Court. As the case was referred as *African Commission v. Libya*,[39] and no communication number is mentioned, it may be assumed that the case was submitted under Rule 118(3) of the Commission's 2010 Rules, which allows the Commission to submit a case based on information which in its view constitutes evidence of 'serious or massive' human rights violations. As this referral route does not necessitate the submission to the Commission of a formal communication, it was possible for the Commission to refer the case immediately, without dealing with issues of admissibility or with the merits of the case. The only question before it seems to have been whether the case met the 'serious or massive violations' threshold. From the available evidence, it appears that the Commission did not regard provisional measures as a feasible option in the circumstances of the case, as the likelihood of actual ability and political will to comply seemed remote.

The African Human Rights Court has an unequivocal mandate to adopt 'provisional measures' in cases of 'extreme gravity and urgency', to avoid irreparable personal harm.[40] Although the Commission did not request the Court to order provisional measures in the case involving Libya, the Court considered the question whether it was competent to do so. Based on the Rules of Court and on the factual grounds that there was a risk of 'imminent loss of human life in the ongoing conflict in Libya' posing a situation of 'extreme gravity and urgency', the Court concluded in the affirmative.[41] It proceeded to issue a provisional order that the government must 'immediately refrain from any action that

AHRLR 212 (ACHPR 1998). However, both these findings illustrate that the States did not comply with the provisional measures.

[38] ACHPR Executive Council, 'Report of the African Commission Fact-Finding Mission to Sudan in the Darfur Region (08 to 18 July 2004)', Twenty-Second Activity Report of the African Commission on Human and Peoples' Rights, AU Doc. EX.CL/364 (XI), 25–29 June 2007, annex III, para. 16.

[39] *African Commission on Human and Peoples' Rights* v. *Great Socialist People's Libyan Arab Jamahiriya, Order for Provisional Measure*, Application 004/2011, 25 March 2011.

[40] Protocol to the African Charter on Human and Peoples' Rights on the Establishment of an African Court on Human and Peoples' Rights, adopted 10 June 1998 and entered into force 25 January 2004, OAU Doc. OAU/LEG/EXP/AFCHPR/PROT (III), art. 27(2).

[41] *African Commission* v. *Libya, Order for Provisional Measures*, paras. 13 and 22.

would result in loss of life or violation of physical integrity of persons'.[42] The government was also ordered to report to the Court, within fifteen days of receipt of the order, on the measures taken to implement the order.[43] There is no indication that the Libyan government provided information about any 'measures' taken in compliance of the Court's order. The reported facts appear to point to a failure to take the required measures, due in part to the fact that the situation prevailing at the time the order was made had largely been overtaken by subsequent events.

The substantive case is yet to proceed, mainly because the Commission requested (and was granted) an extended period, until 31 August 2012, to gather the required evidence.[44] When the case is considered on the merits, the immediate urgency would have long waned, and a new government would have to answer for the actions of the previous regime. The main contribution of the Court's decision would be to curb myth-making by providing a judicially established historical record of events. These circumstances suggest that the Court's orders on provisional measures may be of more importance than its final decision on the merits. Even if the implementation of the provisional order was problematic due to an ongoing armed conflict, it may have added to pressure on the political organs to act, provided the order was widely publicised and backed by the political will of at least some States. However, the Court's order was seemingly lost amidst the disarray and indecisiveness of the AU's political organs.

Spearheading and facilitating R2P interventions by political organs

Article 58 of the African Charter and its 2010 Rules of Procedure allow the African Commission to play an important role as a catalyst for intervention by the AU's political organs, which would include, in the most extreme cases, the actual implementation of Article 4(h) of the Constitutive Act.

---

[42] *Ibid.*, para. 25.   [43] *Ibid.*
[44] *African Commission* v. *Libya, First Extension of Time*, ACHPR, Application 004/2011, 2 September 2011.

Situations of series of serious or massive violations brought to the attention of the political organs

Neither the African Commission, nor the Court can by itself put into operation R2P in its most strident form. However, based on communications submitted to it, the Commission can make recommendations to States, and can report relevant instances of massive violations in terms of Article 58 of the Charter to the AU Assembly, for its action. As the Charter predates the adoption of the Peace and Security Council (PSC) Protocol, it does not accord any role to the PSC. However, as the PSC supplements the Assembly's mandate in respect of peace and security, the PSC should by necessary inference also be made aware of situations in which serious or massive violations occur. In any event, this logic was formalised in the PSC Protocol, which requires the Commission to bring to the PSC's attention all relevant matters.[45] While the Court can make orders, its orders need to be backed up by political action – especially in cases of non-compliance by States.

The Charter requires that the Commission deals with allegations of 'serious or massive violations' confidentially; prescribes that it must draw the attention of the Assembly of Heads of State and Government to the matter; and obliges it to wait for the Assembly's political authorisation to conduct an 'in-depth' investigation.[46] If it is mandated to conduct an investigation, the Commission must submit a report containing its findings and recommendations to the Assembly. The Assembly's decision to 'request' an in-depth investigation is entirely discretionary.

In the first years of its existence, after its request for referral fell on deaf ears, the Commission developed a practice of omitting reference to Article 58(1). Faced with a number of situations of serious or massive violations, and following the wording of Article 58(1), the Commission made a referral to the Assembly on the strength of communications submitted to it, and not on its own initiative. Umozurike, Chairperson of the Commission from 1989 to 1991, recounts that the Commission during 1991 and 1994 communicated such 'special cases' to the OAU Chairperson, after it had 'received communications alleging a series of

---

[45] AU, Protocol Relating to the Establishment of the Peace and Security Council of the AU, adopted 9 July 2002 and entered into force on 26 December 2003, art. 19. See also Kuwali, *Article 4(h) Intervention*, pp. 206–7.

[46] AU Constitutive Act, art. 58(1).

serious and massive violations' in Burundi, Rwanda and Sudan.[47] The first such referral is contained in the Commission's *Seventh Annual Activity Report*, and relates to the DRC (then Zaire).[48] In this case, the Commission, in a one-line statement, merely stated that it 'admits evidence' of a series of serious or massive violations and decided to 'call the attention' of the Assembly to the situation. However, according to Umozurike, nothing 'came out of the contact' in this or any of the other cases.[49] The two findings in the *Chirwa* case illustrate the practice emerging at the time. In its first finding, contained in the Commission's *Seventh Annual Activity Report*, the Commission found violations and referred the case to the Assembly under Article 58(1).[50] Apparently in response to the silence with which this request was met, the Commission decided the case a second time, on essentially the same legal basis. However, in this finding the Commission concluded the matter without requesting a referral under Article 58(1).[51]

Not only in the *Chirwa* case, but in all subsequent cases, the OAU Assembly did not request the Commission to conduct an in-depth investigation, or even pronounce itself in any other way on the information received from the Commission. It would be fair to say that the OAU ignored the Commission, and thus adopted a practice in conformity with the principle of non-interference in the domestic affairs in Member States – even in the face of serious or massive violations.

By the time the AU replaced the OAU, this position had become firmly established. In *Sudan Human Rights Organisation and Another v. Sudan*,[52] the Commission rejected the complainants' request to refer a matter clearly related to serious or massive violations to the AU Assembly in terms of Article 58. Explaining its refusal, the Commission noted that it had already conducted, on its own initiative, a 'fact-finding' mission to Darfur in 2004.[53] By further placing on record that the findings and recommendations emanating from this report

---

[47] Oji Umozurike, *The African Charter on Human and Peoples' Rights* (Leiden; Boston: Martinus Nijhoff, 1997), p. 77.

[48] *Lawyers Committee for Human Rights v. Zaire* (2000) AHRLR 71 (ACHPR 1994).

[49] Umozurike, *Human and Peoples' Rights*, p. 77.

[50] *Achuthan and Another (on behalf of Banda and Others) v. Malawi* (2000) AHRLR 143 (ACHPR 1994).

[51] *Achuthan and Another (on behalf of Banda and Others) v. Malawi* (2000) AHRLR 144 (ACHPR 1995), para. 13.

[52] *Sudan Human Rights Organisation and Another v. Sudan* (2009) AHRLR 153 (ACHPR 2009).

[53] *Ibid.*, para. 225.

'were sent to the Respondent State and the African Union',[54] the Commission implies that a further referral to the Assembly, or any other AU organ, would be futile as the situation had already been brought to the attention of the AU's political organs and political action had already been taken. It should be noted that the AU deployed first its own peacekeepers in 2006 – the AU Mission in Sudan (AMIS) – and later, in 2008, took the unprecedented step to merge its force with that of the UN – the UN Mission in Sudan (UNMIS) – to form the African Union/United Nations Hybrid operation in Darfur (UNAMID).

However, the Commission added that, if no action whatsoever had been taken by the AU organs, a request under Article 58(1) would have been appropriate. In the Commission's view, the measures taken constitute what would most likely have ensued, had an in-depth study been undertaken under Article 58.[55] The Commission further pointed out that it 'has continued to monitor the human rights situation' in Darfur 'through its country and thematic rapporteurs and has presented reports on the same to each Ordinary Session of the Commission, which are in turn presented to the Assembly of the African Union'.[56] The African Commission thus leaves the door open for referrals under Article 58 to the AU Assembly, or the Peace and Security Council, in the absence of any fact-finding mission and report to the Assembly, and peacekeeping measures taken by the AU. By implication, the Commission also identified the desired outcome of such a referral, namely, a peacekeeping operation such as AMIS or UNAMID.[57] In a subsequent resolution,[58] the African Commission welcomed the establishment of UNAMID, called on all role players to ensure the speedy 'operationalisation of the force', and urged African States to contribute troops.

In a very welcome development, the Commission's 2010 Rules of Procedure stipulate that it must 'draw the attention of' both the AU

---

[54] *Ibid.*   [55] *Ibid.*, para. 226.   [56] *Ibid.*, para. 225.

[57] It should be borne in mind that the UN Security Council established UNAMID under Chapter VII of the UN Charter. UNSC Res. 1769, UN Doc. S/RES/1769, 31 July 2007. Its mandate includes the objective to 'contribute to the *protection of civilian populations* under imminent threat of physical violence and prevent attacks against civilians, within its capability and areas of deployment' (UNSG, 'Report of the Secretary-General and the Chairperson of the African Union Commission on the Hybrid Operation in Darfur', UN Doc. S/2007/307/Rev.1, para. 54(b)). See also UNSC Res. 1769, para. 15(a)(ii). Although the language used in that phrase is clearly reminiscent of R2P, it is qualified by the following: 'without prejudice to the responsibility of the Government of the Sudan' (*ibid.*).

[58] ACHPR Res. 117 (XXXXII).

Assembly and the PSC to communications that 'relate to' a series of serious or massive violations.[59] The Rules effectively amend the Charter in two respects. First, relying on the Commission's established practice, the Rules make no mention of the obligation of the Commission to refer such cases to the Assembly, or to obtain its permission to undertake in-depth studies. It could thus be accepted that the Article 58 requirements have fallen into disuse. Second, the Rules add the role of the PSC. This 'addition' is uncontroversial, as it adjusts the position to include the most important and relevant addition to the landscape of conflict prevention, management and resolution in Africa, which has come into being after the adoption of the Charter. This position is also in line with the cooperative relationship envisaged between the Commission and the PSC under the PSC Protocol, and gives effect to the Commission's obligation to 'bring to the attention' of the PSC 'any information rele-vant' to its mandate and objectives.[60]

Urgent situations brought to the attention of the political organs

In addition to the specific communications related to serious or massive violations, the Commission must under Article 58(3) of the Charter also refer 'a case of emergency' to the Chairperson of the Assembly, who may similarly to the Assembly, request an in-depth study. This provision presumably covers action to be taken when the Assembly is not sitting, during the period between sessions, but is not explicitly limited to the inter-sessional period. Juxtaposing the term 'communication' – used in Article 58(1) – with 'case' – in Article 58(3) – it is arguable that 'urgent cases' need not arise from submitted communications, but may be noted by the Commission itself. Given that the Commission did not find the Assembly responsive to Article 58(1) referrals, it is unsurprising that it did not place much faith in the possibility presented by Article 58(3). There is, equally unsurprisingly, no recorded instance in which this provision has been used.

The 2010 Rules of Procedure make reference to the notion of 'matters of emergency'.[61] Reflecting the position under the Charter, these 'mat-ters' do not need to relate to submitted communications. In such sit-uations, which include but extend beyond 'serious or massive violations', the Rules stipulate that the Commission must not only draw the

---

[59] ACHPR, 'Rules of Procedure', 2010, rule 84(1).   [60] PSC Protocol, art. 14.
[61] ACHPR, 'Rules of Procedure', 2010, rule 80.

Chairperson's attention thereto, but also that of the Peace and Security Council, the Executive Council and the AU Commission Chairperson. Although this rule has not yet been applied, it holds much promise for a more proactive approach by the Commission to situations that may bring R2P into play.

Ex post facto accountability for massive human rights violations

By ascribing to States international responsibility for serious and widespread human rights violations, it is anticipated that recalcitrant States would be less likely to engage in similar acts in the future. It is also important to recognise these violations as a matter of historical record. Individual communications to the Commission and cases to the Court provide the two main mechanisms through which responsibility is determined. Although the Commission's on-site visits are more attuned to dialogue and long-term solutions, its findings may also set in motion or support a chain of accountability. In its report on the Darfur visit adopted in September 2004, the Commission recommended that an international commission of enquiry be established to investigate the role of the government forces in 'war crimes and crimes against humanity' and the role of the rebel movements in the same crimes, but also for 'massive violations of human rights'.[62] Although this report was only published in 2007, the engagement between the Commission and the Sudanese government is part of the chain of events that culminated in the decision of the Security Council to establish such a commission,[63] the commission's report,[64] the subsequent Security Council referral of the case to the International Criminal Court[65] and the indictment of prominent Sudanese leaders, including President al-Bashir, initially only on charges of war crimes and crimes against humanity, but later also of genocide.

Findings by the Commission in cases of serious or massive violations

In the absence of any request or other action by the Assembly under Article 58(1) of the Charter, and presumably in order to retain the

---

[62] ACHPR Executive Council, 'Mission to Sudan', annex III, para. 138.
[63] UNSC Res. 1564, UN Doc. S/RES/1564, 18 September 2004.
[64] International Commission of Inquiry on Darfur, 'Report of the International Commission of Inquiry on Darfur to the United Nations Secretary-General', 25 January 2005.
[65] UNSC Res. 1593, UN Doc. S/RES/1593, 31 March 2005.

semblance of relevance and legitimacy, the Commission had little option but to proceed to deal with 'serious or massive' violations as communications under its general protective mandate. Realising that its potential as a conduit to bring R2P situations to the Assembly had no effect, the Commission adopted the practice of holding violator States in such situations accountable under its 'ordinary' violations procedure. Because Article 58(2) of the Charter gives the Assembly discretion to request follow-up action, the Commission should arguably be able to deal with the situation under its 'ordinary' procedure under Article 55 and 56 of the Charter if the Assembly does not request follow-up action. Understood in this way, the distinction between communications alleging 'serious and massive' violations and 'other communications' falls away, as all communications are dealt with in a similar fashion. It is indeed now standard practice for the Commission to deal with 'serious and massive' violations under its ordinary communications procedure. These cases ended in findings of violations and ascribed responsibility to States without prior referral of the matter to the Assembly.

One of the first cases in which this practice became established is *Organisation Mondiale Contre la Torture et al.* v. *Rwanda,*[66] in which the Commission found that events preceding the 1994 Rwandan genocide constituted 'serious or massive' violations, but did not refer the matter to the Assembly.[67] This matter relates to two separate communications, the one submitted in 1990, and the other in 1993, alleging extra-judicial killings and discrimination on the basis of ethnicity, the massacre of a large number of Rwandan villagers by the Rwandan armed forces and extra-judicial executions for reasons of their membership of a particular ethnic group.[68]

The impact of this finding has been constrained by the lack of government participation in the process. Despite repeated requests to file information and provide responses, the government did not respond. This lack of cooperation may at least partly be ascribed to the institutional disarray associated with a post-genocide State coming to terms with the loss of personnel and damage to infrastructure. Quite conceivably, international obligations enjoyed a lower priority at the time due to

---

[66] *Organisation Mondiale Contre la Torture et al.* v. *Rwanda.*

[67] See also *Free Legal Assistance Group and Others* v. *Zaire* (2000) AHRLR 74 (ACHPR 1995), in which the Commission also found the existence of serious and massive violations, but did not invoke Article 58.

[68] *Ibid.,* para. 25.

the new government's disappointment and lack of confidence in the international community – including the OAU human rights system – to come to the assistance of those in the midst of the human slaughter. In addition, it is perhaps understandable that the new government would, despite the principle of continued State responsibility, find it awkward if not absurd to be held accountable for the failures and atrocities of the previous government, under whose watch, and at whose instigation the genocide happened.

A further factor limiting any possible effect of this finding – and any other finding in respect of a situation of massive or serious violations – is the inordinate period of delay between the events and the submission of the case, on the one hand, and the eventual finding and its publication, on the other. In this instance, the Commission only finalised the case at its twentieth session, in October 1996 – some six years after the submission of the first case, and more than two years after the genocide started.[69]

This practice of dealing with 'massive' cases without any attempt to refer them to the Assembly is now consistently followed. In a relatively recent case, concerning the serious and massive violations in the Darfur region of Sudan,[70] the Commission for example did not make a referral to the AU Assembly. Although it is clear from the factual circumstances in the case that the violations occurred on a large scale, involved thousands of victims, and were of a very serious nature, the Commission's finding did not characterise the violations as 'serious or massive'.[71] The 'serious or massive' nature of the case is foregrounded in the remedial 'recommendations' issued by the Commission, which call for official investigations of abuses committed by military and paramilitary forces to be conducted, and for the prosecution of those responsible for human rights violations. Indeed, in one of the recommendations, the State is urged to put a legal framework in place to 'handle cases of serious and massive human rights violations'.[72] One of the reasons for the omission of the 'serious or massive' terminology in the finding on the merits is probably the fact that the Commission rejected the applicants' specific request to refer the matter under Article 58 on the basis that the AU had already taken political action.

---

[69] ACHPR, 'Tenth Annual Activity Report of the ACHPR 1996/97'.
[70] *Sudan Human Rights Organisation et al.* v. *Sudan.*   [71] *Ibid.*, para. 228.
[72] *Ibid.*, para. 229(2).

In the single inter-State communication finalised by the Commission,[73] dealing with massacres, rapes, mutilations, mass transfers of populations and looting by forces from Burundi, Rwanda and Uganda in the DRC, the Commission agreed that it 'cannot turn a blind eye to the series of human rights violations attendant upon such occupation'.[74] However, while finding the three respondent States in violation of the Charter, the Commission did not use the term 'serious or massive' violations in its decision, and did not make a referral under Article 58. The delay in finalising this case further highlights the largely retrospective role of the Commission's protective mandate. Relating to events that took place in 1998, submitted in 1999, decided in 2003 and made public even much later in 2006,[75] this case illustrates the protracted nature of the complaints procedure before the Commission. While accepting the importance of the eventual finding in providing a reliable historical record, in establishing accountability and in preventing future abuses, the Commission's finding evidently did not provide a basis for an international response at the crucial time when the violations were unfolding.

Although the African Children's Charter does not contain a provision similar to Article 58 of the African Charter, or, indeed, any reference to 'serious or massive' human rights violations, the Children's Charter can still be relevant to situations of widespread or large-scale violations. This contention was confirmed by the submission of the first communication to the Committee in 2005.[76] This communication alleges that the Ugandan government failed to act with due diligence to protect the rights of children from widespread human rights violations, including mutilation, torture, sexual violence, abduction and displacement, resulting of the Lord's Resistance Army's (LRA) violent actions in Northern Uganda. In response to this submission, the Committee undertook an on-site mission to Uganda. Regrettably, the report of that visit had not been made public. Some five years after the submission, in 2010, the Committee declared the communication admissible, and in late 2011 considered it on the merits. Due to this delay, the Committee's

---

[73] *Democratic Republic of Congo* v. *Burundi, Rwanda, Uganda* (2004) AHRLR 19 (ACHPR 2003).

[74] *Ibid.*, para. 69.

[75] ACHPR Executive Council, 'Twentieth Activity Report of the African Commission on Human and Peoples' Rights', AU Doc. EX.CL/279 (IX).

[76] The communication, *Children Affected by Lord's Resistance Army (LRA)-related Conflict* v. *Uganda*, has by mid-2012 not yet been finalised (on file with author).

role in this conflict situation has largely been reduced to retrospective apportionment of responsibility. However, in framing a remedy that speaks to more than accountability, and by having regard to subsequent changed circumstances, the Committee may forge for itself a role in the current and ongoing effects of the LRA-related conflict and its effect on children.

Situations of massive violations submitted to and decided by the African Human Rights Court

Under its 2010 Rules of Procedure, the Commission may refer a case *directly* to the Court if a situation of 'serious or massive' violations has come to its attention.[77] This is a significant departure from the Charter in two ways. First, the Charter uses the notion of a '*series of* serious or massive violations'. By omitting the phrase 'series of', the 2010 Rules of Procedure suggest a lower threshold, in terms of scale and duration of violations, which needs to be passed in order to refer such cases to the Court. Second, and more significantly, under the Rules of Procedure referral to the Assembly of situations of serious or massive violations is replaced by referral to the African Human Rights Court. In other words, judicial consideration replaces political decision-making. While this may be lauded as a positive development, as it brings the political organs into the picture on the basis of a Court decision, rather than the Commission's 'recommendation', it should be pointed out that neither the Charter nor the Court Protocol provides the Commission with this competence. Arguably, if it is accepted that referral to the Court leaves it to the Court to *investigate* the matter more fully and take an appropriate decision, the Commission's competence to refer these matters may be derived from its mandate to 'resort to any method of investigation'.[78] In addition, the Court complements the Commission's protective mandate, and if the Commission deems the Court's jurisdiction more suitable than its own, the Commission may at any stage of a proceeding refer a case to the Court.[79] Given their explicitly legally binding status, there should be little controversy about the competence of the Assembly to enforce the Court's decisions.[80]

---

[77] ACHPR, 'Rules of Procedure', 2010, rule 118(3).   [78] AU Constitutive Act, art. 46.
[79] See also ACHPR, 'Rules of Procedure', 2010, rule 118(4).
[80] In cases of non-compliance, the Assembly should impose appropriate measures against recalcitrant States, including sanctions, when appropriate. AU Constitutive Act, art. 23(2).

The African Commission's role in rebuilding and reconstruction

The Commission's potential role in rebuilding societies in the aftermath of massive violations would best be realised through the non-confrontational aspects of its promotional mandate, in particular, promotional visits, special mechanisms and the State reporting process. Thus far, the Commission has not attached much prominence to its role in the process of 'transitional justice'. However, there are some indications that the Commission is integrating issues related to 'rebuilding' into its mandate. In the concluding observations adopted after the examination of the Sudanese State report, in 2009, the Commission called on the government to establish a 'National Commission of Enquiry/Truth and Reconciliation Commission as part of the reconciliation and healing process, and as part of the process of addressing the multiple conflicts currently going on in the country'.[81] One of the problems is that States emerging from periods of trauma often do not prioritise the submission of State reports. Countries like Burundi and Sierra Leone, for example, have not submitted reports since emerging from periods of intense conflict and massive human rights violations. This state of affairs requires that a more prominent role be accorded to promotional visits and special mechanisms.

In the future, the Commission should pay more attention to and better integrate concerns for societies emerging from situations of massive violations in its examination of State reports, in its promotional visits to countries, and in the work of its special mechanisms.

Conclusion

On paper, the African Union leads the way on R2P. Article 4(h) of the AU Constitutive Act, which may rightly be described as the first statutory embodiment of both collective humanitarian intervention and R2P, has received much acclaim. In practice, however, it has remained a dead letter. The African human rights mechanisms – in particular the African Commission – could have done more to prevent this from happening.

---

[81] ACHPR, 'Concluding Observations and Recommendations on the Third Periodic Report of the Republic of Sudan (2003–2008)', 13–27 May 2009, para. 43.

The African human rights system can and must play a much more pronounced role in bringing Article 4(h) to life. In the 1980s and 1990s, under the previous dispensation of the OAU, the African political organs were reluctant to mandate collective action to address massive violations in Member States, as stipulated by Article 58 of the African Charter, prompting the Commission to allow this provision to fall into disuse. However, the African Commission has to shoulder some of the blame for this inaction. One of the factors inhibiting political action was the delay between the time when immediate action was required, and the eventual recommendations to the OAU Assembly. With the advent of the AU, the Commission has not yet explored the possibility of involving the Peace and Security Council to follow up cases of massive violations in which R2P may have found application. The Commission should reinvigorate the Article 58 procedure in the most appropriate cases, involving not only the Assembly, but also the Executive Council and the PSC. The 2010 Rules further emphasise that the Commission should bring all instances of massive or serious violations and urgent cases to the attention of the AU Assembly and PSC. Whether the Commission uses the route of Article 58 or its Rules of Procedure, the African Commission has a crucial role to play in providing a basis for and placing pressure on the AU Assembly and PSC to take action and, if appropriate, to intervene under Article 4(h).

The addition of the Court to the human rights landscape and the Commission's progressive 2010 Rules of Procedure may usher in a new era. The Court's order of 2011 for provisional measures against Libya underscores both the potential role of speedy and binding Court orders to deal with cases of massive violations and the complexities attendant upon judicial resolution of R2P-type situations. By allowing the Commission to refer to the Court urgent situations, including those involving massive human rights violations, outside its formal communications procedure, the Commission's 2010 Rules enhanced the Commission's ability to react to massive violations. In order to use this avenue to become an effective and reliable conduit of crucial information to the political organs, the Commission must prioritise urgent matters in its working procedures and must improve its fact-finding competence.

Questions may be posed about the suitability of the Court to deal with large-scale and widespread violations. Even if a judicial setting is not ideal to deal with highly politicised issues and large-scale violations, relying on the Court may become a more feasible option when there is a political impasse, as in the case of Libya. In any event, it is inevitable that the African Court would have to interpret and make findings on and order remedies related to peoples' rights.[82] The experience of other regional human rights courts shows that judicial institutions are capable of dealing with collective complaints, recurring violations and structural problems.[83]

While both the Commission and the Court have definite roles as catalysts and sources of information to enable possible decisions under Article 4(h), they have a much more far-reaching role in the context of R2P. By improving the quality, visibility and impact of its State reporting procedure and the work of its special mechanisms, the Commission may play a role of increasing importance in the early identification, and ultimate prevention, of situations before the need to invoke R2P arises. By inscribing the issue of transitional justice into its agenda and working methods, the Commission may also promote the rebuilding of societies emerging from a situation in which R2P could have, or had been invoked. Through the application of its quasi-judicial and judicial functions, the Commission and Court remain the most important forums where States can be held accountable, especially if prevention and intervention fails.

So far, the Commission has not been the catalyst it can be, or realised its potential role in preventing and reacting to massive killing, ethnic cleansing and other situations of massive human rights violations. Although there are some indications of improved engagement with these issues, the Commission still seems not to sufficiently prioritise the prevention of massive and urgent violations. In fact, it needs to prioritise its protective mandate, which has become increasingly marginalised at the expense of attention being devoted to the burgeoning array of special mechanisms. In any event, as long as it remains beset by institutional weaknesses, such as a lack of qualified staff, while its response to events is delayed, and if its action remains largely invisible, the prospects of the Commission playing a more effective and meaningful role are remote. The same operational caveats apply to the

---

[82] 'Socio-economic rights' such as the right to education and health are unequivocally justiciable under the African Charter, and are the subject of the Court's broad remedial competence to make any 'appropriate order' and to order provisional measures in cases of 'extreme gravity and urgency' (ACHPR Protocol, art. 27(1) and (2)).

[83] See for example Philip Leach, Helen Hardman, Svetlana Stephenson and Brad Blitz, *Responding to Systemic Human Rights Violations: An Analysis of 'Pilot Judgments' of the European Court of Human Rights and their Impact at the National Level* (Antwerp: Intersentia, 2010).

potential and actual role of the African Human Rights Court and the Children's Rights Committee.[84]

To play a more productive role in the context of R2P, broadly under-stood, some reform of the African regional human rights system is required. The positions of Chairperson of the Commission and Committee have to be made full-time. A permanent and dedicated presence at the seat of the two institutions would enhance the capacity of these institutions to respond more effectively to urgent situations involving massive violations. The African Children's Committee should amend its Rules of Procedure in line with those of the Commission, to allow it to respond more timely and decisively to situations where urgency is required. The Commission, Committee and Court should all maintain a close working relationship with the AU's political organs, and with the PSC, in particular, and should tailor their reports to the political organs to highlight ways in which massive violations may be prevented and reacted to. In the aftermath of such violations, they should do more to ensure that the weight of the AU is put behind attempts to rebuild societies and cultivate a culture of respect for diversity and human rights.

Ultimately, more decisive action by the AU's political organs, and in particular the Assembly and PSC, in response to the recommendations and decisions of the African human rights institutions is required in the future – both to convert the promise of Article 4(h) into reality and to prevent massive human rights atrocities from escalating into situations where this provision would have to be invoked at all.

---

[84] For more on some of these caveats, see Frans Viljoen, *International Human Rights Law in Africa* (Oxford University Press, 2012), chs. 9 and 10.

PART VI

Concluding remarks

22

Sharing the responsibility to protect: taking stock and moving forward

GENTIAN ZYBERI

Introduction

By dealing with a number of key actors engaged in turning the responsibility to protect (RtoP) into practice this book aims to provide a general picture of existing institutional mechanisms and practices relevant to RtoP. Many contributors have also explored and suggested potential ways of improving the current systems of collective security and enforcement of fundamental human rights. The depth of the discussion, its institutional focus, and the possibility to include therein institutional responses to recent RtoP situations as those in Sudan, Kenya, Libya, Ivory Coast and other unfolding situations, as that in Syria, enable us to get a better understanding of the institutional possibilities and limitations of the selected actors in protecting populations from mass atrocities. What becomes evident from the previous chapters is that institutional efforts to operationalise RtoP differ considerably from one organisation to another. Instead of providing a summary of the previous discussions, this last chapter sets out to discuss a number of selected issues which are of importance to RtoP's current status and further development. First, the chapter provides a brief discussion of specific aspects of core crimes falling under RtoP. A number of theoretical and practical issues are addressed in turn, including the multilayered nature of RtoP obligations, early warning and assessment capabilities, entrenching a culture of accountability, timely and decisive response mechanisms and uncertainties and problems arising from sharing RtoP obligations among the different levels and relevant actors.

I am very grateful to Nicholas Turner and Kjetil Mujezinović Larsen for their comments on an earlier draft. Any possible mistakes are my own.

The concept of RtoP epitomises the humanitarian character and central purpose of international human rights, humanitarian law, refugee law and international criminal law, namely protecting populations from mass atrocity crimes. The general principle of humanity and the right of peoples to peace, which permeate these bodies of law, lie at the foundations of RtoP.[1] The concept of 'elementary considerations of humanity', as elaborated by the International Court of Justice (ICJ), lays down both a negative obligation on the part of States and individuals to abstain from committing mass atrocities, as well as the obligation to prevent them from occurring. RtoP creates a political framework for action based on fundamental principles of international law related to preventing and putting a stop to acts of genocide, war crimes, ethnic cleansing and crimes against humanity.[2] It provides a general framework which mainstreams the sometimes dormant power of existing rules and principles of international human rights, humanitarian law and international criminal law which prohibit mass atrocities. RtoP has a political and normative as well as a clear legal dimension. As Hoffmann and Nollkaemper have noted, the change from the original 2001 report of the International Commission on Intervention and State Sovereignty (ICISS) to the 2005 World Summit Outcome Document (WSOD) has resulted in a distinct legalisation of RtoP.[3] The protection responsibilities of the State under pillar one are considered as the least controversial. Amnéus states that this responsibility reflects obligations under international law such as the treaty and customary obligations to prevent and

---

[1] The principle of humanity underlies both human rights and humanitarian law. Simply put, this principle requires States and individuals to conduct themselves in a certain (humane) way, so as not to cause unnecessary serious harm to individuals. The principle is intrinsically linked with the concept of 'elementary considerations of humanity', elaborated further in Common Article 3 to the 1949 Geneva Conventions and the Martens Clause. The right to peace is directly related to the main condition conducive to the fulfilment of other human rights. A corollary of the right to peace is the prohibition of aggression and use of force. The crimes falling under RtoP can be seen also as crimes against peace. See, among others, United Nations General Assembly Res. 290 (IV), UN Doc. A/RES/290(IV), 1 December 1949; and 'Declaration on the Right of Peoples to Peace', UN Doc. A/RES/39/11, 12 November 1984, annex, declaring that the preservation of the right of peoples to peace and the promotion of its implementation constitute a fundamental obligation of each State.

[2] UN Secretary-General, 'Responsibility to Protect: Timely and Decisive Response', UN Doc. A/66/874–S/2012/578, 25 July 2012, para. 59.

[3] Julia Hoffmann and André Nollkaemper, 'Concluding Observations', in Julia Hoffmann and André Nollkaemper (eds.), Responsibility to Protect: From Principle to Practice (Amsterdam University Press, 2012), pp. 355–71, at p. 359.

punish genocide, to respect and ensure respect of international humanitarian law, and the 'duty to respect, protect and fulfil' under international human rights law.[4]

Under paragraph 139 of the 2005 WSOD the UN General Assembly is
charged in terms of its responsibility under the UN Charter to continue
consideration of RtoP. That ensures that RtoP is further developed
through an open and inclusive process, through which all the Member
States of the UN can participate and play their role. Evidently, RtoP is a
concept which has evolved considerably, since it was first announced in
the 2001 ICISS report. Indeed, from that initial report, protection under
RtoP has extended considerably, since the protection responsibilities of
the State have come to include the whole population under its jurisdiction and not only to its citizens. The subject matter has been clearly
confined to the core international crimes, namely genocide, war crimes
and crimes against humanity. Ethnic cleansing, although stated explicitly in the 2005 WSOD, can be properly subsumed under the categories
of war crimes and crimes against humanity. Its separate listing alongside
genocide, war crimes and crimes against humanity has more political
overtones than real legal significance. The original three pillar structure
of the 2001 ICISS report, based on the duty to prevent, duty to react, and
duty to rebuild has been substituted by the three pillar structure developed by the Secretary-General in his 2009 report based on the protection
responsibilities of the State, international assistance and capacity-
building and timely and decisive response. Besides outlining RtoP in
terms of the responsibilities of relevant actors, especially emphasising
the primary responsibility of States, this pillar structure also helps avoid
to some extent the impression that RtoP actions can be easily sequenced.
This structure allocates responsibility under RtoP among relevant stakeholders and institutional and programmatic lines.

RtoP is not to be equated with the concept of protection of civilians in
armed conflict, as endorsed and developed by the Security Council in
Resolution 1265 (1999) and subsequent resolutions and in reports by the
UN Secretary-General. As the Secretary-General has noted, while these
concepts obviously overlap, they retain separate and distinct prerequisites and objectives.[5] Protection under RtoP would apply also outside an
armed conflict situation, while the concept of protection of civilians in
armed conflict, as the term suggests, is necessarily connected with the

---

[4] For more details, see Amnéus, Chapter 1 in this book.
[5] UNSG, 'Timely and Decisive Response', para. 16.

existence of an armed conflict. RtoP is limited to three core international crimes, that is, genocide, war crimes and crimes against humanity, whereas the concept of protection of civilians seems to have a much broader scope. The threshold of harm for triggering the application of military intervention under RtoP's third pillar on 'timely and decisive response' seems to be set higher than that applicable under the protection of civilians in armed conflict.

Limiting protection to the core international crimes

RtoP is based on a 'narrow, but deep' approach.[6] A major source of its strength is the limitation to the three international crimes of utmost gravity, namely genocide, war crimes and crimes against humanity. These crimes give rise to State responsibility as well as individual criminal responsibility. Genocide is widely considered as the crime of crimes, since it denies the existence to entire groups of people based on their national, ethnical, racial or religious affiliation. The Tribunal for Rwanda through *Akayesu* has extended protection to 'any stable and permanent group', besides these four groups enumerated in Article 2 of the 1948 Genocide Convention.[7] However, the International Court of Justice has clarified that a group needs to be defined by 'particular positive characteristics – national, ethnical, racial or religious – and not the lack of them'.[8] The Genocide Convention is the first international instrument which, besides criminalising acts of genocide in time of peace or in time of war, imposes on the States Parties a duty to prevent and to punish. The UN ad hoc tribunals have contributed greatly to elucidating the subjective element of genocide.[9] Thus, the crime of genocide requires the

---

[6] As the Secretary-General noted in his 2012 report, 'From the outset, the importance of a narrow but deep approach has been highlighted – narrow, in terms of restricting its application to the crimes and violations cited in paragraph 138 of the 2005 World Summit Outcome and to their incitement, and deep, in terms of the variety of Charter-based tools that are available for this purpose' (*ibid.*, para. 9).

[7] *Prosecutor v. Jean-Paul Akayesu*, Case No. ICTR-96-4-T, Judgment of 2 September 1998, para. 516. The Trial Chamber held that, 'In the opinion of the Chamber, it is particularly important to respect the intention of the drafters of the Genocide Convention, which according to the *travaux préparatoires*, was patently to ensure the protection of any stable and permanent group.'

[8] *Case Concerning the Application of the Convention on the Prevention and Punishment of the Crime of Genocide (Bosnia and Herzegovina v. Serbia and Montenegro)*, Judgment, ICJ Reports 2007, pp. 124–26, paras. 193–6.

[9] See, among others, Antonio Cassese, 'Genocide', in Antonio Cassese et al. (eds.), *The Oxford Companion to International Criminal Justice* (Oxford University Press, 2009),

specific intent, or aggravated criminal intent, to destroy, in whole or in part, a national, ethnical, racial or religious group, as such. The ICJ on its part has clarified some of the obligations incumbent upon States with regard to preventing genocide in its February 2007 judgment in the *Application of the Genocide Convention* case.[10] Thus, a State's duty to prevent genocide is not limited only to populations within its own jurisdiction, but extends beyond its borders. The ICJ has held that in achieving the aim of prevention of genocide, States should use all reasonable means available, in accordance with international law and in close coordination with other States and with concerned international and regional organisations.

War crimes are serious violations of treaty or customary international humanitarian law committed during an armed conflict, of an international or of a non-international nature. The 1949 Geneva Conventions create the system of grave breaches under which States have a duty to prosecute or extradite suspected war criminals. Substantially, war crimes can be divided in the following categories: war crimes against persons requiring particular protection; war crimes against property and other rights; prohibited methods and means of warfare; and crimes against humanitarian assistance and peacekeeping operations.[11] The deliberate targeting of the civilian population during an armed conflict would be a clear example of war crimes giving rise to an RtoP situation.

Crimes against humanity are not codified in a specific international treaty, as the crimes of genocide and war crimes are.[12] While there is no separate treaty-based obligation for States to prosecute such crimes, crimes against humanity have been part of the subject-matter jurisdiction of international criminal courts and tribunals, starting with the Nuremberg and Tokyo tribunals, and culminating with the permanent International Criminal Court (ICC). Crimes against humanity include murder, extermination, enslavement, deportation, and other inhumane acts committed as part of a widespread or systematic attack directed against any civilian population, with knowledge of the attack. Crimes

---

pp. 332–6. For a more detailed discussion, see Frencken and Sluiter, Chapter 17 in this book.

[10] For a more detailed discussion, see Zyberi, Chapter 16 in this book.

[11] For more details, see Volker Nerlich, 'War Crimes (International Armed Conflicts)', in Cassese *et al.* (eds.), *Oxford Companion*, pp. 566–8; Nerlich, 'War Crimes (Non-International Armed Conflicts)', in Cassese *et al.* (eds.), *Oxford Companion*, pp. 568–70.

[12] See Leila Nadya Sadat (ed.), *Forging a Convention for Crimes against Humanity* (Cambridge University Press, 2011), especially the chapters by Gareth Evans and David Scheffer, respectively pp. 1–7 and pp. 305–22.

against humanity do not necessarily have to be committed in the context of an armed conflict.[13] The attacks on the civilian population have to be widespread or systematic and the term 'civilian population' refers to people who are civilians, and not members of armed forces or otherwise combatants.

Ethnic cleansing is the fourth crime listed in the 2005 WSOD. Although ethnic cleansing that meets the threshold of genocide is likely to be referred to as such, the term remains a popular expression for crimes which are perhaps more likely to fall within the orbit of crimes against humanity or war crimes.[14] In their case law both the International Criminal Tribunal for the former Yugoslavia (ICTY) and the ICJ have been able to clarify and interpret the concept of ethnic cleansing, as being rather distinct from genocide. Thus, the ICTY Appeals Chamber in *Krstić* has held that forcible transfer 'does not constitute in and of itself a genocidal act'.[15] For its part, the ICJ has held that neither the intent to render an area ethnically homogenous, nor operations to implement the policy 'can *as such* be designated as genocide: the intent that characterises genocide is to "destroy, in whole or in part", a particular group, and deportation or displacement of the members of a group, even if effected by force, is not necessarily equivalent to destruction of that group'.[16] From a legal perspective, ethnic cleansing is commonly related to the forceful deportation or expelling of a certain group of people from an area where they usually live and would be properly subsumed under war crimes or crimes against humanity.

The main legal instruments relevant to RtoP have been interpreted and developed over the last two decades by a considerable number of international courts and tribunals. Recent case law by these international judicial mechanisms lays out in some detail the duties of States as well as

---

[13] The International Criminal Tribunal for the former Yugoslavia (ICTY) has held that under customary international law crimes against humanity do not require a connection with an armed conflict. See *Prosecutor* v. *Duško Tadić*, Case No. IT-94-1, Decision on Defence Motion for Interlocutory Appeal on Jurisdiction of 2 October 1995, para. 141.

[14] See Tarun Chhabra and Jeremy Zucker, 'Defining the Crimes', in Jared Genser and Irwin Cotler (eds.), *The Responsibility to Protect: The Promise of Stopping Mass Atrocities in Our Time* (Oxford University Press, 2011), pp. 37–61, at p. 54.

[15] *Prosecutor* v. *Radislav Krstić*, Case No. IT-98-33-A, Judgment of 19 April 2004, para. 33. See also *Prosecutor* v. *Vidoje Blagojević and Dragan Jokić*, Case No. IT-02-60-A, Judgment of 9 May 2007, para. 123; and *Prosecutor* v. *Vujadin Popović, Ljubiša Beara, Drago Nikolić, Ljubomir Borovčanin, Radivoje Miletić, Milan Gvero and Vinko Pandurević*, Case No. IT-05-88-T, Judgment of 10 June 2010, para. 813.

[16] *Bosnia and Herzegovina* v. *Serbia and Montenegro*, para. 190 (emphasis in original).

different aspects of individual criminal responsibility. While that provides a good basis, much work still remains to be done, in order to develop in a sufficiently precise manner the legal obligations to prevent mass atrocities incumbent upon third States, and regional and international organisations.

RtoP as a multilayered system

RtoP is based on a multilayered system of basic protection and human security whereby different important stakeholders as States, regional and sub-regional organisations and international organisations hold obligations which vary in nature and scope. Relevant actors and mechanisms are present in all three levels of protection, namely domestic, regional and international. In the present State-centred system it is expected that in exercising its sovereign rights over a population under its jurisdiction, a State, while acting independently, is conscientious of its legal obligations *vis-à-vis* that population and at a minimum bound to fulfil its RtoP obligations.[17] On an international plane, on its own and in the framework of regional organisations and the UN, a State is expected to require and ensure respect for those obligations on the part of other States through cooperating and offering international assistance and assisting in capacity-building, as well as through contributing to the extent possible to an international response under RtoP's third pillar, 'timely and decisive response'.

The 2005 WSOD represents a solemn pledge on the part of States to fulfil existing obligations and for increased international solidarity and cooperation. The legal obligations on the part of States are enshrined in a number of relevant international instruments such as the 1948 Genocide Convention, the 1949 Geneva Conventions and their 1977 two Additional Protocols, the main international human rights treaties, the statutes of the ad hoc tribunals and the ICC and so on. At the same time, the prohibition of genocide, war crimes and crimes against humanity are also part of customary international law.

Since the establishment of the UN in 1945,[18] there has been a considerable growth in the number of international and regional organisations covering different important fields such as security, economy, and

---

[17] See Amnéus, Chapter 1 in this book.

[18] For a detailed discussion of the establishment of the UN, see Stephen Schlesinger, *Act of Creation: The Founding of the United Nations* (Boulder, CO: Westview Press, 2003).

others. This development means a potential growth in terms of the capacity of these organisations to carry out RtoP obligations, but also implies the need for more cooperation and clarity regarding their respective fields of competence. That cooperation would help avoid unnecessary overlap and confusion, besides saving scarce resources. As the previous chapters show, a lot remains to be done in order to introduce and embed RtoP into the agenda and activity of several regional and security organisations. A noteworthy initiative in providing assistance in this regard is the launching in January 2012 of a Task Force on European Union (EU) Prevention of Mass Atrocities to contribute to the EU's continued efforts to translate its general commitment to RtoP into practice and make the prevention of genocide and mass atrocities a priority of EU foreign policy.[19] Other regional and security organisations could potentially benefit from a similar effort.

The UN remains the only body of its kind with universal membership and comprehensive scope, and encompassing so many areas of human endeavour.[20] The UN is the main international organisation, whose mission is to ensure peace and security, sustainable development and human rights protection. And as the Secretary-General has pointed out, ultimately, the United Nations exists for, and must serve, the needs and hopes of people everywhere.[21] Its main organs and especially the Security Council have an important role to play in protecting populations from mass atrocities.[22] Besides guiding the conceptual development of RtoP, the Secretary-General has continued to play an important role in further consolidating State commitment to RtoP. He has been encouraging national governments to adopt strategies for RtoP and, as proposed by the Special Adviser on the Prevention of Genocide in 2005, to establish focal points for situations related to RtoP, such as the recently appointed Director for War Crimes and Atrocities within the US National Security Council.[23] An important RtoP mechanism is the joint office of the advisers to the Secretary-General on the Prevention of Genocide and that on the Responsibility to Protect, whose mandate focuses on preventing mass atrocities and promoting a culture of prevention. Over the last years the General Assembly has engaged in a discussion and the

---

[19] This Task Force was launched by the Foundation for the International Prevention of Genocide and Mass Atrocities. For more information on this initiative, see www.massatrocitiestaskforce.eu/Background.html.

[20] UNSG, 'We the Peoples: The Role of the United Nations in the Twenty-First Century', UN Doc. A/54/2000, 27 March 2000, para. 8.

[21] *Ibid.*, para. 10.   [22] See Gill, Chapter 4 in this book.

[23] See Turner, Chapter 6 in this book.

charting of a proper doctrinal, policy and institutional life for RtoP.[24] General Assembly powers possibly include recommending forcible military action and sanctions under the 1950 Uniting for Peace resolution.[25] An important intergovernmental advisory body established under the 2005 WSOD as a dedicated institutional mechanism to address the special needs of countries emerging from conflict towards recovery, reintegration and reconstruction and to assist them in laying the foundation for sustainable development is the UN Peacebuilding Commission. The main purpose of the UN Peacebuilding Commission is to bring together all relevant actors to marshal resources and to advise on and propose integrated strategies for post-conflict peacebuilding and recovery.[26] This mechanism which reports annually to the General Assembly also assists the Security Council in considering emerging threats to international peace and security and is following the situation in Burundi, the Central African Republic, Guinea, Guinea-Bissau, Sierra Leone and Liberia. As Evans has pointed out, in contrast to the one hundred or so countries at any given time that are subject of reasonable human rights concern, there will usually be a dozen or so countries that can properly be regarded at any given time as being of RtoP concern.[27] That limited number should allow the different relevant regional and international mechanisms to prioritise and focus their efforts in responding to RtoP situations.

By now regional organisations such as the Arab League and the African Union[28] have dealt with a number of RtoP situations, especially in the cases of Sudan, Kenya, Libya, Ivory Coast and Syria. These first experiences have influenced considerably and to a large extent have shaped the attitudes and the response of these regional organisations to unfolding RtoP situations, including their cooperation with the UN and other relevant organisations. For example, a shared impression among its members on NATO's overstepping of the Security Council's mandate in Libya has led the Arab League to be more careful with the ongoing situation in Syria.[29] That same situation

---

[24] See Ryngaert and Cuyckens, Chapter 5 in this book. [25] *Ibid.*

[26] '2005 World Summit Outcome', UN Doc. A/RES/60/1, 24 October 2005, paras. 97–105. More information on the UN Peacebuilding Commission is available at www.un.org/en/peacebuilding.

[27] Gareth Evans, 'Lessons and Challenges', in Genser and Cotler (eds.), *Promise of Stopping Mass Atrocities in Our Time*, pp. 375–92, at p. 383.

[28] See, among others, Centre for Conflict Resolution, 'Africa's Responsibility to Protect', 23–24 April 2007, at www.responsibilitytoprotect.org/files/Vol-19_R2P_Report.pdf.

[29] For a more detailed discussion, see Aljaghoub, Aljazy and Bydoon, Chapter 13 in this book.

has also pointed out the need for important regional organisations such as the African Union to be more closely linked to the Security Council through their own group members.[30] Independent of their success or lack thereof in a given case, these interactions are quite important in that they help to devise and test the procedures for cooperation between relevant organs of different organisations and expose existing weaknesses in the system. It should be noted that the capacity of regional organisations to deal with RtoP situations differs considerably, and besides the African Union and the European Union, which can and have deployed peacekeeping or peace-enforcing missions, other regional organisations are lagging behind when it comes to capacities necessary for delivering a timely and decisive response. At the same time, the peacekeeping operations in Darfur, Sudan, and the Democratic Republic of Congo have shown the limits of missions which are small, poorly equipped and lack proper logistic support when operating in large countries lacking the necessary infrastructure.

Early warning and assessment

In practice, early warning and analysis of potential RtoP situations is done by States, international organisations, regional and security organisations and a number of non-State actors, mainly large specialised NGOs. Relevant information is contained also in reports prepared by established international human rights NGOs such as Amnesty International, Human Rights Watch and La Fédération Internationale des Ligues des Droits de l'Homme (FIDH).[31] A specialised NGO that plays an important role in the field of early warning and conflict prevention is the International Crisis Group with its analysis and pinpointed recommendations to relevant stakeholders. While there is a wide range of actors that collect and analyse information with regard to conflict areas, cooperation and sharing of such information and analysis is largely unstructured.

The UN has a fairly elaborate system of early warning. Although no special unit has been established to assist the Secretary-General, as recommended in the 2001 ICISS report,[32] specialised parts of the system such as the Office of the United Nations High Commissioner for Human

---

[30] For a more detailed discussion, see Dersso, Chapter 10 in this book.

[31] For more details, see van Steenberghe, Chapter 2 in this book.

[32] International Commission on Intervention and State Sovereignty, *The Responsibility to Protect* (Ottawa: International Research Centre, 2001), para. 3.16.

Rights (OHCHR) and the joint office of the Special Advisers of the Secretary-General play a key role in filtering information and drawing attention to such dangerous indicators as patterns of human rights violations or hate speech, which might otherwise escape detection.[33] Also the Human Rights Council plays an important role through its human rights special procedures mechanisms and by fielding missions of inquiry to investigate situations at risk from imminent or actual serious violations of international human rights or humanitarian law.[34] Paragraph 140 of the 2005 WSOD is quite important in that it supports the mission of the Special Adviser of the Secretary-General on the Prevention of Genocide which is to act as a mechanism of early warning to the Secretary-General, and through him to the Security Council, by bringing to their attention situations that could potentially result in genocide.[35] That function is complemented by the work of the Special Adviser on the Responsibility to Protect.[36] In effect, the joint office of the two Special Advisers to the Secretary-General offers a focal point within the UN system with regard to early warning and assessment of situations concerning mass atrocities.

Also a number of regional and security organisations have developed early warning mechanisms. The High Commissioner for National Minorities of the Organization for Security and Co-operation in Europe has played an important role in this regard by collecting and assessing information and by taking early action in order to defuse tension in several conflicts.[37] Organisations such as the EU and the AU have different mechanisms at their disposal. Through the European External Action Service (EEAS) the EU is able to gather and analyse a large amount of relevant information which would serve to predict arising RtoP situations.[38] The AU has created its own early warning system, the Continental Early Warning System (CEWS), tasked with the responsibility of collecting, analysing and assessing emerging threats to peace and security in Africa. Accordingly, the purpose of the CEWS is

---

[33] UNSG, 'Preventive Diplomacy: Delivering Results', UN Doc. S/2011/552, 26 August 2011, para. 45.

[34] For more details, see Sunga, Chapter 7 in this book.

[35] UNSG, 'Early Warning, Assessment and the Responsibility to Protect', UN Doc. A/64/864, 14 July 2010, para. 6(c).

[36] More information on the work of the Special Advisers is available at www.un.org/en/preventgenocide/adviser/methodology.shtml. For a more detailed discussion of the joint office, see Turner, Chapter 6 in this book.

[37] See Sandole, Chapter 14 in this book.   [38] See Fiott and Vincent, Chapter 9 in this book.

the provision of timely advice, otherwise known as early warning, by availing information and analysis to the Chairperson of the AU Commission on potential conflicts and threats to peace and security.[39] While the Organisation of American States (OAS) does not have a specific early warning mechanism, Ramcharan has put forward a proposal to establish an Inter-American Commissioner on Human Rights and the Responsibility to Protect.[40] Probably that would be a good first step towards including RtoP in the agenda of the OAS and towards its further institutionalisation.

The three gaps identified in the Secretary-General's 2010 report on early warning and RtoP include insufficient sharing of information and analysis among different UN structures, the fact that these structures do not view that information through the lens of RtoP, and the need for assessment tools and capacity to ensure both efficiency and system-wide coherence in policymaking and the development of an early and flexible response tailored to the evolving needs of each situation.[41] As the Secretary-General has pointed out, getting the right assessment – both of the situation on the ground and of the policy options available to the United Nations and its regional and sub-regional partners – is essential for the effective, credible and sustainable implementation of the responsibility to protect and for fulfilling the commitments made by the Heads of State and Government at the 2005 World Summit.[42] As (recent) experience shows, however, the existence of information about mass atrocities impending or being committed does not mean that preventive action will be taken in every situation.

Gareth Evans draws attention to the need to 'mainstream' consideration of RtoP issues by governments and large intergovernmental organisations through focal points, staffed by officials whose full-time day job is to keep track of relevant information, evaluate it, ensure that it gets on to the relevant desks, identify response options and follow them through, and whose status in the systems in question is high enough to ensure that their voice will be heard.[43] Since September 2010 sixteen countries have appointed a national RtoP focal point.[44] That means that less than ten

---

[39] See Dersso, Chapter 10 in this book.
[40] See Lugon Arantes, Chapter 12 and Sobers, Chapter 20 in this book.
[41] UNSG, 'Early Warning', para. 10.   [42] Ibid., para. 19.
[43] Evans, 'Lessons and Challenges', in Genser and Cotler (eds.), Promise of Stopping Mass Atrocities in Our Time, p. 386.
[44] For more information on this particular issue, see www.globalr2p.org/advocacy/FocalPoints.php.

per cent of the Member States of the UN have a national focal point. The Secretary-General has seen the development of a voluntary network of RtoP focal points in a substantial number of capitals around the world as an encouraging trend. Moreover, he has noted that over time, the group could take on a range of communication, learning, policy, capacity-building and mapping functions.[45] It remains to be seen how this initiative and network-in-the-making will develop in the coming years and what role, if any, it will play in further operationalising RtoP.

Entrenching respect for the responsibility to protect through accountability mechanisms

The punishment of mass atrocity crimes through a proper legal process is intrinsically related to the early activity of the two military tribunals established in the aftermath of the Second World War, namely the Nuremberg and Tokyo tribunals. These tribunals tried some of the individuals most responsible for the atrocious crimes committed during the Second World War. Besides these trial processes resulting in the 1950 Nuremberg Principles,[46] detailed international legal standards were developed in order to prohibit certain criminal behaviour, as the 1948 Genocide Convention which was followed only a year later by the four Geneva Conventions. While international human rights and humanitarian law standards have developed significantly over several decades through the adoption of a number of international instruments, enforcement mechanisms for these bodies of law were generally lacking or had considerably limited powers.

The establishment by the Security Council in the early 1990s of the two ad hoc tribunals, the tribunal for the former Yugoslavia (ICTY) and the tribunal for Rwanda (ICTR), followed by the adoption of the Statute of the International Criminal Court in 1998, has emphasised accountability for serious crimes in an unprecedented way. Moreover, a number of other accountability mechanisms have been created over the last two decades as part of cooperation between the UN and the countries concerned, in order to bring to justice perpetrators of gross human rights violations. The net effect of the establishment and activity of these

---

[45] UNSG, 'The Role of Regional and Sub-regional Arrangements in Implementing the Responsibility to Protect', UN Doc. A/65/877-S/2011/393, 27 June 2011, para. 28.

[46] See 'Principles of International Law Recognized in the Charter of the Nürnberg Tribunal and in the Judgment of the Tribunal', UN Doc. A/1316, 29 July 1950.

international or mixed judicial mechanisms is emphasising and consolidating the treaty-based and customary principles that acts of genocide, war crimes, and crimes against humanity encompass serious crimes which States have an obligation to prevent, and otherwise to investigate and punish. Moreover, wherever committed, these crimes of utmost gravity attract strong international condemnation and calls for accountability on the part of governments, international and regional organisations, and the civil society.

A lot of attention has been given in the book to the role of regional human rights systems and the international courts and tribunals. Obviously, the judicial and quasi-judicial mechanisms of the regional human rights systems in existence and in the making have an important role to play in ensuring rights and freedoms of persons falling under their jurisdictions.[47] These mechanisms have been instrumental in interpreting and developing the obligations of States *vis-à-vis* the persons under their jurisdiction. While the regional human rights mechanisms are equipped to deal with individual violations and not with mass atrocities, the activities of the European, Inter-American and African human rights systems have exercised a healthy influence on the domestic systems of the States Parties. Notably, the case law of the Inter-American Court of Human Rights coupled with the democratic changes that took place in the continent paved the way for the transformative processes which made it possible to address widespread and systematic human rights violations committed during the Cold War period. However, the regional human rights systems have no comprehensive 'early warning system' and little prospect of rolling out interim measures forcing a State to cease and desist from carrying out actions of concern.[48] Obviously, in a case where mass atrocities are pending or ongoing, relevant regional or international political organs would be expected to take the lead.

By prosecuting perpetrators of mass atrocity crimes such as genocide, war crimes, and crimes against humanity, the ICTY, ICTR and ICC help in bringing closure to victims and providing them with some sense and measure of redress.[49] The other important function of these

---

[47] For a detailed discussion, see Smith and Mallory, Chapter 19 (European system), Sobers, Chapter 20 (Inter-American system) and Viljoen, Chapter 21 (African system) in this book.

[48] For more details, see *ibid*.

[49] See, among others, Gentian Zyberi, 'The Role of International Courts in Post-Conflict Societies', in Ineke Boerefijn, Laura Henderson, Ronald Janse and Robert Weaver (eds.), *Human Rights and Conflict: Essays in Honour of Bas de Gaay Fortman* (Cambridge, UK: Intersentia, 2012), pp. 367–87, at p. 392.

international judicial mechanisms is their preventative role and helping create and spread a culture of accountability.[50] Moreover, as Deller has pointed out, the preliminary examinations of the ICC and the Office of the Prosecutor's gravity threshold for determining the admissibility of a case might provide some guidance with regard to the necessity of applying pillar three of RtoP, dealing with a timely and decisive response on the part of the international community.[51] The assessment of the gravity threshold is based among others on such criteria as the scale and nature of crimes, the manner of commission and their impact on the affected local community.[52] These criteria would be useful for policy and decision-makers in coming to informed decisions with regard to when action under RtoP becomes necessary.

Obviously, in order for these international judicial mechanisms to be able to fulfil their mission properly and efficiently, State cooperation is a must. As a number of situations pending before the ICC show, ensuring State cooperation from certain States has proven rather difficult. The UN Security Council, regional organisations and other important stakeholders need to do more so as to render sufficient support to the ICC in carrying out its functions. In this regard, the positive influence of the close cooperation between the EU and the ICTY in ensuring the cooperation of the States emerging from the former Yugoslavia with the ad hoc tribunal can serve as a good example.

Timely and decisive response

The intractable situation in Syria has laid bare, even for those who had hoped otherwise, that RtoP does not change the balance of power nor can it necessarily alter the will of a permanent member of the Security Council one way or another. However, and independent of the politically intractable aspects related to delivering a 'timely and decisive response', there is a lot that could be done to improve the system supposed to

---

[50] As acknowledged in the 2012 report of the Secretary-General on RtoP, 'the threat of referrals to ICC can undoubtedly serve a preventive purpose and the engagement of the ICC in response to the alleged perpetration of crimes can contribute to the overall response. More generally, the emergence of a system of international criminal justice has had a positive influence on the development of the concept of RtoP' (UNSG, 'Timely and Decisive Response', para. 29). See and compare Frencken and Sluiter, Chapter 17 and Contarino and Negrón-Gonzales, Chapter 18 in this book.

[51] See Nicole Deller, 'Challenges and Controversies', in Genser and Cotler (eds.), *Promise of Stopping Mass Atrocities in Our Time*, pp. 62–84, at p. 70.

[52] *Ibid.*

deliver that response when there is agreement.[53] That international response is legally based on applying a varied range of measures available under Chapters VI (Pacific Settlement of Disputes), VII (Action with Respect to Threats to Peace) and VIII (Regional Arrangements) of the UN Charter. Those measures range from preventive diplomacy to military intervention with Security Council authorisation under Chapter VII of the Charter. Before authorising a military intervention under Chapter VII in the Libyan situation, the Security Council applied a number of targeted sanctions, which comprised the freezing of financial assets of a number of leadership figures, imposition of travel bans, establishment of a no-fly zone and arms embargoes and the referral of the situation to the ICC for investigation.

Generally speaking, with maybe a handful of exceptions, the military assets of countries are not equipped and trained for the kind of military operations which are necessary in RtoP situations. Moreover, the considerable risks and expenses involved in such deployments as well as domestic politics play an important role in a government's decision to make available and use its military capabilities. From another perspective, it remains unclear how the Security Council can retain control of the military operations and ensure that the countries involved do not exceed its mandate. Regional organisations such as the EU and the AU have taken steps to make available standby military capacities in order to ensure a certain degree of readiness for responding in a timely manner to RtoP situations. Notably, the standby military capacities developed by the EU have not been deployed thus far, despite the possibility to do so in the case of Libya.[54] At the same time, those of the AU will not be operational before 2015.[55] Despite its involvement in the Libya situation NATO still needs to develop a doctrine on how to deal with RtoP situations. But it seems that besides certain cases where the interests and security of members of the alliance are at stake, it is not keen to play a significant role in this regard.[56] So, on the face of it, it does not seem that the international community is either ready or keen to deliver a 'timely and decisive' response, in the sense of launching a military intervention against a sovereign State in order to stop mass atrocities.

---

[53] For a detailed discussion, see UNSG, 'Timely and Decisive Response'.
[54] See Fiott and Vincent, Chapter 9 in this book.
[55] See Dersso, Chapter 10 in this book.   [56] See Prescott, Chapter 15 in this book.

Division of responsibility: shared or diluted State responsibility?

The provisions of paragraphs 138 and 139 of the 2005 WSOD define the authoritative framework within which Member States, regional arrangements and the UN system and its partners can seek to give a doctrinal, policy and institutional life to the responsibility to protect.[57] However, these provisions do not clarify how the different actors composing the international community will share the burden of RtoP. Nor is there much guidance as to which organisation or organ should do what, when and how in the case of an RtoP situation. These lingering uncertainties call for more guidance on the part of the General Assembly. Regrettably, the cases of Darfur (Sudan), the Democratic Republic of the Congo, Somalia and Syria demonstrate *par excellence* the existing gap and the problems encountered when it comes to delivering a timely and decisive response to mass atrocities. These cases also illustrate the failure of the international community to hold accountable the States or the individuals most responsible for gross human rights violations falling under RtoP when this community is divided or largely indifferent.

The sharing of the responsibility at the international level seems to give rise to some institutional apathy, confusion or burden shifting when it comes to enforcing RtoP obligations. The complex and prolonged political and legal processes which usually accompany the taking of concrete steps to address RtoP situations might cause a delay instead of furthering a timely and decisive response on the part of the relevant international and regional mechanisms. Moreover, there seems to be problems at the highest political levels with regard to the understanding of the utility and use of force in conflicts among the people.[58] While RtoP is based on the principle of complementarity, placing the primary burden on the individual States and in case of failure upon the international community, broadly defined, this doctrine does not differentiate between the obligations of neighbouring States and of regional organisations, which are going to be primarily affected, and those of other more distant actors. Among the concepts and variables that need to inform this ongoing discussion are: the concept of contribution to the wrongful act; the economic, political and military resources available to the States involved in an RtoP situation; the institutional competences

---

[57] UNSG, 'Implementing the Responsibility to Protect', UN Doc. A/63/677, 12 January 2009, para. 2.

[58] Rupert Smith, *The Utility of Force: The Art of War in the Modern World* (New York: Penguin, 2006), pp. 332–404.

and the resources made available to international organisations; and relevant institutional possibilities and limitations. Other relevant concepts, which have been discussed in literature and by the ICJ in its case law, are those of due diligence, the duty to prevent and to punish, and the principles of international cooperation and solidarity.

Concluding remarks

Identifying and addressing the roots of the conflict before it escalates is a crucial part of RtoP's preventive aspect. As the UN Secretary-General has noted in his 2012 RtoP report:

> Crimes and violations relating to RtoP often stem from identity-related conflicts, whether the conflicts are between the groups specified in the 1948 Convention on the Prevention and Punishment of the Crime of Genocide, which are 'national, ethnical, racial or religious' groups, or those defined by other factors. Such conflicts emanate not from mere differences between the groups, whether real or perceived, but from implications of those differences, which may cause populations to be subjected to indignities reflected in gross inequalities, namely, discrimination, marginalization, exclusion, stigmatization, dehumanization and denial of fundamental human rights.[59]

Since its launch in 2001, RtoP has gained increased attention and acceptance as a concept which provides a framework for ensuring that populations are protected from mass atrocity crimes.

Despite claims made with regard to its uncertain legal status, including in this book, the concept has a strong basis in treaty and customary international law, namely in binding human rights and humanitarian law standards, some of which like the prohibition of genocide have attained *jus cogens* status. Therefore, RtoP does not create a new norm for the protection of populations from mass atrocities; it just provides an overarching political platform, which is based on the UN Charter and well-established treaty and customary international law norms and principles and supported by the case law of different international courts and tribunals. As Luck has put it, RtoP's goal is changed behaviour on the part of stakeholders.[60]

---

[59] UNSG, 'Timely and Decisive Response', para. 6.
[60] Edward Luck, 'The Responsibility to Protect: The Journey', in Hoffmann and Nollkaemper (eds.), *From Principle to Practice*, pp. 39–46, at p. 39.

Obviously, every RtoP situation has its own specificities and needs to be decided on its own merits. Especially decisions to intervene militarily in a certain country require a careful and thorough analysis, where the involvement and input of regional organisations and interested third countries could be very useful in taking the right decisions. The close involvement of regional organisations is desirable and necessary for a variety of reasons. Oftentimes regional organisations have a better understanding of the local situation and the root causes of the conflict and are generally perceived as more acceptable interlocutors. Avoiding mistakes based on false analogies, faulty analysis, misperceptions and miscalculations can be achieved through cooperation between relevant institutions at different levels, domestic, regional and international. Ensuring the necessary protection for populations at risk of mass atrocities through cooperation between different institutional actors ultimately depends on institutional capacities and limitations and political will.

This book exposes the capacities and limitations of a number of important stakeholders. Those capacities and limitations need to be taken into account while building the necessary structures and models through which to address RtoP situations. Although our society has come a long way in terms of its institutional organisation, as the chapters of the book point out, existing regional and security organisations generally lack the institutional capacity and dedicated institutional structures to deal effectively with RtoP situations. Moreover, some of the institutions dealt with in this book are underfunded and understaffed, which means that the process of institutionalisation of RtoP therein is going to take considerable time and effort. Evidently, the viability, efficiency and effectiveness of the necessary institutional structures focused on implementing RtoP needs to be safely anchored and reflected in the respective budgets allocated to these institutions.

As our society has struggled over centuries in forging its way forward and in developing the necessary mechanisms to ensure as a minimum the protection of populations from mass atrocities, the concept of RtoP encapsulates a fundamental aim of this progressive and piecemeal evolution. Understandably, this concept resonates with a constituency reaching to all corners of the globe and within institutions composed of States and societies that have gone through widely different processes of creation and transformation. While the different experiences and stages of development inform peoples of different backgrounds, there is broad agreement regarding RtoP, as expressed in the 2005 WSOD and the informal debates organised at the General Assembly from 2009 onwards. The proper operationalisation of RtoP necessitates planning and coordinating the action required to be taken by several important stakeholders that have different competences, different capacities and sometimes even different or competing interests.

The UN main organs, regional and security organisations, the international courts and tribunals and regional human rights systems all have an important role to play in operationalising RtoP and ensuring that RtoP is transformed from promise into practice. As Bellamy notes, there is much work to be done to improve the ability of the UN and regional organisations to give early warning of genocide and mass atrocities, use preventive diplomacy effectively, end impunity via international criminal proceedings and human rights monitoring and dialogue, use rapidly deployable peacekeepers to prevent atrocities and to protect civilians, use and develop a range of targeted sanctions to deter abuses and to deny the abusers the means to ply their trade, and transform shattered societies in the wake of mass killing.[61] As the process of building a suitable and acceptable model is currently a work in progress, taking stock of existing institutional procedures and mechanisms and designing and establishing effective procedures and mechanisms to carry out the obligations under RtoP provides not only new challenges, but also new opportunities. The RtoP operational model needs to be a model in which domestic, regional and international mechanisms are well connected and synchronised in their actions, whereby decisions on addressing RtoP situations are taken through well-informed and meaningful deliberations, and the commitment to protect the populations at risk of mass atrocities is matched by the necessary material and human resources and political will.

---

[61] Alex Bellamy, *Responsibility to Protect: The Global Effort to End Mass Atrocities* (Cambridge, UK: Polity Press, 2009), pp. 196–7.

INDEX

Lightning Source UK Ltd.
Milton Keynes UK
UKOW06f1349270916

283903UK00014BA/757/P